D1084415

THE NEW
CAMBRIDGE MODERN HISTORY

ADVISORY COMMITTEE

G.N.CLARK J.R.M.BUTLER J.P.T.BURY

THE LATE E.A.BENIANS

VOLUME XII

THE ERA OF VIOLENCE
1898-1945

THE NEW
CAMBRIDGE MODERN
HISTORY

VOLUME XII

THE ERA OF VIOLENCE
1898-1945

EDITED BY
DAVID THOMSON

CAMBRIDGE
AT THE UNIVERSITY PRESS
1960

PUBLISHED BY

THE SYNDICS OF THE CAMBRIDGE UNIVERSITY PRESS

Bentley House, 200 Euston Road, London, N.W. 1
American Branch: 32 East 57th Street, New York 22, N.Y.

©

CAMBRIDGE UNIVERSITY PRESS
1960

Printed in Great Britain at the University Press, Cambridge
(Brooke Crutchley, University Printer)

CONTENTS

CHAPTER I

INTRODUCTORY SURVEY: THE ERA OF VIOLENCE (*page* 1)

By DAVID THOMSON, *Master of Sidney Sussex College, and
Lecturer in History in the University of Cambridge*

CHAPTER II

THE ECONOMIC MAP OF THE WORLD: POPULATION, COMMERCE AND INDUSTRIES

By G. C. ALLEN, *Professor of Political Economy in the University of London*

CHAPTER III

THE TRANSFORMATION OF SOCIAL LIFE

By DAVID THOMSON

v

CONTENTS

CHAPTER IV

POLITICAL INSTITUTIONS IN EUROPE:
POLITICAL ISSUES AND POLITICAL THOUGHT

By the late SIR ROBERT ENSOR, *Honorary Fellow of Corpus Christi
and Balliol Colleges, Oxford*

CONTENTS

CHAPTER V

SCIENCE AND TECHNOLOGY

By Douglas McKie, *Professor of the History and Philosophy of Science
in the University of London*

CHAPTER VI

LITERATURE, PHILOSOPHY AND RELIGIOUS THOUGHT

By the Very Rev. W. R. Matthews, K.C.V.O., *Dean of St Paul's*

CONTENTS

CHAPTER VII

THE UNITED STATES OF AMERICA

By D. W. BROGAN, *Professor of Political Science in the University of Cambridge*

CONTENTS

CHAPTER VIII

LATIN AMERICA, 1899-1949

By J. H. PARRY, *Principal of University College, Ibadan, Nigeria*

CONTENTS

CHAPTER IX
THE WESTERN QUESTION IN ASIA AND NORTH AFRICA, 1900–45

1. THE NEAR AND MIDDLE EAST AND NORTH AFRICA

By BERNARD LEWIS, *Professor of History of the Near and Middle East, School of Oriental and African Studies, London University*

2. INDIA

By C. H. PHILIPS, *Professor of Oriental History, and Director of the School of Oriental and African Studies, London University*

3. SOUTH-EAST ASIA

By D. G. E. HALL, *Professor of the History of South-East Asia, School of Oriental and African Studies, London University*

CONTENTS

4. THE FAR EAST

CHAPTER X

ARMED FORCES AND THE ART OF WAR

I. NAVIES

By ADMIRAL SIR G. J. A. MILES

CONTENTS

2. ARMIES

By the late FIELD MARSHAL EARL WAVELL

CONTENTS

3. AIR FORCES
By Air Chief Marshal Sir Arthur Longmore

CHAPTER XI

INTERNATIONAL RELATIONS, 1900–12

By J. P. T. Bury, *Fellow of Corpus Christi College and Lecturer in History in the University of Cambridge*

CONTENTS

CHAPTER XII

THE APPROACH OF THE WAR OF 1914

By J. M. K. Vyvyan, *Fellow of Trinity College, Cambridge*

CONTENTS

CHAPTER XIII

THE WAR OF 1914–18

By C. T. ATKINSON, *Fellow of Exeter College, Oxford*

CONTENTS

CHAPTER XIV

THE RUSSIAN REVOLUTION

By Isaac Deutscher

CONTENTS

CHAPTER XV

THE PACIFIC IN THE FIRST WORLD WAR AND IN THE SETTLEMENT

By J. W. Davidson, *Professor of Pacific History in the Australian National University*

CONTENTS

CHAPTER XVI

THE PEACE SETTLEMENT OF VERSAILLES, 1918–33

By ROHAN BUTLER, *Fellow of All Souls College, Oxford*

CHAPTER XVII

THE LEAGUE OF NATIONS

By the late J. L. BRIERLY, *Professor of International Law in the University of Oxford*

CONTENTS

CHAPTER XVIII

ECONOMIC INTERDEPENDENCE AND
PLANNED ECONOMIES

By Asa Briggs, *Professor of Modern History in the University of Leeds*

CONTENTS

CHAPTER XIX

THE BRITISH COMMONWEALTH OF NATIONS

By J. C. BEAGLEHOLE, *Senior Research Fellow and Lecturer in Colonial History, the Victoria University of Wellington, New Zealand*

CONTENTS

CHAPTER XX

EUROPEAN CIVILISATION IN THE TWENTIETH CENTURY

By David Thomson

CHAPTER I

INTRODUCTORY SURVEY:
THE ERA OF VIOLENCE

EUROPE of the mid-twentieth century differed greatly from Europe of the late nineteenth century in its internal political, economic and social structure and in its external relations with the other continents of the world. The present volume is concerned with the processes of change which brought about this transformation in the content and context of European civilisation. It may serve as a bridge between the more long-term historical developments described in preceding volumes and the environment of our own times.

The writing of what is so nearly contemporary history involves the scholar in problems that in some ways are less acute for the historian of ages more remote. He works so close to the frontiers of both experience and knowledge that the historian's usual privilege of informed hindsight is somewhat curtailed. The bugbear of bias, seldom completely absent from the task of historiography, is a particularly insidious enemy when the themes directly involve personal experience, sentiments, and expectations. The contemporary historian, however, enjoys some compensating advantages. His sources, if not complete, are superabundant. He has the feel of the events, the sense of atmosphere, the appropriate presuppositions for sympathetic understanding. The very immediacy of his interpretation may endow it with value for his successors. In any case it is important that professional historians should not shirk the duty of making available to those who must try to shape the immediate future the best understanding of the age that their techniques and skills can achieve: for to abdicate this duty would be to abandon the field to propagandists and soothsayers.

The chapters of the present volume cannot have the same appearance of finality of historical judgment or the same definitive scholarship that come only from standing on the shoulders of countless predecessors. But contributors have attempted a comparable scholarly balance of judgment, and a similar discrimination between verified facts and unproven beliefs. They have been deliberately chosen from the English-speaking world, on the principle that wherever in a co-operative work there may intrude some unconscious bias of national or cultural emphasis it is better that this should be as far as possible consistent. Prejudice is more likely to become apparent, and therefore discountable and harmless, when it has some consistency than when it lurks behind diversity. For the same reason, the editor has not sought to impose any particular emphasis upon contributors, whose authoritative status in their own fields of study entitles them to quite independent judgments, even when these do not at all points agree with the judgments of their colleagues. If history can ever pass 'final verdicts', it certainly cannot pass them within one generation.

The European scene in 1900 presented a medley of forces of unity and diversity, of assimilation and diversification. Mechanisation, industrialism and commerce already dominated European civilisation. The peoples of Europe were subject to broadly similar forces of change, all making for a relatively rapid growth of population, a spectacular increase of productivity, an intensification of national consciousness, a more eager resolve to make the state and its policies correspond to the secular needs and desires of the communities that it governed. Mentally, psychologically, spiritually, the peoples of Europe had reached a condition of crisis when the century began. The age of the masses, of the anonymous multitude, was upon them. The nineteenth-century triumphs of liberal and democratic ideas were still only partial triumphs which the growth of militarism and imperialism seemed likely to imperil. The growth of socialism was marked by a sharp cleavage between the movement's domestication in western and northern Europe and its violent and revolutionary purport in southern and eastern Europe. The speedy overflow of European people, capital, commerce and modes of life into the other continents of the world betokened the coming of a new era when European civilisation would be affected at least as much by the developments and reactions of non-European peoples as by the peoples of Europe itself.

The economic map of the world (ch. II) revealed a new pattern of world relationships in which Europe's fate was now inextricably enmeshed. The older industrial countries and the countries of primary production, whether the newly settled lands or the older populated lands of Asia and Africa, came to have complementary economies, linked together by a large international trade. Until 1914 this pattern remained relatively stable and continuous. But world war disrupted it and contributed, along with other more long-term changes, to its transformation into a different pattern of more separatist and more deliberately planned economies (see ch. XVIII). The intrusion of political purposes and requirements into economic life, which liberalism of the previous century had striven to end, became more continuous and more ubiquitous after the first world war. The most spectacular and wholesale domination of economics by politics appeared—paradoxically enough—in the Soviet Union, where long-term economic planning by a central bureaucracy became a recipe for progress. But the prolongation of war-time controls, the attempts to remedy the dislocations of war, the need everywhere to fight the economic depression of 1929–32, the growth of militarist dictatorships anxious to ensure self-sufficiency in war, conspired to superimpose on the old economic map of interdependence a new politico-economic map of attempted autarky. This pattern prevailed not only among nations within Europe, but spread over all the continents. Freedom of movement of men, capital and goods which underlay the nineteenth-century economy was now largely destroyed in favour of more separatist national economies more mercantilist in spirit. When economic liberalism declined, political liberalism too was thrown on to the defensive.

Despite this transformation of the economic map, the peoples of Europe continued, throughout the first half of the twentieth century, that rapid expansion of industrialism and urbanism, of productivity and material welfare, of democracy and social justice, which had all begun in the previous century (ch. III). The age that opened with the application of great new sources of power (gas, electricity, petroleum) reached its climax after 1945 in the development of atomic power. The chemical and electrical industries in which Germany led the world in 1900 became, by 1950, the foundations of new technologies. In spite of interludes of savage mutual destruction in two world wars, of economic collapse and mass unemployment, of barbaric persecutions in the name of political ideologies, for most European nations during these fifty years the general standards of life and health, comfort and amenity vastly increased. The ideals of democracy and socialism found expression in the Welfare State.

The political map of Europe underwent changes more obvious but no less important than the changes in the economic map: and the demand for greater social security in an era of violence, which gave rise to the Welfare State, was accompanied by a new pattern of states and of government (ch. IV). As the number of independent states in Europe increased, the number of them that ranked as great powers decreased, from six in 1900 to only three in 1950. The great dynastic agglomerations of Russia, Austria-Hungary and Ottoman Turkey that existed in eastern Europe before 1914 were replaced, after 1919, by a number of new or enlarged states claiming to be based on principles of national self-determination (see ch. XVI). By 1950 these mostly survived, though with modified frontiers, but many of them endured avowed or *de facto* subservience to the Soviet Union. The Bismarckian *Reich*, whose economic and military power dominated European affairs throughout the period, had by 1950 come to be divided sharply into two zones, of which the eastern was also under indirect Soviet control. The Italian kingdom, that other beneficiary of mid-nineteenth century crusades for national unification, likewise ranked as a great power until after 1943. Unlike Germany it escaped partition, but it too lost status as a great power. France, wonderfully resilient in her economy after the devastations of each war, did not enjoy a comparable revival in her political or military power. For these reasons the whole distribution and balance of power among states was fundamentally changed. Whereas before 1914 European diplomacy had been preoccupied with tensions between a powerful Germany and her neighbours to the east and the west, by 1950 it was dominated by the world-wide cleavage between East and West and the dangers of a power-vacuum in central Europe. Internal political systems presented a new series of contrasts. The constitutional monarchies of north-western Europe (Great Britain, the Low Countries, Scandinavia) remained throughout the home of liberal parliamentary democracy: and republican France belonged to the same political camp. But whereas before 1914 western and central Europe appeared as the source of nationalist and socialist revolutionary movements likely to disrupt the multi-national dynastic empires of eastern Europe, by 1950 these roles were reversed. From Moscow, Berlin and the other communist-controlled capitals of eastern Europe came encouragement and support for disruptive and revolutionary communist parties within most western states.

The most fundamental of all forces which straddled the economic and political divisions of Europe, assimilating social life into one homogeneous and novel pattern even whilst it contributed immediately to aggravating the tensions and differences between states, was the irresistible development of science and technology (ch. v). These fifty years brought advances in science and technology surpassing those of all former times in extent, rapidity and application. Refined methods of investigation and precise measurement exposed both the complexity of the atom and the living cell, and the vastness of the universe. The atom proved to be almost a cosmos in itself, whilst the hundred million universes of cosmic space seemed to be composed also of atoms. Research in radio-activity revealed affinities between matter and energy, and made possible that controlled transmutation of elements of which medieval alchemists had dreamed. Studies in biochemistry and organic chemistry, genetics and cytology, suggested affinities between the physical and biological sciences, between energy and life. Scientific knowledge reached a phase when conventional distinctions between its sectors meant less and less, and a new synthesis transcending the former fragmentation of the sciences again seemed attainable. Paradoxically, the very dedication to specialised investigation that made this possible and the speed with which new knowledge was acquired made it increasingly difficult for a single human mind, however capacious and flexible, to encompass the whole. Whilst the new knowledge, through the subsidiary sciences of engineering and medicine and the parallel growth of technologies, was having the most far-reaching material consequences for the life and welfare of man, new concepts of scientific thought were assimilated only slowly and very imperfectly into modes of thinking about individual and social life.

European culture and humanistic studies reflected the current crisis in both thought and material civilisation (ch. vi). The development of psychology and the widespread popular interest in it had far-reaching effects on literature and the arts, most notably on the novel, the drama, biography and painting. The environment of scientific ideas and material progress encouraged a new realism and experimentalism, whilst the prevalence of violence and disruption stimulated neurotic introspection and extravagant coteries. The spread of universal suffrage and popular education combined with the facilities offered by the mass media of press, cinema, radio and television, to provide for the arts both new patrons and a new public. Fresh stimulus was given to the co-operative and public arts—architecture, opera, ballet, drama. In current philosophy the schools of positivism and pragmatism tended to prevail, though in Britain and Italy idealist schools of thought retained their influence, and the three paramount philosophers—Karl Marx, Friedrich Nietzsche and Sören Kierkegaard—dated from an earlier age. The impact of science on theology produced the modernist movement, the new psychology questioned the nature of religious experience, and the uncertainty of both the social and intellectual background re-awakened an interest in mysticism.

The changing fortunes of European civilisation must be traced in other continents than Europe itself. The economic, social and political development of the United States of America in these years touched and interacted at countless points with that of Europe (ch. VII). American history, like European, had as its landmarks the two world wars and the Great Depression. The depression destroyed faith in the business class as a ruling class, whilst the authority of the federal government as wielded by such presidents as Theodore Roosevelt, Woodrow Wilson and Franklin D. Roosevelt became dramatic, impressive, popular, and very much more active. American external policy, which at the beginning of the century had favoured isolation and protection, was transformed by the course of events into a policy of world leadership and extensive economic and technical aid to other countries.

The peoples of the southern half of the American continent (ch. VIII) also experienced momentous changes in these years. When the century began, the twenty-odd nations of Latin America combined nominal political independence with heavy economic dependence upon events and movements outside their borders, whether northern or transatlantic. During the next fifty years, as European influence declined North American influence increased, but the major states (notably Argentina, Brazil, Chile and Mexico) moved haltingly towards more complete independence. Pan-Americanism made little headway until the 1930's, but through first the League of Nations and later the United Nations, the states of Latin America assumed an important separate and collective role in world affairs. Economic instability, increased by the dislocations of the two world wars and the Great Depression, was often accompanied by great political instability: during 1930 and 1931 eleven of the twenty republics experienced revolution, usually of a bloodless character. In the 1930's authoritarian governments triumphed in Latin America as in Europe.

Their economic policies, too, were usually autarkic, or at least mercantilist, in spirit and purpose.

Still more fundamentally revolutionary changes took place in Asia (ch. IX). European power was at full-tide at the beginning of the century, and receded to low ebb by 1950. In the Near and Middle East, India and the Far East, British power was predominant in 1900, and along with France and the Netherlands Britain controlled most of South-East Asia. In central and eastern Asia Russia was consolidating her power. By mid-century the western European powers had been ousted from paramount positions in these regions, and even in central and southern Asia Russian hegemony was challenged by communist China and independent India. In the Far East a defeated Japan opened the door to strong United States influences. In the Near and Middle East the old Ottoman empire had disintegrated, leaving behind a mosaic of new nations and states, including a new Turkish state, and a new Israel face-to-face with a series of quarrelsome Arab states. Everywhere a self-assertive nationalism strongly coloured by anti-colonialism was the most explosive product of western influences. Throughout Asia the population grew rapidly, usually more rapidly than the development of economic resources, with consequent increase of poverty for the masses, despite great progress in industrialisation. By 1950 the 'western question' in Asia was no longer a political question of rival imperialisms, but rather an economic and social question of establishing new relationships between the Asiatic and the European and American peoples, based on economic aid, technical assistance, and joint participation in the large network of functional agencies connected with the United Nations. Politically, however, the tensions between the communist and non-communist states of the world cast a long shadow over the whole future of the peoples of Asia. The condition of world crisis known as 'the cold war', which had come into existence by 1950, was the tragic outcome of a half-century of wars and economic upheavals which had forged a completely new relationship between the continents of the world. Relations between races assumed a new importance.

Part of the transformation in the content and context of European civilisation during the twentieth century was the revolution in the art of war and the nature of armed forces (ch. x). That dedication of the major European powers to warlike preparations, which was so striking a feature of their activities in the decade before 1914, remained one of the most constant factors in the development of all European peoples. Application of the new sciences and technologies (and the resources of industrial production) to the art of warfare brought about new modes of military organisation, and supplied armies and navies with new weapons demanding radical rethinking of strategy and tactics. It also produced an entirely new kind of armed service—the air force. Air power, whether used as an independent striking force or in close liaison with sea and land forces, revolutionised warfare as a whole. Its development came too late to exert great influence in the first world war, but thereafter its effects became decisive. Whereas in the first world war the balance of advantage lay with defence, by the second it lay with offence: and the main reasons for the change were the introduction of air power and of highly mobile mechanised armoured columns. If an advantage continued to lie with the offence after 1945 it was because the development of guided missiles, nuclear weapons, and jet propulsion, made still higher speeds possible.

The two great wars which dominate the history of Europe in this period differed from all their predecessors in many ways. The second, if not the first, was virtually world-wide, for it saw prolonged fighting in the Pacific as well as in the Atlantic, in Asia and Africa as well as in Europe. For all major participants both were wars of unlimited liability, in the sense that whole peoples and entire national economies were mobilised on both sides. They were alike, in that both began in eastern Europe; both arose from treaty obligations towards smaller powers; both involved an initial alliance between Britain and France arrayed against a German-dominated central Europe; both implicated Germany eventually in a war on two fronts and were won by a grand alliance of Britain, France, Russia, and the United States; both changed their character and their dimensions as they proceeded until they engaged most powers in the world; both left behind them a series of subsidiary wars and tangled problems of reconstruction and resettlement that taxed to the utmost the ingenuity and resources of mankind. The ultimate similarity between them was that the eventual outcome of each was quite unforeseen and largely unintended when it began (see ch. xx). In their demands on human effort and sacrifice, their dislocation of economic systems, their disruption of old empires and states, their far-reaching social consequences, they were in the nature of major revolutions. Each, indeed, was accompanied or followed by communist revolutions, the first in Russia, the second in China. War and revolution became almost inseparable and indistinguishable phenomena in the twentieth century.

International relations before 1914 (ch. xi) contained all the seeds of the first world war: a complex of ancient dynastic and national hatreds, of insurgent nationalities within the borders of the empires of Austria-Hungary, Ottoman Turkey, and tsarist Russia, of great-power rivalries and fears on sea and overseas. Already there was a tendency for the great powers of Europe to become greater, the small powers relatively weaker: a tendency to be much intensified after the second world war, when two of the greatest great powers, the Soviet Union and the United States, were largely extra-European. With the growing division of Europe into two rival armed camps, the Triple Alliance and (after 1907) the Triple Entente, disputes anywhere tended to arouse suspicions, fears and hopes everywhere. Attempts to restrict competition in the accumulation of armaments (such as the first Hague Conference of 1899) or to settle colonial disputes (such as the Algeciras Conference of 1906) yielded no lasting relief from the crescendo of international tensions. Diplomacy proved powerless to avert war when the whole structure of inter-state relations was determined by the fear-driven policies of the great powers.

By 1912, although all outstanding colonial disputes had been settled or shelved, naval rivalry between the British and German empires had intensified, and the complex rivalries between Austria-Hungary and Russia in the Balkans were kept at fever-pitch by the activities of such restive nationalities as the Serbs and the Bulgarians. The Balkan wars of 1912 and 1913 were preludes to mightier conflicts. Even at this stage it was by no means inevitable that war would ensue, or that if it did it should be from the outset a general war involving Germany, France and Great Britain. Events of the immediate pre-war years (1912–14) can now be very fully documented from the archives of all the great powers (ch. XII). Collation of these sources throws light on the protracted debate about 'war guilt' and makes possible some clearer analysis of the successive steps by which each government's behaviour contributed to the final catastrophe.

The course of the war (ch. XIII) revealed the miscalculations of all governments. Contrary to all predictions it became, within six months, a war of deadlock and attrition on the western front and in the Atlantic. The system of alliances held firm, save for Italy, and embroiled every great power in Europe in a long war of unlimited commitments. Within its first year it produced for every belligerent an acute shortage of munitions and supplies, and this combined with severe losses of life on both western and eastern fronts to impose great internal reorganisation, both economic and political. Germany was eventually defeated, despite her vast preparations for war and her massive efforts to sustain it on two fronts, because of her own initial miscalculations, the fragility of her main allies, the resilience of France and Britain and the persistence of Russia, the overwhelming resources and manpower thrown in the scales against her by the British Commonwealth and, after April 1917, by the United States of America. Even so, she survived almost intact as a territorial unit whilst her allies, Austria-Hungary and Turkey, were shattered. It was in completing the disintegration of eastern Europe and Turkey, and in precipitating revolution in Russia, that the war produced its most immediately apparent and possibly its most far-reaching international consequences.

Of all the war's unforeseen and most momentous consequences, the greatest was its precipitation of the Bolshevik revolution in Russia (ch. XIV). Even so, Russia's vast losses in the war only accelerated a process of collapse which had begun decades before. For this reason the revolution now occurred with dramatic speed and completeness. The classical prelude to other revolutions, attempts to devise a constitutional monarchy, dated back to 1905, and had been played out before 1917. The complex revolutionary situation of 1917 was the accumulated deposit of Russian history, detonated by the explosion of war. It caught government and revolutionary leaders alike by surprise, and it was the masterful revolutionary genius of Lenin which alone took charge of events and steered them resolutely towards the triumph of Bolshevism. The defeat of Germany and the preoccupations of the other great powers made possible the completion of the revolution and consolidation of the Bolshevik party's control over the vast areas of Russia. For two-and-a-half years the new government waged war against White armies and foreign forces of intervention. Bolshevik successes in this war, together with the failure of communist *coups* in Europe, forced the Soviet government to undertake social reconstruction in isolation. Experience of the civil war paved the way for ruthless single-party dictatorship, compelled Lenin to introduce his New Economic Policy which partially readmitted capitalism, and led by 1924 to Stalin's enunciation of the doctrine of 'socialism in a single country'.

The preoccupations of Russia with internal revolution during the immediate post-war years facilitated another unpremeditated result of the war—the hegemony of Japan in the Far East (ch. xv). The Anglo-Japanese Treaty of 1902 had signalled the end for Britain's policy of 'splendid isolation' and the beginning of Japan's rise to power in the Pacific. She had defeated China in 1895 and was soon to defeat Russia in 1905. She annexed Korea in 1910, and expanded her influence into parts of Mongolia and Manchuria. General war in which her effort was slight gave every opportunity for her to strengthen this power, both political and economic. In January 1915 she presented China with her 'Twenty-one Demands'. Though whittled down, they were clear enough indication of Japan's ambitions, and enough of them were accepted to ensure Japan's position in the Far East as a serious economic and naval rival to the western powers. In the post-war settlement Japan and the United States emerged as rival powers likely to overshadow Germany, France, and even the British Commonwealth as predominant influences in the Pacific. Both enjoyed rapid economic growth and enhanced naval power. At the Washington Conference of 1921–2 they, together with Great Britain, France and Italy, agreed to fixed ratios of tonnage in capital ships for their fleets. The same powers, apart from Italy, concluded a four-power treaty which virtually ended and replaced the Anglo-Japanese alliance. The same four, with five other interested powers including China, also made a nine-power treaty vaguely safeguarding the position in China. The Washington Conference did something to prolong peace in the Pacific on the short run. It contributed little or nothing towards a long-term solution of the problems arising from a changed balance of power in the Pacific.

9

The post-war settlement in Europe (ch. XVI) was the outcome of war-time events and post-war conditions, as well as of the deliberations and agreements of statesmen in conference at Paris or elsewhere in the years 1919–23. At Paris the leaders of the major victorious powers virtually dictated the terms to the defeated powers of Germany, Austria-Hungary, and Bulgaria: but the terms were themselves largely dictated by war-time undertakings, the ineluctable conditions of the world in 1919, and the mood of its peoples. Austria-Hungary, the Ottoman empire, and the western fringes of the old Russian empire had already largely disintegrated into component national groups, some of which had provisional governments assuming administrative responsibilities in their territories. This ensured that the Austro-Hungarian empire was parcelled out among half a dozen 'succession states'; that from the Baltic to Galicia ran the *cordon sanitaire* against Bolshevism which consisted of Finland, Estonia, Latvia, Lithuania, and Poland; and that by 1923 the former possessions of Asiatic Turkey became a group of Arab kingdoms and sheikdoms whilst Syria, Lebanon, Iraq, Palestine and Transjordan were administered under mandates by France and Britain. Defeated Germany, by contrast, lost relatively little territory in Europe and remained one single republic, but upon her was imposed a series of disarmament and reparations requirements which provided sources of international tension and friction until they eventually lapsed or were repudiated. Allied occupation of the Rhineland until 1930, the allocation to Poland of the 'Polish Corridor' dividing East Prussia from the rest of Germany, and French occupation of the Ruhr in 1923 in an effort to exact overdue reparations payments, fed the flames of resurgent German nationalism. In Italy the Fascist party led by Mussolini came to power in 1922 on the tide of post-war discontent and disorder, and within four years established itself as a single-party dictatorship eager to assert Italian claims for expansion. The broad effect of the settlement in Europe was to create rival blocs of states, one led by France, Great Britain and the new 'succession states' and anxious to preserve the settlement intact; the other, led by Italy, Germany and Hungary, demanding revision of the settlement and a reversal of those parts of it which they regarded as hostile to their national interests. Though not committed to fixed alliances as in 1914, the powers drifted into hostile camps.

It had been the hope of the peacemakers of 1919 that such a development might be prevented by the machinery for arbitration or negotiation of disputes, and above all by the activities of the League of Nations (ch. XVII). This new experiment in international organisation, provided for in each of the main treaties of peace made after the war, came to be associated closely with preservation of the territorial and political settlement itself. The United States did not become a member, Germany was not admitted to membership until 1926, nor the Soviet Union until 1934.

During its formative years, therefore, its success depended mainly on the co-operation of France, Great Britain and the Commonwealth, as the powers most immediately interested in making it work. The league, in no sense an international government but only a standing facility offered to its members through which they might concert action to preserve peace, seemed in the 1920's to be establishing itself as a normal and necessary part of international relations. Some minor disputes were settled through its intervention, and the mutual confidence fostered by the foreign ministers of the three principal league powers (Sir Austen Chamberlain, Aristide Briand and Gustav Stresemann) during the years of the Locarno pacts bred hopes of its success. The evacuation of the Ruhr and the Rhineland, and the virtual abandonment of claims for reparations, eased European tensions. But the time of hope was short. Before the National Socialist party of Hitler gained power in Germany (1933) the prestige of the league, as well as of its leading champions, was challenged by Japan in her attack on Manchuria, and by the failure to enhance security by an agreed programme of disarmament. In the economic blizzard of the Great Depression which began in 1929, action through the league proved equally ineffectual. In 1935 Italy's attack on Ethiopia, a fellow-member of the league, destroyed any hope that the system of 'collective security' envisaged by the Covenant could stand the test of resisting aggression by a major power. Henceforth, except for the expulsion of the Soviet Union in December 1939 for her attack upon Finland, the league remained a passive witness of the aggressions of the single-party dictatorships. In its work on social and economic problems the league helped to widen and deepen that embryonic international society which was already coming into existence by 1900. But upon the actual policies followed by the major powers of the world—several of which either never joined or quickly left the league—it proved unable to exert much influence: and in the policies of the powers war had its roots.

If the connecting links, politically, between the two world wars can be found in the alignment of European states into revisionist and anti-revisionist states, the rise of a militant and aggressive Japan, Italy and Germany, and the collapse of international organisation designed to keep the peace, the economic links are to be sought in the disruption of the former world economy by the aftermath of the first war, by processes of economic change themselves, and by the failure of the powers to achieve a total expansion of world trade (ch. xviii). Before 1914 the central place in an economically interdependent world was occupied by Europe (see ch. ii). Half of the world's trade consisted of the imports and exports of seven European countries—the United Kingdom, Germany, France, Belgium, the Netherlands, Switzerland, and Denmark. The central network of European trade depended on the regular supply of raw materials and foodstuffs from other continents, and Europe was both the world's main workshop and its main banker. Already, however, it knew periods of stagnant trade and unemployment, and these prompted some experiments in control and even planning. The experience of war greatly extended and intensified regulation and planning, most impressively in Germany, and during the 1920's it was not only the Soviet Union which embarked upon planning whole sectors of its economy. The Great Depression compelled the most reluctant governments to adopt far-reaching control of economic activities (see ch. VII). To refrain from deliberate regulation and planning in conditions of acute economic depression and mass unemployment meant abandoning national welfare to the hazards and cruelties of blind economic forces; and this no government subject to sectional or popular pressures could afford to permit. The rearmament measures of the later 1930's, and the growing international tensions, moved most European states on to a near-war economy. The still more violent upheavals of the second world war left post-war Europe largely dependent on external aid and even more rigorous governmental planning, and prompted fresh experiments in economic co-operation between nations.

Pending completion of the extensive civil and military histories of the war being compiled from official sources, it has been decided not to attempt an account of the second world war comparable with chapter XIII. The main technical developments have been described in chapter X. The repercussions of the war have been only briefly indicated where appropriate: they would, indeed, merit a volume to themselves. But one major consequence was already clear in 1945. The fact that so much of the material for war was produced outside Europe—in the United States, the Commonwealth or Asiatic Russia—whilst so much of Europe was devastated and dislocated, tipped the whole balance of the world's economy more decisively against Europe. During its post-war convalescence Europe was dependent on external supplies and aid, and joined with the industrialised countries overseas to extend economic and technical aid to the more underdeveloped areas of the globe, mainly in South-East Asia and Africa.

The fortunes of the British Commonwealth of Nations in the twentieth century (ch. XIX) may serve as an epitome of the forces which have shaped contemporary history. When the century dawned the British empire covered roughly a quarter of the earth's surface and comprised a quarter of humanity. By 1914 it owned nearly half the world's tonnage of merchant shipping, and through its naval power it controlled most of the seas. Never had it been more unpopular in the world than during the Boer War. A sharp difference in both political and economic status was emerging between the settled and self-governing 'Dominions' in Canada, New Zealand, Australia, and South Africa, and the 'colonial empire' of mainly coloured peoples in the West Indies, India, Africa, the Far East, and the southern Pacific. The events of the generation after 1914 completely transformed this structure in both extent and substance. The two world wars, the decline of world trade, the growth of nationalism and of industrialism overseas, the changed economic and political balance of the world's economy after 1945, all of which reshaped the content and context of European civilisation in the ways already described, had their corresponding repercussions on the British Commonwealth. The older dominions gained still more complete independence, and were joined after 1947 by two great states in the Indian sub-continent, India and Pakistan, as well as by Ceylon. Some parts of the former empire, notably Eire and Burma, separated themselves from even the elastic framework of the new Commonwealth. Malaya, Central Africa, the West Indies, developed federal systems of government and won a high degree of political independence. Other African colonies, notably the Gold Coast (Ghana) and Nigeria, moved decisively towards self-government and eventual independence. The pattern of the new Commonwealth was no less variegated than that of the old; and there remained within it a comparable balance between forces of cohesion and common action and forces of separatism. It remained, even more conspicuously than in 1900, an organic and dynamic entity, guided by principles of liberalism and partnership and a readiness to share in wider international co-operation. That its future path would not be without stones and thorns was shown by active unrest in Cyprus, Malta and Kenya.

The phase of European history which is analysed in this volume has, therefore, a character and an internal coherence which make it possible crudely to summarise it as 'an era of violence' (ch. xx). To label it thus is not to minimise the important role of violence in all earlier periods of history, nor to neglect the persistence of men and peoples in this half-century in seeking safeguards against the use of violence in human affairs. It is merely to emphasise that the capacity of modern nations and governments to generate power, to accumulate resources of power in more mighty agglomerations than ever before, has in these years far exceeded their ability to harness such power for creative and constructive ends alone. Violence may be defined as the abuse of power: and abuse of power can be defined only in relation to its proper use for promoting prosperity, welfare, security, freedom and justice. The capacity of science, technology and mechanisation to produce material wealth, the ability of administration and organisation to produce greater welfare and social justice, result also in the enhanced power of modern societies to destroy one another and in a greater facility for modern dictators to establish inhuman despotism. Perhaps, with so much power at man's disposal, the marvel is that its abuse has not been even more persistent.

All these things have happened, simultaneously, in the remarkable half-century whose history constitutes the theme of this volume.

CHAPTER II

THE ECONOMIC MAP OF THE WORLD: POPULATION, COMMERCE AND INDUSTRIES

DURING the nineteenth century the growth of population, the spread of industry, the migration overseas of persons and capital and the expansion of international trade were all closely linked in Europe's economic development, and the pattern of economic relations which these brought into being became ever more strongly marked as the century drew to its close. Industrialisation provided the higher real incomes which made possible the survival of larger numbers living in improved conditions, and rising populations in turn stimulated investment in new capital goods and so opened the way to the economies of large-scale production. Specialised industrial populations, living at a higher standard of life than hitherto, called for increased supplies of food and raw materials which could be obtained only by fostering the primary industries of overseas countries and by creating new transport services to move the products. These developments were greatly assisted, and often initiated, by European enterprise and capital, enterprise that called to its aid the results of scientific and technical progress, and capital that was derived from the increased savings of the business and professional classes born of the urban industrial civilisation. The rising demand for the products of new lands and the availability of capital for investment in the primary industries created abundant opportunities in those countries for the emigrants which Europe, because of its rapidly increasing numbers, could supply. The older industrial countries and the countries of primary production, both the new regions that were being settled by men of European race and also the older and often densely populated lands of Asia, came to possess complementary economies. As each pursued its special advantages, a great international trade grew up among them, a trade which took, though by no means exclusively, the classical form of an exchange of finished manufactured goods for raw materials and foodstuffs.

This world economy, with its complex system of relationships, was required to undergo adjustments whenever, as was inevitable, one of the quantities in the cosmic equation changed. As the new lands filled up, for example, or as industry spread from its original centres, the simple pattern of international exchange was bound to alter. Thus, the United States passed during the last quarter of the nineteenth century from a situation in which she exported raw materials in exchange for finished manufactures to one in which her exports of the latter class of commodity exceeded her imports. During the same period the United Kingdom was forced to make profound adjustments in her industrial structure in response to competition from abroad; the fall in the importance of textiles among her exports and the shift in the location of her main textile markets from North and South America to the East were symptoms of this change. Within the circle of the industrial nations, moreover, there was a tendency towards increased specialisation, and consequently the exchange of manufactured goods among those countries (between Germany and the United Kingdom, for example) became a prominent feature of international trade. Experience showed that the relative industrial importance of particular areas was liable to be rapidly transformed by technical discoveries, such as those which in the 'eighties made it possible to smelt economically the ores of Lorraine and so gave rise to the great German basic steel industry.

Mutability in particulars, however, proved to be consistent with stability in the system as a whole. In spite of many innovations that were in themselves momentous, during the period from 1900 to 1914 the general pattern of economic relations which had appeared in the nineteenth century did not alter. Continuity rather than change was the outstanding feature of the time. The staple industries of western Europe and the United Kingdom greatly expanded. International trade and investment grew very fast, and between 1900 and 1914 overseas emigration from Europe was greater than ever before. If the nineteenth-century economic system rested upon a precarious basis, this was certainly not apparent in the first decade and a half of the present century. Indeed, the most characteristic features of that system became more strongly marked than at any other time, and the rise of new centres of economic power did not affect the position of western Europe as the pivot of the system.

In the course of the next thirty years the structure that had been built up in the preceding century crumbled, and the foundations of western Europe's economic life were undermined. It is fruitless to debate whether this change is to be directly attributed to the two world wars and to the Great Depression of 1929–32, for opinions will differ about how far these, especially the last, are to be regarded as exogenous factors. Certainly many profound changes occurred which did not arise out of the political catastrophes of the time, while others were only partially affected by them. Industrialism, as was inevitable, continued to spread from western Europe and from the United States, and altered the content of international trade. Advances in technique and shifts in demand affected the relative importance of the different regions of supply. Emigration dwindled, partly because the western populations were ceasing to grow, and partly because the new lands were less ready to receive immigrants. Overseas capital investment diminished or changed in character, because the former chief suppliers of capital suffered a decline in their capacity to provide it and because risks increased with political changes. These are the chief trends which are to be examined in this chapter.

POPULATION

The great increase in the world's population during the nineteenth century was brought about in the main by a fall in the death rate. In Europe and in countries inhabited by persons of European descent this fall was attributable chiefly to the advance of science and industry, with consequential effects on medicine, sanitation and nutrition, and in Asia to the establishment, usually by European governments, of order and settled political conditions. By 1900, however, it was becoming apparent that in certain countries, where the increase had been most noteworthy during the previous century, the forces responsible for it were losing their strength. In the exceptional case of France, the birth rate had dropped from early in the nineteenth century. After 1880 it began to follow the death rate downwards in England and Wales, Norway and Sweden, and by the turn of the century a sharp decline in the birth rate spread to all northern and western European countries (except Holland) and to many overseas countries that had been peopled from Europe. Although death rates in these countries also continued to fall, the effect was to slow down the rate of natural increase and to bring some of the populations within sight of an actual decline. From 1900 onwards the largest proportionate increases in European population came from the eastern and southern parts of the continent where the fall in the death rate was steep, while the birth rate, though falling slightly, still remained high. The contrast between the experience of north-west Europe[1] and that of eastern Europe can be brought out by examining the average annual rates of increase. For the former area the average annual rate fell from 0·861 per cent in the period between 1850 and 1900 to 0·671 per cent in the period between 1900 and 1930, whereas for the latter area the rate, which was higher in both periods, scarcely changed; it was 1·062 per cent between 1850 and 1900 and 1·056 per cent between 1900 and 1930.[2]

Throughout the world this contrast in demographic experience could be observed, for though the movements in the death rates and birth rates followed similar courses in many countries after 1900, there were wide differences among those countries in the extent of the changes and in their timing. On the whole the reduction in the birth rate, and so in the rate of natural increase, occurred earliest and went farthest in countries which had been drawn most completely within the orbit of modern industrial civilisation, including the countries which, though still largely agricultural, used highly capitalistic methods of farming. These countries included the United Kingdom, the states of western and northern Europe (except Holland), the United States, Australia and New Zealand. In this group

[1] By north-west Europe is here meant Great Britain, Sweden, Denmark, Norway, Germany, Switzerland, Holland and Belgium.
[2] See A. M. Carr-Saunders, *World Population* (1936), p. 21.

16

of countries the annual rate of natural increase had by 1939 become very small (0·15 per cent for Belgium, 0·27 per cent for England and Wales, 0·49 per cent for Ireland, 0·09 per cent for France, 0·34 per cent for Switzerland, 0·39 per cent for Sweden, 0·57 per cent for Norway, 0·67 per cent for the United States and 0·78 per cent for Australia). The decline in the birth rate was brought about chiefly by a fall in the specific fertility rate,[1] except in Ireland where later and fewer marriages were responsible. A second group of countries may be distinguished where the rate of natural increase began to fall during the second quarter of the twentieth century, although it was still high in 1939. This group includes the late-comers to modern industrialism, the countries of southern and eastern Europe, the U.S.S.R. and Japan. Here, in 1939, the annual rates were 1·05 per cent for Greece, 1·07 per cent for Poland, 1·19 per cent for Russia, 1·01 per cent for Italy, 0·97 per cent for Roumania and 0·94 per cent for Japan. Canada, with a rate of 1·07 per cent, and Holland, with a rate of 1·2 per cent, came within this group and so stood out in contrast with their neighbours and their peers in economic and cultural development. Germany, with a rate of 0·81 per cent, came within the second group rather than the first, but this was the result of a sharp revival of the birth rate after the early 'thirties when it had been very low. The third group consists of countries in which the rate of natural increase probably rose after 1900, namely India, South-East Asia, Egypt, parts of Latin America, and some others. In some of these regions greater security and economic development led to a fall in the death rate but left the high birth rate unaffected; in others an originally high rate of increase was maintained. For Egypt where in 1939 the rate was 1·62 per cent, for the Argentine where it was 1·28 per cent, for Mexico where it was 2·16 per cent, and for Yugoslavia where it was 1·5 per cent, the situation was comparable with that of the most prolific European countries in the nineteenth century. Caution is needed in dealing with figures for Asiatic countries, for the statistical data are not very reliable, and much that has been written about their populations is partly based on conjecture. This is particularly true of China which would appear to have been in a stage corresponding to that of Europe before the eighteenth century, for high birth rates were there matched by high death rates, with the result that the population was comparatively stable.

These divergences in the growth of population altered substantially between 1900 and 1940 the distribution of world population. So far as the proportionate distribution among continents is concerned, the figures in Table 1 scarcely bear out this assertion, since the European share in 1940 was only slightly smaller than in 1900, while Asia had a significantly smaller share.

---

[1] This rate is found by referring all births occurring among women of a given age to the total number of women of that age.

The paradox is to be explained partly by the fact that the continents contain regions with contrasting experience in the growth of numbers, and partly by the fact that the trends in the rate of increase had not had time by 1940 to exert their full influence upon the relative magnitude of the different populations. Thus, Europe maintained her share because of the rapid growth in Russia. If Russia be excluded from the European figures, then Europe's share would fall during this period from 20 per cent to 18 per cent. Again, the countries of western and northern Europe[1] in 1900 had 26 per cent of the total European population; by 1940 the proportion had fallen to 23 per cent.

Table 1. *World Population*[2]

	Numbers in millions		Percentage distribution	
	1900	1940	1900	1940
Europe (including European Russia)	401	530	24·9	24·6
North America	81	141	5·1	6·5
Central and South America	63	129	3·9	6·0
Australasia	6	10	0·4	0·5
Africa	120	150	7·4	6·9
Asia	937	1200	58·3	55·5
Totals	1608	2160	100·0	100·0

The second part of the explanation is more intricate. Changes in fertility and mortality rates reveal themselves in alterations in the age structure of a population long before the total numbers are seriously affected. Those who are concerned not merely with the immediate and obvious results of those changes but with their ultimate effect use a measure known as the net reproduction rate. This rate measures the extent to which a population reproduces itself from generation to generation provided that current rates of fertility and mortality remain unchanged. At the beginning of the twentieth century it is probable that European net reproduction rates were everywhere, except in France, well above unity, that is to say, above the rate at which one generation exactly reproduces itself. The net reproduction rates shown in Table 2 demonstrate both the dramatic change that took place in western Europe after 1900 and also the contrast that had come to exist by the later 'thirties among the several countries. It should be observed that for many countries there are no data available to permit an estimate of the net reproduction rate to be made, and for others it is not possible to carry the comparison very far back in time.

It is not necessary here to consider the prognostications based on these rates, which are reliable guides to the future only on the assumption that

[1] Includes the United Kingdom, France, Belgium, Switzerland and the Scandinavian countries.

[2] These figures are estimates and are subject to a wide margin of error, especially for Asia and Africa.

fertility and mortality rates continue unchanged. Recent experience suggests that it is rash to make this assumption. Birth rates have risen sharply in the United States and in several European countries since the second world war, and the very pessimistic forecasts made during the 1930's about the probable trends of certain populations have had to be revised. But whatever the future has in store, the main effect of the changes so far has been to alter profoundly the age distribution in the countries that have experienced them. Where the net reproduction rate has for some time been low, the proportion of the total population in the older age groups has substantially increased. During the 'thirties and 'forties the population of western Europe had not merely a low rate of growth, but it was also ageing; whereas in those countries in which the rate was high, the population was young and its age structure such as to promise a large increase in the future. To make an illustration from England and Wales, in 1901 32 per cent of the population was in the age group 0–14, and 20 per cent in the age group 45 and over; by 1940 the proportions had been almost exactly reversed—21 per cent in the first age group and 32 per cent in the second. The ageing of western populations had become by the 'thirties a problem that was casting shadows on social and economic well-being. It is true that the first effect of a decline in the proportion of children in a population is likely to be an increase in income per head, since the proportion of non-producers is diminished. But the change presently makes itself felt in shifts in demand which require structural adjustments in the economy, and these are not easy to bring about in ageing populations whose occupational mobility is low. Furthermore, a prospect is perceived when the burden of maintaining a large body of aged people has to be shouldered by a relatively small active population. This prospect troubled the social scientists of western Europe in the 'thirties, but it had scarcely been realised by the majority and its influence on social and economic policy was still negligible.

Table 2. *Estimated Net Reproduction Rates for Certain Countries*

Country	Period	Rate	Period	Rate
England and Wales	1921	1·087	1938	0·80
France	1906–13	0·930	1940	0·82
Germany	1901–12	1·480	1940	0·98
Norway	1901–12	1·556	1940	0·81
Sweden	1901–12	1·429	1940	0·81
United States (white population)	1920	1·14	1935–40	0·98
Australia (white population)	1920–1	1·319	1939	0·99
European Russia	1896–7	1·65	1926–8	1·7
Poland	1927	1·3	1934	1·11
Italy	—	—	1935–7	1·13
Bulgaria	1901–5	1·88	1933–6	1·19
Japan	1930	1·57	1937	1·44

An important influence on the growth of population that has not yet been mentioned is that of war. The full effects are very difficult to measure. Direct losses in war-time occur not only by the death of men in battle and the rise of the death rate among civilians through privation and other causes, but also by the reduction in the birth rate because of the absence of men on military service. It has been calculated that in the first world war Europe (excluding Russia) lost from 20 to 22 million people through these causes, the equivalent of the natural increase between 1914 and 1919. In Russia the loss during the war and the Revolution may have been about 28 millions.[1] The total loss in Europe (excluding Russia) thus represented about 7 per cent of the total population, and in Russia about 18 per cent. A comparable estimate for the second world war is not yet possible.

The expansion of numbers in particular countries and the changes in the geographical distribution of world population as a whole cannot be fully explained without reference to migration. Just as during the nineteenth century immigration was responsible for a substantial part of the growth in the population of America and the British dominions, so in the twentieth century it did much to offset the effects of the fall in the rates of natural increase in those regions. The migrations of the present century fall into several distinct categories. By far the most important movement was the inter-continental migration from Europe to North and South America and the British dominions, and this dwarfed other movements which, absolutely, were very large. Examples of these other movements are the flow before 1914 of Poles to Germany, France and Russia, the influx into France between 1920 and 1930 of nearly 3 million foreigners, mainly from eastern and southern Europe, the great migration from European Russia to Asiatic Russia which between 1900 and 1914 amounted to over $3\frac{1}{2}$ millions, and the large outflow from India to Burma, Malaya and East Africa, and from China to South-East Asia and Manchuria.

In the first decade and a half of the century the number of European emigrants, mainly to the New World, was far greater than in any corresponding period in the nineteenth century; between 1906 and 1910 the average annual number was about 1,450,000 and between 1911 and 1914 it was 1,650,000. These figures are of gross outward movements. The net emigration was less than the gross figure, possibly by as much as a third, since many emigrants returned to their home countries after a short period abroad. Emigration occurred mainly because of the opportunities provided in the New World for improved incomes, and so it was usually high during periods of good trade in the receiving countries and low during periods of slump. The United States remained the chief country of immigration and received in the first decade of the century $8\frac{3}{4}$ million immigrants, nearly all from Europe. Other countries of immigration were, however, becoming important, notably Canada, Brazil and the

[1] F. W. Notestein and others, *The Future Population of Europe and the Soviet Union*, ch. III.

Argentine, and this led to a fall in the proportion of the total immigrants going to the United States. The most significant change of the period was in the supplying countries. During the latter part of the nineteenth century the predominance of northern and western Europe as a source of emigrants declined, and in 1896 for the first time the number of emigrants from that region (the region of the 'old emigration') was exceeded by that from southern and eastern Europe (the region of the 'new emigration'). This tendency persisted. Although all European countries showed an increase in the first decade of the new century, the largest contribution came from countries of the 'new emigration'. The change in the racial composition of the emigrants affected mainly the United States. Canada still looked chiefly, and Australia almost exclusively, to the British Isles for its immigrants. Immigrants into Central and South America came chiefly from Italy, Spain and Portugal.

The first world war put a temporary stop to migration, and although the movement was resumed on a large scale during the 'twenties, it did not attain the magnitude of the first decade of the century. The countries of the 'old migration' had now, because of the fall in their birth rates, fewer people to supply, and the considerable number of emigrants who in fact left their shores during the 'twenties bore a higher proportion to the natural increase than in pre-war days. In the case of Great Britain, for example, net emigration represented one-fifth of the natural increase in 1921–31, compared with one-ninth in the forty years before 1911. During this decade, moreover, acts of policy put an end to the virtually unrestricted migration of the pre-1914 era. In this connection the most notable measure was the United States Immigration Act of 1924. This carried further a policy already in operation by which quotas were imposed on the supplying countries, and it had the effect of diminishing the importance of the United States as a country of immigration.[1] The form of the control was such as to make it much less restrictive for the countries of the 'old emigration' than for those of the 'new emigration'. Consequently, the stream of migrants from southern and eastern Europe not merely declined, but was also diverted to countries other than the United States. Brazil, the Argentine and Canada rose to greater prominence as countries of immigration. Most of the British emigrants during this period went to the Dominions.

While post-war policy had a disturbing effect on migration, the Great Depression almost destroyed it. For a time, indeed, the movement in the case of some important receiving countries (e.g. Australia and New Zealand) was reversed, and even when economic recovery set in, the great outward flow of European peoples was not renewed. Not merely did it appear that opportunities had declined in the New World, which was

[1] Immigration into the United States was drastically limited for the first time by the Quota Act of 1921.

submerged in depression, but several of the chief countries of emigration in Europe began to pursue autarkical economic policies and obstructed the movements of their citizens. North-western Europe, with a rate of natural increase in 1936–8 only half that of 1911–13, could no longer supply large numbers of persons in the acceptable age groups. Moreover, while the countries of that region continued to suffer during the 'thirties from unemployment, their recovery from the effects of the Great Depression was on the whole more rapid than that of the United States or of the primary producing countries. It is significant that the United Kingdom, which between 1901 and 1921 suffered a direct net loss of population by emigration of 1,730,000 persons, and which even in the 'twenties lost 670,000, actually gained over half a million during the 'thirties. During the same decade gross immigration into the United States barely exceeded that figure, about one-seventeenth of its total immigration in the first decade of the century. In the 'thirties the Argentine took nearly as many immigrants as the United States, and Argentine and Brazil together far more. The slowing down of emigration had some important economic and social consequences. On the one hand it intensified the over-population of the land in the agricultural countries of eastern and southern Europe, and on the other hand it tended to redress the balance of the sexes in Europe, since the majority of the emigrants had always been young men.

The second world war and the subsequent disturbances led to large movements of population both within Europe and between Europe and other countries; but these had little in common with the large, and on the whole steady, streams that flowed westwards before 1914. Migration had passed increasingly under the organised control of governments, and whatever the number of migrants may be in the future it is unlikely that we shall see a return to the regime of *laisser-passer* under which the thriving new nations of the western hemisphere and Oceania were created. The great migrations had not merely raised the living standards of those who moved, for by opening up new areas of primary production they also improved the terms on which the urban populations of the old world could obtain the food and materials they required. That migration should decline was inevitable. It had been an integral part of a particular period of world economic development, and its fall marked the shift to a new phase.

The conclusions may now be summarised. Before the first world war the population of Europe (excluding Russia) was growing at the rate of about 10 per cent per decade, in spite of emigration which caused a net loss between 1900 and 1910 of over 7 millions. The war had the effect of reducing the increase between 1910 and 1920 to 2 per cent. After the war the rapid growth was temporarily resumed and, because the net loss through emigration was less than 3 millions, the rate of increase in the post-war decade was nearly equal to that of the pre-war period. There had, however, been striking regional changes. The rate of growth was lower in western Europe and higher in eastern and southern Europe than it had been before the war. Between 1930 and 1940 the population of Europe grew by about 7 per cent. That the rate was as high as this is to be explained partly by the absence of a large emigration, and partly because the abnormal age-distribution helped to keep the number of births high and the number of deaths low. The ageing of the population, however, meant that the time would come when the rate of natural increase would decline substantially and populations would cease to grow. Most of the countries settled by Europeans had by 1940 entered upon a similar demographic stage. Since many non-European populations, as well as the Russian population, were still growing as fast as that of Europe at the beginning of her period of rapid expansion, there was a pronounced tendency for Europe's share of the world population, especially western Europe's share, to decline.

COMMERCE AND INDUSTRIES

In the decade before the first world war industrial and commercial development was along paths which, though they disclosed new vistas, were familiar. In spite of some increase in tariff barriers during the 'nineties, the system of multilateral trade was not seriously impeded and the international division of labour was carried further. Between 1900 and 1913 the quantum of world trade in manufactured goods doubled and that in primary products increased by two-thirds, while the annual average export of capital from western Europe to the less highly developed countries reached about £350,000,000, an amount far in excess of that in any previous period. The process of industrialisation proceeded very fast, and world manufacturing production is estimated to have been two-thirds greater in 1913 than in 1900. This progress was widely shared. In western and central Europe there was a great expansion of industry, especially the metallurgical industries; but the most noteworthy advance occurred in the United States where, ever since 1870, the growth of manufacturing enterprise had been very rapid. Between the turn of the century and the outbreak of war the volume of United States industrial production nearly doubled, and the proportion of her occupied population engaged in manufacturing and mining rose between 1900 and 1910 from 26 per cent to 30 per cent. In Japan, India, Russia, the British Dominions and other primary producing countries large-scale industries began to appear, although even in 1914 the comparative industrial importance of these countries was still very small. These advances occurred without apparent damage to the trades of the oldest and most highly specialised of the industrial countries, the United Kingdom, and in this period her great staple industries, cotton, wool, coal, iron and steel, engineering and shipbuilding, reached new peaks of production and successfully extended their exports.

The growth in manufacturing output could not be explained wholly by the expansion of the trades which were associated with the rise of industrialism during the nineteenth century, nor by the spread of those trades over a wider range of countries. Invention and technical innovation had by this time given birth to new industries which now became prominent: the electrical generating and apparatus industries, the motor industry and certain branches of the chemical industry. These industries, as well as the new steel industry, made especially rapid progress among the United Kingdom's chief rivals. The United States took a leading part in all of them, and Germany in the electrical and chemical industries. The United Kingdom, of course, obtained a share of this new production; but her industrial life still remained specialised to the great staples of the nineteenth century.

Although all the leading industrial countries enjoyed a large absolute advance in their manufacturing output, the rate of progress naturally differed from one to another, and between 1900 and 1914 there was in fact a significant shift in industrial importance. This was not due to the industrialisation of countries that were formerly engaged mainly in primary production, but rather to the rapid growth of manufacturing in the United States. By 1913 that country, it is estimated, was responsible for over a third of the world output of manufactures, a proportion not far short of the combined shares of the United Kingdom, Germany and France.[1] The United Kingdom, as the oldest of the industrial countries, naturally lost some of her relative importance through these changes, and her proportion of world manufacturing production declined from nearly 20 per cent to 14 per cent during this period. The shares of Germany, France and Belgium also fell slightly. Thus the general advance of production was accompanied by a movement of the industrial centre of gravity from the old world to the United States; this, of course, was the continuance of a tendency which had begun before 1900.

The growth and spread of manufacturing activity, far from damaging world trade, enlarged it—not merely trade between agricultural and manufacturing countries but also trade between the great manufacturing specialists. In 1913 Germany, besides being the United Kingdom's chief competitor, was also one of her best customers, and the United Kingdom in turn bought largely of the German manufactures, notably dyestuffs, chemicals and miscellaneous consumer goods. Even within the same group of industrial products, there was mutual exchange between these nations. For instance, the United Kingdom exported pig-iron and acid steel to Germany and took in return semi-manufactured steel products. With other parts of the world, the classical pattern of international trade

[1] League of Nations, *Industrialisation and Foreign Trade* (1945), p. 13.

persisted. Further industrialisation meant a heavier demand by western and central Europe for raw materials and food, and both the old, densely settled areas of Asia and the new countries of the western hemisphere enlarged their output and exports of these commodities and became better customers of European industries. The United Kingdom, the chief exporter of manufactured goods, found her most rapidly expanding markets among the primary producers, and even when overseas industrial developments forced her to alter the destination of her exports, they aided rather than checked the growth of her trade as a whole. This was because the increased demands exercised by continental and other industrial countries on the primary producers raised the latters' demands for British exports, and at the same time permitted the United Kingdom to buy greater quantities of continental manufactures. This flourishing system of international commerce depended upon the absence of serious barriers to the movements of goods and to the transmission of funds across the exchanges. In other words, it depended upon the existence of almost unfettered opportunities for multilateral trade. Thus, the United Kingdom had a credit balance in her dealings with the primary producers, who settled their balance of indebtedness by their export surplus to the continental industrial countries and to the United States. The continental countries in turn financed their import surpluses with the primary producers and the United States by their export surpluses to the United Kingdom.

The pivot of the system was the London capital and money markets. A large part of the world's trade was financed by means of sterling bills of exchange, and the operation of the international gold standard, which provided the conditions for the smooth conduct of international trade and investment, depended to a large extent upon London's power and skill as a world financial centre. Here international debts could be set off against one another, and funds were usually available to relieve temporary disequilibria in balances of payments. The development of the resources of overseas countries had been accelerated during the nineteenth century by the export of capital from the United Kingdom. By 1900 other countries, particularly France and Germany, had also become international lenders on a large scale; but the United Kingdom still remained far in the lead. In the first decade of this century international lending reached its zenith. At this time the United Kingdom annually invested abroad a sum equivalent to her total current receipts in interest and dividends earned on her accumulated overseas capital holdings.

It was not only by providing capital that the western countries helped in the development of the world's resources, for western enterprise took a direct part in that process. British merchants, banks and industrial firms continued, as they had done in the past, to initiate and manage enterprises in manufacturing, mining and trading in India, the Far East, Africa and South America. In the same way the Dutch were actively engaged in calling into use the vast resources of the Netherlands East Indies. The Americans played the same part in the Philippines, the French in Indo-China and North Africa, and the Germans in eastern Europe. Usually, the activities of western entrepreneurs and lenders were determined by commercial motives and were not directly guided by their governments. In the same way, the economic changes that occurred in overseas countries resulted, for the most part, from the impact of western enterprise, in search of profitable investments, on the older societies. In the countries settled from Europe these developments occurred without giving rise to any serious social and political strain, for many of them formed, as it were, an agricultural hinterland of the European industrial areas from which they drew much of their population and capital. But in Asiatic countries, the old social systems were disrupted as they were drawn within the orbit of western enterprise, and immense new political forces were engendered. These were becoming apparent in the first fifteen years of the present century in China and India, as, under different political circumstances, they had become apparent in Japan a generation earlier.

In Europe itself the spread of the urban industrial civilisation had far-reaching effects on agriculture. The improvement in the standard of life led to an increased demand for animal products, and this, in association with cheap supplies of grains and oil seeds from overseas and from Russia, produced striking structural changes in European agriculture. In the west and north of Europe in particular, animal products, fruit and vegetables became more important, and this meant an intensification of farming. At the same time, the technical equipment of agriculture was improved and scientific methods extended. The results were a fall in the amount of land in fallow and an increased yield per acre of the staple crops. For this reason, in part, the Continent's dependence on overseas imports of basic foods remained comparatively small, in spite of the growth in its population and the increasing concentration of its own farmers on producing the higher-priced foods. In the years immediately before the first world war, continental Europe (excluding Russia) imported only about 12 per cent of its grain consumption, and most of these imports came from Russia. Within Europe itself there was a considerable movement of grain, especially from the Danube basin, to the industrial countries. Great Britain stood out in contrast to the Continent. Her agriculture had steadily declined after the depression of the 'seventies, and her dense population became increasingly dependent upon a wide range of foreign countries, both near and far, for its food supply. Thus, whereas continental countries had tried, on the whole successfully though at considerable cost, to reconcile industrialism with the preservation of agriculture, Great Britain in these years had carried industrial specialisation to an extreme limit. This was to the advantage of her standard of life; but it meant that on the eve of the war the number of persons engaged in agriculture represented only 8 per cent of her occupied population, compared with 35 per cent in Germany, 43 per cent in France and 22 per cent in Belgium.[1]

The major effects of the first world war on long-term economic development are sometimes considered to have been limited to the strengthening of certain tendencies perceptible in the pre-war economy and to the sharp stimulus given to changes which would otherwise have occurred by gradual adjustment. An observer of the scene in the late 'twenties would certainly have found ample evidence for this view, and as he traced the process of recovery after the economic disturbances of the immediate post-war period, his main impression was likely to have been of continuity with the pre-war world rather than of a sharp and disastrous breach with the past. This judgment would hardly be accepted today, when it is possible to perceive that the apparently successful reconstruction of the pre-war economic system during the 'twenties concealed serious damage at the foundations.

The immediate effect of the war was to cripple the economy of Europe which had played such a large part in sustaining the commercial, industrial and financial life of the world. Between 1914 and 1919 there was a steep fall in Europe's agricultural and industrial production and in her export trade, heavy damage to her economic organisation, and a loss of her wealth at home, by the destruction of capital equipment, and abroad, by the liquidation of many of her assets. In many parts of the Continent, moreover, inflation had brought about financial chaos. Outside Europe, however, there had been little physical damage. New industries had developed in many countries, such as India and Japan, which had been deprived of their normal sources of supply, and there had been a massive growth of production, both agricultural and industrial, in the United States. The return to the pre-war system depended, therefore, on the revival of Europe, and a condition of this was the restoration of financial stability. In the early 'twenties policy was directed to the re-organisation of monetary systems, and by deflation or devaluation governments tried to return to some version of the international gold standard which should bring with it stability in rates of foreign exchange. The United Kingdom led the way when she returned, in 1925, to the gold standard at the pre-war parity to the dollar, and she was followed by others. Although currency depreciation continued in Belgium, France and Poland, during the next two years these currencies also were stabilised on gold after devaluation, and by 1928 the process was virtually complete.

Besides disorganising currencies, the war had also interrupted overseas capital investment. The world economy was geared to a steady annual

---

[1] Owing to differences in the classification of the occupied population, the figures available are not strictly comparable; but they are sufficiently free from error to illustrate the broad contrasts among these countries.

outflow of lending from the older European countries, and the economic life of those countries themselves had been accommodated to their receipt of great sums as interest on past investments. In 1914 the outstanding foreign investments of the United Kingdom are estimated to have been $18,000 million, of France $8700 million, and of Germany $5600 million. The United States, though itself an overseas investor, had a net debit on capital account of some $3000 million. The war tore up this fabric of claims. European countries sold their securities to the United States and contracted new American loans. The investments in Russia, held mainly by the French, became valueless. By the end of the war the value of British foreign investments had fallen by a quarter, and of the French by more than a half. Germany had lost practically all her foreign assets. On the other hand, the United States had become a large creditor and was now the chief capital-exporting country. One of the most remarkable features of the post-war period was that European countries were able to resume capital exporting on a substantial scale. But in the early 'twenties it differed in character from pre-war investment. In the first place, the bulk of the lending was to Germany and other European countries, where the capital was used to finance reconstruction and to cover deficits in balances of payments. In the second place, much of the lending by European countries took the form of short loans to governments, especially those of eastern Europe, which could not raise long-term loans, and the lenders obtained their funds by borrowing in the United States. After 1925 capital movements began to assume their pre-war form, inasmuch as a larger proportion of the funds raised were for investment in industrial and commercial enterprises. The relative importance of the supplying countries had, however, changed. The United Kingdom had by then returned to her former position as a major overseas investor; but her lending was on a much smaller scale than before the war, and, except for a single year in the period between 1924 and 1929, she was outstripped by the United States. France was able to resume foreign investment only to a small extent, and Germany had changed from a lender into one of the chief borrowers.

The alterations in international capital movements were even more profound than appeared on the surface. It was not merely that the distribution of investment and the importance of the investing countries had changed. Long-term capital movements, though almost as large in the later 'twenties as before the war, were far less steady. For instance, the net export of capital from the United States was $500 million in 1927, over $1000 million in 1928 and only $233 million in 1929. The fluctuation in the foreign investments of the chief lending country was a source of instability, for international equilibrium in balances of payment depended upon a steady flow of capital from creditors to debtors. Further, some of the investment was not accompanied by the creation of revenue-earning assets in the receiving countries, but had been used rather for consumption purposes. Finally, international financial relations were complicated by the rise in the proportion of short-term loans which were liable to be called in if any loss of confidence occurred. The organisation of international finance had, moreover, seriously deteriorated. London, having lost its dominating position in the market for both long and short loans, now shared the leadership with New York, where traditions and experience were different. There was no longer, therefore, a concentration of decision in moments of crisis. It would seem that the apparently successful reconstruction of Europe had obscured permanent changes in underlying conditions and was not well adapted to them. In particular, the existence of serious economic difficulties in the United Kingdom, as shown by the weakness of her export trade, was hardly compatible with the resumption of her role as a great international lender. These flaws in the structure were clearly revealed with the onset of the Great Depression at the end of 1929.

Nevertheless, during the 'twenties the main troubles could be regarded as a temporary legacy of the war, or, at worst, could be attributed to structural changes which, it was reasonable to expect, could ultimately be accommodated within a progressive economic system. By 1925 the world, taken as a whole, was probably richer than it had been in 1913, for the output of foodstuffs and raw materials was then about 16 per cent above the pre-war level, while the population was only 6 per cent greater. There had, however, been a striking change in the geographical distribution of production. Europe's output of food and raw materials by 1925 had only just attained the pre-war volume, while by then Oceania and Asia had increased their output by a fifth, North America by a quarter, and South America and Africa by still more. These changes in primary production, though they might be regarded in some degree as symptoms of a permanent shift of economic power away from Europe, were for the most part a direct consequence of temporary war-time conditions. To the extent that this was so, the expansion overseas was insecurely founded and so endangered stability. This argument needs further development.

The war had led to a sharp fall in the European production of cereals (except in the United Kingdom), and output remained low for several years after 1918. Russian supplies, moreover, were no longer available for export. To meet the deficiency overseas, exporting countries, stimulated by the rise in prices, greatly enlarged their output. Wheat and barley farming was extended to semi-arid zones of the eastern Rockies, and to the northern territories of Canada. In the Argentine the pampas were ploughed, and in Australia and New Zealand the number of sheep was much increased. The rise in the output of agricultural products was brought about not only by an extension of the area devoted to the crops, but also by the increased application of capital to the land and by more scientific methods of farming. The mechanisation of agriculture, particularly the substitution of tractors for horses, was an example of this change. The result was that in the early 'twenties the grain production of the United States and Canada was 16 or 17 per cent above the annual average of 1900–13, and later in the decade more than a third greater. In the immediate post-war years grain exports were double their pre-war exports, and the grain exports from the southern hemisphere were a fifth greater. The same upward movement in output and exports was experienced by the dairy trade of New Zealand, the chilled meat trade of New Zealand and Australia and the sugar and vegetable-oil trades of several overseas countries. The output of industrial raw materials, such as cotton and wool, also expanded. There was an immense increase in rubber output during the 'twenties, and large specialised rubber plantations were developed in the East Indies. In Europe agriculture recovered slowly and it was not until 1925 that the pre-war cereal output of the Continent (excluding Russia) and the size of the livestock herds were restored. As population had increased during the previous ten years, reliance upon imports, especially upon grain, had become greater. Yet, although Russia no longer furnished substantial supplies, the growth in imports from overseas, after the initial post-war scarcity had been overcome, was less than might have been expected; for consumption of grain per head remained lower than in 1913. This was partly because of the change in diet which led to a substitution of dairy products for cereals.

As European agricultural output recovered and overseas output advanced further during the 'twenties, the world's primary producers met with difficulties. World prices of raw commodities had fallen sharply in 1920 and, compared with other prices, they remained low throughout the decade. The opening up of new low-cost areas was not accompanied by a withdrawal of high-cost producers from the market, except in the case of the United Kingdom. Consequently, agriculture began to suffer from surpluses and excessive capacity, and the attempts of governments or of organised groups of producers to meet the situation by introducing valorisation schemes or by holding supplies off the market failed, in the absence of a universal control over production, to remove the surpluses. Stocks steadily accumulated; for instance, the world's year-end stocks of wheat rose from 8·8 million tons in 1925 to 15·9 million tons in 1929. Agriculture was not the only branch of primary production to be affected by these conditions. Mining, especially coalmining, shared the same experience and for not dissimilar reasons. New sources of supply were opened up; substitutes—for instance, oil and lignite—were introduced; and economies were effected in the use of solid fuel. Throughout the world coal prices and the wages of coalminers were low, and in countries which bore the brunt of this chronic depression, particularly Great Britain, there was heavy unemployment in the industry.

In manufacturing industry experience during the first seven years of peace was much the same as in agriculture. By 1925 the world output of manufactures was probably 20 per cent above that of 1913. This advance was wholly attributable to the great expansion of production in the United States and to the development of manufacturing in countries previously in the early stages of industrialisation. The chief event of the next period, from 1925 to 1929, was the remarkable recovery of industrial production on the continent of Europe, especially in Germany, France and Russia; while in other parts of the world progress continued. On balance, in spite of the disturbances of the war years, the period between 1913 and 1929 showed a marked persistence of previous trends. This applies particularly to the increase in the relative importance of the United States as an industrial producer. In the late 'twenties that country was estimated to have been responsible for nearly two-fifths of the world output of manufactured goods. Other overseas countries, late starters in industry, Japan, Canada and India, had also increased their share of the output, although that share was still quite small.

These relative changes were at the expense of the older industrial countries of Europe, especially the United Kingdom, whose industrial importance diminished in comparison not only with the United States but also with other European countries. The most obvious symptom of this failure on the part of the United Kingdom to keep pace with the advance of industry elsewhere was the chronic depression in the staple trades which began after the collapse of the post-war boom in 1920. This depression in turn could be ascribed to the failure of those trades to maintain their export markets. The world demand for the types of goods on which Great Britain specialised rose comparatively little during the post-war decade, and because of the growth of domestic production in the importing countries and of successful competition from other exporters, the United Kingdom's share of the trade in these goods declined. The depression among the primary producers to whom Great Britain sent a high proportion of her exports compelled them to seek cheaper sources of supply, to reduce their total purchases, or to manufacture for themselves. India, the major British textile market before 1914, had substantially raised her own output of cotton goods and at the same time bought large quantities from Japan. Again, the substitution of oil for coal in the shipping trade damaged the British coal exports which depended largely on that source of demand. At the same time, the United Kingdom failed to obtain in compensation an adequate share either in the production or in the exports of the newer manufactures in which the greatest developments took place during the 'twenties. For instance, the world output of motor vehicles grew from about half a million in 1913 to over $6\frac{1}{4}$ millions in 1929, and this led to the extension of numerous industries that provided materials, parts or fuel for the motor manufacturers and the users of their products.

Motor transport was among the most important innovations of the first few decades of the century. It was accompanied by widespread changes in the structure of demand, and it called into being a variety of new industries while it damaged several old ones. The United States took the major share of this trade, and in 1929 that country was responsible for over four-fifths of the world output of motor vehicles and for most of the export trade. The United Kingdom produced only one-tenth of the American output and her export trade was comparatively small. In some other new industries, such as electrical apparatus and rayon, the United Kingdom did not display the same superiority as she had done in the older staples to which her industrial life was still specialised. It was these new industries, however, which were engaging a rapidly increasing share of the world's industrial resources and which were contributing lavishly to world trade. The result was that while international trade as a whole was considerably greater in 1928–9 than it had been before 1914, and while continental Europe had by then recovered its former place in that trade, the volume of British exports was about a tenth less.

The weakness of the export trade and the strain of adjustment to a less favourable economic environment did not prevent the United Kingdom from sharing in the rise in real income per head. In all the advanced industrial countries, and even in some others, e.g. Japan, real income per head in 1929 was well above that in 1913. Increased productivity in industry and the improvement in terms of trade with primary producers were mainly responsible for this advance. The rise in income altered the structure of demand and so affected the occupational distribution of populations in the industrial countries. The changes in the relative importance of different manufacturing industries has already been referred to. An even more important consequence was the expansion of industries that provided services rather than goods—entertainments, catering, professional and personal services of all kinds. As personal incomes rose, a larger part of them was spent on these services, and all western countries saw the growth in the proportion of the occupied population engaged in industries which, in Adam Smith's sense, were 'non productive'.

The economic position in 1929 was, on the surface, satisfactory. Currency stability had everywhere been restored. Agricultural and industrial production and foreign trade had risen above their pre-war levels. If Europe's position in the world economy had receded before the advance of the United States, this could be regarded as a continuation of a pre-war tendency. And Europe had regained in fact much of her old importance, while the world economic system which she had created seemed to have become adjusted to the new circumstances. It was easy for a contemporary observer to miss the deeper changes that had shaken the foundations of economic society. These were revealed with the onset of the Great Depression which began in the autumn of 1929. Everywhere prices, output and trade declined rapidly and steeply; unemployment rose to levels never previously reached; international financial obligations were repudiated; and in most countries policy became concerned primarily with insulating the national economy from the effects of the world-wide slump and with finding local remedies for the general disaster. When in the autumn of 1931 a financial crisis occurred, the achievements of the previous decade in the field of monetary stabilisation were quickly swept away, and the international gold standard was destroyed.

The steepness of the fall in prices between 1929 and the early months of 1933, when the lowest levels were reached, is clearly illustrated by the movements of wholesale price index numbers. In the United States the Bureau of Labour's Index fell from 100 in 1929 to 63 in March 1933, and in the United Kingdom the Board of Trade's Index fell in the same period from 100 to 72. It was on primary products that the incidence of the depression was heaviest. This is illustrated below by the gold prices in January 1933 of certain commodities, expressed as a percentage of their prices in January 1929:

Wheat	42	Rubber	13	Timber	55
Rice	41	Copper	29	Linseed oil	45
Wool	22	Sugar	50	Coffee	41
Cotton	34	Tin	47		
Silk	28	Coal	71		

Countries that specialised in these products suffered a corresponding decline in their incomes and were faced with serious disequilibria in their balance of payments. They were obliged to reduce their imports of manufactured goods, with depressing effects on the industrial countries, and to abandon the servicing of their foreign debts. The output of primary products was also affected. It is true that the production of agricultural goods did not decline; but the output of certain industrial raw materials, especially minerals, dropped sharply. This was because the organisation of mineral production, in contrast with that of agriculture, makes it possible to contract output in response to a fall in prices. In the industrial countries the depression showed itself chiefly in a heavy decline in production and a rise in unemployment. It has been estimated that in 1932 manufacturing production in the world as a whole (excluding the U.S.S.R.) was about one-third less in volume than in 1929. The extent of the decline varied widely from country to country. In the United States the index of industrial production for 1932 stood at 54, in Germany 53 and in Canada 58, whereas it was 84 for the United Kingdom, 69 for France and 98 for Japan.[1] This disparity could be explained both by the differing extent to which countries had been responsive to the preceding boom and also by their varied success in the use of measures for insulating themselves from the general depression, often at the expense of others. The

---

[1] Production in 1929 equals 100 in each case.

33

course of unemployment in the several countries is difficult to compare because of differences in definition. But in almost all the industrial countries the rise was very steep. In March 1932 the unemployment figures for the United Kingdom, United States and Germany were 2,800,000, 13,700,000 and 5,600,000 respectively.

International trade and investment were thrown into disorder. In the third quarter of 1932 the volume of world trade was only two-thirds of the quarterly average for 1929, and the fall in the exports of the industrial countries was particularly steep. In 1932 British exports were only 63 per cent of those of 1929, American exports 53 per cent, and French and German exports only 59 per cent. The industrial countries were, however, able to maintain their imports of primary products at a relatively high level, chiefly because of the disproportionately steep decline in the prices of those imports. This mitigated the effects of the depression on the real incomes of such industrial countries as were large buyers of raw materials and food. It has been estimated that the real income per person in work for the United Kingdom was nearly as great in 1932 as in 1929, and that even if the unemployed are included, the average real income per head was only 10 per cent less.[1] The more favourable terms of trade thus to some extent offset for the industrial areas the damage caused by the depression; but this meant, of course, that the specialised primary producers had to sustain a crushing burden.

The collapse of world trade was accompanied by a virtual cessation of international lending. The flow of capital from creditor to debtor countries dried up, and the financial crisis that came to a head in the autumn of 1931 was largely the result of efforts by various countries to increase the liquidity of their resources. This led to a withdrawal of the funds invested on short term in London and drove the United Kingdom off the gold standard in September 1931. The subsequent fall in the sterling rates of exchange intensified the depression outside the United Kingdom and brought about exchange depreciation in a succession of countries. In 1933 even the United States, though remaining on gold, revalued her currency downwards. The monetary systems which had been so carefully re-built in the 'twenties were thus swept away.

Recovery, which set in after 1933, went at a different pace and took different forms from country to country. Its course was affected everywhere by acts of policy designed to deal with disequilibria in balances of payments, to control output or prices in the interests of particular groups of producers, or to create additional employment in particular regions. In the United States efforts were made to raise prices by a reflationary monetary policy, by great projects of public works, by curbing competition through the Industrial Codes instituted under the National Recovery Act, and by removing surplus capacity by schemes introduced under the

[1] Cf. Colin Clark, *National Income and Outlay*, p. 208.

Agricultural Adjustment Act. In Germany and Japan rearmament played a major role in economic recovery, and in the United Kingdom cartelisation was officially encouraged, or required, in order to lift the incomes of the more seriously depressed groups of producers, as in the cotton industry, coalmining, the iron and steel industry and agriculture. In the chief primary producing countries organisations of producers, often supported by governments, assumed control over marketing, and this was sometimes associated with schemes for destroying excessive capacity or stocks. Many of the so-called rationalisation schemes in industry had a similar purpose, notably those introduced into the British cotton-spinning and shipbuilding industries. In the sphere of international economic relations government intervention was widely extended, and obstructions to the movement of goods and to the remittance of funds across the exchanges became formidable. The raising of the United States tariff in 1930 made it more difficult for debtor countries to settle their accounts with the chief creditor. Elsewhere, import duties were supplemented by quantitative restrictions of various kinds. The flow of trade between countries was often influenced strongly by bi-lateral agreements which set out the types and quantities of goods to be exchanged by the parties over a given period. In Germany and in some other countries, control over foreign trade was assisted by the practice of varying official rates of exchange for the currency according to the type of transaction. This was merely an extreme example of methods of exchange control that were very widely practised. One great country carried this state control of economic life much farther than the others. The U.S.S.R., working with a succession of central plans, sought to govern the whole course of its economic development and foreign trade.

The course of economic recovery was deeply influenced by these autarkical or self-regarding policies, which naturally altered the distribution of resources within each country. Old high-cost industries, which would have declined under the stress of international competition, were maintained or enlarged, and at the same time new industries were created which could be justified only because they were held to serve a political or strategic end. Certain branches of the British iron and steel industry provide an example of the former; the industries established in Germany and elsewhere to provide substitutes for imported strategic materials, such as the synthetic rubber and the staple fibre industries, are examples of the latter. The volume of industrial production as a whole, so far as it can be adequately measured in these circumstances, recovered very slowly from the depths of the depression; but by 1937, the best year of the 'thirties, it was probably one-quarter greater than in 1929. This improvement was very unevenly spread. In the United States, France, Italy and Belgium industrial production in 1937 was still less than in 1929, while in Germany, the United Kingdom and in Sweden the pre-depression output had been surpassed, by 17 per cent, 24 per cent and 49 per cent respectively. The most striking advances occurred in certain of the newer industrial countries, particularly the U.S.S.R. and Japan; indeed, the quickened pace of industrialisation in the U.S.S.R. was the outstanding feature of the decade in this sphere. The effect of these changes on the distribution of manufacturing output throughout the world is significant. Up to 1929 the importance of the United States as an industrial centre had grown from decade to decade and, as we have already seen, by that year she was probably responsible for 40 per cent of the world's output of manufactures. The sudden rise of Russian production in the 'thirties, accompanied as it was by stagnation in the United States, brought the American proportion down to about 30 per cent.

The production of primary products, while it fluctuated less between 1929 and 1939 than that of manufactured goods, grew comparatively little. This was particularly true of foodstuffs; for the output of industrial raw materials, especially minerals, responded after the middle 'thirties to the increased demand from industry. World prices of these goods recovered very slowly from the depths to which they had descended during the depression, and even in 1937 the ratio of the price of foodstuffs to that of manufactured goods was some 10 per cent lower than that of 1929, and after then it worsened. Industrial countries, therefore, continued to enjoy favourable terms of trade *vis-à-vis* their suppliers of primary goods, and this helped the large buyers in the world market to improve their standard of life. But for many countries world prices of raw commodities were no longer so relevant to the terms of international exchange as they had formerly been. Policies of agricultural protection were adopted or extended in varying degrees by most industrial countries during this period, while sources of supply were frequently determined not by price differences but by the provisions of bi-lateral treaties. Hence, industrial consumers were obliged to pay higher prices for their food than would have been necessary under a regime of free imports. This applied particularly to Germany, but the United Kingdom and other importing countries were affected in the same way, though not to the same extent.

Commercial policy during the 'thirties had important consequences for the volume and the nature of international trade. Recovery in world production was not matched by a corresponding recovery in world trade, and even in 1937 the volume of trade was barely equal to that of 1929. This was in sharp contrast with developments in the past when the advance in production and the advance in trade had proceeded *pari passu*. It is true that the disparity during the 'thirties was in part attributable to the fact that the country in which industrial growth was most rapid concerned itself very little with foreign trade. But this is not the whole explanation. The contrast between advancing industrial output and stagnating commerce was present almost everywhere. In the United Kingdom, for example, the increase of 24 per cent in the volume of industrial production between 1929 and 1937 was accompanied by a fall in the volume of her exports of no less than 16 per cent. The constituents of world trade had also altered. In 1937 the quantum of trade in foodstuffs was about 7 per cent below the 1929 level and in manufactured goods 14 per cent below, whereas in raw materials it was 12 per cent above. The explanation lies in the fact that the increased national self-sufficiency which was secured in industrial countries by the protection given to the food producers, and in agricultural countries by that given to manufacturers, could not be extended, without great loss, to raw materials, many of which came from specialist producing areas. Rearmament in Europe also contributed to this demand for industrial raw materials. The changes in the geographical distribution of foreign trade were as significant as those in its composition. Before the depression the United Kingdom had an import surplus both with Europe and with the United States, while the countries of the British empire in which the United Kingdom had heavy investments had an export surplus with those regions. The servicing of the empire's debts to the United Kingdom and the settlement of the United Kingdom's import surplus were thus achieved by a multilateral transfer. The depression shook this system. The empire was not able to earn as much as formerly by selling its materials in Europe and the United States, while manufactured goods from Europe were shut out of the British market. The result was that bilateral exchanges between the empire and the United Kingdom increased greatly in importance. The Ottawa Agreements of 1932 helped to strengthen this tendency.

Bilateralism and exchange control were fatal to the resumption of foreign investment of the old type, for these practices hindered the transference of capital yields and made investment abroad precarious. Throughout the 'thirties international lending, except where political or strategic considerations were important, was on a very small scale. Apart from the increase in risk, the economic condition of the two chief lenders was very unfavourable to a resumption of large outward capital movements. The United Kingdom, it appeared, had come to the end of her great career in foreign lending. After 1920 the weakness of her export trade had made it difficult for her to resume her traditional role, and whereas before 1914 she had invested annually about the same amount as she received in interest and dividends on her outstanding holdings, in the late 'twenties her capital exports were only about two-fifths of her receipts from these sources. In the 'thirties she faced a deficit on current account because of the further decline in her exports and the reduction of her earnings on existing foreign investments. On balance, between 1930 and 1939 the United Kingdom imported capital, and the same is true even of the United States and of other countries that had formerly been important capital exporters. There was no place in the autarkical world of the 'thirties for foreign lending of the old type, and it was reasonable to expect that investors should try to liquidate their outstanding investments even at a loss.

In spite of the economic disorder, technical progress continued. Improved methods were introduced into the older industries, such as the mining, textile and metal trades, and these resulted in a rise in the quantity of output per person employed in them. Many of the industries which first achieved some importance in the early years of the century had come, by the 'thirties, to occupy leading positions in the economies of the chief manufacturing countries. Among these industries were the motor, electrical, chemical, and rayon manufactures, together with many auxiliary trades that served them or used their products. Other new industries, such as the aircraft and light alloy industries, were becoming substantial. The autarkical policies of the 'thirties stimulated the development of some of these new trades, such as the synthetic-textiles industry, and preparation for war brought about the enlargement of the aircraft and synthetic-oil industries. Technical progress is not, of course, to be confused with an increase in economic welfare, and some of the new industries made little contribution to that end. On balance, however, there can be no doubt that the advance in technical efficiency was accompanied by improvements in material well-being, and that it was, indeed, a major cause of them. For instance, although there were several factors at work, the rise in the British standard of life during the inter-war period was, in part, made possible by the substantial increase that took place in productivity; industrial output per man-hour in Great Britain was probably about 50 per cent greater in 1938 than it had been just before the first world war. In some other countries the advance was at an even higher rate. This meant, in a comparison between British and American industrial productivity, the widening of an already large gap, and recent estimates suggest that on the eve of the second world war output per man-year in manufacturing industry was more than twice as high in the United States as in Great Britain.[1] For certain other countries in which productivity had formerly been lower than in Great Britain, the gap was narrowed during the inter-war years. This disparity in rates of improvement explains some of the United Kingdom's economic difficulties in that period.

The world's inhabitants, or at any rate those who made up western society, were certainly better off on the eve of the second world war than they had been in the first decade of the century. Economic instability had not meant economic stagnation. Whether real income per head was higher in 1938 than in 1929 is more difficult to judge. It is estimated that the quantum of manufacturing production rose during that period much

[1] Cf. L. Rostas, *Comparative Productivity in British and American Industry, passim.* Comparisons of productivity involve some intricate statistical and economic problems; but when full allowance has been made for the qualifications to which such comparisons must be subject, the correctness of this broad conclusion is not disturbed.

faster than world population and that the quantum of primary production, though not of foodstuffs, rose at a slightly faster rate. But the resulting improvements in the standard of life were not evenly shared, and the statistical conclusions themselves are difficult to evaluate. In the United Kingdom there was certainly a substantial rise in real income per head which was made possible partly by the improvements in productivity and partly by exceptionally favourable terms of trade. It must be remembered, however, in any comparison with former times, that in this decade the United Kingdom had not merely ceased to export capital, but was on balance a net importer. In the United States, where 1929 had been a very prosperous year and where the subsequent depression proved to be more intractable than in Europe, real income per head probably increased very little. In many of the specialist raw-material producing countries the position had worsened. In Germany and Japan, where income per head certainly grew considerably, the increased output included a large volume of munitions and strategic materials. In France there was probably a deterioration. The estimates on which these judgments rest are open to criticism, and the whole question of the measurement of changes in material welfare is beset with difficulties. What can be said with assurance about the period from 1929 to 1939 is that many of the benefits that were conferred by improvements in technique and productivity were thrown away by failure to solve the economic problems of the time, especially the problems of economic adaptation, unemployment and international economic relationships (see also ch. III).

The second world war found the economies of the world very differently organised from those of 1914, and for many of the belligerents the step from a peace economy to a war economy was a short one. Several countries, Germany, Japan and Russia, had been creating a war-preparation economy for some years before the outbreak, and in them a high degree of centralised control already existed. Elsewhere the old liberal economic system had been profoundly modified by government intervention during the 'thirties. Nevertheless, the changes brought by the war were immense. The mobilisation of resources went much further than in 1914–18 and governmental direction of the economies was more detailed and comprehensive. Among all European countries the rationing of consumer goods was extended to all the necessities of life, and the supplies of other peace-time goods were steeply reduced in order to free resources for war. Government control over production everywhere extended to agriculture, mining, transport and to most branches of manufacturing industry, as well as to foreign trade, prices and the use of materials. The most influential of all controls was, of course, that over manpower, and among the chief belligerents the whole population of working age, including women, was subject to direction. In the United Kingdom the government's expenditure in 1944 represented over three-fifths of the national income. As in the first world war certain industries in all countries greatly expanded—the aircraft, engineering, metallurgical and chemical industries—while others, textile, clothing and consumer goods in general, declined. New capital equipment was created in the munitions trades, but elsewhere both fixed and working capital was run down, leaving serious problems for the reconstruction period. Since the content of foreign trade was determined wholly by the needs of war, it ceased to bear any resemblance to its peacetime structure. In the case of the United Kingdom, for example, exports sank to one-third of their pre-war volume, and imports were financed, first by the sale of overseas assets and by foreign borrowing, and later under the United States Lend-Lease programme.

By 1945 Europe no longer had a viable economy; that is to say, it could not maintain for its people a standard of life approximate to that of 1939 without help from outside. With capital assets at home destroyed or depreciated, with industries disorganised and the production of many essential goods low, she lacked the capacity to import what was needed for re-equipping herself and for feeding her population. A large part of her foreign assets, especially British foreign assets, had been sold to finance the war, and she had passed from being the world's creditor to being a debtor. At the same time, the economy of Germany, on which had hinged the economies of many neighbouring states, was in ruins, and trade between eastern and western Europe was impeded by the political division of the Continent into the regions within the sphere of the western Allies and those over which Russian and communist influence had triumphed. Economic change and political disorder in other parts of the world (for instance, in South-East Asia) deprived western Europe not merely of a source of raw materials, but also of a means by which, through the processes of triangular trade, she had been able to finance her import surplus from the United States. For Asia herself the war had been as great a disaster as for Europe. Japan's economy had been brought almost to a standstill; China, including Manchuria, was in economic and political chaos; and many other Asiatic countries were unable, because of political upheavals, to resume production or trade on a pre-war scale. South America and the British dominions had escaped physical damage, and their industrial development had been greatly stimulated by the war. Even there, however, a continuance of prosperity was threatened by the economic disorders among their former customers and suppliers, and by the weakened financial position of countries with which their economic development had been closely linked. The main oasis in the desert of economic distress was the United States. That country, unlike the other belligerents, had been able to create huge armies and munitions industries, to turn herself into the chief source of supply for the allied war effort, and yet to maintain her standard of life. This was possible through the immense increase in production in American industry and agriculture, and through calling into employment the large reserve of resources unused during the 'thirties.

The second world war thus had the effect of carrying much farther the tendency for an increasing proportion of industrial production to be concentrated in the United States, a tendency that had been strong during the first three decades of the century and had been interrupted during the 'thirties. The shift of economic power to America, which was perhaps the most important single tendency of the twentieth century, was confirmed. It had been mainly at the expense of Europe which, between 1939 and 1945, suffered an absolute as well as a relative decline. Whether this is to be regarded as permanent cannot yet be decided. Europe showed great powers of recuperation after the first world war, and the changes in her position during the inter-war period were less decisive than once seemed likely. But she could then call to her aid favourable factors on which she can no longer count. She could rely, for the settlement of her adverse trading balance with the rest of the world, upon income received from overseas investments built up in the years of her supremacy, and her recovery was assisted by the very favourable terms on which she was able to buy food and raw materials from abroad. These advantages were enjoyed particularly by the United Kingdom as the largest buyer of overseas materials and as the chief beneficiary from foreign investments; but the continental countries shared in these benefits, both directly, and also indirectly through the processes of multilateral trade. The second world war destroyed both these buttresses of Europe's economic structure. Her investment income was no longer sufficient to make a substantial contribution towards meeting the deficit on her commodity trade, while the terms of trade had moved sharply against the industrial countries. These changes occurred at a time when, because of the condition of many of Europe's former suppliers, she became more than ever dependent upon imports from the western hemisphere. Adaptation to these changed circumstances created intricate problems not merely for Europe but for the countries which inherited her former functions and position. The transference of economic leadership to the United States, which is the outstanding feature of twentieth-century economic history, would doubtless have come about even if war had been avoided. But the two great wars both accelerated the movement and also, through the disorganisation which they caused, reduced the capacity of the world economy to adjust itself smoothly to it. After 1945 the strains of adjustment became so great as to threaten not merely the reconstruction of Europe, but also material progress in general and, with it, the whole system of economic relationships which arose in the period when Europe was an education to the world.

CHAPTER III

THE TRANSFORMATION OF SOCIAL LIFE

THE first half of the twentieth century brought far-reaching changes in the ways of life and standards of living of all European peoples. This transformation was so vast and so complex that it is possible to explore only its main aspects. The four aspects selected are the growth of industrialisation and urbanisation, with the consequent changes in standards of living and habits of life; the spread of democratic ideas and organisations, most fundamentally universal suffrage, general education and social services, and the quest for greater 'social justice'; the development of labour organisations and parliamentary socialist movements; and the rise and fall of the revolutionary movements of communism and fascism. Although these four aspects of social change may be distinguished for purposes of examination, it is their interaction and correlation that are especially important. They are but four of the larger facets of the same polyhedron; they are carved by the action of similar historical forces; all involve a like process of interplay between human will and aspirations and the new conditions of concentrated power and violence which characterise the twentieth century (see ch. I). They are infinitely complex, varying in significance from one decade to another and from one country to another. Yet the complexity is reducible to some kind of pattern, and that pattern reveals something of the nature and development of European civilisation.

The spread of industrialisation in twentieth-century Europe is described elsewhere (chs. II and XVIII). The new phase of industrial change which began towards the end of the nineteenth century and lasted until the beginning of the atomic age in the middle of the twentieth century, originated in the United States and Germany. Its main features were the techniques of 'mass production', subdivision and specialisation of the processes of production within one great 'assembly line' comprising workers, materials, and machines; the development of oil and of electricity as new sources of power for manufacture and transport; and the production in chemical laboratories of new materials such as oil, rubber, dyes, rayons and plastics.

When the century began Germany led the world in the chemical and electrical industries. The United States, also rapidly developing these industries, led in the techniques of mass production. Just as the steam engine had made coal and steel the bases of the old industrial revolution, so the internal combustion engine and the diesel engine made petroleum and oil vital for the new industrial revolution. Britain, France and Belgium, which had been pioneers in the first, were confronted with

42

problems of modernisation and adjustment in the second. Since coal, steel, engineering and ship-building remained of great importance, Britain still ranked high among the industrial powers. But there came into existence, within a single generation, a civilisation built on the automobile, aviation, the tractor, the power-station, and the laboratory (see ch. v). Soviet Russia based its industrial development on these foundations. Hydro-electric power helped to free countries like France, Italy and Switzerland from reliance upon coal and oil in which their natural resources were deficient. The balance of economic power in the world shifted rapidly in favour of Germany and Japan, and of large continental areas that were rich in the new foundations of wealth, especially the United States and the Soviet Union; though older industrial countries, such as the United Kingdom and France, still enjoyed great advantages.

The total result was a vast enrichment of Europe's productive capacities which made possible a general and rapid rise in the standard of living. Without the benefits of the new technologies European civilisation could hardly have survived the extravagance of two great wars within a generation. They enabled Europe to recover with remarkable speed from war's devastations and dislocations. By 1928 the belligerent countries were more prosperous than they had been in 1913; by 1950 they had mostly exceeded their industrial and agricultural production of 1929. The new abundance made poverty seem unnecessary and therefore more intolerable, and was itself a stimulus to social reforms. It was the bedrock of all social change.

The speed of change varied greatly as between different countries, and its variations had important social consequences. At the beginning of the century Great Britain retained her position, won during the nineteenth century, as the world's most highly industrialised country. In 1910 the Board of Trade estimated that whereas 48 per cent of the population of England and Wales were engaged in manufacturing and mining, only 40 per cent of Germans, 33 per cent of Frenchmen and 30 per cent of Americans were so employed. But already Germany and the United States were fast overtaking Britain's lead in total industrial production, and they produced goods which had been among Britain's chief exports— coal, iron and steel, and ships. The spread of industrialism brought closer economic interlocking of the nations, and each came to depend more on imports for essential elements in its economic life. By 1914 Great Britain imported four-fifths of its wheat, France a third of its coal, Germany nearly all its wool. On the other hand, such interdependence was accompanied by more intense commercial and colonial rivalries between nations, and by the dangers that domestic dislocation and unemployment would be caused by forces outside the control of national governments. Mass unemployment, destined to be one of the greatest threats to social stability in modern Europe, first made its appearance in modern guise in Britain at the beginning of the century. William Beveridge produced his pioneer study of the problem in 1909. In England, in the decade before 1914, the percentage of unemployment was estimated to vary between 3 in the best years and 8 in the worst. Persistent unemployment on a considerable scale could now threaten national prosperity, the standard of living of the workers, and the social order itself.

In 1914 European economies to a large extent hinged upon Britain and Germany. British exports went almost as much to Europe as to the countries of the commonwealth. As J. M. Keynes later pointed out, 'We sent more exports to Germany than to any other country in the world except India, and we bought more from her than from any other country in the world except the United States'.[1] Germany was the best customer of Russia, Austria-Hungary, Italy, Switzerland, Belgium, Holland and Norway; and the third best customer of France. Every country to the east of her in Europe did more than a quarter of its whole trade with her. Russia was rapidly becoming linked with the economies of western and central Europe. Her heavy industries and railways were built largely with the use of foreign capital. By 1913 she was producing half as much pig-iron as France, and nearly two-thirds as much steel. She, too, suffered an industrial depression, especially in her heavy industries, at the beginning of the century. It lasted until 1908. But from 1910 onwards her industrialisation proceeded at a rate of progress comparable with that later planned by the Soviet government. The amount of coal mined in the Donetz basin doubled between 1905 and 1913, and by 1910 Russia's mileage of railways exceeded Germany's. Even so, eight out of ten Russians still lived on farming and their methods remained backward.

After the first world war, the economic power of the United States in the world overshadowed that both of Germany and of Great Britain. Japan, too, appeared as a new industrial power of formidable strength. For some years Soviet Russia was almost cut off economically from the rest of Europe. She endured famine and immense social distress, followed by a great experiment in economic planning designed to expand her industries and reorganise her agriculture (see ch. XVIII). The economies of eastern Europe underwent a dramatic change after 1918. Political emancipation (see ch. XVI) was accompanied by a social revolution based on breaking up the estates of big landed proprietors into small peasant holdings. More than three-quarters of the population of Roumania, Bulgaria, and Yugoslavia were peasants; Austria, Czechoslovakia, and the Baltic states all felt the influence of the same movement. This 'green revolution', distinct from the 'red revolution' of Russia, gave a new predominance to small-scale farming by owner-cultivators.

But it was a social more than an economic revolution. Less successful 'land reforms' in Hungary and Poland left big landed estates predominant. Whatever was gained in political independence and social emancipation

[1] J. M. Keynes, *The Economic Consequences of the Peace* (1919), p. 15.

was partially lost by the raising of new impediments to more intensive and efficient farming. By 1939 the output per acre in Roumania and Yugoslavia was still less than a third of that in Denmark, and less than a fifth of that in Switzerland. In eastern Europe farming was still mostly the growing of grain and other foodstuffs for the family's own consumption, plus a small surplus for the market: in Denmark and Switzerland it was mostly intensive pig-keeping and dairy-farming for sale in urban markets. The rapid increase of population in proportion to the amount of land available, the backward methods of small peasant farming, the tariff barriers erected by the new national states, the distractions of corrupt politics, all helped to keep down the standard of living in eastern Europe. Investigations which the League of Nations carried out in the Danubian countries in 1936–7 revealed a prevalence of diseases due to malnutrition. Infant mortality rates were three or four times higher than those of western Europe. Tuberculosis was a scourge. Housing was generally bad, and by western standards often appalling. In such conditions new democratic constitutions did not long survive, and unstable governments fell prey to extremist tendencies and to foreign influences, whether fascist or communist. By 1939 democratic governments survived in most of the dozen countries of the world that had the highest income per head of the population—and hardly anywhere else.

Industrialisation in eastern Europe continued throughout the period, and in Czechoslovakia, Poland and Hungary it reached important dimensions. But it was often on an unsound basis. Artificial industries were created by high protective tariffs at the expense of the consumer, or on foreign capital for purposes quite unrelated to the economic needs of the country and to its native resources of materials and labour. Industrialisation advanced most in those areas of Czechoslovakia and Poland where industry and trade had been firmly established before 1914, as in Bohemia and Galicia, and where a strong experienced middle class already existed. There both middle classes and industrial workers enjoyed better standards of living, but were exposed to economic depressions comparable with their counterparts in western Europe. In the same three industrialised states of Czechoslovakia, Poland and Hungary, trade unions prospered in the skilled trades of textiles, metallurgy and printing. They maintained standards of living for their members largely at the expense of the unskilled and the peasants. All three countries suffered serious unemployment in the Great Depression. Elsewhere in eastern Europe trade unions were weak and were constantly repressed, often with considerable violence. The Great Depression in Poland, Hungary and Roumania widened the gap between rich and poor peasants and checked such developments as improved education. One consequence of the growth of population and the spread of industrialisation was an increase in the number and size of towns. This naturally varied as much as did the degree of industrialisation: but cities like Athens, Salonica, Sofia, Belgrade, Bucharest, Budapest, Lodz and Warsaw grew greatly in size. Many towns, especially in the Balkans, were subject to a periodic influx of peasants as unskilled workers. This had the effect of depressing industrial wages for all but the most skilled workers.

Everywhere industrialisation bred big towns. The uprooting of people from village life and rural pursuits, their concentration into urban areas and their subjection to the disciplines of factory life, were constant features of twentieth-century change. More precisely it meant, in a period of rapidly expanding population, that the numbers engaged in agriculture frequently remained static or dwindled, while the increased numbers were almost totally absorbed into expanding industries and created the new towns. In Germany, for example, the number engaged in agriculture in 1914 was little more than in 1850, although the population of these territories had grown meanwhile from 35 millions to 65 millions. If communities of 2000 and more are classed as urban, three Germans out of every five lived in towns by 1910, as compared with only two in every five a generation earlier. The extent of large-scale urbanisation may be roughly indicated by the number of towns with more than 100,000 inhabitants each, and by the proportions of the whole population living in such towns. By the later 1940's, as compared with the early 1880's, the population of London, Glasgow, Amsterdam, Vienna, Naples doubled or nearly doubled; that of Birmingham and Lisbon nearly trebled; that of Madrid, Hamburg and Milan grew fourfold; that of Barcelona, Rome and Prague grew more than fivefold. In 1951 more than 38 per cent of the population of the United Kingdom lived in 71 towns of more than 100,000 inhabitants. In Italy 20 per cent lived in 25 big towns; in France less than 14 per cent lived in 22 big towns. In Germany, whereas in 1910 there were 48 such towns housing more than a fifth of the population, by 1951 there were 56 housing 28 per cent. (In 1840 there had been only two such cities in Germany.)

Towns of this size usually exclude all primarily agricultural centres: they are almost entirely industrial centres, large ports and capital cities. People living in such communities enjoy all the amenities but incur all the hazards of modern urban civilisation. They are subject to many different mass-pressures. They are the first to feel the impact of an industrial slump and unemployment. They are most at the mercy of processes of inflation and of administrative control. At the same time, they are also more susceptible to forces of mass-suggestion and social unrest, more open to new ideas and better able to make effective organised protests against bad conditions than their country cousins. Townspeople, because they are more exposed to the fluctuations of the modern economic system, are also more likely to support ideas and movements which can provide them with greater security against the hardships of such fluctuations. It is these urban masses in twentieth-century Europe which have given the main momentum to movements of social reform, as well as to the building of labour organisations, trades unions, and socialist parties. They have also been the main seed-beds of movements of social unrest and revolutionary violence. There have been few peasant revolts in Europe in the twentieth century.

It is probable that before the first world war the disparities between town life and country life were sharper than after the second world war, despite the growth meanwhile of still larger urban and suburban areas. Until the appearance of cheap and fast road transport and the popularisation of radio, the countryman was often virtually cut off from the amenities of the town in his daily life. Even the railways did not provide the great ease of movement which came with the internal combustion engine; and the cinema, unlike radio and television, was an amusement mainly of the towns. The tendency since the 1920's has been for agriculture to become more mechanised and for the villager to share more easily in the material facilities of the towns: for him to become more assimilated, thereby, to the outlooks and patterns of behaviour previously peculiar to townsmen. At the same time many things have conspired to take the townsman more into the countryside: the growth of annual holidays with pay and of cheap rail and road transport; a nostalgic 'return to nature'; the cult of the bicycle in France, of the *Wandervogel* in Germany, of youth hostels in Britain, of the Boy Scout movement everywhere; the upheavals and evacuations of war; the institution, even, of compulsory national service in peace-time, which almost every continental country had established by 1914 and which Britain accepted after 1939. Whether the final effect was to impoverish or to enrich rural life, it certainly helped to soften the differences between rural and urban populations and to create still greater homogeneity in national life. Where, as in France or Spain, or in much of eastern Europe, massive urbanisation was comparatively rare and the distinctive interests and methods of agriculture were more tenacious, disparities between rural and urban people remained both clear and significant. It is doubtful whether the impressive increase in international travel during these years greatly affected the matter. Travel across frontiers, whether for business or pleasure, is mainly between large towns, between ports and airports, or directed towards 'tourist centres'.

The consequences of both industrialisation and urbanisation for the standard of living of Europeans are difficult to measure in detail, though they are obviously of great importance in general. No completely satisfactory test of 'standard of living' has been devised. Real wages are little guide in a rural society where a large part of income is in kind; or in a highly developed welfare state where a large part of real income takes the form of free social services; or in a period when married women are increasingly taking employment. Such vital matters as the general standard of housing and the kinds of food customarily eaten must enter into any comparison of standards of living in different countries, or even in one country at different times. So, too, the frequency of unemployment or of under-employment, and the degree of security against sickness and old age, are important components of any realistic criterion of well-being. Above all, since a standard of living is of no use without life itself, such data as the infant death rate and expectation of life are useful indications of the medical services available, conditions of housing and nutrition, and the amount of human suffering endured.[1]

Measured by the tests of vital statistics, the United Kingdom made great and steady progress. In 1900–2 infants under one year old died at the rate of 142 per thousand; in 1920–2 at the average annual rate of 82; in 1930–2 at the rate of 67; in 1938–9 at the rate of 54.[2] By the same test France made equally rapid progress but at a lower standard. Her infant death rate averaged 161 per thousand in 1896–1900; 97 in 1920–4; 80 in 1930–4, and 71 in 1935–9. Although it was as high as 112 again in the critical year 1945, it more than halved (to 52) by 1950. In both countries the most striking improvement came after 1945. In the United Kingdom it fell from 49 in 1945 to only 31 in 1950. In 1950 Sweden, with only 21 per thousand, could claim the lowest infant mortality rate in the world. In most European countries it at least halved during the first half of the century, and dropped especially markedly between 1930 and 1950. Similar improvements in the general expectation of life occurred during the period. Within the hundred years, 1850–1950, western civilisation added a full generation to the average length of life. In a number of the more advanced countries, during the fifty years before 1900, the expectation of life increased by about 2 years each decade; during the fifty years after 1900 increase was accelerated to about $3\frac{1}{2}$–4 years each decade. As a result, and as some index of this new tenacity of life, the population of Europe excluding Russia grew from roughly 310 to 396 millions between 1900 and 1950. In this way Europe continued into the twentieth century, though with diminished momentum, its remarkable propensity to grow in population, despite declines in some national birth rates and despite the heavy losses and dislocations of two world wars.

It was industrialisation, world trade, and improvement in methods of agriculture and transport that made it possible to maintain this increased population on a generally improving standard of living. Because the speed and the extent of industrialisation and the use of more scientific methods of production varied considerably from one country to another, there remained wide disparities in their average standards of life: differences almost as great as those between European and non-European countries. In

[1] Infant death rate is the number of infants, per thousand born alive, who die during the first year of life. The expectation of life is the average age to which a person is likely to live if the death rate of the year when he or she was born remains unchanged.

[2] *Annual Abstract of Statistics*, no. 94, p. 35.

Spain the expectation of life at the age of one year in 1940 (52·4 for males, 58·8 for females) was still lower than that in France had been in 1900: and the infant mortality rate of Roumania in 1940 (188 per thousand) was about the same level as that of France a century before, and higher than that of India in 1940. In 1948 the Department of Economic Affairs of the United Nations surveyed such differences in standards of living, and attempted to assess them in terms of the national income per head of the population in 1938, computed in United States dollars. The comparative figures showed as wide a range as 481·2 for the United Kingdom, 321·8 for the Netherlands, 243·9 for France, 131·8 for Italy, and 78·9 for Greece. The report added that 'the evidence at hand indicates that international disparities have been further intensified during and immediately after the war'.[1]

Few valid generalisations can be made about standards of living in Europe as a whole, save that broadly (though unevenly) there was notable improvement in physical health and length of life, and a general advance in the material well-being of the masses. This improvement included a general shortening of the working day and the working week, and even a contraction of the working life brought about by the tendency to raise the school-leaving age and to introduce a conventional age for retirement and superannuation. But material betterment was uneven for many diverse reasons. Whereas the large-scale migrations of the early decades improved both the standards of living of the migrants and the conditions of trade available to those who remained in Europe, the scale of migration overseas shrank considerably in the decades after 1914 (see ch. II). In the Soviet Union under the first Five-Year Plan, and in the 'people's democracies' of eastern Europe after 1945, deliberate emphasis on capital investment for expanding heavy industry, at the expense of agriculture and immediate consumer goods, kept down the standard of living. Everywhere heavy expenditure on armed forces and armaments competed with consumer demands in the great dilemma of 'guns or butter'.

The general increase of the national income in most countries, and the larger share of it enjoyed by the middle and working classes, were reflected in a growing expenditure on amenities and luxuries: on motor-cars and radio sets, on entertainments of all kinds, particularly the cinema and sports, on gambling and alcohol, tobacco and confectionery. Even countries with a relatively low standard of living came to be lavishly equipped with cinemas: so that by the end of the period Italy had nearly 9000 cinemas with a seating accommodation for nearly $3\frac{1}{2}$ millions, Spain had nearly 4000 cinemas with accommodation for 2 millions. The spread of popular amenities changed social habits and exposed ill-educated people to a multitude of new influences. Entrepreneurs, quick to meet the demands of the working classes, now made effective by their greater purchasing

---

[1] *Salient Features of the World Economic Situation, 1945–47*, Economic Report, Department of Economic Affairs, United Nations (January 1948), p. 243.

power, built up vast businesses and made immense profits. Lever Brothers made a fortune by meeting the new demand for soap and margarine, the Cadbury Brothers by making sweets. The whole structure of industry and business, especially of retail business, was deeply affected by this expansion of popular demand for non-essential consumer goods. Multiple stores multiplied, but so did small shops. Since life itself was more assured, trivialities assumed a new importance.

If wealth was more abundant, property was more insecure. The half-century was studded with wars, revolutions, and economic crises, each of which in turn wrought havoc with the previous distribution of wealth and social structure. The first world war brought the collapse of the old dynastic empires of Austria-Hungary, Turkey and Russia. This collapse involved the overthrow of much of the aristocracy and landed nobility. Throughout eastern Europe the old order went down in the violence of war and revolution. Within Russia, after the Bolshevik Revolution, land, factories, property of all kinds were confiscated. Power and control of wealth fell to new ruling cadres of party and state. In Germany land-owners joined with the army and the new industrialists to retain political and economic power in their own hands; or, as in Hungary, they stemmed the tide of revolution by violent reaction. The great currency crash in Germany in 1923 ruined the bulk of the middle and *rentier* classes, and effected social upheaval at a level at which it had been evaded in 1919. During the world economic crisis of 1929–32 bankruptcies and mass unemployment brought ruin to many who had previously known prosperity. After 1933 the National Socialist regime confiscated the property of Jews and all who fell victim to the charge of political opposition. After 1939 the process was extended to all German-occupied territories. It was reversed by the post-war governments, who attacked collaborators and those who had profited from national misfortunes. In eastern Europe the new communist regimes after 1945 repeated much of the story of Russia after 1917. Meanwhile both world wars, and the political and racial persecutions of the inter-war and post-war years, resulted in a vast uprooting of millions of displaced persons and refugees who were left homeless and often destitute.

Which social classes gained or lost most by these upheavals it is difficult to determine. It is probable that the peasantry, still the substructure of much of Europe's economy, on balance gained from the changes. In eastern Europe they gained more land. The economic depression of the 1920's provoked government assistance for agriculture, greater mechanisation and more intensive cultivation. The 1930's were a period of steadily rising food production, and by 1939 agriculture was in a healthy state in most countries on the Continent. The upheavals of war, German occupation, and liberation, were accompanied by a steep decline in production and often by hunger and starvation. But except in the battle-areas these upheavals tended to hit urban rather than rural populations, and the strenuous efforts made, with American help, to restore European prosperity after the war brought a quick return to pre-war levels of production. The world shortage of food after the war meant high prices, official subsidies and encouragement, and frequently (as in France) a positive raising of the standards of living of the peasant above pre-war levels.

Landowners, though suffering less from inflation than the middle classes and less from currency collapse than the *rentier* class, suffered more from drastic confiscations. Industrialists, traders and shippers suffered from the world economic depression and from war-time confiscations, controls, and destruction. During the profound social revolution which occurred in Germany between 1923 and 1933, members of the middle classes whose incomes derived from salaries, pensions, small shops and businesses, the rental of real estate or interest on bonds or mortgages, were usually reduced to great poverty. Meanwhile others gained: debtors, employers on a large scale, speculative investors, and farmers who, because they paid a fixed rent or owned their land, could benefit from rising prices. Industrial and agricultural workers, and many black-coated workers, suffered most acutely from mass unemployment during the world economic crisis. In most countries there appeared a persistent and growing army of unemployed. In Germany it approached 5 millions in 1930 and exceeded 6 millions by the beginning of 1933. In Great Britain it numbered 2 millions at certain times during 1921 and 1922, and reached nearly 3 millions in the years 1931–3. No European country suffered from mass unemployment more than Germany. France, being less dependent on foreign trade for her national prosperity, suffered less and later than either Germany or Britain. Between 1945 and 1950 only western Germany experienced unemployment on any important scale.

The human anxieties, deprivations and destitution which these events caused are the other side of the coin to the new abundance which modern technology made available to Europe. Amid plenty, poverty seemed more intolerable. This helps to explain the intensity and universality of the demand that the state should provide greater social security and undertake a more systematic redistribution of wealth. Repeatedly the normal hierarchy of wealth was violently upset. The divorce of economics from politics, which had underlain mid-nineteenth-century doctrines of *laissez-faire* and free trade, could not survive such experiences. From the years before 1914 derived a more insistent demand for 'social justice', and with it a repertoire of devices by which greater social justice might be attained. The adoption and extension of these measures was, accordingly, the second main aspect of social change in this period.

The demand for social justice involved several interlocked procedures. It meant, first, completing that democratic revolution of the previous century which had moved towards universal suffrage and the extension of civic liberties and rights to all citizens. It meant, secondly, achieving greater social equality: an attack on extremes of wealth and poverty, a concern for greater equality of opportunity in education and for careers open to talents. It meant, thirdly, greater social security: protecting the individual and the family against the hazards and vicissitudes of an industrial society and an unstable world economy; providing safeguards against the poverty that could come from sickness or disability of the wage-earner, from periodic or chronic unemployment, from old age. It meant, finally, a new code of behaviour between different communities: extending self-government and civic rights to colonial peoples; co-operating with other nations in a rich variety of international bodies for promoting higher standards of living everywhere. So intense and so persistent was the general demand for greater social justice that by 1950 every European government was committed to such measures. The old division between economic and political activity was totally abandoned, and every state was engaged in implementing programmes of social security, economic regulation, and full employment. That intimate reciprocal relationship between state and society, government and nation, which was the outcome of both nationalism and democracy in the nineteenth century, was elaborated and carried very much farther in the first half of the twentieth.

By 1900 most states of western Europe had either established universal suffrage or were approaching it. All Frenchmen of 21 and over had had the vote since 1870; all men in Germany since 1871, in Switzerland since 1874, in Belgium since 1893, in the Netherlands since 1896, in Norway since 1898. Although the minimum age varied the principle was generally accepted. Universal male suffrage was introduced in Sweden and Austria in 1907, Turkey in 1908, Italy in 1912. In Finland and Norway even women gained the vote in 1907. After 1918 the fashion for democratic government prevailed, and all the new states of Europe adopted democratic constitutions with universal suffrage. In 1918 women over 30 gained the vote in the United Kingdom; in 1919 women over 20 gained it in the German Republic. Turkey enfranchised women in 1934. By 1950 equal female suffrage became general throughout Europe. It was attained in Russia in 1918, in Britain in 1928, France in 1945, Italy in 1946, Belgium in 1948; and Switzerland remained the only outstanding exception. The general acceptance of equal political rights for both sexes had far-reaching but somewhat incalculable effects on representative government. It usually more than doubled the size of the electorate within a single generation. It compelled political parties to compete for the female vote in a way which may partly explain enthusiasm for systems of pensions for the widowed and aged, national health services and family allowances. The new electoral pressure of women reinforced other tendencies promoting the Welfare State.

The social revolution of twentieth-century Europe, which in most countries resulted in a new status for women, went much deeper in its causes than the agitation for female suffrage and much wider in its consequences than the extension of electorates. It was closely linked with the democratic ideal of equality, which emphasised the basic claim of every human being to equal civil and political rights. It was also part of a more comprehensive change of outlook in social life. This came with the decline in the infant mortality rate which freed women from the burden of frequent pregnancies; with more scientific facilities for birth-control and the fashion for smaller families; with opportunities for the employment of women (including married women) in offices, factories, restaurants and retail stores; with the extension of popular education to girls as well as boys; with a general demand for greater leisure and comfort. In Britain the average number of children per family was over five in the 1870's, but about two in the 1930's. With the growing demand for female labour in factories and offices, domestic servants became more scarce, but the demand for them also declined. As housewives, women found their drudgery diminished by a host of labour-saving devices and by more abundant supplies of cheap soap, cheap furnishing materials and more modern homes. Women in Britain and in some European countries supplied a large additional labour force in both world wars. Less economic dependence on their fathers or husbands made them more independent in spirit, more assertive of legal and social rights which legislatures, increasingly anxious to satisfy the demands of the new female electorates, readily granted. In the whole process cause and effect were usually indistinguishable. Again the change varied greatly in extent from one country to another. It was often resisted by the influence of the Roman Church. The dictatorships of the inter-war years, especially the German, discouraged it and tried to raise the birth rate and force women back into the kitchen and the nursery. In deference to this policy, the National Socialist regime in Germany failed to mobilise women for the war-effort as thoroughly as did Great Britain.[1]

Whilst the enfranchisement of the whole people gave a new basis to government, the fashion for republics and for weakening second chambers helped to give popular opinion a more direct impact on the directing of policy. Out of some twenty-six states in 1950, only eight were monarchies[2] and those were mostly old constitutional monarchies. Upper houses were either abolished, as in Finland in 1919 or Turkey in 1925, or were weakened in legislative power as in Britain in 1911 and 1949, Germany in 1919 and

[1] The number of women employed in the German civilian labour-force actually declined by about a quarter of a million during the first two years of war, and fell from 14,626,000 on 31 May 1939 to 14,437,000 three years later. See *Hitler's Europe*, ed. Arnold Toynbee and Veronica M. Toynbee, Royal Institute of International Affairs, 1954, pp. 8, 226 and 234.

[2] They were the United Kingdom, Belgium, the Netherlands, Luxembourg, Norway, Sweden, Denmark and Greece.

1948, France in 1946, Italy in 1948. Constitutional impediments to full democratic government were in general removed. Systems of plural voting which gave greater weight to favoured sections of the electorate were abolished in Belgium, Sweden, and in the United Kingdom. Some countries, including Belgium, the Netherlands, Sweden, Germany under the Weimar Republic, and France under the Fourth Republic, experimented with schemes of proportional representation (see ch. IV). Methods of direct democracy, especially the plebiscite and referendum, were popular for such purposes as determining the future of disputed territories by consulting the inhabitants (as in the Saar in 1935), or for deciding upon the future constitution of the state (as in France and Italy after 1945).

So great was the prestige of democratic government that even the dictatorships ostentatiously used the institutions of democratic government, whilst they took equal care to keep real power in the hands of a single party. Both Hitler and Mussolini followed Napoleonic precedents by seeking the approval of plebiscites for their major strides to power. They preserved a system of 'representative' assemblies and popular elections, whilst destroying any forces of opposition; they claimed that their dynamic leaders and monolithic parties infallibly expressed the will and defended the interests of the nation as a whole; and the 'Soviet democracy' and 'people's democracies' of eastern Europe claimed to be achieving more completely the democratic ideals of equality and fraternity.

It was a doctrine of democracy everywhere that voters must be educated. By 1914 all Europe was being sent to school. Free compulsory education, at least at the primary level, was accepted as the normal or desirable arrangement in most countries. In France instruction had been free in all state primary schools since 1881, and compulsory for all children between the ages of 6 and 13 since 1882. In England a law of 1870 empowered local school boards to require attendance at primary schools; in 1881 compulsion became general, and ten years later elementary education became free. Comparable measures were passed during the same decades or earlier in most countries of north-western Europe, so that after 1900 their peoples were becoming increasingly literate. During the twentieth century literacy was similarly promoted in the Soviet Union after 1917, in Turkey under Mustafa Kemal, and throughout southern and eastern Europe, though often without complete success. In Portugal in 1950 more than 40 per cent of the population over the age of seven could not read or write: in Bulgaria in 1946 nearly a quarter of the whole population was illiterate.

The increase of literacy everywhere was accompanied by a great development of secondary and technical education and by expansion of university education. In Britain the Board of Education came into being in 1900, and the Act of 1902 prepared the way for a rapid growth of secondary education under central stimulus. This in turn generated a demand for expansion of the universities, and for provision of a ladder of educational grants which would make it possible for an able child of poor parents to have access to even the highest levels. The Education Acts of 1918 and 1944 went far towards providing a complete national system of education at all levels. In 1911 no university students received aid from the central government, and only 1400 received grants from local authorities: in 1950, 32,940 were receiving aid from the Ministry of Education (which had replaced the Board in 1944), and 34,621 from local authorities.[1] In several countries these years saw establishment of new universities on a scale unknown since the sixteenth century. The Portuguese universities of Lisbon and Oporto were founded in 1911. In 1924 new Italian universities were founded at Bari, Florence, Milan and Trieste, and in 1944 at Salerno. The Danish university of Aarhus was founded in 1928, the Norwegian university of Bergen in 1946. In Britain the University of Wales was formed in 1903, and seven new English universities were founded, at Birmingham (1900), Liverpool (1903), Leeds (1904), Sheffield (1905), Bristol (1909), Reading (1926), and Nottingham (1948). As a result of this remarkable growth and of expansion (especially in scientific departments) at the older universities, the student population at British universities by 1950 ran at about 85,000 each year, as compared with only half that number in the 1920's: and although this figure was not high as compared with some continental countries, the ladder of opportunity was probably more complete in Britain than anywhere in Europe. The enrichment of national life was incalculable.

In many countries, notably France, Germany, Italy and Belgium, this rapid expansion of state-provided or state-aided public education involved conflict between the state and the church, which had previously been the chief provider of education. This conflict was particularly acute where the Roman Catholic Church predominated, and in France it precipitated the separation of church from state in 1905. In such countries the education provided in state schools and in teachers' training colleges was usually positivist and secular, imbued with a strong spirit of anti-clericalism. A similar conflict revived under the dictatorships, which strove to indoctrinate the whole youth of the nation with their own secular ideologies. It recurred from time to time in the democracies, as in Britain after the Act of 1902, in Alsace and Lorraine after their return to France in 1919, and in France of the Fourth Republic in 1950 (see ch. IV).

These triumphs of liberal democracy in Europe were accompanied by a fundamental challenge to it. Even in the first decade of the century it became apparent that the developments already described might in aggregate move in either of two possible directions. They might tend, as liberal democrats expected and believed, towards the creation of a well-informed and thoughtful public opinion, seeking to use the power of the vote

[1] *Education 1900–1950: The Report of the Ministry of Education*, June 1951, pp. 100–102.

critically and reasonably, and in conformity with democratic ideals as these had been inherited from the rationalist democratic movement of the late eighteenth century. Or they might move in the direction of mass emotion, the subjection of public opinion to the power of propaganda, and the manipulation of the irrational impulses inherent in crowds and mobs. Popular education, movements for adult education,[1] the more responsible sections of the press and the provision of free libraries encouraged the tendency towards thoughtfulness and responsibility. Commercial advertising eager to capture the rising purchasing-power of the working classes, the sensational press made cheap by the support of advertisers, the more aggressive movements of nationalism, encouraged the contrary forces of irrationalism and mass excitement. Before 1914 it was clear that the second tendency was at least as probable and inherent an outcome of the new democracy as the first. Social theorists like Gustave Le Bon in France and Graham Wallas in England explored these questions with apprehension.[2] Popular hysteria and violence of feeling, such as were induced in Britain by the Boer War, in France by the Dreyfus Case, in Germany by the agitation for colonial and naval expansion, and in the United States by the Spanish-American War, revealed something of the capacities for violence endemic in the urban, nationalist and more literate societies of 1900.

What was new after 1900 was not human susceptibility to the arts of persuasion and propaganda. Great leaders in all ages had shown how opinion could be moulded. The popular associations of the nineteenth century had discovered all the arts of mass agitation. Nor was it novel for nationalist pride and aggression to capture popular enthusiasm. The novelties were the exposure of semi-literate urban populations to more intense pressure from propagandists of business and press, and the enhanced importance of the reactions of these populations because of universal suffrage, state activity and international tensions. The immense physical and emotional strains imposed by the four years of the first world war were quickly followed by the further expansion of media of mass persuasion in the form of the cinema, the radio, and large public meetings made possible by electrical amplification. Between the two wars it seemed that democracy had merely made the world safe for dictatorship. The monolithic parties of Soviet Russia, Fascist Italy, National-Socialist Germany, and their counterparts in some other states, seized and kept power by

[1] In Britain the universities of Cambridge, Oxford and London began extra-mural activities in the 1870's: the Workers' Educational Association was founded in 1903, its Swedish counterpart in 1908, and the French *universités populaires* between 1899 and 1903. The famous Danish People's High Schools dated from as early as 1844.

[2] Gustave Le Bon's *Psychologie des Foules* appeared in 1895, Graham Wallas's *Human Nature in Politics* in 1908. Psychologists like William McDougall and sociologists like Gabriel Tarde developed, in the years before 1914, the more scientific study of social behaviour which then continued to make headway throughout the period.

skilful manipulation of all the latest means for exploiting the irrational, pathological impulses of men and women in modern society. These forces, harmlessly expressed by fashion, the hero-worship of sports favourites and film-stars, and the phenomena of song-crazes and best-selling novels, came to be harnessed to politics and (as in the propaganda which accompanied the five-year plans in the Soviet Union) to economics. By 1950 television opened up still further possibilities of the same kind: and even in the most stable parliamentary democracies electioneering by film, radio and television became no less important than electioneering by poster, press and public meeting.[1]

States that were becoming increasingly democratic in structure and spirit also became providers of social services. Here, too, a certain pattern had been inherited from the later nineteenth century. By 1914 every European country outside Russia and the Balkans had relatively well-developed codes of factory and labour legislation. In the 1880's Bismarck had introduced legislation which equipped Germany with a comprehensive national system of social insurance against sickness, accident, and incapacity in old age, and in 1911 it was codified and extended to various classes of non-industrial workers, such as agricultural labourers and domestic servants. By 1913 some $14\frac{1}{2}$ million people were thus insured, and codes of factory legislation and of child labour were added. Germany's neighbours, impressed by these measures, were quick to imitate them in whole or in part. In 1911 the United Kingdom introduced its first National Insurance Act, setting up a contributory scheme insuring a large part of the working population against sickness, providing for free medical attention, and insuring some categories of workers against unemployment. Belgium and Denmark, like Britain, imitated Germany's scheme of insurance against accident, sickness, and old age. Austria introduced accident and sickness insurance in the 1880's, Italy and Switzerland in the 1890's. In these years, too, Britain, France, Norway, Spain and the Netherlands passed legislation which obliged employers to compensate their workers for accidents which occurred during work. This expansion of state responsibility for the safety and well-being of its citizens, combined with the urbanisation of much of European society, brought about a general overhaul of local government and administration. By 1914 democratised and active municipal governments had endowed Europe with a great new equipment of public utility services of sanitation, water, gas, electricity and transport, and of hospitals, markets, laundries, slaughter-houses, labour exchanges, museums, recreation grounds, parks, libraries, schools, and all the other amenities of modern urban life.

The increased activities of government, both national and local, called for new fiscal policies. Until after 1871 direct income tax had been a

[1] See R. B. McCallum and A. Readman, *The British General Election of 1945* (1947), ch. VII; H. G. Nicholas, *The British General Election of 1950* (1951), ch. VI.

device almost peculiar to Great Britain. With electorates of consumers indirect taxes became unpopular, and progressive direct taxation, scientifically assessed and collected in proportion to income or wealth, came into favour. In his budget of 1909 Mr Lloyd George included the whole gamut of fiscal devices which had been evolving in Britain for some years: heavy duties on tobacco and liquor, heavier death-duties on personal estates, which had first been introduced by Sir William Harcourt in 1894, graded and heavier income tax, an additional 'super-tax' on incomes above a fairly high level, a duty of 20 per cent on the unearned increment of land-values, and a charge on the capital value of undeveloped land and minerals. During the 1890's, *pari passu* with the great expansion of governmental expenditures on armaments as well as on social services, Germany and her component states, as well as Italy, Austria, Norway, and Spain, all introduced or steepened systems of income tax. French governments repeatedly shied away from it, though they resorted to progressive death duties in 1901, and it was 1917 before a not very satisfactory system of income tax was introduced. The great fiscal burdens of war accustomed people to heavier taxation. In 1920 the French ambassador, M. Paul Cambon, could remark to Mr Churchill: 'In the twenty years I have been here I have witnessed an English Revolution more profound and searching than the French Revolution itself. The governing class have been almost entirely deprived of political power and to a very large extent of their property and estates; and this has been accomplished almost imperceptibly and without the loss of a single life.'[1] If M. Cambon was exaggerating in 1920, he was perceptively prophetic, for his description became undoubtedly true after the second world war. Already in 1937 it was calculated that 5 or 6 per cent of the national income was being redistributed from rich to poor. In 1939 people in Britain whose net incomes, after paying taxes, were £6000 or more a year, numbered about 7000. In 1949 they numbered only 70.[2]

A landmark in the history of social services in Europe was the *Report on Social Insurance and Allied Services* published by Lord Beveridge in 1942. It won wide international acceptance as a social creed for the post-war world, even when the methods he proposed were unacceptable. It found fullest embodiment in the British National Insurance Act of 1946, the National Health Service Act of the same year, and the National Assistance Act of 1948, all passed by the Labour government. These measures unified the previous systems of insurance against sickness, disability, unemployment and old age into a national scheme of social security organised by the state, though leaving room for further voluntary provision; extended universally the provision of free medical and dental services; and ended the old poor law. A system of family allowances, also advocated in the

[1] Winston S. Churchill, *My Early Years* (1930, new ed. 1947), p. 90.
[2] *91st Report of the Commissioners of Inland Revenue*, table 32.

Beveridge Report, was instituted in 1946; and on a much more lavish scale in France in 1945–6, as part of her General Scheme of Social Security. Comparable provisions had existed in Spain since 1939, and were instituted in Belgium in 1944 and Norway in 1946. Social security, the notion of public protection for the individual and the family against sickness, poverty, unemployment, squalor and ignorance, 'from the cradle to the grave', was the social ideal generated by the bitter experiences of the inter-war years.

These aims involved not only the provision of minimal social services such as public education, health services and old-age pensions, but the adoption by governments of a policy of 'full employment'. This policy was designed to forestall and prevent, by measures of currency and trade regulation and public investment programmes, a return of unemployment on a massive scale. Without full employment it was unlikely that social services could be maintained. By 1950 it was widely accepted in Europe that extremes of wealth and poverty should be avoided; that whilst national standards of living depended largely on world trade, the average standard of living in any country should be maintained at as high a level as possible by deliberate state action and regulation. The whole climate of opinion was completely changed from that of 1900, which outside Germany had distrusted state action. In most countries of eastern Europe more drastic policies of collectivisation were followed by the communist governments which held power after the second world war. The yearning for social security no less than for national security, which President Roosevelt in 1941 described as the desire for 'freedom from want and from fear', was a major result of this half-century of violence and insecurity.

Major national resources and industries were increasingly taken into public ownership or management. Although this tendency was greatly stimulated in the twentieth century by revolutions, wars, and economic crises, as well as by the growth of socialist movements, it was not a novel trend. In the nineteenth century Germany and Italy had nationalised railways, several countries had nationalised posts, telephones and telegraphs, and in France the production and sale of tobacco, matches and gunpowder had for long been state monopolies. In 1918 the Alsatian potash mines became state property, when the province was restored to France. Between the two wars all the single-party states, headed by the Soviet Union, established either public ownership or extensive state control over many of the major industries and services. In western countries, where municipal enterprise had become a favourite method of exercising public control, various forms of 'public corporation' were devised to meet new needs. In the United Kingdom the Port of London Authority dated from 1908, the British Broadcasting Corporation from 1927, the London Passenger Transport Board from 1933, the British Overseas Airways Corporation from 1939. In France the Popular Front government of 1936–7 nationalised railways and munitions factories, and created in the *Société nationale des chemins-de-fer français* (S.N.C.F.) a 'mixed corporation' in which the state held 51 per cent of the stock. Aircraft factories were also entrusted to a mixed corporation. In eastern Europe state ownership of railways and mines became common between the two wars.

After 1945 the urgent needs of economic reconstruction and the power of trade unions and socialist parties carried these tendencies very much farther. In the United Kingdom the Labour Party government of 1945–50 passed in 1946 the Bank of England Act which made the bank a governmental agency in name as well as in fact, and the Coal Industry Nationalisation Act which gave the management of coal to a National Coal Board. The Transport Act (1947) set up the British Transport Commission to supervise all forms of public transport; and corresponding authorities were created for gas and electricity. Such bodies, though ultimately accountable to government and parliament for the efficient conduct of their concerns, emphasised business methods rather than bureaucratic regimentation, and made possible flexible management and considerable regional or functional decentralisation. Post-war French governments likewise nationalised civil aviation, coal mines, gas and electricity services, the Renault motor works, and some of the large insurance companies, and completed the nationalisation of the Bank of France. They, too, used the device of the 'public corporation' for managing such industries as coal mining, gas and electricity; the directorate being composed of representatives of employees, consumers, and government. Between a fourth and a third of the nation's productive capacity became state-owned. Industry as a whole was re-invigorated by the Monnet Plan for the Modernisation and Equipment of French Economy, launched in 1946. It concentrated on the six basic sectors of coal, steel, power, transport, building materials and agriculture. By 1950 its main objectives had been mostly, but unevenly, reached.

Partitioned Germany marked the contrast between western and eastern Europe. Whereas in the western Federal Republic most industry was left to private enterprise, buttressed temporarily by help from the Allied military government and by Marshall Aid from the United States, the eastern German Democratic Republic left little more than a third of its economy outside state control. Communist governments in several other eastern states also nationalised their main industries and set up planned economies on the Russian model, until by 1948 over 90 per cent of industrial production in eastern Europe, apart from Roumania, was state-owned. Even anti-communist Turkey nationalised her railways, shipping, banking, and many other industries. Collectivisation of the land also proceeded fast, though often by the circuitous route of breaking up the remaining large estates and establishing peasant co-operatives.

The social and economic antithesis of the mid-twentieth century was not between systems of free enterprise and systems of collectivism, but between western nations wherein certain public enterprises were organised for the benefit of the community as determined by democratically elected governments, and the 'people's democracies' of eastern Europe wherein almost the whole national economy was controlled by single-party dictatorships operating within the orbit of Soviet power. Nearly all European states, whatever their political structure or ideology, had become different in social function and in normal activities from their predecessors of 1900. The modern state, whether multi-party democracy or single-party dictatorship, became more ubiquitous in action, more collectivist in method, more socialistic in purpose and ideals. In western and central Europe, indeed, industrial and farming activity was still mostly that of private individuals, families, or companies. In 1950 the private sector of British economy still included four-fifths of industry. But everywhere private enterprise operated within a complex framework of state regulation and subsidies, and governmental control of credit and trade. In Britain the recently nationalised industries employed some two million people, or about 10 per cent of those in civil employment. The large size of the nationalised concerns, such as the National Coal Board that employed a staff of more than 700,000, posed a host of new organisational and human problems. The modern state everywhere engaged no less than before in the 'government of men': it also busied itself immeasurably more with the 'administration of things'.

These transformations of the modern state were so much due to the exigencies of war and the experiences of economic crisis that it is difficult to assess the part played in them by the direct influence of socialist movements in politics. It could even be argued that the growth of labour organisations and of socialist parties was as much a consequence as a cause of the new collectivism that prevailed throughout Europe. But whatever the relationship between human intentions and actual conditions, the rise of organised labour and of socialist parties must rank as the third aspect of social transformation in the twentieth century. In number, size, functions, character, and outlook they also underwent great changes in close correlation with the wider social and political trends already described.

It was evident by 1914 that wherever industrialisation was well advanced, the national standard of living high, national cohesion strong, and democratic institutions effective, there too trade unions tended to be large and strong, and socialist movements could find in parliamentary politics an arena for effective activity. In the United Kingdom and the Scandinavian countries close links were established between trade unions and parliamentary socialist parties, and their joint influence grew on the solid basis of the expanding working-class organisations of the late nineteenth century. In 1900 the British Trades Union Congress, Fabian Society, Independent Labour Party, and Social Democratic Federation combined to set up a Labour Representation Committee. Renamed the Labour Party in 1906, it sent twenty-nine representatives to the House of Commons. Similar developments took place in the British Dominions, notably in Australia and New Zealand. In Norway, Sweden and Denmark parliamentary labour parties likewise enjoyed the backing of trade unions and made rapid gains in parliamentary strength: in the Danish elections of 1913 the Social Democrats won more votes than any other party.

In France and Italy, where the pace of industrialisation had been slower and democratic government worked less smoothly, the pattern of development was different. In both countries trade unionists and socialists remained greatly divided, although before 1914 they were already moving towards greater national unification. Trade unionism was less strong than in Britain, Scandinavia, or Germany, for it attracted a smaller proportion of the total labour force. Small units of production were less favourable than large for the growth of solid unionism, and national traditions kept apart, in suspicious separatism, catholics and socialists, syndicalists and communists. Socialist movements were likewise divided by doctrinal and tactical differences, and were distrusted by trade unionists who tended to prefer economic methods of collective bargaining and strike action to political methods of parliamentary electioneering and persuasion. The French *Confédération générale du travail* (C.G.T.) was formed in 1895, and in 1902 combined with the federation of the *Bourses du travail*. It held aloof from the socialist parties which, under Jean Jaurès, formed in 1905 the 'Unified Socialist Party', and in 1914 won 103 seats in the Chamber of Deputies. In 1906 the Italian socialist unions founded the General Italian Federation of Labour, but there too political socialism found real unity impossible.

The trade unions and socialist movements of Germany and Austria developed according to yet a third pattern, combining the political solidity of the British with the doctrinal divisions of the French. The German Social Democratic Party, dating from the socialist congress at Gotha in 1875, developed under the leadership of August Bebel into the most highly organised and best disciplined socialist party in Europe. By 1912 it mustered $4\frac{1}{4}$ million votes and returned 110 representatives to the Reichstag. Even so, the party conference held at Jena a few weeks after Bebel's death in August 1913, revealed a threefold division within it. There were dogmatic Marxists, a moderate centre which backed the party machine, and an opportunistic 'revisionist' wing led by Eduard Bernstein. These divisions in varying degrees characterised social democracy everywhere in Europe before 1914. The Austrian Social Democratic Party, held together by Dr Victor Adler, had eighty-seven members in the Reichsrat of 1914, though it was divided not only by doctrinal and tactical differences of policy, but even more deeply by national divisions into German, Czech and Polish groups. The Social Democrats of Germany owed much of their strength to the backing of the main trade union organisations. By 1913 these had a total of nearly 3 million members, of whom $2\frac{1}{2}$ millions in the Free Trade Unions almost solidly supported the socialists. In this they resembled the British Labour Party. Austrian trade unions were weaker and smaller, and divided along both national and religious lines: the membership of non-Catholic unions totalled about 400,000. Despite apparently more successful unification than in France and Italy, these working-class organisations in Germany and Austria suffered from special fundamental weaknesses. The German Reichstag rested on universal male suffrage, but it had little effective power in the state: and until 1907 the energies of the labour and socialist organisations in Austria were spent in the fight to win universal suffrage and democratic rights. The German Social Democratic Party looked monolithic and tended by sheer weight to dominate the activities of the Second International. Yet its concrete legislative achievements in Germany by 1914 were very meagre. The major social reforms of pre-war Germany were bestowed upon it from above, by Bismarck and his successors. It was only in the Weimar Republic of 1919–33 that socialists came to exercise a more positive influence on national policy.

In eastern Europe trade unions still struggled for legal status and freedom of action, and socialism was dominated by a more extremist and violent revolutionary tradition. Since democratic institutions were unknown or weak, social discontent found expression not in parliamentary agitation but in conspiracy and revolution. Nationalist divisions, as in Austria, cut across socialist loyalties. The contrast with all other European movements became plain enough in the nature of the programmes formulated by the different parties.

It became common for European social democratic movements to distinguish between their minimum and maximum aims. The minimum programme included universal suffrage and civic liberties wherever these had not been attained, and a list of such social reforms as could be elicited from parliamentary governments. The maximum programmes stated the long-term objectives of social democracy, often couched in more doctrinaire and Marxist terms. When the main French socialist groups combined in 1905 they declared that 'in parliament the Socialist Party must dedicate itself to the defence and extension of political liberties and the rights of workers, to the promotion and realisation of reforms which will ameliorate the conditions of life and of the class struggle of the working classes'. They also protested that the new 'unified' party was 'not a party of reform but a party of class struggle and revolution', and professed the ultimate aim of socialising the means of production and exchange. Only thus could Marxists and moderate socialists be reconciled within one movement. The German Social Democrats' Erfurt Programme of 1891 served the same purpose. Its minimum programme included demands for 'universal, equal, and direct suffrage, with vote by ballot, for all men and women of the Empire over twenty years of age'; 'a people's army in place of standing armies'; free expression of opinion and the right of union and meeting; secularisation of education; free medical services; and 'effective national and international protective legislation for workmen'. Its theoretical basis was stated in more thoroughly Marxist terms, declaring that 'private property in the means of production is incompatible with their rational application and full development'.

Wherever socialist parties were committed to attracting majorities in order to win parliamentary power it was inevitable that the minimum programme of immediate reforms should predominate. Such programmes were drafted to attract the maximum number of votes, and so had to be a list of reforms attainable without revolution within the existing framework of capitalist economy and liberal democracy. To enter into competition with other political parties for winning votes, and to elicit from governments concessions of immediate benefit for the working classes, was a procedure that enmeshed every social democratic party, however stern its protestations of ultimate proletarian purposes, in more nationalistic ways of thinking and behaving. They had to think less in terms of classes than of individual voters and majorities, not of class war but of national policy. Their working-class supporters, benefiting increasingly from legislation in their interests passed and enforced by the national state, likewise thought more in national and non-revolutionary terms. The growth throughout western and central Europe of social democracy, parliamentary labour parties, and successful trade unions, brought about a domestication and nationalising of socialism which increasingly disrupted the sessions of the Second International.

The contrast with socialism in eastern Europe becomes clear when these tendencies are compared with the development of the Russian Social Democratic Party after 1903. Its programme adopted in that year was, in accordance with European precedents, also divided into minimum and maximum aims. But since it was not exposed to the Italian, French or German temptation to exalt the minimum at the expense of the maximum, both were of necessity revolutionary. The minimum political aims of 1903 began with the revolutionary overthrow of the tsarist regime and its replacement by a democratic republic. The minimum economic aims were those normally included in the minimum programmes of western socialists: an eight-hour day and a six-day week; effective factory inspection; state insurance against sickness and old age; the confiscation of church lands. But these too, in Russia before 1914, were revolutionary demands, and were not essentially different from programmes of proletarian social revolution.[1] The most important decision taken by the congress of the Russian Social Democratic Party in 1903 was not about objectives of policy but about the future organisation of the movement as a militant force, geared to revolutionary struggle against the whole established order. Lenin ensured that socialism in Russia should be undiluted by liberal procedures and compromises (see ch. xiv). Since liberal democracy made so little headway, even after the revolution of 1905–6, Russian socialism remained inherently revolutionary and violent, devoted to fighting the class war and hostile to any compromise.

Nor had the industrial and political condition of Russia permitted the rise of strong trade union organisations. In 1905–6, although the first trade union conferences were held, the strikers tended to organise themselves not in trade unions but in soviets, which had a political revolutionary character. Unions again went into abeyance until 1917. In June of that year the first All-Russian Central Council of Trade Unions was elected. It played no important part in the revolution of October. The unions, coming into existence only after industrial organisation was on a large scale, now took shape as big industrial unions, more comprehensive and generalised than in the West and claiming to represent the workers as a whole. These facts determined the relationship which grew up between trade unions and the Bolshevik Party. By the beginning of 1918 the unions were charged with the administration of the new system of social insurance for all workers. Despite efforts of their leaders to retain political independence for the unions, alliance between unions and party led remorselessly to the domination of party over unions. In this respect the development of labour organisations in Russia contrasted sharply with that in Britain and Germany. In Britain the trade unions had been older than the Labour Party and closer relations between them brought more effective control of unions over party. In Germany, where unions and social democracy had grown more or less simultaneously, there was first rivalry and eventually equal partnership.[2]

By 1914 both labour organisations and socialist parties had made considerable headway throughout Europe. They existed even in Spain, Portugal, and the Balkan states, though there they were weak. In all the more industrial countries socialist parties doubled or trebled their numbers during the decade before 1914. In the United Kingdom, Scandinavia and Germany their advance had been swift and solid, and close relationship was established between the economic and the political organisations of the working classes. Although nowhere had socialist parties won control of government, the prospect of political power no longer seemed remote. In the many congresses of the Second International the frequent

[1] See E. H. Carr, *A History of Soviet Russia: The Bolshevik Revolution 1917–1923* (1950–52), vol. I, p. 28, vol. II, p. 14; and V. I. Lenin, *What is to be Done?* (1902).
[2] Carr, *op. cit.* vol. II, p. 102, note 5.

cleavages along mainly nationalist lines showed that this prospect weakened rather than enhanced the international solidarity of socialism. When war began in 1914 the social democrats of each country mostly lent support to their own governments, voting for war credits and accepting the allegiances of nationalism. Only four years before, at the Copenhagen Congress of the International, they had solemnly resolved not to do this. But in 1914 national feeling proved to be stronger than class cohesion or socialist doctrine. In France, Belgium, Denmark, Sweden, and eventually Britain, socialists entered into war-time coalitions. Trade unions were no less patriotic. General strikes to stop the war and precipitate a proletarian revolution did not occur anywhere.

During the war the importance of trade unions in the national effort brought them enhanced power, but socialist parties suffered further splits and vicissitudes. In 1915 most socialist parties split between supporters and opponents of the war. After the first flush of warlike enthusiasm, when only a few outright pacifists or extremist revolutionaries opposed war, larger numbers began to join them in opposing its continuance. The International split in September 1915. The anti-war socialists from all the major countries (including Lenin) met at Zimmerwald in neutral Switzerland, and a majority of them signed a manifesto denouncing the war and urging peace without annexations or indemnities. The conference set up a permanent International Socialist Commission, separate from the surviving secretariat of the Second International which had been transferred from Belgium to neutral Holland. This new commission became, in 1919, the nucleus of the Third (Communist) International, or Comintern.

During the last year of war the repercussions of the Bolshevik Revolution combined with the consequences of war's upheavals to produce a surge of revolutionary movements in which socialist and communist aims were inextricably mingled with agrarian unrest and insurgent nationalism. Throughout much of eastern Europe and parts of central Europe, governmental collapse favoured the spread of violence. Strikes and agitations helped to precipitate revolutions in Bulgaria, Austria, Hungary, and eventually Germany. In disillusioned Italy, war-torn France, impoverished Britain, social discontent was great. While the peace-makers met in Paris two conferences met in February at Berne: one of trade union delegates from sixteen former belligerent and neutral countries, to draft a Labour Charter embodying labour's demands for social reforms and to revive in stronger form the pre-war international organs of trade unionism; the other of socialist delegates from twenty-six countries, intending to revive the Second International. The first of these led to the creation, in July 1919 at Amsterdam, of the International Federation of Trade Unions (I.F.T.U.). Within a few months of its formation it emerged as representative of organised workers in twenty-two countries. The second found itself as deeply divided as ever, and bitterly opposed by a new rival body, hastily formed at Moscow in March 1919, the Comintern. Whilst the Second International proclaimed its loyalty to the principles and methods of democracy and the aims of social reform, the Third called on workers to form revolutionary councils, turn the 'imperialist war' into a civil war, socialise industry and credit, and set up a 'dictatorship of the proletariat' on the Russian model. By 1921 the Comintern also created a Red International of Labour Unions (R.I.L.U.) to fight the unions of the I.F.T.U. There thus began, in 1919, a bitter struggle for leadership between the champions of democracy and reformist socialism and the adherents of revolutionary dictatorship, which for the next twenty years continued to divide both trade unionism and socialism. The small communist groups that formed separate political parties in most European states during 1920 became inevitably the voice of Moscow, and the rift in socialism was carried into the heart of every country.

Between the two world wars the relative strength of the three main international organisations varied greatly according to circumstances. The I.F.T.U. won its first major triumph in October 1919, when it was accepted as the world spokesman of organised labour by the first conference of the new International Labour Organisation (I.L.O.), set up by Part XIII of the Treaty of Versailles. By the end of 1921 the membership of the national centres affiliated to it exceeded 23 millions: and even after the many vicissitudes of trade unions in Germany, Austria, Spain, and Czechoslovakia, the figure in July 1939 was still some 19 millions.[1] It established especially close relations with the Labour and Socialist International (L.S.I.), formed in May 1923 by a merger of the Second International with those dissident left-wing movements which had, since February 1921, constituted the International Working Union of Socialist Parties, the so-called Vienna or 'Two-and-a-Half' International. In principle the L.S.I. engaged in only political activities, the I.F.T.U. only in industrial activities; but the frontier between them was inevitably blurred, and they shared the same fluctuations of fortune between the wars. The vogue for democratic constitutions after 1918 favoured their cause; in 1920 there were socialist or partly socialist governments in Germany, Austria, Sweden, Czechoslovakia, and several other countries; and the demands and need for social reconstruction after the war gave socialist parties their first great historical opportunity. Electorates, more broadly based on universal suffrage and habituated to war-time controls, were more receptive than ever before to socialistic proposals.

Even these highly favourable conditions, however, produced results

---

[1] J. Price, *The International Labour Movement* (1945), pp. 52–3, and Lewis L. Lorwin, *The International Labor Movement: History, Policies, Outlook* (New York, 1953), ch. VII. In every country a high proportion of workers remained outside trade union organisations.

that were disappointing for socialist hopes. In Britain the Labour Party formed only minority governments in 1924 and 1929, and the intervening general strike of 1926 left a legacy of unwonted bitterness in British politics. In Germany the Social Democrats, led by Hermann Müller, Friedrich Ebert and Philipp Scheidemann, were kept in power only by alliance with the nationalist and imperial authorities of army and bureaucracy. In the manner of the French democrats of 1848 they crushed the extreme left, the Spartacists, with the help of the conservatives and the reactionary Free Corps. In 1925 the election of Marshal von Hindenburg to the Presidency of the Weimar Republic began that abdication of democracy to authoritarian nationalism which was completed, eight years later, by the abdication of Hindenburg to Hitler. The Austrian Social Democrats, in many ways the model of a strong, disciplined, democratic socialist party, contrived until 1927 to hold their reactionary enemies at bay. But thereafter they were challenged by the *Heimwehr*, a private army consisting mostly of sons of wealthier peasants, led by aristocrats and backed by big business and the Catholic Church. Even so, the Social Democrats won 72 out of 165 seats in the parliamentary elections of 1930, and it was March 1933 before the Christian Social Chancellor, Dr Engelbert Dollfuss, overthrew parliamentary democracy and governed by emergency decrees. Five years later his successor, Dr Kurt von Schuschnigg, was forced by Hitler to acquiesce in the *Anschluss* between Austria and Germany. Six months after that the hitherto successful social democratic regime of Czechoslovakia succumbed similarly to Nazi pressure and to the fatal concessions of territory forced upon the Czech government at Munich. In central Europe the chief destroyer of socialist governments was authoritarian nationalism, whether in the guise of Italian Fascism, Austrian clericalist-militarism, or German National Socialism. These anti-socialist forces fed on fear of communism, discontent with parliamentary democracy, and the upheavals of the world economic crisis of 1929–32.

In western Europe the emphasis was different. There the reverses of socialism were due more directly to the consequences of the world economic crisis, and to the failures of socialist parties to devise economic policies and political strategies adequate to the needs of capitalism in crisis. Internal fascist movements existed in Belgium, France and Britain, as in most other European countries, but they failed to overturn these well-established democratic regimes. In Spain they succeeded only after prolonged civil war and with foreign aid. Western socialism cherished particularly the axiom that the class war could be contained within the bounds of democratic procedures and conducted by non-violent methods. So long as national production was expanding, as during the boom before 1921 or after 1936, the tensions between classes were eased. But when, as between 1921 and 1924, or between 1929 and 1934, employers, workers and peasants competed for larger shares in a contracting national output just as nations competed for shares in a shrinking world trade, then tensions between them came nearer to breaking-point. Economic depression particularly discredited social democrats because they were committed to 'administering capitalism', to making the system of competitive private enterprise work within a framework of national controls. Every example of its breakdown was, therefore, fresh ammunition for their communist or fascist enemies. In this way the fate of socialism depended directly on the interplay of the other three themes considered in this chapter: the development of industrialism and a world economy, of democratic government, and of revolutionary movements.

For socialist parties to assert a more independent control over their own destinies, they needed to do two things, neither of which any except the Swedish Social Democratic Party proved able to do. One was to modify profoundly the economic policies of monetary and fiscal orthodoxy (and in Britain free trade) which they had usually taken over from liberalism, and to cling less resolutely to the panacea of nationalisation which they had derived mainly from Marxism. The other was to shed the outlook and impulses of a pressure-group, which they had acquired during their early phases as small minority movements, and to develop the fully responsible national policy that a democratic system requires of its major political parties.[1] In the most advanced industrial democracies of Belgium, France, Britain, and to some extent the German Weimar Republic, the close bonds between parliamentary socialist parties and large national trade-union organisations, which were a source of electoral strength, proved to be in this respect a source of weakness. Trade unions were necessarily concerned with the immediate material interests of their members. They turned most readily to demands for concrete social ameliorations and improved labour conditions within the existing framework of society and industry, and so impelled any party that they supported into the tactics of a pressure-group and away from basic fiscal experiments. For this reason, the characteristic response of western socialist parties to the Great Depression was to take part in broad national coalitions. This impulse produced the British National Government led by Mr Ramsay MacDonald in 1931, the Van Zeeland coalition in Belgium in 1934, the Spanish and French 'Popular Front' governments of 1936. Faced with acute economic crisis, the strongest natural impulse of parliamentary socialist leaders was to seek, through participation in a national coalition, some concessions for the interests they represented. The compromises dictated by this action inhibited them from challenging the orthodox economic principles and policies that proved, in the event, impotent to overcome the depression.

The outstanding exception was the Social Democratic Party of Sweden,

---

[1] This thesis has been cogently argued by A. Sturmthal, *The Tragedy of European Labour, 1918–1939* (New York, 1943; London, 1944).

led by Per Albin Hansson, Rickard Sandler, Ernest Wigforss and Gustaf Moeller. Assuming all the key posts in the government of 1932, the party tackled the economic crisis by expanding public investment, budgeting for a deficit, and carrying out a programme of major public works financed not by taxation but by borrowing. It reduced unemployment to vanishing point. Much of the necessary re-thinking of economic principles and policies, done for Sweden by Professor Gunnar Myrdal, was along lines closely similar to the revolution in economic thought brought about by Lord Keynes in Britain. By thus devising a bold and coherent policy of economic recovery, and by refusing to behave as a pressure-group rather than a mature political party, the Swedish socialists won for themselves an initiative and measure of self-determination that were rare in Europe. It was 1945 before the British Labour Party and left-wing coalitions in post-war France and Italy found themselves in a position to undertake comparable basic reforms.

There remained, throughout, a deeper sense in which socialism differed from communism. The contrast was not merely one of urgency and immediacy of aims, or one of methods and tactics. The two creeds were not just different responses to the same problem: they were responses to different problems. Socialist literature from Charles Fourier and Joseph Proudhon to William Morris and Jean Jaurès, and through them to western parliamentary socialism, contained countless criticisms of industrialism itself, and not merely of capitalist industrialism. Socialist movements, like trade unions, sprang essentially from attempts to rescue workers from the effects of fast and unfettered industrial growth: hence their constant emphasis on factory legislation, improved housing, social security and the 'right to leisure' as well as the 'right to work'. The literature of communism, from Marx and Engels to Lenin and Stalin, contains hardly a breath of criticism of industrialism itself.[1] The central complaint against capitalism is that it is an inefficient and wasteful means of ensuring the abundance that a collectively organised industrialism could achieve. The socialism of labour parties, as of trade unions, was inspired by a desire to humanise industrial society and to achieve a more just distribution, among consumers, of the amenities of high productivity. The communism of Lenin and Stalin, as of the five-year plans, was designed to industrialise a primitive economy, and to attain maximum productivity even by the sacrifice of immediate consumer goods and by perpetuating great inequalities of wealth and of privilege. This profound difference of purpose and spirit underlay the history of these decades.

The inter-war record of communist parties in Europe, outside the

[1] Marx and Engels shared in the characteristic mid-Victorian admiration for the achievements of science and industry in bringing about spectacular material progress. Cf. *Communist Manifesto* (1848), Part I, with many later Stalinist glorifications of the material achievements of the five-year plans.

Soviet Union, was even more barren of achievement than that of the socialists. Committed in principle to the overthrow of capitalism and the eventual destruction of existing parliamentary democracies, they won a few short-lived triumphs in 1919 and 1920 and thereafter incurred a series of defeats that continued unbroken until 1945. The Soviet republics of Bavaria and of Hungary lasted only a few months; the attempted *coups* elsewhere in Germany failed; in France, Spain, and Austria, as in Italy and Germany, communist tactics succeeded only in weakening socialist parties and strengthening the appeal of fascist movements. Fluctuating between open warfare with social democrats and pleas for 'united fronts' with them, the communist parties of Europe came to be increasingly regarded as the puppets of Moscow. It took four years of alliance in war between the Soviet Union and the western powers, and experience of prolonged underground resistance to fascist invasion and occupation, to give communism its next chance of gaining political power in Europe. Only after 1945 did communism in France, Italy, and parts of south-eastern Europe become a mass-movement, attracting a fifth or more of the popular vote, and exerting widespread influence over labour organisations. There was probably no moment between 1921 and 1945 when communist revolution had a serious chance of succeeding in western or central Europe. It was communist misunderstanding of British politics that gave to the British general strike of 1926 its surprising significance in the history of European communism. It was never intended by its leaders as a revolutionary bid for power. In conformity with the pressure-group traditions of western labour, it was intended as a means of pressure on government and employers, and when it failed as that it failed completely.

The combination of conditions favourable to the growth of a violent revolutionary movement has been listed as 'a social structure based on a primitive and poor peasantry and a small unskilled working class little if at all less primitive or poor; a political system based on bureaucratic despotism; an educational system producing an intelligentsia ideally rebellious and personally dissatisfied; the habit of religious persecution and support by the Church to political tyranny; the diversity of nationalities within one state'.[1] It was in Russia, Hungary, Spain, and some of the Balkan countries that such a combination of conditions most nearly prevailed. It was there, and in Austria, Italy and Germany where some of these conditions existed, that violent revolutionary movements succeeded or came nearest to succeeding. In Britain, Scandinavia, and to a lesser extent France and the Low Countries, where labour organisations were large and relatively prosperous, parliamentary democracy was strong,

[1] H. Seton-Watson, *The Pattern of Communist Revolution: A Historical Analysis* (1953), p. 11. On the special place of a discontented intelligentsia in the leadership of communist movements see *ibid.* pp. 8–9 and 337–56, and the tentative sociological inquiry by G. A. Almond, *The Appeals of Communism* (Princeton, 1954).

the level of education was high, and there was considerable religious tolerance, extremist movements could make headway against such unfavourable circumstances only in times of acute economic depression. It was for these reasons that the course of politics in twentieth-century Europe was correlative to the transformation of social life, and to the recurrence of economic depression. Socialism and communism can be understood only in relation to the interplay of those other central themes of modern history: the growth of industrial society and an interdependent world economy, of liberal democratic government and nationalist enthusiasms.

The same is true of revolutionary fascist dictatorships. Violent fascist movements, hostile to liberal democracy and free labour organisations, to socialism and communism alike, arose from the same combinations of circumstances that favoured communism. Between the two wars scarcely a country in Europe failed to produce its indigenous fascist or semi-fascist movement, and they flourished most during the economic depressions of 1923 and 1929–32. Their opportunities came from political instability, aggrieved national pride, social unrest, and economic dislocation, all of which their behaviour helped to aggravate. After the coming to power of fascist parties in Italy and Germany, such movements drew encouragement and often direct aid from these countries: but their roots remained deep in native soil, and the fortunes of fascism in different countries varied largely according to the strength of these roots.

Politically and constitutionally, the most striking feature of Europe between the two world wars was the conflict between democracy and dictatorship, between multi-party and single-party states. This conflict was complicated by the ideological warfare between communism and fascism. But in the longer perspectives of history, a more significant theme is the impact upon all nations and states of the basic transformations in social life and structure brought about by economic change and total war. In this perspective the 'welfare state' of liberal democracy and socialism, the economic planning and collectivism of communism, and the 'corporative state' of fascism may be regarded as variant national responses to the needs of an industrial society, and of a mass civilisation based on science and technology.

CHAPTER IV

POLITICAL INSTITUTIONS IN EUROPE: POLITICAL ISSUES AND POLITICAL THOUGHT

IN 1900 Europe, if we ignore a few midgets like Monaco and Andorra, included no less than twenty independent states. Six of them were the great powers, all with populations over the 30 million mark. Twelve were the little powers, all well below the 10 million mark. Only two states held anything like an intermediate rank—Spain, still with less than 20 millions, and Turkey (the bulk of whose population was Asiatic) with perhaps 23 millions.

One of the great powers was a republic—France. So was one of the little powers—Switzerland. The remaining eighteen states were all monarchies. During the nineteenth century, when a new small nation was constituted, it was sooner or later provided with a monarch, as a rule from among the reigning families of Europe. Belgium, Greece, Roumania and Bulgaria were the cases in point, followed as late as 1905 by Norway and in March 1914 by Albania.

In 1919, after the first world war, the situation was much changed. The number of European states was further increased; it had risen to twenty-six. The number of great powers had declined to five through the disappearance of Austria-Hungary. Turkey retained only a bare foothold in Europe and had been pared down elsewhere from an empire to a nation-state. But on the intermediate level, that is between 10 and 30 millions, Spain had been joined by no less than four other countries—Poland, Roumania, Yugoslavia and Czechoslovakia. The ratio between monarchies and republics had also greatly altered. Now only two of the five great powers remained monarchies, and all the six new states set up in consequence of the war, together with the re-conditioned Russia, Germany, Austria, Hungary and Turkey, took shape as republics. Only in the expanded states of Roumania and Yugoslavia, in each of which the nucleus-territory had long been a monarchy, did that form of constitution remain. The kingdom of Montenegro disappeared. Yet the list of monarchies still included all those European states (except Switzerland) in which democracy worked best—Great Britain, Belgium, Holland, Sweden, Denmark and (since 1905) Norway.

In 1945 the picture was widely different again. The European great powers were reduced to three—Great Britain, France and Russia. Italy's siding with Germany in the second world war had altered her status; while Germany—disarmed, deprived of large territories on her eastern frontiers, and for the rest bisected between Russia and the western occupying powers—was temporarily in a category apart. Of the smaller powers Russia had annexed three (Lithuania, Latvia and Estonia); and besides absorbing other large accretions of territory at the expense of Germany, Poland and Roumania, she had reduced eight countries (Finland, Poland, Czechoslovakia, Hungary, Roumania, Yugoslavia, Bulgaria and Albania) to the position of 'satellites', which in every instance but Finland and Yugoslavia came eventually to imply total subjection to Moscow. In western Europe no such imperialist changes occurred; on the other hand, two small countries (Southern Ireland and Iceland) had by different stages become independent republics.

To the external changes as between 1919 and 1945 a series of internal changes corresponded. The republics set up in 1919 had been democracies, designed to be governed by the popular will as expressed through impartially conducted general elections. But in the sequel the system failed to work satisfactorily in any of those republics, and before 1938 had in all but Finland and Czechoslovakia been replaced by another. The model for this was provided by Russia; where already since the Bolshevik Revolution of November 1917 representative government had been discarded, and in its stead the direction of the state had been committed to the arbitrary dictatorship of a single party—the only one permitted by law to exist. Between the world wars a constitution on similar lines came into force in every one of the new republics, except the two mentioned above, and in at least three of the monarchies—Italy, Yugoslavia and Greece. These movements, though copying the Russian constitutional model, were not necessarily communist or pro-Russian; on the contrary, both Fascism in Italy and National Socialism in Germany were in origin anti-communist and anti-Russian. But after defeat in the second world war had brought to an end the anti-Russian types of totalitarian government, the pro-Russian type remained. Promoted from Moscow by force and by a very active propaganda, it was ready to Russia's hand as a simple device for effecting the conversion of Poland, Czechoslovakia, Hungary, Roumania, Yugoslavia, Bulgaria and Albania from independence to subjection. (Yugoslavia returned to independence in 1948, although her constitution remained that of a communist dictatorship.) Formal democracy, which in 1900 had appeared likely before long to become general throughout Europe, had thus shrunk back to certain countries on the western sea-board together with Switzerland, Italy and Greece.

The war-induced changes in Europe's map, though in themselves part of the foreign history of the countries concerned, affected at the same time the whole framework of their internal history. It is therefore impossible to trace the movements of European home politics consecutively over the whole of our period. Rather we must think in terms of three sub-periods punctuated by the two wars. Two other cataclysmic events also modified profoundly the stream of evolution. One was the world economic crisis (1929-32), which was nearly as subversive in its politico-social effects as war had been. The other was the rule in Russia (from November 1917 onward) of an ultra-Marxist school of socialism. This not only supplied other countries with the model for a totalitarian regime, but by advertising the success of a doctrine based on the cultivation of class-hatred and violence considerably modified the tone of socialist politics even in lands where socialism till then had largely been utopian, philanthropic, libertarian and constitutional. That does not mean that the western socialist parties embraced the Russian form of socialism (officially called communism from 1920 onwards), but that, especially before 1939, they were considerably influenced by it, as in turn was the anti-socialist reaction.

Movements from democracy to dictatorship had a negative as well as a positive side. In 1900 it was common in England to assume that the future lay everywhere with parliamentary institutions. During the previous seventy years one European country after another had set up a parliament, until Russia, Turkey and Montenegro were the only states devoid of one in any form. Even where, as in Germany under Bismarck's constitution, the advent of a parliament had not meant the advent of parliamentary government, the common supposition had been that in course of time it would. If we ask why these hopes were falsified and why thirty years later the lamp of representative government had gone out in so many countries, we shall find a great part of the answer in the differences between British parliamentarism and continental. They were two distinct systems of government, not merely unlike, but at many points directly opposite to one another. It is essential to grasp the nature and origin of the difference.

The British parliament, the 'mother of parliaments', was organised on a two-party system. This was due to the mode of election employed; any number of candidates might stand for a seat, but the one who polled most votes would win, irrespective of whether he had an absolute majority or not. A moment's thought will show that this mode exerts very strong pressure to reduce the number of candidates for any given seat to two, since serious competition from even a third candidate, let alone from five or six, 'spoils the running'. Transfer that polling-day logic from the single seat to the totality of them, and you get the two-party system. At the end of the nineteenth century it functioned on this basis in every English-speaking country, but in few other countries save Sweden and Alfonsist Spain, both of which had the British mode of election, but with excessively narrow franchises.

By contrast nearly all of the continental parliaments were organised on a many-party system. This was partly due to a mode of election, known as second ballot, which France had originated and other countries had copied from her. Second ballot means that unless on the first polling in a constituency one of the candidates polls a majority of the votes cast, there is a second poll a week or a fortnight later, at which the voters can concentrate on those shown by the first ballot to have the best chance. On the first round the tendency to limit the field is in abeyance; seven or even ten candidates may stand for one seat, and nobody minds. And any one of them, if by extremism or some other aid to prominence he can make his personality stand out amid the jostling crowd of competitors, may hope to acquire on the first ballot a lead which will win him the second. In all but one of the many countries practising it, this mode of election regularly led to a multitude of parties—as a rule, six main ones, with a considerable fluidity of policies and membership as between some of them, and usually with some small 'splinter parties' besides. None of the parties had, or ever expected to have, a majority in the nation or in the parliament. Government was always carried on by temporary coalitions—usually weak, venal, irresponsible, and short-lived.

Down to 1899 every election in Europe had been conducted on one or other of these lines—single ballot immediate election (the British mode) or second ballot (the French mode). The first had invariably tended to produce a two-party system. The second produced a many-party system in every country save Belgium, where owing to the consolidating effect of block voting in the four great cities a two-party parliament functioned in spite of second ballot. But in 1899 Belgium had become still more peculiar; for in that year she was the first to institute a new mode of election—a form of proportional representation. Down to 1893 she had had a very narrow franchise, and the two parties in her parliament were catholics (conservatives) and liberals. But in the 'eighties there grew up among the voteless workers outside parliament a strong but mainly voteless socialist party, which in 1893 forced the introduction of a wide franchise. The immediate result was confusing; the new wine burst the old bottle; and before things had time to sort themselves out, the nation in 1899 replaced second ballot by proportional representation. The particular form of it adopted was one which allowed an extra party to come into the picture if (but only if) there were an exceptionally strong demand for it. The result of the change was a parliamentary structure till then very unusual in modern history—neither a two-party nor a many-party system, but a three-party system.

Thus at the beginning of our period all the parliaments in the world were elected and organised in one or other of three different ways. The third was too recent for its workings to be mapped with certainty, but the bearings of the other two were already unmistakable. The two-party system was a success. In Britain it had enabled an ancient state to be modernised and democratised without revolution. In the United States it had saved the national politics of a vast country with scattered and widely divers populations from the total incoherence which might else have overtaken them. When in the nineteenth century one British colony after another was given self-government, the same mode of election ensured government on the same two-party pattern, and it was their almost automatic success which clinched the British belief in the inevitability of parliamentarism. The wide gulf dividing this system from the many-party systems of the Continent was not sufficiently appreciated on either side.

The working difference between the British and French systems of parliamentary government might be seen in this way. Suppose a government was outvoted by the parliament at Westminster, what would happen? Parliament would willy-nilly have to be dissolved (a most restraining thought for its members, who would incur the cost and risks of an electoral contest); while the government, at least for the time, might normally remain. Suppose a similar conflict at the Palais Bourbon? Invariably the government would be dissolved and the parliament would remain. Thus at Westminster power was with the cabinet, but in Paris it was with the individual members of parliament, who could destroy governments whenever they pleased at no cost to themselves. Where power is, there alone can there be responsibility—in London, with the cabinet, but in Paris, with the members of parliament. But while it is possible to bring home responsibility to the score or so of individuals composing a cabinet, it is far less possible to bring it home to the multitude composing a parliament. And the thing went farther. Under the two-party system the bulk of the government's opponents belong to a single party, which must be ready to take over the administration if the government fails. That readiness compels some measure of responsibility even among opposition critics. How different from the French system, under which there was little to deter a critic from behaving irresponsibly; since he knew that, even if he became a minister, it would be in a fleeting coalition government, where he would have a thousand excuses for not implementing what he had said. Meanwhile under a many-party regime the ministers, daily liable to overthrow, had daily to buy support from individual parliamentarians, especially by letting them influence appointments to offices, but often by concessions of larger scope. Thus jobbery, inefficiency and corruption, together with extremism, pervaded public life.

So while in the English-speaking world representative government was generally assumed a success, a growing question-mark stood against it in the continental countries with second ballot. There were, of course, degrees in its failure, corresponding to the tempers and cultures of the people concerned. The Dutch made a better thing of it than the French, the French than the Italians, while the lowest level may have been reached in some parts of eastern Europe. But everywhere the success or failure of the many-party system tended to be regarded as the success or failure of representative government, and not (as it was) merely that of a particular form of representative government. The phenomenon of a two-party system in Great Britain and Canada (not to mention the United States, where there were other important differences in the form of government) was attributed, not to its real cause, the mode of election, but to some fancied idiosyncrasy of the British political genius. It was therefore thought irrelevant; and whenever the evils in French public life appeared intolerable, the remedy mooted was not to copy Great Britain, but to copy Napoleon III, and to revert from representative government to plebiscitary absolutism.

Similarly in Germany, where the Bismarckian constitution of 1871 had set up a parliament without parliamentary government, the natural tendency to develop from the one to the other was stopped dead by pointing to the example of France. The German federal parliament, being elected like the French chamber by second ballot, had already by 1900 developed much the same number and quality of parties. As early as 1902 a French writer, Antonin Lefèvre-Pontalis, comparing the French Chamber and German *Reichstag* of that day, showed how remarkably similar were the frameworks, or patterns of their parties (see his *Les élections en Europe*). The *Reichstag* could therefore plausibly be argued too irresponsible to be entrusted with supreme power. It is true that in Austria (where the usual ill effects of the many-party system were accentuated by the chaos of nationalities) the Emperor Franz Joseph did concede to a federal parliament, elected by manhood suffrage from 1907 onwards, the powers of a theoretically sovereign legislature. But in case the arrangement should in practice not work, it was provided that under a special article of the constitution the emperor might still, if necessary, legislate over the parliament's head. In the sequel down to 1914 it was only by action under this article that the country was kept afloat. Indeed, in March 1914 the Austrian parliament was adjourned *sine die*, and was still not functioning when four months later Austria-Hungary took so prominent a part in launching the 1914–18 war.

Meanwhile between 1899 and 1914 the new Belgian system—a three-party parliament based on the d'Hondt system of proportional representation—came to work with remarkable success. The reason why this system did not produce more than three parties (as some of its leading promoters had hoped that it would) was that under it every party's surplus votes were lost, whereas if two parties united and their surplus votes in each constituency were added together they might with them obtain in many cases an additional seat. The pressure of this logic soon over-rode the nascent dissensions between liberals and radicals in the Liberal Party and those between non-catholic conservatives and non-conservative catholics in the Catholic-Conservative Party. But it could not over-ride the difference between the socialists and both the other parties; and so a triangular parliament resulted, with no one party commanding a majority. To work this satisfactorily it was necessary that any two of the three parties should be capable of combining to form a ministry, while on occasions even a three-party national cabinet was not excluded. These conditions were satisfied in Belgium, with the aid from 1909 onwards of a remarkable king, Albert I. Meanwhile the early success of the system had caused it, in 1907, to be imitated in Sweden. Sweden till then had the British mode of election, but the conditions there were very like what they had been in Belgium earlier—a narrow franchise, a two-party system, and a third (socialist) party developed on a large scale among the voteless masses. Only, whereas in Belgium there had been two stages of change—first the franchise-widening and later the proportional representation—in Sweden the two were telescoped into a single reform. The form of proportional representation differed only at minor points from that used in Belgium. The feature which had saved the Belgian system from freely multiplying parties—viz., that each party's surplus votes were wasted—was reproduced, possibly without anyone being fully aware of its significance. And another remarkable king, Gustav II, helped to make the triangle a success.

The next phase was a peculiarly unfortunate one for Europe. In 1918, while the first world war was still in progress, Holland, which under second ballot suffered from the usual multiplicity of parties and had seen the Belgian system working well next door, decided to instal proportional representation. She copied the two existing models, but with, as was supposed, an improvement. Regarding it as unjust that any votes should seem wasted, the theorists devised a plan whereby the votes left over in each constituency were collected into a 'national pool', from which by again applying proportional representation further members were returned to the parliament. This plan was adopted, its sponsors not appreciating that the feature which it removed from the Belgo-Swedish system was really its keystone. For the creation of the 'national pool' took away all incentive to keep the number of parties small. Indeed, it went to the other extreme and opened the door wide to 'splinter' parties. Even a party which could not win a seat in a single constituency might yet hope to enter parliament by collecting small votes from many constituencies to yield a quota in the national pool. It is true that some of the countries eventually concerned (notably Germany and Czechoslovakia) tried to correct this by making a party's claim to 'pool' seats depend on its having already won an ordinary constituency seat. But this, while checking party atomism in its extremest form, left the general effects of the system unaltered.

The working of a new constitutional feature is seldom apparent immediately, and for a short time after Holland had adopted the national pool it could still be generally regarded as an improvement on the Belgo-Swedish plan. And during that brief interval it befell in 1919 that no less than eight new republics, essaying democracy, had to frame parliamentary constitutions and determine how their parliaments should be elected.

They were the German republic, Poland, Austria, Czechoslovakia, Finland, Lithuania, Latvia and Estonia. Every one of them adopted proportional representation of the Belgian type, but with the Dutch alteration. Consequently every one of them in the sequel developed parliaments with an unmanageable multiplication of parties; and the many-party system, which had originated in Europe as the outcome of second ballot, became actually aggravated by the substitution of proportional representation with a 'national' pool. Even in sober Holland a parliament of only 100 members came to include ten parties; while in the Reichstag of the German republic before its destruction by Hitler the number of parties exceeded forty. Meanwhile France herself abandoned second ballot, but only for two elections (1920 and 1924), after which it was resumed. The system substituted during the interval (one of so-called, but very peculiar, proportional representation) was rather more consolidating than second ballot, but not enough so to induce a fundamental change.

The first country in which the breakdown of the many-party system led to a dictatorship was Italy. The dictator, Benito Mussolini, obtained supreme power by a kind of *coup d'état*—the so-called 'March on Rome' of 22 October 1922. His system copied pretty closely that evolved by the bolsheviks in Russia, while both he and they owed much to the nineteenth-century example of Napoleon III. The Italian 'Fascist' Party began as a combination of local gangs resembling the 'cudgel-men' on whom Napoleon III had relied, and not very unlike those of Clodius or Milo in the last years of the ancient Roman republic. Mussolini, a blacksmith's son, who began his political life as a socialist and for some time edited the Italian socialist party's chief newspaper, *Avanti*, had many qualifications for a demagogic role—a strong physique, a bold and bombastic eloquence, and above all a deep familiarity with the temper and moods of the Italian people. But he owed his success (which was broken only by defeat in war) above all to two policies, both copied from Soviet Russia. The first was complete control and ceaseless exploitation of all his people's channels of information—newspapers, books, radio, films, stage, schools and platform; the only exception was the pulpit which, however, he largely won over following the concordat concluded by him with the Vatican in 1929. The second was the working of the 'one party'. This was formed by consolidating his various local gangs (each called a *fascio di combattimento*) into a national 'Fascist' Party, which came to number about a million members, or about 2½ per cent of the population. The function of the party, to which most men in important positions had to belong, was to act as the guardian of the regime throughout the country. The despotic system, instead of resting solely on the police, was given the appearance of a popular movement upheld by a vast network of voluntary action. The fascists in Italy thus closely reproduced the role of the communists in Russia, although their doctrinal policies differed and fascism in fact regarded itself as a counterblast to communism. But since so many evils in Italian politics could be fairly attributed to the multiplicity of parties, there was an appearance of logic in attempting to cure them by reducing parties to one.

Mussolini, who in home (though not in foreign) affairs knew his ground well, took the title of Leader (*Duce*) and sought to make it appear that the party and not the individual was the wielder of power. Thus the 'Grand Fascist Council' was declared the supreme authority of the regime. But in fact the Duce controlled it, and all the appointments to posts of any importance throughout the country were subject to his approval. Another development was that of 'corporativism', whereby for economic purposes the greater part of the population was grouped according to its occupations into corporations purporting to represent both employers and employed. Corporativism had some value as helping to mask dictatorship.

Between the first and second world wars this system of government came to be adopted by a great many countries as a substitute for parliamentarism. It need not actually dispense with parliaments, but reduces them to ciphers. The usual method came to be that at elections only candidates of the one party were allowed to stand, and the voters were put under strong compulsion to vote for them, in order that the endorsement which their vote was supposed to furnish for the regime should be as imposing as possible.

The first important country to copy the Italian example was Poland, where in May 1926, not quite four years after the march on Rome, a dictatorship under Pilsudski was set up by a *coup d'état*. This was directly due to the faction and failure of a many-partied parliament elected under the Dutch system of proportional representation. Pilsudski, who in 1923 had retired from public life as the hero of his people, was a most unwilling dictator. For many years he refused to form 'one party', preferring to obtain support from a loose *bloc* of sympathisers. As time went on, however, he had to move closer to the Italian model; and from his death in 1935 to the outbreak of war in 1939 Poland was ruled under a new constitution by one party at whose head stood not an individual, but a small *camarilla*.

The greatest trigger-puller for the change was, however, yet to come. This was the world economic crisis, which spread to Europe from the United States in the latter half of 1929 and lasted for the greater part of four years. It was similar in kind to the 'cyclical' economic crises which had first defined themselves a century earlier; but it was more widespread and vastly more severe than any of its predecessors. Prices and wages fell catastrophically in nearly all countries, and unemployment reached unprecedented heights. In one way or another almost every country save those already under dictatorships changed its government. In those with a stable democracy like Great Britain and the United States the change came constitutionally by a switch-over at or before elections—from

Republicans to Democrats in the United States and from Labour to Conservatives in Great Britain. Taking a wide view over the countries concerned, it cannot be said that the effect of the economic crisis was either radical or conservative; what happened was that in each case the existing government, no matter of which complexion, was turned out. But those changes which, though made in a constitutional way, would not have happened but for the crisis, led on in some cases to changes of constitution. A good illustration was that of the Irish Free State, in which the government of Mr Cosgrave, which for ten years had successfully upheld the Anglo-Irish Treaty of 1921, was because of the crisis defeated by Mr De Valera, with the result that Mr De Valera in the sequel got rid of the treaty and converted what had been a dominion into a republic. But his policies were all ratified by the Irish parliament, and the sovereignty of that parliament remained.

It was otherwise with the countries of eastern and southern Europe, among which there was a wide-spread tendency to replace democracy by the dictatorship of a single party on the Russo-Italian pattern. The example of this which had, in every way, the most importance, occurred in Germany. Prior to the economic crisis there had long been among the thirty or forty parties in Germany two which aimed at dictatorship, and organised 'private armies' for that end (there were other 'private armies' in Germany, notably the *Stahlhelm*, but none so entirely subservient to a political racket). These parties were the Communist, which took its inspiration from Russia, and the National Socialist, which copied the model of Italy. Neither had ever made much headway; and the National Socialists, led by Adolf Hitler, seemed definitely declining. But the economic crisis gave them new life. Ten months after it had extended to Germany occurred the general election of September 1930, when the party of Hitler enlarged its representation in the Reichstag, which at the previous election in 1928 had been only 12, to 107, thus becoming for the first time a leading force there. Even so, nearly two years and a half elapsed before Hitler obtained the post of German Chancellor; nor might he then have done so but for the demonstration which the Reichstag had afforded of a many-party parliament's impotence and irresponsibility. This became critical in 1931–2, when the Reichstag could not be got to vote a budget and the state's necessary revenue had to be obtained by presidential decrees—a course which led President Hindenburg to dismiss from the chancellorship the Reichstag's majority leader Dr Bruening, and to take the disposal of that office entirely into his own hands.

Hitler's one-party dictatorship in Germany, Mussolini's in Italy and Lenin's or Stalin's in Russia had much in common beside their form. All three were what the ancient Greeks called 'tyrannies'; that is, they were systems of absolute government based not on law or inherited right, but on forcible seizure of the reins. And since what force wins force must hold, they inevitably were in the modern sense tyrannical. This was not a new experience for any of the peoples concerned. A century earlier all three had lived wholly or mainly in police-states without the rule of law. Two of them had in the interval moved away from that—the Italians to a constitutional monarchy and a fairly liberal regime, the Germans to a stage at which they claimed that their state, although not a democracy, was a *Rechtstaat*, that is, one subject to the rule of law. Even tsarist Russia, though it could never dispense with severe and arbitrary police methods, usually confined their harsher application to comparatively few persons. The new despotisms set the clock right back. The rule of law they undermined by the rule of the torture-chamber—an institution which in Germany and Russia was used on an enormous scale to inflict the extremest cruelties. Hardly less inhuman were the concentration camps and forced labour camps, to which even greater numbers of people were sent by the secret police on political charges, and there done to death by starvation, overwork and brutal treatment. By these methods or by plain murder political opponents were said to be 'liquidated'. Political trials were rare, except in Russia; where, however, they were used, not to give a prisoner any chance to prove his innocence, but only to advertise a guilt which he had previously been forced to 'confess'.

In Italy there was less savagery than in Russia and Germany, but the principle of tyranny was the same; and so in the other dictatorships. The most humane were the Portuguese, under General Carmona and Dr Salazar, and the Polish, under Pilsudski. With those exceptions the dictatorships represented for Europe a startling retrogression alike in humanity and in morality. The idealism of the nineteenth century gave place to a cynical outlook glorifying force and aggression; while all the older loyalties of family and friendship were undermined by ubiquitous espionage.

The dictators, as has been mentioned, relied very much on controlling the minds of their subjects. The method was both negative and positive— to exclude criticism of the regime and to create enthusiastic support for it. And since the early years are the most impressionable, a special effort was made to win the allegiance of the young. In all the principal dictatorships 'youth' organisations, borrowing many features of the 'boy scouts' but developing a far more militaristic character, became a leading feature. Where, as in Russia and Germany, the party doctrine paraded anti-religious tenets, it was chiefly over this question of training the children that conflict became acute between the regimes and the churches.

In particular the Roman Catholic Church, which had always tried to assert the principle that Catholics should be educated only by Catholics, offered conspicuous opposition to a system which subjected their children to the teaching and leadership of professed unbelievers. In the nineteenth century and early in the twentieth the Roman Catholic Church had, with some exceptions, been usually ranked among the conservative forces of continental Europe, with the liberal forces aligned against it. But now its role changed. In face of dictatorship it was seen as a champion of liberty. The political consequence was that after the second world war, when the dictatorships had been crushed in Italy and Germany and those bodies which had stood against them enjoyed prestige, the governments which came into power in Rome and in Bonn had at their heads 'Christian Democrats'; that is, the leaders of a party which in both countries represented the new bond between Roman Catholic religion and democratic politics. A similar party, the *Mouvement Républicain Populaire* (M.R.P.), was able for similar reasons to occupy a similar position in France.[1] On the other hand, in Russia and in the countries forcibly compelled to become Russian satellites the revived conflict between totalitarian dictatorship and the Roman Catholic Church speedily became acute, and the bishops and clergy of that Church were singled out for systematic persecution, even in countries which had been so predominantly Catholic as Poland, Czechoslovakia and Hungary.

From the dictators' standpoint the dictatorships were uniformly successful. Not one was overthrown by its own subjects during peace. Partly this may be explained by the drastic 'liquidation' of their opponents and the bloody 'purges' in which any subsequent discords within the one party were obliterated. But even more effective perhaps was the mental control, which amounted to something like a new technique of government. Hitler in his book *Mein Kampf* puts no limit on what can be done by propaganda; people will believe anything, provided that they are told it often enough and emphatically enough, and that contradicters are either silenced or smothered in calumny.

The possibilities of such a control were enormously enlarged, within the period that we are considering, by new techniques and inventions. Alfred Harmsworth's two London dailies, the *Evening News* (1894) and *Daily Mail* (1896), were the precursors in Europe of a technically new kind of journalism, which in two decades acquired a footing in most continental countries. Its first aim was circulation, and it reached a far wider public than the earlier press. Next, in 1905, the first European cinema was opened in London. In a few years every country had them; and whereas the cheap newspaper reached people who could barely read, the film reached those who could not read at all. Its usefulness to a tyranny was further increased when the problem of synchronising sight and sound was solved, and from 1927 onwards films became 'talkies'. In the 'thirties the Hitler regime in Germany made very great use of this medium. Every-

---

[1] France after the second world war abandoned second ballot and resorted to different experiments in proportional representation. The first, which elected the constituent assembly, narrowed the field to three substantial parties; the second widened it to four, and the third to five. Governments were precariously based upon combinations of the middle parties.

thing which the government did or wanted to do was explained by special films; but in addition small newsreels brought the 'leader' and his chief associates before their subjects every evening. They were seen and heard at work and at play and in popularity-courting aspects of all kinds; being exhibited, of course, more uniformly at the top of their form than would be possible in real life. Thus a great part of the popular hero-worship, which in the cinema age came to be lavished on 'star' performers, was in Hitlerite Germany, and later in the east European countries, canalised to glorify and endear the dictators.

Last but not least came the invention of broadcasting. The first American broadcast was in 1920; the first British, 1922; the Continent followed. In Russia and elsewhere in eastern Europe the development took a form peculiarly convenient for despotism. The listeners had not each, as in the west, a wireless receiver of his own, but were connected by telephone with a group receiver. Thus they could not use their apparatus to hear foreign broadcasts, or indeed any but their government's. It is difficult to measure the contribution made by each of the above factors to the success of dictatorship, but that of broadcasting was very large. At the same time the dictators did not neglect much older expedients—processions and marches with banners, bands, slogans and oratory, and (a special feature in communist countries) huge portraits of the leaders borne aloft many times life size. Nor did books cease to play a part as 'scriptures'—in Hitlerite Germany Hitler's *Mein Kampf*, and in Russia the works of Marx, Lenin and Stalin.

By using all these devices at once the dictators were able to subject the minds of their peoples to such a battery of persuasion as no human beings had ever undergone before. At the same time they did what they could to prevent any opposed ideas from circulating. In Hitlerite Germany, which till September 1939 retained many commercial and cultural contacts with the West, this was naturally more difficult than in Soviet Russia. After the second world war Russia succeeded in secluding not only herself but all her Sovietised neighbours behind the so-called 'Iron Curtain'. This covered for many purposes the Russian-occupied part of Germany; while the remaining two-thirds of the German people were organised by the western powers on parliamentary lines as a Federal Republic.

What were the principal issues which during this half-century divided the politicians of Europe, each within their several countries? In dealing with so many lands (and such a changing list) large allowance must be made for local peculiarities. Yet there were also marked parallel movements, about which we can usefully generalise.

The most widespread of these may be considered under the following six heads: (1) nationalism; (2) conflicts concerned with the form of government; (3) conflicts between wealth and poverty, giving rise to particular movements like socialism and syndicalism, and also to a wider drift of social reform towards the ideal of a 'welfare state'; (4) agrarian problems, prominent everywhere, but above all for the semi-feudal land-owners and depressed peasantries of eastern and southern Europe; (5) other economic issues—currency, tariffs, quotas; (6) controversies over religion. Of these the second has been dealt with in the preceding pages of this chapter, and the third in the preceding chapter. We shall therefore here be mainly concerned with the other four.

Of course they did not always present themselves separately but often were tangled together. In particular the issues arising out of poverty, grouped above in the third category, affected the shaping of most other issues. It may be said that in the twentieth century economics replaced religion as the issue in politics around which the rest usually revolved. For in this period for the first time it became usual to formulate definite 'standards of living', and the state came to be regarded as responsible for their maintenance and improvement. This conception, which was only nascent in the nineteenth century, emerged originally from the work of statisticians and social enquirers; but it derived much added impetus from the successive wars of 1914–18 and 1939–45, and perhaps even more from the world economic crisis of 1929–32 (see ch. III).

Let us start then with nationalism. In its clearest-cut form it is a claim by a body of persons who consider themselves a nation, that on that ground they are entitled to the position of an independent sovereign state. The claim is generally (though not always) supported by allegations that their nation enjoyed independent statehood in the past—perhaps a misty past. Sometimes the independent sovereign state is already there, but the claim is that blocks of its co-nationals who are still forced to live under other flags ought to be brought under that of their nation. This form of nationalist agitation, which is commonly termed irredentism, was in this period especially to the fore in southern and south-eastern Europe, where the Italians, the Yugoslavs, the Greeks, the Bulgars, the Roumanians, and after the first world war the Magyars, were particularly affected by it.

The number of possible 'nations' in Europe is extremely large, but in practice since the break-up of the medieval unity their multiplication had been limited, not merely by the acquisitiveness of the large states, but by the acquiescence of the smaller units themselves on grounds of defence and economics.

At the beginning of the twentieth century, powers directly affected by nationalist unrest were three—the Ottoman empire, the Austro-Hungarian monarchy, and the Russian empire. The principal subject groups were—under Ottoman rule the Albanians, and the Greek, Serb and Bulgar irredentists in Macedonia; under the Dual Monarchy as such, the Serbs of Bosnia-Herzegovina; under Austria, the Czechs, part of the Poles, some irredentist Ukrainians, and the Slovenes; under Hungary, the Croats, the Slovaks, the Serbs of the Banat, the Roumanians of the Banat and of Transylvania, and some Ukrainians; under the Russian empire, the Finns, Estonians, Letts and Lithuanians, the largest block of Poles, the great bulk of the Ukrainians, and the Roumanians of Bessarabia.

Among the subject peoples the Poles occupied a special position, because they had no longer ago than the eighteenth century been not only an independent nation, but a great power, and because their present subjection was to as many as three of the pre-1914 great powers—Russia, Germany and Austria-Hungary. Of these, Austria-Hungary held the smallest portion, but her rule was notably more sympathetic than that of either Russia or Germany. In Russian Poland a kind of guerrilla warfare between nationalists and police was endemic. In German Poland from the beginning of the century antagonism increased. In 1901 occurred the much-publicised Wreschen incident, when Polish schoolchildren were flogged for refusing to say the Lord's Prayer in German. In 1902 Prince Bülow, then German Chancellor, carried a law expanding an existing scheme for buying up Polish-owned land and settling Germans on it. Further measures against Poles in Silesia were taken in 1904.

Beside all these conflicts of nationalism under the more or less despotic empires of eastern Europe, there were two notable cases of it in the West— the Irish and the Norwegians. In 1905 Norway revolted from Sweden (with which she had been associated in a dual monarchy not unlike that which combined England and Scotland before the Act of Union), and became by peaceful agreement a separate state with a monarchy of its own. In Ireland the agitation of the Roman Catholic native elements, which from the time of Parnell onwards had developed upon increasingly nationalist lines, culminated in 1922 in an Anglo-Irish treaty, whereby all but six of the Irish counties were constituted a 'dominion' (entitled the Irish Free State) within the British Commonwealth of Nations. By two stages (1937 and 1948) this state left the Commonwealth and became the entirely separated 'Republic of Ireland'.

Liberal opinion, which was dominant in Great Britain and France between 1900 and 1914, generally favoured the claims of nationalism. In Britain the great name of Gladstone could be invoked on behalf of those struggling against the Turk or the Austrian. In the United States the stream of sympathy flowed still stronger; for emigrants from the subject races had settled there in large numbers, and in great centres like New York or Pittsburgh or Chicago were formed into organised blocks of voters. Among the immigrants Jews were a numerous body, and thus it was that Zionism—the policy of re-converting the Jewish race into a nationality with a historic soil of its own—won early support in the American Jewries.

The Balkan wars of 1912–13, which expelled Turkey from Macedonia and from all but a corner of Thrace, left the dual monarchy of Austria-Hungary in the invidious position of being the leading obstacle in Europe to nationalist claims. The war of 1914–18 (of which the nominal starting-point, at all events, was an ultimatum by Austria-Hungary to Serbia, then the 'Piedmont' of Yugoslav nationalists) put in question the whole structure of a regime in which the two ruling races added together formed rather less than half the population. Internally the nationalist conflicts had been growing steadily more acute, ever since the settlement of 1867 emancipated the Hungarians while leaving the other subject nationalities in subjection. Yet the powers of the Triple Entente did not in the beginning adhere to a policy of breaking up Austria-Hungary. Partly this was due to the attitude of tsarist Russia, who had nationalist problems of her own, and partly to a recognition, widespread among older diplomatists, that the maintenance of one great power in south-eastern Europe had advantages over a plethora of little ones.

But when the war reached the year 1917 two important changes occurred. One was the Russian revolution—in its two phases, March and November—and the other was the entry of the United States into the war under the leadership of President Wilson. As a result of the first, after some vicissitudes, Finland, Russian Poland, Estonia, Latvia and Lithuania, which were all in German occupation, became detached from the Russian empire. The effect of the second was to bring into the councils of the western powers a statesman who preached the right of self-determination for small peoples. Even so he did not at once draw the full conclusion. In his 'fourteen points' speech (8 January 1918) he merely said that the peoples of Austria-Hungary should be accorded the freest opportunity 'of autonomous development'. But on 18 October 1918 the American note addressed to Austria-Hungary through the Swedish minister, after recounting Washington's recognition of the Czechoslovaks and Yugoslavs, declared that the President was 'no longer at liberty to accept a mere "autonomy" of these peoples as a basis of peace', but must insist 'that they and not he' should be 'the judges of what action on the part of the Austria-Hungarian government will satisfy their aspirations *and their conception of their rights and destiny as members of the family of nations*'.

In the European re-settlement which followed the war Austria-Hungary disappeared. Its dismembered territory went to seven different states—a small Austria, a small Hungary, a much enlarged Roumania, a much enlarged Serbia (called officially the kingdom of the Serbs, Croats and Slovenes, and more popularly Yugoslavia), a new state called Czechoslovakia, a reunited Poland, and Italy. Wilson was guided by two principles, which his colleagues generally accepted: (1) the formerly subjected nationalities should become sovereign; (2) their constitutions should be republican, not monarchical. A few practical exceptions were allowed. Thus the Serbs, Croats and Slovenes were formed into one state, not three;

and the Czechs and Slovaks into one, and not two. Also the established monarchical constitutions of Serbia and Roumania were allowed to survive the great enlargement of these countries (see ch. xvi).

The triumph of nationalism had in the sequel both good and bad results. Frustrated nationalism works like a poison in a community, paralysing the progress that otherwise might be made towards higher standards of life and education. Freed from this paralysis the new states went ahead much faster than they had under Russian or Austro-Hungarian rule. They came, as we have already seen, to be badly handicapped by the chaotic many-party parliaments, to which the form of proportional representation so popular in 1918 condemned them. Nevertheless, much material progress was made in some of them—notably in Poland, in Czechoslovakia, in Finland and in the little state of Estonia. Elsewhere, unfortunately, the enthronement of one nationality too often involved the dethronement of another. The worst case was Hungary, large numbers of whose people found themselves inside the new Roumanian, Yugoslav, or Czechoslovak boundaries, while the surviving core, consumed by a spirit of fierce irredentism, settled down after a brief communist interlude to a reactionary regime, which appeared a standing threat to its neighbours and allowed little progress among its own people. Yugoslavia, again, was torn by conflicts between Serbs and Croats; Roumania had little skill in dealing with the Hungarians and Germans who had become her subjects in Transylvania; and even Czechoslovakia, whose relative success has just been noted, failed to win reliable support from either her Germans or her Slovaks. The rise of an adjacent revolutionary force like Hitler's quickly disclosed all these fissures.

In the 'Balkanised' Europe which resulted, economic policies conformed to the nationalist bias. Each of the new political units aspired to be an economic unit as well, and every new frontier became a new barrier to the movement of goods and services. Not merely were the areas, within which there was internal free trade, much smaller on the average than before, but the tariff walls dividing them were generally much higher; and to tariffs were now added direct restrictions upon imports in the form of licences and quotas. These barriers were raised especially high in most of the east European countries. There very large percentages of the populations were engaged in peasant agriculture, with low living standards and too little spare land or available capital to support higher ones. To relieve this peasant congestion it was sought to develop manufacturing industries; and it was thought necessary to protect them heavily against foreign competition.

The same problem had long confronted Russia, in which down to 1914 so many of the so-called 'succession states' had in whole or in part been included. The policy of industrialisation had been notably developed towards the end of the nineteenth century by the tsarist statesman,

Count Witte, to the accompaniment of a specially high tariff and very low wages. Soviet statesmanship, as it gradually developed after 1917, embodied similar ideas. Great plans were formed to industrialise the country, and it was sought to find capital for them by appropriating nearly the whole margin of the country's increased production, the workers being exhorted and compelled to tolerate for the time being standards not much higher than before. This policy took shape under a system of state collectivism which (save for a brief reversion to freer enterprise—Lenin's so-called 'New Economic Policy' of 1921) embraced the whole industry and commerce of the country. Foreign trade became centralised in the hands of co-operative organisations closely controlled by the government; it was limited to bulk sales and purchases of what were considered essentials, and embodied as a rule in barter agreements. The aim was 'autarky' —to render the Soviet empire independent of supplies from outside; and the consequences for the rest of Europe was a shrinkage of its eastern market. Till 1914 Germany and Great Britain had each an important Russian trade; but under the Soviet system most of it came to an end. Russian Poland, again, had under the tsardom developed a large textile industry, whose goods were sold especially to Russian purchasers. But the reunited Poland after 1919 was no longer inside the Russian tariff, and found the old market for Polish textiles closed.

Economic separatism was further accentuated by the world economic crisis of 1929–32. This began in America, but crossed the Atlantic towards the end of its first year. In 1930 and 1931 its ravages were phenomenal; they first affected the producers of primary commodities, then industry and then banking. The whole conformed to the general picture of a cyclical economic crisis; but none previously recorded had been anything like so severe. The one country not affected by it was Russia, whose state-directed machine went on functioning in autarkic isolation. True, the value of her immunity was offset by her low living-standards; but her government was not overthrown, whereas elsewhere in the world nearly every government was—in constitutional countries at the hands of the voters, and elsewhere by *coups d'état*.

Although many economists at the time attributed the severity of the 1929–32 crisis in part, at least, to the economic fragmentation of Europe, the reaction of governments to it was generally towards increasing, not relaxing, the effort to achieve autarky. In this they were influenced, not only by the motives already described, but by the desire to support their respective currencies. Before the first world war the task of relating national currencies to world trade devolved mainly on the City of London. Great Britain was the chief creditor and lender country; and with her own currency firmly anchored to a gold standard she maintained a working adjustment of currency exchanges throughout the world. That system was destroyed by the first world war, at the close of which all the major

European countries, including Great Britain, had come down to having currencies of inconvertible paper. The change had been accompanied by inflation, the degree of which varied widely from one country to another.

In the decade between the end of the first world war and the beginning of the world economic crisis, different currency developments occurred in different countries, but two may be cited as opposite extremes—the British and the German. Great Britain, at the cost of depressing her trade, pursued a deflationary policy, until in 1925 she brought the pound back to gold at the pre-war parity. But this proved still too high, and the attempt to maintain it caused British trade to remain depressed, while the Continent enjoyed a temporary boom. Then came the world depression; and when in 1931 it had reached the stage of wrecking many continental banks, the Bank of England was heavily shaken and Great Britain returned to a currency of inconvertible paper. Thus all the sacrifices which she had made for the gold standard appeared to have profited her nothing, and other European countries were not tempted to follow her example.

But neither were they tempted to follow Germany's. Her case was complicated, her situation being affected not merely by her recklessly top-heavy war finance and huge losses, but by the reparations payments imposed on her under the Treaty of Versailles. This is not the chapter in which to trace the course of the resulting international controversies, which led in 1923 to the occupation of the Ruhr by French troops (see p. 465). But the tactics employed by the German government involved the unlimited inflation of the German mark, and this provided all Europe with an object-lesson in what unlimited inflation may mean. Money in Germany so completely lost its value that all wealth held or payable in money form virtually disappeared. The blow fell heaviest on the middle and professional classes, whose savings were wiped out, and whose earnings could never keep pace with the inflation. The catastrophe was felt the more, because Germany was orderly and the inflation did not, as it had done earlier in Russia, form only one revolutionary feature in a situation revolutionary all over. With the material effects went moral effects at least as important. The stability of money in any society is needed for the stability of contracts, and that, again, for the stability of moral obligations. Thus any gross instability of money saps the very foundations of social conduct; people affected lose their old bearings and drift at the mercy of any new tide or current. It was the demoralisation of Germany by the great inflation of 1923–4 that made possible nearly ten years later her people's acceptance of Hitler (see also above, ch. III).

The German currency crisis was eventually ended for the time being by the creation of a new currency, with substantial help from abroad, including the readjustment of reparations payments under the Dawes Plan. But it for long influenced the rest of Europe as a warning. Pressures making for inflation existed in nearly all European countries, and especially in those where many-party parliaments produced weak governments liable to be blackmailed into overspending. But in most cases, before the situation had quite passed beyond control, awareness of the German precedent would bring a recoil. Meanwhile the persistency of the currency problem constantly stimulated the autarkist policies already noted.

The world economic crisis in the three years of its course (1929–32) occasioned unemployment and economic misery on an unexampled scale, and so led, as has been said, in nearly every country but Russia to a change of government. Some of these changes, like that in Great Britain in 1931 or that in the United States in 1932, involved no change of regime, and might have occurred in any case through swings of the pendulum. Others, like that in southern Ireland in 1932, had revolutionary results, and completely diverted the stream of history. But in the revolutionary class by far the most important case for Europe and the world was that of Germany. In 1928, a year before the economic crisis, a German general election was held, at which Hitler's National Socialist (commonly abbreviated to 'Nazi') party polled only 800,000 votes. Two years later, after Germany had endured the crisis for less than a year, they polled at the general election of 1930 some 6½ million votes. This startling rise first made Hitler a serious candidate for office, which he never had been before; and though in 1931 and 1932 his prospects fluctuated, on 30 January 1933 he became Chancellor. Once his hand was on the controls, the revolution began, which led eventually to the second world war.

Hitler was fortunate in attaining power just as the economic crisis showed signs of waning. But its disappearance from Europe was accelerated by his policy of rapid rearmament. This he had always advocated; and its effect on the economic situation in Germany, and indeed throughout Europe, was that of 'priming the pump' on an enormous scale. Business was stimulated directly or indirectly outside Germany's borders, while inside them the problem soon became, not to find employment, but to adjust the claims of the armament industries with those of the industries sustaining the nation's life. Hitler's lieutenant, Goering, crystallised the antithesis as 'guns versus butter'. In the upshot it proved possible to keep Germany well provided, while finding for armaments larger sums than she had declared herself able to find for reparations.

For the continent of Europe the period 1933–9 was under these conditions prosperous economically; but it was darkened by deepening fear and foreboding. The violence and bloodshed which accompanied the German revolution were on a far smaller scale than the Russian, but they came much nearer home to western Europe; and the barbarous vendetta against the Jews inspired particular horror. Moreover, Germany's fast-reviving army was obviously intended for fighting, and every one of the ten countries then bordering her had reason to dread becoming its battlefield. The threat began to affect their home politics; new Fascist parties (like the Belgian 'Rexists') appeared as forerunners of German invasion; while in Spain for $2\frac{1}{2}$ years the three totalitarian powers—Italy and Germany on the one side, and Russia on the other—fought a war which was of limited liability for themselves, but unlimited for the Spaniards, of whom over a million perished in the 'civil' struggle. Political refugees from the dictator-ruled countries thronged into the remaining democracies, living evidence of the advancing terror. Under such conditions the issue of totalitarianism versus free government came to overshadow all others, and the politics of ordinary progress were slowed down before it.

One of the most characteristic features of the time was the development in many countries of 'private armies'. Probably the first (1919) was Mussolini's 'blackshirts', who carried him into power in Italy in October 1922, and were then expanded into a nation-wide organisation. Similar para-military bodies sprang up in Germany and Austria, where every large party or group of parties tended to form its para-military equivalent. The movement spread widely elsewhere, though in constitutional countries like France and Britain it was kept within bounds. Linked to each 'army' was usually a 'youth movement', which taught to boys in their teens the gospel that violence gives a better political title than votes.

There followed the war of 1939–45, during which the whole continent except Spain, Portugal, Switzerland, Sweden, Turkey and parts of Russia fell for varying periods under the control of totalitarian Germany. Germany's chief care was to exploit their economic resources for her war purposes—which she did skilfully and on the whole successfully—and to suppress the guerrilla warfare organised by 'resistance' movements. Guerrilla warfare is a demoralising experience for all concerned in it; and when peace came back in 1945, the evil legacy of lawless violence and the claims of war-time 'resistance' leaders to become peace-time political leaders bedevilled the politics of a great many European countries, including France and Italy. Russia annexed the three Baltic states, and put an end to their separate existence; and besides other large direct annexations contrived to impose communist constitutions on six states— Poland, Hungary, Roumania, Bulgaria, Yugoslavia and Albania. They had all in 1919 been set up as democracies, though all had subsequently experienced dictatorships. Czechoslovakia, though also bound to Russia, was at first allowed to remain democratic; but a *coup d'état* in February 1948 caused her to become communist. A little later Yugoslavia, while remaining communist, threw off the Russian yoke; which, however, remained effective for the others, and was rigorously enforced by periodical 'purges'—first of opposition leaders, and later of communist leaders who had incurred Moscow's disapproval. State trials and death penalties crushed independence.

Let us now cast our eyes back over the half-century and trace briefly the courses taken in it regarding two issues which we noted at the outset: the agrarian and the religious.

Agrarian questions shaped themselves differently according as a particular country was an importer or an exporter of farm products. Countries like Germany and France, which consumed more food than they grew, could and did help their farmers materially by imposing tariffs on imported food. Countries like Russia, Roumania or Denmark, which were exporters of food, could not. In the latter, therefore, the question of food tariffs seldom arose; but in the former it engendered much opposition between urban and rural interests. In France the rural interests won, because the peasants were the largest class in the nation. In Germany they also won (against the opposition of the Social Democrats and the Left parties in general), because the landowners of the north and east were the pillars of Prussia and Prussia was the pillar of the Reich, and because down to 1914 it was generally held that country dwellers were better material for an army than town dwellers.

Another important contrast was that between large-scale farming and peasant agriculture. In some areas of Europe one of these patterns prevailed; in others, the other; and again in others the two were found side by side. In the last case there was apt to be discontent and political ferment, the peasants hungering for more land, and subdivision of the large estates seeming the only obvious way to obtain it. Cases in point were Spain, Italy, Sicily, Roumania, Galicia and above all Russia down to the revolution of 1917. France, the Low Countries and southern Germany were predominantly peasant; northern and eastern Germany was mainly cultivated in large farms. So was Hungary, where the Magyars practised some of the best farming in Europe.

In Russia at the beginning of the century a third system was still widely prevalent—cultivation by the *mir*, a kind of village collectivity. This did not make for efficiency and was associated with low standards of living. After the revolutionary outbreak of 1905–6 had been suppressed, Stolypin, one of the few real statesmen whom tsarism employed in its last decades, pursued a policy of dissolving the *mirs* and substituting individual ownership. This might have achieved even more than it did, had not the murder of Stolypin in 1910 and the outbreak in 1914 of the first world war operated to restrict its effect.

Subdivision of the large estates always stood in the background as a policy which could be relied on to make a revolution popular; and it was one of the two policies (peace with Germany being the other) which enabled Lenin and his associates in and after 1917 to rivet their rule upon Russia. But it had one grave drawback. The large farms were far more productive per acre than the peasant holdings, so that the change always tended to create shortages of food. For that reason the communist rulers of Russia were led to abandon peasant ownership and substitute a policy of state-controlled 'collective farms'; in this way it was hoped to secure the economic advantage of large-scale farming without creating a powerful class of large landowners. Under Stalin the policy, preluded by the 'liquidation' of the richer peasants (*kulaks*), was ruthlessly insisted upon. A large manufacture of tractors was also organised to equip the new farms.

The other topic, religion, had during the nineteenth century played a very prominent part in European politics. This was especially so in countries where the dominant church was the Roman Catholic; including France, Italy, Austria and the southern and western areas of Germany. Religious conflict in Germany receded after 1880, following Bismarck's abandonment of the *Kulturkampf*; but the century opened with a sharpening of the issues in the Latin countries. There Catholicism faced the hostility not only of liberals, radicals and freemasons but of the rapidly rising socialist movement.

France had just been through the drama of the Dreyfus case, and the turned tide ran heavily against the church. In 1901 the remarkable cabinet (1899–1902) of Waldeck-Rousseau passed an Associations Law closing down all monasteries, convents and religious orders save such as the state might authorise. But the rising waters of anti-clericalism did not stop there. In 1905 a more extreme premier, Émile Combes, carried a Separation Law, which abolished Napoleon's 1802 concordat between France and the Vatican and at once disendowed and disestablished the church. This proved not entirely to the church's disadvantage; but the legacy of bitterness continued, survived the first world war, and helped to increase the political confusion of the inter-war period. One of the issues was state help for the maintenance of the Catholic schools; it was a dogma of the Left that none should be given.

In Italy there were similar cleavages, in addition to the special conflict arising out of the state's refusal to the pope of temporal sovereignty over any Italian soil. A *non expedit* issued by Pope Pius IX in 1867 advised Italian Catholics not to vote in the state's elections. That was not strictly an order, and early in the present century bold spirits disregarded it. But it was not until November 1918 that Pope Benedict XV withdrew it, and opened the way for full Catholic participation in Italian democracy. The 'popular party' then formed disappeared, like the other parties, under Mussolini; but in 1929 the next pope, Pius XI, concluded with the dictator a concordat which ended the strife between church and state, and recognised the pope as temporal sovereign of a token area, the Vatican City. The agreement contained other points in the Vatican's favour.

Thanks to it, and to Mussolini's awareness of his countrymen's regard for the papacy as an Italian institution, no such conflict subsequently arose in Italy between the church and the dictatorship as in Germany and Russia. The communists and the national socialists were each anti-religious, though in form both allowed freedom of religious worship. Where they primarily came into conflict with the churches was over the training of youth. Each had its 'youth movement' designed to indoctrinate the rising generation with the party's aims; and as these in both cases negated Christianity, the churches, Evangelical as well as Catholic, resisted. Later, when the German dictatorship fell, their resistance gave them in countries which it had ruled a title to popular favour, and so helped to account for the new prominence in post-war Germany, France and Italy of popular 'Christian Democrat' parties. In the communist-ruled east it was different. There the churches resisted; but dictatorship did not fall.

It is early to conclude that the half-century was poor in great political thinkers; for often the importance of a particular teaching only becomes manifest in the practical world after some generations. The period reviewed in this chapter witnessed in the academic sphere a large expansion of political studies—notably in France, Great Britain and America, but also in Germany and Switzerland; the last being specially stimulated by the installation of the League of Nations at Geneva. But political practice still drew its guiding impulses from earlier theorists—on the Continent from Rousseau, Hegel and Marx; in Great Britain from Burke, Bentham and John Stuart Mill. And even if to the first trio we add Comte and Bismarck and to the second Bagehot and Sidney Webb, we still scarcely emerge from the nineteenth century, only the last-named having lived on into the twentieth.

The dominant issue of the period was that between representative government and (in one form or another) dictatorship. If free institutions based on free voting will not work (and in many countries such seemed to be the case, whatever might be its true explanation), can an unfree dictatorship solve the unsolved problem of government, and if so by what methods and on what principles? The leading dictators of the period—especially Lenin, Hitler and Stalin—differed from their prototype, Napoleon III, in that they were all copious and forcible writers; and their books, which attained fabulous circulations, were directed to answering those questions.

Between the Russian dictators and the Italian and German there was a theoretical difference. The Russian despots were Marxists, while the Italian and German were not (though Mussolini had entered public life as one, and Hitler called his party 'National Socialist'). But this made little difference to their versions of dictatorship. Each rejected government by free votes; each relied on a small governing junta, appointed by the dictator and in the last resort responsible to him alone. Ruling in Italy, Mussolini judged it expedient to make a concordat with the Vatican. But the other three were hostile to Christianity, which their most trusted supporters were not allowed to profess. For each of the four, might was right; moral scruples were ruled out; and the injustice of any policy or the falsity of any propaganda was immaterial provided that it succeeded. Each relied on three main agencies to uphold their regimes: an intense and monopolistic propaganda; a secret police, backed by torture-chambers; and 'the party'. The second was not a new invention, but the other two were. The concept of a 'party', originally developed in connection with voting, was twisted to cover the enrolment of a ubiquitous corps of pledged supporters, who became the unpaid but privileged props of a system from which free voting had disappeared. The chief motive for political doctrine was to indoctrinate these 'party members'.

The writings of Lenin pre-suppose the infallibility of the Marxist dialectic, and represent a blend of Marxian thought with some later accretions— notably a theory of 'imperialism' derived from the English economist J. A. Hobson (1858–1940). Stalin's writings also are usually, in form, comments on the Marxian oracles. Conversely Mussolini and Hitler each tried to give an air of system to their unsystematic ideas by tying anti-Marxist labels to them. Mussolini's writing seldom rose above ephemeral journalism; but Hitler in his *Mein Kampf* produced perhaps the most significant book of the period. Tawdry in style and loosely flung together, it yet impresses by its flaming conviction, by its mastery of the dynamics of hatred, and by the brutal sincerity with which it negates ordinary values and erects a kind of idealistic satanism in their place.

In their overthrow of eighteenth- and nineteenth-century traditions the dictators were helped, if not prompted, by a broad current of thought. One might instance the late nineteenth-century influence of Nietzsche (1844–1900) and the early twentieth-century writings of Oswald Spengler (1880–1936). The latter, whose *Untergang des Abendlandes* appeared in 1918, when the disillusionments of the first world war were already rife, gave powerful expression to the view that the nineteenth-century ideals had been mirages and the society corresponding to them was breaking up. The weakening of the popular hold of many Christian churches in the more advanced countries had a parallel effect; in decade after decade from about 1880 the size of their congregations tended to fall. Parallel too was the switch-over in the philosophical schools (very marked in England) from the so-called idealism of the later nineteenth century to the so-called realism of the twentieth. The new doctrine, so far as it affected any springs of action, did so in the direction of sanctioning materialism and weakening morality. So, on the whole, did the writings of the two great British socialist men of letters—G. Bernard Shaw and H. G. Wells; neither of whom really believed in democracy (see also ch. VI).

Yet the advocates of dictatorship were far from having things all their own way. Great Britain, the mother-country of representative government, remained firmly attached to it; and her example, powerfully reinforced from overseas by that of the United States and those of the British Dominions, was never interrupted. Elsewhere it was possible in Switzerland, the Low Countries and Scandinavia for writers, like statesmen, to take democracy for granted.

Of democratic theories during this period the most striking feature is the number of new (or partly new) fields of speculation which were opened up. Sociology, psychology (with psychiatry and psychoanalysis), anthropology and economics were all brought to bear on political thinking; while the increased number of states with democratic constitutions greatly widened the possibilities of comparative politics.

Three sociologists who were closely contemporary—T. Veblen (1857–1919) in the United States, Graham Wallas (1853–1932) in England, and E. Durkheim (1858–1917) in France—illustrate the variety of results to be obtained from that approach; though the last two had a common background in the radicalism of the nineteenth century. Another English sociologist of that period, L. T. Hobhouse (1864–1929), blended utilitarian with evolutionary thought and found new applications of the latter. Wallas also took a part in applying psychology to politics. But there the period's greatest figures were the Viennese Freud (1858–1939) and the Swiss Jung (1878–), both of whom influenced political thought (not everyone, for instance, who spoke of an 'inferiority complex' knew that he was employing a category of Jung's). In their bearings on politics the tendency of both psychology and anthropology was to draw attention to the large part played by custom and habit, the sub-rational and the non-rational, the subconscious and even the unconscious, in the build-up of societies and states. These discoveries widened men's outlook, but the actual constitutions of the democracies were little affected by them. The dictators, on the other hand, used them extensively in their policy of governing by propaganda.

In the study of political obligation an interesting contribution was that of the 'pluralists' (H. J. Laski, Bertrand Russell, G. D. H. Cole). Widening an argument originally developed by churchmen, they denied the state's right to override all other loyalties, for example those to a church, a trade union or a guild.

Of the vastly increased importance which economics had for politics in this period, something has been said above. Earlier and much fuller recognition of it accounts mainly for the growth of the socialist school at the expense of the liberal. The British conception of the Welfare State sprang, inevitably perhaps, from the final widening of the franchise in a mainly industrial country. Its theory, however, owed a great deal towards the beginning of the century to Sidney and Beatrice Webb; while both its theory and its practice came eventually to be shaped by W. H. (later Lord) Beveridge, whose *Report on Social Insurance and Allied Services* (1942) may be claimed as one of the seminal writings of the century.

In the field of comparative politics the names of James (Viscount) Bryce and Esmein still led. Bryce's last great work, *Modern Democracies* (1921), appeared only a year before he died, but pointed the way for much useful work on similar lines. Nevertheless, it is remarkable how little attention, on the whole, was paid to such study by statesmen, and how often constitutional or electoral changes were made, whose results were not intended, yet could have been anticipated.

CHAPTER V

SCIENCE AND TECHNOLOGY

As the nineteenth century drew to its end, the mechanism and pattern of Nature seemed to have been revealed to the scientist in broad outline; and his researches appeared to some degree, especially in the physical sciences, to have assumed the form of investigations into a structure that was more or less known and established by the work of those who had gone before him. Scientific thought had already undergone three great changes that are properly described as revolutions, since they were no mere changes of emphasis but fundamental changes in outlook. They had all been effected in modern times and in western Europe. The seventeenth century had seen the revolution in mechanics and the foundation of modern physics, begun by Galileo and completed by Newton and marked particularly by the publication of Newton's *Principia* in 1687; in the eighteenth century there came the revolution in chemistry, brought about by Lavoisier's classic experiments and associated, so far as such events may be dated, with the publication of his *Traité élémentaire de Chimie* in 1789, a date which still conveniently marks the foundation of modern chemistry; the revolution in biology was more recent, introduced by the publication of Darwin's *Origin of Species* in 1859. Biology had not kept pace with the physical sciences, but it too now seemed at last to have set out on its modern road; and the scientific mind appeared to be concerned at this period with what may be described in general terms as an increasingly refined anatomy of Nature. The world around us, it was considered, was made up both in its living and in its non-living forms of a number of chemical elements. About seventy-five were already known, and it was recognised that there were probably others not yet discovered. The elements consisted of eternal and indestructible atoms: the atoms of any one element were alike and had the same weight, different from that of the atoms of every other element. The protean nature of energy was understood and its transformation from one form into another of its numerous manifestations, into mechanical or thermal or chemical or electrical energy, had been quantitatively determined in exact and refined experiments. The framework of the world was apparently known.

In the last few years of the century, however, the situation suddenly changed. In 1896 Becquerel discovered radio-activity and in 1899 Mme Curie concluded that radio-active atoms were unstable and that in the radio-active processes observed they were undergoing disintegration with release of energy; and meanwhile in 1897 Sir J. J. Thomson showed that the so-called cathode rays, discovered by Plücker in 1859, consisted of sub-microscopic particles carrying negative charges of electricity: since they were produced in identical form from many different kinds of atoms, these particles, which he called 'corpuscles', and which were later renamed 'electrons', were a common constituent of atoms. Atoms, therefore, were not simple but composite; and some of them were unstable and disintegrating at measurable rates. These two discoveries, made at the very close of the century, ushered in the fourth revolution in science in modern times and opened to us the new world of atomic physics.

Science had, of course, been applied to some extent in industry even in the seventeenth century and still more in the nineteenth, but such application was not general and the links between science and technology were not close. Many of those engaged in politics realised the importance of scientific knowledge and its application in the modern world. Before the nineteenth century closed A. J. (later Lord) Balfour remarked of scientists: 'They are the people who are changing the world and they don't know it. Politicians are but the fly on the wheel—the men of science are the motive power.' But it was the first world war that effectively demonstrated to the modern nation-states and their governments the necessity of applied science for their economic and military survival.

So the nineteenth century ended with a fundamental and revolutionary change in the physical sciences and with some recognition that it was science that was moulding the world of the future.

The first half of the twentieth century proved to be a period of advance in science surpassing that of all preceding times in extent, in rapidity and in application; and in these fifty years the harvest of four centuries of modern science was reaped so thoroughly that it changed the whole aspect and outlook of our civilisation as well as our daily lives and our habits of thought. When men began some four hundred years ago to abandon the older ways of thinking and speculating about Nature and her workings, and to give up the practice of constructing systems of the world prematurely on shreds of evidence, they turned instead to the limited objective. They turned also to the 'explanation' that was to be accepted as 'true'—and this merely in the provisional and scientific sense—only if it agreed with indisputable and verifiable experimental fact. They had embarked upon a new adventure, much as other men went on voyages of discovery; and none could have foreseen that the knowledge that would ultimately be gained would presently outstrip their organised political capacity to control its application and to limit its use to beneficent ends, or that the customary freedom enjoyed by scientists for centuries in the publication of their discoveries would finally have to be taken from them in certain fields in the interests of military security and national survival. In the period now being discussed the invention of the internal combustion engine solved the problem of heavier-than-air flight and so gave us the aeroplane with its terrible powers of destruction in war; the advance of atomic physics has given us the atomic bomb, by which humanity holds in its own hands the very means of its extermination, perhaps of the destruction of 'the great globe itself' with 'all which it inherit', or perhaps of the mutation of living forms into new and monstrous evolutionary species. Man has for the first time become the master of his fate.

From its very beginnings, of course, modern science has been of consequence outside the study and the laboratory, beyond its immediate frontiers and often far beyond them. In the physical sciences, the heliocentric theory of Copernicus, set forth in his *De Revolutionibus Orbium Cælestium* in 1543, displaced the habitation of man from the centre of the universe, about which the sun was believed to revolve for his benefit, to a minor planet in the solar system and gave him a less dignified and less important place in the material scheme of things; and, more recently, in the biological sciences, Darwin's theory of evolution as propounded in the *Origin of Species* in 1859 demonstrated man's remote and humble animal origin and removed him from his proud and privileged spiritual position of being 'a little lower than the angels'. From Copernicus to Darwin, however, these and similar advances, with such consequences on human thought and life as they might have, affected the minds of only a very small minority of men and the daily lives of probably none of them. The first half of the twentieth century brought great change in this respect; through the spread of education and the multiplication of a great variety of means for the popularisation and dissemination of scientific and technical knowledge, men and women of all classes everywhere, at least among the democracies, became aware that their survival and alike their destruction depended on the progress of science, or on how their rulers or the rulers of other peoples decided to apply that progress. These matters became clearer, however, and grimmer in their dread reality at the end of the second world war. We turn for the moment to earlier years and other fields in the half-century.

In the last fifty years there has been an unparalleled increase in our knowledge, not only of the complexity of the atom but also of the vastness of the universe, not only of the infinitesimally minute but also of the incomprehensibly great. When the century opened, the distances of only about twenty stars were known with any reasonable accuracy. As a result of the construction of new telescopes and of developments in photography the distances of several thousands have been determined accurately in the last half-century, and much has been learned thence about the size and structure of the cosmic system. The completion of the great 100-inch reflector telescope at Mount Wilson in California provided an instrument with greatly increased light-gathering power; and it soon became clear that there are galaxies other than our own, the so-called 'island universes' to the number of about a hundred million, all about the same order of size and all receding apparently from our universe, the Galactic System. The nearest is some 500 million light-years distant from us, that is, at the distance that would be traversed in 500 million years by light, which travels at a speed of 186,000 miles per second. The astronomer has, indeed, had to devise and adopt a new yard-stick for his measurements, namely, the 'light-year', the distance travelled by light in one year, in order that he may be enabled to handle these huge and incomprehensible figures conveniently. The expansion of our world in these fifty years is enormous; its vast dimensions cannot be visualised by the human mind, and man, though the astronomers may show him to be 'a citizen of no mean city', finds his imagination incapable of realising its gigantic and colossal grandeur. Our own 'universe' has a diameter now calculated at about 100,000 light-years.

Cosmic space, therefore, so far as the great modern telescopes have probed, has been shown to contain an enormous number of 'island universes', all more or less of the same size and more or less evenly distributed. Some of them appear to be still in process of condensation and formation from glowing gaseous matter, or were so when the light by which our telescopes detect their existence and their state left them hundreds of millions of years ago on its long journey to our planet. Inter-stellar space, for long thought to be void, appears to be far from empty, since it contains much highly tenuous matter, this inter-stellar matter being comparable in amount with the stellar matter of the cosmos.

Much knowledge was gained during this half-century about the stars and about their chemical constitution and their evolution. The existence of 'giants' and of 'white dwarfs', which consist of very dense matter, as much as 10 tons to the cubic inch, and of variables of different kinds has been detected. It has also been shown that, in general, the main sequence stars consist in all probability mainly of the element hydrogen, from which there are other reasons for supposing all the other chemical elements to have been formed. The process of probing space continues with ever more powerful telescopes, but the present century has already revealed much of the structure of the vast universe, or system of 'universes', with some knowledge of its evolution and its composition.

So far as this century has gone, these advances have brought an even greater sense of the vastness of the world and have reduced mankind, at least on the physical plane, to a creature of still more microscopic minuteness, yet taking such courage as he may in this awful immensity in which he finds himself from the circumstance that it is his mind that has penetrated to some extent its remote depths.

The hundred million universes, it has been shown, are composed ultimately, like man himself, of atoms, of those sub-microscopic particles which the present half-century, after some beginnings at the close of the nineteenth century, has revealed as minute and complex worlds in themselves. Almost until 1900 the atom, in spite of the rise of a chemical atomic theory under John Dalton in the first decade of the nineteenth century, was, so far as science was concerned, merely a hard solid unstructured sort of infinitesimal billiard-ball, or, as Lucretius had described it two thousand years earlier, *solido atque æterno corpore*. In 1897–9 Sir J. J. Thomson detected the first component to be known in the structure of the atom. This has since become familiar as the *electron*. Electrons were identical in all atoms from which they were obtained; and they proved to be particles carrying a negative charge of electricity, and possessing a mass very much smaller than that of a hydrogen atom, a mass presently shown to be about 1/1850th of that of a hydrogen atom. The identification of a constituent common to all atoms recalled the dreams of the alchemists about the transmutation of the elements, and such changes were indeed effected later.

Shortly afterwards another particle was discovered in the structure of the atom, a particle charged with positive electricity equal in amount to the negative charge on the electron, and with a mass the same as that of the hydrogen atom. It was called a *proton*. It appeared that the atoms of the different chemical elements were formed of differently ordered assemblages of electrons and protons, the number of electrons in the atom of a particular element being the same as the number of protons, since the atom as a whole was electrically uncharged.

Then in 1911 Lord Rutherford introduced, to quote Sir Arthur Eddington, 'the greatest change in our idea of matter since the time of Democritus'. In his researches on radio-activity Rutherford had shown that the alpha-rays, as they were called, which were emitted like beta-rays and gamma-rays in radio-active disintegration, were, in fact, not rays, but positively charged helium atoms. Their mass was four times as great as that of a proton and they carried a charge double that of the proton. Also they moved at high speeds and had a high kinetic energy. They were known to pass through matter easily because of their great velocity and high energy, but Rutherford found that in so doing they occasionally suffered very large deflections. He concluded therefore that the inside of the atom was mostly empty, which would account for the observed fact that alpha-particles in general passed through matter without deflection, but that the occasional deflections had been caused when the alpha-particles had, in traversing the atoms, approached near a small central and positively charged nucleus or core. Thus the ancient solid atom, accepted from Democritus to Dalton and even for a century after Dalton had propounded his theory, was now revealed as a structure largely empty and consisting of a minute but massive central nucleus, with a positive electrical charge, surrounded at a distance by a peripheral shell of negatively charged electrons—a kind of solar system in miniature. Matter seemed, therefore, to be mostly empty space.

It appeared at the same time that protons and electrons, in some instances, might form two slightly different structures with slightly different atomic weights and, therefore, that the atoms of a given chemical element might exist in two forms with slightly different atomic weights. Up to this time the atomic weight of an element had been one of its supposedly invariable characteristics; but for such chemically identical atoms, with slightly different atomic weights but otherwise chemically indistinguishable, as now appeared to be possible, Soddy coined the name 'isotopes' in 1913 when he discovered the two isotopes of lead produced by the radio-active decay of uranium and of thorium respectively. In the same year J. J. Thomson in a study of positive rays discovered the isotopes of neon; and by means of the ingenious mass-spectrograph F. W. Aston showed in 1919 and in later years that most of the chemical elements were mixtures of isotopes.

The discovery that all atoms possessed two constituents, and that atoms differed chemically because of the different numbers of protons and electrons of which they were composed, brought science back to the long rejected idea that matter was transmutable, a theory over which the alchemists had spent their lives and their fortunes, or some part of the fortunes of their patrons. Studies on radio-activity had already shown that certain elements were gradually undergoing change and disintegration, that uranium slowly passed into lead through a very long period of time and that thorium also underwent the same change. In other words, certain elements were being 'transmuted', but neither by the methods of the ancient alchemists nor according to their dreams; for, whereas they had hoped to convert base lead into noble gold or silver, Nature was slowly turning precious uranium into base lead. The first modern 'transmutation' was achieved by Rutherford in 1919, when he succeeded in obtaining hydrogen by bombarding certain light elements with alpha-particles, and thus in producing a simpler atom from a more complex one. In 1922, however, Blackett concluded from similar experiments that oxygen was produced in the bombardment of nitrogen atoms with alpha-particles, in this case a more complex atom being obtained from a less complex one by a 'transmutation' in which there was a building up rather than a breaking down. The rapid development of this work, by means of the cyclotron and later the atomic pile, has brought about many other transmutations: it has even led to the production of new elements, the so-called 'trans-uranic elements', those that fall beyond the heaviest element, uranium, in the chemist's Periodic Table. These new elements, such as neptunium, plutonium, americium, curium, berkelium and californium, were first produced in the laboratory; some of them have since been detected in minute proportions in pitchblende. The significant advance, however, is that the atomic physicist has, in this half-century, not merely transmuted elements but also produced artificial or synthetic ones.

Further striking advances in this field have led to the production of a number of radio-active, that is, unstable, isotopes of known elements, a result that has found many valuable applications. One that may be specially mentioned in passing is the use of radio-active carbon, or radio-carbon as this isotope of carbon is often called, in physiology and in medicine, whereby this substance may be traced in its passage through the organism by means of the external photographic detection of its radio-activity.

The use of radio-carbon has led also to the remarkable discovery that animal tissue shares with plant tissue what was long regarded as a unique function of the latter, namely, the utilisation of carbon dioxide, previously regarded as a waste product, in the building up of more complex substances; and it has also been shown that the oxygen evolved in photo-synthesis by green plants under the action of light does not come, as was formerly supposed, from the decomposition of the carbon dioxide absorbed by the plant, but from the decomposition of water.

Since atoms, therefore, appeared to be assemblages of electrons and protons, every atom being electrically neutral because it was composed of an equal number of both kinds of particles, and since the proton had a mass about 1800 times as great as that of the electron and, in fact, a mass that was practically equal to that of the hydrogen atom, it seemed that the proton, or perhaps the hydrogen atom, might be akin to the *protyle* or primary matter of the Greeks, from which all matter and therefore all atoms were made. A form of this ancient idea had been revived in the second decade of the nineteenth century by William Prout, a London medical practitioner, who had based his views on the somewhat inadequate evidence at his command that the atomic weights of the elements were whole numbers on the scale in which the weight of the atom of hydrogen was taken as unity, whereas, in fact, many of them were not integral. Prout thought that he had discovered in hydrogen the stuff of which all atoms and therefore all matter was composed, but for the moment the facts were against the acceptance of his hypothesis, although much time and exact experiment were given to further determinations of such important numbers as the atomic weights of the chemical elements. But in 1911 Barkla, in his studies on the scattering of X-rays, showed that the number of electrons in a particular atom corresponded to its place in the chemist's Periodic Table, in which the elements fall into well-defined series and groups when arranged in the ascending order of their atomic weights. In 1913–14 Moseley showed that the number of units of positive electricity (protons) on the nucleus of the atom of a chemical element gave its 'atomic number', which was, with certain exceptions—all long-standing anomalies—nothing more or less than its numerical position in the Periodic Table. In the modern form of the Periodic Table, subsequent to Moseley's work, the elements are arranged not in order of their atomic weights, but in that of their atomic numbers, since the latter are more fundamental, different isotopes of the same element having the same atomic number, and there are no anomalies.

Already, in 1901, Strutt had been attracted to Prout's hypothesis; and he had examined the eight most accurately determined atomic weights and shown mathematically that the probability of the total deviation of these atomic weights from a whole number being as great as found by experiment was about 1 in 1000. He then examined in the same way a further eighteen other atomic weights which could not be so reliably determined and concluded: 'A calculation of the probabilities involved fully confirms the verdict of common-sense, that the atomic weights tend to approximate to whole numbers far more closely than can reasonably be accounted for by any accidental coincidence. The chance of any such coincidence being the explanation is not more than 1 in 1000, so that, to use Laplace's modes of expression, we have stronger reasons for believing in the truth of some modification of Prout's Law, than in that of many historical events which are universally accepted as unquestionable.'[1] The discovery of the electron and the proton as common constituents of all atoms, with the consequent revelation of atomic structure, and the remarkable discovery by Moseley of 'atomic numbers', seemed in the 1920's to have proved the truth of that 'modification of Prout's Law' foreshadowed in Strutt's conclusion, that the hydrogen atom in the form of its nucleus, the proton, was the primary stuff, so far as mass was concerned, of which all matter was made. And later came the conclusion that the main sequence stars consist, in all probability, mainly of hydrogen, which therefore began to reveal itself as the *protyle* of the Greeks, the basis of all matter, terrestrial and celestial, although, of course, the Greeks excluded celestial matter as being of a different and permanent and unchanging nature. But, so far as the atom was concerned, simplicity soon disappeared with the discovery of fundamental component particles other than the proton and the electron, namely: the neutron (Chadwick, 1932), an uncharged particle with a mass equal to that of the proton; the positron (Anderson, 1933), with a mass equal to that of the electron, but a positive, instead of a negative charge; a variety of mesons, particles with a short life and positively or negatively charged with electricity or even neutral; and, possibly, the neutrino, a neutral particle of very small mass. The structure of the atom, at first apparently simple, has since proved to be complex; and, although the atom now seems to be almost a cosmos in itself, its complex constitution and its fine structure have in these fifty years become subjects of experimental investigation.

Increasing knowledge of the atom and of its structure has largely broken down the barriers between the sciences of physics and chemistry. The terms 'atomic physics' and 'chemical physics' have come into use for special fields that overlap two sciences that are really but one, while at the

[1] *Philosophical Magazine*, 1901, vol. I, series vi, pp. 313–14.

same time mathematics has entered into the science of chemistry to play almost as great a part as it plays in that of physics. Other developments associated with the study of living matter have brought into being the sciences of biochemistry and, more recently, biophysics. In biochemistry, in its brief half-century as an off-shoot of chemistry, probably the most important advance was Gowland Hopkins's discovery of what were at first called the 'accessory food factors' and later known as the vitamins, those substances without which a diet, although it may supply ample energy to the organism, is inadequate for the maintenance of health. The vitamins, in small amount, are necessary ingredients of our daily bread; their absence causes what have been called the 'deficiency diseases', such as rickets, scurvy and so on. It is now known, for example, that Scott's South Polar Expedition (1910–12) was equipped with a diet satisfactory with regard to the energy that it would provide, but deficient in vitamin content, and that the expedition's tragic end was due to this cause. The results of the discovery of the vitamins and of wide development of know-ledge in this field have brought inestimable benefit to the health of nations. Today some of these substances are, in fact, produced on the manufacturing scale. Another important group, essential to life and health, the hormones, produced in certain glands in the body and carried by the blood-stream to their points of action, was also discovered in this period by Bayliss and Starling (1902). Adrenaline was isolated by Takamine in 1901 from the supra-renal glands and thyroxine from the thyroid gland by Kendall in 1915. Insulin, isolated by Banting and Best from the pancreas in 1922, proved of great value in the treatment of diabetes mellitus; cortisone, from the adrenal cortex, isolated by Kendall in 1936, is being applied in the treatment of rheumatoid arthritis; and there are others, and some have been synthetised and some prepared on the manufacturing scale.

While the germ theory of infection had satisfactorily established itself, it now became clear that there are other and more minute agents of disease, namely, the ultra-filterable viruses, which can reproduce them-selves only in living tissue. Some of these viruses, from plants, were isolated by Stanley in 1935 as crystals; they were found to be mostly complex protein substances or nucleo-proteins. The question of whether they are living matter is not yet capable of clear decision.

In organic chemistry, progress continued at an ever increasing pace. The characteristic work of the 'classical' organic chemist advanced farther in the isolation of substances that occur in or are associated with living matter, in the determination of their structure and their subsequent syn-thesis in the laboratory, and often in their production on the manu-facturing scale if they proved of industrial or medical importance. Other organic chemists successfully applied the electronic theory of valency and molecular structure to chemical changes in order to explain the mechanism of the reactions between organic substances, which had previously found little or no explanation in the electro-chemical terms that had long been used and applied in inorganic chemistry. Thus, the nineteenth century closed with the science of chemistry, the science of which it is justly said that it affects our daily lives more than any other science does, divided into two distinct fields, organic chemistry on the one hand, and physical and inorganic chemistry on the other. The first half of the twentieth century, by this wide application to organic chemistry of the methods and theories of physical chemistry, has seen a unification of these two great fields of chemistry, which is but part of that wider unification of the sciences of physics and chemistry that characterises the period.

A number of investigators in this half-century succeeded in the preparation of new drugs with the property of being deadly to bacteria and other organisms of disease infecting the higher animals, while being generally harmless to the host. The problem was approached deliberately and it was clear that it would be difficult. The component that would deal with the bacteria or other organisms must be combined with some other molecular group to form a new molecular grouping that would be innocuous to the host but yet retain the bactericidal properties of the first component. One of the first of these new drugs to be prepared was salvarsan, obtained by Paul Ehrlich in 1909. It was fatal to the spirochaete of syphilis, but harmless to the subject; it revolutionised the treatment of this disease. Salvarsan was an organic compound of arsenic; the long and patient research involved in the prosecution of a problem of this kind is indicated by the fact that Ehrlich prepared over six hundred compounds by elaborate syntheses before obtaining a product possessing the requisite properties. Other similar drugs for the treatment of such tropical diseases as sleeping sickness followed: but it was not until 1935 that Domagk showed that streptococcal infections could be treated in a similar way by means of prontosil, a red organic dye-substance. After it had been realised that the effective part of the prontosil molecule was the sulphanilamide group, the new drug, known as 'M and B 693', or sulphapyridine, was synthetised by Ewins and Phillips and applied in 1938 in the treatment of pneumonia and other 'killing diseases'. It has so greatly reduced the mortality from pneumonia that Osler's term for this formerly dreaded disease, 'Captain of the Men of Death', a phrase which he derived from John Bunyan, is no longer applicable. The sulphanilamide drugs have also proved an effective remedy in puerperal fever. The discovery of the antibacterial properties of penicillin by Fleming in 1929, and its successful development as an antibiotic by Chain and Florey in 1940, placed another powerful weapon in the hands of the physician. It was presently produced on the commercial scale. Other antibiotics followed, including streptomycin, chloramphenicol and aureomycin, which have been used with success in the treatment, respectively, of some forms of tuberculosis, of typhus, and of virus diseases.

In the realm of crystallography, the chemical architecture of the molecule has been laid bare by physical methods in the pioneer work of Sir William Bragg and his son, Sir Lawrence Bragg, who devised the method of using a crystal as a diffraction-grating for X-rays. From the spectra thus given, the arrangement of the atoms in the crystal molecule could be deduced. In this fascinating revelation of the patterns in which Nature builds, physics and chemistry have again combined; and the work of the Braggs and their pupils and other crystallographers has shown once again that these two sciences have become so closely linked as to be essentially one.

The discovery of the hormones, secretions of the ductless glands, as well as advances in our knowledge of the detailed chemical mechanism of the process of respiration, have been important developments in physiology in these fifty years. In neuro-physiology progress has been equally striking, especially Sherrington's researches on the integrative action of the nervous system, Dale's on the humoral transmission of nervous impulses and Adrian's on peripheral nerves. In physiology, and in the related science of histology, the instruments of the physical scientist have been partly responsible for the increased rate of progress; of these we may mention only X-ray diffraction methods and the improvements in microscopic technique, especially the ultra-microscope in the earlier part of this period and more recently the electron-microscope.

Geology is another science in which the techniques of physics and chemistry have been widely brought into use in this present century, on the purely scientific side in elucidating the problems of geochemistry, and on the practical side in locating sources of valuable raw materials beneath the earth's crust. Today the geologist is called upon for scientific advice on many problems of our modern civilisation, apart from the location of new sources of raw materials for industry: water-supplies, building materials, the nature of soil and its suitability for various purposes, the sites for roads and houses. The study of the atmosphere by sending up carriers of recording instruments ranging from kites to the more recent powered rocket has shown that it consists of three very different layers: the troposphere, or lowest layer, a region of much movement and not of uniform temperature extending from the surface of the earth to a vertical height of about six miles; the stratosphere, above the troposphere and at a uniform temperature; and, above this, the ionosphere, beginning about thirty miles above the earth's surface and extending a further one hundred and twenty miles, increasingly ionised towards the upper layers and affecting the transmission of wireless waves, which it reflects. The circulation of the atmosphere and the formation of clouds have been increasingly studied, together with the many changes in this complex system. It appears that the causes of rain and snow and the formation of ice are not as simple as they were once supposed to be.

The search for sources of power, for coal and oil, has needed the services of the geologist, once the haphazard exploitation of former days had exhausted obvious supplies. The use of physical methods, such as the reflection of percussion or electromagnetic waves (wireless waves), or measurement of the minute changes in electric or gravitational fields, has been introduced to locate oil, water and a variety of minerals beneath the earth's surface. An interesting development in geological thought, in geophysics, was propounded in Wegener's theory of continental drift in 1915, to explain the distribution of the great land masses, the continents, on the earth's surface. Evidence was adduced to show that the various continents had in remote times gradually separated and drifted apart from one original land mass. The theory long remained a subject of lively debate but its acceptance was far from general.

However, it was the study of radio-activity that in the early years of this century provided the geologist with a reliable means of dating the formation of many of the strata that he studies. By laboratory measurements the physicist had established the rate of disintegration of radio-active substances, for example, into helium and radium-lead (an isotope of ordinary lead). It remained only to measure the proportion of lead and helium in radio-active minerals to establish the age of the rocks in which these minerals occurred. By this means, the geologist was shown to be correct in the estimates that he had made on purely geological data for the great age of many of the rocks, namely, hundreds of millions of years; indeed, the 'geological time' that he had demanded was in some cases now granted to him in overflowing measure without the scepticism that had on occasion formerly accompanied it. The passing of the half-century has also seen the geologist concerned in the location of sources of uranium and other elements of high atomic weight. The production of the atomic bomb at the close of the second world war, and the hopes of applying and developing the use of atomic energy, have led to an almost world-wide search for the necessary basic materials.

Meteorology is another science that calls to its aid the instruments of physics and chemistry; with these, more reliable daily weather forecasts have been made available, and mariners can be fore-warned of bad conditions and farmers advised of good. State meteorological stations have been established by all civilised nations, and are a necessity for air travel, while the increased rapidity of communication brought about by means of wireless telegraphy has made more immediately available the data necessary for accurate forecasting of weather conditions.

But it is in physics itself that the most profound changes in scientific thought have occurred. While the nineteenth century closed with a firm belief in Newtonian mechanics, the researches of Max Planck on the radiation of heat disproved the older belief that energy was equally distributed among the different wave-lengths in which it was radiated by a black body; and energy appeared to be not continuous, as had been supposed, but discontinuous, discrete, almost corpuscular, so that it might be regarded as released in units or *quanta*. Where *v* is the frequency of the emitted radiation and *h*, a universal constant, which Planck called the 'quantum of action', the amount or quantity of energy emitted by a radiating body might be represented as the product of *h* and *v*, or *hv*. Planck's quantum theory and his constant *h* have revolutionised the physicist's ideas on energy. Moreover, the development of the Special and the General Theory of Relativity by Einstein has shown that the energy (*E*) of a body is proportional to its mass (*m*) according to the relation $E = m.c^2$, where *c* is the velocity of light *in vacuo*. Mass and energy have therefore lost their once so obvious difference and are now seen to be one and the same thing, or perhaps both imperfect expressions of one and the same incompletely understood idea, so that the laws of conservation of mass and of energy—the establishment of the latter being one of the great triumphs of the physics of the second half of the nineteenth century—really express the same idea from two different points of view. Indeed, the energy received from the sun may be largely due to the loss of mass that occurs when helium is formed from hydrogen, the change occurring in the sun which is considered to produce the energy that it radiates.

With the rise of the Special Theory of Relativity, absolute space and time, together with the old mechanical ether, have been abandoned; and under the Special Theory of Relativity, gravitation and electromagnetism (and light also, which was shown to be an electromagnetic phenomenon by Clerk Maxwell in 1873) have been unified in a new form of 'field physics'. The Newtonian world has been replaced by the four-dimensional space–time continuum; and thus the whole physical picture of the world has been changed, but rather by an extension than an abandonment of Newtonian principles. The emission of light, too, since it is essentially a radiation, is discrete and it is emitted in units named photons. Since, however, earlier in this century light was considered to have the properties both of a wave and a particle, there was considerable development in the study of wave mechanics with the consequence that wave phenomena were recognised as statistical probabilities, as had also appeared in the study of heat radiation. Indeed, the statistical view, the view that a phenomenon occurs because it is the most probable among a number of possibilities, became widely applied in physics during the period with which we are here concerned.

The biological sciences have exhibited during this half-century a proliferation similar to that of the physical sciences: and genetics, which is concerned with heredity and variation, has developed so extensively that it is to be regarded as a science in itself, especially since, unlike physiology and biochemistry, it does not depend on the techniques of the physical sciences. When the century opened, it was realised that Mendel, whose work had begun at least as early as 1857 and had subsequently escaped the recognition that it properly deserved, had already discovered and established the principles of heredity experimentally. The situation was interesting. Darwin in his *Origin of Species* in 1859 had expanded the idea that he had put forward in collaboration with Alfred Russel Wallace in 1858 about a mechanism of organic evolution, namely, natural selection: it was in fact embodied in the full title of his book, *The Origin of Species by means of Natural Selection or the Preservation of Favoured Races in the Struggle for Life*. But Darwin's theory had been expressed in terms of small continuous variations and, before the nineteenth century closed, biologists had turned preferably to discontinuous variations or, as they were named, mutations. The theory of natural selection, over-simplified as 'the survival of the fittest in the struggle for existence', was presently supplemented by the explanation that 'particulate' inheritance, or Mendelian inheritance, is conveyed and controlled by the mechanism of *genes*— inherited factors or units existing in any individual in pairs, one derived from each parent. The *genes* are carried in the *chromosomes* of the cells and follow the Mendelian laws of inheritance. Probably the most important development in biology in this half-century has been the subsequent integration of Mendel's principles of heredity with the theory of natural selection.

In Mendelian genetics the hereditary units have been shown to maintain their identity, whereas Darwin had supposed that these factors blended. The advances of the recent half-century have now made it clear that evolution is governed by selection acting on Mendelian or 'particulate' inheritance, and in this way Darwinism has been more widely accepted in a new form. As for such theories of evolution as that of Lamarck, who based his ideas on the inheritability of acquired characters, such as might be produced by use or disuse, and who supposed that it was these changes induced in organisms that controlled the process of evolution, these views have in the second quarter of this century found wider acceptance in the Soviet Union for political reasons and not for their scientific validity.

In the last quarter of the nineteenth century an increasing number of finds of the fossil remains of Neanderthal man helped to establish the fact of human evolution. Then *Pithecanthropus* was found in Java in 1891 and afterwards *Sinanthropus* near Pekin; in 1900 it was generally considered that Neanderthal man arose at some point between *Pithecanthropus*, the most ancient fossil form recovered, and *homo sapiens*, or modern man. In 1912 the famous Piltdown remains were found, since shown to have been the greatest scientific hoax ever perpetrated. The Steinheim skull, found in 1933, and the Swanscombe (Kent) skull found in 1935, together with numerous other finds, led to the rejection of Neanderthal man from the line of descent of *homo sapiens*, and to his relegation as an extinct off-shoot. Many other varieties of human remains have come to light in this half-century, notable among these being *Australopithecus* from South Africa, found in 1925 and combining in remarkable ways the characteristics of man and ape. The descent of *homo sapiens* has, however, remained a problem.

The applications of science to medicine have been many and various in the period that we are here surveying. At the beginning of the century Ronald Ross had demonstrated that malaria was carried by mosquitoes that had bitten malaria patients and Reed in 1900 showed that the deadly yellow fever was similarly transmitted. These discoveries led to the control of the breeding places of the mosquito as a means of preventing these diseases and opened up large territories to cultivation and settlement: a spectacular result of the work on yellow fever was that it arrested the disease that had prevented the construction of the Panama Canal. In the treatment as opposed to the prevention of malaria, many new anti-malarial synthetic drugs have replaced quinine. Artificial immunisation was greatly developed also in this period: typhoid fever, hitherto the scourge of armies, had a negligible incidence in the first world war, and since then diphtheria has been similarly reduced. From 1940 onwards blood transfusion became a normal hospital procedure through improve-ment in the system of determining the blood group of the patient. One scientific discovery after another has been pressed into the service of medicine, notably X-ray photography.

The most significant change in our half-century from the point of view of technology is probably that we have separated ourselves from the horse and taken to the internal combustion engine in the motor-car and the aeroplane. The motor-car dates from the last decade of the nineteenth century, but it came into general use only after the first world war. The first aeroplane flight powered by petrol was that made by the Wright brothers in 1903; they flew 284 yards. In 1909 Colonel Bleriot flew across the Straits of Dover. The first world war provoked development and design in aircraft; and in 1919 Alcock and Brown flew the Atlantic from west to east, while in the same year a passenger service between London and Paris was started. Successful helicopters and jet-engined aircraft date from the second world war, the demands of which, like those of the first world war, led to intensive development of this still novel and promising weapon.

In 1947 an aeroplane first flew faster than sound travels in air; and in the same year a flight of about 20,000 miles was made around the world. Long flights became common and large passenger aeroplanes were built. In another development of flight during the second world war flying bombs and rocket bombs were devised. Researches on rockets led to further speculations on the possibilities of flight to the moon, and of inter-planetary and even of space travel; and the sending out of artificial earth-satellites carrying recording instruments fitted with radio-transmitters was planned.

The internal combustion engine has replaced the horse where he was most familiar, namely, on the farm; and in this half-century, more particularly in the later part of it, the plough and all other agricultural implements have been powered by tractors. Much toil and drudgery have thus been avoided both for men and animals. In the home similar saving of labour has been achieved by the aid of electricity, especially in the working of the suction cleaner or so-called vacuum cleaner, and the washing machine, and also by the use of gas and of electricity for heating in place of coal. The same period has seen the devising of refrigerators operated either by gas or electricity.

Electricity has replaced gas as an illuminant in this period both in the home and in the factory, where also it has become the usual source of power. Its production on the large scale in hydro-electric plants—the so-called 'white coal' from 'falling water'—is now widespread where there is a sufficient supply and 'head' of water, that is, in hilly or mountainous rainy districts. Such schemes have carried electricity to the remote countryside as well as to the great cities; and in the later part of this half-century many countryfolk have in their homes passed from wood or coal or oil as fuel, and oil as an illuminant, to the use of electric power, without passing through the intermediate use of gas as did their fellows in the towns. In the same period electricity has brought broadcasting and television to town and country. The advance was rapid. In 1897 Marconi sent a message by wireless telegraphy a distance of eighteen miles, and in 1901 signals were successfully passed across the Atlantic. In the 1920's radio-broadcasting became general and it was followed by television after the second world war.

Wireless telephony was but another of those scientific inventions that men have misused. It might have been applied to break down the misunderstandings across frontiers. It all seemed so remarkable at first, and 'nation shall speak to nation' seemed about to be realised. When the nations did speak to each other by this medium, however, it was frequently the propaganda leading up to the second world war that they spoke, and the 'air' was often filled with raucous argument or, as some of them ensured by a warped sense of technology, noisy with the hideous blare with which they 'jammed' their rivals to prevent them from being heard by their own nationals. Statesmen and political leaders used this new method of communication to speak to audiences of nations; by its means messages could be passed to and from ships at sea and many lives were thus saved; and it had much to do with the urbanising of the countryman. Radio and television have proved valuable aids to education in the schools. They have brought the music, literature and art of the ages into the home and within the reach of the individual, even to his bedside when he is ill or old. But the control and the use of these great inventions with their almost boundless possibilities for the improving of men's minds have been and still are challenged and fought over by those who are more concerned with mass entertainment than with the preservation and dissemination of man's cultural inheritance. Science and technology, at last closely linked in our time, have lavished their gifts on a civilisation too immature to appreciate and use them properly.

The rapidity of modern technological advance, following the equally swift strides of modern science, is nowhere so evident as in the tapping of the vast source of energy in the atom. When Rutherford, first of the modern alchemists, in 1919 succeeded in transmuting certain light elements into hydrogen by bombarding them with the swift alpha-particles emitted in the disintegration of radium, and Blackett in 1922 effected a similar transmutation of nitrogen into oxygen, these changes took place on a minute scale, because only a very small proportion of the atoms subjected to the bombardments underwent transmutation. But in 1931 Cockcroft and Walton in Cambridge developed an improved method for effecting such changes by means of a high-voltage apparatus; and Lawrence, working in the University of California, devised the cyclotron, the justly so-called 'atom-smasher', for obtaining charged particles with a high energy without the difficulty of using correspondingly high voltages. This ingenious contrivance was most successful. In 1932 Chadwick discovered the neutron as a further component in the structure of the atom, electrically neutral and with a mass equal to that of the proton. Fermi in 1933–4 showed that neutrons were very effective in atomic transmutations and that many new radio-active elements could be produced by bombarding various atoms with neutrons: and it was found that radio-active isotopes could be produced for all the chemical elements. In January 1939 Hahn and Strassmann in Germany reported that by bombarding uranium with neutrons they had obtained an isotope of barium, an element far removed from uranium and with an atomic number of 46, whereas that of uranium was 92. These atomic numbers, as we have seen, represent the nuclear charges of the atoms. It therefore appeared that something entirely new had been observed. This bombardment had not produced the usual result of merely removing from or adding to the bombarded nucleus one of the familiar particles such as a proton or an electron or an alpha-particle: on the contrary, it had split the nucleus into two parts—atomic fission had at last been achieved.

The significance of this discovery was at once realised by scientists throughout the world. The opening of the second world war brought with it, however, the usual precautions of military secrecy, although the full possibilities of what had happened were not at first appreciated by the governments involved in the conflict. Within three years complete secrecy had been imposed and a team of physicists, American, British and Canadian, was officially organised to exploit the discovery of atomic fission for use in war. This application was no longer a scientific but rather an engineering problem. The first atomic bomb was dropped on Hiroshima on 6 August 1945, and the second on Nagasaki three days later. The governments of the United States, Great Britain and Canada had kept secret the technical information necessary for the manufacture of these atomic bombs; they had kept it from their allies, including the Soviet Union, and there was much criticism and resentment shown by the latter when this policy became clear and when it was maintained even after the conclusion of the war. Those who had been allies now split into two camps, one struggling to overtake the other's technical advance; and there were some 'leakages' of secret information and deliberate breaches of trust for political reasons. In six and a half years the application of the discovery of atomic fission, expedited by the exigencies of total war, divided the world in a race for technological superiority in the perfection of an offensive weapon capable of measureless material destruction and of shearing off whole nations in swift extermination. The democracies, comprising the United States of America and the nations of the British Commonwealth and of western Europe, were well ahead in 1945; but within another five years the Soviet Union narrowed this lead, and made and tested the first of a series of atomic bombs. In this uneasy tension civilisation faced a menace that seemed irremediable.

On the other hand, the sudden discovery of the availability of atomic energy brought a new source of power within the reach of those nations whose scientists were equipped to deal with such a problem and whose resources included the necessary materials, particularly uranium. Here again advance has been rapid; and, shortly after the close of the period with which this chapter is concerned, power stations supplying atomic energy were in operation.

The discovery of atomic fission had another and a quite different consequence, but this time within the world of science itself. From the beginnings of modern science in the sixteenth and seventeenth centuries scientists had published their work without any interference or censorship or ban by their rulers or governments. Now matters stood differently, and for the first time. Knowledge in a particular field of science, a branch of atomic physics, became of such vital interest to governments for the survival and military security of their peoples that it was declared secret, and those who worked in this field, mostly, of course, in special establishments and laboratories set up for that work, were forbidden to publish or communicate their work to others. Science, which had long and rightly boasted that it knew no frontiers, had to adjust itself to changed circumstances.

Developments in technology have been so numerous and so varied that any attempt at an inclusive summary would soon degenerate into a mere catalogue of invention, and so we shall refer only to a few of the more important. Metallurgical progress, for instance, has been most marked, especially in the production of a great variety of alloy steels. The special use of silicon steel in the cores of electromagnets dates from 1903 and effected considerable economies in electric power. Stainless steel, an alloy with chromium, has saved much domestic labour and has been of great benefit to the surgeon. Alloys with manganese, tungsten, nickel, vanadium, cobalt and molybdenum, have added to the variety of metallic products necessary to our complex modern engineering; and in their different proportions there are some thousands of such alloys of steel with these different metals. This half-century has seen also a considerable development and application of the alloys of the light metals, notably of aluminium alloys for the aircraft industry. Aluminium, apart from its valuable quality of lightness, is particularly useful because of its further property of resistance to atmospheric corrosion by means of the thin film of protective oxide that is immediately formed on the clean surface of the metal when it is exposed to the air.

The pneumatic tyre, with all that it has meant to motor transport, has been mainly developed in this period; and a wide range of synthetic rubber substitutes with different properties was produced from 1930 onwards.

The first commercially-produced plastic, bakelite, was made in 1908 and its production marked the beginning of what became a considerable industry: these plastics, or synthetic resins, are now so widely applied for many purposes to replace stone and wood and metal that one has only to look around to see them almost everywhere. Perspex, the first plastic to replace glass, was discovered in 1930, and polythene, a flexible plastic, came into production in 1939. Other plastics have been found useful as wrapping materials and electrical insulators.

Nylon, which can be formed into a thread and which replaced artificial silk as a fabric, dates from 1935. The earliest of these artificial fabrics, rayon, dates from the beginning of the century; it was followed in turn by cellulose acetate and then nylon; and towards the end of our period terylene proved successful.

Atmospheric nitrogen has been fixed by various industrial processes either in the form of nitric acid or of ammonia. The success of these processes proved of great benefit to agriculture and to the explosives industry, and brought to an end their dependence on such natural sources as the mineral nitrates of Chile. The successful invention of one of these processes in Germany is said to have been a factor in the decision to make war in 1914, since it appeared to indicate that an adequate future supply of nitric acid for the manufacture of explosives was assured even if imports from Chile were cut off.

Many new and improved dyestuffs have been manufactured in this period and they have added colour and variety to fabrics. Photography has been greatly improved with plates and films of varying sensitivity for different purposes; and what was at first a difficult and complicated process has passed successfully into the hands of countless amateurs. Insecticides in great variety have been invented, the best known probably being DDT, but careless or too general use of such remedies is said to destroy the pollinating insects as well as those that prey on the crops to be protected. Selective weed-killers, that destroy the weeds and leave the crop undamaged, have also been devised.

While the volume of agricultural production has steadily increased in this half-century by the application of scientific knowledge, the human race has multiplied even faster, and frequent warnings have been sounded that in a world populated by over 2000 millions of people, increasing annually by 20 millions, a mere 1 per cent, disastrous shortages of food may well lie round the corner. In the West food supplies have so far proved adequate for an increasing population: in the East, however, this is, in general, so far from being so that birth-control has been recommended as the only solution against a threat of famine. The bringing into cultivation of hitherto untilled land has proceeded steadily, especially in those marginal areas where rainfall and temperature are only just sufficient for agriculture: and remedies for loss of soil by erosion, as in the 'dust-bowls' of America, have been scientifically and successfully applied. In the later years of this half-century, however, surplus stocks of food have been amassed in some countries, with the threat of dangerous or even ruinous falls in prices, while at the same time the populations of whole tracts of the world have been underfed.

In the preservation of food, an important discovery in the refrigeration of meat carried in ships was applied in 1934. Two methods had long been in use: either the meat was frozen about ten degrees below the freezing-point of water, in which state it could be conveyed satisfactorily for great distances, for example, from Australia and New Zealand to Europe; or it was chilled to just below the freezing-point of water, and then it could be carried only for shorter distances, such as from America to Europe. Frozen meat deteriorated rapidly on being thawed, while chilled meat retained its quality and flavour but not its colour. It was discovered, however, that if 10 per cent of carbon dioxide was added to the air in which the chilled meat travelled, the length of time in which it might be stored in this way was doubled, while the addition of a proportion of oxygen prevented the change of colour. This useful discovery was applied to other cargoes than meat in suitably adjusted atmospheres at the temperatures found necessary for these different products.

The domestic refrigerator is another invention that has come into common use in this period; and the so-called 'deep-freeze' for fruit and vegetables has followed it in preference to drying methods, the frozen materials preserving much of their freshness although only for a short time after thawing.

Ships have passed from coal to oil and from the steam engine to the steam turbine, which was first applied to drive a ship in 1894. The change from coal to oil has reduced the number of stokers to one-tenth. Time signals broadcast by wireless telegraphy have greatly helped the navigator since it is no longer necessary to calculate Greenwich mean time in order to determine the longitude of his ship's position. Other radio aids to navigation, particularly radar, which was first applied in 1936 to locate aircraft in flight, were developed during the second world war and these have, in effect, linked the ship with the shore for the purposes of controlling the direction of its course, while radar itself has reduced the perils of fog, darkness and icebergs.

Among many developments in communications the two most striking were the thermionic valve, which effected a fundamental change in method in wireless telegraphy and which came into general use about 1920, and the multiplex working of cables, by which a number of messages, often several hundreds, could be sent at the same time, an improvement dating from about 1930.

Colour cinematography and sound films were introduced in the late 1920's (see also ch. III).

The progressive assembly technique in manufacture on conveyor lines or belts, with which Henry Ford was specially associated in America, originated in 1913 and later became a characteristic of modern industrial practice.

The world shortage of animal fats led to greater use of vegetable oils and fats; and the shortage of soap, arising from the shortage of fats, led to the production of 'synthetic' detergents in a great variety.

And so we might continue, enumerating one technological advance after another. The important thing for us to observe, however, about this half-century is that these advances have been made through a far closer alliance between science and technology than that seen in any previous age; and it is in this sense that our modern civilisation is properly described as scientific or technological. While the chance invention has still occasionally played its part in this period, it has been a part that is seen to be ever decreasing, both in extent and in quality, when contrasted with the conscious and deliberate exploitation of new scientific knowledge and its application to practical ends. That new knowledge has been won and its application has been effected in this half-century by the labours of one who has but lately come upon the scene, namely, the professional scientist; and to him it is now necessary to refer in greater detail.

The men who founded modern science were amateurs, not professionals; they were often churchmen interested in what was called 'natural philosophy' or they were men of wealth and social position with a similar attraction to the study of Nature, and their education had in general been in classics and in mathematics and in theology; and some others had studied medicine for a profession. The universities did not teach science in our sense of the term and still less its applications. In the eighteenth century there were, however, a few special colleges in France and Germany for training in military and civil engineering and in mining, but the École Polytechnique, founded in Paris in 1794 during the Revolution, was the first college concerned with the application of science. Developments in the nineteenth century were gradual. Germany led the way in multiplying technical schools of increasing standard, although it was not until 1899 that these institutions were raised to university status. In Great Britain, home of the Industrial Revolution, there was a similar slow progress towards technical education, and the teaching of science itself developed only gradually during the nineteenth century. The slow rise and growth of the newer university colleges and universities, after the foundation of University College, London, in 1826 had introduced the teaching of the different sciences into higher education, indicate lack of national alertness to the possibilities of applied science among the countrymen of Watt and Faraday. Gradually scientific studies were organised, even in the older universities. Both in Europe and in the United States there was scientific as well as technical education and young men, in small numbers, went into industry after such training. The idea of scientific research with the object of applying its results was not yet common, and scientists, outside the scientific departments of the universities, were not numerous. Further, higher education was regarded as education in the arts, and education in science, even in a university, was something that did not rank as high in the intellectual and social scale.

The twentieth century opened, however, with scientific education in the universities well established in Germany, and with the resounding recognition of technical education at the usual high standards of the German universities. In France the situation was much the same, science and technology having been long allied. Generally there was a deeper realisation of the necessity of science to industry, as voiced by A. J. (afterwards Lord) Balfour, who was quoted at the beginning of this chapter. In the earlier part of this century, however, there was a much keener realisation of this necessity in Germany than in any other country; and it was only as a result of the application of science in certain war industries during the first world war, coupled with a better understanding of the part that scientific research had played in the technical advances of German industry, that steps were taken in other countries for the promotion of similar advances and for the establishment of official or semi-official encouragement and financial aid for such technical or industrial research. In Great Britain the Department of Scientific and Industrial Research was instituted under a committee of the Privy Council while the war was still in progress; later a number of research associations were formed for different industries, the government subscribing 'pound for pound' with the different industries to finance these research associations; various research boards were organised; and the National Physical Laboratory was taken over. In the United States, the British reaction to the pre-war neglect of scientific and industrial research was not only understood and admired, but also imitated: a National Research Council was set up and National Research Fellowships were instituted. In France, since the close connection between science and technology was no new thing, there was less need for these new departures. In the Soviet Union, after the reorganisation that followed the revolutionary period, great attention was given to the setting up and equipping of technical colleges in great numbers. The general object of these movements in all these countries was the stimulation of industry to new developments by means of fundamental research and its application; and emphasis was laid on the connection between science and industrial efficiency and progress. For a time, however, the increasing number of young scientists trained in this way was not very considerable, and it was not realised that a new profession was in process of being formed, that of the professional scientist or the industrial scientist or the technologist, as he has been variously called: and it was only at the end of our period, during and after the second world war, that the professional scientist in large numbers found his place in industry and in the scientific branches of the civil services of the various governments. The nations had learnt that scientific knowledge and research were vital for their survival, and this gave the professional scientist an established place in the state. The state itself was often the only possible source for the heavy expenditure that scientific research required. Much of this had to be carried out in university laboratories; the staffs of university scientific departments had to be greatly increased; many industries had to set up their own research laboratories, often of a considerable size and with large technical and scientific staffs; research in pure science or academic research went on at the same time at an increasing rate, since science itself must progress in fundamental knowledge, and the advance of science and technology proved mutually stimulating; and the undergraduate and postgraduate student in science was no longer merely studying a particular science or sciences, but preparing himself for the practice of a profession much as the medical student had always done. At the beginning of our period, the chances of his doing so were small indeed; but such had become the life of the young scientist as the mid-point of the century approached.

Another development closely followed these changes. At the beginning of our period a graduate in science with inclinations towards research might work for two years with his professor or with another either at home or abroad, and with or without (but much more probably without) one of the few scholarships or grants then available; and then, if opportunity offered, he might find a place in some university department where he would be able to carry on with such research as his duties might give him time for. But it would normally be individual research, done by himself in the spare time left after his teaching and other duties; and it would be done at his own cost. Sir William Ramsay, as is well known, financed his classic researches on the inert gases from the fees that he earned as a consultant. In the early 1920's, however, the beginner in scientific research received a grant from one or other of such bodies as have been mentioned above; and it was given for a specific research under his professor or supervisor, and that research might or might not constitute a part of the attack on a large problem on which others might be working in the same laboratory. Later, after these beginnings, the young scientist might be one of a team working together on a problem, and it became less and less likely that he would be engaged in individual research. The organisation of such teams was a marked feature of much scientific research in the later part of our period. In Great Britain, for example, much of this kind of academic research was financed by the Department of Scientific and Industrial Research, the Medical Research Council, the various research associations and individual industrial companies. Often the problem was precisely stated and the research organised as needing a staff of so many and as likely to take so long, but more often these details were not calculable. The speed and the urgency of much scientific research changed greatly in the times we are discussing: and the services of a variety of scientists trained in different sciences were often needed in collaboration on one problem. Such were the organisation and practice of science at the mid-point of the twentieth century.

Of the organisation of these great numbers of scientists throughout the world into their specialist societies in every country, it is scarcely necessary to mention any detail except that these scientific societies provided in their journals, maintained by the subscriptions of their members, the media for the publication of the bulk of the world's scientific research. In conjunction they organised also a service that compiled for publication classified abstracts of the latest memoirs in the journals dealing with each particular science. By this means the researcher was enabled to keep in touch with the latest advances in his own field and in any other in which he might be interested. Societies multiplied with the increasing complexity of science in this half-century, and their publications greatly increased. *The World List of Scientific Periodicals* gives valuable information on this point. The first edition of this useful work covered the period from 1900 to 1921 and included all journals published up to 1900 or brought out between that year and 1921, except those that might have escaped its net: the total was about 25,000. The second edition brought these details up to 1933: the number had increased to 36,000. The third edition brought them up to 1950: the number exceeded 50,000. As for the scientific books published and translated from one language into another, it would be difficult to form any estimate of the increase in their publication.

It will be noticed that between 1921 and 1950 the number of scientific periodicals doubled. Scientific periodical literature originated in the middle of the seventeenth century with the publication of the proceedings of the first national scientific academies; the number of such journals steadily increased. The data from the *World List* indicate that the total had reached 25,000 by 1921; much of this increase, it is known, occurred in the nineteenth century. It will be noted, however, that the number of scientific journals rose from 1921 to 1933 by 11,000 in twelve years, and then by a further 14,000 from 1933 to 1950 in seventeen years, from which six years of war should be deducted. This is characteristic of the whole period; and, looking a little farther back, to a century ago, we may say that, when the advances of the last hundred years are studied closely, it is found that by far the greater part lie in this half-century, and, similarly, when the progress of this half-century is analysed, it is evident that the greater part of it fell within the second quarter. The pace has steadily increased through these hundred years.

The historian of science surveying these fifty years, if he can detach himself from contemporary disputation and argument about the ethics of the application of scientific discovery to the waging of war, about remedies against the narrowness of scientific education, about the perils of technocracy, and about the urgent need for more and more scientists, looks upon a period of unparalleled and ever accelerated progress in science and technology. By far the greater part of it fell within the second quarter of the century, and much of it was expedited by the needs of two world wars and of the so-called 'cold war' as well. He will reflect sorrowfully that science, which began as the study of Nature for its own sake, became in this age vital to the survival of nations in arms, and that in its disinterested pursuit of truth it was forced for the same cause to halt at frontiers where hitherto it had recognised none.

CHAPTER VI

LITERATURE, PHILOSOPHY AND RELIGIOUS THOUGHT

IN this chapter we essay the impossible task of surveying the literature, philosophy and theology of the first half of the twentieth century. The immense amount of material to be considered is beyond the power of any single mind to grasp or estimate and for this reason alone it will be necessary to concentrate attention mainly on the English scene with some glances at the wider field. This is perhaps not so disastrous a limitation as it would be in some other periods, for it is a characteristic of our time that its literature and to a less degree its philosophy and theology have developed on national lines.

The cause of the multiplication of books and other writings is the establishment of universal education in the civilised countries of the world and the consequent sudden increase of the reading public. We are concerned here with the ideas which were current and the manner in which they were expressed and communicated. We are therefore bound to consider the audience and its capacity to understand. Though the law of supply and demand has not the sovereign power in the realm of mind which it still possesses in the economic sphere, it has considerable influence and very much of the mass of writing which lies before us is mainly a commercial product designed to meet the requirements of the new literate class. Thus many of the most widely read books, the 'best-sellers' of the day, have no claim to be regarded as literature. They are nevertheless not negligible for the purpose of the historian, because they mirror probably better than greater writings the emotional and intellectual tendencies of the population. It would not be a waste of time to reflect upon the difference between the best-sellers in the five decades since 1900 and on the significance of Charles Garvice, Ethel M. Dell and Edgar Wallace as symptoms of the spiritual state of the nation.

The development of popular journalism, a direct result of the large increase in the reading public, had some influence on literature. The demand for short, stimulating essays on general subjects called forth a host of competent writers and provided a platform for some of the most eminent men of letters. G. K. Chesterton came into notice by reason of his brilliant contributions to the *Daily News*; Bernard Shaw and Hilaire Belloc are among those authors who did not disdain the opportunities offered by the 'cheap' press. Any estimate of the influence of the newspapers ought to take into account the fact that they have been the medium through which many people have acquired an interest in literature and ideas.

We have to record, however, a decline in the vogue of the longer essay. The deplorable cessation of the *Edinburgh Review* was a sign that the new conditions were unfavourable to this type of composition. It seems that the effort of sustained attention is more irksome to the men of the twentieth century than it was to those of the nineteenth. Whatever the cause of this phenomenon may be, its effects can be observed in many aspects of life. It is a serious loss to literature that essays such as Macaulay's or Carlyle's could no longer find a large audience, or indeed a periodical which could print them. This has not meant that the serious essay has entirely ceased; in fact the period has been rife in able essayists who through volumes of detached studies have swayed opinion. Dr W. R. Inge's *Outspoken Essays* are a notable example among many others.

The spate of books which pours from the publishers every year has been of doubtful advantage to the cause of literature or of sound learning, and one might often wish that some plan could be devised by which, without the hateful tyranny of censorship, a check could be put upon the flood. No doubt this is impossible, but the evil is real. The general reader is overwhelmed by the number of works competing for his attention and is often quite unable to distinguish between the competent and the merely silly. The attempts which have been made to draw up reading lists and to signalise really important books have done something to mitigate the inconvenience and might become more effective if the experts in various subjects were more aware of the importance of an instructed public opinion. The really good author has suffered from the excessive supply of reading matter. It has become more difficult for a serious writer to obtain recognition and a new temptation has arisen—or rather an old temptation has grown more formidable—that of writing too much. This was, of course, potent in the nineteenth century but has on the whole increased in force since then. A writer, once established, feels the pressure to retain his hard-won foot-hold on eminence by never giving his public time to forget him. Of more than one writer it could be said that he had bartered greatness for copiousness.

Some of the technical achievements of the time have affected literature, and, to a small degree, philosophy and theology. Broadcasting has been a major factor in the social change of the century and has not been without influence in cultural activities. In those countries where the radio has not been captured for propaganda, talks and discussions have been a popular and effective part of the programme. The 'Brains Trust' was for a time of great importance in the life of Britain. The tendency of these talks has been mainly beneficent. They have stimulated rational reflection and initiated many into the process of responsible argument. Perhaps, however, they have also encouraged a mood of satisfaction with superficial understanding and an undue respect for snap judgments pithily expressed. However that may be, it is certain that broadcasting has helped to change literary style. The 'fireside talk' is more effective on the wireless than the older style of oration and all public speaking, on platform and in pulpit, has tended to assimilate the 'talk' technique and in the long run the spoken word modifies the written. We should not exaggerate this, however, to the point of holding that rhetoric is doomed, for the prime ministers in the two world wars, Lloyd George and Winston Churchill, were masters of the older style of eloquence.

The cinema has perhaps less importance but is not negligible. The art of script writing is a new literary form and has evolved a new kind of drama, while the novel has been both directly and indirectly modified by its rivalry. Long descriptions of scenery and persons tend to disappear and many novels are plainly written with a view to the film rights. This remark applies only to the inferior novelist and, on the whole, it is to be hoped that the two forms of art, the novel and the film, will pursue independent paths, for they have in fact quite different aims.

It will not be irrelevant here to comment on a feature common to cinema, wireless and popular literature—the vogue of the crime story in its two forms of detective story and 'thriller'. Much ingenuity and literary skill have been devoted to this *genre* and a few of the best examples are not beneath the notice of the historian of literature. The phenomenon is not confined to one country but appears in all the nations embraced in the term 'western civilisation', and in each talent of a high order has been deflected from the ordinary novel to this specialised type of narrative. Agatha Christie, Dorothy Sayers and many others are known probably to more people than any of the poets of the period. Nor has the addiction to this kind of story been the pastime of the unlearned alone; it has attracted, both as authors and as readers, the lettered and the sophisticated. One feels, like Tennyson contemplating his 'flower in the crannied wall', that if one could penetrate to the hidden causes of this odd fact, the secret of the inner life of our times would be revealed at least in part. Of course the crime story is itself no new thing; it has existed since men began to tell tales; the remarkable fact is its immense elaboration and expansion. It may be that the obvious causes are enough to account for this. Suspense, a puzzle to be solved, vicarious adventure, are all fascinating to human beings in every age.

It has been plausibly suggested that in modern civilisation we become bored with the monotonous security of our lives and welcome the escape into imaginary fear and danger; but when we reflect that two world wars, in which most people had their fill of real excitement and peril, have not in the smallest degree abated the demand we may doubt whether the cause alleged is adequate. Very tentatively we might conjecture that the deepest source of this type of story is rather more sinister. It springs from and ministers to an unconscious drive towards destruction and violence of which there are other signs. Some corroboration of this conjecture may be found in the sadistic taint which is evident in some of the 'tougher' school of crime novelists.

The difficulty of selecting a few authors from among so many as the significant writers of the time is in any case acute, but it is complicated by the need to distinguish between those who have permanent value and those who were 'persons of note in their day' but are not likely to be read in later times. The second class may often be more valuable as symptoms of the trends of thought and emotion than men of greater genius. Anyone who, in the Elizabethan age, wished to estimate the forces which were at work in society shaping the future would have gained comparatively little information from the works of Shakespeare but very much from the now unreadable diatribes of Puritan divines. So now poets such as Walter de la Mare will certainly be quoted in anthologies for centuries to come but have no place among the writers who changed public opinion or reflected it. To be 'not for an age but for all time' involves a certain detachment from history.

The century opens with a work which has unquestionable significance from both points of view. Thomas Hardy's *Dynasts* appeared in the years 1904-8. The flowering of the 'second spring' of Hardy's genius, it proved to be prophetic of the mood which events would induce in many during the coming years. It was remarkable that its author should, after establishing a position as one of the great novelists, late in life strike a new and resounding note in poetry. In the *Dynasts*, which is one of the longest and most sustained works in English verse, he universalised the vision of life which is implicit in most of his novels—pessimism combined with a pity which feels itself to be impotent. The vast drama of the life of Napoleon I is exhibited, not as a personal tragedy, but as the tragedy of a large part of the human race. Destiny, presented as an unconscious will, carries the central figure and millions of men and women forward on a path which they did not choose and cannot deflect. In the main, the gleam of hope hardly lights the scene except in the last Chorus of the Pities, which hints that 'consciousness the will informing' may in some unimagined future 'fashion all things fair'. The philosophy of this great poem, if philosophy it can be called, was one which was to be only too plausible to the coming generations, who felt themselves to be swept onwards by historical forces which they could neither understand nor control to catastrophes which engulfed millions of simple folk, and who suffered from the frustration of impotent sympathy.

These notes are to be heard in many voices throughout this age of violence. All sensitive spirits were tortured by the contradiction that a period in which slaughter, cruelty and destruction reached an unprecedented height was notable for the spread of humane impulses, so that the efforts to relieve suffering, including that of animals, were never more sincere. Another poet who belongs perhaps mainly to the previous century,

Rudyard Kipling, was producing work which reflected an aspect of the mind of the first decade. Kipling is a more considerable writer than the Georgians allowed, and his imperialism and racial self-complacency are only one side of him, but he stands for the hopes and ideals of the time which was passing away and his drums and trumpets which were not amiss in the South African War were drowned by the thunder of Armageddon.

The development and function of poetry in this half-century is, in more than one respect, paradoxical. The poets have been numerous and prolific, they have given the world some great poems and have made new departures in poetical technique, many of them have been passionately concerned with the social distresses of their times and have sought to utter some prophetic word to the people, but, compared with the nineteenth century, the twentieth century so far has been a period when poets have declined in power to move the masses. No poet comparable in influence on the thought of the nation to Tennyson or Browning has arisen and many of the poets who most ardently wish to speak to the common man have adopted a mode of utterance which is apt to seem to the common man to be neither poetic nor intelligible. It is probably true that poets of the older tradition, such as Alfred Noyes and Masefield, have been the most widely read. This is not, of course, to say that poetry has not been a significant factor in the culture of the time or that it has had no importance in forming public opinion. Writers such as Auden in England and George in Germany have no doubt been creative influences within somewhat restricted circles.

The most interesting literary form, both from the point of view of the development of technique and from that of reflecting the spirit of the age, has been the novel. To it the most distinguished minds have been devoted and in it have been expressed the most formative ideas. A period which includes Wells, Bennett, Conrad, Galsworthy, Proust, Thomas Mann, Lawrence and James Joyce is evidently a great flowering time of the art of the novelist. It happens that the fifty years under review are almost covered by the career of H. G. Wells, and his writings are a mirror not only of the development of his own mind but of the mind of a considerable part of the more intelligent population of Europe. His novels have been read in almost every civilised country and have had some recognisable influence on the social thinking of all of them. Wells began to write in the nineteenth century and some of his most effective work is satirical description and criticism of the social conditions of that time. Though he would have been a better novelist had he been less of a propagandist, he would have been less important for the historian. He combined the art of story telling with social criticism and the novel of ideas in one masterpiece, *Tono Bungay*, but in the rest of his later works the prophet and the sociologist have the upper hand. The succession of his writings is a picture of the tragic experience of the intellectuals. He begins with the firm conviction that a rational and scientific organisation of society is the one thing needful and, though he is aware of some of the dangers, he believes that the advance and application of science and the spread of scientific thought is the sure way of advance. The last writings, *The Shape of Things to Come, The Fate of Homo Sapiens* and *Mind at the End of its Tether*, represent a rapid process of disillusionment ending in despair. It is interesting that the place which Wells occupied in the minds of the young intellectuals in the first quarter of the century was, for a time, taken by Aldous Huxley. His novels of the earlier phase, which are deri-sive of values and teach the doctrine 'Do what you will', chimed with the scepticism of the generation which had begun to doubt the gospel of scientific humanism; and his most characteristic book, the savage satire on scientific utopianism *Brave New World*, signalises the extreme revulsion from the Wells type of optimism. The subsequent pilgrimage of this admirable writer, which has led him to a quietistic form of mysticism, has had a few but not many companions.

Arnold Bennett wrote not as a critic but as a contemplator of the human scene, but Galsworthy and many others used the novel as the means of exposing the injustice which the order of society sanctioned. There were others, however, who wrote to express a philosophy or a vision of life as a whole. The strange and tormented genius D. H. Lawrence is the outstanding figure among these writers and perhaps his deep anti-rational-ist feeling and mysticism of the life-force and of the sex impulse could have been presented in no other medium. He is noteworthy as the first great author to be consciously affected by the psychology of Freud—though not the last. A very different development of the novel, so far as form is concerned, is found in the work of Ivy Compton Burnett, who evolved an individual style of narrative through dialogue couched in a level tone, which conveyed a somewhat cynical view of human motives. Virginia Woolf, Kafka, and James Joyce, though very diverse in aims and manner, were alike in attempting to carry the novel into new forms and to use it for new purposes. The symbolic narrative, with symbolism which the reader must interpret for himself, and the representation of the 'stream of consciousness', if not entirely new departures in the novel, have never been so wholeheartedly tried before. James Joyce went one step farther. In *Ulysses* he presented the flow of conscious experience, in *Finnegan's Wake* he tapped the unconscious. For this purpose he invented a new vocabulary, which to the mass of readers is unintelligible, though the experts claim that it is a deeply significant utterance. It is too soon to judge whether this is an important enlargement of the scope of literature or an interesting experiment which will have no sequel, but we may regard Joyce as an outstanding symptom of the revolt against reason which is a feature of the age. The novel is to be no longer a representation and interpretation of life through a narrative controlled by reason. Men feel that reason distorts and they seek to get beyond, or below, reason to 'life', to the experience as it wells up from the dark recesses of the unconscious.

Though, on the whole, the drama has been of less importance than the novel, the drama of ideas has had eminent practitioners in all European countries. Beyond any competitor, George Bernard Shaw has had the widest influence and, along with Wells, has had the best claim to be a world-figure. Though he has always had a positive message, probably his chief effect has been that of a solvent of accepted ideas and values. A great dramatic genius and a first-rate writer of polemical prose, he has shaken many out of dogmatic slumbers and started questions on the foundations of society. Perhaps it is not altogether by chance that his one certainly immortal work, *St Joan,* is the one in which he is least concerned with contemporary problems. The positive doctrine which he preached was a blend of socialism and authoritarianism on a background of Nietzsche and Bergson, the 'Superman' and the 'Life Force'; and here it is to be observed that the prophetic voices of the age were almost unanimously hostile to democracy. Though it has been called 'the era of the common man', the leaders of thought had a poor opinion of the common man's wisdom, ability and honesty. Shaw looked for the 'Superman' and Wells played with ideas of a new 'Samurai' or scientific, governing elite. The writers who were genuinely in favour of democracy were those who defended the Christian position, such as G. K. Chesterton.

Biography and autobiography form a large section of the literary productions of the period and a change of spirit and technique can be observed which was due in part to a revolt against the long and somewhat euphemistic official biographies of the Victorians, and also to the influence of psychology. Even those 'lives' which carried on the tradition of the nineteenth century tended to be shorter and more lively and to admit that the hero sometimes made mistakes. Lytton Strachey, in his *Eminent Victorians* and *Queen Victoria,* introduced a new note. He was the master of a pointed and allusive style which he employed to reveal the imperfections of some Victorian worthies. On the whole the result was salutary, though he reacted in more than one instance from adulation to excessive denigration. For a time this method and style became a model for writers who, not possessing Strachey's talent, frequently gave the impression of impertinence. The 'picturesque' biography, however, which employs the art of the novelist to present a living image of the subject, has evidently established itself and has had eminent practitioners. Aldous Huxley's *Grey Eminence* is an example of a picturesque biography which includes an exposition of a philosophy of the spiritual life woven, as it were, into the story. In the last decade a series of volumes by Osbert Sitwell, beginning with *Left Hand Right Hand!* struck out a new line combining biography, autobiography and a fascinating description of a whole section of society of the recent past in one continuous narrative. This may well be one of the most durable works of the age. It cannot be said that much light has yet come from those who have brought modern psychology to the aid of biography in spite of many ingenious essays, but the attempt will no doubt continue and possibly when there is a greater measure of agreement among the psychologists will be more illuminating.

In France the literary expression of the spirit of the age was, in many respects, analogous to that in England, though with important modifications. It must be sufficient here to mention three great writers who represent phases of the evolution. The stark and sordid realism of Émile Zola marks the opening of the century—a reflection in literature of the prevailing materialism. Anatole France is in the tradition of Voltaire. He wrote a charming and lucid prose which was the perfect vehicle for a mocking scepticism. But there was something more. There was pity and sympathy for the weak. In his most profound and most shocking work, the *Revolt of the Angels*, he touched with wit and imagination upon the corruption which accompanies unlimited power. Though he would have been happier if he could have wrapped himself in an Epicurean indifference, the evils of the society which persecuted Dreyfus enlisted his satirical pen against them and he might have claimed, like Heine, whom he a little resembled, to be in his fashion a 'soldier of the spirit'. The long life of Romain Rolland (1866–1945) included much and various activity, but he emerges as a figure in the literary scene only at the beginning of the century. In a long series of novels he speaks for the idealists who hoped that the conflict which overshadowed the years before 1914 could be avoided and the antagonism between France and Germany be healed by good-will and understanding. The failure of this hope left him and many others in an impossible position which he held with courage, attempting to be 'au-dessus de la mêlée', and to preserve an objective attitude towards the war in which the very existence of his country was involved. At the end of his life he was in sympathy with the mystic Charles Péguy, for whose genius he helped to secure recognition. Marcel Proust began to be an important influence after 1918 and his reputation has grown steadily ever since. He is the most significant writer of the period in France and has added a new territory to fiction. The picture of a section of society in dissolution and of the inner corruption of outwardly reputable persons may be read with approval by Freudians and by believers in original sin, but the historian may note that the whole of Proust's work is the expression, by a man of genius, of distrust of and revolt against reason, and the recognition of the reign of instinct and desire. The literature of France is more deeply troubled than that of England. The danger of catastrophe and the feeling that there is no security are more insistent, and the divisions in the nation are more profound. The two Frances, that of the Catholic tradition and that of Voltaire and the Revolution, still confront one another and lend, even to serious fiction, the air of a debate.

Poetry since 1900, like the arts of music and painting, has been remarkable for the attempt to find a new technique. In music the search for a new idiom has been due no doubt partly to the idea that the older idiom has been exhausted and that there is nothing more to say in it, but probably still more to the need for expressing a different kind of emotion or vision. Much the same may be said of poetry. In England, France and Germany, fresh rhythmical patterns have been employed, and the poetical vocabulary and imagery have been modified. Here, too, the cause of this has been not only the thirst for originality but the sense that the smooth metres of the established poetical forms were out of harmony with the vision of unrest, uncertainty and insecurity which the poet wished to convey. The greatest poets, however, have not been the greatest innovators. W. B. Yeats, who is certainly one of the most considerable of them, has no very startling innovations. T. S. Eliot stands out as the poet who has exercised the greatest influence on the conception of the nature of poetry and its possibilities in the scientific age. He is a curious combination of the revolutionary and the conservative. In his free verse he has succeeded in writing a poetry which, untrammelled by traditional metrical structure, yet is obviously poetical in form as well as content and which could not be taken for poetical prose. In his earlier poems, such as *The Waste Land* and *The Hollow Men*, he was felt by his readers to convey with undeniable force a mood of disgust and disillusionment. Eliot, however, is really not a revolutionary and in his later poems, without any loss of power, he has employed his verse technique for the exposition of Christian themes. The exploration of the possibilities of new types of verse rhythm has been carried forward by many others, among whom we may mention Edith Sitwell and Auden. Sometimes these poets have been concerned with the social problems and hopes and fears of the contemporary world, in reaction against 'the accepted order and the complacency of the comfortable', and some have an interpretation of life to offer which negates the relative optimism of Christianity. But there seems to be no necessary connection between eccentricity of prosody and unorthodoxy of thought, for out of these troubled years there comes a voice singing the most unmitigated pessimism in the simplest and most exquisite of strains. A. E. Housman's small sheaf of poems will remain when much has been forgotten to remind succeeding centuries that there were some who in the twentieth century faced life on the 'firm foundation of unyielding despair'.

One of the functions of the poet is to impart a vision of the eternal basis of life and thus to offer consolation and peace amid the storms of existence. Here the poet has an affinity with the philosopher and the prophet. In the confused and bewildered days of this half-century few were able to rise to the calmness of assured utterance, but one poem, Robert Bridges' *Testament of Beauty*, a sustained reflection upon the significance of beauty, ranks among the few great philosophical poems of the world. For the purpose of his exposition Bridges devised a form of blank verse with a standard twelve syllable line which was admirably adapted to the slow meditative movement of his thought.

Any survey on so limited a scale even of the poetry of one nation must be unjust to many excellent authors and give an imperfect view of the activity of the creative impulse; enough perhaps has been said to indicate the multitudinousness of poetic voices and the persistence of the poetic vocation in an unpropitious world. One sign of the vigour of poetry is the revival of verse drama. John Masefield, T. S. Eliot, Gordon Bottomley, W. H. Auden, Dorothy Sayers, Charles Williams, are only a few of the names which deserve mention. The modern verse drama has broken from the strict following of the Elizabethan and Victorian pattern and made a relatively fresh start. Much of this drama has been religious in inspiration and performed at church festivals and indeed it is worthy of note that some of the most accomplished and original poets of the period—Eliot, Bottomley, Bridges, Dorothy Sayers and Charles Williams—were not only Anglicans but ardent members of that church.

Philosophy since 1900 baffles description. On the one hand the interest in philosophical problems has grown and its debates have, largely by means of the wireless, been brought into the market-place. The number of intelligent amateurs of the subject has greatly increased. But on the other hand, when philosophers have come into the market-place they have been found to be disconcertingly at variance not only in their conclusions but in their methods, aims and vocabulary. During the second world war complaints were heard that the philosophers had no guidance to give to minds perplexed—complaints which were treated with proper contempt by the professional thinkers. A significant change may be observed in the character of philosophical discussion. Controversy has a less central place at the end of the half-century than it had at the beginning. In the first decade the controversies between positivists and idealists and between F. H. Bradley and the pragmatists were real and fundamental. They were between men who understood each other's language and respected each other's point of view. At the end of the period there seem to be no such debates and the schools of thought have drawn so far apart that what to one appears obvious truth to another seems obvious nonsense. Somewhat strangely this lack of real contact is most evident in the sphere of logic, and the adherents of the current 'atomistic' logic treat the idealistic logic as simply 'outmoded'. There can be little doubt that the disruption of the philosophical tradition is not only a symptom but a cause of the distraction of the mind of the age and of its distrust of reason.

Nevertheless, three thinkers of the past, each of whom was rejected by the master-builders of his day, have overshadowed our time—Karl Marx,

Friedrich Nietzsche and Sören Kierkegaard. Of the two latter we shall have something to say hereafter, but of the first we may dispose at once. In one sense Marx has dominated the half-century. As a creed Marxism has produced, and is still producing, prodigious effects, nor can we deny that in the realm of social philosophy and the philosophy of history it has had important consequences. No writer on those subjects could afford to leave his position with regard to Marx undefined. The economic interpretation of history is admitted, even by opponents of Marxism, to be at least a partial truth. There is, however, nothing to record of the development of Marxism as a general philosophy of existence. Unfortunately the original text has been elevated to the position of a dogma and does not lack its infallible interpreters. When development is likely to be treated as 'deviation' with disagreeable results for the deviator it is not likely to happen. It cannot be said that any light has come from authoritative sources on the obscurities of the Marxian philosophy and, in particular, the question how a philosophy can be, in any intelligible sense, both materialist and dialectical remains without an answer.

When the century dawned Herbert Spencer was alive and his synthetic philosophy still a force to be reckoned with, at least in Britain and America, while positivism was a powerful influence in most European countries. The idea that scientific truth is the only real truth and that the task of the philosopher is mainly to establish the hierarchy of the sciences and, if possible, to weave out of their results a general view of the universe, was prevalent and had an exponent of great popularity in Ernst Haeckel, whose *Riddle of the Universe* was a 'best-seller'. It is a truism to remark that the period is dominated by the progress of natural science, and the theory of 'naturalism' in various forms makes its appearance throughout. In its later years, however, the scientific experts, particularly the physicists, found that the progress of their own researches raised questions which were not susceptible to treatment by the scientific method, and the more confident type of naturalism waned. In 1900 these questions were not insistent and it was more plausible than it is today to hold that scientific knowledge is, as Comte thought, the only kind worthy of the name. Those who saw in naturalism a negation of the life of the spirit and a threat to religion and morality exerted themselves to refute its presuppositions. James Ward in his *Naturalism and Agnosticism* and Rudolf Otto in an early work were two of the many critics who struck doughty blows. It was not enough to expose the errors of naturalism; an alternative view was required and, in the main, the critics defended some type of idealism. In the case of Ward it was a pluralistic idealism inspired by Leibniz, but the philosophy which for a time made the greatest headway against naturalism was absolute idealism. This is true of the English-speaking nations, but not of Germany or France. For a time most of the important philosophers in England, Scotland and America were absolute idealists.

This Anglo-Saxon school of idealism owed a debt, which was readily acknowledged, to the German idealists of the Romantic movement and particularly to Hegel, but few of its members were in any strict sense disciples of Hegel. It was adorned by one man at least who must rank among the greatest philosophical writers in the English language—F. H. Bradley, who united the gifts of dialectic with a style worthy to be compared with that of Berkeley or Hume. Bradley is, in the proper sense of the word, a rationalist and holds with Hegel that the real is the rational. In *Appearance and Reality* he applies this test to all possible claimants to reality and argues that nothing which involves relations can be completely real, because, in the end, relations are not intelligible. He concludes that the only fully real being is the absolute, which must be a perfectly coherent and harmonious experience. Within the absolute there are degrees of reality, and though neither the God of religion nor finite persons are mere illusions, they are not, in so far as they fall short of the absolute, fully real. B. Bosanquet, who held the same fundamental convictions, contributed to the development of the theory in logic, ethics and social philosophy. Even within the school, however, there were differences, or at least hesitations. The position of the finite self, and indeed of all finite existence, in Bradley's philosophy seemed to need further elucidation, and it was feared that in fact the absolute swallowed up and abolished all freedom and responsibility. Josiah Royce in America attempted, while remaining within the fold of absolute idealism, to show that finite existence need not be 'transmuted' in the absolute. The direct influence of Hegel was much more evident in the thought of J. M. E. McTaggart, who accepted, with modifications, the Hegelian dialectic and maintained that the absolute was a plurality of timeless beings united by perfect love. It is too soon to say that absolute idealism as taught by Bradley is a philosophy of the past because it is still held and there are eminent defenders of its thesis today, but it has ceased to hold a position of authority. It was the last of the purely rational philosophies which proceed on the assumption that the intellect contains within itself the principle by which we may know reality, that thought and reality are one.

In America, and in the university of Josiah Royce, there arose the most tireless critic of 'absolutism'—William James. An eminent psychologist who contributed much to the advancement of that infant science, he was also deeply interested in philosophical problems and a vigorous writer. He reacted violently against the 'block universe', which was, in his view, the conception implicit in the metaphysics of Bradley, on the ground that it destroyed freedom, removed the sense of adventure and was false to our experience. In place of the block universe he proposed a view which may be described as an inchoate pluralism. The elements of this manifold, he argued, were not related in a thoroughly determined manner, but 'strung along'. It must be owned that his theory was never very clearly

136

thought out and is expressed largely in metaphorical terms such as that quoted. His real importance lies in the theory of knowledge. Developing some suggestions of his friend C. S. Pierce, he became the leader of the pragmatist group. The essential truth, as these thinkers saw it, was the primacy of the will and, over against the intellectualist logic and epistemology of the absolute idealists, they elaborated a voluntaristic view. The controversy, which was lively and conducted with a demure acrimony, turned on the meaning of truth. To the two recognised theories on this subject—the correspondence theory and the consistency theory, held by realists and idealists respectively—the pragmatists added a third, the formula of which is, 'truth is that which works'. The discussion was confused, because it was never quite clear whether the pragmatists meant that 'working' was the sign of truth or the only significance of the word, nor indeed was the answer to the question, 'works for what end?' easy to answer. Considerable thinkers are to be counted among the pragmatists, among whom F. C. S. Schiller is remembered for his controversial power and his drastic attack on formal logic. The pragmatic school is not extinct. One of the most influential philosophers in America during the past and present generation, John Dewey, is a pragmatist with a difference. He is concerned with social experience and connects 'working' with the viability of a social complex.

It is evident that pragmatism was, as it claimed to be, a type of radical empiricism and, in a sense, the assertion that life is superior to logic. Contemporary with James was a greater figure who struck even fiercer blows at intellectualism. Though Henri Bergson was hailed by James as an ally, he was certainly far more than a pragmatist. The voluntaristic strain in French philosophy found in Bergson its prophet, for he possessed an eloquence in writing and speech which carried his doctrines far beyond the circle of professed philosophers. He became a social and literary force. The two books, *Les Données immédiates de la conscience* and *Matière et mémoire*, which laid down his fundamental principles, were published before the beginning of the century, but the works in which he developed them into a philosophy of existence, *Introduction to Metaphysics*, *L'Évolution créatrice* and *Les deux sources*, all fall within our period, the last of these appearing in 1932. Like James, Bergson will have no block-universe. He rejects any theory, whether materialistic or idealistic, which would present us with a world where 'tout est donné'. 'The gates of the future', he proclaimed, 'are wide open' and freedom is a fact. The intellect, which would persuade us otherwise, is not adapted to grasp reality. It is evolved for practical purposes and distorts the living experience of the 'life-force' which we can feel and know within ourselves only by an effort of deep intuition. Durée, which is not the 'time' of science, is the life-force itself in its forward movement. In the work on evolution which was most widely read, Bergson, with great art, painted a picture of the life-force making its way through the opposing obstacles of matter and mechanism towards the goal of ever-greater freedom. Though Bergson has fallen into comparative neglect, we have not heard the last of him. His difficult theory of time may have something still to contribute to our understanding of the universe as physics proceeds on its unpredictable course; his impact on social theory is not exhausted, and in his last book, where he dealt with morality and religion, he has something important to say on the mystical experience.

The impulse to form a comprehensive system did not fade away with the recession of absolute idealism, and two English philosophers, Samuel Alexander and A. N. Whitehead, have added chapters, or at least paragraphs, to any future history of philosophical systems. They differ, however, in a significant way from the older systems. Whereas the absolute idealist alleged that, if our minds pursued the inquiry resolutely and consistently, they must conclude as he concluded, Alexander and Whitehead ask us to admit certain postulates, or hypotheses, and offer to show that, on that basis, an intelligible view of reality can be built. Alexander in his *Space, Time and Deity*, given the concepts of space-time and emergent evolution, will show us how the universe develops and will account for the experience of religion. His postulates have not been universally accepted and his idea that God is the next stage in the evolutionary process has not commended itself to theologians, but *Space, Time and Deity* remains one of the great books of the time and a stimulus to thought. Whitehead will probably rank with Bradley as among the giants. Beginning with a sustained research into the foundations of mathematics and the philosophy of natural science, he proceeded to a larger enterprise and in his *Process and Reality* gave the world an outline of general metaphysics in the form of a 'philosophy of organism'. This highly complex and difficult work cannot be characterised in a sentence. It must suffice to say that, though Whitehead is a realist, he comes in the end to a conclusion not wholly different from that of Bradley, though he is much nearer to Plato. His highly original conceptions of the 'primordial' and 'consequent' nature of God and of creativity as apparently an independent factor in the universe have still to be thoroughly criticised.

The reaction against idealism and towards realism began in England in 1903 with the publication of G. E. Moore's essay *The Refutation of Idealism* and gathered force until in 1910 a notable group in America produced a programme for work on realistic lines. It cannot be said that this led to any definite results; indeed, it soon became clear that realism was a very vague term which might apply to any theory which held that some objects are not mind-dependent. The discussion of the nature of the objects which are real led to long and inconclusive disputes on 'sense data', so that what had started as a return to 'common sense' tended to remove itself even farther from the realism of the plain man. The work of G. E.

Moore on ethics, *Principia Ethica*, applied the realistic method to the problem of value and made a contribution of lasting importance to the philosophy of morals. Bertrand Russell is beyond question one of the formative influences of the period and it would be hard to estimate the impetus which he has given to philosophical thinking, but his importance lies rather in criticism than construction. In so far as he has permitted himself metaphysical speculation he holds 'neutral monism'—a view which has affinities with Herbert Spencer's 'unknowable'—but his main interest is in analysis of the methods and concepts of science. A pupil of Russell's, Ludwig Wittgenstein, published in 1922 his *Tractatus Logico-Philosophicus*. It elaborates the theory of 'logical atomism' and argues against the possibility of rational metaphysics. There is an element, however, of mysticism in Wittgenstein with which Russell disagrees.

The latest phase of the reaction against rationalism and idealistic logic is an empiricism even more radical than that of William James. Logical positivism, whose chief representative in England is A. J. Ayer, works out to the end the conceptions of Carnap and other writers and also the empiricism of David Hume. A short way with metaphysics and theology was discovered in the 1930's; it consisted in showing that all propositions of a metaphysical or theological character are unmeaning, because incapable of verification in sense experience. Thus the theist and the atheist are reconciled, because both are talking non-sense.

The development of philosophy in Germany took a different line. The vogue of the great idealistic philosophies had waned before the opening of the century and there were many and various essays in going 'back to Kant' to make a new beginning. The most fruitful work, however, was that of a man who saw a new problem. Wilhelm Dilthey wrote his most important works in the nineteenth century, but he survived for some years into the twentieth and may be regarded as a thinker of the present age. The humanistic studies and cultural history were the subjects on which he reflected deeply and, abandoning the ambition to construct a world-view, he concentrated on the effort to seize the spiritual content of the great periods of human culture and to realise, in living experience, the spirit that was in them. Other eminent philosophers, among whom R. Eucken and Ernst Troeltsch are worthy of mention, pursued the same general line, the latter with special reference to the relation between religion and social forms. Max Weber may be included here; his *Protestant Ethic and the Spirit of Capitalism* is the best known of his works on the 'spirit' of different societies.

Meinong and Husserl are thinkers who have made a stir in their time and whose permanent place in history is hard to assess. The former set out to classify the objects of thought and held that the realm of such objects is far wider than that of existence. The distinction between 'existence' and 'subsistence', which has been useful to realists of every type, is due to him. Husserl is the founder of 'Phenomenology', which is not by any means the same as Phenomenalism; he believed that a steady contemplation of the departments of existence, particularly of those investigated by the special sciences, would disclose their logical structure, and since this contemplation is without presuppositions, it is phenomenal in the sense that it allows the phenomena to convey their own meaning.

After the end of the second world war the 'existentialist' philosophy made many converts and inspired, if that is the right word, eminent authors such as J.-P. Sartre. It is not, however, easy to say what they have been converted to, for the existentialists march under many banners, from catholicism to atheism. They have one characteristic in common—that they are indebted to Kierkegaard and, in a smaller degree, to Nietzsche. Kierkegaard opposed to the systematic philosophy of Hegel a personalist theory or rather a personal experience. Writing from a deeply Christian standpoint, he insisted that all genuine thought is thought of a particular person in a given situation, and moreover that it is always against a background of 'Angst', of fear and trembling. Nietzsche who, as we have remarked, was a ferment in the general mind of the educated classes through most of the period, had preached the need for the superior and creative individual and the transvaluation of all values by the will of the superman. Both these ingredients enter into existentialist philosophies in various proportions. For the atheist the 'Angst' of the person in a situation where decisive action has to be taken is due not only to the lonely responsibility of choice but to the fact that he has to make, by his act, the values themselves. In the case of a theistic existentialist such as Jaspers the 'existential moment' is the transcendence of the routine and commonplace by the free choice of the individual and the participation in an experience which is not his own creation. In all its forms existentialism seems to be an enemy of intellectualism and one more symptom of the revolt against reason, for all agree that it is not by detached thinking that man knows reality.

In Italy two idealists exercised an influence beyond the boundaries of their own country. Benedetto Croce, who came to philosophy from the study of history, revised the dialectic of Hegel in order, as he believed, to expel the last vestige of transcendence and to reach a theory of purely immanent spirit. In the end, he held, history and philosophy and history and reality are one. In the course of explaining and defending this paradoxical position he has given us some profound insights into the nature of history and of historical writing. His doctrine, that religion is philosophy couched in images and destined to vanish when the concept appears, has obvious importance for theology, though few theologians have given it the attention it deserves. Croce has always been a stout defender of liberty, but Giovanni Gentile, his pupil, became Minister of Education under Mussolini. In his brilliantly written *Theory of Mind as Pure Act* he presented an activist idealism of the most thoroughgoing character which, he claimed, was the truly Christian philosophy. He has the distinction among continental philosophers of taking Berkeley seriously and his doctrine that there is nothing but thought (*cogitans* and *cogitatum*) owes more to the English idealist than to Hegel.

We should have a distorted picture of an age which, on the whole, was marked by a trend away from reason and towards reliance upon some intuition or immediate experience, if we omitted to notice the steady and growing power of the rationalism of Thomas Aquinas. The concentration of attention upon St Thomas in the Roman Church has borne fruit not only in the seminaries but in the larger world. Two laymen of high ability, Étienne Gilson and Jacques Maritain, have devoted their powers of exposition to the scholastic philosophy, with the result that it once more counts as a 'live option'. The confident assertion is made that this is the true *philosophia perennis* and that thought since Descartes has been on the wrong track. Though much of the energy of this school has been expended on the elucidation of particular points in the work of the master, it is by no means true to say that the movement is a mere revival. Real efforts are made to develop and criticise the system of St Thomas and to apply his principles to new problems. The sustained and impressive argument of Maritain's *Degrees of Knowing* is only one example of essays aimed at showing that modern science can be understood from the standpoint of St Thomas's epistemology.

In this brief sketch much of real significance has to be passed over. We have not referred to the important work on ancient philosophy by A. E. Taylor, W. D. Ross, W. R. Inge and many others, nor to the deeper understanding of Indian thought which has come to us through men like Radhakrishnan who have been trained in the wisdom of both the East and the West, nor have we been able to do more than hint at the reconsideration of ethical problems which has been going on since the opening of the century, but we cannot altogether ignore the emergence into the centre of attention of the philosophy of history and of civilisation. It was a matter of course that at a time when our culture was threatened with collapse questions about the meaning of history and the nature of civilisation should present themselves to every reflective person. R. G. Collingwood, who had affinities with Croce and was probably a more seminal thinker than was recognised in his lifetime, has left some penetrating studies of history and culture. Of more immediate effect, however, have been the writings of Marxists and the strange book by Oswald Spengler published at the end of the first world war, *Der Untergang des Abendlandes*. In this work, filled with learning and fantasy, Spengler elaborated a theory of civilisation based on biological analogies. A culture, he thought, passed inevitably through the stages from birth to death like a living organism. Unlike most philosophers of history, Spengler has a fulfilled prophecy to his credit, for he predicted that western civilisation was about to enter on a phase of dictatorships. The work of Arnold Toynbee, *A Study of History*, treats of the same problem of civilisation and makes the same assumption as Spengler, that civilisations or cultures can be regarded as individual entities. He looks, however, to spiritual and moral tendencies rather than to biological analogies for the clue to the reasons for their rise and decay and suggests that the fate of any civilisation is determined, in the main, by its response to the 'challenges' which it has to meet. In contrast with Spengler, Toynbee approaches the problem of history from a Christian standpoint. Though some of his fundamental positions are controverted and will doubtless be discussed critically for a long time, his book by reason of its massive learning and its wide sweep of generalisation is one of the most remarkable products of the past fifty years.

The foregoing account of the philosophy of the period has perhaps not sufficiently indicated the close relation between philosophy and theology which was a characteristic of its first half. Very much of the best thinking of the time was directed towards the question of the nature of religion, the conception of God in the light of modern science and the bearing of new knowledge on the traditional doctrines of Christianity. Pringle Patterson's *Idea of God*, which restated the doctrine of theism from the idealist point of view, had considerable influence and was a distinguished essay in interpretation. Clement C. J. Webb devoted a long life of reflection to the study of the history of natural theology and the philosophical aspects of the belief in divine personality. Dr Tennant, in his *Philosophical Theology* and other shorter writings, brought an acute and analytic intelligence to bear on the central dogmas of religion, approaching them with the presuppositions rather of the realistic Cambridge school than with those of idealism. Hastings Rashdall, in his *Theory of Good and Evil* and his *Doctrine of the Atonement*, gave to the world two substantial works in which deep theological and philosophical knowledge were blended. Though an idealist, he was opposed to absolute idealism and held the empirical idealism of Berkeley. To these names we may add that of W. G. de Burgh whose writings on the relation between morality and religion and on the place of reason in religion, *The Life of Reason*, came at the end of the period and have the interest of summing up a tendency of thought in which many thinkers had taken their part. Nor may we forget two philosophers who concentrated attention on the moral argument for a religious view of the world—Professor W. R. Sorley and Professor A. E. Taylor. The latter, who had begun his philosophical career as a disciple of Bradley, illustrates a movement of religious thought which had wider significance than the development of an individual mind. He abandoned the pantheistic conclusions of absolutism and ended with a view which was at least not far removed from that of Thomas Aquinas.

All the authors mentioned in the preceding paragraph were concerned to maintain the validity of religious experience and the essential truth of the central affirmations of Christianity, but it cannot be said that in all cases the theologians were grateful for the services of the would-be defender of their science. The modifications and limitations which some of the philosophers of religion would have introduced into the accepted doctrines appeared to many to be dangerous departures from revealed truth and to this feeling we must ascribe the fact that two of the best minds of the Anglican Church in these years, Dr Rashdall and Dr Tennant, were not given the recognition and influence they deserved. The times in fact were not propitious for the calm discussion of religious ideas, for from the outset of the century the Christian religion was passing through a severe crisis in which, as it seemed, there were more urgent problems than those which the detached thinkers debated. The leaders of the churches were confronted with a wide falling away of the people from public worship and from any serious allegiance to 'organised religion'. Though this fact is not the only important factor which affected religious thought from 1900 to 1950 it is one to be constantly borne in mind.

Religion, being a social activity as well as a subjective experience, is necessarily more directly linked than philosophy with the vicissitudes of history, and the crisis of western civilisation which culminated in the two world wars is reflected very clearly in the somewhat abrupt changes in theological currents which have occurred. The nineteenth century bequeathed to the twentieth two unsolved theological problems. The first was how to reconcile the results of natural science with the world-view which seemed to be implied in the Christian faith, and the second was how to assimilate the results of the historical criticism of the Bible and the conclusions of the students of comparative religion. Somewhat later another source of disquiet appeared in the 'new psychology' which, in the opinion of its pioneer, Sigmund Freud, showed that religion was an illusion.

When the century began, a powerful and earnest body of protestant Christians in Great Britain, America, Germany and most of the European states had adopted a theology which is named, chiefly by its critics, Liberal Protestantism. The principal features of this type of Christian belief were a minimising of the supernatural and dogmatic aspects of Christianity and a 'return to the Gospels'. In them, it was thought, the dominant idea was that of the Kingdom of God. Liberal Protestantism, therefore, placed the Kingdom of God at the centre of its interpretation of the religion of Christ, but it concentrated attention on the coming of the Kingdom in this present world excluding, so far as might be, those elements in the Gospels which suggest the 'other-worldly' aspect of the Kingdom. The 'social gospel' became identified in the minds of some with the idea of progress, which, in the first decade of the century, was regarded as almost certain, if not inevitable. The greatest name associated with Liberal Protestantism is that of Harnack, whose *History of Dogma* is one of the major influences in the intellectual ferment of the time. In this work, distinguished by wide learning, Harnack sustained the thesis that the original Christian experience which created the New Testament had been so interpreted by Greek philosophy that it had been transformed from its primitive simplicity into a series of theological propositions and an elaborate sacramental and hierarchical system. The popular *Das Wesen des Christentums*, which reproduced lectures given by Harnack to students in Berlin, was an eloquent plea for a simplified Christian faith consisting in two fundamental affirmations—the fatherhood of God and the brotherhood of men. It would be unjust to Harnack and the very numerous 'liberal' theologians who were in sympathy with him to say that they ignored such weighty matters as sin, redemption and the Incarnation; they aimed rather at a revaluation of these doctrines in the light of what they supposed to be the simple message of Jesus. T. R. Glover's *The Jesus of History*, which was widely read in England and America, is an attractive example of the writing produced by this type of Christian scholarship. The study of the religions of the Hellenistic age, to which Glover also contributed, was an additional factor in the problem. The researches of Reitzenstein, Cumont and others led to a clearer understanding of the importance of the 'mystery cults' and the question was raised how far the transformation of the primitive Christian gospel was due to the influence of the mystery religions and whether the process had not already been begun by St Paul, who was alleged by some to have borrowed ideas and phrases from pagan rituals.

The writings of Harnack were in part the occasion of the modernist movement in the Roman Catholic Church. Catholic scholars in France, Germany, England and Italy were conscious of the need for relating the teaching and practice of the church with modern scientific and historical knowledge, and some at least were dissatisfied with the intransigent attitude of ecclesiastical authority to all concessions to the thought of the new age. At the same time, they were firmly convinced that the church was the providential bearer and protector of the life of the spirit. The Abbé Loisy, meeting the challenge of Harnack and Liberal Protestantism, attempted to develop a new kind of Catholic apologetic in his two short but effective books, *L'Évangile et l'église* and *Autour d'un petit livre*. Accepting a criticism of the sources at least as drastic as Harnack's, he tried to show that the gospel and the church were inseparable and that the living tradition of worship in the church was the substance of the Christian religion. In England two eminent theologians were associated with the modernist movement, George Tyrell and Baron F. von Hügel. The latter, though certainly a modernist in his critical views, was probably not a philosophical modernist; and he escaped the papal condemnation which overtook his friends. For the Roman church, or at least the Vatican, repudiated the new apologetic and the programme of accommodation to modern knowledge. Modernism was banned as a heresy in 1907 and there followed a drastic 'purge' of the seminaries and the parochial clergy. To all appearance the movement was defeated in the Roman Church and perhaps it had in the end its greatest influence on the liberal wing of the Anglo-Catholic section of the Anglican Church. Loisy and Tyrell continued to write. The former became more agnostic than believing and his *Birth of Christianity* would be hard to reconcile with his *Gospel and the Church*.

The social gospel had a different complexion in the Anglican communion. Its exponents, the so-called Christian Socialists, Charles Gore and Henry Scott Holland, based their teaching on the Incarnation and on the Catholic doctrine of the Incarnation to the defence and explanation of which Gore's principal books were devoted. Bishop Gore represents one of the chief trends of Anglican thought in the first thirty years of the century and was one of the outstanding personal influences. The liberalism of his earlier period, when he contributed to *Lux Mundi*, was always of a strictly limited character and in later life he stood for an orthodoxy which was prepared to silence those clerics who went farther in criticism of traditional doctrines than the acceptance of the positions of *Lux Mundi*. Nevertheless, he was always half a liberal and it is interesting to note that his 'kenotic' theory of the Incarnation is now repudiated by Anglo-Catholic theologians who find this leader of the Catholic party of yesterday too liberal for today.

The first world war was a heavy blow to the optimism of liberal protestantism. The dream of the permeation of society by the principles of Christianity was clouded though not destroyed. The League of Nations was, in great measure, the creation of Christian idealism and it failed chiefly because the spiritual power which made it was not sufficient to sustain it. The hopes of the 1920's and the disillusionments of the 1930's had their repercussions in religious thought, but there were also other disturbing causes which arose within theology itself.

The 'historical Jesus' who leads mankind into the Kingdom is the central figure of idealistic Christianity. He is a universal figure, modern at any rate in the sense that He speaks in language which has significance for our time. This figure had been constructed by selecting from the Gospels those traits and words which are consonant with our ways of thinking and dismissing the rest. The Apocalyptic school of New Testament interpretation protested against this picture on the ground that it left out the most important element in the story. They pointed out that the first three Gospels are deeply imbued with the ideas and imagery of Jewish Apocalyptic. Albert Schweitzer caused the greatest perturbation with his book *The Quest of the Historical Jesus*, in which he insisted that Jesus was 'a Jew of the first century'. Other works, *The Mysticism of St Paul* in particular, followed the clue of Apocalyptic and the striking and attractive personality of Schweitzer, together with his devoted labours as a medical missionary, have made him one of the most important religious spirits of our time. The extreme Apocalyptic view of the Gospels has been criticised and eminent scholars still reject it altogether, but on the whole it may be said that the contentions of Schweitzer and those who agreed with him in his principal positions, such as Professor Burkitt, have left a permanent mark on New Testament interpretation and on the conception of the Kingdom of God in the teaching and experience of Jesus.

The question of the nature of the religious experience was raised, as we have seen, by the new psychology and much active theological discussion was directed to the refutation of the fundamental scepticism of the Freudians. A positive contribution to the problem was made by Rudolf Otto's *The Idea of the Holy*, in which he developed a theory of 'the numinous' as a distinctive feeling which exists at all levels from that of unreasoning, shuddering dread to that of awe and reverence. Otto linked his theory with the theology of Schleiermacher, the philosophy of Fichte and the religion of Luther and carried his line of thought farther in a penetrating study of *Mysticism, Eastern and Western*. For reasons not easy to discover he had a larger following in England and America than in Germany. He is one of the authors of the time whose writings will probably be of permanent value and his doctrine of the 'irrationality' of the divine has not yet been placed in its proper perspective.

In the ferment of conflicting theories perhaps the systematic theologian is at a disadvantage, because he finds no firm ground of accepted presuppositions under his feet, but noteworthy efforts were made to restate the orthodox doctrines for contemporary minds. Dr Gore, at the end of his career, returned to the defence and exposition of the Christian beliefs about God, Christ and the Church; Dr A. C. Headlam, beside books on the *Life and Teaching of Jesus* and *The Atonement*, produced the first volume of a system of theology which he did not live to finish. William Temple, archbishop of Canterbury, was through most of these years probably the most effective exponent of a liberal kind of orthodox theology. His wonderful powers of memory and of lucid statement enabled him to pour out books in spite of his absorption in the practical work of the church. Three of his books, *Mens Creatrix, Christus Veritas*, and *Nature, Man and God*, contain the essence of his thinking and display the movement of his mind from a 'broad Church' to a more traditional standpoint.

We have already observed in passing that an interest in mysticism appeared in more than one quarter and it may be suggested that one of the causes operating to quicken this interest was the uncertainty both of the social and the intellectual background. Men sought for some basis for life and found no reassuring answer in the idea of progress or in the dogmas of the church. They looked within for the foundation and many found it there. The list of distinguished students of mysticism is long and we can notice only a few of them. Dr W. R. Inge, in his *Christian Mysticism* and in his lectures on *The Philosophy of Plotinus*, did much to widen the understanding of mysticism and to persuade those who were suspicious of it that it was worthy of serious attention. Evelyn Underhill, in her *Mysticism* and many other books, brought the words of great mystical writers home to the general reader and had an influence on wide circles through her spiritual conferences. Baron F. von Hügel was a religious thinker who brought a unique acquaintance with contemporary continental scholarship and philosophy to the service of a liberal Catholic theology, but his most memorable book, *The Mystical Element of Religion*, was a detailed study of St Catherine of Genoa on which was based an investigation of the nature and significance of the mystical experience. The London Society for the Study of Religion, which von Hügel founded, was a meeting-place for some of the finest spirits of the 1920's and 1930's. Two of its members, Claude Montefiore, the Jewish scholar and student of the Gospels, and Edwyn Bevan, the expert on Hellenistic culture and author of a valuable book on *Symbolism*, must be named.

In the year following the end of the first world war Karl Barth came into prominence and since that time his 'dialectical' theology of crisis has been a major feature in Protestant thought. Though it can hardly be said that Barth has any disciple or colleague who accepts all his positions and he has conducted lively controversies with some who were at one time members of his school, such as Gogarten and E. Brunner, his influence may be discerned in the majority of Protestant theologians since about 1925 either by way of agreement or of criticism. At the beginning of our period there were those who placed so much faith in the philosophy of religion that they expected it to take the position formerly occupied in the church by dogmatic theology; at the end we find a powerful movement which repudiates all connection with philosophy and presents a dogmatic based on the Bible as the only divine truth open to men. The conception of the Word of God is central for Barth and he draws a sharp distinction between it and all the wisdom and spiritual experience of humanity. The Word of God comes into the world as a direct and unrelated act of God. It is not to be criticised or validated by human reason which, being corrupt through the Fall, is incapable of passing judgment on the Word. The root of Barth's hostility to every form of philosophical theology is his denial of the 'analogia entis', that is of any 'image of God' in man from which he could rise by a process of analogical inference to any knowledge of God. The Barthian theology represents the extreme form of the reaction against liberal protestantism and 'rational' religion. It is, as the name 'Theology of Crisis' implies, a movement evoked by the menace of the historical situation, but it may have more permanent importance than that, for it is, on one side of its doctrine, a revival of elements in Christianity which have their origin in St Paul.

A brief reference is all that space permits to the contribution of Russian and Eastern Orthodox writers. The exile of many Christian scholars from their native land has enriched the religious thought of the West. The names of Franks and Bulgakov must be passed over with a bare mention though the former has given us an excellent exposition of a philosophical type of mysticism which is not afraid of the idea of the church. Nicolas Berdyaev, in a long series of books, presented a philosophy of religion and a theology which attracted attention partly by its difference in method and inspiration from all western religious thought. Neither the Scholastic logic and metaphysics nor the Reformation are among the fundamental sources of his thought, which is moulded chiefly by the tradition of Orthodox theology, Marxism and German philosophy. He writes rather as a prophet than a philosopher though his works are full of references to philosophy of all ages and many nations; he does not argue but states his conclusions in an oracular manner. Towards the end of his life he was interested in the permanent value and truth of the Apocalyptic vision of history, a subject which he had approached through his two most significant studies, *The Meaning of History* and the *Destiny of Man*. Probably his really important contribution was his frank recognition of the necessity of 'mythological thinking' in religion and his attempt to elucidate the nature of myth in Christian belief. It is remarkable that many orthodox theologians hailed Berdyaev as an ally in spite of the obvious tendency of his mind towards positions which would be distasteful to the traditional dogmas both of Protestants and Catholics. Many reasons may have contributed to this, the stimulating character of Berdyaev's thought, the obscurity of his writing and the obtuseness of the orthodox.

Even so brief and inadequate a sketch as the present must have made it clear that any attempt to sum up the tendencies of the first half of the twentieth century as manifested in its literature, philosophy and theology must be futile. No one who is himself a part of the stream can detach himself from it sufficiently to judge its direction and its volume. It may be making for some glorious sea, or it may be dispersing and losing itself in the sands. The most that can be expected from an author is that he should state the impression which the phenomena leave on his mind for what it may be worth. One has then the sense of a growing loss of confidence in the universe. The sombre vision which Hardy projected at the beginning of our period has not been dissipated—it has spread and deepened. The world has appeared to be less intelligible and less friendly to human aspirations than our fathers imagined. To many it has seemed that the solid ground is giving way beneath them and that the primal certainties on which they relied have melted away. Even the men of faith, the exponents of religion, have recognised the necessity of examining again the foundations of belief and have sought for some basis which would be beyond and beneath the contemporary crisis. But at the same time one would add that there is no sign of the failure of the human mind and spirit. Sustained surely by some deep, unconscious faith the human intelligence has never been more active. Distracted by the catastrophes of the age of violence and by fear of the future, it has continued to probe, to construct, and to dream. Though its outstanding victories have been in the sphere of natural science, the age has been prolific in poets, novelists, philosophers and theologians of note, and if there are no figures among them which strike us as being certainly among the immortals that may be due to our lack of perspective. To the historian of the future the age will be deeply interesting not only for the shattering events which mark its course but for the extraordinary ferment of ideas which opened new paths for the mind; he will know, what is hidden from us, whether it was a chequered gleam of light before the great darkness or the prelude to a new age of peace and human amity.

CHAPTER VII

THE UNITED STATES OF AMERICA

I N the last year of the nineteenth century the American people re-elected William McKinley as President. By doing so, they ratified the liberation of Cuba and the annexation of Puerto Rico and the Philippine Islands. Probably not knowing what they were doing, and certainly unwilling to accept the full implications of their new situation, the American people had moved out on to the world stage, little better prepared for their new role than the Japanese had been when Commodore Perry's 'black ships' broke the centuries-old, self-imposed blockade of the island empire.

William Jennings Bryan, who had fought for the economically unfortunate, above all for the angered and impoverished farmer in 1896, had fought in 1900 against 'imperialism'. But the sharp edge of discontent had been blunted by the flow of gold from South Africa and the Yukon, by a natural turn in the trade cycle, and the vague issue of 'imperialism' was not an adequate fighting theme. Flushed with an easy victory over an impotent Spain, and moving into a new boom period, the American people was convinced that it was living in the best of all possible republics, that it had nothing and no one to fear.

The politicians who felt this mood had no need to worry about re-electing the President and some of them took the chance to get out of the way an obstreperous hero of the brief Spanish-American war, Theodore Roosevelt, who had won the governorship of New York on the strength of his achievements with a regiment of irregular cavalry in Cuba. Possibly against his will, he was nominated for the vice-presidency. In Washington his great and unused energies were turned, for the moment, to the study of law. On 6 September 1901 the President was shot by a probably mad 'anarchist', Leon Czolgosz, and died on 14 September. Theodore Roosevelt was President of the United States.

The new President was just under forty-three, the youngest man ever to enter the White House. He was exceptional in other ways. Born in 1858, the Civil War was a vague memory for him, not a great crisis lived through as it had been for every one of his predecessors since Lincoln. He was the first Republican President since Johnson who was not a Civil War veteran and, although he was a vehement party man, his mother's family were Georgia Democrats and a paternal uncle was, and remained, a Cleveland Democrat. Not of a rich family by the new standards, he yet belonged to a stable and prosperous element in New York society. Graduating from Harvard, he had had a varied experience as state legislator, as ranch owner, as Police Commissioner, as Civil Service

Commissioner, as Assistant-Secretary of the Navy. But although active in politics he was not a politician as McKinley understood the term. He was the most versatile President since Jefferson and, if much of his knowledge was superficial, his interests, curiosity and sympathies were genuinely wide. His talent for dramatising himself was his greatest gift. His mannerisms were the delight of cartoonists and satirists. They were also the delight of the voters. Almost at once he made the presidency the centre of the political system as it had not been since Lincoln's time. He knew how to manœuvre, how to conciliate congressional leaders; he did not quarrel for quarrelling's sake. And until he was re-nominated and re-elected in 1904, he avoided a show-down with the conservative elements who had hoped to bury him in the vice-presidency.

The impress on the American mind made by Theodore Roosevelt was greater than the positive achievement of his administration. Indeed, that impress was the main achievement of the administration. He made the federal government dramatic, impressive, popular. He also made it more modern. The new President had ideas on nearly all topics. He had plans for reforming the coinage on Greek models; he revived L'Enfant's plan for the development of Washington. He gave jobs to poets and naturalists as well as to former 'Rough Riders'. He exposed (with the help of a celebrated novel, *The Jungle*, by Upton Sinclair) the filth of the Chicago meat-packing plants. Although far from radical in his economic views, Roosevelt had none of the automatic sympathy with and admiration for the businessman that all his predecessors since Johnson, including Cleveland, had shared. Thus he intervened in the great Pennsylvania coal strike, but on the side of the miners. The effectively dramatised presidential attitude was a novelty in the White House and a welcome novelty. For the discontent that had exploded and died away in the Bryan campaign had taken a new and more relevant form. The Sherman Anti-Trust Act of 1890 had been a dead letter since the Cleveland administration had failed to enforce it in a prosecution that, some said, it had not pressed very effectively. The trusts had certainly flourished. Standard Oil, the best known and most hated, was stronger than ever and not only did the creation, in 1901, of the United States Steel Corporation unite all the great steel producers in one vast combine, but that corporation was capitalised at $1,400,000,000, just about the total of the national debt. And as it was notorious that the assets taken over were not worth this sum, it was concluded that the promoters, J. P. Morgan and Company, were discounting the future profits of monopoly. When, therefore, the same banking house arranged peace between the warring Harriman and Hill railroad interests by the creation of the Northern Securities Company in 1902, public alarm was great and it was a triumph for the administration when the Supreme Court ordered the dissolution of the company in 1904, an election year.

The Roosevelt administration was marked by the development of two policies that were, among other things, presidential hobbies. Roosevelt had spent impressionable years in the west and he was deeply convinced of the necessity for conservation of natural resources. The policy of withholding national lands from mere exploitation went back as far as Cleveland, but Roosevelt extended the policy, especially the policy of preserving the forests, built up the forest service and dramatised the issue with a success that deeply marked future federal policy.

From his youth, Roosevelt had been fascinated by military affairs and, although protesting his love of peace, was deeply impressed by the reality of war. He supported the efforts of his war secretary, Elihu Root, to reform the army, but nothing could make the United States a great military power. The navy was another matter. Roosevelt begged, pleaded, argued for a big navy and he got it; and he watched the development of that navy with the keenest personal attention. As a gesture for peace through strength, he sent it on a cruise round the world, with only enough funds voted to send it half way, thus imposing on a reluctant Congress the duty of voting the funds to bring it back.

But not all his acts were mere gestures. When he came to office he re-opened negotiations with Britain for a new treaty dealing with the 'Isthmian Canal' question. The second Hay–Pauncefote treaty permitted the United States to fortify the canal. It was now necessary to decide between the Panama and Nicaragua routes: Panama was chosen and the Hay–Herran Convention was negotiated in 1903. But the Colombian senate refused to ratify the Convention and the canal might have been held up, or built in Nicaragua, had not a revolution conveniently broken out in the province of Panama. American recognition was given within three days and, a fortnight later, the Hay–Bunau–Varilla treaty gave the United States the right to construct a canal in the territory of the newborn nation. Later, Roosevelt was to boast that he 'took the Canal'. Although American complicity in the convenient revolution was never proved, the episode poisoned the relations of the United States with Latin America for many years. In other ways Roosevelt wielded what, in one of his telling phrases, he called 'the big stick'. He interpreted the Monroe Doctrine to mean that the United States, if it kept European powers from using normal coercive measures to secure redress from the fleeting governments of the turbulent republics of the Caribbean, was bound, in turn, to impose a minimum of decorum on these republics. Thus the Dominican Republic was put under American supervision, not by a treaty, but by an 'executive agreement', and Olney's dictum in the Venezuela dispute, that the 'fiat' of the United States was law, was made to look like the truth, in this area at least.

Nor were greater issues avoided. The great struggle over the balance of power in the Pacific that led to the Russo-Japanese war saw American official, like unofficial opinion, deeply pro-Japanese. But Roosevelt, acting the part less of the honest broker than of the candid friend, persuaded the Japanese, who were, economically at least, at the end of their tether, to be moderate in their peace terms, and the Treaty of Portsmouth was concluded under American auspices in 1905. The balance of power was threatened in the Atlantic, too, and although less openly than at Portsmouth, Roosevelt supported the Franco-British position at the Algeciras conference of 1906. Not since the end of the Napoleonic wars had the United States been of such importance in world politics; but then it had been as a patient, now it was very much as an agent.

There was no doubt (at any rate after the death of Mark Hanna, McKinley's manager) that Roosevelt would be re-nominated. The Cleveland Democrats capitalised on Bryan's discomfiture in 1900 and hoped to capitalise conservative discontent with Roosevelt, by nominating a conservative and little-known New York judge, Alton B. Parker, but 'big business' was not frightened enough of the President to back Parker; it contributed handsomely (although Roosevelt did not know or preferred not to know this) to the President's campaign funds. Parker lost many of the supporters of Bryan and gained little from the disgruntled Republicans. The campaign was a great personal triumph and, in the moment of victory, Roosevelt announced that he would not be a candidate for re-election. He was the first President in American history to be elected in his own right after coming to the presidency by mere succession, and he might have accepted the interpretation of the third term taboo pressed on him— that it meant two *elective* terms. But he burnt his boats and, all through his second term, suffered from the congressional knowledge that he would be out of office in 1909. His friends hoped and his enemies feared that he might change his mind, but he was determined to keep his word and even persuaded himself that a little less than eight years in the White House was enough for him and the country.

The second term was not sterile. A beginning was made with effective federal control of railway rates. Relations with Japan, which had rapidly deteriorated with the disappointment of the Japanese people with the terms of the Treaty of Portsmouth and with their resentment of anti-Japanese legislation in California, were nursed back to convalescence, if not health, by the President and his Secretary of State, Elihu Root. Work on the Panama Canal was pushed vigorously ahead after a great deal of initial confusion and squabbling. The President, when he quarrelled, managed as a rule to get the public on his side. His popular prestige was as great as ever and he was able to choose his successor. He had considered Root, but Root's corporation connections were considered too great a handicap and Roosevelt's choice fell on his Secretary of War, the vast William Howard Taft. The Democrats nominated Bryan, who did much better than Parker, showing where the Democratic strength still lay, in the south and west. But the country, seeing in Taft the heir of Roosevelt, voted for the President in choosing his successor.

The new President had never held an elective office before he entered the White House. As a federal judge, as Solicitor-General, as Governor-General of the Philippines, as Secretary of War, Taft had held high but subordinate office. He was now on his own. And he must have been conscious that he was only President because Roosevelt had chosen him as his successor. He began badly by getting rid of the whole Roosevelt cabinet. He went on by taking the risk (one never taken by Roosevelt) of raising the question of tariff revision. The senatorial leaders, who had smarted under Roosevelt, began to take the measure of his successor and what they saw reassured them. For Taft believed in the separation of powers; it was not his function, he thought, to dictate to Congress or even to lead it. As a result the tariff bill (the Payne–Aldrich bill) which was finally presented to him was a parody of a revision. Taft might have stopped it earlier, might have forced modifications, but he accepted it and defended it. That part of his trade policy which might have redounded to his credit, the Reciprocity treaty with Canada, was rejected by Canada. This was not Taft's fault; if it was anybody's in the United States it was the fault of brash Democratic orators like Champ Clark, now Speaker of the House of Representatives. For the Democrats had capitalised on Republican disunion and had carried the House for the first time since 1892. In the House the middle-western insurgents had already combined with the Democrats to depose the autocratic Speaker Cannon. Even if the President had been willing to lead Congress, it was too late. And Roosevelt had returned from Africa and Europe suspicious and soon to be angry.

The wave of discontent with the old order, with the 'stand-patters', was far from spent. All over the country the voters were looking for a leader and Taft was not that. He felt, rightly, that he had not betrayed the trust that Roosevelt had placed in him. He resented warmly the charge that he and his Secretary of the Interior, Ballinger, had carelessly or corruptly alienated valuable parts of the public domain. He knew that his administration had been more active and more successful in prosecuting the trusts than had Roosevelt's. But Taft was a man of judicial temper and of physical and, to some extent, of mental lethargy. The revolting western radicals would have none of him. For a moment, it seemed possible that they would rally round Senator Robert Marion La Follette of Wisconsin, but La Follette could not compete with Roosevelt as a dramatic figure. And Roosevelt, still young, feeling like 'a bull moose', as he was to say, was under great pressure from his friends and his temperament to break with Taft. Shooting lions in Africa, visiting kings and emperors, receiving the Nobel prize for peace, or even giving the Romanes lecture in Oxford, were not enough for a man of such physical and mental energy, still only a little older than Lincoln had been when he entered the White House. Submitting to both pressures, Roosevelt became a candidate for the Republican nomination.

It is certain that he was the first choice of the average Republican voter, and it is probable that he was the only candidate who could have held the deeply divided party together. But Taft was resolved to fight and with him was most of the high command of the party, including such close friends of Roosevelt as Henry Cabot Lodge and Elihu Root. And the high command were ready to lose with Taft rather than win with Roosevelt and see the control of the party pass into dangerously radical hands. A President in office can always secure his renomination and Taft did so; but Roosevelt and his supporters, protesting that he had been robbed of the nomination, hastily founded the Progressive party and it nominated its hero.

This made a Democratic victory certain and, from the politician's point of view, the obvious candidate was the Speaker of the House of Representatives, Champ Clark of Missouri. But Bryan, although even he had come to see that a fourth nomination was almost, perhaps quite, impossible, saw in Clark the nominee and ally of his old conservative enemies, the people who had nominated Parker in 1904. He threw his strength, which was still very great, to the only serious rival of Clark, the Governor of New Jersey, Woodrow Wilson, who overtook the Speaker's early lead and was nominated.

The Democratic candidate was as unusual a phenomenon in American politics, in his way, as Roosevelt was in his. He had been in active politics for only two years when nominated. He had been a distinguished professor of political science and a famous President of Princeton University. He had been a standard southern, conservative Democrat, opposed to Bryan and Bryanism. But he fought and fought unavailingly to make Princeton 'democratic'. He became, to many, a martyr; he also became impossible as President of Princeton. He accepted the offer of the Democratic bosses to run for Governor of New Jersey and was triumphantly elected. Again he became a national figure by quarrelling with the bosses, by defeating them and by advancing increasingly radical views. And it was as a radical, or at any rate as an advanced liberal, campaigning for 'the New Freedom', that he was triumphantly elected.

The new President was a devoted admirer of British constitutional practice. He saw himself both as President and as Prime Minister. When he was still President of Princeton University he had written that 'if he (the President) led the nation, his party can hardly resist him. His office is anything he has the capacity and force to make it.' He practised this doctrine. He disregarded the precedent set by Jefferson, who was no orator, and instead of sending a long, written—and ignored—message to Congress, he addressed it in person, and Wilson was an orator. He had prepared and now pushed through a coherent programme of legislation. A bill reducing the tariff was introduced and passed by effective and dramatic appeals to the public and effective public and private pressure on Congress. The long debated question of a reformed banking system was dealt with by the creation of the Federal Reserve System that provided for a far more elastic currency and a much better organised federal banking system. It also, in form, gratified the hostility to bankers of the agrarian radicals, whose leader, Bryan, Wilson prudently made Secretary of State.

He gratified Bryan in other ways: by tolerating, and to some extent gratifying, his desire to reward the faithful 'deserving Democrats' with patronage and by withdrawing support from the American bankers who had been encouraged by the previous administration to meddle in the already troubled affairs of China. 'Dollar diplomacy' was deemed to be dead. True, Wilson was unlucky. In Mexico a real revolution was continuing. No Mexican government could carry out the normal obligations of a sovereign state. Many Americans had very real grievances against Mexico and Wilson was forced, he thought, to intervene and occupy Tampico to secure reparation for an insult to the flag. But he did succeed in getting rid of the 'usurper', Huerta, and, by accepting the mediation of Argentina, Brazil and Chile, he conciliated Latin-American opinion. He proclaimed that the Monroe Doctrine was not a form of protectorate and, although he continued intervention in the Caribbean, he steadfastly refused full-scale intervention in Mexico, contenting himself, in 1916, with sending a punitive expedition after Pancho Villa who had raided American territory. The grant of greater autonomy to the Philippines, like the granting of American citizenship to the inhabitants of Puerto Rico, was proof of the same liberal, anti-imperialistic attitude.

But the war of 1914, as Wilson feared, pushed him, the longer it lasted, into the field of foreign affairs for which he was not prepared. It caused the resignation of Bryan from the cabinet. The question of the American attitude to the two sides more and more preoccupied the President and the public. Legislation was not stopped. Labour unions were exempted (it was thought) from the anti-trust legislation; a Federal Trade Commission was set up to control business in the spirit of 'the New Freedom'. One of the most effective critics of big business, Louis Brandeis, was put, after a bitter fight, on the Supreme Court. The demand of the railway workers for a federal limitation of hours was granted in the Adamson Act and, at the end of his first term, Wilson could look back at a record of successful domestic leadership that few presidents have ever equalled.

The reunited Republicans nominated Charles Evans Hughes who resigned from the Supreme Court to run. Hughes was a stiff and tactless candidate and alienated some Progressive supporters he might have won. But Wilson's record was his chief asset, not only his domestic record, but the belief, summed up in a famous convention speech, that 'he kept us out of war'. It was to be an ironical reason for victory.

The Democrats elected their President but barely kept control of Congress. Wilson, once re-elected, attempted to mediate between the warring powers, but the future of German-American relations was being settled in Berlin, not in Washington. The German high command decided to ignore the risk of American intervention which, they decided, would come too late to be effective and, a month after his second inauguration, Wilson led the American people into war. Wilson the reformer became Wilson the war leader. True, the United States was not an ally, only an 'associated power', but Wilson was the chief spokesman to his own people, to the allied peoples, to the German people, to the Russian people. Necessarily, the 'New Freedom' was neglected and the administration devoted more and more exclusively to the war. No American war had ever been run so efficiently, with so few scandals, with such a rapid mobilisation of the power of what was now the world's greatest industrial nation. The American people had reason to be grateful, but their gratitude, unlike their patriotism, was limited. The famous speeches that were heard round the world, culminating in the 'fourteen points' speech of 8 January 1918, had more enthusiastic audiences in tormented Europe than in a comparatively immune America.

The internal impact of the war was, by the standards of the time, very great. Conscription for service overseas was an unprecedented innovation. So were the economic controls like the imposition of limits on farm prices, the assumption of a general direction of the railways. The campaigns for the 'victory loans' were propaganda efforts unknown even in the Civil War and they were accompanied by a repression of dissent also unknown in the Civil War and more severe than anything found in Britain, France or Germany. The two 'Espionage Acts' seemed, to many, a gross breach of American tradition. German-Americans were the subject of an imbecile campaign of hostility, and radical dissenters began to suffer from legal and extra-legal repression. The President, absorbed in the conduct of the war and inclined to see in criticism and scepticism a reflection on his own moral purpose, was not as wisely magnanimous as Lincoln. He was, however, less inclined than Lincoln had been to act on a vague 'war power'. He went to Congress for his authority, but equally refused to countenance anything like the Civil War 'Committee on the Conduct of the War'. The Republican opposition, for the most part, supported all the war effort zealously; indeed, its most vocal members deplored the mildness of the President's language in his addresses to the German people and professed fear of a 'soft peace'. Wilson's refusal to give high command in the overseas army to Roosevelt and to Leonard Wood embittered their numerous Republican friends, and the President neglected to encourage, by close association with the administration, the numerous Republicans who wanted something more than victory. In the autumn of 1918 victory was in sight. So were the congressional elections and Wilson was induced to issue an appeal for a Democratic Congress. It is commonly asserted that this was a mistake. That cannot be proved or disproved. At any rate, the Republicans carried both houses.

Quite early in the war many Americans had pondered the problem of a 'League to Enforce Peace', and the President was determined to make that the basis of the new peace treaty. The war had been represented to the American people simply as a crusade for perpetual peace. That it might be that, and other things as well, had not been stressed and candid discussion of war issues was difficult under the regime of the Espionage Acts. Yet the loss of control of Congress did not shake Wilson's confidence in his mandate or his mission. He decided, against the advice of some close friends, to go to Europe himself. He neglected to take with him any of the eminent Republicans, like Taft, who might have carried weight in the party that now controlled Congress. Wilson in Europe was a Messiah at the very time that he was being disowned at home. For the American people was demobilising, psychologically as well as materially. The artificial character of much of the support for the war effort was now made manifest; so was the folly of imposing conformity. Germans, Irish and then Italians turned against the administration.

The Republican leadership took full advantage of the change. The new chairman of the Senate Foreign Relations Committee, Henry Cabot Lodge, packed the committee and led the campaign to impose reservations on the Covenant of the League of Nations that the President would refuse. Wilson, finally returning from Europe with a treaty of peace indissolubly tied up, he thought, with the Covenant, began a speaking tour to re-convert the country. Without the aid of wireless, Wilson undertook a task beyond his power and collapsed in Denver. He refused to compromise and any chance of American adherence to the League was over.

It was evident that the tide was turning against the Democrats, that the referendum that Wilson had called for would be hostile to his great design. The stroke which the President had suffered kept him from exercising either his functions as President, or as party leader, and a sharp economic recession in 1920, the election year, further blighted the faint Democratic hopes. They nominated a former Governor of Ohio, James M. Cox, an able and responsible newspaper owner little known outside his state, and, as a running mate, gave him the handsome and energetic young Assistant-Secretary of the Navy, Franklin D. Roosevelt. In the far more important Republican Convention the leading candidates cancelled each other out and the small senatorial group and some astute party managers imposed on the tired delegates an empty, idle, Ohio senator, Warren Gamaliel Harding. The platform was highly ambiguous, and eminent Republicans who had supported entry into the League could persuade themselves that the way to do it was to vote the Republican ticket. The managers of the campaign knew better. As a last and sole gesture of independence the convention nominated the Governor of Massachusetts, Calvin Coolidge, for the vice-presidency. The election was a walkover; the Republicans carried every state outside the 'solid South' and carried Tennessee in it. The exile of the party that thought it alone was fit to govern was ended. So was intrusion into the affairs of other nations. Once in office, any serious attempt to carry out the vague promises of the platform was abandoned and instead a separate peace was made with Germany. The 'great crusade' was over and disowned.

The years between the inauguration of Harding and the stock market crash of 24 October 1929 became, in retrospect, one of the least admired periods in American history, only comparable with the years that followed the Civil War. Each was a 'gilded age'. And because the second era coincided with a profound change in the folkways of the American people, affecting domestic life, education, religion, sport, because a whole host of new forces attacked the older American ways, it was an era far more disturbed than the era of Grant. It lay between two catastrophic wars, in an age of change at least as profound as the age of the French Revolution and Napoleon. It would have been strange if the leaders in politics, in business, in religion, in education, had all been adequate in the crisis. Many were not and none were fully adequate. But they suffered a double condemnation since many of them claimed a competence that it was soon tragically demonstrated that they did not possess, and the outer world, on which a majority of the American people had gladly turned its back in 1920, refused to be excluded, refused to limit its sins and follies to those which did not affect the United States.

The landslide character of the Harding victory in 1920 was an affirmation of a nostalgia for the safe, stable American past that men thought, rightly, was threatened. It was a triumph for those sections of the Republican party which resented the concessions to 'progressivism' that had been forced on the party since the death of President McKinley. Yet the federal government did not quite go back to the old ways. A higher degree of control of the railroads was entrusted to the Interstate Commerce Commission and new obligations were imposed on the railways. Other instruments of federal control might be emasculated, as was the Federal Trade Commission; the spirit of the Republican administrations might be far more friendly to business rights (often disguised as states' rights) than had been true of the Wilson administration; but federal power could not but grow, if only because the new industries spreading into previously rural regions, the greater financial integration produced by the working of the Federal Reserve banking system, produced a 'more perfect union' that only the doctrinaire could ignore. The mere necessity of servicing the national debt, which had increased nearly twenty-five-fold since

1914, extended federal power and gave to questions of tax policy a new intensity of interest. It was possible to pass a temporary and then a permanent tariff law (the Fordney–McCumber Act of 1922), but this return to the principles of high protection did not merely, by being enacted, make the United States again a debtor nation or provide the dollar-hungry countries of Europe with means of buying American exports, above all of buying the products of the extension and intensification of American agricultural production that the war had fostered. Nor was it possible to limit the effects of the immigration restrictions that cut down to a trickle what had been a flood, and discriminated (as they were intended to do) against the 'new immigration' from eastern and southern Europe. 'America', said President Coolidge, 'must be kept American.'

That was also the view of less eminent persons. In the south there was a revival of the Ku-Klux-Klan. It was not, for long, confined to the southern states, although it tended, in the north, to be strongest in states like Indiana with a strong southern element in the population. Nor was its sole enemy the negro. Its members had to be 'white, Gentile, Protestants'. It enforced the standards of fundamentalist Protestant morality by whipping, branding, castration, murder.

The uneasiness that led to the creation of the new Ku-Klux-Klan found other manifestations. It inspired legislation against the teaching of Darwinian evolutionary theory in the schools of several states; it inspired violent controversies within Protestant churches in which 'fundamentalists' (the term dates from this time) fought 'modernists'.

Politically, the most important achievement of this defence of the old American standards was the adoption of the eighteenth amendment to the constitution in 1919. It provided, not for the extension of the powers of Congress over the liquor traffic, but for the prohibition of 'the manufacture, sale or transportation of intoxicating liquors within, the importation thereof into, or the exportation thereof from the United States and all territory subject to the jurisdiction thereof'. It also provided that 'the Congress and the several States shall have concurrent power to enforce this article by appropriate legislation'. All states but Connecticut and Rhode Island finally ratified the amendment. Many states began by passing legislation reinforcing the main federal law, the 'Volstead Act', but zeal evaporated as it was discovered that mere law had very serious limits. Within a few years the administration of prohibition legislation, then the whole question of the wisdom and efficacy of the amendment, were one of the two or three burning themes of politics and one of the most significant lines of division between the old America and the new: the America of the countryside and the small towns, mainly north European in origin and Protestant in religion; and the America of the great new urban centres, where most of the population was of fairly recent immigrant stock, Catholic or Jewish in religion, and, in ways of life, ignoring some of the most cherished traditions and prejudices of the countryside.

Behind the fears for the American way of life lay equally potent discontent with some aspects of that life. The artificial markets created by the war had led to a fantastic over-estimate of the permanent demand for American foodstuffs and raw materials like cotton. The prices of land soared as these expectations were discounted. Arable settlement moved in the war years and immediately afterwards into areas unsuited for ploughing except in exceptionally favourable seasons. Money was borrowed to buy land, to pay for improvements, to build schools and roads. The slump of 1920 wiped out many hundreds of millions of investments, turned many owners into tenants, wrecked the hopes of becoming owners of many more and left all the western and some of the southern states with a permanent grievance. They alone were not sharing in the golden stream that was flowing so freely in other regions. An alliance between the representatives and senators of both parties, the 'farm bloc', weakened party discipline. Behind and below the formal Republican triumphs there was this pool of discontent. And no Republican administration committed to the *ethos* of business could give the farmers what they wanted: some real, tangible, cash equivalent of the benefits flowing to industry from high tariffs. The new Republican administration had good fortune in its first year or two. The business recession of 1920 passed away and what was, with some minor lapses, an unprecedented boom began. The great American mass production automobile industry, personified by Henry Ford, was the delight of Americans and the wonder and envy of the world. Poverty was boldly asserted to be disappearing, the immense wealth produced by business was lavishly if not equally distributed.

Even the outside world seemed, for a moment, to be returning to sanity and solvency. The American government carefully avoided all commitments in Europe or Asia, but the two 'settlements' of the German reparations question were made under American auspices; the Dawes plan in 1924, the Young plan in 1929. The American government denied any moral or legal connection between the reparations debts owed by Germany to Britain, France, Italy and the debts these countries owed America, but the funds with which Germany paid the victors were provided by the American private investor and, in turn, were in the main paid over to the American government as part of the war debt settlements negotiated in these years; settlements that, admitting the desirability of such payments, were in the presumed economic state of Europe generous—a view more strongly held in America than in Europe. In the Far East the Washington treaty of 1922 which settled, for the time being, the ratio of naval power, seemed, to the optimistic, to deal adequately with the situation created by the absence of Russian power, the decline of British and French power, the chronic civil war in China and the temptations that this situation offered to an economically expanding but hard-pressed Japan. Even when the stability of this settlement was open to more and more doubt, the Kellogg Pact of 1928, in which all the great powers, except Russia, renounced 'recourse to war...as an instrument of national policy', seemed to a legalistically-minded people to mean the end of the threat of a renewal of the follies of 1914–18. It also made the disputes over armament conventions more unintelligible, more easily explicable in terms of the crude interests of bankers and munition makers. The discomfited Democrats themselves abandoned the cause of the League of Nations. And it was significant that, despite support from every President right down to the outbreak of the second world war, all attempts to get the United States to join the World Court broke down in the Senate.

Good fortune also attended the Republicans in a grim form, for the death of President Harding in 1923 relieved them of a burden that might have been fatal to their chances in 1924. Harding was unfit to be President and suspected it; he had no executive experience; he had not been a working senator, active in committees or investigations. His closest friends were machine politicians, very ready to share his good fortune. Soon rumours then more than rumours of corruption began to spread. And they were rumours of corruption on a great scale, of corruption abetted by the Attorney-General and the Secretary of the Interior as well as corruption affecting lesser federal officers. Harding died before the storm broke. The Senate investigated scandals connected with the alienation of federal oil lands, with the administration of the Department of Justice, with the Veterans Administration. The evidence was abundant and conclusive; there had been no such plundering of the public assets since Grant's time. The new President hesitated but gave way. Three cabinet officers resigned; one was later imprisoned; the new administration cleaned house and the evil was interréd with the bones of Harding.

The new President, Calvin Coolidge, was of a very different type from the lush orator and small town editor who had been foisted on the American people. He was a dry, Yankee lawyer, with experience of administration as Mayor of Northampton and Governor of Massachusetts and with a record of party regularity that had not involved him in being the dupe or accomplice of politicians like Harry Daugherty or Albert Fall. He gave to the White House, in an age of dissolving standards, a reassuring air of Yankee thrift, caution and taciturnity. The Republicans soon noticed that their new President was an asset and all the resources of publicity were devoted to building him up.

Inside the Democratic Party the feud between city and country, the old and the new, took dramatic and suicidal form. The two chief candidates for the nomination in 1924 were William Gibbs McAdoo, Wilson's Secretary of the Treasury (and son-in-law), and Alfred Emmanuel Smith, who was serving his second term as the phenomenally popular Governor of New York. One was the candidate of the rural, evangelical, 'dry' sections of the party, the candidate favoured by William Jennings Bryan; the other was of Catholic Irish origin, a son of Tammany Hall, a wet, most manifestly a child of the 'sidewalks of New York'. The partisans of the two wrecked the convention and the chances of the Democratic Party. The nominee, chosen almost in despair, was an eminent corporation lawyer, John W. Davis, who campaigned on the issue of corruption. It was not only that the issue was not very effective in a boom year, but a great part of the radical discontent of the country was drawn off to support the 'Progressive' candidacy of Robert Marion La Follette, the famous radical senator. In these circumstances, the victory of the Republicans was inevitable.

Coolidge, as much as Walpole, wanted to let sleeping dogs lie. The business boom continued and the Secretary of Commerce, Herbert Hoover, both encouraged the rationalisation of internal business, the standardisation of technical and of commercial practice, and encouraged American business to look abroad for ever-expanding markets. There were dark patches. The textile towns of New England were harder and harder hit by southern competition. Many coalfields faced crippling competition from fields either newer or easier to run because the miners' unions were weak or absent. The hopes of an expansion of organised labour that had risen high in the war were seen to be baseless. The unions barely held their own. In some areas they did not do even that. The radical forces that had rallied round La Follette were disorganised and demoralised. Communist zealots were active in fomenting strikes, in starting rival unions, in all kinds of agitation and propaganda, but what was the use in a country like the America of Coolidge?

As the presidential campaign of 1928 approached, there was only one doubt in the minds of the observers, would President Coolidge run? In an ambiguous statement he conveyed that he would not and that made it certain that the two candidates would be Herbert Hoover, the successful personification of the businessman in politics, and 'Al' Smith, now serving his fourth term as Governor of New York. They were duly nominated and the campaign was of more significance than it seemed. For the nomination of a Catholic brought into the open the forces that had hidden behind the Ku-Klux-Klan. In no campaign in modern times had word-of-mouth slander played a greater part. And, with one important exception, in no campaign in modern times had the two candidates been closer in their programmes. Each asked for a mandate to carry on the business of the United States as it was being carried on. The one exception was that Governor Smith was hostile to the zeal with which, formally at least, the federal government was enforcing prohibition, while to Secretary Hoover it was 'a great social and economic experiment, noble in motive and far-reaching in purpose'.

Again, there was little doubt of the issue. Prosperity was too widely spread, the 'golden expectation' of an even more rapid increase in wealth and in general well-being too generally shared, for an opposition candidate, even if he had not been a Catholic, Tammany, New Yorker, to defeat the party that had wrought so well. And formally the Democratic party did worse than ever before, even losing five states of the solid south. But some observers noted that Smith got more votes than any Democrat had ever got, that he carried Massachusetts and Rhode Island and that everywhere in the great cities he showed a strength that no Democratic candidate had known for a generation. But the business candidate was elected and prepared to lead a business civilisation to greater heights. In less than six months the bubble burst. It is possible that earlier 'panics' were as severe as that which began with the break in the New York Stock Exchange. Earlier panics, too, had had marked political results. But the 'Depression' of 1929 which lasted, in one form or another, though with diminishing severity, until 1940, was more revolutionary in its impact than the previous 'panics' had been. It produced changes in American political and economic life as important as those produced by the Civil War, and more important than American intervention in the first world war or possibly even in the second.

In the first place, it accelerated developments in American governmental functions and in state and federal relations that would no doubt have come anyway. Isolationism had taken more forms than the drawing of American skirts away from Europe. It had been based on a belief that, inside America as well as outside it, dangers threatened the American way, dangers of state intervention in favour of labour, dangers of rudimentary state socialism, dangers of the use of the taxing power to redistribute income in accordance with some idea of social justice. It was not accidental or insignificant that the unions started and controlled by the great corporations should have been dubbed by the sponsors 'the American plan'. The same forces that produced political support for prohibition, for immigration restriction, that produced laws against 'radicalism', were at work in saving the United States from the contagious example of Europe. But seen over a longer perspective, the forces, social and political, that were at work in the presidencies of the first Roosevelt and of Taft and during the first term of Wilson were only stayed, not stopped. They were stayed because the Republicans and their business allies claimed, plausibly, to be the natural, beneficent and successful leaders of the American people. 'The business of the United States is business', said Coolidge in an unguarded moment, but, taken out of its context as it was, the phrase did represent what most Americans thought. It was discovered, between 1929 and 1933, that the business leaders did not understand or could not control the great economic machine that they had claimed to have made and to know how to operate with more and more skill.

The inevitable result of the depression was to weaken, then to destroy faith in the business class as a ruling class. Even as far as it was merely a matter of liquidation of speculation, it was serious enough and faith-destroying enough. Millions had been encouraged to speculate—in German securities, in Latin-American securities, in many much-touted American securities—and these investments proved of no more permanent value than losing tickets at a race meeting. Nor had most of these securities been marketed by fly-by-night entrepreneurs (although there were enough of them), but by great banks and by great bankers. Even had there been no more speculation, the credit structure was top-heavy. The long farm depression had, for years before the crash, been putting a strain not only on local banks, which failed in thousands, but on insurance companies, on loan companies, on holders of farm mortgages. The railroads were not in good shape, and even when well managed (and not all were) were under the strain of competition from the automobile, car and truck alike. As pressure continued, as banks insisted on payment of loans, as brokerage houses insisted on payment of margins, as money was lost in 'safe' banks and 'safe' securities, cautious and secure citizens found themselves as badly off as the mere gamblers. And, as scandal after scandal was revealed; as it was learned how the tax laws made it easy and legal for the rich-and-well-advised to avoid payment of income tax; as it was learned how the markets had been rigged; as fraudulent pyramids of cards like the Insull utilities 'empire', or the less scandalous but equally insolvent Van Sweringen railroad 'empire' collapsed, discontent and distrust swelled into fear and anger. The American people, or many millions of them, had been betrayed by their natural leaders, so they turned to other leaders.

It was possibly unjust that this loss of faith should have been most visible in the change of the popular attitude to the new President. Herbert Hoover's reputation for ability, probity, industry, special competence, was not fictitious. But he had not only to deal with a world crisis, he had to deal with a domestic crisis for which his party, if not himself, was in part to blame, by its tariff policy, by its blind faith in the wisdom and trustworthiness of big business, by its illusion that the outer world could be ignored. Thus the only Republican answer to the crisis in America's balance of payments was to raise the tariff yet higher in the Smoot–Hawley Act of 1930, a piece of monstrously ill-timed legislation. Many were willing to believe that the two congressional authors of the act did not know what they were doing, but could not believe that the President, the former energetic Secretary of Commerce, who had so pushed external trade, did not know it. Whether positive American co-operation in liquidating the war debts, reparations and the whole tangled web of inextricable financial deals made in the boom years would have saved Europe from the final crash no one knows. But the President could not do more than offer a temporary moratorium. Congress and public opinion would not let him do more. And even if it was true, in part, that America's troubles came from Europe, the American people had been taught for over a decade to disregard the powers for mischief of the outside world. It was too late to blame Europe now. The administration was blamed instead.

It was blamed for many things, for some of which it had no responsibility. It may be doubted whether any administration would have dared rigorously to limit the supply of money for speculative financing, thus bringing an end to a boom that most Americans expected to last and whose cessation they would have blamed on the politicians, not on the bankers and businessmen. Believing, at first, that the collapse of the market was merely a market collapse, a healthy shaking out of speculators, the Hoover administration placed too much faith in faith, in reassuring messages, in prophecies of speedy recovery 'just around the corner'. And there were, in 1930, short periods of recovery, short periods of minor booms, and the congressional elections of that year were less disastrous than had been feared. The Republicans just lost the House and just held the Senate.

It was in the second half of President Hoover's term that the rot set in. It set in because, as the depression stayed and deepened, the problem of what to do about it became the main theme of politics and one that brought out sectional, party and class differences. After a decade of budget surpluses there was a series of deficits. How were they to be met, by higher income taxes, by closing the gaps revealed in the existing tax laws or, in part, by a sales tax? A revolt of Democrats and insurgent Republicans defeated the sales tax in the House of Representatives. The insolvency of many railways, the threatened insolvency of many banks and the many disastrous bank failures, the drying up of local credit, left the federal government no choice but the underwriting of the credit structure. One instrument of that underwriting was the creation of the Reconstruction Finance Corporation. But, for the insurgent members of Congress, the theory behind the new corporation was exactly what the country had been wrecked on. It was the theory of wealth and well-being percolating down from above. They wanted aid for the unemployed to be provided by the federal government, aid provided for bankrupt municipalities and for states whose tax resources were drying up. Poverty was no respecter of state lines and some of the poorest states had the most poor. It was not until 1932 that the barriers the Hoover administration had set up against 'raids on the treasury' began to go down. It was noted, bitterly, that they did not go down until the depression had finally reached the possessing classes. For the great corporations which had cut wages and dismissed workers also maintained dividends, dividends not earned and not necessarily spent when received. The owners of tax-free securities (which successive Secretaries of the Treasury had tried to have abolished) still drew their interest, while all public services were cut—libraries, schools, roads, even prisons suffered from a wave of drastic economy that was thought, by many 'responsible' people, to be the drastic cure for the economic disease.

But not all voters or politicians were 'responsible'. A few listened to the heretical theories of John Maynard Keynes; others revived the old inflationary panaceas; the veterans, or most of them, wanted to be paid a bonus, now. Thousands of the veterans descended on Washington; the 'bonus army' was like Coxey's army of 1895. The veterans were finally expelled from their camp by troops using gas bombs. It was the equivalent of Cleveland's use of troops to break the Pullman strike in 1894. But it got far less applause and was one of the many burdens the administration had to bear in an election year.

Despite all the activity of communists, of socialists, of radicals of all types, it was to the regular opposition that the voters were turning. The Democratic nominee would be elected; the only question was his identity. The obvious candidate was Franklin Delano Roosevelt. Roosevelt had been elected Governor of New York in 1928 when his chief, Al Smith, failed to carry his own state. He was re-elected in 1930 with the greatest majority in the state's history. He was the most 'available' candidate and, despite bitter opposition, he was nominated and broke all tradition by flying at once to the Convention and accepting the nomination on the spot. This disregard of tradition gave a welcome impression of energy and gave proof that the infantile paralysis, from which the candidate suffered, had not destroyed his energy. The Democratic platform, above all its double promise of a reduction in federal expenditure and support for the repeal of prohibition, won millions of voters away from the Republicans; for, to add yet another mill-stone to their burden, the Republicans had hedged about the fate of what the public insisted, wrongly, that the President had called 'the noble experiment'. Roosevelt carried forty-two states, including all the large states save Pennsylvania. The Democrats swept both houses of Congress and nearly all state offices and state legislatures. There was a mandate to do something, but there was then an interval of four months between the election and the inauguration of the new President. President Hoover stubbornly stuck to his policies, above all to measures designed to keep the dollar on gold. The President-elect, equally firmly, refused to underwrite the policies of the repudiated administration and party. The world situation grew worse. Hitler took power in Germany; an assassin almost succeeded in killing Roosevelt in Florida. The long-promised revival of business was postponed again because, said the Republicans, uncertainty about the policies of the new administration destroyed confidence. But that had been destroyed at least a year before.

The crisis that the new administration had to deal with had only been equalled, if ever, by the crisis that faced Lincoln in March and April 1861. Three years of deepening economic distress had undercut the foundations of many once strong and respected institutions. Few governmental units, cities, counties, states, were solvent. Social institutions designed for a rural society, charitable institutions designed for minor economic catastrophes or personal disasters, had had to face an ever-increasing strain. Under that strain they were breaking and what threatened to become an unmanageable mass of misery was poised like an avalanche. Social habits which had made for stability and discipline had been worn down. The 'bonus marchers' in Washington had been, for the timorous, only the precursors of the storm. If the angered veterans, if the desperate unemployed once began to move *en masse*, what could the local authorities, often bankrupt, with their reduced police forces, with their sullen citizens all around them, do? What meaning in this context had the traditional slogans of Americanism, the traditional precepts of self-help, of thrift, of sturdy independence? Indeed, the wonder was not that these attitudes were wearing out, but that they had lasted so long. The winter's discontent faced the new administration, and its situation was made dramatic, and the need for a dramatic solution made evident, by the collapse of the banking system. Banks had failed in increasing numbers; little country banks, great city banks. But now the machinery of banking and credit was grinding to a stop. More and more bank holidays were proclaimed until, on the eve of the inauguration, banks were closed in forty-seven states. And one of the first acts of the new President was to close all banks in the United States by presidential proclamation. Congress hastily ratified this action; no banks could be re-opened except by permission of the federal government. The federal reserve banks were re-opened first, then the solvent private banks. The first shock of the crisis had been met.

It is impossible to understand the 'New Deal' without bearing in mind the character of the crisis with which the new administration was faced. In his inaugural address, Roosevelt had said that there was 'nothing to fear but fear itself'. But the old sources of faith, trust in the regular way of doing things, in the businessman as the natural custodian of the governmental machinery, all these supports of faith had gone. They had to be replaced by new faith, faith in new ways of doing things, faith in the energy and audacity of the new administration. That faith was given abundantly and uncritically; it was near treason to be critical. Franklin D. Roosevelt began his administration with a greater share of the confidence of his countrymen, especially but not exclusively of his electors, than any president had ever had, except possibly Jackson, Grant and Hoover.

The first months of 'the New Deal' came to be known in retrospect as 'the Hundred Days'. But it was not a hundred days ending in Waterloo, but a hundred days ending in a feeling of hope and energy that the American people had not known since 1930. Again, in immediate retrospect, the period seemed to be completely dominated by the leadership of the new President; it was dominated by him, but not completely. He had been nominated by a coalition of the west and south, the same coalition that had nominated Wilson in 1912 and re-elected him in 1916. And that coalition still hankered after the old remedies, above all inflation by the use of silver or the issue of paper currency. The banking policy of the new administration was thus, in part, forced on it by the knowledge of the strength of the inflationary forces, by the knowledge that 'sound banking practice' meant for many, perhaps most Americans in 1933, an ingenious system of robbery. So the sprawling banking system was left unrationalised, for although many hundreds of banks never re-opened, the local banking system remained unaltered. The one great change was the imposition of a system of federal guarantee of deposits (at that time up to $5000), a measure that shocked the orthodox, but which was essential if restoration of faith in banking and the restoration of the credit structure were to be possible. In the same way, the embittered farmers had to be given something tangible. The 'revolving funds', the marketing schemes with which the Republicans had attempted to cure the earthquake that was threatening to bring the rural credit structure down and which threatened to produce something like a *jacquerie*, were swept aside. Farmers were to be paid *not* to produce the excessively abundant crops which were driving down the prices below the bankruptcy level and the A.A.A. (Agricultural Adjustment Administration) came into being. In the field of industry, a corresponding effort was made to put an end to the much denounced evils of 'cut-throat competition'. This effort took shape in the most controversial experiment of the first New Deal, N.R.A. (the National Recovery Administration). N.R.A. lumped together, in a hastily and badly drafted statute, a number of remedies not necessarily consistent with one another. Like some other legislation of this time, it was in part designed to head off more radical measures, such as the Black–Connery bill that proposed to spread employment by imposing a thirty-hour week. Originally N.R.A. was to provide public works (carrying farther a remedy tried by the Hoover Administration); its functions included the relief of agriculture. But by the time the law was enacted, these two fields of action had been allotted to others. The device by which the N.R.A. became best known, the 'codes of fair competition' were, again, originally planned only for the great, well-organised industries. But every type of business insisted on sharing in the guarantees against 'unfair competition'. Labour, too, wanted its share in guaranteed wages, in limitation of hours, in recognition of the sickly trade unions. Even the consumer was to be represented and protected. N.R.A. was launched under General Hugh A. Johnson with all the publicity that had been used for the 'Victory Loans'. The emblem of the 'Blue Eagle' was sported by great businesses and little.

And since one object of N.R.A. was the raising of prices, people bought against the anticipated rise and caused a reversal of the long, downward spiral.

It was not only that this precautionary buying came to an end in a few months, but that not all firms played up, notably the great and, until recently, sacred firm of Henry Ford. Many minor businesses which had gladly sported the 'Blue Eagle' now began to repent it. Evasion of its obligations became more and more common, the hastily drawn-up codes were harder and harder to enforce. Labour, too, found that employment did not noticeably increase, and where it did it was not obvious that the codes deserved the credit. And the protection given to the unions, in the Act and in the codes, turned out to be illusory. By the time that the Supreme Court unanimously condemned the original act in *Schechter Poultry Corporation* v. *The United States* (1935) N.R.A. was already moribund. Few regretted its death except the President, and his public regrets may not have represented his real thoughts.

In other ways, the new administration turned its back on the policy of its immediate predecessor. That the new administration would tamper with the currency had been a resented Republican charge. But it promptly did so; the United States went off gold and the President 'torpedoed' the London economic conference by his refusal to discuss stabilisation, a decision that put further severe pressure on the remaining gold-standard countries, notably France, and acted both as a tariff barrier to European imports and a bonus to American exports. The new currency policy, if it horrified the orthodox, gratified that much more numerous group, the creditors, who had seen their real obligations rise steadily since 1929. The foreign economic policy of the new administration, indeed its whole foreign policy in this period, was what came to be called 'isolationist'. The new Secretary of State, Cordell Hull, was a fervent Wilsonian, a believer in low tariffs and in international co-operation but, as yet, he had not the ear of the President.

The American people had discovered how little paper barriers to aggression meant when Japan destroyed the last remnants of Chinese authority in Manchuria over the heated protests of President Hoover's Secretary of State, Henry L. Simson, not backed up, even verbally, with any warmth by the British Foreign Secretary, Sir John Simon. The temper of the people was revealed in the Johnson Act of 1934, which forbade all credits to countries which had defaulted in payments on their war debts to the United States. A special Senate committee, headed by Senator Nye, seemed to the uncritical to prove that one of the main causes of war was the selfish interest of bankers and munitions makers, the 'merchants of death'. A series of 'Neutrality Acts' prohibited trade in arms or the extension of credit to belligerents. The administration resisted, as far as it could, attempts to limit executive discretion, but it had to accept legislation designed, as was later said, to 'keep the United States out of the war of 1914'.

A more positive policy was inherited from the Republicans in the Latin-American field. A series of Mexican revolutions had further complicated the problems that plagued and perplexed Wilson. Confiscation of American property was answered by vehement demands for redress, to be obtained by force if necessary. The worst of the tension with Mexico was ended by Coolidge's ambassador, Dwight Morrow, although a formal settlement of American claims was not completed until 1942. Intervention in the Caribbean republics was ended (except in Haiti) and $25,000,000 was paid to Colombia in 1921 for unspecified losses, which meant the damage done by American policy at the time of the Panama 'revolution'. The Roosevelt administration carried farther the 'good neighbour' policy. After a revolution in Cuba, it consented to an abrogation of the Platt amendment of 1901 authorising American intervention to preserve order in the newly liberated republic. Haiti was evacuated and Pan-American conferences were used by Secretary Hull to build up a policy of 'hemispheric solidarity'. In the Philippines, where the Wilson policy of self-government had been to a large extent reversed by the Harding administration, the Roosevelt administration moved towards complete independence (a movement made easier by American pressure-groups hostile to competition of Philippine products inside the American customs barriers). The Commonwealth of the Philippines was created and it achieved complete independence in 1946.

Next to the bankers in public disesteem were the great power companies, and it was easy to get through Congress a measure, vetoed by several Republican presidents in a simpler form, for using federal installations of the late war at Muscle Shoals on the Tennessee River to produce power. But the Tennessee Valley Authority had more to do than improve navigation and, as an ostensible side-line, produce power. The whole valley was to be rehabilitated by a government corporation, secured from political interference, with a broad commission to promote the general welfare of an especially backward region where the normal motives of capitalist development did not work. Attacked in the courts and shaken by internal feuds, the T.V.A. survived and throve, becoming one of the show-pieces of the administration.

There were other new federal organisations created, like the Securities and Exchange Commission invented to police the stock markets. The powers of the Interstate Commerce Commission and the functions of the Relief Finance Corporation were extended. The foundations were laid of systems of unemployment insurance, administered by the states but largely financed by the federal government. The practice of 'grants in aid' was not new, but it was now vastly extended; children, widows, the unemployed, the blind, benefited. Behind the often inefficient and often bankrupt local units stood the federal government. Promises of cutting down federal expenditure, which had led to actual cuts in salaries and payments to veterans in the first few months of the new administration, were forgotten by the administration and remembered by its enemies; such enemies, including eminent Democrats like Al Smith, as those who founded the 'Liberty League'. But the tide was running one way. At the mid-term elections of 1934 the administration scored an unprecedented triumph; it increased its majorities in both houses. Republican chances were dim for 1936. Nor were they made brighter by the action of the Supreme Court in killing not only the unregretted N.R.A., but the A.A.A. and other social legislation. The conservatism of the majority of the Supreme Court had long been a source of resentment in the breasts of those who wished to use state or federal power to reduce economic inequality and temper the harshness of competition. The court seemed determined to prevent either the states or the Union from legislating in fields long occupied by European governments.

The Republican nomination in 1936 was not much worth having. It went to one of the few Republican politicians who had survived the deluge, Alfred M. Landon, the Governor of Kansas. Landon was an old Progressive of 1912 with a good local record, but he was a bad speaker and he had bad luck. A terrible drought in 1934 was followed by an equally severe drought in 1936; the farmers were in no mood to hear sermons on government extravagance or states' rights. An overwhelming majority of the press, of business leaders, of sound, conservative opinion was against the President but when the results were in, he had carried every state but Maine and Vermont, with a percentage of the popular vote only exceeded by Harding's in 1920. And in Congress the Republicans were further reduced until they found it difficult to do their share of the manning of committees.

The American people more definitely than in 1932 had given a commission to Franklin D. Roosevelt to reform the Republic. How would he interpret it? On 4 February 1937 the Democratic leaders in Congress were told; the 'court bill' was shown to them. It purported to be a bill for the general reform of the federal court system and many of the reforms were overdue. But the gist of the bill was a provision allowing the President to appoint not more than six new justices of the Supreme Court for every justice of seventy and over who had served ten years and did not retire; or, as its enemies put it, it was a bill to 'pack the Supreme Court'. It was bitterly fought; the Republicans wisely left the fight to revolting Democrats and it was discovered that, even after the election of 1936, there were institutions that the American people still treasured, no matter how bitterly they criticised them.

The threat to the court came, too, at a moment when moderate public opinion was alarmed by the wave of 'sit-down strikes' that had marked

THE UNITED STATES OF AMERICA

the great drive to create effective trade unions in the mass industries. This had been undertaken by the Committee for Industrial Organisations set up by the American Federation of Labor, headed by the leader of the miners, John L. Lewis. There were threats and rumours of revolution and disorder everywhere. There had poured into Washington, with the new administration, not merely the usual crowd of hungry office-seekers, but many thousands of young, ardent men and women anxious to have a hand in the saving of American society. And there had come others whose desire was to have a hand in the total reconstruction of American society on Marxist lines. They did not advertise their presence, but it was suspected in Washington, in Detroit, in Pittsburgh. But the great strikes, however suspect the leadership, succeeded. United States Steel, that had resisted attempts at unionisation so successfully in 1919, made peace with the new steel union. One after the other the other steel companies, and the automobile companies, recognised the unions. Only the stubborn individualist, Henry Ford, held out. But long before he gave way the Supreme Court had transformed its own position, and that of the unions, by validating the 'Wagner Act', passed in 1935, which had put the power of the federal law and administration behind the unions. Its constitutionality was contested, but by a majority of one the act was upheld; a victory for organised labour that outweighed the split in the labour movement, for the American Federation of Labor expelled its committee and the unions which supported it. The 'Committee for Industrial Organisation' became the 'Congress of Industrial Organisations', keeping the now magic letters C.I.O.

Equally important was the effect of this and comparable decisions on the court fight. If the court was no longer an obstacle to social legislation, much of the driving force behind the 'court plan' would disappear. With each favourable decision, it did; the bill was rejected and the administration, within six months of its prodigious triumph, was defeated. Or was it? For justices now began to retire under new pension provisions and before the end of his years as President, Roosevelt had nominated every member save one, and that one, Harlan F. Stone, he had promoted to be Chief Justice. The court ceased to be an obstacle to federal legislation and most of the original legislation of the New Deal was re-enacted, barring the unfortunate 'codes of fair competition'. Child labour, minimum wages, hours of work were now subject to federal legislation. A silent revolution in federal–state relations was accomplished.

But if the New Deal triumphed in the courts, it did not triumph in all fields. Disastrous unemployment had been one of the main causes of the overthrow of the Republicans and although the new administration or the flux of time had reduced the number of the workless, millions still depended on charity or on state or federal aid. In the first years of the New Deal, various temporary bodies were set up to create work. One of these, the Civilian Conservation Corps, took young unemployed men into camps

173

run, on a non-military basis, by the army, fed them, paid them and re-habilitated them. The C.C.C. was soon the only New Deal experiment that had hardly any enemies. Relief for older unemployed took two forms. In what came to be called the Works Progress Administration, temporary jobs were provided, some of them intrinsically useful, some not. And the head of the 'W.P.A.', Harry Hopkins, was suspected of diverting his resources into fields that were politically likely to be fruitful as well as beneficial to the unemployed. The other great spending agency, the Public Works Administration, under the vigilant and irascible Secretary of the Interior, Harold L. Ickes, was run on very different lines. Its projects were all long-term and of intrinsic value, and never in American history had such vast sums been spent with so little whisper of political or financial scandal.

But the unemployed remained. A drop in government expenditure brought about a 'recession' and in the congressional elections of 1938, although Democratic majorities remained abnormally large, the moribund Republican party of 1936 showed itself full of life and fight. And in the new Congress the President had to cajole, persuade, beg, instead of ordering.

Now the thoughts of the President were more and more turned outward. The economic and political isolation of the first years was abandoned. The efforts of the Secretary of State, by the system of reciprocal trade agreements, to make a breach in the lofty tariff wall, were supported by his chief. As the League of Nations collapsed before Italian aggression in Abyssinia, as Hitler occupied the Rhineland, as the Spanish Civil War presaged a greater, the President began to test American public opinion. In a speech at Chicago in October 1937 he advocated an economic quarantine of the aggressors. But public opinion firmly refused to follow. Munich shocked that opinion but did not change it, and all the President's efforts to get the Neutrality Acts amended failed. But as the second world war drew nearer, the political aspect of the United States changed and what had only been a device of politicians fearful of losing the next election if the master politician was not in the field, became a more serious possibility. Men who had no liking for the innovation and were not necessarily worried about the election, began to worry about the fate of the United States and began to talk, more and more openly, of an unprecedented solution to the internal and external problem, a third term for the President.

That talk grew louder as the war came. In November 1939 the President forced through an amendment of the Neutrality Acts permitting the belligerents to buy war supplies on a 'cash and carry basis' and that, in 1939, meant that Britain and France could buy the war supplies they could pay for and take away in their own ships. It was an alteration of the law to the disadvantage of Germany. The great German victories of the spring and summer of 1940 made the renomination of Roosevelt a certainty. Great sums were hastily voted for armaments; two eminent Republicans were brought into the cabinet as Secretaries of War and the Navy; the President began to consider how best to aid Britain, now alone and soon to be beleaguered.

The chief Republican candidates for the nomination had, unfortunately for themselves, committed themselves to a policy of strict neutrality before Hitler upset the confident expectation of a certain if slow allied victory. Senator Vandenberg, Senator Taft and the young District-Attorney of New York, Thomas E. Dewey, were, to the surprise of all the professionals, beaten by Wendell Wilkie, perhaps the darkest horse in American history. A few years before he had been a Democrat. He had only come into public notice as a vigorous defender of the utility companies, which he headed, against the T.V.A. The presidency was the first public office he had ever aimed at. Wilkie made a gallant campaign and it is possible that if the war had ended before the election he would have won it. But the war went on; the British stand excited admiration and anxiety. The President, by a series of agreements, aided Britain with destroyers, weapons, supplies in return for bases in the western hemisphere. Roosevelt won, and in the new Congress produced the scheme of 'Lend-Lease' in the form of a bill happily and deliberately numbered '1776'. If this was neutrality, it was neutrality of a totally novel kind. When Russia was attacked Lend-Lease was extended to her; but still the Germans held their hand. It was the Japanese who precipitated the decision and saved the administration from a more and more difficult situation. Refused any concessions by the United States, convinced that American support to China was the main reason why China could still resist, the military party in Japan took the same decision as the military party took in Germany in 1917. On 7 December 1941 the main Pacific fleet at Pearl Harbor on Oahu was wrecked from the air. A few hours later the main air force at Manila was wrecked on the ground. The United States was at war with Japan and, in a few days, with Germany and Italy which supported their ally.

The role of the United States in the second world war was very different from that in the first. Then she had been an active belligerent for only a few months. Now she was in action from the day she was attacked and underwent a series of disasters with few parallels in her history. The loss of Corregidor ended resistance in the Philippines and, until the battle of Midway (June 1942), it was by no means certain that the Japanese could not successfully attack the Hawaiian islands, if not the mainland.

The manner of American entry into the war produced a far more real unity and energy than had existed in 1917. The scale of the war imposed a far more rigorous control of the American economy, a far more severe call on manpower. By the end of the war over 12,000,000 men were in arms and the United States was by far the greatest naval and one of the two greatest military powers in the world. The war was fought, too, with a more serious sense of the possibility of defeat and with less ideological emphasis than the first war had been. Roosevelt was in any case not such a master of the great oration as Wilson had been and neither the 'Four Freedoms' (January 1941) nor the Atlantic Charter (August 1941) had the effect of Wilson's speeches. And after America was a belligerent she had as an ally Soviet Russia, whose ruler had no intention of letting Roosevelt take the propaganda lead that Wilson had assumed in 1917–18.

Roosevelt's greatest achievement was as a war leader. Unlike Wilson, he had pondered the problems of war and of defence. He had built up the navy, even before 1939, as much as Congress allowed him to. He had, with great boldness and skill, managed to get Congress to agree to conscription in time of formal peace in 1940, and he chose and supported his war leaders with good judgment and resolution. Yet the first year of their participation in the war was one of frustration for Americans, and this was reflected in the near defeat of the Democrats in the congressional and local elections of 1942. But the tide had already turned. Allied armies landed in North Africa just after the elections; Guadalcanal was at last won in the Pacific; soon the Russians were to capture a German army at Stalingrad.

Public opinion was now prepared for American participation in a peace settlement; everyone was anxious to avoid or to forget the mistakes of 1919. A 'bi-partisan' foreign policy was preached and, to some extent, practised. At a series of allied conferences, the higher strategy of the war was planned and the character of the peace outlined. Again, as 1944 approached, there was no question of who would be the Democratic candidate. The only change since 1940 was the dropping of the Vice-President, Henry A. Wallace, in favour of Senator Harry S. Truman of Missouri. The Republicans nominated Thomas E. Dewey, now Governor of New York. By the time the election came, victory, as in 1918, was in sight, but it was not so near. Roosevelt was again elected and, in February of 1945, went with the British Prime Minister to Yalta to meet the Russian ruler, Stalin. Hitler's Germany was on its last legs; Mussolini's Italy existed only as a ghost. The net of American naval and military might was drawn, closer and closer, round Japan and already it was probable that the Americans would soon have in their power the most destructive weapon in the history of mankind, the atom bomb. Suddenly, to the surprise even of his intimates, Roosevelt died at Warm Springs in Georgia on 12 April 1945, a month before the end of the Third Reich.

Few presidents have been more loved and hated. After his first few months, his support came mainly from the economically distressed or discontented; to the wealther classes he became an object of hatred surpassing that evoked by his hero, Andrew Jackson. Under his administrations, if not solely or even mainly because of him, the whole economic and political balance of power in the United States was altered and, probably, the balance of power in the world; for a less bold and ingenious leader might have been at a total loss in the desperate year 1940. By his greatly extended use of the press conference and of wireless, above all in the 'fireside chats', he continually and effectively appealed to the people over the heads of Congress. Few presidents have so completely overshadowed their colleagues and, indeed, opponents. Roosevelt's successor was hardly known to the public, but it fell to him to deal with the other allied chiefs in the ruins of Berlin, to receive at Potsdam the news that the atom bomb tests had succeeded, and to authorise the use of the bomb against Japan. Already (26 June) a new international organisation, the United Nations, had been launched at San Francisco. On 14 August the Japanese surrendered.

The United States was the most powerful and richest nation in a world which her armies, navies, air fleets literally engirdled and all parts of which were, in various fashions and degrees, involved in American economic life and were dependants of American wealth and bounty. But it was not a confident and assured nation that looked back on its unprecedented achievement and power. For the old world in which America could live to and by herself was gone for ever, gone if for no other reason because of the bombs dropped on Hiroshima and Nagasaki. There was exultation, as in 1865 and in 1918, that 'the dreadful trip was done' but, underlying the euphoria of victory, a knowledge that nothing could now minister to them 'that sweet sleep which they owed yesterday'.

CHAPTER VIII

LATIN AMERICA, 1899–1949

THE independence achieved by the states of Latin America in the
nineteenth century was political only. These twenty-odd new nations,
varying greatly in size, in peoples and in resources, suspicious of
their former rulers and of each other, had one characteristic in common:
a heavy dependence upon events and movements outside their own
borders. As specialised primary producers, they had to rely on foreign
markets to dispose of their goods and on foreign investment to develop
their resources. As heirs of revolution and often victims of political and
financial instability, many of them experienced active foreign intervention.
In the nineteenth century the intervening powers were usually European;
except for the episode of the Texan war, and the period of impotence
during the American civil war, the United States government upheld
Latin-American independence. It not only disapproved of European
interference and influence; on the whole it refrained from interference
itself. In the twentieth century, however, there was to be a dramatic
exchange of political roles. European influence declined; North American influence increased; and some of the major Latin-American states
began to move haltingly towards a real independence. The process was
punctuated and accelerated by two world wars and a world depression of
unexampled severity.

In 1898 Spain, after a brief war with the United States, lost the last
fragments of a great American empire—Cuba and Puerto Rico. No
longer feared and hated as an 'imperialist' power, Spain was to become
the object of sentimental respect and affection and the centre of Pan-
Hispanic feeling. Great Britain, though a colonial power, still by far the
largest investor in Latin America, the principal source of manufactured
goods and the biggest single market for food and raw materials, showed
less and less inclination to political interference, especially since the growing naval power of Germany made it necessary for British governments
to court North American friendship. France, despite a long record of
interventions in the nineteenth century, seemed even less likely than
Spain or England to become involved politically in Latin-American affairs.

In the United States, on the other hand, a rising national feeling, a
growing sense of power, created a desire for a more aggressive interpretation of the Monroe Doctrine. The Venezuelan boundary dispute in
1897 had been made the occasion for strident pronouncements by
North American statesmen. In inter-American affairs the United States
was taking a resolute lead. The first Pan-American conference had met

178

at Washington in 1889; a second was convened in Mexico in 1901. Pan-Americanism might appear to offer more solid advantages than a sentimental Pan-Hispanism or than vague proposals for a purely Latin-American league.

Pan-Americanism, however, with its assumption of common sentiment and common interests throughout the hemisphere, rested to some extent on an illusion. Most Latin-American states had closer kinship with Latin Europe than with Protestant North America, and for many South Americans Europe was physically more accessible than the United States, or indeed than other Latin-American countries. Pan-Americanism was largely the product of North American policy; it was long suspected of being an instrument of North American political and economic power, and for the first three decades of the new century it made little headway.

Among Latin-American states in 1900, four stood out from the rest as leaders in power, wealth and political stability. In Brazil, by far the largest state in area and in population, a military revolution in 1889 had ousted the Braganza monarchy. The resulting constitution, in 1891, had inaugurated a federal republic in which the several states enjoyed wide autonomy, including power to levy export taxes and to raise military forces, and in which the federal authority was relatively weak. Political leadership was shared between São Paulo and Minas Geraes, the coffee-growing and mining states of central Brazil. Government rested not upon the popular vote, nor upon party organisation, but upon a convention of balance of power between these two states, each of which provided four presidents between 1894 and 1930. Subject to this convention, a president could usually contrive to nominate his successor by an understanding with the governors of the states and with the majority in Congress, which first helped to manage the presidential election and then acted as arbiter of its legality. The system succeeded, as a rule, in raising men of marked ability to the presidential chair.

The political conventions of Brazil directly reflected the current economic trends. The country's prosperity, once based on sugar and tobacco, now depended upon the export of vast quantities of coffee, supplemented by wild rubber and other forest products from the Amazon basin. The coffee industry demanded the construction of ports and railways and, for this, capital was needed. A £10,000,000 loan, negotiated with the Rothschilds during a presidential visit to Europe, tided the country over a financial crisis in 1899. Rio de Janeiro and Santos grew from squalid waterfront towns into fine modern harbours in the early years of the twentieth century. The coffee economy of Brazil was built up by a steady flow of British, French and German capital, and of Portuguese, Italian and German labour; while most of the coffee was sold in the United States.

What coffee was to Brazil, beef and wheat were to Argentina. Much of the beef was exported to Great Britain. The production of beef suitable for the British market required enclosed pasture, good transport arrangements and elaborate processes of preparation. Barbed wire, the railway and the *frigorífico* were the instruments of Argentine prosperity, and for the most part British investors provided the capital, British and North American manufacturers the machinery. Rural society was patriarchal, with immense areas of good land in the hands of relatively few owners. It was this business-like land-owning oligarchy, with its characteristic pride in good stock, which imported English pedigree bulls and developed the high quality, as well as the vast quantity, of Argentine beef production.

The large-scale export of grain began considerably later than the export of beef, but by 1904 its value was even greater than that of beef. The development of arable farming created a great demand for labour; and like Brazil, Argentina attracted large numbers of immigrants, mostly Spanish and Italian. Many of these immigrants were seasonal visitors—*golondrinas*—who returned to Europe after each harvest; but more than three million of them made permanent homes in Argentina between 1880 and 1913 (see also ch. 11).

As in Brazil, government, while adhering to constitutional forms, depended largely upon deals between members and groups of the land-owning oligarchy. Subject to these deals, the presidents nominated not only their successors, but provincial governors, members of Congress, and most of the important officials. In Argentina, however, unlike Brazil, there was no longer a balance of influence between semi-autonomous states. Wealth and political power were more and more concentrated in the humid pampa area surrounding Buenos Aires, and in the capital itself. A radical party existed, which clamoured for free elections and occasionally staged revolts, provoked by the consistent manipulation of political affairs. These incidents were all confined to the capital, none aroused much popular interest, and none caused serious alarm. Conditions in general were stable. A series of conservative governments provided adequate and orderly administration in a time of rising prosperity, and appeared in little danger of being unseated by elections, financial crises, or accusations of corruption and extravagance.

Chile, the third of the so-called 'A.B.C.' powers of South America, was by far the smallest in area and in population. Most of the people lived by farming in the beautiful and fertile valleys of central Chile. As in Argentina, a small number of families owned most of the productive land; but methods of farming and estate management were conservative, paternal, somewhat feckless, and Chile, though an agricultural country, imported food. Most of the public wealth came from the copper mines of the western Cordillera, and above all from the northern coastal desert provinces, which yielded the world's chief supply of natural nitrates. The nitrates were dug and exported to the wheat-growing areas of the world by companies employing Chilean labour, but financed mainly by British, and later North American capital. There was thus a serious and growing division between political power and economic reality. Political power, as in most Latin-American states, was in the hands of the land-owning aristocracy, who controlled a Congress elected by a narrowly restricted franchise. Moreover, as a result of the civil war of 1891, the power of the executive had been so severely curtailed that Congress could always either control or frustrate the policy of the president. Inevitably the ruling oligarchy split into many shifting factions. Most governments were coalitions, most cabinets short-lived and unstable. Meanwhile the steady activity of the nitrate trade encouraged the growth of a commercial and professional middle class and of a small industrial labour force. The export tax on nitrates enabled social services and popular education to develop more rapidly than in most other Latin-American countries. In the long run these would inevitably prove powerful solvents of aristocratic government; but so long as the nitrate market remained firm the business of the country could be carried on, if not with conspicuous efficiency, at least with moderation and due regard for law, by a cultivated and, on the whole, remarkably public-spirited aristocracy.

Mexico, like Chile, depended for most of its revenue upon the export of minerals. The chief mineral products included gold, silver, lead, zinc, copper, antimony and, in the present century, petroleum; the first successful oil well was drilled in 1901. In Mexico as in Chile, mineral resources were developed, railways and harbour works built, with foreign capital, by foreign engineers and managers and native labour. The great majority of Mexicans, however, lived by agriculture, upon the relatively small area of cultivable land afforded by an arid and mountainous country. The ownership of land was concentrated, to an even greater extent than in Chile, in a small number of very large, self-contained estates. Mexico lacked the racial homogeneity of Chile; persons of mixed blood formed a majority of the population, but the big *hacendados* were often of European descent, while most agricultural labourers were either Indians or *mestizos* in whom Indian blood predominated. Many landlords were absentees. Labourers were bound to the estates by a deep feeling for the land on which their forebears had lived, but which they no longer owned; and by *peonage*, a species of serfdom based upon truck payments on credit, keeping the *peón* in a condition of debt-slavery which, in custom if not in law, was usually hereditary. The land hunger of these dispossessed *peones* was the most striking characteristic of Mexican society, and was to prove in the twentieth century a powerful explosive force.

Mexico had been governed since 1876 by an efficient and ruthless dictatorship. Porfirio Díaz throughout his reign observed most of the forms of a federal constitution; but effectively he ruled his wild and heterogeneous country through an intricate network of jobs and personal loyalties. Judges, state governors, deputies in Congress, were all his men, and so were the *rurales*, the highly efficient but arbitrary irregular police. A *mestizo* himself, he was not without a genial intuitive sympathy with his Indian subjects; but he did not seek, and could not afford, to offend the great landowners, and the incorporation of *ejidos*—village common lands —in private *haciendas*, whether by purchase, fraud or force, reached its peak in his time. He was no demagogue, and preached no military nationalist aggrandisement. His regular army, or at least its rank and file, was largely fictitious. His foreign policy included friendship with the United States, scrupulous service of acknowledged debts and adherence to treaties, and enthusiastic participation in schemes of international co-operation. The second Pan-American Conference met in Mexico in 1901–2; and in 1906–7 Mexico collaborated with the United States in an ambitious and statesmanlike plan for peace-making in Central America. At home, Díaz sought above all to exploit the most remunerative resources of Mexico, and to build impressive public works, by offering the most tempting terms to foreign investors. Mines, harbours, railways, factories, oil-fields developed under foreign control and much farm and pasture land in their neighbourhood passed into foreign ownership, British, North American and German. Don Porfirio made himself famous, and his country liked and respected, abroad. At home he allowed his people to become strangers in their own land.

The chief economic and political characteristics of these four great states were present in varying degrees in most of the twenty-odd republics. Latin America in the early twentieth century was a land of promise, a magnet for the enterprise, the capital and the skill of more industrialised peoples. It was becoming a major source of a number of vitally important commodities. The government of most of its larger states was orderly, effective, sympathetic to investors. Its prosperity, if measured in terms of production, of exports and of public revenue, was rising steadily. All the Latin-American states, however, suffered from dangerous, but for the time hidden, economic and political maladies. They all depended for their revenues upon the export of one or two commodities, either food-stuffs or raw materials for industry. They were therefore extremely vulnerable to changes of price in the world market. They had nearly all become deeply indebted, through constant public and private borrowing from foreign sources, often at high rates, sometimes for unproductive purposes; and the willingness of European investors to throw good money after bad made it difficult to call a halt to this financial rake's progress. Most Latin Americans lived by agriculture, usually employing primitive and wasteful methods; they derived no direct and obvious benefit from the inflow of foreign capital or from the proceeds of the specialised export trades. They did not, as a rule, own the land they worked; if tenants or share-croppers, the terms of their tenure were often harsh and insecure. They had, therefore, a ready grievance.

Of those Latin-American countries which practised constitutional government, the majority were governed by somewhat theoretical constitutional rules, mostly borrowed from the constitution of the United States, owing little to the realities of Latin-American history and circumstances, commanding little general respect. The extremely artificial nature of 'federalism' in many states was an obvious example. The letter of the constitution often gave no indication of where real power lay. Constitutional remedies were so ineffective against powerful groups or personal interests that only revolution could effect a real change of administration; and 'revolution' often meant no more than an extra-legal demonstration calling for a change. The chief concession to realism in most Latin-American constitutions was the emergency power of suspending constitutional 'guarantees', entrusted to the president precisely to enable him to forestall such 'revolutions'. In many states constitutional government was a brittle façade; in some of the smaller states it hardly existed.

As in public affairs, so in more individual realms of spirit and mind the Latin-American peoples showed the symptoms of dependence upon imported and imperfectly assimilated ideas. Catholic Christianity was the outward religion of most people; but in many of the republics great numbers of Indians and *mestizos* hung between half-understood Christianity and half-forgotten local pagan cults. Among such people, as for instance in Mexico, a revolt against Christianity, once begun, was likely to be extreme. Even among people of European descent, with a few notable exceptions, the vital elements in Latin-American Catholicism were—and are—the foreign religious orders and foreign currents of Catholic thought. There had long been difficulty in maintaining the numbers and standard of the priesthood. The church, moreover, as a great land-owner and a conservative force in politics, was disliked and feared by reformers, who tended throughout Latin America to be anti-clerical and sometimes anti-religious; though it is fair to add that most of them greatly underestimated the church's hold upon men's loyalty, and the secularising theories which they advocated, from positivism down to communism, were themselves mostly imported from Europe. Avowedly religious people had long felt a vague sense of frustrated nationalism; some of them were uneasy in their allegiance to a church whose roots in America seemed uncomfortably shallow; but no satisfying alternative appeared. The Vatican was undoubtedly justified in regarding Latin America as a field of missionary endeavour; but no effort directed from Europe could, by itself, give to Latin-American Christianity the indigenous character which it lacked.

Many of the capital cities of Latin America were centres of vigorous intellectual life. Intelligent appreciation and discussion of serious literature, and to a lesser degree of music and the visual arts, had long been characteristic of educated town-dwellers. Poetry never lacked an audience in any part of Latin America; but outside the towns literate people were very few. For the most part, literary activity was confined to relatively small groups of people and followed European models. It is true that *Facundo* or *Martín Fierro* could have been written nowhere but in Argentina, *Os Sertoes* nowhere but in Brazil; but apart from exceptional works of genius, there had been little attempt at a development of independent culture, which would have meant a fusion of Indian and Iberian patterns of thought and expression. On the contrary, the liberal Latin tradition led to France, and French cultural influence was dominant at the end of the nineteenth century. For those who disliked French liberalism and French anti-clericalism, the most tempting alternative lay in a return to the Hispanic tradition.

In short, Latin America in 1900 was intellectually, economically and politically dependent upon the outside world. Its cultural life, though varied and active, lacked native self-confidence and drew its inspiration from abroad. Its economic and political life, though occasionally turbulent within its own area, assumed peace and stability elsewhere. Neither the national economies nor the national political structures were designed to withstand general adversity.

There was, indeed, no obvious reason for expecting adversity. Between the turn of the century and the outbreak of the first world war, the prosperity of Europe continued to overflow into Latin America. Progress was especially rapid in Argentina. The introduction of lucerne as a fodder crop, the substitution, from 1907, of a chilling process for crude freezing, the meticulous grading and pricing of fine stock, together built up an export trade in good beef unparalleled in the world. Buenos Aires became the greatest city of the southern hemisphere, and the centre of a railway system almost equal in extent to that of the United Kingdom.

In this period of rapid economic progress, however, three striking and significant developments took place which proved portents for the future. They were a peaceful but radical constitutional change in Argentina, an extremely violent social and political revolution in Mexico, and a remarkable growth of North American power and assertiveness in Central America and the Caribbean islands.

The Radical Civic Union, the precursor of the Radical party of modern Argentina, had been formed in 1892, and for twenty years devoted itself to the apparently hopeless task of electoral reform. Yet reform, when it came, was not directly the work of the Radicals, but of a member of that aristocratic caste which the Radicals wished to unseat—Roque Sáenz Peña, President from 1910 to 1913, a distinguished lawyer and a statesman of exceptional probity and devotion. Sáenz Peña, apparently from motives of pure conviction, insisted in 1912 on the passage of the electoral law which bears his name, providing for universal male suffrage and secret, compulsory voting. This revolutionary enactment—for so it was in the circumstances—by enfranchising the industrial and largely immigrant population of Buenos Aires, changed the whole basis of Argentine politics. Assisted by a daily press distinguished for responsibility and moderation, it promised a progressive liberalisation of government. It was also to reveal in time the dangers attending a sudden injection of democracy into a body politic largely unprepared for such treatment. Its first result was the election of Hipólito Irigoyen to the presidency in 1916, and the inauguration of a period of Radical rule broken only by revolution in 1930.

The Mexican revolution of 1910–11 was far more drastic and far-reaching. Its immediate causes included a financial depression in 1907, crop failures in 1907 and 1908, brutality in the suppression of the consequent strikes, and a wave of anti-foreign feeling and of political agitation. The armed rising which, in a few months, hounded Porfirio Díaz from office and from the country, was led by a liberal theorist, Francisco Madero, with the conventional battle-cry of 'no re-election'; but it quickly threw up a host of other leaders—agrarian rabble-rousers such as Zapata, bandits like Pancho Villa, military adventurers like Huerta, the murderer and successor of Madero. Mexico suffered ten years of almost continuous civil war, and since all parties looked to the United States as a source of arms, President Wilson's government was soon drawn into the conflict, supplying weapons to the self-styled constitutionalists under Carranza and denying them to Huerta. The inevitable incident occurred— an affront to American marines at Tampico; and in 1914 the United States intervened and seized the port of Vera Cruz. The intervention helped to remove Huerta, but failed to place the 'constitutional' party in power; and naturally it provoked universal resentment. An offer of mediation, however, made jointly by the 'A.B.C.' powers, enabled Wilson to withdraw without undue loss of dignity. The fighting went on; and eventually Carranza secured the presidency not by North American help, but by publicly accepting a programme in which he certainly did not believe—the agrarian reform programme of Zapata and his Indians. Thus in the midst of destruction, and almost unnoticed abroad because of the greater war then raging, a remarkable blue-print of a nascent new order was produced in the constitution of 1917, which is still the constitution of Mexico. Its political provisions contained little that was new; they repeated and expanded the radical and bitterly anti-clerical constitution of 1857, which the astute manipulations of Díaz had rendered ineffective. The most striking innovations were in the economic clauses. In article 123 a comprehensive, and for the time extremely generous, industrial labour code was written into the constitution. Article 27, more revolutionary still, proclaimed a reversal of the whole trend of Mexican agrarian history. It declared all land, water and minerals to be national property, private ownership existing only by an implied and conditional public grant, and certain types of mineral-bearing land, including oilfields, being inalienable. It restricted the regions in which foreigners might acquire land and the terms on which they could hold and use it. It limited narrowly the area which might be owned by a single person or corporation, and forbade ecclesiastical bodies to hold land. It promised the restoration of all village common fields alienated since 1854, and authorised grants of land—presumably to be confiscated from private estates—to villages which possessed no commons. Agrarian bitterness had by that time reached such a pitch, and fighting was so widespread, that this drastic programme of redistribution was probably the only way of securing any semblance of peace. As it was, the opportunist Carranza failed either to govern or to keep his agrarian promises. He was driven out by his lieutenant, Obregón, in 1919, and soon afterwards murdered. Peace of a kind was achieved with the election of Obregón to the presidency in 1921; but nearly twenty years more were needed to enforce the new order, and an unpredictable length of time to make it work.

Meanwhile revolutions of another kind were shaking the small republics of Central America. The Spanish-American war had started the United States on a career of intervention which might become a career of colonial aggression. Puerto Rico was annexed in 1899. Cuba, the largest and richest of the Caribbean islands, after a short period of North American occupation, became politically independent in 1902; but the United States retained a base at Guantánamo and, under the Platt amendment, a right to intervene in the event of serious disorder. North American attention was drawn to the political affairs of the Caribbean countries by the prospect of a ship canal through Central America, and by the desire of the United States government to control the canal approaches. Shortly after the end of the Spanish-American war, two obstacles to the building of the canal, one diplomatic, the other territorial, had been removed. The diplomatic obstacle was the Clayton–Bulwer treaty of 1850. The British government agreed, after some discussion, to replace that instrument by the Hay–Pauncefote treaty of 1902, which provided for a canal controlled and fortified by the United States. The territorial obstacle was the attitude of Colombia to the project of a canal through Colombian territory. An opportune revolt broke out in the Panamá province of Colombia in 1903. United States naval forces were employed to prevent the intervention of the Colombian authorities; and the new republic of Panamá, hastily recognised, agreed to a treaty giving the United States virtual sovereignty in the Canal Zone. This stroke of policy, while clearing the way for the canal, caused bitter and lasting resentment in Colombia, and did not pass unnoticed in the rest of Latin America (see also ch. vii).

While Theodore Roosevelt was 'taking the Isthmus', the problem of defending the Caribbean approaches was complicated by the decision of the Hague Court of Arbitration in the Venezuelan debt dispute. This decision, by upholding the legality of the British, German and Italian blockade of the Venezuelan coast, placed a premium on the use of force as a means of collecting debts. It suggested the possibility of further European armed interventions, sanctioned by international law, in areas where American control was vital to the defence of the United States. The only hope of forestalling this possibility seemed to lie in police action by the United States government, to prevent defaults on just debts and disorders affecting foreigners. Accordingly in 1904 Theodore Roosevelt announced his so-called corollary to the Monroe Doctrine: a warning that the United States might be compelled to intervene in the affairs of Latin-American states in order to remove grounds for intervention by others.

The United States government already controlled, in effect, the affairs of Panamá. In 1905 it negotiated an agreement with the Dominican Republic whereby the customs of that country were to be collected by North American officers, in order to remove occasion for European action. In 1906, to prevent a dangerous internal crisis, Cuba was reoccupied in accordance with the Platt amendment and the relevant provisions of the Cuban constitution. This second occupation lasted only until 1909, when an elected administration was duly installed; but advice, often unwelcome, continued to be proffered to the Cuban government. In the turbulent region of Central America a conference, in which Mexico took part, was convened at Washington in 1906–7 to formulate proposals for peace-making. The chief task of this conference was to prevent the kind of quarrel which arose from revolutions in one state being hatched in the territory of another. Its main result was an ingenious agreement to withhold recognition from governments which seized power by revolution. Thus within a few years the Roosevelt policy produced benevolent supervision in Panamá, sporadic meddling in Cuba, and in Central America a new policy of non-recognition generally regarded—and resented—as a form of indirect intervention. These measures were not enough to keep the peace to the satisfaction of the United States, and President Taft, Roosevelt's successor, soon found his Central American policy drifting from a warning diplomacy towards the use of force. In 1909 Zelaya, the dictator of Nicaragua, whose aggressive designs abroad and xenophobia at home had repeatedly threatened the peace, was expelled in a revolution backed by North American commercial concerns. In 1912 American marines were landed in Nicaragua to prevent Zelaya from starting a counter-revolution. Nicaragua remained under North American tutelage, with one brief interval, until 1933. Two more armed interventions followed, both provoked by acute internal disorder, in Haiti and in the Dominican Republic. Haiti was occupied from 1915 to 1934, Santo Domingo from 1916 to 1924.

A naïvely cynical interpretation of these moves has applied to them the phrase 'dollar diplomacy'. It is true that Taft's Secretary of State, the egregious Knox, believed that a transfer of the public debts of the Central American republics from European to North American holders would be in the interests of peace; but he had great difficulty in persuading New York bankers to make loans to such governments as Haiti, Nicaragua, and the Dominican Republic. Only in Cuba were North American investments considerable at that time. No doubt the missionary zeal of conscious efficiency impelled North Americans to 'tidy up' these small, disorderly republics; but the principal considerations were strategic. In order to forestall possible European threats to the canal approaches, successive secretaries of state were prepared to risk the alienation of Latin America. Of course, the policy of the United States was resented; it was unpopular at home, where it ran counter to deep-rooted traditions; it was naturally disliked in Central America, and over Latin America as a whole it gave rise to deep and lasting suspicion. In Argentina especially, journalists with ambitions for Argentine leadership in South America made the most of evidence of Yankee imperialism. The circumstance chiefly responsible for the strategic anxieties of the United States was the rise of German naval power. When, in 1914, the first great war against Germany began, the United States had hardly a friend in the Americas.

Latin America in 1914 was already far more important in world affairs than it had been in 1900. Politically, the participation of Latin-American delegates at the Second Hague Conference in 1907, and the intellectual qualities which they displayed there, had opened the eyes of Europe. The greater states of Latin America had become known and generally respected. Above all, their economic importance had greatly increased. Europe could not easily do without the food and the raw materials of Latin America, and Latin-American friendship became a valuable prize of belligerent diplomacy. In particular Germany, which in peace had ranked third among nations trading with Latin America, embarked upon an assiduous courtship backed by elaborate and costly propaganda. The most powerful counter-arguments were also provided by Germany, however, in the form of sinkings of neutral ships.

The Americas had no common policy towards the belligerents. The governments of Mexico and Venezuela were pro-German throughout, and in Chile, whose army was German-trained, there were many German sympathisers. These three states, with Argentina, Colombia, Paraguay and El Salvador, remained neutral throughout the war, maintaining diplomatic and—as far as possible—commercial relations with all the belligerents. Chile, the most formidable naval power in South America, was subjected to a test of patience in 1915, when British warships sank the cruiser *Dresden* in a Chilean harbour—a gross infringement of neutrality for which the British government apologised. Argentine neutrality, though strictly correct, was distinctly favourable to the Allies, and especially sympathetic towards Italy, as was natural. Argentina won a notable diplomatic victory in 1917, when the German government made full apology and reparation for the sinking of three Argentine ships. In the latter half of 1917 Irigoyen had some difficulty in maintaining relations with Germany in the teeth of mass meetings and resolutions of Congress demanding rupture. Both Argentina and Uruguay gave material assistance to the Allies in the form of credits for the purchase of food.

The entry of the United States into the war inevitably affected the Latin-American position. Nearly all the states of Central America and the Caribbean joined the United States in making formal declarations of war. Peru, Uruguay, Bolivia and Ecuador broke off relations with Germany, and handed over to the Allies all German ships in their harbours. Brazil, whose foreign policy for years past had been conspicuous for statesman-like moderation and respect for international law, independently declared war on Germany in October 1917. This decision was immediately provoked by the sinking of Brazilian ships; but throughout the war most Brazilians had sympathised with the Allies, especially with France, which they regarded as the pattern and guide of Latin civilisation. Brazilian warships operated with the ships of the Allies in the Atlantic, though no military forces were sent to Europe. One important internal result of the war was a sustained attempt to 'Brazilianise' the German colonies in southern Brazil.

Politically, the chief effect of the war upon the Latin-American countries was their closer participation in international affairs. All the Latin-American states sooner or later joined the League of Nations, and most of them were original members. Membership fluctuated somewhat, disputes over the distribution of council seats being the occasion of several resignations; but many Latin-American states remained steadily loyal. The League appealed strongly to Latin-American idealism, and afforded a platform on which relatively weak states could make their voices heard. It is true that the presence in the Assembly of a large number of small states, with a voting power out of proportion to their physical strength, contributed to the air of unreality often characteristic of the deliberations of that body. It is true also that some states regarded the League as a counterpoise to the power of the United States and a substitute for the Pan-American system which the United States favoured. Naturally the absence of the United States from Geneva made political action by the League in the Americas extremely difficult. Nevertheless, Latin-American membership of the League was important and valuable. The technical organs of the League achieved a considerable degree of success in Latin America, and on one occasion the League was responsible—this time with the co-operation of the United States—for settling a serious dispute, between Colombia and Peru in 1933-4, over the Leticia territory.

Economically the war had administered a sharp but temporary shock to Latin America. The supply of European capital and the stream of immigrants suddenly ceased. Exports to Europe dropped temporarily, through the diversion of shipping to other tasks, and then quickly recovered, thanks to the urgent demands of the Allies for food and raw materials. On the other hand, imports of manufactured goods from Europe dropped heavily, as European industry concentrated upon warlike needs. One result of this excess of exports over imports was a tentative industrial development in the A.B.C. states, especially in the manufacture of textiles for the home market, and the canning and preserving of food. This effort to achieve greater diversity and self-sufficiency in supplying home markets has continued persistently, though not steadily at the same speed, ever since. Another important result was a great increase, both absolute and relative, in imports from the United States. North American trade with Latin America held and further increased its war-time gains after the war, despite strenuous efforts by French and British firms, in the 1920's, to recover lost ground. On the whole, capital followed trade. In 1913 British investments in Latin America amounted to some $4983 million; North American investments totalled $1242 million, and were nearly all in Mexico and Central America, only $173 million being held in South American countries. In 1929 British holdings were $5889 million, North American holdings $5587 million including $3102 million in South America.[1] North American investments followed much the same lines as British, but were more widely spread, less heavily concentrated in railways and other public utilities. Direct investment predominated. Most of the capital went into concerns such as mines, producing raw materials for export to manufacturing countries, and into transport developments ancillary to such concerns, rather than into industrial undertakings producing finished goods. Throughout Latin America the shifts of trade and finance during the war years and after thus produced not economic independence, but a partial change of masters, an overall increase in foreign capital invested, and a continued rise in apparent prosperity.

One or two important exceptions to this general trend require to be noticed. The war caused serious dislocations in the economic life of at least two of the leading states. Chile, though remote from the conflict, suffered heavily from its indirect results. Sodium nitrate is not only a fertiliser, but an ingredient in the manufacture of nitro-glycerine. During the war the Allies bought vast quantities of Chilean nitrate; but the Germans, cut off from Chile by the blockade, turned to the manufacture of synthetic nitrate and succeeded in supplying most of their own needs. After the war the use of synthetic nitrate became general. It was more expensive than the natural product; but the governments of the great powers all disliked dependence upon a remote source for an important

---

[1] M. Winkler, *Investments of United States Capital in Latin America* (Boston, 1929), pp. 275–83. *The Republics of South America*, Royal Institute of International Affairs (Oxford, 1937), p. 182.

munition, and preferred to make farmers pay more for fertiliser, in order to produce the raw material of explosives within their own territories. The Chilean share of world nitrate production fell from about 70 per cent at the turn of the century to 35 per cent in 1924 and to 11 per cent in 1931.[1] It continued to fall in the 'thirties. At the same time the world market for copper was extremely unreliable. The population of Chile was too small to provide a market for extensive industrial production, and the drop in value of its two principal mineral products presented a prospect of economic decline for which no adequate remedy has yet been found.

The war had a serious effect upon the Argentine and Uruguayan beef industry. During the war the demand for chilled beef had been supplemented by a greatly increased demand for tinned or frozen beef. The product of the tinning process is of equal insipidity whatever the quality of beef used, and the high demand encouraged the breeding and sale of inferior animals. At the same time, a series of disastrous failures of the lucerne crop in the early years of the war made the production of good beef more difficult and expensive. The cattle industry was still in this disorganised state when the European slump of 1922 produced a sudden break in the market and made all but the best beef unsaleable. By 1925 the rubbish had been cleared and the industry was once again paying its way; but even then it had to make another re-adjustment to meet a demand for smaller beef joints resulting from the decline in the size of families in most parts of Europe. The chilling companies began to demand smaller beasts. The big shorthorn bullocks which had hitherto commanded the highest prices fell from favour and had to be replaced by stockier breeds such as the Aberdeen-Angus. This change was still in progress when Argentina, with the rest of Latin America, received the staggering blow of the 1930 depression.

Apart from these troubled industries, Latin America throughout most of the 1920's was peaceful and prosperous. In Brazil cotton appeared alongside coffee as an important export crop and cattle (though of poor quality) increased considerably in numbers in the southern states. There was steady development in mining and in industry; Brazil, though lacking convenient coal, possesses large quantities of iron ore. In the arid northern states, post-war governments spent large sums on dams for water storage. There was a steady overall growth of population, both by immigration and by natural increase; and in the south, a slow but steady advance in state-sponsored colonisation. The most remarkable increase in wealth during this period, however, took place in the republics of the northern Andes, especially in Venezuela, where immense oil-fields were discovered. Venezuela was—and outside the oil-fields and the capital city still is—a backward pastoral and agricultural country. The export of

[1] C. A. Thomson, 'Chile struggles for national recovery', *Foreign Policy Reports*, IX (1934), p. 288. See also above, p. 118.

oil began in 1918; by 1930 Venezuela was producing rather more than 10 per cent of the total world supply, and thanks to petroleum royalties was the only Latin-American state unencumbered by public debt. Nearly all the oil produced was exported, and nearly all production was—and is—in the hands of foreign firms, British and North American. The national economy depends almost entirely upon the price of oil in the world outside.

Peru, Colombia and Ecuador also developed oil-fields in the 'twenties, and all granted concessions to foreign capital for this purpose as well as for the development of public services. None of these countries, however, reached anything approaching the Venezuelan level of production, or became so dangerously dependent on oil. Colombia in particular enjoyed a period of very considerable prosperity and progress. The foreign trade of the country more than doubled, and expanding exports included coffee, cacao and sugar as well as oil. Two commercial and industrial cities, Cali and Medellín, in valleys far from the capital, grew rapidly, Medellín especially becoming an important centre of mining and textile manufacture in this period. Peru was more centralised than Colombia, more dependent upon its capital, Lima, and the near-suburban port of Callao. Peruvian society, moreover, was dangerously split between the isolated highland population, Indian and agricultural, and the people of the coast, largely European in outlook, concerned with commerce, mining, and to some extent industry. Despite these disadvantages, considerable development and diversification took place in the 'twenties. Peru exported copper, cotton, sugar and various other agricultural products as well as oil; and as in the neighbouring countries, its economic life was largely and increasingly controlled by foreign capital.

One characteristic common to nearly all Latin-American countries in this prosperous era of the 'twenties was concern over the wages, working conditions and general welfare of industrial labour. The attention of governments was directed to problems of labour by the general desire to speed up the slow process of industrialisation. International discussion of such problems through the International Labour Organisation of the League of Nations stimulated interest, and so, no doubt, did the Mexican constitution of 1917. An advanced labour code became a matter of national prestige, a badge of membership of the comity of civilised states. Moreover, in most parts of Latin America mines, oil-wells and factories were foreign-owned. Pressure brought upon foreign employers to raise wages and improve conditions was popular, patriotic, and politically safe. There could be no doubt of the need, by European or North American standards, for very considerable improvement of labour conditions. Argentina, Brazil and Chile all set up separate ministries or departments of labour, and they and several other states enacted labour codes, including such principles of social legislation as the eight-hour day, the right to strike, the minimum wage, and protection of women and children.

Uruguay—once a battle-ground of *gaucho* armies, now one of the most prosperous and stable states in South America—and Chile embarked on schemes of national insurance. The volume and quality of legislation is impressive, but much of it is based on European and North American ideals and does not necessarily correspond to local needs. In most countries it has hardly touched agricultural life, where employers are native and the personal relation between *patrón* and *peón* is strong. Even in industrial centres much legislation is ineffective through lack of adequate inspection. The activity of legislative bodies in Latin America is often in inverse proportion to the ability to put the legislation into effect.

The movement to improve labour conditions came chiefly from above—from governments—rather than from below. Trade union organisation was weak everywhere; socialist movements, where they existed, were in infancy, and sometimes proscribed. A distinctive feature of the whole movement, however, has been the connection between industrial labour and the student population. Latin-American universities for the most part offer professional and technical training rather than general education; students are numerous; their organisations have considerable solidarity, and are often very active politically. Their activity usually issues in a vague clamour for reform rather than in support of a definite party programme, but it can be extremely vociferous and sometimes violent. In some countries it became in the 'twenties, and has since remained, a considerable political nuisance.

The governments which inaugurated all these programmes of social betterment in the 'twenties varied greatly in political form. In some countries, notably Colombia, the pre-war pattern of a land-owning oligarchy governing through a discreetly manipulated constitution survived with little change. In Brazil the pre-war routine went on, though it was troubled by several abortive military outbreaks. In a few countries, constitutional radicalism was temporarily in the ascendant. The Radical party in Argentina ('Whig' would perhaps be a more descriptive title) had come to power as a result of the Sáenz Peña electoral reform. In Chile an analogous change of government took place in 1920. Alessandri, the new president, came from the northern province of Tarapacá and was avowedly the representative of labour and middle-class interests. The economic plight of the country and congressional opposition to proposals for reform compelled Alessandri to abandon the old 1833 constitution and to introduce a new one, ratified by plebiscite, which greatly increased the powers of the President. The outcome was a series of *coups d'état*, and from 1927 a military quasi-dictatorship, which carried into effect most of the provisions of Alessandri's reform programme. A pronounced characteristic of the radical parties in general was the intensely personal nature of their organisation. Irigoyen, the Argentine radical leader, who served twice as President, was known as the last of the *caudillos*; his personal control over every detail of party organisation and national government, his heavy-handed intervention in provincial government, recalled the methods of the old *caudillos*; but at least his actions came within the letter of the constitution. Several republics in the 'twenties, on the other hand, were governed without any serious pretence of constitutional forms, and carried through considerable programmes of development and reform by means of undisguised dictatorship. Unscrupulous politicians were learning the uses of an industrial proletariat as a support for unconstitutional power. Leguía, ruler of Peru from 1919 to 1930, was a man of humble origin whose seizure of power was supported by middle-class and labour interests, and whose programme included legislation for the protection of labour, general education, and re-distribution of land, as well as the usual elaborate public works. A considerable part of the programme, especially in public works and in education, was put into effect by means of public loans raised in the United States. The perfect pattern of the radical dictator, however, was Juan Vicente Gómez, the uneducated *mestizo* who for twenty-six years, under various official titles, dominated the affairs of Venezuela. Gómez's armoury included all the now-familiar weapons of censorship, of secret police, of torture, of imprisonment without trial for political offences, of the distribution of responsible offices among those of the dictator's relatives who showed capacity and loyalty. Gómez ran Venezuela with ruthlessness and shrewd business efficiency. Like Leguía, he specialised in education and costly public works; but he was preserved from financial difficulties by the revenues from the oil industry. He died in his bed in 1935, still in office, immensely wealthy and universally respected. His nominated successor took over without serious commotion and the Gómez system lasted until 1945, when a revolution placed the Democratic Action Party—a constitutionalist, middle-class body—in power.

Constitutional government, then, was by no means universal in Latin America even in the peaceful and prosperous 'twenties. On the other hand, the habit of revolution seemed to have been broken in most countries. To have broken it in Venezuela was Gómez's proudest boast. In leading states such as Argentina, which had known no violent change of government for half a century, stability and order were taken for granted. Everywhere great advances had been made in replacing the rule of force, of interest or of caprice, by the rule of law. Yet the underlying weakness, the excessive dependence upon the outside world, the failure to develop indigenous creative power, remained. World forces over which the Latin Americans had little control were to launch them into a period of disorder and distress.

The great depression of world trade which set in towards the end of 1929 struck Latin America almost immediately and with disastrous results. The Latin-American countries were more vulnerable, perhaps, than ever before. They depended upon foreign sources for many essential goods and services; they relied upon the export of a few basic commodities to pay for their very varied purchases. They were in many cases under contractual obligations to supply their customers, and the burden of their contracts was greatly increased by the fall in prices. Most of them were saddled with a heavy load of public and private debt. Their public revenues, out of which interest had to be paid and administration maintained, were drawn largely from export and import duties, which shrank alarmingly as trade declined. Faced with economic crisis, all governments except Venezuela and Argentina defaulted on their interest payments abroad; and all, perforce, reduced expenditure at home. Spending on works of capital development, on public health, on education, was drastically reduced. Governments and private concerns reduced their staffs. There was widespread unemployment—a new phenomenon in Latin America—followed by labour unrest, rioting and political revolts.

During 1930 and 1931 eleven of the twenty Latin-American republics experienced revolution; or, more accurately, experienced irregular changes of government; for these outbreaks were alike not only in their success, but, in most instances, in their relatively bloodless character. In some countries criminal proceedings were started against outgoing rulers—Leguía died in prison—but there were few assassinations or massacres. In general the revolutions took the civilised but extra-legal course of demonstration —ultimatum—resignation. It would be an over-simplification to attribute the outbreaks entirely to the depression. Bad business helped to make bad government intolerable. In every case there already existed social and political grievances to which the depression gave an opening. The commonest complaints were dictatorship, real or alleged, in some states; radicalism and pampering of labour in others; over-liberal terms offered to foreign capitalists; administrative waste and corruption; and the perennial grudge of the 'Outs' against the 'Ins'.

In Argentina the administration of Irigoyen was disliked by conservatives for its radicalism and by almost everybody else for its personal character, which concentrated a totally unmanageable mass of administrative detail in the hands of an upright but self-willed and narrow septuagenarian. It was not a dictatorship, but a creeping paralysis of administration, against which resentment grew. Irigoyen had forfeited labour support by an uncompromising attitude towards strikes in 1930. In September of that year an immense but well-organised and orderly demonstration in Buenos Aires compelled Irigoyen to resign. The demonstration was staged by students and the military. Its immediate consequence was a year of military rule under General Uribusu. An election was eventually held late in 1931, and General Justo took office as the head of an elected National Democratic—that is, conservative—government. The times were

unpropitious for a conservative policy in the ordinary sense, and government tended to drift away from constitutional practice towards oligarchic
rule of the old type. Finally, during the second world war, the oligarchy
was displaced by a regime which bore at least a superficial resemblance
to European fascism.

The revolution in Argentina was followed six weeks later by a widespread
insurrection in Brazil. The coffee industry of Brazil had for some time
been controlled by a valorisation scheme under which the government
restricted the amount of production, bought the crop, stored it, and
released quantities appropriate to the demand, in order to maintain the
price. The scheme broke down inevitably and disastrously early in 1930,
and the only way of disposing of vast quantities of unsaleable coffee was
to burn it. To the resulting discontent the reigning President, Washington
Luis of São Paulo, added a political grievance by giving official support to
a Paulista candidate in the presidential election of 1930. As was customary in Brazilian elections, the official candidate was returned, and the
conduct of the election gave great offence in Minas Geraes, the state
which would have provided the next president according to long-standing
political convention. The situation, with its threat of permanent Paulista
government, was seized and exploited by the candidate of a third state,
Rio Grande do Sul, which had been growing in wealth and population
and now claimed a greater share in central government. Dr Getulio
Vargas embarked upon civil war supported by Minas Geraes as well as
by his own state of Rio Grande, defeated the forces of São Paulo, drove
out the President, and set up a form of modified dictatorship, bolstered
by two extensive constitutional changes designed to strengthen the power
of the President and to reduce that of Congress and the state governments. The second of these enactments, in 1937, inaugurated a 'corporative' organisation reminiscent of fascist Italy; but Vargas was no Mussolini. His rule, though centralised and authoritarian, was neither arbitrary
nor—except in dealing with revolts by alleged communists—repressive.
He himself displayed an engaging geniality and studied moderation. The
great emperor Pedro II used to call himself the best republican in Brazil;
Dr Vargas might similarly have said that, had he not the misfortune to
be a dictator, he would have been a very democratic fellow.

The revolution in Chile was exceptional in being a successful revolt
against military dictatorship. Chile probably suffered more severely than
any other country from the depression; its export trade, already depressed,
was for a time almost killed. Yet the Chileans, remote, poor, proud,
eminently civilised, selected the inauspicious year 1932 for a return to
constitutional government. The President inaugurated in that year, after
two disputed elections and considerable disorder, was again Alessandri,
liberal, upright and able, by far the most respected of Chilean statesmen.
He governed for six years of modest recovery and careful administration,

moving steadily away from this old radicalism towards a conventionally conservative policy. In his last years he adopted measures of active repression against socialists and communists, which drove them to compose their differences and join with the radicals in a joint election campaign. Alessandri was thus succeeded in 1938 by Aguirre Cerda at the head of a 'popular front' coalition—itself a new and disturbing portent in Latin-American politics.

In Mexico there was no revolution in the ordinary sense. Mexicans considered that their country had been undergoing a continuous revolution since 1910. In the 'twenties, however, the process had slowed down. The old revolutionaries had become the new conservatives, and except for their anti-clericalism had forgotten much of the revolutionary programme. Obregón's successor, Calles, who either as President or as a power behind the President dominated Mexican politics from 1924 to 1934, publicly announced his opinion in 1929 that the land reform programme had gone far enough. In the early 'thirties distribution almost ceased. It is true that the industrial labour laws grew somewhat beyond what industry could safely afford; but the labour movement, like the government, was susceptible to jobbery, and trade-union leadership became a road to affluence and power. Meanwhile there had been several armed revolts in the 'twenties, and the gun-toting tradition of Mexican politics was still alive. The general political tone of this phase of the Revolution is best expressed in the nickname given to Calles. He was called the *Jefe Máximo*—the Big Boss. Yet even in these circumstances the emotions supporting the Revolution were too ardent to be chilled by the economic blizzard from abroad. The depression produced not counter-revolution, but impatience with the slow progress of the Revolution. With the election of General Cárdenas to the presidency in 1934 the scene changed abruptly. During his six years of office most landowners possessing any considerable extent of good arable land were dispossessed of all but a small area. The expropriation was no longer confined to owners who had acquired land by illegal means, who farmed inefficiently, or who had given political offence. The mere size of an estate, and its proximity to a village which wanted land, was enough to justify seizure, and it became much more difficult to stave off expropriation by the payment of bribes. Forty-seven million acres of land were distributed among more than a million peasant families between 1936 and 1940, compared with some 20 million acres granted to three-quarters of a million in the previous twenty years.[1] Cárdenas's policy, much influenced by some aspects of communism (Trotsky found asylum in Mexico), favoured the grant of *ejidos* to villages in common, rather than of plots in permanent ownership to individuals, who often used their plots to produce crops for

---

[1] P. E. James, *Latin America* (London, Cassell, 1943), p. 602. Detailed tables are collected in N. L. Whetten, *Rural Mexico* (Chicago, 1948).

immediate subsistence, and nothing more. The hasty re-distribution, necessarily based on inadequate surveys, caused widespread disorganisation and, temporarily at least, a serious drop in production. The development of communal peasant farming posed urgent problems of capital and management. A land bank system was started to lend money to *ejidatarios*; but the collection of interest in small sums from many scattered borrowers demands a costly and elaborate organisation, and the operations of the bank have been mostly confined to promising villages in favoured localities. The management problem is even more difficult of solution. Few *peones* have experience of management, and since *ejido* managers are elected, they are often chosen on grounds of personal popularity rather than of business ability. Nevertheless, some villages, particularly in the now celebrated Laguna cotton-growing district, have achieved considerable success under the new system. Difficulties of leadership may prove easier of solution as the determined efforts of government to provide general education begin to bear fruit. Meanwhile the price of revolution had to be paid in high cost of living, shaky national credit, and uncertainty. What is certain is that an agrarian revolution of the Mexican type cannot conceivably be reversed.

The revolution was avowedly nationalist as well as agrarian. One of the most spectacular acts of the Cárdenas administration was the expropriation of the foreign oil companies in 1938, on terms of compensation which could only be called derisory. A move to achieve native control of so important a resource was understandable; but whether through exhaustion of existing wells, or inexperienced management, or intractable labour, or lack of capital for exploratory work, productivity declined for a decade after expropriation. Recovery began in the 1950's, but exports remained small, barely enough to pay for the import of necessary machinery.

The nationalism of the revolution was more than economic. The plunder of the *hacendados* wrought havoc in the cultivated social and intellectual life, urban in character, French in tone, which their wealth had supported. A new and remarkable cultural development has to some extent taken its place, self-consciously indigenous, based largely upon Indian artistic tradition. Modern native Mexican art is best known in the fields of painting and sculpture, and is less evident in literary work. At present if suffers from a close pre-occupation with immediate social problems; but it represents genuine and original creative effort, and may be a presage of the growth of mental independence which Latin America as a whole urgently needs.

To carry through the drastic changes of the 'thirties more than ordinary powers were needed, and President Cárdenas, supported by the army, industrial labour and the peasantry, was virtually a dictator. There was only one political party, the Party of the Mexican Revolution. The dictatorship, however, was one of creative enthusiasm rather than of repression.

Except in its persecution of the church and its ruthless invasion of property, it was tolerant of divergences of opinion and permitted outspoken public criticism of its policy. Most significant of all, when Cárdenas's term came to an end he attempted neither to seek re-election nor to evade the constitution by interfering in the administration of his successor.

Most Latin-American states in the 1930's showed a marked tendency to adopt more authoritarian forms of government. These forms could not fairly be called 'totalitarian'; most educated Latin Americans possess too strong a sense of personal dignity to tolerate extreme dictatorship and too keen a sense of ridicule to be deceived by the cruder forms of racial myth. Governments, moreover, lack the detailed administrative machinery which the 'totalitarian' state requires. There was, nevertheless, a very evident growth of self-conscious nationalism. In internal affairs it took the form of agitation and sometimes of financial discrimination against foreign capital—against the English railways in Argentina, against the nitrate concerns in Chile, and of course the oil companies in Mexico. Many of these undertakings had become notoriously unremunerative, and clearly the great days of foreign—or at least European—investment in Latin America were past. In some countries, legislation intended for the protection of labour was used as a means of discrimination against foreign employers. Most governments enacted anti-alien employment laws, limiting the number of foreigners who might be employed in industry or commerce. At the same time, the open-door immigration policy which had existed over most of Latin America came to an end. Restrictive legislation began in Brazil and on the Pacific coast with quota regulations aimed against the immigration of Japanese, who presented a difficult problem of assimilation and were generally disliked; but most governments wished also to protect the industrial and agricultural labour market, in a time of unemployment, against an influx of European wage-earners. In Argentina and Brazil, the principal immigration countries, restrictive legislation reached a peak of severity in 1938. Both countries still contained immense areas of empty land, and exceptions were made in favour of farming settlers; but few immigrants in the 1930's were of this class. Pioneer settlement was—and still is—hampered by lack of capital. Today there is little prospect in any part of Latin America of a revival of indiscriminate mass immigration.

Throughout Latin America renewed and strenuous efforts were made, particularly in developing industries, to achieve a greater degree of economic independence. Governments attempted to control the production of staple products—Brazilian coffee, Argentine wheat, Chilean nitrate, Bolivian tin—in the hope of maintaining prices. In foreign trade, barter agreements between governments began to replace the competition of the open market. Prominent among these was the Roca–Runciman agreement between Argentina and Great Britain in 1933, followed by other similar pacts which, whatever their economic justification, caused considerable resentment in the United States. Nationalism also took overt political forms. There were several acrimonious disputes between states, and one serious war between Paraguay and Bolivia over possession of the Gran Chaco. Bolivia, land-locked and disorderly, dependent for revenue upon the product of its foreign-owned tin mines, was defeated and suffered yet another loss of territory. Bolivian irridentism would, no doubt, be a serious menace to the peace, but for Bolivian weakness. As it is, the country offers a standing temptation to aggression by its neighbours.

Nationalism, however, was clearly no panacea for Latin-American difficulties, and most governments knew and admitted that autarky, even if desirable, was out of the question in any foreseeable future. In many countries—though not in all—the 1930's saw a striking growth of enthusiasm for the Pan-American idea, and an elaboration of Pan-American arrangements for meeting and discussion. To some extent this was due to the decline in the prestige of the League of Nations, to Latin-American disappointment with the League's achievements, and disinclination to become involved in European quarrels which seemed to be passing beyond the scope of international discussion. In great measure, however, the revival of Pan-Americanism was assisted by changes in the foreign policy of the United States.

The Union of American Republics is an entirely voluntary association of theoretically equal sovereign states. It has no centralised administration and no constitution; few of its organs rest on formal conventions. Since 1910 it has maintained a permanent Bureau at Washington, which is a centre of research and propaganda as well as a secretariat for the periodical Pan-American conferences. The chief function of the Union is to facilitate the open discussion of matters of common interest to the American republics. The United States has always been the Union's chief sponsor; the chief obstacle to the work of the Union has been Latin-American suspicion of the United States. Many North American statesmen, notably Woodrow Wilson, insistently proclaimed their country's respect for the sovereignty of all its neighbours. These pronouncements appeared to be contradicted by the interventions in Mexico in 1914 and 1916–17, followed by a decade of uniformly bad relations; by the presence of United States forces—however few in number and helpful in intention—in Haiti, Santo Domingo and Nicaragua; by the Platt amendment; by the non-recognition policy; by the economic power exercised in Cuba by the sugar corporations, and throughout the Caribbean by the United Fruit Company, an organisation far wealthier and more potent than the little republics in which it operated.

After the first world war it was generally thought that the strategic excuse for North American intervention in the Caribbean had disappeared. Resentment against the political and economic policy of the United States flared up in public speeches at the Havana Conference in 1928. The hostility then displayed gave a considerable shock to public opinion in the United States, and the year of the Conference saw the beginnings of a determined effort to improve relations with Latin America. The policy of the 'good neighbour' is closely associated with the name of Franklin Roosevelt. He was not responsible for the Clark memorandum, published in 1930, which explicitly repudiated the 'Roosevelt corollary'; nor for the appointment of Dwight Morrow, who as ambassador in Mexico did much to create friendly feeling and to postpone the Mexican onslaught on foreign property. The new policy reached its fullest expression, however, after Roosevelt became President in 1933. In that year, at the seventh Pan-American Conference at Montevideo, the United States accepted a resolution denying the right of any state to interfere in the internal affairs of any other state. The Buenos Aires Conference in 1936, which was opened by President Roosevelt himself, re-affirmed this principle in more explicit terms, and drew up a pact providing for consultation in the event of any threat to the peace of the Americas. The administrative organisation and procedure for carrying out this consultative pact were created by the eighth Pan-American Conference at Lima in 1938.

During this period of frequent conferences the United States government withdrew the last of its forces from Nicaragua and Haiti, rescinded the Platt amendment in 1934, and in 1936 voluntarily gave up its treaty right of intervention in Panama. Evidence of a radical change of policy was afforded not only by the actions of the State Department, but by its abstentions from action. North American investors abroad were left to shift for themselves. There was no intervention in Cuba during the anarchy of Grau San Martín's administration, and when the Mexican government confiscated the foreign oil wells, the British Foreign Office was left alone to make futile protests and to break off diplomatic relations. Meanwhile a new and more liberal trading policy, initiated by Mr Cordell Hull under the Reciprocal Trade Agreements Act of 1934, found an effective sphere of operation in Latin America. By the end of 1939 agreements had been made with eleven Latin-American states.

The success of the 'good neighbour' policy was not universal. The Buenos Aires Conference, for instance, resolutely refused to endorse the neutrality legislation of the United States. There were sharp differences of opinion between Argentina and the United States over the procedure to be adopted to bring the Chaco war to an end, and over Argentine proposals for non-aggression pacts in which European states might be invited to participate. Not only were Argentine governments jealous of North American political leadership; the Argentine economy was complementary to that of Europe and directly competitive with that of the United States. Argentina today easily holds a record among American states for the non-ratification of international agreements.

Nevertheless, the Pan-American movement grew in strength, and its value became evident in 1939. Within three weeks of the outbreak of war the American foreign ministers met to establish a 'zone of neutrality' in the Americas and to set up a financial and economic advisory committee designed to reduce the economic consequences of the war in Latin America. In 1940, the emphasis having shifted from neutrality to defence, they met again at Havana, and devised a scheme for taking over the administration of European colonies in the western hemisphere in case of German victory in Europe. The Havana Conference also passed a resolution declaring that any attack by a non-American state would be considered an act of aggression against all the Americas.

An act of aggression against the United States took place towards the end of 1941, and early in 1942 the American foreign ministers met again, at Rio de Janeiro. This meeting—after a severe struggle in which Argentina led the opposition—recommended all American republics to sever relations with the 'Axis' powers. The co-operation of Latin America was now vital to the Allied cause, since the Japanese had possessed themselves of the chief sources, in the East, of tin, rubber, quinine, and a whole range of tropical products. The Latin-American states rose to the occasion. Mexico and Brazil declared war in the summer of 1942. Both in due course sent forces abroad. All the republics except Chile and Argentina broke off relations with the 'Axis' before the end of the Conference. Chile made the break in January 1943. Argentina broke off relations in 1944 and declared war in January 1945, obviously with a view to securing a place at the United Nations Conference. By that time Argentina was almost isolated politically, and its relations with the United States were deeply embittered. Argentina was not represented at the fourth conference of foreign ministers in 1945, but it eventually acceded to the final Act of Chapúltepec. This Act repeated the principle of common American resistance to aggression, and made it clear that the principle was to include aggression by one American state against another. Further, it provided for the first time a working definition of aggression, and committed states, if necessary, to the use of economic and military 'sanctions'. The Act of Chapúltepec thus marked, on paper, the metamorphosis of the Monroe Doctrine from a unilateral declaration of policy to a reciprocal system of regional security, within the proposed framework of the United Nations.

The strength and permanence of this system depend to a great extent upon the policy of the United States. The successes of the 'good neighbour' policy were achieved through the readiness of the United States to exercise exceptional restraint, and to make important concessions of immediate interests. There was still, however, considerable latent hostility towards the United States in Latin America. It broke briefly into clamour in Peru and Ecuador during the war, over the North American attitude towards a dispute between those countries about territory on the Upper

Amazon. Hostility might become more general if the United States relaxed its 'good neighbour' efforts, or appeared for any reason unable or unwilling to undertake the defence of the Americas. The United States government, on its side, might feel obliged to abandon its policy of non-intervention if, for instance, there were a widespread development in Latin America of pro-Russian communism.

There seems little likelihood of such a development. Communist groups exist in most republics, and are habitually made the scapegoats of disorder; but they are small and unimportant. It is true that the thought of the Mexican Revolution owes much to Marx; but *agrarismo* is a peculiarly Mexican phenomenon, and really has little in common with contemporary Russian totalitarianism. The same is true of *Aprismo*, the very interesting left-wing movement which came into power in Peru at the election of 1945. *Aprismo* purports to be Marxist in political and social philosophy, but it appreciates the importance of religion in social life and recognises the need for the support of the middle class in the reform of society. *Aprismo* is hostile to the influence of foreign capital, stresses the importance of the Indian races in American affairs, and supports the idea of Pan-Latin-Americanism; but all these points of policy tended to slip into the background as a result of the war and of the attainment of power by the *Apra* party. The *Apra* government was overthrown by a military insurrection in Peru late in 1948; but *Aprismo*, though outlawed, remained the most vigorous indigenous social movement in South America. Its chief political characteristic, the combination between the middle and professional classes and labour, was common to many moderate radical movements in Latin America. A number of successful post-war governments in Latin America were based on coalitions of this kind. Communism, which would not as a rule accept such a coalition, remained weak.

One of the major states of Latin America was until 1955 governed by a radical dictatorship of a fairly extreme kind. Argentina resembles Australia in that, although its wealth comes from its immense rural resources, three-quarters of its population live in towns. Immigrants have always tended to seek employment in or near the towns, and urbanisation was accelerated by industrial development before and during the war. One-fifth of the population live in the capital. During the war, through the greatly increased demands for industrial production, especially (as in 1914) for tinned beef, labour in Buenos Aires received very high wages and became very powerful. After the war, with the falling-off of temporary demands and the attempt to resume normal pre-war trading, the labour in the canning factories and other concerns became extremely unruly. General Perón came to power as a result of a military *coup* in 1943 and a tumultuous election in 1945. His strength rested upon labour and the army, and was due to his gift of talking to the workers of the capital in language which they understood—simple, emotional and violent. His theme was an extreme left-wing nationalism, a promise to lead the workers against the capitalist and the foreigner. His success in 1945 was probably assisted by the attempts of the United States ambassador in Buenos Aires, Mr Spruille Braden, to rally opposition against him. This helped to explain the attitude of the government towards the United States. Unwillingness to compromise hindered trade negotiations with other states, notably Great Britain. National feeling insisted on the purchase in 1947 of the very unremunerative English railways—*el pulpo inglés*, the English octopus—as they were called in the Peronista press. The failure of the meat companies to deliver the beef which was to pay for the railways was due, not so much to ill-will or bad faith, as to labour trouble and general disorganisation in the trade. The economic life of Argentina was, indeed, in some disorder in 1949, despite its great potentialities.

Dictatorships of the *Peronista* kind remained rare in Latin America, at least in the greater states. In Mexico the revolution lost its fierce urgency and constitutional government seemed, for the time, firmly established. In Brazil the Vargas administration ended in 1945, and President Dutra correctly described his own government as one devoted to 're-constitutionalising' the political system. Meanwhile Latin America, while still depending to a great extent on the purchasing power of Europe and the United States, was modestly prosperous. The second world war, with the expansion of Latin-American productive activity and the curtailment of the usual sources of supply, gave a fresh and powerful stimulus to industrial development and to agricultural diversification. Both these movements received powerful financial and commercial support from the United States. Heavy industry made a beginning in Brazil, in Mexico and in Peru. In Brazil the building of the great Volta Redonda steel works was hailed as a declaration of economic independence. It would be rash to assert, as some Latin Americans did assert, that South America in 1950 was on the threshold of a development analogous to that which took place in North America in the second half of the last century. Nevertheless, Latin America now represented beyond question a political, economic and cultural force which the world at large could not afford to ignore.

CHAPTER IX

THE WESTERN QUESTION IN ASIA AND NORTH AFRICA, 1900–45

IN the first half of the twentieth century the peoples of Asia underwent revolutionary changes. At the beginning of the period European power in Asia stood at its zenith. From the seaward side Britain held undisputed sway over the key position of the Indian empire. In the Near and Middle East, and in the Far East also, hers was the dominant influence, though these regions, unlike India, were the scene of great power rivalries. Along with France and the Netherlands Britain also controlled South-East Asia, which had been clearly demarcated into spheres of interest. From the landward side Russia, through assiduous colonisation, consolidated her position in central and east Asia.

By the close of the period the change in the position of Europe in Asia was striking. First and foremost the paramountcy of Britain had disappeared. She had quitted the Indian empire; and had quietly given way to the United States in the Far East. Along with the Netherlands and France she was also beginning to yield her position in South-East Asia; and in the Near and Middle East her much-weakened and indeed tenuous position rested mainly on the presence of her forces in the Suez Canal zone. Of the external powers Russia alone had maintained her position and was firmly ensconced in both central and east Asia.

Equally remarkable were the internal changes that had taken place. Many new, independent Asian states had emerged. The Ottoman empire had broken into its constituent parts and Israel had fought its way into existence. Farther to the east, Pakistan, India, Ceylon, Burma and Indonesia had become sovereign powers. In the Far East the ruthless, expansionist policy of Japan had at last brought down on her the full might of the allied western powers, especially the United States, thus allowing a reunited, resurgent China to emerge.

In this half-century European domination gave rise everywhere in Asia to nationalist movements. Capitalist enterprise and higher-education policies brought into existence small but influential middle classes, who understood and respected the full force of the scientific and industrial revolution which had already transformed the West and was in process of transforming Asia. These middle classes, at first slavishly copying the West, formed the spearhead of nationalist movements in their own countries. They sought to establish the political and economic institutions of the West, but at the same time to reject its political and economic supremacy. Everywhere in Asia nationalism and anti-colonialism formed the co-ordinates within which these movements grew to maturity.

Although the presence and dominance of European powers had tended to isolate the Asian countries in self-contained units, the individual nationalist movements had acted and reacted on each other. The anti-western Boxer rebellion in China in 1899 and the victory of Japan over Russia in 1904 lit a spark throughout Asia. The rise of the Swaraj movement in India encouraged parallel developments in Ceylon, Burma and Indonesia: the revival of Islam in the Near East after the first world war influenced Muslim thought in India and South-East Asia: and the triumph of communism in China after the second world war caught the attention of all Asians and set the pattern of events in Indo-China and Malaya. The responses to the application of western political practices in Asia were by no means uniform in the different countries. In the Indian empire, which had come directly and firmly under European control, the most determined attempt was made to establish liberal forms of government after the British fashion. One of the first consequences was the partition of India, and the emergence of Burma as a sovereign state. Nevertheless, the constituent parts persisted in applying representative and responsible forms of government. In China, which had come under the direct influence but not the organised rule of the West, a similar attempt was made, though with less understanding and preparation. Attacked from within by a succession of war-lords and from without by Japan, it ultimately failed in a welter of corruption and inefficiency. Inspired by Soviet Russia, by this time established on China's borders, the Chinese accepted the failure of western forms of democracy and turned to communism.

Economic and social developments unfortunately had not kept pace with the rate of political change. Throughout Asia an enormous increase in population occurred during the period, and the mass of the people were probably poorer at the end than they had been at the beginning. The disparity between them and their new middle-class rulers had become more glaring. Most of Asia was neither capitalist nor communist, but peasant. Everywhere land was in demand and land reform was overdue. Slow-moving traditional systems were faced with the need for quick change.

In short, the influence of the West had created revolution in Asia and in this period had further complicated, not simplified or clarified, the problems facing Asians.

In the sections which follow on the Near and Middle East, on India, on South-East Asia and on the Far East, these developments are discussed in greater detail.

THE WESTERN QUESTION IN ASIA AND NORTH AFRICA

I. THE NEAR AND MIDDLE EAST AND NORTH AFRICA

During most if not all of this period the paramount western power in the Near and Middle East was Great Britain, and it is through the evolution of British interests and policy that the development of the 'western question' in the area can most conveniently be treated.

Towards the end of the nineteenth century British policy underwent a major change. Until then the dominant British interest in the area had been the safeguarding of the Middle East sea and overland routes to India from threats by rival European powers—an objective pursued by the famous policy of 'maintaining the independence and integrity of the Ottoman empire'. From the middle of the century onwards a number of new factors combined to make this policy increasingly out-of-date and inadequate. The rapid modernisation of the transit routes—between 1851 and 1880 over 1000 miles of railway were built in Egypt, and in 1869 the Suez Canal was opened—and the steady growth of direct economic interests, especially in Egypt, where the foreign debt reached £98,000,000 by 1880, gave the area a vastly increased importance requiring closer supervision. At the same time, the Ottoman empire was becoming less and less satisfactory as a shield from outside penetration. French and, to a lesser extent, Russian penetration continued, and from 1880 onwards Germany, already Britain's main imperial rival, showed ever greater interest in the Near East. Ottoman governments, the young Turks no less than 'Abd al-Ḥamīd II, displayed a disquieting acquiescence in German ambitions. German banks and combines obtained concessions, German officers trained and reorganised the Ottoman army, German scientists and archaeologists explored the Asiatic territories, and the whole empire seemed in a fair way towards becoming a German Protectorate. In 1889 work was begun on the famous Anatolian railway, intended, ultimately, to link Berlin with the Persian Gulf via Constantinople, Aleppo, Baghdad and Basra.

The first sign of a new British orientation came with the occupation of Egypt in 1882. This occupation, undertaken unwillingly and without any intention of maintaining it permanently, was aimed in the first instance at restoring order and protecting the interests of European investors and creditors. As the German threat to the north increased, British governments became more and more unwilling to put an end to what seemed to be the only satisfactory way of protecting British interests in and through Egypt, the more so since the Entente with France and the new-found friendship with Russia relieved Britain for the time being of her other European concerns. In 1907 an Anglo-Russian agreement divided Persia into Russian and British spheres of influence, and seemed to exclude the further expansion of Germany eastward from Ottoman Iraq.

On the outbreak of war in 1914 Ottoman suzerainty over Egypt was

207

declared at an end, and the country placed under a British protectorate. The campaigns against Turkey and the secret inter-allied agreements of the war years prepared the way for the final elimination of the Ottoman empire and the extension of direct British and Allied rule to many of its Arabic-speaking provinces. The rise of the Kemalist nationalists in Turkey after the war and their successful defence of the Turkish core of the empire in 1922–3 prevented the complete fulfilment of these plans, while the collapse of the tsarist empire and the consequent withdrawal of Russia from the arena involved some readjustment. By the agreement of San Remo in 1920, confirmed by the League of Nations in 1923, Iraq and Palestine-Transjordan were placed under British, and Syria under French mandates. Britain thus obtained control of the northern approaches to the Suez Canal and Egypt and of the Euphrates route to the Persian Gulf.

As the smoke of battle and the mists of diplomacy cleared from the Middle Eastern scene in the post-war years, it became apparent that great changes had taken place and new forces arisen. In the long run they made the position of the western powers in the area untenable. Politically, the situation at first seemed favourable. The Ottoman empire had gone, and the new Turkish republic, after its successful defence of the Turkish homelands, showed little disposition to interfere in the Arab lands to the south. The Austrian, German and Russian empires were all *hors de combat* and Italy was still too weak and disunited to play an active part, leaving a clear field to Britain and France. Despite a number of ominous clashes, more especially on the lower levels of officialdom, the Anglo-French entente still seemed to be working fairly well, and the partition of the area between the two powers was accomplished without open conflict. Economically perhaps the most significant changes came from the discovery, exploitation and use of mineral oil. First in Persia, then in Iraq, later in Arabia, great new fields were opened up, and the Middle East soon became one of the major oil-producing areas of the world. This new development affected the area in a number of ways. The use of the internal combustion engine revolutionised overland communications. New roads linked the major centres, making possible the exchange of persons, commodities, newspapers and ideas on a hitherto undreamt-of scale, and the gradual replacement of ass, horse and camel by car, bus and lorry, coupled with the rapid economic development of the period and the spread of other western innovations like printing and popular education, began a far-reaching social transformation.

These changes greatly accelerated the major internal political development of the period—the rise of nationalism. The first impact of western armed power on Near-Eastern Islam at the end of the eighteenth century, shattering the age-old conviction of the innate superiority of Islam over the infidel West, had engendered a profound *malaise* that found its first expression in a series of reform movements aiming at the modernisation of Muslim society and the adoption of western achievements, especially in technology. This was followed by a religious reaction, expressed politically in pan-Islamism, which sought to defeat the encroaching West by a return to a pure Islamic tradition in a unified Islamic society. The advent of direct western rule, following on the introduction of the western ideas of nation and fatherland through education and translated literature, gave rise to a new movement—nationalism. The new nationalisms of the Middle East were still profoundly affected by the older Islamic ideal of religious unity, but—and herein lay their novelty—aimed primarily at the liberation of a specific territory or nationality from foreign rule and the achievement of limited, national political objectives. The first active nationalist movement arose in Egypt, and was dedicated to the struggle against the British occupation. In Turkey, after a period of underground activity during the pan-Islamic interlude of 'Abd al-Ḥamīd II, nationalism burst into the open in 1908 with the Young Turk revolution. In Syria, partly inspired by the Turkish and Egyptian examples, partly by the literary revival begun by American and French missionaries working among the native Christians, small nationalist clubs were formed as early as the nineteenth century, and first became active from 1905, when the defeat of a major European great power by Japan had revived hopes and restored confidence in most parts of Asia. In 1916 the British government, disturbed at the possible effects in India and elsewhere of the Holy War proclaimed in Constantinople, entered into negotiations with Sharīf Ḥusain, the Arab ruler of Mecca and, in return for immediate material support and the promise of Arab independence in a vast but vaguely defined area after the war, induced him to begin an Arabian revolt against his Ottoman suzerain. The Arabs of the Hijaz rose against the Turks and played some part in Allenby's campaign in Syria.

In the frustration of Arab hopes after the war and the forcible establishment of British and French rule over peoples just acquiring the taste for freedom, the seeds were sown of the many troubles of the inter-war years. By 1922–3 outbreaks of violence in almost all the Arab lands made it clear that a simple policy of direct rule was unworkable, and a new British policy emerged, the main tenor of which was the creation of new Arab states and the concession to them of a degree of independence, coupled with the signing of treaties safeguarding the privileged position of Great Britain and the right to maintain armed forces on their territories. On the whole this policy was a failure. The concessions made to nationalist demands were always too small and too late to satisfy; they were received as expressions of weakness rather than of goodwill, and a situation arose in which nationalist politics were conducted as a competition in extremism, making it impossible for local leaders to accept anything less than their maximum demands. Where treaties were achieved, they were signed either with unrepresentative governments without the support of the politically active classes, or under the pressure of an urgent external threat—as the Anglo-Egyptian treaty of 1936, signed in the shadow of the Italian advance into Ethiopia.

In two areas the situation was especially difficult. Zionist colonisation in Palestine had begun in the late nineteenth century, and in 1917 received the formal support of the British government in the Balfour Declaration of that year. The reconciliation of this promise, solemnly reiterated in the League of Nations mandate for Palestine, with the expectations aroused among the Arabs, presented the British government with an impossible task and made Palestine a running sore infecting the whole Arab world. In Syria the French faced difficulties of a different sort. They had begun badly. Unlike the British in Iraq and Palestine, they had conquered the country, not from the Turks, but from an Arab nationalist government set up by Prince Faisal, later king of Iraq, during the interlude that followed the Ottoman withdrawal. During the whole period of their rule they never succeeded in overcoming the hostility of the Syrian Muslims, and only in Lebanon, with its important Christian population, could they count on any extensive local support. The French proceeded along parallel lines to the British in Iraq, setting up constitutional machinery and native administration. But owing to the relative weakness of their position they could not go even as far as Britain in appeasing nationalist aspirations, the more so since any encouragement of Arab nationalism in the Near East might have dangerous repercussions in their North African territories. An attempt to negotiate the long-delayed treaty in 1936 foundered in the French Chamber of Deputies, and by 1939 Franco-Syrian relations were still tense and dangerous.

Only in the really independent states of the area can western policy be said to have achieved any real success. The consolidation of the Saudi Arabian kingdom over the greater part of the Arabian peninsula in the 'twenties was followed by close and friendly relations with Great Britain, while the Turkish republic, after a brief period of virtual outlawry, maintained ever closer relations with the West, culminating in the Anglo-Franco-Turkish alliance of 1939. In Persia the anarchy of the war years, when British, Russian and Germano-Turkish agents and levies roamed at will over the country, gave way in the early 'twenties to a new and highly centralised national monarchy. The dictatorship of Riza Shah, though by no means always friendly to Great Britain, for long served the main interest of British policy in Persia by acting as a strong barrier to Russian expansion towards the borders of India.

Italy had obtained the suzerainty of Libya as a result of the Italo-Turkish war of 1911–12. Her direct control was, however, limited to the coastlands, and it was not until the middle or late 'twenties that a series of campaigns established effective Italian government over the whole province. The Fascist government conducted a vigorous propaganda against Anglo-French rule in the Near East, and made no secret of its desire to expand both there and in East Africa. For a while British policy towards the Near Eastern peoples was largely determined by the need to counter Italian threats and blandishments.

From 1933 onwards Britain and France in the Middle East faced a new and more dangerous threat. To the relatively minor menace of Fascist Italy was added the far more potent threat of Nazi Germany, powerful, aggressive, and seemingly bent on resuming and extending the eastern plans of imperial Germany. Nazi propaganda of every kind flooded the Near East, wooing the nationalist movements with promises with which the powers in actual occupation could not compete; playing in particular on the Palestine problem, to which, by their anti-semitism, they had themselves in no small measure contributed. Nazi agents made contacts with politicians, army officers and journalists; German trade missions, more especially in Persia and Turkey, made barter agreements which subordinated the economies of the countries concerned in large measure to that of Germany.

The war of 1939–45 brought great disappointments to both sides in the Middle East. Despite the lavish Axis effort, the response was small. Some facilities in Vichy-occupied Syria, the pro-Axis Rashīd ʻAlī *coup* in Iraq in 1941 were the only major positive results. On the British side too the effort to win the friendship of Arab nationalism proved a failure, and the Allies could at best count on a sullen neutrality. Apart from the Jews in Palestine and the Arab Legion in Transjordan, only in Turkey was there any sign of active pro-Allied sentiment, and that did not reach the point of active intervention at a time when it might still have been effective. In Iran, the hostile attitude of the government, coupled with the Allied desire to control the trans-Iranian supply route to Russia, led to a joint Anglo-Soviet military occupation of the country in 1941. Meanwhile war again brought rapid and significant change. Axis and Allied propagandists competed with one another in flattering nationalist self-esteem and encouraging nationalist aspirations; Axis and Allied armies camped and fought on Arab soil, employing thousands of Arab artisans and labourers and bringing with them the economic stresses and dislocations that are inseparable from modern war. For the first time local political controversy ceased to be chiefly concerned with political matters, and dealt in such topics as shortages, high prices, and other indications of an economy under strain. The war brought two important measures of regional unification, the one economic, the other political. The Middle East Supply Centre, at first a British, then an Anglo-American organisation, attempted with marked success to integrate the economies of the Middle Eastern countries into a planned whole. The Arab League, founded in 1944, grouped all the Arab sovereign states of the Middle East for the joint pursuit of common political objectives.

The end of the war revealed a new international political alignment. Italy and Germany were eliminated by defeat. France, after a tumultuous last act, withdrew from Syria in 1945, and the two republics of Syria and Lebanon were added to the number of Arab sovereign states. In the place of those which had gone, new powers had arisen. Russia, after a long absence, had once more returned to the Middle Eastern arena, with occupation forces in northern Persia, diplomatic and consular representation in all the major centres, and an active policy. America too had arrived at last as an active participant, at first mainly interested in economic and strategic considerations, but with growing and unavoidable political responsibilities.

In this situation Britain found herself gravely weakened. Her economic weakness—she was now a debtor to most of the countries concerned, and could no longer supply their main import requirements—her military weakness, which made it impossible to maintain her pre-war military position in the teeth of growing local resistance—imposed a new orientation of policy. The main objective now was the preservation of the area, with its strategic routes and centres and its economic resources, from Russian penetration. Direct rule had failed. Occupation by treaty was impossible, as the failure to negotiate post-war treaties in Iraq and Egypt showed. And so the outlines of a new policy emerged, similar in principle to the old policy of 'maintaining the integrity and independence' of the paramount local power. The search began for a substitute for the defunct Ottoman empire.

2. INDIA

By the close of the nineteenth century British power in India had reached its zenith. The whole sub-continent from the seas to the mountains had been pacified and unified. The provinces under direct British rule—comprising some three-fifths of the whole country—were functioning under a uniform, paternal and efficient administration; and the Indian princes, nominal rulers of the remaining territories, had found and by this time fully understood their status as 'junior partners in Empire', wholly dependent on the British. India as a whole had become a large and safe field for British investment, and through her Britain reached out to consolidate a great arch of political and economic power in the Indian Ocean from the Cape of Good Hope on the one side to Australia on the other.

Lord Curzon, Governor-General and Viceroy of India (1898–1905), in his own person exemplified the merits and defects of contemporary British rule. India in his view was incapable of ruling herself and had been entrusted to Britain as a sacred charge by Providence. It was necessary for Britain to govern India 'as if...for ever'. She was to be ruled honestly, impartially and efficiently, and no sacrifice, no labour, was too great. But by taking such an exalted view of his office, he confined his field of view and obscured his vision. He was over-conscious of his right-ness, intolerant of the shadow of a slight and exclusive in his attitude. There was no important place in government, in his view, for the rising Indian middle classes, who had in fact been called into existence by the economic, political and educational policy of Britain. The main task as he saw it was economic and not political.

The leaders of Indian middle-class opinion were diametrically opposed to Curzon. They saw his viceroyalty not so much as the beginning but as the close of an era. Indian reaction to British rule and to the full force of European civilisation had been slow to take shape. The former Muslim rulers—a minority in the land—appeared a spent force, economically dispossessed by the more flexible and responsive Hindus and politically discredited by the British. The majority Hindu community was at first interested neither in its own past nor in the facts of political power. In a plural society, largely Hindu and Muslim, each part of which was dominated by religious awareness, it was certain that opposition to wes-tern rule would have to assume a religious form before it could find expres-sion in popular and political ways. In the course of the nineteenth century Hindu and Muslim thinkers began to re-examine their beliefs and practices and new Hindu and Muslim reformist movements sprang up. Some reached out tentatively to come to terms with the West, some recoiled to gain strength and in the process became more stubbornly aware of themselves.

At first the rising middle classes, largely Hindu in composition yet drawing their inspiration from Britain, seized the political initiative and through the Indian National Congress began to ask of the British some share in government. Their proposals were modest, their methods strictly constitutional. They wanted more say in the Legislative Councils and a greater share of the appointments to the Indian Civil Service, and they pressed their point of view both in India and England, where some of their members, like Dadabhai Naoroji, were returned to Parliament. They admired the force and direction of British liberal policy and it was clear that they sought for India a position and a form of government compar-able with that of Britain. They envisaged India as a united nation with a parliamentary form of government. Their policy and methods were in fact a tribute to the essential success of British policy in India.

But at this crucial stage the British government faltered. For their part they doubted whether India ever could become a nation in the western sense and they were increasingly aware that the economic, political and educational development of India had increased the disparity between Hindus and Muslims. Indeed, western educated Muslims such as Sayyid Ahmad Khan had already declared that they were opposed to any attempt to apply a British form of representative and responsible government because it would permanently subordinate Muslims to the more numerous

Hindus. Unable and sometimes even reluctant to see a way through these difficulties, the British, and in particular Curzon, presented an apparently inflexible and inscrutable front to the Indian moderates. As might have been foreseen, the Indian response became tougher, more active and more vocal. A proposal in 1905 to divide the overgrown province of Bengal for administrative reasons produced a spontaneous agitation in which the moderates took full part. Indian commercial interests—already a discernible force—also joined in sponsoring a *swadeshi* movement to encourage the use of home-made as against foreign goods. Just as significant, those Hindu and Muslim reformist groups, whose activities had been somewhat concealed by the quicker and noisier reaction of the moderates, began to come into the open. In the National Congress extremist revolutionary Hindu groups, inspired by Bal Gangadhar Tilak, began to challenge the supremacy of the moderates, and terrorist outbreaks became widespread in northern India, especially in Bengal.

It was a situation which government had to face and in 1908–9 Curzon's successor, Minto, along with his colleague Morley, the Secretary of State, acted promptly. He took extreme powers to combat the terrorists, meanwhile devising with Morley's help reform proposals to regain the support of the moderates. These took a significant form. Agreeing that the problem was essentially that of giving Indians greater opportunities of advising, but quite definitely not of controlling the government, they conceded non-official majorities in the provincial legislatures while retaining an official majority at the centre. They formally recognised, too, the principle of election, but in the face of Muslim opposition shrank from creating territorial constituencies of the British type and instead extended a system introduced in 1892 of representation by special interests. Moreover, to Muslims and Muslims alone were granted separate electorates. In effect, the number of Muslim representatives was to be based on the importance rather than on the size of their community.

Under this provision Muslim electors were bound to think of themselves as Muslims rather than as Indians and would thus become more politically aware of their distinctiveness, and the charge is often made that in this way the British government deliberately applied a 'divide and rule' policy. Indeed, Morley and Minto were not unaware of the possible advantages of this course, but their horizon was not as limited as this charge implies. Had they set themselves to introduce parliamentary government of the English kind into India, their recognition of separate electorates would have been a truly mischievous act. But they had no such intention in mind. As Morley said, they had acted in this way because they did not 'think it desirable or possible or even conceivable to adapt English political institutions to the nations who inhabit India'. In their view India was set on a different course, and it behoved the British government to move cautiously.

This was small comfort to the Indian moderates who had striven so long and hard to equip themselves to apply the whole of the British political and liberal tradition. The decline of their position and influence dates from this period.

The Morley–Minto reforms of 1909 marked the close of the first phase of Indian politics. The British had set out to create 'a class of persons, Indian in blood and colour, but English in taste, in opinion, in morals, and in intellect'. In political terms they had succeeded. The moderates stood ready to serve, but were in effect fobbed off. However, it was not until after the outbreak of the first world war that they began to realise that they had walked into a kind of political blind alley. Their protests and British second thoughts, no doubt inspired by the strong currents of European and American opinion in favour of national self-determination, produced in 1917 a reconsideration of the political situation and future. The Government of India Act which followed in 1919 indicated that Britain had reversed her policy. India was accepted as a nation in the making, for which parliamentary government of the English kind and dominion status within the Commonwealth were feasible.

As a beginning the central government and the nine provincial governments of British India were remodelled. Although at the centre the Viceroy remained responsible to the Secretary of State and Parliament in London, he was to be assisted by a legislature with a majority of elected members. This was envisaged as the germ of an Indian parliament. By its side a Chamber of Princes was constituted, as a purely consultative body, which was to represent the Indian States and which in time, it was hoped, would join in creating an all-India union. Steps towards responsible government were more obvious in the sphere of provincial government. The governor of each province was to be assisted by a group of Indian ministers chosen by him from the provincial legislature. Under him the departments were divided into two categories, those like law and order, revenue and finance, which he 'reserved' under the control of his own officials, and those like education, public health and economic development, which he 'transferred' to Indian ministers, who were responsible for them to the legislature. In time it was hoped that in each province all departments might be 'transferred' to ministers who would then form a wholly responsible cabinet. The franchise for the central and local legislatures was extended to about 7,000,000 voters, divided into the already accepted classes of 1909.

From the British point of view it was a bold plan, and probably in their position the right kind of plan. They assumed that the difficulties— especially those of the heterogeneous and ignorant population, the un-democratic, Hindu caste society, the existence of separate electorates— would sooner or later be overcome, and that it was wisest to apply a system, which although not quite suited to India yet was at least well understood by the British themselves. This policy was first given a trial of ten years, and then persisted in until 1937, and it might well have succeeded had not the major part of Indian political opinion worked so strongly against it. For by the 1920's Indian politics had been revolutionised. The moderates, who were willing to work the Act of 1919, had been steadily but surely pushed into the background by the more extreme groups, which whilst aware of the British political tradition, yet drew their inspiration from Indian reformist movements. Mohandas Karamchand Gandhi, later known as Mahatma ('great soul'), emerged to take the lead of the National Congress. Essentially an Indian, more particularly a Hindu, figure he persuaded the Congress to adopt his technique of passive non-violent resistance to oppose the British. Through his undoubted spiritual exaltation, his masterly skill in symbolising his aims and methods, and his appreciation of the effectiveness of non-violent resistance against a civilised government, he succeeded in producing a mass revolutionary movement with the National Congress as its political fulcrum.

The Act of 1919, which had been devised to meet the political ambitions of a growing western-educated class, was quite inadequate in this situation. The battle was being waged not in the legislatures but in the towns and villages, and even in the legislatures the two-party system, one of the most important conventions of parliamentary government, had not evolved. Much devoted and useful work was done by the new ministries but the swift descent of the trading countries of the world into the economic depression of 1929–32 helped to make their task impossible. Retrenchment was the order of the day, planning was 'on the cheap' and rarely looked effective or caught the imagination. It was clear that a new approach was needed, and the British government actively began to discuss this in 1929. But the political situation continued to change rapidly.

The evident intention of the British to move towards some form of responsible government had juxtaposed the distinctive Muslim and Hindu communities in an underlying political rivalry, of which the existence of separate electorates was a constant reminder and reinforcement. Already in competing for the public services the Muslims had become aware of the Hindus' numerical superiority and stronger tradition of western learning, and over the whole economic field they knew themselves to be on the defensive. Their strength lay among the peasants and land-owning classes and not in the banking and industrial interests which were steadily falling under the control of those Hindu groups whose hereditary occupation for centuries had been commerce and finance. Throughout India the contrast between Hindu wealth and progress on the one side and Muslim poverty and backwardness on the other was becoming plain. The dominance of the Hindus in the Indian National Congress became increasingly evident, and new extremist organisations sprang up, like the Mahasabha, which set out to suppress the Muslims. In response, the All-India Muslim League and other Muslim parties began not only to grow in strength but also to close their ranks.

The complex nature of the political problem, exaggerated by the chaotic effects of the Gandhi movement, prolonged the reform negotiations and it was not until 1935 that the British were able to present their revision of the constitution. This new Act envisaged a federation of the Indian states and of the provinces of British India. It provided straightway for Indian self-government in each of the eleven provinces. Separate electorates were retained and the franchise was extended to thirty-five millions. At the general election which followed, Congress, the active lead of which had passed to Jawaharlal Nehru who had assumed the mantle though not necessarily the methods of Gandhi, demonstrated its commanding position by not only carrying the six Hindu majority provinces but also the predominantly Muslim North-West Frontier Province. Although it had taken part ostensibly 'not to co-operate in any way with the Act but to combat it and seek the end of it', Congress decided to take office by forming one-party ministries in all seven provinces. It flatly rejected Muslim proposals for coalition governments. Understandably the Congress ministries tended to look for guidance to the central Congress committee rather than to the new, untried provincial legislatures, and it was noteworthy that the senior Congressmen, like Pandit Nehru and Rajendra Prasad, themselves chose to remain outside the ministries and to direct affairs from the Congress centre at Wardha. In this way a remarkable, country-wide coherence of policy emerged in the Congress-dominated provinces. Equally noteworthy was the fact that this major attempt by the British government to establish in India a responsible system after the British pattern had produced a system which in practice was not recognisably British.

Most significant of all was the Muslim reaction to Congress policy. Never for long reconciled to any one of the various stages in the growth of Congress, Muslim leaders became alarmed by the scale of the Congress electoral victory, and by Congress's subsequent rejection of the idea of coalition governments. These developments, accompanied by the reiterated Congress claim fully to represent all Indians including Muslims and therefore ultimately to be the sole heir of British power, recalled to Muslim minds the dire prophecies of Sayyid Ahmad Khan about their likely fate under a Hindu *raj*, and as if to confirm their worst fears rumours soon came pouring in of Congress discrimination against Muslims. Whether the rumours were based on fact or not, the Muslims believed them to be true, and they at once raised the cry that their culture was under attack and that to attack their culture was to threaten their life. This modern communal struggle, in essence arising through a middle-class Hindu and Muslim rivalry for political and economic power, naturally tended to take the simplest expression of a more general religious conflict, and riots began to break out in the towns with such frequency that it seemed as though a sporadic civil war had begun.

The All-India Muslim League, under its forthright president, Muhammad Ali Jinnah, stood out as the champion of Muslim views and swept forward on a great, spontaneous wave of Muslim excitement into the position of *the* representative Muslim body. Congress policy had changed it almost overnight into an effective political force. Simultaneously its own policy underwent a revolution, swinging right over to reject the Act of 1935 and with it a British form of parliamentary government which, it argued, with its emphasis on majority rule and the maintenance of a strong centre, would permanently subordinate the Muslims to a Hindu Congress. 'There are in India', Jinnah declared in 1940, 'two nations,' and therefore only a separate, national homeland would remove Muslim fears and satisfy their demands. An independent state called Pakistan (meaning 'Land of the Pure') was demanded consisting of the Muslim majority regions of the north-west and of Bengal in the north-east. With this formal declaration the Muslim reaction to the Congress was complete and partition had become the fundamental issue of Indian politics.

Throughout the war period of 1939–45 the hostility between the Congress and the Muslim League hardened into deadlock. Both sides withdrew from government and several British attempts during and immediately after the war to produce a compromise constitution for a united India failed. But there was no longer any doubt that Britain intended to hand over power, and Congress in 1947, amid scenes of grave communal disorder, at last reached the conclusion that if the unity of India could be preserved only through civil war and the exercise of Congress force, then the price was too high to pay. The partition of India was agreed on and Britain handed over power to an independent Pakistan and an independent Indian Union. Both new states elected to remain within the British Commonwealth. Almost simultaneously Ceylon, which had waged its nationalist struggle more quietly and had gained from the struggle in India itself, also became an independent member of the Commonwealth.

Thus the British promise to free India had been fulfilled. But the British attempt to maintain a united India had failed because Indian society lacked a sense of coherence and did not wish to remain united. In these circumstances the application of British political ideas accompanied by British reluctance to face the task of creating a socially stable community had opened the way to division. Britain had fostered economic development, thus creating the conditions in which a middle class emerged. Yet, as soon as the struggle for economic and political power began, this middle class, lacking social unity, had acted in such a way as to make the partition of India inevitable.

3. SOUTH-EAST ASIA

At the beginning of the twentieth century control over the vast area of mainland and islands now known as South-East Asia was almost monopolised by the Netherlands, Britain, France and the United States of America. Of the four the Dutch had been established the longest and possessed by far the richest empire. With its centre at Batavia, founded by Jan Pieterszoon Coen in 1619, Netherlands India, the 'girdle of emerald flung round the equator', comprised the whole Malay archipelago except the Philippines, parts of Borneo, New Guinea and Timor. It stretched for nearly three thousand miles from the north-west point of Sumatra to the eastern limit of Dutch territory in New Guinea, its breadth from north to south was roughly thirteen hundred miles, and it had a total land area of nearly 735,000 square miles. In 1900 the reduction of the whole area to Dutch rule was still incomplete. Ever since 1873 they had been engaged in a costly struggle with the turbulent chiefs of Achin in north-west Sumatra which was not to end until 1908.

The British empire in South-East Asia was mainly continental. Its largest territory was the former kingdom of Burma, which it had absorbed piecemeal during the period 1824–86. To the south of it lay British Malaya, comprising the Straits Settlements of Singapore, Penang and Malacca, the four Federated Malay States of Perak, Selangor, Negri Sembilan and Pahang, and the five unfederated states of Trengganu, Kelantan, Kedah, Perlis and Johore. Two large portions of the island of Borneo were British protectorates—Sarawak, ruled by the nephew of the original raja, Sir James Brooke, and North Borneo, administered by the chartered company of that name.

On the Mekong River and along the shores of the South China Sea France had been busy, from 1859 onwards, carving out for herself an extensive Indo-Chinese empire. It comprised the colony of Cochin-China in the extreme south, together with the protectorates of Annam and Tongking, Cambodia and Laos. Over the last-named her control was still incomplete in 1900. The United States was the last western power to acquire any considerable territorial dominions in South-East Asia. After the Spanish-American war of 1898 Spain had been forced to cede the entire Philippine archipelago. Not until 1901, however, was American control finally established after intensive guerrilla warfare against a vigorous Filipino independence movement, which the Americans themselves had previously nourished and armed against Spain.

The kingdom of Siam was the sole remaining independent state in the whole area. For years it had maintained an uneasy, precarious existence between the expanding empires of Britain and France. King Thibaw's attempts to play off France, then conquering Tongking, against Britain had led to the extinction of the Burmese monarchy and the annexation of Upper Burma. Siam's hour of crisis arrived when France used her new position in Vietnam to snatch the Laos kingdom of Luang Prabang from Siamese suzerainty and push the Siamese out of all their territories east of the Mekong. British administrators in South-East Asia were convinced that the French regarded their empire in Indo-China as a base for further advances, into China on the one hand and the Menam valley on the other, and even into the Malay Peninsula. The 'Paknam incident' of July 1893 was undoubtedly staged in the hope that Siam would lose her head and present France with a plausible pretext for another forward move. Actually it brought Britain and France to the brink of war, for British policy was to maintain an independent Siam as a buffer state between the Indian empire and French Indo-China. Prince Devawongse's admirable handling of the situation and British diplomatic pressure on France preserved Siam's independence for the time being. Then in 1896, after Anglo-French relations had again been strained almost to breaking-point over a quarrel between their respective boundary commissioners on the Upper Mekong, the two powers agreed to a joint guarantee of the independence of the Menam valley. But not until the Entente Cordiale of 1904 was Siam safely out of the wood.

In 1900 a new age of colonial exploitation had begun which was linking the East more closely than ever before to the productive system of the West. With the arrival of the internal combustion engine the tin, rubber and oil of South-East Asia became vital to western economy. Private capital, directed by a few powerful corporations, was insisting upon the more efficient exploitation of colonies. Efficiency, in fact, was becoming the new administrative watchword, with Lord Curzon in India as its major prophet. But to the new generation of colonial administrators that was arising it was efficiency not merely for the sake of the profits of 'big business', but equally for the welfare of subject peoples. Kipling's 'white man's burden' had its Dutch counterpart in the 'ethical policy' of Van Deventer, whose article 'Een Eereschuld' (A debt of honour) in De Gids (1899) marks the beginning of the great change in the Dutch attitude towards their colonial peoples. Prosperity, however, was the pre-requisite of social progress. The potentially rich but undeveloped countries of South-East Asia were too poor to support the heavy cost of improved social services. Hence in making them a happy hunting ground for private capital, colonial governments provided themselves with means for undertaking large-scale public works and promoting higher standards of public health and welfare.

The native responded to all this activity, in which his own interests and those of capitalist enterprise did not often coincide, by developing a new national self-consciousness and a discontent with western domination, which became in time one of the most potent factors in world affairs. Western education played a preponderating role in this movement. The welfare state needed a large supply of western-trained natives in its administrative services, as also did expanding industry and commerce. The consequent development of secondary and higher education, based on western methods and using western languages as its media of instruction, produced all the effects that its opponents had woefully predicted.

External stimuli also were not lacking. The anti-western Boxer rebellion in China in 1899, the rise of Japan as the alleged champion of the rights of the Asian and her victory over Russia in 1905, the Chinese revolution and consequent end of the Manchu Dynasty in 1912, the rise of the Swaraj party and its struggle to dominate the Indian National Congress from 1906 onwards, all had marked effects upon the minds of the relatively small groups of *literati* in the different countries of South-East Asia. It was from their ranks that the leaders of the various native movements sprang. They taught the native that the much-paraded '*mission civilisatrice*' was a hollow pretence to cover up his own exploitation, and they substituted for it the rallying cry of 'Asia for the Asians'.

In the Philippines the awakening process had already begun before the American conquest, in spite of all the efforts of Spain to keep the islands *incommunicado*, hermetically sealed against the revolutionary ideas of the western world. The Americans loyally stood by their initial promise of the 'amplest liberty of self government'. From the start Filipinos were given high places in the administration, while a liberal degree of representative government was introduced both at the centre and throughout the local divisions of provinces, municipalities and townships. This entailed permission for the formation of political parties, most of which began at once to agitate for immediate independence. From the first meeting of the Philippine Assembly in 1907 until the Japanese occupation one party, the Nacionalista, maintained complete dominance, chiefly through the leadership of three outstanding personalities: the American-trained lawyers Sergio Osmeña (b. 1878) and Manuel L. Quezon (1878–1944), and the brilliant Manuel Roxas, a product of the University of the Philippines.

By the 'thirties opinion in the United States began to veer strongly in favour of Philippine independence, and in 1934 Congress provided for a ten-year period of preparation for self-government and permitted the summons of a Philippine Constituent Assembly to draft a written constitution. In return for these concessions the United States was to retain its military and naval bases, until full independence was achieved.

No sooner, however, were the Philippines well and truly set on the road to complete self-government than the international situation began to darken both in Europe and the Pacific. The Japanese invasion of China caused such alarm that Philippine policy took a sharp turn in the direction of closer association with America, and General Douglas MacArthur, appointed military adviser to the Philippine Commonwealth, began to raise and train a native army with the assistance of American funds.

During the first two centuries of their rule in Indonesia the Dutch were so eager to maintain their commercial monopoly that they paid no heed whatever to its effects upon native institutions. The *cultuurstelsel*, inaugurated in the first half of the nineteenth century, became the most effective system ever devised for the exploitation of native production, and yielded a vast colonial surplus, the *batig slot*, to the home government. Liberalism's prescription for the remedy of the evils which this wrought in Java was to open the door as wide as possible for private enterprise, again with no guarantee for the interests of the Indonesians. Hence the 'ethical policy' of the early twentieth century came as a sort of eleventh-hour repentance. Decentralisation was to be the method and the village community (*desa*) the chief means for enhancing native welfare. Little by little an elaborate village administration was built up. But so great was the degree of Dutch paternal control that it was impossible for anything of the nature of real village autonomy to develop.

The first signs of Indonesian nationalism showed themselves early in the century in the activities of the gifted Raden Adjeng Kartini, daughter of the Regent of Japara, whose letters, published in 1911, stimulated the release of a native spiritual energy which was a new phenomenon in Netherlands India. Both she and Dr Waidin Soedira Oesada, a retired medical officer, who began a campaign for the advancement of Java in 1906, looked to the spread of western education as the means of salvation. In 1908 he founded the first nationalist association, Boedi Oetimo, 'High Endeavour', with a membership mainly of intellectuals and officials. It was soon followed, in 1911, by an association of a very different character, Sarekat Islam, a popular movement which, beginning as a combination of Javanese *batik* traders against Chinese exploitation, became within a few years a revolutionary political party holding national congresses, organising strikes and demanding independence. The Communist Revolution in Russia in 1917 had immediate effects upon the situation in Java. An energetic communist section ('Section B'), closely in touch with Moscow, attempted to gain control over Sarekat Islam. Failing in this object, it formed the Perserikatan Komunist India (P.K.I.) and broke away from the parent body, which, although socialist in outlook, remained firmly attached to nationalist and religious ideals. In 1922, under the influence of native graduates from Europe discontented with the status of natives in the government services, Sarekat Islam established relations with the Indian National Congress and adopted a policy of non-cooperation.

The post-war depression with its crop of industrial disputes presented the extremists with just the kind of opportunity they required for bringing about the maximum dislocation of political and economic life. Moscow regarded Java as a strategic centre of the highest importance. Through agents in Singapore, contact was made between the P.K.I. and the Chinese communists. From 1923 onwards a series of revolutionary strikes, culminating in November 1926 in a sudden revolt, chiefly in west Java but also in the neighbouring parts of Sumatra, led the Dutch to take severe repressive measures. The communist leaders and hundreds of their followers were interned in New Guinea and the movement petered out. In the following year Dr Soekarno's Perserikatan Nasional Indonesia (National Indonesian Party), which had attempted to imitate the Gandhi technique, was also broken up and its leader imprisoned. Firm repression and a strict censorship of the press checked the Indonesian political movement.

Much of the trouble of these post-war years was the result of disappointment at Dutch unwillingness to effect any real transfer of power. Their high-sounding promises meant very little in practice. During the first world war, in response to insistent nationalist demands for a greater share in the government, a Volksraad was brought into existence in 1917, but it had a European majority, half its members were nominated, and its powers were narrowly limited. This development was associated with a general scheme of decentralisation in the provinces but the new system was slow in taking shape, and was completed only shortly before the Japanese invasion. It represented the utmost concessions the Dutch were prepared to make.

The rapid expansion of the motor industry after 1900 revolutionised South-East Asia's position in world affairs. In 1938 the Netherlands East Indies, Malaya, French Indo-China, Siam, Burma, British North Borneo and Sarawak produced practically the whole of the world's rubber and more than half of its tin, with the United States as the chief purchaser and Malaya as the principal producer of both commodities. The great expansion in Malaya's rubber and tin production was achieved by British and Chinese enterprise and capital. It involved so large an influx of Chinese and Indian immigrants that by 1941 Malays formed no more than 41 per cent of the population and were outnumbered by the Chinese. They remained for the most part tenant farmers growing rice, too proud to be interested in the economic progress which transformed their country, and too shiftless to use the more modern methods placed at their disposal by the British.

It has been said that there has never been a race less politically minded and less interested in economic development. Hence the main problem that emerged was, in the words of Professor L. A. Mills, 'how to reconcile the legitimate interests of foreign capital and the immigrant races with the equally valid claim of the Malays to a larger share in the government of their own country'. As most of the Chinese and Indians were only temporarily in the country, the Malays alone developed any sort of Malayan patriotism. Before the Japanese conquest this was limited to a very small middle class, which had absorbed a certain amount of western education. Resentment against Chinese and Indians played its part, as also did the religious revival which occurred throughout the Muslim world after the first world war.

Indirect rule in the Federated States was a façade behind which the Chief Secretary at Kuala Lumpur and his dependent civil service ruled as it were a single unit, and with immense efficiency. In the Unfederated States advisers had to promote co-ordination of policy by means of advice and persuasion. The Straits Settlements were under a Governor assisted by an Executive Council and a small Legislative Council, all the members of which were appointed up to 1924, when two British members, elected by the Chambers of Commerce of Singapore and Penang, were added. The non-official members included one Malay and three Chinese. There was always an official majority which was bound to support the Governor's policy. In practice, however, much deference was shown to the views of the non-officials. There was strikingly little demand for any change in this form of government. British and Chinese economic interests feared the results of any relaxation of control by devolution of power to the sultans, but British administrators were not happy about the situation, and in the 'thirties a very stiff controversy raged around it. Finally a decentralisation policy was adopted; the Chief Secretaryship was abolished in 1935 and some additional powers transferred to the State Councils of the sultans. In this way the responsibility for the co-ordination of policy passed to the High Commissioner and his 'mouthpiece', the Federal Secretary, while the prestige of the sultans was enhanced. Up to the Japanese invasion the Colonial Office in London remained firmly wedded to the policy of decentralisation, and further steps in that direction only awaited judgment of the effects of the changes introduced in 1935.

At the beginning of the twentieth century Burma was a province of the Indian empire under a lieutenant-governor. Its administration was very much like that of any other Indian province, with a handful of British civil servants at the top directing the efforts of a hierarchy of native subordinates, among whom there was a high percentage of Indians. The urge for modernisation and efficiency was making itself felt in a great expansion of governmental functions involving the creation of specialist departments, which inevitably transformed the older paternal system into a bureaucracy.

The Burmese are a friendly people, devoted to sport and to the enjoyment of their many national and local festivals, and their British administrators were on better terms personally with them than with any other people in the dependent empire. But they are also a very proud people with a strong national sentiment, nourished upon the stories of past greatness recounted in their Court Chronicles. Hence when in 1921 the provinces of India proper received new constitutional powers in the form of dyarchy, but Burma's case was deferred for further consideration on the grounds that her people were not ready for western democratic institutions, national sentiment was outraged and displayed itself with a suddenness and force which took everyone by surprise. The British government hastened to extend the measure to Burma. In 1923 she received a new Legislative Council of 103 members, 79 of whom were elected on a democratic franchise.

Within limits dyarchy proved a success. The new House had a solidly nationalist majority, but it was controlled by moderates, and the ministers drawn from their ranks were keen to use their new powers to promote measures of social welfare. But the nationalists were by no means satisfied with dyarchy; their insistent demand was for immediate self-government and separation from India. In 1937, when India achieved provincial autonomy, Burma's goal of separation was gained. At the same time her democratically elected government received so much additional power that, even allowing for the Governor's 'reserved' powers, the Burmese cabinet, composed of ministers responsible to the Legislature, had effectual control over practically the whole range of the country's internal affairs. The nationalists were still unsatisfied, but had it not been for the menace of war in Europe and the growing danger from Japan in the Pacific, Burma might have gradually and unobtrusively achieved dominion status without any major change in the framework of her constitution.

National pride gave the initial stimulus in the creation of French Indo-China. It began with the chauvinism of the Second Empire and continued as a reaction against the humiliation of the Franco-Prussian war. The French never felt quite the same sense of responsibility for the welfare of their subjects as the British and the Dutch. They were bent on exploiting the wealth of the region for the benefit of France. Next to that, but a long way behind, and largely through force of circumstances, came the desire to spread French culture. Any idea of training the natives for ultimate autonomy was utterly repellent. The royal houses of Annam, Cambodia and Laos were left with a semblance of authority, but all real power was in the hands of the French Governor-General, who was the head of a highly centralised administration.

There was a curious inconsistency about Frency policy; for while few French officials spoke the languages or could appreciate the outlook of the people they governed, a comparatively small coterie of French oriental scholars in the École français d'Extrême-Orient, established at Hanoi in 1899, carried out the most remarkable researches into the languages, customs, history and archaeology of Indo-China, to use the term in its widest possible application.

But against that undoubtedly great achievement must be set the ruin of the native land economy over large regions in order to promote French agricultural colonisation, and the creation of a rich landowner class exploiting the labour of an ignorant, apathetic peasantry. Under French rule Indo-China became, along with Siam and Burma, one of the largest rice-exporting areas of the world. It became the most profitable of all

France's overseas possessions. But the wages of the great mass of the people remained pitifully low, and it is small wonder that communism developed stronger roots in French Indo-China than anywhere else in South-East Asia.

The Annamites, with a Chinese civilisation, are the most advanced culturally of the peoples of the Indo-Chinese Union. Annamite nationalism began largely as the product of the French-vernacular schools established for the training of native subordinates. To counteract it the French injected stronger doses of French culture through the higher schools and the University of Hanoi. But the opposite effect took place, and it was commented that the bitterest opponents of the French were those who knew the language best. Thus when in 1907 Paul Beau as a concession to nationalism founded the University of Hanoi, such an outburst of the disease it was intended to cure resulted, that in the following year it was closed, and was not reopened until 1917. The French made the same mistake as the British in Burma of neglecting vernacular education. As early as 1910 an observer noted significantly that the 'curves of crime and European education rose concurrently'.

The Annamite nationalist movement became a serious embarrassment to the French after the first world war, when the educated official class was stirred alike by the western doctrine of self-determination and the Indian Swaraj movement. Communism also became a potent force, and by 1925 there was a revolutionary party, mainly composed of students who imbibed their communism from the Cantonese. In 1930 and 1931 there were small nationalist and communist risings in Tongking, which the French ruthlessly suppressed with hundreds of executions. For years the anti-French movement was driven underground and largely lost its effectiveness.

In 1938 Japan, having delivered China a series of staggering blows in her second great offensive, which had begun in July of the previous year, announced the 'New Order' in East Asia. As publicly proclaimed it had two facets, the one anti-communist, the other anti-western. Two years later, at the moment of German military triumph in western Europe, she announced the creation of a 'co-prosperity sphere', and invited the various countries of South-East Asia to participate in it. South-East Asia had by that time become, in the production of the food and raw materials required by modern technological civilisation, incomparably the richest region in the world for its size. Of all its parts Netherlands India was the one most coveted by Japan, but all her attempts to persuade the Dutch to participate in the co-prosperity plan failed, and Japan realised that only by war could she achieve her objective.

It is a fact of some significance that up to the time when she committed herself to her great southward offensive in 1941 Japan had failed to stimulate in South-East Asian countries anything of the nature of a nationalist rising against the western powers. Nor were the Japanese campaigns materially assisted by the nationalist movements in the various countries which they overran: nowhere were they welcomed as liberators. There were collaborators such as Ir. Soekarno and Mohammad Hatta in Indonesia and Ba Maw and Aung San in Burma; but there were equally sincere nationalists, such as the Sumatrans Amir Sjariffoedin and Soetan Sjahrir, who would have nothing whatever to do with the Japanese. The great mass of the people saw the tide of conquest roll over them with a sort of bewildered helplessness.

The astounding rapidity and ease with which the Japanese overran South-East Asia caused the western powers a loss of prestige that was in many ways decisive. But it was not long before Japanese arrogance and brutality, and still more their ruthless exploitation of native manpower and economic resources, made them feared and detested. Everywhere resistance groups sprang up, often led by European officers left behind by the retreating armies or parachuted into the various countries. During the counter-invasion of 1945 the Burma National Army, largely organised by the Japanese, went over to the Allies and played a useful part in harrying the retreating Japanese.

The capitulation of the Japanese in August 1945 came so suddenly that in two regions where the Allied armies were not operating, French Indo-China and Dutch Indonesia, there was a hiatus before Allied occupation could be carried out, and nationalist movements seized control, largely with Japanese assistance. Ho Chi-minh and his followers gained control over the puppet Annamite government, the emperor Bao Dai abdicated and the Republic of Viet Nam was proclaimed. In Indonesia there was an unavoidable delay of over a month after the Japanese surrender before South-East Asia Command could begin the occupation of Java. Moreover, the Netherlands had been so recently freed from German occupation that the home government was unprepared to deal with the situation created by the sudden Japanese collapse. The way was open therefore for Soekarno, supported by Sjahrir and Hatta, to proclaim the Indonesian Republic. Neither France nor the Netherlands would recognise the authority of the new revolutionary governments in their pre-war empires, and both made preparations to regain as much as possible of their lost power.

In Burma and Malaya the British were welcomed as liberators and within a very few weeks were able to restore civil government. In both countries, however, the experiences of the war years had created a new political atmosphere. In Burma the commander of the national army, Aung San, with the support of the majority of the people, demanded independence, which the British in 1947 granted, but in Malaya the divided state of society and the lack of a majority view left the British in control.

This survey ends with the year 1950, but the revolutionary changes that took place in the South-East Asian scene during the ensuing period were of such importance in world affairs that the years 1945–57 must be viewed as one phase. In 1946 the United States granted to the Philippines the independence promised in the Tydings–Macduffie Commonwealth Act of 1934. In 1947 Britain concluded a treaty with the Burmese, granting them complete independence, and on 4 January 1948 the Union of Burma was inaugurated. In 1949 the Netherlands and Indonesia reached an agreement which resulted in the establishment of the latter as an independent republic. In 1954, as a result of an international conference at Geneva, French Indo-China was divided into four independent states, the republics of North and South Vietnam, the kingdom of Laos and the kingdom of Cambodia. Finally, on 31 August 1957 a new Federation of Malaya came into existence as a fully independent member of the British Commonwealth.

4. THE FAR EAST

The nineteenth century saw the collapse of China before the impact of the West. The feeble defences she set up to defend her way of life were broken down in two disastrous wars—the Opium and the Arrow wars—and no sooner had she succumbed before the onslaught of Europeans approaching from the sea than the appearance of Russia on the Amur and the building of the Trans-Siberian railway brought a new menace on her landward frontiers. Russia clearly intended to absorb Manchuria and Mongolia and had designs on Korea which threatened the national existence of Japan. In 1894 Japan made war on China in order to forestall Russia in Korea, but her victory precipitated the Battle of the Concessions. European powers intimidated China into granting leases of ports and territorial footholds, concessions for building railways and special rights which would have had the effect of dividing China into spheres of influence. France and Russia together embarked upon a scheme for dominating the whole of China by means of railways owned and operated by foreign governments. During the previous fifty years bitter resentment had been roused by the privileges conferred on foreign merchants and by the constant use of gunboats to protect Chinese Christians and to enforce the treaty rights of missionaries. When to these wrongs were added the humiliations suffered during the Battle of the Concessions, resentment broke out in a last desperate but vain attempt to drive the foreigner out of China. The movement known as the Boxer rising culminated in the summer of 1900 in the siege of the foreign legations in Peking and the massacre of many thousand native Christians and many hundred foreign missionaries at a number of places north of the Yellow River. The legations were soon relieved by an international force of 18,000 men, of whom 8,000 were Japanese.

The punishment inflicted on China was a heavy one. The indemnity imposed on China was fixed at £67½ millions, the legation quarter was converted into a fortress and the foreign powers assumed the right to station troops at various points for the maintenance of communication between the capital and the sea. By the provisions of the protocol, combined with those of the unequal treaties of the nineteenth century, China was deprived of many of the attributes of a sovereign state.

The Boxer rising marked a turning point in China's relations with the West. The scramble for spheres of influence was felt by both Great Britain and Japan to be detrimental to their interests—but for different reasons. It was more advantageous to Great Britain that the whole of China should be kept open on equal terms for the enterprise of all, but Japan already aspired to the leadership of Asia in a movement of revolt against the domination of the West. Few, however, realised the extent of Japanese ambitions. There seemed, therefore, to be a community of interest between Great Britain and Japan; but after the Boxer rising the menace to their interests came, not from the scramble for concessions, but from the advance of Russia southward from the Amur. China, with incredible folly, had turned to Russia to protect her against Japan. In 1895 she gave Russia the right to build the Chinese Eastern railway from west to east across Manchuria, so that she might come more quickly to the rescue should Japan attack again. Then, when the Battle of the Concessions began, Russia joined the ranks of the despoilers, and secured the lease of the Kwantung promontory, including the naval base of Port Arthur and the commercial port of Dalny, together with the right to build a railway connecting these places with the Chinese Eastern railway. During the siege of the legations Russia took military possession of the whole of Manchuria. The British government then signed a treaty of alliance with Japan (30 January 1902) the tenor of which was that if Japan became involved in war with Russia and was attacked by a third power, Great Britain would enter the war on the side of Japan.

The decision to enter into an alliance with Japan was based on ignorance of Japanese ambitions and on a miscalculation of the relative strength of Russia and Japan. It was hoped that the alliance would deter Russia from attacking Japan and thus help to establish stable political conditions in the Far East. It was not foreseen that Great Britain's promise of support made it certain that Japan would attack Russia, that the war would result in a resounding victory for Japan and precipitate revolution in Russia, that her victory would make Japan the leader of a movement of 'Asia for the Asiatics' which, in the course of one generation, would bring about the end of western domination in Asia. It was not foreseen that Japan's aggressive attitude would embarrass Great Britain in her relations with both China and America and that the alliance would come to be regarded as directed against America.

America began by warmly approving the policy of the alliance, but after Japan's victory in 1905 the question of immigration into California suddenly became acute; and it was then realised that the Philippines, annexed in 1900, were something of an Achilles' heel. From 1905 until the attack on Pearl Harbour in 1941, the U.S.A. sought to divert Japan from the Philippines. She gave assurances that she would not oppose Japanese ambitions on the mainland of Asia but, with the rise of the national movement in China, it became increasingly difficult to reconcile this attitude with her traditional policy of friendship for China.

The primary aim of the national movement was to throw off the servitudes imposed on China by the unequal treaties of the nineteenth century. During the first two decades of the twentieth century the leaders of the movement were influenced to an overwhelming degree by the example of Japan who, in less than forty years, had transformed herself into an industrial-military state and was now recognised as one of the great powers. The Chinese nationalists sought to follow the example of Japan and set up a parliamentary democracy, with institutions of centralised control, in place of the traditional system under which each province, with its Viceroy and large body of mandarins, was practically as independent in its administration as a federal state in America.

In 1901, even before the signing of the Boxer protocol, the first imperial decrees were issued modifying the traditional system of education. Thousands of students flocked to Japan and America and—in smaller numbers —to France, Germany and England, and their influence soon made itself felt in the popular attention now for the first time paid to national affairs. In 1903 popular clamour compelled the resumption of the concession granted to American interests for the Canton–Hankow railway; in 1904 a nation-wide boycott of American trade was organised as a protest against the violation of treaties and the cruel treatment involved in the application of the immigration laws to Chinese, and in the same year the British expedition to Lhasa was the occasion of a most surprising display of skill and determination in the prompt and effective measures taken by the Chinese government to meet what they believed to be a threat to China's security. In the following year Japan's victory over Russia electrified all Asia and the Chinese national movement began in earnest. In September 1906 the first decree was issued on the subject of constitutional reform and eventually a decree of 27 August 1908 laid down an elaborate nine-year programme promising full constitutional government and an elected parliament by 1917.

At this stage the nationalist movement was still under the control of the moderate wing, led by Yuan Shih-k'ai, which aimed at setting up a constitutional monarchy on the English model, but in November 1908 the access to power of an ignorant, corrupt and inefficient group of Manchu nobles, consequent on the deaths of the Empress Dowager and the Emperor Kwang Hsu, caused the movement to take on an anti-dynastic and revolutionary character. Sun Yat-sen, the founder of the national movement and the leader of its revolutionary wing, had never wavered in his determination that the Manchus must be driven out. This had the unfortunate consequence that hostility to the Manchus became identified with hostility to centralised direction and control by the government in Peking. China's most urgent need was a strong central government without which there was no hope of securing the abrogation of the unequal treaties. Nevertheless, the extremists who followed Sun Yat-sen became fanatical supporters of provincial autonomy and it was this confusion of purpose that was mainly responsible for plunging China into the dismal period of warlordism and civil wars that followed the abdication of the Manchu dynasty in 1912.

The immediate cause of the fall of the dynasty was the issue of an imperial edict on 9 May 1911 placing all trunk railways under the control of the central government and leaving only branch lines to be built by provincial administrations or by private enterprise. This attempt at centralised control provoked armed rebellions which quickly became merged in a general revolutionary movement. Yuan Shih-k'ai, who favoured a constitutional monarchy, made a loyal but unavailing effort to save the dynasty. An abdication edict was issued on 12 February 1912 and Yuan Shih-k'ai, with the support of Sun Yat-sen, became the first President of the Republic of China. The enthusiastic supporters of the revolution naïvely believed that immediately the Manchus disappeared China would become a great power accepted as an equal by western nations. In fact she fell more deeply under tutelage than before and in two important matters—the Chinese Court in the International Settlement at Shanghai and the collection and disposal of the customs revenues—there was an immediate loss of sovereign rights more serious than anything suffered under the unequal treaties of the nineteenth century. Particularly the decision to allow foreign commissioners to collect the customs on behalf of China had far-reaching consequences.

The recognised government of China was the only Chinese authority to whom this customs revenue could be released or who could use the revenue for the purpose of raising foreign loans. The revenue increased greatly during the first world war so that any warlord who succeeded in gaining control of the machinery of the central government of Peking found that he was in possession of a prize of great value. Conversely it was a standing grievance with the Cantonese that, through the agency of the western powers, revenues collected in Canton were used against them by northern warlords in the civil wars that had now become endemic. The foreign control of customs revenues made it a matter of vital importance for Yuan Shih-k'ai to obtain the recognition of his government by western powers. He consequently abstained from raising the question of the unequal treaties but signed instead a document confirming all the privileges hitherto enjoyed for foreigners and in 1913, against the violent protests of the left wing faction under Sun Yat-sen, he negotiated a loan for £25 millions sterling from the international banking consortium organised to make loans to China. About one-third of the proceeds of this loan (the Reorganisation Loan) was used to suppress the short-lived 'second revolution' which broke out in the summer of 1913.

When the first world war broke out in 1914 Japan rightly judged that both Europe and America would be too fully occupied to interfere with her plans for expansion on the mainland of Asia. She first ejected Germany from Kiaochow and then presented demands (the Twenty-one Demands) designed to reduce China to the status of a vassal. When the Russian empire fell to pieces in 1917 she sought to extend her control over the whole of Manchuria, Mongolia and Siberia from Lake Baikal to the Pacific; but in 1920 her position began to crumble rapidly away. The defeat of Germany left her isolated in a world in which it seemed that aggression would no longer be allowed, while further military adventures had in any case been made impossible by the onset of the post-war slump.

This seemed to be a favourable opportunity to persuade Japan to abandon her grandiose ideas of empire and join with England and America in a comprehensive plan for the permanent and peaceful settlement of all the problems of the Far East. A conference of all the powers with interests in the Far East assembled at Washington in the autumn of 1921 and the plan was duly embodied in the famous Nine Power Treaty signed early in 1922 (see ch. xv). The gist was that the powers agreed to abandon aggression and competition for special rights in favour of a policy of friendly collaboration for the economic and political rehabilitation of China. This plan was based on the illusion that China would gratefully accept the tutelage of western powers. It was not realised that the leaders of the national movement had already turned to Soviet Russia and that in their eyes the Washington Agreement formed a convincing proof of the futility of seeking help and inspiration from the West. The treatment meted out to China at Versailles had paved the way, for on 3 May 1919 the news had descended like a bombshell on Peking that, in accordance with the terms of secret agreements with Japan, the treaty of peace with Germany contained a stipulation that the German rights in Shantung were to be transferred direct from Germany to Japan. From that day the national movement took a new turn, and by the time the Washington Conference met, the nationalists had already been attracted by the blandishments of Moscow. Soon afterwards Sun Yat-sen met emissaries from the Comintern who pointed out that the nationalists' attempt to achieve their aim by copying western institutions had plunged China into chaos, that reliance on the western powers had meant that China, after being abandoned at Versailles to the aggression of Japan was now, under the agreements signed at Washington, to be kept indefinitely on leading strings, and that Moscow was ready to show China how she might escape from both the domination of Japan and the patronising tutelage of England and America.

The effect of Soviet influence was seen in the reorganisation of the Kuomintang (the Nationalist party) on the lines of the Communist party in Russia and the rapid progress at last made towards national unity and the abrogation of the unequal treaties. Great Britain was the first western power to realise that the time had come when definite measures should be taken to meet the legitimate aspirations of the Chinese people. These views were expressed in a memorandum—known as the December Memorandum—which was communicated in December 1926 to all the signatories of the Nine Power Treaty. The memorandum urged that the idea that the economic and political development of China could be secured only under foreign tutelage should be abandoned and that foreign control should not be forced on China against her will; and that the nationalist movement which aimed at gaining for China an equal place among the nations should be met with sympathy and understanding, and a beginning should immediately be made by the relinquishment of foreign control and the abandonment of foreign privileges wherever this could be done without the negotiation of formal treaties. Without waiting for replies the British government immediately proceeded to take action on the lines laid down, including rendition of the leased territory of Wei-hai-wei, the return to Chinese control of the concessions at a number of treaty ports and, in particular, the relinquishment of foreign control over the Chinese court in the international settlement at Shanghai and over the collection, custody and disposal of the customs revenues.

This action coincided with the ending of the flirtation between the Kuomintang and Comintern. Sun Yat-sen had accepted the proffered help of Moscow on the express understanding that there was to be no attempt to introduce communism into China. But though the agents of the Comintern came with the professed object of assisting the Kuomintang in the struggle for the recovery of sovereign rights, their real aim was to help the Chinese communists gain control of the party machine, swing the national movement over into communism, drive the British and other western imperialists out of China, infiltrate from China into India and thus, it was hoped, start in eastern Asia the world revolution which had miscarried in Europe. This conspiracy was discovered just after the issue of the December Memorandum and the combined effect of these two developments was that the leaders of the national movement broke with Soviet Russia and adopted a more friendly attitude towards the West. There was no renewal, however, of the attempt to set up the forms of parliamentary democracy. The Comintern advisers were expelled, but the nationalists continued to profit by the ideas they left behind them—the ideas of the single party state and the dictatorship of a single party; the doctrine that the Party (Kuomintang) should establish and control the government, and itself be controlled by a small Central Executive Committee; the committee system of administration in both party and government; intensive political training for both military officers and civilian officials; the formulation of a definite set of political principles and the use of slogans, posters, cartoons, stage plays and other methods of propaganda employed in Soviet Russia. By the adoption of these methods the Kuomintang succeeded in gathering the whole of China into the nationalist fold with very little fighting. Opposition faded away and—on 10 October 1928—within two years of the issue of the December Memorandum—a Kuomintang government, the National Government of the Republic of China, was established with its seat at Nanking. Negotiations for the revision of the unequal treaties then began, but all hope of carrying them to a successful conclusion was destroyed by the renewal of Japanese aggression in China in September 1931.

Ever since she emerged into the modern world Japan had been obsessed by a desperate anxiety to prove that she was the equal of the great nations of the West. She felt it keenly that her people and her manufactures were excluded from the western world, and she therefore concluded that it was necessary to establish political control over adjacent areas in Asia which might serve both as a source for the needed supplies of raw materials and as markets for her manufactures: by 1931 the decision had been reached that the heavy industries that her empire demanded should be established, not in Japan itself, but in Manchuria, and in September of that year she resumed her attempt to occupy Manchuria. Without interference from outside she succeeded and in the Amau Declaration of 17 April 1934 announced that, as she alone was responsible for the maintenance of peace in East Asia, no other power or powers were to attempt to give assistance to China without first obtaining Japan's approval. The British government, nevertheless, made a last effort to induce Japan to return to the line of conduct proposed at the Washington Conference— the line of friendly collaboration with western powers to secure the economic and political restoration of China. The Japanese, however, had a quite different plan of their own for ensuring peace and stable political conditions in the Far East. This plan, which was foreshadowed in the Amau Declaration and which was to be known later as 'the New Order in East Asia', was the exact opposite to that propounded at the Washington Conference. The whole of East Asia, or Greater East Asia, was to be a co-prosperity sphere, with Japan at the centre surrounded by a ring of satellite states. The commercial and industrial development of these states (including of course China) was to be so controlled that their industries became complementary to and not competitive with those of Japan; and in order to make sure that the satellites would agree that their own best interests would be served by becoming members of the co-prosperity sphere a considerable measure of political control would be necessary.

A China that became prosperous and united independently of Japan could not be made to fit into this picture. The renewed approach of the British to restore China convinced the Japanese that no further time should be lost in bringing into operation the New Order in East Asia. On 7 July 1937 an incident was manufactured at the Marco Polo bridge, some ten miles from Peking, and the hostilities that then began were only brought to a close at the end of the second world war by the surrender of Japan on 14 August 1945.

It soon became clear that neither collective nor individual action against Japan would be taken by the interested powers, and in fact for the first four years of the war the U.S.A. retreated into isolationism and continued to supply Japan with two-thirds of the war materials she required for her war of aggression against China, a state of affairs which was brought to an abrupt end by the Japanese attack upon Pearl Harbor on 7 December 1941. China then became an ally in the war against Germany and Japan, and in December 1943 both Great Britain and America signed new treaties with her abrogating the unequal provisions of all previous treaties. The lead among western powers in the Far East had now passed definitely from Great Britain to America, but nothing they jointly or separately could do prevented the national government under Chiang Kai-shek from sinking deeper into apathy, incompetence and corruption. During the last four years of the war the communist movement, with no material aid from Russia but drawing great encouragement from the presence of Russian forces in contiguous territories, rapidly gained ground.

In a quick trial of strength after the war the communists easily ejected the Chiang Kai-shek government and in 1949 brought the mainland of China under their control. On 21 September 1949 the 'People's Republic of China' was proclaimed in Peking, and during 1950 this new communist regime extended its hold over most islands off the coast. Chiang Kai-shek retained power only in Taiwan (Formosa) and a few small island groups. At mid-century the people of China embarked upon a completely new phase in their long history.

CHAPTER X

ARMED FORCES AND THE ART OF WAR

I. NAVIES

THE nineteenth century had seen the transition from sail to steam for the motive power of ships, and from wood to steel for their construction. The designers of guns had produced the rifled barrel with cordite as the propellant to replace the muzzle-loader with its powder charge. These advancements resulted in greater accuracy and longer ranges, which in turn made it necessary for ships to be protected by increasing thicknesses of armour.

Underwater weapons were also making progress and the torpedo was steadily increasing its range, speed and accuracy. Most ships were fitted to fire torpedoes, but the greatest danger was from torpedo-boats—small, relatively high-speed craft—which could attack larger ships at night. These small ships, at this time greatly favoured by the French navy, were replied to by the British torpedo-boat-destroyers—really larger versions of the torpedo-boat, which eventually replaced their smaller antagonists and abbreviated their name to 'destroyer'. Mines, chiefly of the moored contact type, were the subject of much experimental work. The submarine also was still very much in the experimental stage and at the turn of the century was generally considered to be of no great potential danger to the larger surface ships. In the realms of communications, wireless telegraphy was just beginning to be introduced into ships and it was recognised that it would in the future play an important part in naval warfare.

While all these changes and improvements in naval construction and armaments had been taking place there had been an era of peace and—except for the Spanish-American war—no naval engagements had been fought. It was, therefore, a matter of profound naval interest when the Russo-Japanese war started on 8 February 1904.

The two fleets in the Far East were approximately equal in strength on paper, but the morale of the Japanese was far higher than that of the Russians. The Japanese task was to keep open the sea communications between Japan and Korea in order that their troops might be sent there. The Russians, conversely, should have done all they could to prevent this, but in fact they remained on the defensive with the false idea of keeping their fleet in being until reinforcements arrived from home. The Japanese made three attempts to block the entrance to the harbour at Port Arthur which was the Russian naval base—but all their attempts failed, as did their efforts to torpedo the Russian battleships at anchor. The Russians sank two of the six Japanese battleships by mines and themselves lost one with their Commander-in-Chief on board. When the Russians eventually learnt of these Japanese losses, instead of seizing the initiative, they still remained passive in Port Arthur. The Japanese sea communications therefore were not cut and the Russian fleet eventually suffered the in-dignity of being sunk in harbour by the guns of the besieging Japanese forces which they had failed to stop crossing to Korea. Later on a reinforcing fleet from Russia came out. This was numerically and materially superior to the Japanese fleet, but the morale of its sailors was even lower than that of the Port Arthur squadron. It was completely annihilated by the Japanese in the Battle of Tsushima on 27 May 1905. This battle was fought in poor visibility, mostly at very close ranges.

The main lessons learnt were the great potentiality and psychological effect of the mine and the torpedo, although the latter had not in fact achieved much success. This war gave a stimulus to the Royal Navy, and a drive to increase its efficiency was started. In particular, gunnery prac-tices were made more realistic and the art of fire-control came in for intensive study. Hitherto the general naval practice had been to build battleships with a mixed armament: in the Royal Navy this was usually a main armament of 12-inch guns and a secondary armament of 6-inch guns. This mixed armament added to the difficulties of fire-control.

The Entente Cordiale with France came about in 1904, and from then on Germany became the most likely enemy for Great Britain in a future war. Germany was already making a bid for naval supremacy by means of large shipbuilding programmes. This situation, coupled with the fire-control problem, led to the laying down by Great Britain of H.M.S. *Dreadnought*, which had an all-big-gun armament of ten 12-inch guns, and no real secondary armament. This ship outmoded all existing battleships. Except for increases in the size and the number of guns mounted the *Dreadnought* type remained the fashion for capital ships until after the second world war.

Between 1906 and 1914 British naval policy was gradually to withdraw ships on foreign stations—especially capital ships—and concentrate them in home waters. Much time at sea was spent in exercises designed to solve the problem of how a fleet with a large number of battleships, which whilst cruising was formed into many columns, could quickly be deployed into line of battle when the enemy was sighted, perhaps in poor visibility and on an unexpected bearing.

Another problem that occupied the mind of naval tacticians was how, once the ships were deployed into line of battle, it was possible to make a concentrated attack on a portion of the enemy's fleet. Lord Nelson had achieved this at Trafalgar by actually sailing through the enemy fleet and cutting off the van from the remainder. A similar manœuvre in modern times was impossible by reason of the speed and manœuvrability which steam had given to ships and the fact that with the new long-range guns naval actions were no longer fought at point-blank range. The tendency now was to deploy the battle-fleet into a long single line and hammer it out in a gun duel in much the same way that the old sailing ships of the line did for many years before the advent of tacticians such as Lord Howe and Lord Nelson, and before the production of a signal book made a breakaway from old traditions possible.

One method of effecting a concentration of gunfire on a portion of the enemy fleet was to manœuvre one's own fleet across the van of the enemy, thereby allowing the ships to fire their broadsides whilst the enemy could only bring the ahead-fire of a few of his ships to bear. This manœuvre was known as 'crossing the T', and at one period of the Battle of Tsushima the Japanese fleet brought it off. But on that occasion the discrepancy in speeds was pronounced and the Russian morale was already broken. With a nearer equality in speeds, an alert admiral should always be able to avoid having his T crossed by gradually circling away. It was generally considered that a tactical solution to this problem was unlikely to be found. A solution whereby two or more ships fired at the same target was therefore sought. To this end an experimental firing at the old battleship *Hero* was carried out in November 1907, but with the fire-control instruments then in existence it was unexpectedly found that a single ship obtained more hits than when two ships were firing together under similar conditions. Many years were to pass before this problem was satisfactorily solved and it became possible for as many as four ships to concentrate their gunfire on one opponent.

Connected with this problem was another—'director firing'. Ever since it had become possible to elevate and train a gun mounted in a ship, irrespective of the motion on the ship, it had been the duty of the gun-layer to keep his gun pointing at the target, and to fire it at the moment his sights were on. When a number of guns were firing this resulted in ragged salvoes and added to the difficulties of fire-control. With the advent of the *Dreadnought* type of ship it became highly desirable that the guns should fire accurately together, and to this end 'director firing' was experimented with and gradually introduced into the Royal Navy from 1912 onwards. By this method there was one master gunlayer, known as the 'director layer', who virtually laid, trained and fired the guns simultaneously from a sighting position on the mast, where he was clearer of funnel- and gun-smoke than the gunlayers in the turrets.

While solutions to these and many other gunnery problems were being sought, the possibilities of the submarine were beginning to capture the imagination of naval authorities. The opening years of the twentieth century had seen the experimental stages of the very small early craft, which were fitted with petrol engines. These submarines had met with disaster at times, but the general feeling was that they might one day be useful for the defence of coasts and harbours. Larger craft with longer endurance and fitted with heavy oil engines were built, and by 1912 there was even a school of thought which proclaimed that the day of the capital ship was over. The majority of naval officers, after seeing the good results obtained by submarines in the 1912 manœuvres, were of the opinion that the submarine was a valuable vessel which could be used offensively and would play an important role in any future war. All the navies of the world, whether small or large, included some submarines.

In 1903 the first aeroplane flew; but no immediate interest was created in naval circles. In Germany Count Zeppelin was by this time already building and flying lighter-than-air craft known as 'airships'. The British Admiralty were at first attracted to this form of flying and it was thought that airships might provide a means of long-distance reconnaissance. In July 1908 a rigid type of airship which was to be called 'Mayfly' was ordered, but she broke her back in 1911 and was never brought into service. In the spring of that year the Admiralty called for volunteers to fly heavier-than-air craft, for in the past eight years much progress had been made in the performance and reliability of this type of aircraft. Four out of many volunteers were accepted and started their training. These were followed by more, and in May 1912 the naval wing of the Royal Flying Corps (R.F.C.) was formed. Two years later this naval wing broke away from the R.F.C. and became the Royal Naval Air Service (R.N.A.S.), and remained as such until 1918. There was no very definite policy on the duties of naval aircraft in war. It was clear that they could undertake reconnaissance from the coasts, but only to a very limited extent, as their endurance was as yet small. It was also thought that they had special possibilities of sighting submerged submarines; but no offensive role was foreseen for the good reason that no aircraft had so far been armed with a gun or bomb. It was, however, expected that one day aircraft might be useful with the fleet at sea, and the first successful flight off a ship was made in December 1911, when an aircraft flew off a specially built runway on the forecastle of H.M.S. *Africa* (an 18,000-ton battleship with a full speed of 18 knots). This flight was, of course, purely experimental and the special runway put the fore turret of the battleship completely out of action.

The rivalry and competition among the navies of the world had the inevitable effect of spurring on designers continuously to build warships bigger and better than those of a potential enemy. For some years the design of battleships in the Royal Navy had changed little except for minor improvements. Their tonnages gradually rose from 15,000 tons to 18,000 tons, but their armaments of four 12-inch guns and twelve 6-inch guns and their nominal speed of about 18 knots did not change radically until the building of the *Dreadnought*, and until the probability of war with Germany became evident. The size of main armament guns then rose from 12 inches to 13·5 inches, and ships with 15-inch guns were already laid down by 1914. Speeds also advanced from the original 18 knots to about 22 knots, and in the case of battle-cruisers to 25 knots.

The older ships had for many years used coal in their boilers to produce the steam to drive their reciprocating engines. The first main change from this procedure was in the engine-room, brought about by the invention of the turbine. This enabled higher speeds to be obtained and reduced vibration, which in turn assisted in the accuracy of gunfire. The next important innovation was the change-over from coal to oil-fired boilers. It was natural that this should be tried first of all in the smaller ships, and in 1909 some destroyers were so fitted. When it had been proved successful in these the decision was taken in 1914 that all ships—including capital ships—of the Royal Navy would in future burn oil fuel only. The results of these two major decisions in ship design were to simplify maintenance, reduce the fatigue of the boiler- and engine-room staffs and thus enable ships to steam at high speeds for very much longer periods. Finally, it was possible to burn oil fuel without making any smoke, which not only had hitherto often given away the presence of a ship when she did not wish to be sighted, but was also a severe handicap to the accuracy of gunfire.

Such therefore was the progress in warship design in the early years of the twentieth century, before the first world war.

It has been stated already that the building of the *Dreadnought* with her all-big-gun armament had the effect of making all previously designed battleships obsolescent. This led to a shipbuilding race between Great Britain and Germany. The pace set by Great Britain was too hot—indeed in one year she laid down eight battleships—so that Germany was never able to catch up. Other nations changed over to the *Dreadnought* type of battleship in their normal replacement programmes in due time. Great Britain's naval estimates rose year by year and there were tentative proposals put forward for a 'building holiday' between her and Germany. These came to nothing; indeed in England, where the Royal Navy had for years been looked upon as the first line of defence, it was more a question of public clamour for the government to build more ships than of governmental cajoling.

When the first world war broke out on 4 August 1914 the relative strengths of the Royal Navy and the German High Seas Fleet in *Dreadnought*-type capital ships were:

British	German
20 battleships ⎫ in home waters 4 battle-cruisers ⎭ 3 battle-cruisers in the Mediterranean	13 battleships 3 battle-cruisers

Some of these ships would inevitably at times be absent from their fleets, undergoing refits or periodical docking, but it was realised that the

German Admiralty could select their most favourable moment for striking a blow and arrange that at that moment all their ships should be with the High Seas Fleet, thus reducing or even eliminating their inferiority in numbers compared with the British Grand Fleet.

We must now consider the main problems facing the British Admiralty and Commander-in-Chief. The first and chief decision to be made was 'What is the object of the Navy in war?' A school of thought had grown up during the long period of peace before the war that the function of the navy was to seek out and destroy the enemy's fleet. In previous wars this had not been so, but the invariable practice of the Royal Navy had been to place its main fleet in a strategical position such that if the enemy fleet moved out from the cover of its harbour defences it could be brought to action. The enemy fleet was thus prevented from interfering with British commerce on the high seas or providing cover behind which its light forces could work to this end. For example, in the wars against France the British Grand Fleet's strategic position was in the mouth of the English Channel, where it could intercept the French fleet from Brest if it was reported by frigates to be putting to sea, whilst the British light forces attacked French trade and gave protection to British trade. To support the fleet in this role many naval bases had been constructed along the south coast of England. The object of the Royal Navy in war was to secure the lines of sea communications upon which Great Britain was dependent for survival. The defeat of the enemy fleet was only one means towards this end.

In the first world war the Germans were obsessed with the idea that the British Grand Fleet would try to destroy their High Seas Fleet. The British Admiralty, on the other hand, had appreciated that the object of the Grand Fleet was no different from that in previous wars, which was to confine the High Seas Fleet to its harbours and be in a position to bring it to action if it should leave the security of its bases.

The second problem was therefore 'Where should the Grand Fleet be based in order to attain this object?' Whereas in previous wars the enemy had had his bases to the southward and westward of Great Britain, in this war he was to the eastward of the English Channel. There were no protected bases on the east coasts of the British Islands in August 1914, except Chatham, which was unsuitable for a large fleet. Rosyth was being developed but was not yet ready, so the decision was made to use Scapa Flow in the Orkney Islands as the Grand Fleet's operational base. A glance at a map will show that this base was well placed if German forces should try to break out into the Atlantic to the northward, either from the Baltic or the Heligoland Bight. The only other way out from the North Sea was through the Straits of Dover, which could be constantly watched, and the passage of which could be made very hazardous by mines and submarines.

Now let us consider the effects of these two decisions. Before the outbreak of war there were a number of British cruisers and smaller ships stationed in various parts of the world, and likewise Germany had a cruiser force in the Far East and one or two others also overseas. British and German merchant ships were ploughing the oceans all over the world upon their lawful business. When the war started all German overseas trade was immediately brought to a standstill. The British Admiralty took over control of the movements of British shipping and instituted certain precautions for their safety.

In peace-time merchant shipping of all nations tends, from natural causes, to flow across the seven seas on fairly well-defined routes which have the effect of producing lanes of traffic. Moreover, two or more of these lanes frequently converge into the same area when they approach land, and these are known as 'focal areas'. Such focal areas must obviously be the best destinations for an enemy raider or cruiser whose object is to attack trade, as he is likely to find more shipping there with less steaming about the ocean than if he searches in the wide, open seas. This assumption formed the basis on which the British Admiralty made their traditional counter-measures.

First of all, there are never enough cruisers on the outbreak of war to guarantee complete safety to merchant shipping against sporadic attacks by cruisers or raiders as well as to provide adequate forces to hunt down and destroy any enemy cruisers which are abroad and which may be trying to work their way home. The first step taken, therefore, is to order merchant shipping to break away from the well-defined peace-time traffic lanes and to proceed by routes which scatter it over a wider area. Not only is the commerce raider's task of finding merchant shipping thereby made more difficult, but he is not likely to sight more than one ship at a time. This procedure is known as 'evasive routeing'. It is not always possible to move the position of focal areas, as these are usually determined by geographical considerations—for example the mouth of the English Channel or the approaches to the Straits of Gibraltar. Therefore any cruisers available for trade protection patrol these areas as being the most likely places for an enemy commerce raider to be found.

In due course all German cruisers outside their home waters were sunk or destroyed and all German merchant ships (except in the Baltic Sea) were either captured or interned in neutral ports. British cruisers, under the cover provided by the Grand Fleet, had thus gained complete command of the seas. As a result of this, and the various skirmishing actions which had taken place in the North Sea, the German High Command then made two important decisions: (1) they would not risk the High Seas Fleet in a full-scale action with the Grand Fleet, but would keep it in being as a threat and possibly as a bargaining factor at the end of the war; (2) they must by some means destroy British merchant shipping.

We will consider here only the second decision, as this had the effect of altering all preconceived ideas on the waging of warfare against trade. By international law it was generally agreed that in war-time, first, neutral shipping had the freedom of the seas; that is, they could continue to carry on trade and were free from capture by hostile men-of-war outside the territorial waters of the belligerents provided they were not carrying contraband goods to a belligerent. A list of contraband goods, which broadly consisted of goods necessary to a belligerent for the prosecution of the war, was published by the belligerents on the outbreak of war.

Secondly, by international law a hostile man-of-war had the right to visit and search a merchant ship on the high seas, and if she was found to be carrying contraband then either she could be escorted to one of the belligerent's harbours or a prize crew could be put on board to ensure that she proceeded there. If the contraband was confirmed by a prize court she could then be seized in prize. It was also recognised and laid down that if this procedure involved danger to the safety of the man-of-war she might occasionally depart from the rules and sink the ship, if she could subsequently justify that this was done 'in face of an exceptional necessity'. A very important clause then added that in this event the man-of-war was responsible for the safety of the merchant-ship's crew.

As a result of British retaliatory measures imposed as a consequence of certain violations of international law by Germany, added to the fact that Germany had not the forces to conduct the war against trade within these legal limits, she made the momentous decision to attack shipping with her submarines. Because of her small size, and because she does not carry a boat, it is not possible for a submarine to carry out the procedure of visit and search or to put prize crews on board. At first the crews of merchant ships were ordered to take to their boats before their ship was sunk, but later the German submarines were ordered to 'sink without trace', which in effect meant that the merchant ship was attacked without any warning, as though it were a warship. This novel form of attack on merchant ships called for new methods of defence.

A submarine which wishes to make an unseen attack approaches her target submerged, but has to raise her periscope periodically during the final stages of the attack in order to adjust her course and to decide the moment when she must fire her torpedoes. This is the time when she is most vulnerable to counter-attack. In the early part of the war the only two defence measures possible for a large warship were either to zig-zag—that is, to make fairly large alterations of course at intervals on either side of her mean line of advance—or to have a screen of destroyers. These were placed in the best positions for them to see the submarine's periscope in the final stages of her attack.

These measures certainly made the submarine's task more difficult, but even then the only means of destroying her was by ramming. This was not often successful, owing to the deep submergence of the submarine and the inability of a destroyer to turn quickly enough. It was impossible to provide all merchant ships with destroyer screens. They were, however, gradually fitted with a gun in the stern when it was found that the German submarines attacked on the surface, using their gun, in order not to expend their limited supply of torpedoes too quickly. Smoke-making apparatus was also fitted to help a merchant ship to escape.

These were defensive measures which did not call for extra weapons. Meanwhile every effort was made to find some form of attack. The first problem was naturally to devise some means of detecting the presence of a submerged submarine. Hydrophones for listening under water were experimented with but were never really successful in a ship, as it was very difficult to insulate the instruments from extraneous noises caused by the passage of the ship through the water and those made internally by the ship's machinery. This problem was not solved until the end of the war, when a means of sending out a directional supersonic wave under water and receiving back an echo was discovered. These detecting devices were known as 'asdics'.

When a submarine had been found, the next problem was to destroy it. Many ideas were tried, such as towed nets with explosives attached to them, and paravanes with explosive heads. The best weapon in the end proved to be the 'depth-charge'. This consisted of a steel drum with a large content of high explosive fitted with a hydrostatic pistol which could be set to explode the charge when it had sunk to any given depth. Depth-charges could either be dropped over the stern of a ship or projected on either side by a 'thrower'. The usual practice at the end of the war was to drop a large number at a time over the suspected position of the submarine. Important harbours and anchorages were defended against submarine attack by boom defences from which hung heavy nets, by deep minefields which could be exploded from the shore if a submarine was thought to be in one, and by patrols of surface ships to seaward in order to force the submarine to submerge.

In 1917 merchant ships were being sunk by submarines at a greater rate than new ships could be built to replace them, and unless something drastic could be done it looked as if Germany might win the war by means of this unorthodox and illegal form of warfare. The effect was cumulative, because the more that merchant ships were sunk or damaged the more the shipyards were strained to replace and repair them, and the more the same shipyards were called upon to redouble their efforts to build ships, such as escort and patrol vessels and mine-sweepers, to combat the submarine and to convert more and more fishing craft to undertake these duties. It was not until Great Britain found herself in this plight that she turned to convoys as a means of defence.

There was nothing new about the idea of convoys. They were a time-honoured reply in the sailing era to attacks on merchant shipping by frigates and privateers. There was, however, a heated controversy as to whether the introduction of convoys would, in fact, meet the situation under modern and extraordinary conditions. The arguments in favour of convoys were three. First, it was not possible to provide every single, or even certain specially selected, merchant ships with an escort. Second, although evasive routeing undoubtedly made the submarine's task of finding her quarry more difficult, the fact remained that there still were the same number of targets to be found, and a too large percentage of these were met and attacked. Third, when merchant ships sailed singly it was difficult for the Admiralty to keep control over them even while they were still in wireless communication, and once they had passed outside this range control became impossible. All these disadvantages of the then-prevailing system, it was claimed, could be overcome by the use of convoys. First, each convoy could be provided with sufficient escorts to give it protection from submarine attack while in the danger area; second, the task of the submarine in finding a convoy of say twenty ships would be much more difficult than that of waylaying some of these twenty ships if they were scattered about on evasive routes. Although a convoy when actually seen appears to be covering a big area, it is in fact an infinitesimally small pinpoint when plotted on a chart of a large ocean. Third, as the wireless apparatus in an escorting ship would be better than that in a merchant ship, it would be possible for the Admiralty to keep control over convoys at sea through the senior officer of the escort, and to divert them from areas on their route which had been thought to be safe when they sailed but which subsequent intelligence reported to be dangerous from submarines or mines.

The arguments against the introduction of convoys were mainly four. First, the flow of trade would be slowed down, and this could be ill-afforded at that time. The reasons put forward to support this point were cogent. The normal procedure for a merchant ship on arrival at a port was to discharge her cargo as soon as possible. Her new cargo would then be loaded without delay, and when ready she would sail on her new voyage. If ships were in convoy a large number would arrive at a port at the same moment and might have to wait before they could be berthed for discharging and embarking their cargoes. There would also be a delay after a ship was ready for sea while she waited for a convoy to be formed. It was also held that there would be alternately congestion and slack periods at the ports which would adversely affect the internal flow of trade. Second, it was argued that there were not enough escort vessels to provide adequate protection. Third, masters of merchant ships were not trained to keep station on other ships, especially at night when all ships were darkened and showed no lights at all. Finally, merchant ships were not provided with the communications between the bridge and the engine-room which were considered essential for station-keeping in a warship. It was thought that the combined effect of these last two facts might be to increase losses by collision.

Experimental convoys were started between Great Britain and Gibraltar, and when these had proved successful a general system of convoys was introduced. The rate of sinkings immediately began to fall and eventually was so reduced that the danger of Germany's winning the war was completely removed.

Convoys were started as a measure of defence, but they were found to have an offensive value too. A submarine wishing to sink a merchant ship was now compelled to attack a convoy, and it was here that she found her greatest enemy—the escort vessel fitted with depth-charges. The rate at which German submarines were sunk rose.

During the first world war various actions were fought in the North Sea between battle-cruisers, but there was only one major action between the British Grand Fleet and the German High Seas Fleet in which ships of all types, with the exception of submarines, took part. This was the Battle of Jutland, which started in the afternoon of 31 May 1916 and continued into the early hours of the following day. The result was inconclusive, except that it confirmed the German naval authorities in their decision not to risk their fleet in another action but to keep it intact as a bargaining factor when it came to making peace terms. The command of the sea thus remained in British hands.

Some points of interest arose out of these actions. In the matter of tactics the British Commander-in-Chief, with Admiralty approval, had decided early in the war that if the High Seas Fleet was met it would probably refuse a gun duel and turn away in the hopes that the Grand Fleet would follow it. German destroyers would then attack the advancing British fleet with torpedoes. It was considered that the design of British battleships at that time was not sufficiently good to risk their being hit by more than one torpedo, and if the Germans employed this manœuvre the Grand Fleet would not accept the risk and would if necessary turn away to avoid the torpedoes. During the Battle of Jutland the High Seas Fleet employed these tactics twice. The Grand Fleet, in accordance with the agreed policy, did not accept the risk and the gun action was thus twice broken off. It had also been agreed that a night action between large ships would not be sought. Apart from the difficulty of recognising friend from foe, it was thought that the element of luck was too great and would outweigh any superiority in numbers, morale or material. It was found in fact that the German navy had made a considerable study of night fighting and had starshells, better searchlights and personnel well-trained in their use. Darkness fell after the High Seas Fleet turned away for the second time at the Battle of Jutland and the main action was then broken off.

It was only natural that after a prolonged period of peace failures in material would come to light under the testing conditions of war; an important example of this was the pre-war design of British shells. As we have seen, the range at which the Battle of Tsushima was fought was very short—from 5000 to 3000 yards. Gunnery practices by 1914 were carried out at a range of about 7000 to 8000 yards and it was thought that an action would probably be fought at about 10,000 yards. But the experience of war showed capital ships opening fire at 18,000 yards and even longer ranges. Now at shorter ranges a shell hits the armour on the opponent's side nearly at right angles, but the longer the range the higher the shell has to go in its flight, and when it arrives at its target it is falling at a steep angle. It therefore hits its adversary at an angle oblique to the face of the side-armour.

The first result of this was that the pre-war design of shell did not penetrate the armour but broke up on impact. This was not fully appreciated until after the Battle of Jutland. The designing and production of a new shell is a long process and the Grand Fleet was not fully equipped with better shells even by the end of the war in 1918. The second result was the corollary to the first, and was reflected in ship design. If a ship is to stand up to short-range attack by a shell which is thus travelling nearly horizontally, then the best position for fixing her armour protection is vertically on her sides. If, on the other hand, she is to be protected from gunfire at long range by a shell which as we have seen is descending at a steep angle, then it is desirable to place the armour horizontally on her decks. With the comparatively short-range outlook before the war the greatest protection was provided by side-armour. Ships were consequently often destroyed by shells which penetrated the insufficiently protected roofs of magazines and exploded their contents. As ships were taken in hand for refit more horizontal armour was provided, but even so they were considered to be obsolescent compared with ships laid down after the experience of the war had been absorbed and could be incorporated into their design.

At the end of the Russo-Japanese war the mine appeared to have an important role in a future war. German minelayers did in fact lay mines off the east coast of England on the day the war started and the Germans gradually developed a large mine-laying programme. The British naval authorities did not embark on a similar programme until much later, when it was decided to lay mines to prevent the egress of German submarines from their harbours. In order to achieve this, mines were laid in the Straits of Dover, off various harbours frequently used by U-boats and across the Heligoland Bight. Some were laid at a depth that would endanger a ship on the surface and others were laid more deeply to make it dangerous for a submerged submarine to pass. After the entry of the United States of America into the war a still more ambitious plan—to lay a mine barrage across the northern exit from the North Sea from the Shetland Islands to Norway—was started. It is doubtful whether the results obtained from laying mines on this scale are worth the enormous effort required both in manpower employed in their production and in ships and manpower in their laying. However, apart from the number of ships which may be sunk or damaged by mines, there is another very important aspect which has a considerable effect on the war effort of the enemy. In order to provide as safe a passage as possible for shipping, an extensive mine-sweeping organisation has to be created to search many hundreds of miles of channels daily. Such an organisation absorbs a very large proportion of the available manpower and a great quantity of shipping (mostly fishing craft) has to be taken up and converted to mine-sweeping purposes in the already busy shipyards.

With the end of the first world war in November 1918 came the surrender of the greater part of the German High Seas Fleet to the Allies. This left Great Britain with the largest navy in the world, closely followed by the United States of America and then by Japan, France and Italy. Both Great Britain and the U.S.A. had large shipbuilding programmes in hand, including capital ships up to 45,000 tons. All the powers considered their existing warships, which had not had the technical experience of the war embodied in their construction, as being out of date. There were thus all the signs of another shipbuilding race starting, which with the vastly increased cost of building would have been economically unsound in the exhausted state in which most countries found themselves as a result of the war. The Treaty of Versailles had moreover indicated that the great powers would have to consider disarmament at some later date, and this led to discussions as to whether it was possible to divide weapons into offensive or defensive types, with a view to banning the former. For example, was a submarine built for offensive or defensive purposes? Naturally no agreement could be found. The era of conferences for the limitation of naval armaments thus started, the more important of which were those held at Washington in 1922 and in London in 1930.

As a result of these conferences Great Britain renounced her former policy of a 'two-power standard'—that is, of maintaining a navy equal to the combined strength of the two navies next in order of strength— and agreed to parity with the United States of America. The strength of the navies was fixed as the ratios Great Britain 5, America 5, Japan 3, France 1·75, Italy 1·75. The size of a capital ship was limited to 35,000 tons, with guns of not more than 14 inches calibre; and similarly the maximum size for cruisers was fixed at 10,000 tons with guns of not more than 8 inches calibre. There were various other limitations imposed, such as numbers of, and in some cases the total tonnage allowed for, certain classes of ships; other types of ships, such as repair ships, depot ships and so on, were exempted, provided they conformed to certain rules. All countries had to scrap ships in order to comply with these treaties, but Great Britain was the chief sufferer in this respect (see also ch. xv).

One important effect of the imposition of maximum sizes was the decision of all nations to design their new ships up to these maxima, regardless of whether the resulting warship was really the most suitable for their requirements. It must be remembered that the design of a warship has to be a balance between the conflicting requirements of offensive power (guns, torpedoes, etc.), defensive qualities (armour and under-water protection), speed, and endurance (the amount of fuel carried). With the final displacement fixed at, say, 10,000 tons, only a percentage of these tons can be devoted to each of these requirements. Before the Washington and London naval treaties a naval staff could say they wanted a ship, for example, with twelve 6-inch guns, four torpedo-tubes, six inches of armour, a full speed of 28 knots and an endurance of 8000 miles. The ship designer would then inform the staff that the resulting displacement of such a ship would be, say, 11,500 tons. There is no doubt that during the era of 'Treaty-designed' ships many bad and unbalanced warships were built.

Efforts were also made to codify rules for the conduct of war against trade with particular reference to submarine warfare, after proposals for the total abolition of submarines had failed to get general agreement at the various naval limitation conferences. A convention which declared that submarine warfare as conducted by Germany in the first world war was illegal was in fact internationally agreed upon, but had not been ratified by all the signatory powers by 1939.

The Royal Naval Air Service (R.N.A.S.), which was formed just before the outbreak of war in 1914, had taken part in operations in home waters, France, the Dardanelles and Mesopotamia. Seaplanes were the usual type of aircraft flown, and successful attacks were made on Zeppelins, airship sheds and U-boats. Owing to the short endurance of the seaplanes of that period they were taken in ships (usually cross-channel steamers specially converted) to their flying-off positions, where they were hoisted out. This was not a satisfactory method because it was necessary to have a calm sea both for taking off and landing, and such conditions could seldom be depended upon. It is of historical interest that one reconnaissance seaplane flew during the Battle of Jutland and actually reported some ships of the High Seas Fleet. She was thus the first aircraft to take part in a naval battle.

A considerable amount of thought and effort was expended in trying to solve the problem of taking off and landing on the deck of a ship. It was soon found possible to fly the forerunner of the modern fighter aircraft—the Sopwith Pup—off quite a small platform erected on a cruiser. The landing problem took longer to solve. An old Cunard liner, the *Campania*, was converted in 1916 into an experimental aircraft-carrier and in 1918 H.M.S. *Furious* was likewise converted. The latter had a hangar and a flight-deck built into her, but she still retained a funnel and superstructure in the centre-line of the ship which divided the flight-deck into two parts. This was not satisfactory and after more experiments in H.M.S. *Argus*, which was the first aircraft-carrier to be produced with a completely flush flight-deck with no obstructions, H.M.S. *Furious* was taken in hand for similar conversion; but she was not ready before the end of the war. Broadly, the advent of aircraft into naval operations during the first world war caused no profound change of ideas in tactics or strategy, but a great deal of experimental work was carried out in a much shorter time than would have been possible under peace-time conditions. The foundations of future aircraft co-operation with the navy were firmly laid, although the relative importance of the various roles in which aircraft could assist was still open to considerable argument.

In 1918 the Royal Flying Corps was reconstituted as the Royal Air Force (R.A.F.) and this also embraced the old Royal Naval Air Service (R.N.A.S.). The Fleet Air Arm (F.A.A.) was composed of approximately 70 per cent R.A.F. and 30 per cent naval personnel. On the other hand, in the U.S.A. the navy and army each had its own air component. This led to a certain amount of controversy in Great Britain, but nevertheless considerable progress was made in the co-operation of aircraft with warships. By 1937, when it was decided that the Royal Navy should once more have its own air component, a high degree of confidence and reliability in aircraft as part of the fleet imbued most naval officers.

Aircraft-carrier design eventually became stabilised in the 'island' type. This design provided the whole length of the ship as a flight-deck with the funnel and bridge superstructure built on the starboard side in the form of an island. The possible naval uses for aircraft were: first, reconnaissance; second, the spotting of the fall of salvoes fired by ship's guns; third, the carrying of a torpedo or bombs; and finally, fighting. After much experience in peace-time exercises requirements for the first three tasks were combined in one type of aircraft, called a torpedo-spotter-reconnaissance (T.S.R.) aircraft. The re-equipping of the Royal Navy with T.S.R. and fighter aircraft was only partially completed when the second world war started in September 1939.

We must now consider the chief changes and developments in naval warfare which took place during the 20 years of peace between the two world wars. The first in importance was the reduction in the size of fleets imposed by the various limitations of armaments treaties. Great Britain and America were allowed fifteen capital ships each and Japan nine—a very large reduction from the seventy possessed by Great Britain in 1918. The numbers of cruisers, destroyers and so on were also reduced proportionately. The likelihood of ever seeing again a fleet comparable with the British Grand Fleet of 1914 appeared small. However, the principle remained unaltered that the battle-fleet, small though it might be, formed the hard core. This battle-fleet when cruising required an advance screen of cruisers to give it warning of the approach of enemy ships, but with the improvement of naval aircraft and experience gained in air navigation over the sea, this duty was more and more becoming the role of reconnaissance aircraft. Air reconnaissance had the advantage that it was capable of being pushed out to a greater penetration and over a wider area than was possible with surface ships, although it failed in bad visibility. From an aircraft the range of visibility for spotting a ship at sea has been found in practice to be no greater than that from a crow's nest on the mast of a ship. Moreover, it is not possible for an aircraft to prevent an enemy's cruiser from sighting a battle-fleet. A combination of air reconnaissance and cruiser screen was therefore considered to be necessary.

The Royal Navy changed its policy about seeking a night action; and after considerable improvements in the efficiency of starshells and searchlights and their control had been made, it was decided that a night action would be considered to be as normal an operation as a day action. Experience in the Dardanelles campaign in 1915 gave rise to intensive study of 'combined operations' not only in the realms of planning and command, but in the design of specialised material necessary to assist the navy in safely transporting and landing the army against opposition under modern conditions. Every country with a navy studied this highly complex problem and carried out exercises. The Japanese navy in its operations against China had the benefit of obtaining actual practical experience.

One of the deficiencies shown up in the Dardanelles and other places was the inability of naval guns, with their high velocity and low trajectories, to provide the army with a bombardment of the enemy's positions comparable with that which they normally expected from their own artillery, with its low-velocity guns and high trajectories. Whereas on shore the artillery knows its own position exactly and that of its target with tolerable accuracy, a warship whilst bombarding may have to be steaming about at fairly high speed, if it is suspected that submarines are in the vicinity: moreover, although charts gave a ship accurate information about the sea, the topography shown on the small amount of land normally depicted on a chart is a bare minimum necessary for navigation. This problem of naval bombardment, which plays an important part in a combined operation, was successfully solved with the help of all three services.

Since great progress had been made in the co-operation of aircraft with fleets, it was only natural that the counter to this—anti-aircraft measures—also received much attention. This problem was a new one, with two aspects, the offensive and the defensive. The first was the problem of destroying an attacking aircraft before it endangered a ship. This could be done by intercepting it at some distance from its target by fighter aircraft, but the technique of directing fighters on to an enemy aircraft in the air requires a highly skilled organisation, and this was not satisfactorily evolved until after experience had been gained in the second world war and more advances had been made in radar. Failing destruction by fighters, a ship had to rely on her anti-aircraft guns. This also is a very complex technical problem, and again was not satisfactorily solved until after considerable progress in ranging by radar had been achieved, and the actual experience of war conditions had been obtained. All ships had anti-aircraft guns and control added to their armament during peace-time, but the experience of war showed the need for more and more equipment; it was even eventually found necessary to remove some of a ship's main armament in order to allow more anti-aircraft guns to be fitted. The defensive aspect of the problem was partly material—for example, the fitting of more horizontal armour to prevent bombs penetrating the vitals of a ship—and partly tactical. Ships when operating together adopted a less compact formation than hitherto, and were individually given complete freedom to take whatever avoiding action they thought fit.

The last important development to notice is radar. This was produced with great secrecy, in the first place in Great Britain, to get the range and bearing of an aircraft by the reflection of a directional radio impulse. It was subsequently developed to give warning of surface ships as well; and later, as a very accurate rangefinder, was incorporated into the gunnery fire-control systems of main and anti-aircraft armaments. On the outbreak of war in 1939 there were only two ships in the British Home Fleet fitted with the early type of aircraft warning set.

On 3 September 1939 the second world war started. Again the British Main Fleet took up its strategic station at Scapa Flow. No German cruisers were stationed overseas, but it was thought that Germany's main effort would be directed against British seaborne trade. This proved to be correct, as from time to time German warships were sent out into the Atlantic Ocean for this purpose, and her submarines started sinking ships indiscriminately on the first day of the war, notwithstanding her agreement to respect merchant shipping. The British instituted the convoy system at once and this led to the continuous and bitter struggle between the German U-boats and the convoys' escorts throughout the war which became known as the Battle of the Atlantic.

At the outset the U-boats employed tactics similar to those of 1918, which were to sight a convoy in daylight and attack it after dark, usually on the surface. Later, after Germany had overrun the Low Countries and France, the 'pack' tactics were introduced. In this form of attack U-boats, spread across the likely convoy routes, would wait until one of them or one of their aircraft reported the position of a convoy and would then concentrate ahead of it and make a concerted attack on it, possibly some days later. Initially they gained some devastating successes, as there were not enough British aircraft able to operate long distances over the Atlantic to attack the German aircraft or to keep the U-boats submerged by day, thus preventing them from getting into the position of concentration in time. Nor, when the attack did develop, were there sufficient escort vessels to beat the U-boats off.

In 1942, as in 1917, the situation for Great Britain was extremely serious. More aircraft were then made available and the number of escorts steadily began to increase as the large shipbuilding programmes came to fruition. By this time, too, great advances had been made in the efficiency of radar, and in fitting it priority was given to ships and aircraft taking part in the Battle of the Atlantic. It then became possible to detect a submarine on the surface at night and in poor visibility by day, both from the air and from surface ships. The tide turned in favour of the Allies, the number of U-boats sunk increased, and the Battle of the Atlantic was won. Radar also played an important part in night actions. The enemy, invisible to the human eye, could be accurately plotted until a suitable tactical position had been gained, and then, by the use of radar gunnery range-finding sets, fire could be opened. Examples of this technique were the Royal Navy's successful battles against the Italians off Cape Matapan in 1941, and the sinking of the German ship *Scharnhorst* in 1944.

Perhaps the most interesting form of warfare in the second world war was the 'combined operation'. It was realised after the collapse of France in 1940 that final victory could be achieved only by sending Allied armies into Europe again. Since the Dardanelles campaign in 1915 the requirements of a modern army on landing had grown enormously; and it was now necessary for the navy to transport and put ashore heavy equipment such as tanks, big guns, large vehicles and a prodigious weight of ammunition, petrol and stores, as well as the personnel. The Air Force was also a new commitment, and apart from their petrol and stores it was usually necessary to land all the heavy equipment required for making airfields, such as bulldozers and metal tracks for runways. At the same time the strength of an enemy's opposition had been greatly intensified by the increase in fire-power possible with modern weapons, by land mines, by the possibility of using gas, by underwater obstructions off the beaches, as well as by air attack.

A large variety of special ships and craft was devised and built, and before the landings in Normandy in 1944 much experience was gained in operations in Madagascar, North Africa, Sicily and Italy. In the Pacific the Americans developed a slightly different technique in retaking the many islands occupied by the Japanese. These islands were mostly of the low-lying coral atoll type having steep beaches with jungle behind them, unlike the gradually shelving beaches backed by houses and cultivated land to be found in Europe.

Combined operations can be divided into two broad types: first, the overseas operation where large ocean-going transports have to be used for the sea voyage between the ports of embarkation and the enemy's beaches; and second, the shore-to-shore type, such as the Normandy landing, where it was possible for many of the special small craft to proceed, ready loaded, across the Channel under their own power instead of having to be transported to the scene of operations in a ship. Obviously, the greatest secrecy has to be imposed to prevent the enemy from knowing the destination and date for the operation and, if it is of the overseas type, the date of sailing and routes of the many convoys involved. No two operations will be similar, but the following moves would probably be necessary in most cases. Local superiority in the air would have to be achieved before the landing. This might be done by aircraft operating from carriers, or might involve a subsidiary earlier operation to capture a suitable airfield within striking distance of land-based fighter aircraft. There would then probably be a heavy bombing attack in the area behind the beaches, and a bombardment of certain strong points and of the beach defences by warships and specially designed shallow-draft gun-vessels. Parachute troops would then capture any landing-strips or airfields, and underwater obstructions would be cleared by specially trained men, such as frogmen. The beaches would be bombarded by rockets, carried in special craft, just before the landing of the first flight, which according to circumstances might be commando-trained men or swimming tanks. The army's immediate task after landing would be to push inland as quickly as possible and secure their first objective. This is normally selected with the object of preventing direct artillery and machine-gun fire on to the beaches. During this phase, and indeed until the army has sufficient artillery on shore, warships might be required to carry out bombardments of enemy positions at short notice. As long as ships and craft were unloading reinforcements and stores over the beaches, the navy's task would be to protect them from surface ship or submarine attack and to keep approach channels swept clear of the enemy's mines.

At sea the day of large battlefleets had passed and the dawn of the era of war by carrier-borne aircraft had arrived. Particularly was this so in the Pacific, where islands, often thousands of miles apart and occupied by the Japanese, had to be recaptured. This developed into a series of separate operations, all of which were part of one concerted plan for the final defeat of Japan. The American navy divided their ships into what were termed 'task forces', each consisting of a number of aircraft-carriers with some battleships, cruisers and destroyers as support. At the same time, because of the great distances separating their bases from the scene of operations, they decided that these 'task forces' must remain at sea for very long periods, often months at a time. To achieve this the technique of the 'fleet train' was developed. The fleet train consisted of a number of ships which carried stores, ammunition and fuel, for ships as well as aircraft, and which were specially fitted for discharging their cargoes to the men-of-war whilst still at sea. The American navy had given some thought to this problem in peace-time, but it was new to the Royal Navy, which had usually had a number of bases from which to operate. By the time the war in Europe had ended, a British task force complete with its own fleet train was sent to augment the American naval forces in the Pacific.

The Japanese Air Force towards the end of the war produced what were known as 'suicide bombers'. These were aircraft with a large charge of explosive, which were actually flown into a ship by a pilot. When operated in large numbers it was inevitable that some were not shot down and found their mark, which was usually an aircraft-carrier. Before the second world war Great Britain had designed her later carriers with an armoured flight-deck as well as some side armour. The American carriers on the other hand were not armoured, which meant that with the same tonnage they were able to carry considerably more aircraft than their British counterparts. As a result of the war-time experience of ordinary bombs and suicide-bombers the British design was amply vindicated, since after being hit British carriers were usually able to operate their aircraft again within a short time without having to return to a base for repairs. American carriers, on the other hand, usually had to leave the task force, and were sometimes destroyed.

In this 'era of violence', in which two world wars have been fought, the principles of sea warfare have not changed, although the methods of applying them have altered with the advances made in the design of ships and weapons. Above all, the second world war has re-emphasised the absolute interdependence of all arms, whether naval, military or air.

2. ARMIES

At the beginning of the present century the most considerable armies of the world were modelled on the system devised by Prussia in the middle of the nineteenth century and proved in the wars of 1866 and 1870. The chief features of this system, which was sometimes referred to as 'the nation in arms', were: universal liability to military service without exceptions or substitutions; as short a period of active service in the standing army as was consistent with efficient training, so that the maximum numbers could be passed to the reserve with the minimum dislocation of industry; and the perfection of arrangements for rapid mobilisation in the event of war, so that the largest possible army could be put into the field in the shortest time. These changes, which involved the practical disappearance from the battlefields of Europe of the long-service professional soldier and his replacement by the whole able-bodied strength of a nation, less fully trained perhaps but more conscious of national unity and purpose, were made possible only by the development of communications, railways and roads, which permitted the deployment and supply of such large numbers. The nature of armies in fact altered as a result of the economic changes wrought by the industrial revolution. Just as the hand-made article was replaced in industry by the machine-made, so it may be said that the hand-made soldier was replaced by the machine-made—cheaper, more numerous, but lacking a little in quality.

Of all the states which had standing armies of any size, only Great Britain and the United States maintained the principle of voluntary enlistment and long service. While it was the temperament of their peoples that rejected compulsion for military service, it was the fact that sea-power was their first line of defence which made this possible. For Great Britain the chief problem was that of finding large garrisons for her overseas possessions in India and elsewhere, for which long service was inevitable. Field-Marshal Lord Roberts's campaign, after the Boer War, for some form of national service for the defence of the home country was a complete failure, in spite of his personal reputation and popularity. Japan, although an island and dependent on sea power, had adopted the Prussian principles and maintained a large standing army, a fact which might have been held to indicate aggressive intentions on the mainland.

Rapid improvement in weapons and warlike materials was being brought about by the progress of science. The invention of smokeless powder changed the whole character of the battlefield; the small-bore magazine rifle greatly increased the accuracy and rapidity of small-arms fire, which was soon to be made much deadlier by the development of the modern machine-gun; and artillery fire had far longer range, accuracy and power. The effects of the internal combustion engine and its application to warfare were only just beginning to be realised when the first world war broke out in 1914; armies still moved on their feet, and were supplied by horse-drawn transport; the air arm was still in its infancy.

The two principal wars between 1900 and 1914, the Boer War of 1899–1902 and the Russo-Japanese War of 1904–5, had little general effect on the organisation of armies or the theory of war. The conditions of the war in South Africa were held by continental experts to be abnormal and the British army out-of-date; while the Japanese victories in Manchuria were considered to be a triumph for German methods, on which the Japanese had modelled themselves. The warning conveyed by the protracted nature of the operations went unheeded. The reforms instituted in the British army as a result of the experiences in South Africa were timely, and enabled Great Britain to put into the field in 1914 an expeditionary force equal in organisation and equipment, and superior in training, to any in Europe. In South Africa, too, dominion forces came into the field in support of the mother country for the first time and inaugurated the preparations which made possible the great effort of the dominions in the world wars. The casualties in the South African War from disease, chiefly enteric, much exceeded the battle casualties and showed the need for a greater application of medical science to armies in the field.

Meanwhile, the theories on war of Jean de Bloch, a Warsaw banker, had been attracting some attention.[1] He predicted the likelihood of trench warfare, but considered that the power of the small-bore rifle would make the storming of entrenchments too costly for troops to face, and that any such war would therefore end in a stalemate. His estimation of economic and other material factors showed insight, but he underestimated the blind determination of governments once committed to war and the resolution and endurance of the fighting man in the face of unprecedented losses.

The chief feature of the quarter-century before the outbreak of the first world war in 1914 was the struggle between the principal European armies for predominance in numbers. Germany set the pace: in 1874 she had had a peace establishment of some 400,000; by 1914 it had risen to 850,000 and there were available for war nearly 5,000,000 trained men. France with her smaller population strove desperately to keep on the heels of her rival; she trained every available man while Germany could still afford to exempt large numbers; in 1913 by a final spurt she increased the period of active service from two to three years, and the total liability for service from 25 to 27 years. Russia, with her almost inexhaustible resources in men, trained a smaller proportion with a longer term of service, yet had a peace strength of nearly 1,500,000 and about 6,000,000 trained for war.

The system which the spirit of Prussia—ruthless, efficient but unimaginative—had imposed on the armies of Europe had in fact made peace almost as tense a military struggle as war. The general conception was to place in the field the largest possible host of men in the shortest time and to overwhelm the adversary at once by sheer weight of numbers. Little manœuvre was possible once the great masses had been launched to cover every road leading to the objective. Thus the skill of the administrator in peace, who by minute improvement of mobilisation arrangements and railway time-tables could gain a day or even half-a-day's advantage in the initial concentration and deployment, might count for more than the genius of the commander on the battlefield. This meant also that the order for mobilisation was practically equivalent to a declaration of war, since no nation could afford to waste a moment in negotiation once one of its adversaries had set a light to the mobilisation fuse that led without a check to the explosion of millions of men from railway centres across the enemy frontier.

[1] J. de Bloch, *La Guerre* (6 vols. Paris, 1898–1900).

The German plan of operations, which was the logical result of their peace-time organisation, only just failed to bring them speedy and complete victory in 1914. They deployed enormous masses in a wide sweep through Belgium round the French left wing. The fortress of Liége, reckoned almost impregnable to assault, fell at once through the initiative of Ludendorff (then Chief of Staff of Bülow's Second Army and afterwards famous as Hindenburg's Chief of Staff) and the surprise production of the 17-inch howitzer from the Austrian Skoda works, the heaviest piece of artillery yet used in the field. The French plan, which involved a wild unskilful thrust at the German centre, was based on a supposed Napoleonic legacy of fierce assault that must always succeed if pressed with sufficient vigour. It failed disastrously with such losses as had seldom if ever before been incurred in so short a period. At this critical moment the calm resolution of Joffre brought about a quick re-grouping of the French forces and 'the miracle of the Marne', which showed that a little unexpected grit was sufficient to check the great war machine of the Germans and that the Germans were slow at improvisation to meet an unforeseen emergency. The British Expeditionary Force, small but efficient, was the grit thrown into the machine, which thereby probably saved Europe from German domination.

Long before the end of 1914 the stagnation of trench warfare foreseen by M. Bloch had set in on the western front: it was to continue for four years, which he had considered impossible. Neither side was prepared for this form of warfare, nor for a long war. For the Germans it meant what they had dreaded, war on a double front. They had intended to strike down the French in a short ruthless campaign while holding off the more ponderous Russians, and then to turn with full weight on their eastern enemy. Now they had to divide their forces. Their tactical insight was, however, surer than that of their opponents and they were quicker to grasp and exploit the essentials of the new situation, which was in fact siege warfare on a gigantic scale, and which should have been treated as such, instead of as open warfare at the halt, as most generals on the Allied side seemed to regard it.

Machine guns and barbed wire were the two new factors that gave such power to the defence; and the problem to which the attackers sought a solution throughout the war was to destroy the barbed-wire entanglements with which the defenders protected their trenches, and to subdue the fire of the machine guns sufficiently to enable the infantry to advance and assault the trenches. Some rusty old expedients were dug out from past wars and refurbished for modern use—the mortar, the grenade, and Greek fire, under the modern aspects of poison gas and the flame-thrower. Mining and countermining became a common feature of trench warfare as they had been of siege warfare. Besides offensive mining, defensive mining to protect the front line troops from the heaviest bombardment was initiated by the Germans, and copied less effectively by the Allies. Of all these contrivances, gas warfare was the most important. Its use violated international law, but it was employed by the Germans in April 1915, and subsequently by all combatants. Gases were asphyxiating, lachrymatory or vesicant, and were discharged by cylinders, shells or projectors. The most effective was mustard gas, which penetrated clothing and blistered the skin; its effect persisted long after discharge and could render an area untenable except with heavy casualties. The protective gas mask became an essential part of the front-line soldier's equipment. Though the Germans almost won a decisive success by the surprise, and in some instances the panic, caused by their initial discharge of a gas cloud in the Ypres salient, they were in the end the heaviest sufferers from gas casualties.

But it was chiefly by weight of artillery fire that the attackers sought to force a way through the trench system. The number of guns brought into the field was greatly increased, high explosive was substituted for shrapnel, which had been the principal projectile for field guns in open warfare, and heavy guns of a calibre up to 18 inches were introduced. In fact the 'siege train' of former days was brought up. But it was found that the prolonged and concentrated artillery fire necessary to destroy the enemy defences so cut up the ground as to make any rapid advance or deep penetration impossible. The solution was eventually found in an expedient that had practically vanished from the battlefield some three hundred years before, bullet-proof armour. It was the use of petrol as a motive power and caterpillar tracks as a means of cross-country movement that made the tank (a name originally applied for purposes of secrecy) possible. The designing and introduction of this bullet-proof vehicle armed with machine guns, or later with small quick-firing guns, with considerable power of cross-country movement, stand to the credit of the British. H. G. Wells, in an imaginative story written some ten years before the war, had foreshadowed the use of these land ironclads. The new arm was developed as a result of the initiative of Colonel E. D. Swinton (later Major-General Sir Ernest Swinton) and was backed by Winston Churchill, then First Lord of the Admiralty. It first appeared on the battlefield in September 1916, but it was not till nearly two years later that its influence became decisive.

Other new developments in methods of warfare were the use of smoke shells to screen the movements of troops and the introduction for the same purpose of camouflage or protective mimicry; improvements in wireless telegraphy for intercommunication; the use of sound-ranging apparatus to locate the position of enemy guns; and a number of other similar contrivances.

Such were the main developments in weapons and material, apart from the use of the air arm, which is dealt with in another section. As the war went on, the motive power of petrol became more and more the key to military strategy and tactics. The war had begun on a horsed basis; it was the last war to be fought on the motive power of the horse, which after 1918 disappeared from the field as an effective agent of man's death struggles with man. Petrol not only made possible the aeroplane and the tank, the two weapons which were to dominate the next great war, but also revolutionised the whole problem of movement and supply. At the beginning there were no more than a handful of motor vehicles in any army. But gradually the motor lorry was used more and more to transport the huge mass of material used in this static war. Motor transport did not at any time affect the pace or range of operations, since the great belt of fortifications across Europe proved an almost impenetrable barrier to the end; and the motor vehicles of the day had no power of cross-country movement but were confined to the roads. Even in the final advance the pace was that of the marching foot-soldier, and the range of a day's operations was that of his day's march, except in Allenby's great cavalry manœuvre in Palestine in 1918.

In this siege warfare on the western front generalship was at a discount. There were no flanks to turn or threaten, no manœuvre was possible, and the art of the commander was confined to selection of the front on which to mass guns and troops in an effort to break through by sheer weight of men and metal. The possibilities of the new weapon, the tank, and the best means to make use of it, were not fully realised by any commander. On the eastern front—Russia against Austria and Germany—much the same situation developed, though the fronts were less closely locked. It was only the campaigns against Turkey, in the Caucasus (Russia), and in Mesopotamia, Palestine and Syria (Great Britain), that gave some scope for manœuvre and mobile warfare and for exercise of the art of generalship. Allenby's campaigns in 1917 and 1918 for the capture of Jerusalem and for the final advance to Damascus and Aleppo were the most remarkable. These campaigns included the last great exploits of cavalry and showed the value of mobility, both tactical and strategical, that the course of the warfare in Europe had tended to obscure.

Amphibious warfare, the landing of troops from the sea on open beaches to seize areas of tactical advantage, had always been a feature of British strategy. It was represented in this war by the two landings on the Gallipoli Peninsula, at Helles and at Suvla Bay. Although on both occasions the troops effected a landing, the campaign was a failure. The only new method introduced was the running ashore of a large steamer, the *River Clyde*, filled with troops, at the point of Cape Helles.

The problem of co-operation or combined command between the Allied forces caused much difficulty and considerable friction. The French regarded themselves by reason of their greater numbers and military reputation as entitled to take the lead in direction. But for a long time the British

Expeditionary Force remained an independent army responsible only to its own government. In 1917 the British Prime Minister, Lloyd George, attempted to place the British forces in France under French command for Nivelle's ill-starred offensive. After its failure the British army resumed for all practical purposes its independent status. Later the Supreme War Council was established at Versailles. It served as a useful clearing-house for the plans of the Allies, which now included the United States and Italy; but the attempt by an Executive War Board of the Council to direct operations in the field was a failure. It required the crisis of March 1918, caused by the German break-through, to produce unity of command under Foch. There was, however, no integrated staff, and Foch's control was general and indirect.

On the other side, the Germans attempted to ride rough-shod over their Turkish allies, and to place German generals and staff in direct control of their operations. The result was great resentment and ill-feeling.

Developments in the manpower problem which took place in the 1914–18 war were far-reaching. The war started on the assumption by all the powers concerned that it would be a short one; and that it would be decided before the trained reserves of young men had all been employed and before the stock of munitions accumulated in peace-time had been exhausted. The Germans, in the hope of a quick ending, used their surplus reservists at once to form new corps to add to the weight of their first blow; and this was almost decisive. But as the war went on and the hopes of a speedy end were falsified, the whole manpower of the nations engaged was drawn into war work, either in the field or in the factories. Long before the end, war had ceased to be an affair of the armed forces alone; it had become the business of the whole nation. And for the first time women also were organised on a large scale for war purposes, and played a considerable part. All sections of the nation and all classes were affected. Industry was harnessed to the making of munitions on an unexampled scale. Chemistry was enlisted for new explosives, new poison gases or their antidotes, and similar inventions. Even the press and literature took part in the spreading of propaganda, which grew into a deadly weapon aimed at men's minds and morale.

The replacement of casualties in the field and the formation of fresh units was a comparatively simple matter for nations which had already a system of compulsory service in peace, although the battle wastage was on a much higher scale than had ever been expected. For Great Britain and her Dominions, and later the United States of America, the problem was more complicated. Great Britain, after raising over 2,000,000 men by voluntary enlistment, passed reluctantly to conscription, after the compromises of national registration and what was called the Derby Scheme, early in 1916. Canada retained the voluntary principle till May

1917; Australia never adopted conscription during that war. The United States passed a compulsory service act on her entry into the war in April 1917.

In the raising of new units and formations, Great Britain neglected the plain teaching of history that it is better to expand an existing force than to create a new one. It would have saved much difficulty of administration had expansion taken place on the Territorial Force (which in July 1914 had a strength of just on 270,000), through the medium of the County Associations, as Lord Haldane its creator had intended. But in 1914 the Minister of War, Lord Kitchener, formed an entirely fresh force, the New Army. Another mistake was made in not preserving as many as possible of the trained officers and non-commissioned officers to instruct the new levies. It was of course inevitable that the regular divisions of the original Expeditionary Force should go forth fully manned; and the losses of trained officers and men in the first months had to be accepted, though grievous. But in the first winter, many precious lives of fully trained men were squandered in the mud and blood of trench warfare when they might have been saved to guide and instruct the new armies. Also many young men of the experience and education to fit them as officers and leaders were allowed to enlist in the ranks and to be lost prematurely. The selection of officers was made by the War Office on the recommendation of superior officers or of civilians of high standing. Men were not required to pass through the ranks before being commissioned; but a large number of senior non-commissioned officers were promoted to commissioned rank. The system was simple and on the whole worked well. The Officers Training Corps at schools and universities, which had been established as part of the Haldane reforms after the South African War, proved invaluable. Its strength in 1914 was some 27,000.

The circumstances of the war, the deadlock in the main theatre, were favourable to the formation and training of new forces, in that they could be introduced gradually into the conflict, instead of having to be thrust hurriedly into battle, as for instance were the new French levies of 1871. In addition, the conditions of trench warfare did not demand as high a standard of training as open warfare.

Casualties reached unprecedented numbers. In a single day's battle, the opening of the Allied offensive on the Somme on 1 July 1916, the British Army had nearly 60,000 casualties, of whom almost 20,000 were killed; while the losses of the French and Germans on the same day were also very heavy. In the five months that this battle lasted the British casualties were over 400,000, those of the French some 200,000; their adversaries the Germans probably lost nearly 500,000 in the same period. The approximate figures of those who were killed or died of wounds in this deadly war are as follows:

British Empire	1,000,000
France	1,500,000
Italy	500,000
Russia	2,000,000–3,000,000
U.S.A.	100,000
Germany	2,000,000
Austria-Hungary	1,250,000
Turkey	500,000

The above figures are largely conjectural, especially as regards Russia, Turkey and Austria-Hungary, where no complete records are available. At least 10,000,000 men of all nations lost their lives, and three times as many were wounded, of whom many were maimed for life.

It can be argued with some reason that the British loss was the most grievous of all; not only was it higher in proportion to population than that of the other combatants, but since the British clung to the voluntary principle for the first part of the war, it fell more unevenly on the best part of the nation, those who had at once volunteered for service in combatant units. It is doubtful whether Great Britain has ever wholly recovered from the holocaust of her best and most gallant sons, the greater part of a complete generation being lost or maimed in the grim struggle by sea and land and air.

For the first time in history coloured troops were used in warfare on the continent of Europe; the French used their Senegalese troops in large numbers, the British brought to France in 1914 an Indian Expeditionary Force of two divisions.

An interesting innovation in discipline was brought into the British army by the Suspension of Sentences Act in 1915, whereby a soldier's sentence by court-martial might be suspended, and might eventually be reduced or cancelled as a result of good service. It was originally introduced to check an unnecessary waste of fighting manpower; it was found to be a success and was retained in peace-time.

The changes in the organisation of armies were less marked than the developments in weapons and equipment. The division, the army corps and the army underwent no great change in functions or composition other than came naturally from the stagnancy of the operations. In the proportion of fighting arms, artillery was almost doubled and rose to approximately 10 guns per 1000 rifles, while the numbers and value of cavalry declined. Infantry remained the principal arm, but it was a lame infantry, overwhelmed with equipment (such as grenades, gas-masks, sandbags, entrenching tools in addition to the normal rifle, ammunition and rations), able only to hobble slowly forward on the crutches of artillery or tanks and propped up by machine-guns in defence. By 1916 the weight of the infantryman's load had risen to 66 lb, often more than half his body-weight, while that proverbial beast of burden the army mule was expected to carry only one-third of its body-weight. The British made their machine-gunners and tank personnel into separate corps. The proportion of engineer units was also greatly increased.

Behind the fighting troops the proportion of rearward services grew abnormally owing to the static and complex nature of the war. Units were formed for such duties as camouflage, salvage and repair of equipment, cleaning and disinfecting men and clothing, meteorological forecasts and other purposes not formerly part of the war machine. The health and comfort of the soldier were cared for as never before. As a result the proportion of men in administrative services to the fighting troops greatly increased. Of a little over 2,000,000 American troops on the western front at the time of the armistice, over 650,000 were employed on the line of communications.

As was only natural after so tremendous a struggle, the period following the end of the war was unfavourable to any further development of armies or of the art of war. The defeated armies of Germany, Austria, Turkey, Bulgaria had to comply with the dictates of the conquerors, who were determined to reduce them to the lowest possible level in numbers and armament. The victorious nations were anxious to reduce their own military commitments for the sake of economy. Demobilisation of armed forces was rapid, except in Russia where civil war continued for a further two years. The British Chiefs of Staff Committee, set up in 1924, was the main improvement in organisation resulting from war-time experience.

There is interest from the social and psychological point of view in the demobilisation scheme of the British forces. An elaborate plan had been prepared before the end of the war, mainly with a view to the rehabilitation of industry as soon as possible, priority being given to the release of those most useful for restarting commercial activities. On paper the plan had much merit, but in practice it meant that many of those who had been last to enter the armed forces, and that only by compulsion, stood higher for release than others who had volunteered and had served for longer periods. The men still serving showed unmistakably that they considered such discrimination unfair, there were disturbances in some centres, and the scheme had to be drastically modified. The human factor had been under-rated by the bureaucrats.

Great Britain and the United States returned almost at once, like swords dropping back into their scabbards, to their former practice of voluntary service—a small professional first-line army and a half-trained citizen force as the second line. The principle of voluntary service was also forcibly applied to the defeated, with the idea of eradicating the 'nation in arms' theory; long service of not less than twelve years was imposed with the idea of preventing a reserve being built up; numbers were strictly limited, the German forces were not to exceed 100,000; and aircraft, tanks and heavy artillery were forbidden. Disarmament com- missions of Allied officers were formed in the conquered countries to enforce these terms and to destroy all military equipment above the scale allowed. The German General Staff was declared to be dissolved. As became evident later, the Germans showed much skill and purpose in evading the terms of disarmament both in spirit and in letter.

The French army became the dominant military force in Europe. France had suffered German invasion too often and too recently to trust her neighbour. When she failed to secure the frontier of the Rhine at the peace battle, and when the United States refused to ratify the guarantee of assistance given by President Wilson as a substitute, France deter- mined to remain on guard fully armed. She also armed and to some extent trained the new 'successor states'—Poland, Czechoslovakia, Yugo- slavia, Greater Roumania—as allies against a German revival.

In the peace treaties the principle was implicit that universal reduction of armaments to the lowest level should be the sequel to the disarmament of the defeated nations. The story of the long discussions in the League of Nations is political rather than military, and hinged mainly on the problem of security.[1] But the difficulties of finding a practical standard of comparison between the forces maintained by various states and of deciding on the means of limitation were clearly shown. In the first place modern war involves the whole strength of a nation and factors which obviously cannot be limited, such as industrial development, financial strength, resources in raw material, growth of population. There was much argument as to how far the ultimate war potential of a nation was to be taken into account in calculating the armaments and forces to be maintained in peace. It was also difficult to find an agreed standard of comparison between personnel (for instance, whether a long-service volun- teer was to count more than a short-term conscript) and between the various forms of armament (such as, how tanks should be compared with artillery). It was also found practically impossible to reduce to a common denominator the sums actually spent by the various nations on their armed forces, or to arrange for an acceptable system of investigation and supervision of each country's preparations for war. Generally speak- ing, France had no intention of reducing her armaments so long as there remained the least danger from Germany; Great Britain and the U.S.A. had already reduced theirs to even less than their pre-war strength; Russia, though exhausted by civil war, was organising large forces; and Germany, while making every effort to secure the disarmament of the nations which had defeated her, was secretly preparing to re-arm as soon as opportunity arose. A scheme of 'qualitative' disarmament, that is, the prohibition of weapons most likely to give the aggressor the advantage (for example, tanks and heavy artillery), almost won acceptance; but after years of

[1] See below, ch. XVII.

265

fruitless discussion all hopes of universal disarmament had practically ended by 1933 when Germany left the League of Nations. Both statesmen and military experts had failed to solve the problem of limitation of armed forces.

Meanwhile progress in the art of war also remained stagnant. With the eclipse of the German General Staff, the French were accepted as the arbiters of military progress; and the logical mind of the French is apt to run to extremes. Twice in the first world war, at the very beginning and in Nivelle's offensive in 1917, they had put their faith in an 'all-out' attack designed by its very fury to sweep all before it after the Napoleonic pattern; and had on each occasion suffered the most shattering and costly defeat. Now they went to the other extreme, concentrated heavily on the defence, and decided that any advance could be made only by the most deliberate methods, after the concentration of an overpowering artillery at the point of attack. Rapid manœuvre seemed to be ruled out of their conception of warfare. Their defensive obsession culminated in the building of the Maginot Line of permanent works, begun in 1930 to cover their eastern frontier, but never fully completed.

Some British commanders and a number of junior officers had a livelier and more imaginative prevision of future tactics, and advocated the development of the armoured vehicle, the tank, a British invention which had done much to win the war. They succeeded in so far that in 1927 the first armoured force was formed on Salisbury Plain; and a little later an experimental infantry brigade, wholly mechanised and with armoured carriers for machine-guns and mortars, was formed at Aldershot. But the dead hand of finance, especially after the crisis of 1931, and a lack of imagination in the higher ranks, prevented any real development of mechanised warfare, and the British army lost the lead in tactics which the invention of the tank might have given it. The experimental armoured force was broken up in 1928; a tank brigade was formed in 1934; but it was not until 1937 that the formation of an armoured division took place. This was still incomplete and ill-equipped when war broke out in 1939. Meanwhile the United States army was also making experiments in armoured warfare, its handicap being the smallness of the regular army and the national lack of interest in the armed forces.

It was left to two nations which had suffered defeat in the war to put into practice fresh ideas in tactics and equipment. The Russian army was the first to experiment with airborne troops and parachutists, to be dropped behind the enemy lines or far in advance of the normal troops to secure some point of great tactical importance, though it was the Germans who first put the idea into practice in war. Russia also developed the manufacture of tanks on a large scale. It was in Germany that the conception of 'Blitzkrieg' was developed, of a break-through and rapid penetration by an entirely armoured force, supported and partly supplied from the air, which was to change the whole character of warfare, and was to make the second world war as remarkable for swift deep strokes as the first war had been for sluggishness. The Germans, admittedly, owed their ideas largely to the experiments which had been made in the British army, and to the works of British military writers, such as Captain B. H. Liddell Hart and Major-General J. F. C. Fuller.

Progress in equipment during this period consisted rather in development and improvement of the weapons of the first world war than in the introduction of any fresh ones. The speed, armour, and armament of tanks were increased; and as a consequence anti-tank guns were included in the organisation of formations, either as infantry weapons or in special artillery units. Mortars which had been used in trench warfare were adapted for use in the field to give the infantry additional close support. To meet the increasing menace from the air, the number of anti-aircraft guns was greatly increased and their performance improved. Dispersion and camouflage also received much attention as means of lessening the danger from the air. It was believed that the weapon of poison gas would be used on a much larger scale, and means of protection received extensive study. Transport was mechanised in the armies of those countries which could afford the expense, and a high capacity for cross-country movement was given to mechanical vehicles by such devices as the provision of six wheels instead of four.

On the human side, two developments in the British army deserve mention. The death penalty for desertion in the field, cowardice in the face of the enemy and one or two similar military crimes was abolished. During 1914–18 some 3000 death sentences had been imposed for these offences, of which about 350 had been carried out. This mitigation of the military code was undoubtedly in accord with public opinion, though it resulted in a very large increase in the number of desertions in the second world war. The second development was the increased impetus given to the general education of the soldier by the formation of the Army Educational Corps in 1920. The British army had for a long time past paid considerable attention to education, which was now emphasised and extended by the new corps, instituted on an ambitious scale though it subsequently suffered reduction because of financial restrictions.

In all countries with large military commitments the question of industrial mobilisation in the event of war received close attention, since it was realised that modern war demanded the rapid development of the whole potential of a nation. Preparations were also made for the protection of the civil population against attack from the air. The only fighting during this period that could throw any light on future tactics and equipment took place in the Italian invasion of Abyssinia, in the Spanish Civil War, and in the Japanese aggression in China. The rapid success of the Italians showed how greatly the application of science to war had widened the gulf between the forces of civilised and uncivilised nations. The Abyssinians, in spite of their fighting qualities and the natural advantages of the terrain, were quite unable to prevent the Italians quickly overrunning their country; the use of poison gas, against which they had no protection, demoralised them badly. In the Spanish Civil War, the Germans and Italians on the one side and the Russians on the other intervened more or less openly; and the Germans undoubtedly used the opportunity to test new equipment and methods. The war in China seemed to show the Japanese army in an unfavourable light, since the ill-equipped Chinese forces were able to offer very considerable resistance; and this led to a depreciation of Japanese potentialities which was to have unfortunate results. It also led the Japanese to revise their tactical procedure, which had been based on their methods of 1904–5 in Manchuria.

To sum up the period, the armies that had been victorious in the first world war made little progress in military art during 1920–39, partly in the hope of a long period of peace and partly in misplaced confidence that the methods which had served them in the last war would also bring success in any future conflict. They tended to concentrate on defence, which had been so powerful in 1914–18 and had, they believed, been increased in power by the further development of automatic weapons. Meanwhile in Germany the stimulus of defeat had heightened the grim genius of that people for war, to which they had since 1933 devoted practically their whole economy and policy. When war broke out in 1939 Germany was the only nation up-to-date in war equipment and with fresh ideas on the conduct of war. The Soviet Union, actuated mainly by fear of Germany, had devoted a very large proportion of its national effort to the equipment and training of the Red army, and had a formidable force at her command, though inferior to the German in all but numbers.

The French army, though impressive on paper, had made little progress in equipment or tactics; that its morale was so low was realised only later. Great Britain at last, a year or so before war broke out, realised her danger, cast off the hampering shackles of the Ten Years Rule,[1] and began too late to set her military house in order. In May 1939 an Act for compulsory military service was passed; and the Territorial army was doubled by a stroke of the pen, though it would obviously take very considerable time to give effect to this. In the United States military authorities held a very shrewd watching brief, and made plans for a rapid development of America's immense resources when necessary.

---

[1] The Ten Years Rule, which laid down that no major war need be expected for that period, was first laid down in 1919, for financial reasons, and at that date was reasonable. But after the expiry of the original period in 1928 it was renewed from year to year without any reduction of the period until it was obviously inappropriate and dangerous. Even after its cancellation in 1932, hopes of agreement on disarmament at Geneva were allowed to become a fresh hindrance to re-armament.

In 1796 an unknown young general called Bonaparte had changed the whole style and tempo of war by his invasion of Italy. The chief features of this new style were pace, vehemence of attack, and disruption of the enemy's communications. Nearly 150 years later, on 1 September 1939, Hitler's generals again inaugurated a new-style war, which became known as '*Blitzkrieg*', by the invasion of Poland. The chief features were once again a bewildering pace, ruthless and vehement offensive action and immediate disruption of the opponent's system of communications and command. The weapons of this new style were of course quite different from those of Bonaparte, who trusted for speed to the marching powers of his soldiers and their ability to live on the country. In 1939 petrol had replaced 'long boots'; it was armoured vehicles, supported by air action, that overwhelmed the Polish forces almost before they knew that war had begun. Attacks from the air on airfields and headquarters paralysed the Polish system of command at once; and the advance of the armoured and motorised forces was comparatively easy and rapid in spite of a gallant resistance by the old-style forces. The topography of the theatre favoured strategical encirclement; and the doom of the Polish armies was evident very early.

On the other side of Germany the French, obsessed by their twenty-year-old theories of the overwhelming strength of the defence, and of a methodical advance backed by great masses of artillery as the only antidote, had missed the opportunity offered by the engagement of the bulk of the German forces against Poland, and had failed to attack. Even in defence the incomplete Maginot Line obviously did not afford full protection; or even fulfil the only true purpose of fortifications, to release large forces for the offensive. The defensive shield was extended by entrenchments in an endeavour to cover the north as well as the east of France. The British army, smaller at first than the original Expeditionary Force of 1914 and lacking much modern equipment, was in no state to undertake the offensive, and was only too glad of time for training and equipping. Nearly nine months went by without a serious move on either side on the western front, a period called at the time the 'phoney' war.

This period of inaction was ended in the spring of 1940 by the German invasion of Denmark and Norway. The British attempts to go to the assistance of Norway were ineffectual, and emphasised two lessons of warlike operations, one old, one comparatively new. The old one was that hastily prepared overseas expeditions against a country occupied by an active enemy almost invariably end in failure; the new one, which was only gradually being realised, was the great difficulty of operations by land forces without air superiority or at least a considerable measure of air support.

The German invasions of Holland, Belgium and France followed in May, and again the new-style '*Blitzkrieg*' triumphed rapidly over the old-style defence. Holland was overwhelmed before she had even time to be ready; the Belgian defences crumbled at once.[1] The pace of the armoured thrust by the Germans through the Ardennes at the hinge of the Allied defences in France was such that the counter-measures devised by the Allies were always out-of-date before they could be put into action. The moral effect of the German 'Stukas' (dive-bombers) was considerable; and the masses of refugees fleeing from the terror of German war methods created a serious traffic problem for the Allied armies.

The reasons for the collapse of the morale of the French armies in so many instances were partly civil and partly military. The civil reasons were the instability of French governments between the wars, much communist and pro-German propaganda, and the lack of determined leadership; the military reasons were lack of modern equipment, an out-of-date military organisation and theory of war, and lack of air support. The fall of France was in fact a Jena in reverse: just as Napoleon's swiftness in movement and determination in attack had routed the stiff Prussian army of 1806, so the ruthless speed and boldness of Hitler's forces over-turned the defensive system in which the French had put their trust. The neutrality of Belgium had also hampered Allied defence measures.

The escape of the British army from Dunkirk set Hitler an entirely new problem, an overseas invasion on a large scale against a determined enemy, perhaps the most difficult of all operations of war, for which he had made no adequate preparation. In the end he and his generals refused, perhaps wisely, to accept the risk. Meanwhile in Great Britain the peril of invasion caused the creation of a force peculiarly and uniquely British, the Home Guard (originally known as Local Defence Volunteers). All were volunteers, unpaid, from men under or over the age of military service. The force was completely democratic, and included in the ranks men of all classes and positions. Their work often involved long hours and exposure to hard conditions. At first they had only shot-guns or home-made weapons. In the end the force amounted to nearly 2,000,000 men, reasonably well armed and equipped. The Home Guard never went into action, but its formation enabled other troops to be sent abroad. It thus performed an invaluable role; but above all it represented the determination to resist invasion at all costs.

While Britain was re-arming and training, and bearing grimly but indomitably the ruthless German air attack on London and other cities, the only theatre of active military operations on land was the Middle East.

The campaigns in the Middle East were remarkable for producing a novel form of warfare in which large armies fought for two-and-a-half years in an area which was mainly desert, stretching along the north

---

[1] Just as the fortress of Liége had fallen abruptly in 1914 to new methods, so the frontier fortress of Eben Email, with all the latest devices for defence, fell suddenly in 1940 to a carefully prepared and rehearsed attack, which included new methods and weapons.

coast of Africa from the Nile Delta to Tunis, near the site of ancient Carthage. Until now deserts had been regarded as obstacles which armies crossed as rarely and as rapidly as possible and where large-scale engagements were almost impossible, owing mainly to the difficulties of water supply. Napoleon in the first of his military maxims laid down that a desert was the most difficult of all obstacles to the march of an army, more so than mountains or rivers. The British campaigns across the Sinai Desert into Palestine in 1916–17 had shown that by modern methods, such as rapid railway construction and pipe lines, the difficulties of desert warfare could be overcome; but in these campaigns the great number of animals in the armies made the water problem always a very serious one. In the desert campaigns of 1940–3 the only animal whose presence on either side is recorded was the white horse on which Mussolini proposed to enter Cairo in triumph, had the battle of El Alamein gone otherwise. With motor transport capable of traversing the desert practically anywhere, the water and supply problems were much simplified; and the size of the armies put into the field was limited only by the number of motor vehicles available.

The strategy of these desert campaigns was simple. One flank of either army was protected by the Mediterranean, the other was in open desert. The only points of any strategical value were the ports, such as Tobruk, Bengazi and Tripoli. Neither side had sufficient naval and air superiority to support landings in any strength behind the enemy lines on the sea flank; consequently the almost invariable manœuvre was to launch the largest available mass of armoured troops round the desert flank of the enemy. It was almost impossible to hold a fixed line of defence for long—the only exceptions were the fortifications of Tobruk, which were held by British and Dominion troops for some eight months in 1941, and the position of El Alamein, where the practically impassable Qattara Depression enabled a line to be formed with both flanks protected. But Tobruk fell twice after a short resistance, to the British in January 1941 and to Rommel in June 1942; and generally speaking warfare in the desert was speedy and fluid. It bore in fact some resemblance to sea warfare in its independence of fixed defences, its rapid manœuvres, and its decisions by superiority in gun-power and armour. Certain stretches of desert impassable to armoured vehicles represented the shoals and rocks of sea navigation. As at sea, minefields took the place of the barbed wire of the 1914–18 trench warfare. In superiority of gun-power, armour and equipment the balance changed more than once. In the first campaign against the Italians, the British forces though greatly inferior in numbers were better equipped and trained. When the German Afrika Corps first appeared the British, though superior in numbers, suffered serious reverses. Later at El Alamein the appearance of American Sherman tanks in large numbers turned the scales again in favour of the Allies.

In certain other respects German equipment showed more foresight. The supply and distribution of petrol was a vital factor, and the German containers (known to the Allies as 'jerrycans') were immeasurably superior to the original rather flimsy British tins which caused so much unnecessary waste of the precious fluid. The Germans were also first in the field with tank-transporters, large wheeled machines which could carry tanks long distances and prolong the life of the tank tracks, which were the components most subject to wear. On the whole, German tank design was simpler and stronger than British, and German guns more effective. In one respect, guerrilla warfare against the lines of communications, the British showed much greater enterprise and ingenuity. The long-range desert patrols, which from the hitherto almost unexplored depths of the Sahara sand dunes raided effectively and constantly the airfields and depots of their enemies, were the equivalent of submarines in naval warfare, a constant menace, usually hidden till the launching of their attack.

The other campaigns in Africa—in Somaliland, in Eritrea, in Abyssinia, in Tunisia—served to emphasise that modern armament and equipment had again made the offensive stronger than the defensive; although where the terrain was favourable, as at Keren in Eritrea and in the mountains to the south-west of Tunis, it proved long and costly to overcome the defence of a resolute enemy. The advance from the borders of East Africa by Kismayu, Mogadischu and Harrar to Addis Ababa was a remarkable example of the mobility given by motor transport to a pursuit.

The theatres of war in Europe, after the overthrow of France and the British escape from Dunkirk, were Greece, Crete, Russia, Sicily, Italy, and North-West Europe. The main tactical features of modern warfare in these theatres were the amphibious operations of the Allies, illustrated by the landings in Sicily, at Anzio in Italy, and finally in Normandy; the need by land armies of strong air support; the employment of airborne troops; the combination of tanks and infantry in attack and defence; and the use of anti-tank and anti-personnel mines as a means of defence.

Landing operations against a prepared enemy have always been hazardous. Hitler, as has been seen, refused to launch his armies against the shores of Great Britain. The British, after the disastrous failure in August 1942 of the Dieppe raid made mainly by Canadian troops, rightly insisted on the most elaborate preparation for the final landing in Normandy. No more carefully planned and staged operation of war has ever taken place on such a large scale. At Gallipoli, nearly thirty years before, the landings had been made mainly in a style centuries old, by rowing-boats or launches from warships or merchant ships brought in as close to land as was deemed advisable. The Normandy landing was made in a variety of special craft—vessels for landing infantry, vessels for landing tanks, vessels to give supporting fire, vessels for stores—which could run straight up on to the beach, enabling the assault to take place within the minimum time. Combined operations became in fact a highly specialised form of war, demanding much special equipment.

The use of airborne forces in Europe falls under two heads. In two instances, the German invasion of Crete and the British attempt to establish a bridgehead at Arnhem, the airborne operation was the main one. In others, such as the German invasion of Holland, the attack by the Germans on the bridge over the Corinth Canal during the Greek campaign, the Normandy landing and elsewhere, the airborne detachments were a subsidiary part of the main operations, briefed to seize some important point or to create a diversion. On a number of other occasions individuals or small parties were dropped behind the enemy lines, to get information or to make contact with guerrillas acting against enemy communications, as in the Balkans. In the large-scale operations, considerable numbers of troops (about four divisions in Crete, two at Arnhem) were landed in enemy territory by parachute, glider or transport aircraft— that was the intended sequence if all went well. The German airborne forces succeeded in capturing Crete, but at such heavy cost that they never employed an airborne force again. The Arnhem operation after some success failed, partly because of unfavourable weather. Although airborne forces can hardly claim an unqualified success during the war, they undoubtedly exercised a considerable moral effect, and established themselves as a powerful strategical and tactical weapon in the hands of bold and skilful commanders. The Russians, who had been the pioneers of this form of warfare in peace, made no attempt to profit by their experience; and it was British individuality and adventure that made best use of the new arm.

British enterprise also showed itself in what were known as 'commando' operations, usually overseas raids on important objectives by men specially picked and trained. The word 'commando' comes from the South African war memories of Winston Churchill, who was an enthusiastic supporter of these enterprises. At first the men were all drawn from the army, but it was recognised later that the marines were specially fitted by their training to take part. There may be two opinions as to the advisability of forming units from men of many different regiments and of withdrawing from regiments some of the boldest and most ardent spirits; but the success of the commandos is unquestioned, and the damage they inflicted on the enemy may perhaps be best judged by Hitler's infamous order that they should be shot out of hand if captured.

While war in Europe during the period 1941–5 never suffered from the long stagnation of trench warfare as in 1914–18, and while the attack generally overcame the defence, operations were never so rapid as in the '*Blitzkrieg*' of 1939 in Poland or 1940 in France, or as in the North African desert. By trading space for time the Russian armies were able, as in 1812, to avoid defeat by the more highly trained and equipped armies of their enemies, and eventually, aided by American and British equipment, to overcome them by sheer weight of numbers. The combination of all arms was the deciding factor on the battlefield; but tanks and armoured cars had taken the place of the cavalry rather as it had been used in the Napoleonic wars, both as heavy cavalry to intervene in the actual battle and as light cavalry for reconnaissance and pursuit. There was considerable argument by experts and commanders on whether all these roles could be performed by a single type of tank, or whether two or more types were required. The Germans on the whole kept their lead in tank design, and nothing as powerful and formidable as their Panther and Tiger tanks was produced on the Allied side.

The difficulty of bringing troops into battle and manœuvring them on the battlefield against overwhelming air superiority was most strikingly shown in the battles in Normandy when Allied command of the air rendered the movement of German reinforcements so slow and hazardous as to cripple their strategy and tactics.

Portable mines, laid rapidly in large numbers, took the place that barbed wire had played in the first world war and often caused heavy casualties to personnel and vehicles. The clearance of minefields became one of the chief tasks of the engineers.

The entry of Japan into the war at the end of 1941 brought two novel elements into the conflict of large armies—one human, one material. The human factor lay in the fanaticism of the Japanese soldier, who would fight to the last and invite or contrive his own death rather than surrender. The material factor was the nature of the eastern jungles, in which large-scale modern armies had never manœuvred before. On the Allied side Japan's intervention led to a remarkable phenomenon in the history of war, the richest and most powerful manufacturing nation in the world taking off its coat and putting all its resourcefulness and resources into the business of war—a war which it had not provoked or desired but was now determined to carry through to the end. When the United States of America had entered the first world war in 1917, the nation and army had been unprepared and had had to organise and equip forces hurriedly and with little basis of experience. In 1941 the foundations had been well laid, both on the personnel and equipment side. A Selective Service Act passed in September 1939 had authorised the enlistment and training of up to nearly one-and-a-half million men. An officer reserve of 100,000 had been trained in the period between the two great wars. After the outbreak of war expansion proceeded smoothly and purposefully on a well-thought-out system. By the end of the European war in 1945 the American army (which included the Air Force) had reached a strength of nearly eight-and-a-half million men: and no army has ever been more lavishly equipped. The American army produced too a large number of forceful and competent commanders.

The strategy and tactics of the eastern war were conditioned by the nature of the terrain. In Malaya and Burma the British and Indian troops had to fight in thick jungle with poor communications. The Japanese tactics of sending small lightly equipped detachments through the jungle to take up a position astride the communications, from which they could only be dislodged when their last man was killed, proved most effectual at first against troops whose training had been mainly for open warfare. When means were found of countering these tactics, by special training and by the use of air supply to troops whose land communications had been cut by the enemy, the Japanese were not found to be resourceful soldiers, though their skill in entrenchment (their trenches for some reason received the name of 'bunkers') and their fanatical resistance-to-the-death made them formidable to the end.

With the lack of adequate land communications, supply of troops by air became a highly developed feature of the eastern campaigns. It began with the supply of the Chinese armies by American transport aircraft from Assam 'over the Hump' to western China, after the Burma Road had been lost. Later, the Chindits (a name given to forces organised by General Wingate for operations behind the Japanese lines) were landed by air and supplied entirely by air. The reconquest of Burma by British and Indian troops also depended largely on air supply.

The American operations across the Pacific against Japan involved a series of landing operations to secure island bases for a further advance. Thus the development of the technique of amphibious warfare or combined operations became a very marked feature of the second world war. The final landings in Japan itself, which had been prepared on a great scale and would have been the culmination of this technique, were rendered unnecessary by the use of the atom bomb.

The question of co-operation between allies has always been a difficult problem. In this war the arrangements made between the American and British armies for co-operation and command reached in the final stages of the war in Europe the closest integration between the forces of two proud and powerful nations that history has yet recorded. Beginning with the campaign in North Africa in the autumn of 1942, an organisation was built up for the invasion of Europe, in which a Combined Staff under a single Supreme Commander directed the operations of both armies throughout the landing and subsequent campaigns. That such an arrangement worked with the minimum of friction was partly due to the fact that the two nations had a common language and a similar heritage of ideas and traditions, and partly to the personality of the Supreme Commander, General Eisenhower.

The second world war was the first war fought on an almost entirely mechanised basis. The motive power of the horse practically disappeared and the American 'jeep' replaced the traditional army mule. The war was won in the laboratories of science and in the workshops of industry as much as by manœuvre and battle in the theatres of war. The result of the Battle of the Atlantic which placed the manufacturing power of the North American continent at the disposal of the Allies in Europe and Africa was really the deciding factor in those theatres; and it was strength in vessels and armaments of every kind that enabled the Americans to undertake so successfully difficult operations against Japan, at such distances across the Pacific. First-class war may be said to have become the prerogative only of first-class powers with unlimited industrial strength.

There was no radical change in the organisation of land forces; and the composition and size of brigades, divisions, corps and armies varied only in the proportion of the arms. Armoured units took the place of cavalry and played a far more important role than cavalry had done in the first war, though infantry still remained one of the principal arms. Since operations were more mobile, less heavy artillery was brought into the field, and the proportion of anti-aircraft and anti-tank artillery was greatly increased. The German 88 millimetre gun which could play the role of a field piece, anti-tank or anti-aircraft weapon was the most effective artillery weapon. Rocket artillery began to be developed towards the end of the war. Anti-aircraft artillery employed many new devices with greatly increased power and range. Contrary to expectation, no army used the weapon of poison gas which had been such a feature of the first world war. Preparations for an even deadlier weapon, bacteriological warfare, were made but not put into effect.

The developments in amphibian warfare (or combined operations) and the first use of airborne troops were the most marked strategical changes; while the evolution of the tank from its tentative use in 1914–18 to the position of one of the three principal arms and the use of the landmine as a defensive weapon were the chief tactical developments. The effect of partisan and guerrilla activities against the lines of communication should also be noted. These 'resistance movements', as they were called, were a feature of the war in Russia, in France (the 'Maquis'), in the Balkans, and to some extent in Malaya.

Casualties, though heavy, were on a lesser scale than in the trench warfare of 1914–18 with its continuous daily fighting and constant murderous assaults against entrenchments. The tendency of civilised troops to surrender when surrounded rather than to continue a hopeless resistance was marked; the 'less civilised' Japanese presented a difficult problem by their refusal to surrender in any circumstances. The marked reduction in death and disablement in spite of the increased range and accuracy of weapons, and in casualties from disease, was due largely to great advances in medical science. Amongst these may be mentioned blood transfusion and the discovery of penicillin, which undoubtedly saved the lives of many wounded, and the use of drugs such as mepacrine and D.D.T. which made warfare possible in the malaria-haunted jungles of Burma and elsewhere. The immediate evacuation of casualties to base hospitals by air was a feature of the concluding campaigns, and undoubtedly saved many lives and much suffering.

The scale of rations and the arrangements for the alleviation of discomfort for the troops engaged at the front reached an unprecedented height in the American army; and those of the British army were only a little less lavish. The result was a very high proportion of personnel employed on non-combatant duties, a danger of obstruction or retardation on the lines of communication, and, of course, an enormous addition to the expense of war. Troops less accustomed to demand the comforts of civilisation in the field, and trained to live harder, such as the Japanese and Russians, undoubtedly gained some advantage over their opponents in mobility and comparative independence of communications. This was usually counterbalanced by an inferiority in the supply of weapons, munitions and warlike stores of all kinds. The whole history of war down the ages has shown that while the less civilised force may win successes for a while by superior mobility and hardiness, the nation with the greater reserves will always win in the end, provided it retains its fighting spirit and determination for victory.

3. AIR FORCES

The world showed no great interest when the experiments by the Wright brothers at Kitty Hawk, California, led to the first successful power-driven flight by an aeroplane in December 1903. Though the value of air observation for military operations was recognised, it was to the lighter-than-air balloon and airship that development was primarily directed. As early as 1878 the first Army Balloon School was formed at Woolwich. In Britain, France and Germany airship construction had started. In January 1909 the Committee of Imperial Defence stated that it was 'imprudent and dangerous to neglect the precaution of air defence'. The statement resulted from the progress of the Zeppelin airship developments in Germany and sums for airship construction were included in British naval and military estimates.

France was the first power to recognise the potential value of the aeroplane for military purposes. From 1908 onwards progress in that country was rapid. Military trials and competitions revealed steady technical development. Speed, range and reliability increased. Bleriot's crosschannel flight in July 1909 was a significant event and aroused much interest in Britain. Could it mean that some day Britons would no longer remain secure behind the shield of a strong navy? If that possibility was realised by some, two years were still to elapse before any move was made by the British government to develop aeroplanes for use in war or to train personnel to operate them. It was left to private enterprise to build the machines and to enterprising amateurs to learn to fly them. Meanwhile, during 1911, long-distance races in Europe—Paris–Rome, Paris–Madrid and Circuit of Britain—showed great progress in aerial navigation. These races were invariably won by French pilots in French aeroplanes.

In Britain, by December 1911, official recognition was given to the potential military value of the aeroplane. Impressed by the great progress abroad, in France with the aeroplane and in Germany with the Zeppelin, the Committee of Imperial Defence began to elaborate the details of a Flying Service. As a result the Flying Corps was formed on 13 May 1912. It was originally intended that both naval and military wings should be included, but developments in the use of aeroplanes for purely naval purposes led to the creation of the Royal Naval Air Service in July 1914 under the sole direction of the Admiralty, leaving the Royal Flying Corps to the army.

On the outbreak of war in August 1914 the normal performance of aeroplanes of the opposing forces was limited to a speed of 70–75 miles per hour and an endurance of 2–3 hours' flying. It was a stage of development in which effective employment was practically confined to tactical and short-range strategical reconnaissance for armies in the field. Seaplanes employed from ships converted to seaplane carriers or from coastal bases had similar limitations. In the Zeppelin, Germany possessed an airship capable of extended flight with a load of bombs: Britain and France had smaller types of airship suitable for sea reconnaissance under favourable conditions. Two outstanding examples of the value of air reconnaissance occurred in the early stages of the war. The wheeling movement of Von Kluck's First Army to the south-east in August 1914 was first reported by the Royal Flying Corps air observers: a German Taube monoplane observed the disembarkation of the British 7th Division at Ostend and Zeebrugge in October 1914. In the mobile warfare of this early phase of the campaign such information was vital.

The year 1914 saw the start of air fighting. Air reconnaissance ceased to be free from interference by opposing aircraft. Machine-guns took the place of rifles strapped to struts. The new German fighter, a Fokker monoplane with a machine-gun firing through the airscrew, made its first appearance in the summer of 1915 and seriously interfered with Allied reconnaissance planes. It became evident that air support for the army would depend on the degree to which an enemy air service could be dominated. Formation flying by flights or squadrons was introduced and fighter squadrons were formed. The battle for air supremacy on all fronts increased in intensity as the war continued. At times technical development of a new plane, numerical superiority or some fresh tactics gave advantage to one side or the other. The first real fight for command of the air opened during the Verdun battle of February 1916. Over the Somme battlefield in the autumn of that year the R.F.C. established a local superiority over the German air force never to be surpassed during the campaign.

Before the end of 1915 the use of air-to-ground wireless telegraphy for artillery observation had become general, and air photography of enemy positions a matter of routine. Other uses in support of the land campaign were introduced as time went on. Early efforts in the launching of improvised bombs by dropping them by hand over the side of the plane were succeeded by the development of release racks and sights. At the Battle of Loos in September 1915 a successful attack was made on two German munition trains by the R.F.C. The bombs were 100 lb. and 20 lb. and incendiaries. The future possibilities of aeroplanes as a primary striking weapon became evident. Over the sea, naval planes fitted with bombs searched for submarines and escorted coastal shipping convoys. Raids on German airship bases and German-occupied ports in Belgium were made by seaplanes from carriers or by aeroplanes from shore bases in France. The Royal Naval Air Service played an important part in the Dardanelles operations as well as in the Mediterranean and the Aegean.

Independent of the sea and land campaigns German Zeppelins began operations against Britain in 1915. The intermittent night bombing of London and the other cities and towns continued for some two years before home defence night-fighters and anti-aircraft guns were sufficiently effective to render this form of attack too costly for these vulnerable airships. However, in 1917 technical development had provided Germany with a new type of twin-engined bombing plane. A formation of these Gothas raided London in daylight in June 1917 and again in July. These raids, which were to be followed by frequent moonlight night attacks on the city, created a profound impression in Britain. Counter-measures seemed slow in effectively preventing this new form of attack. For over a thousand years no invader had attacked the British civilian population on its native soil. Public opinion in Britain led to agitation in Parliament for a more effective counter to these attacks from the air.

What became known as the Smuts Committee was formed to report on air defence. In the general's memorandum of August 1917 reference was made to the fact that an air service could be used as an independent means of war operation, and nobody who witnessed the attacks on London could have any doubts on that point. 'As far as can at present be foreseen there is absolutely no limit to the scale of its future independent war use and the day may not be far off when aerial operations with their devastation of enemy lands and destruction of industrial and populous centres on a vast scale may become the principal operations of war, to which the older forms of military and naval operations may become secondary and subordinate.' The report of this committee was accepted by the government, the Air Force (Constitution) Act received the royal assent in November 1917, and the Royal Air Force came into being in April 1918.

Strategic bombing of German industrial centres had been discussed by British and French authorities as early as 1915 but the need for maximum support to the armies in the field prevented the allocation of air forces for this purpose until late in 1917. By May 1918 a British formation under General Sir Hugh Trenchard and known as 'the Independent Force' was equipped with day and night bombers and began an offensive against German railway systems, blast furnaces and air bases in the Rhine area. Though the material damage was not great, petitions to the German government from the cities and towns attacked bore testimony to the dislocation caused to munition production and to the depressing effect on morale generally. A special group of Handley-Page night bombers with four engines, a bomb load of thirty 250 lb. bombs and an endurance of 14 hours was formed in England during October 1918 for attacks on Berlin, but the war ended before their operations began.

During the final Allied offensive in France in September 1918 the bombing effort of all air units of the Independent Force was switched from industrial targets to enemy rail systems and to the general dislocation of rear communications. In Palestine in the same month the Turkish retreat from Jerusalem to the north was turned into a complete rout by air attack. These were examples of the flexibility of the new air arm and of the use of its striking power in relation to the main battle. Four years of war had shown the need for air supremacy in a land campaign and the contribution which could be made by aircraft in the war at sea. It had also given some idea of the value of air power in an offensive role independent of forces on land and sea.

This short summary of the early growth of air power has so far been mainly concerned with British and German developments. Other Allied and enemy air forces composed of aircraft with similar limitations were principally employed as ancillaries to armies. Britain and Germany were the first to use the new arm in an independent role. Britain alone had formed a special service distinct from navy and army.

At the time of the Armistice in November 1918, the R.A.F. was exerting a powerful influence on the conduct of operations. In four years it had grown from a few aircraft and personnel to a total of 22,000 aircraft (of which 3300 were first-line strength) and nearly 300,000 officers and men. It was, in fact, the most powerful air arm in the world until the pressure for rapid demobilisation soon reduced this lead, leaving France as the strongest air power for some years after the war. The League of Nations gave promise of a prolonged peace or at least of no major war. Money voted by the British Parliament for the services would be limited. At the same time there were many oversea commitments and the R.A.F. would be required to play its part in operations and garrison duties. For these purposes the surplus aircraft remaining from war-time production would suffice. The aircraft industry built up during the war years could not be kept alive by small orders for experimental war types alone: however important research and development might be, production orders were necessary to sustain the firms concerned. The question was whether the demands of civil aviation would fill the empty production lines and absorb at least some of the redundant trained pilots and ground crews.

When peace came, Britain, the United States and France turned their attention to the future possibilities of air transport. Some of the larger types of service aircraft were capable of being converted for limited commercial purposes, and short-distance air-routes were started in most countries. A London-to-Paris service was inaugurated, mostly for mails. British private enterprise led to various long-distance pioneer flights in converted war-time bombers: Captain John Alcock flew the Atlantic in June 1919 and before the end of the year Captain Ross Smith had reached Australia in a similar machine in twenty-eight days. These were the first of many flights to develop air communications throughout the world by various nations, principally Britain, the United States and France. Great technical developments resulted in aircraft design, accessories and in aids to navigation which were to influence the growth of air power. By 1934 a British plane (De Havilland Comet) had flown the 11,000 miles to Australia in under seventy-one hours. The design of the Mosquito, built by the same firm seven years later and used for a variety of war purposes, was largely influenced by the performance of the Comet. Similarly, the British Supermarine monoplanes fitted with floats, which won the Schneider Trophy on three successive occasions and, in 1933, raised the world speed record to over 400 m.p.h., gave the necessary lead to the design of the Spitfire eight-gun fighter produced by the same firm and used throughout the war of 1939–45.

Airships, which had proved too vulnerable for use in war in areas where they were liable to be intercepted by fighters or shot down by anti-aircraft fire, were still considered to have a future for commercial purposes. Britain built two which flew in 1930. One of them made a successful flight to Canada and back but the other, R 101, crashed in France *en route* to India, after which airship construction in this country was abandoned. Only in the U.S.A. did the airship survive and the U.S. Navy continued to use a small type for coastal patrol work.

The use of air power for the control of undeveloped countries was first considered in Britain in 1919 after successful minor operations by an R.A.F. squadron in Somaliland to counter the influence of the 'Mad' Mullah. Working with a small force of the Camel Corps the R.A.F. were credited with having been the main instrument and the decisive factor in the overthrow of the Mullah's power which had defied military measures of varying intensity since 1900. The operations lasted only three weeks and were completed at comparatively small cost. At the Cairo conference in March 1921 a scheme for the air control of Mesopotamia (renamed Iraq in September 1921) was approved in principle. Air control implied the use of aircraft as the primary arm to support the administration of the country in order to restore or to preserve law and order. The supporting land forces, large or small according to conditions, might be imperial troops, locally raised levies or police. The scheme came into operation in October 1922, the command of all forces being vested in an air officer.

After successful land/air operations in the Mosul Vilayet and Kurdistan during the spring of 1923 the British and Indian battalions were reduced until finally only levies and well-organised police remained. A feature of these operations was the employment of Vickers-Vernons as air transports for conveying stores, spares and rations to the mobile columns. Over 200 casualties from the area of operation were evacuated by air the 200 miles to Baghdad. Before the Iraq government assumed responsibility under the Anglo-Iraq Treaty of 1930 air power alone dealt with incidents on the Turkish frontiers and in the south against raiding tribesmen from Saudi Arabia. As a result of the experience gained in Iraq, air control was introduced in 1928 as a means of garrisoning Aden.

Reference has already been made to the problem of keeping alive the nucleus of an aircraft industry in Britain: one that could be rapidly expanded in emergency. Though development orders were placed with as many firms as possible for prototypes of advanced design, production contracts for modern military types were on a very modest scale: this was particularly the case during the Disarmament Conference which opened at Geneva in February 1932. For over two years British support for the principle of disarmament prevented any substantial orders being placed for military aircraft towards the expansion to fifty-two metropolitan squadrons proposed some ten years before. Nor were the orders for commercial aircraft forthcoming. Though progress with civil air transport had been made by Britain the scope for any large extension did not, as yet, exist. Internally distances were too short and too well served by railways and good roads. Empire air routes remained in the development stage until 1935. In contrast, the United States had numerous regular services running by 1926. The statistics of 1933 showed the U.S.A. in the lead with over 54 million miles flown on established air routes: Britain came fifth with just over $2\frac{1}{2}$ million miles. To provide up-to-date commercial types for the various air lines America had several large private aircraft firms building in keen competition. A healthy industry was thus maintained. It was evident that a nation with a thriving air transport service requiring a regular supply of modern equipment was in a favourable position for expansion in emergency and for conversion to war types.

It followed that both the U.S. army air force and the naval air arm could rely on substantial production of aircraft at relatively short notice. For the time being a variety of types including fighters and bombers were in service, none of them with outstanding performance. On the other hand American civil air-transport planes were ahead of European types by 1938 and were capable of being converted for certain war purposes, as indeed they were when Britain placed large orders in the United States in 1939, to the great advantage of the production capacity of the firms concerned.

When Hitler proclaimed in 1935 that Germany already possessed air parity with Britain, a programme of considerable expansion of the R.A.F. was announced in both Houses of Parliament. The decision about the proportion of bombers to fighters which should be built presented some difficulty. Air exercises in 1934 had shown that successful interception by fighters of raiding bombers required more accurate information from the ground as to movements of hostile formations than was, at the time, available. Particularly at night was this the case, and it resulted in a high percentage of bomber formations reaching their target. The conclusion reached, therefore, was that counter-bombing of hostile air bases might be a more effective method of defence than to rely entirely on interception fighters. This influenced the construction programme to the extent that, of the orders placed to achieve the target of 1500 first-line aircraft by 1937, no less than 1000 were to be bombers. To reach this figure the 'shadow factory' scheme was introduced whereby the works of certain large motor-car firms were to be extended to start construction and assembly of aircraft and engines of standardised types. Many difficulties were encountered. The change from wood and fabric air-frame construction to metal meant accurate jigs and tools. These took time to make and any modifications of the original design retarded progress. Effective air power could not be built up at short notice or under conditions other than of extreme urgency, which, even as late as 1937, were not felt to exist.

Meanwhile a system of ground observation was organised to give accurate reports of aircraft movements. In addition, early experiments with radio location gave some promise of further aid in the interception of raiding aircraft. By 1938 these measures and the radar experiments had reached a stage which improved the chances of interception by fighters both by day and night. In the further expansion scheme, then decided upon, the figure for fighters was raised to 800 and that of the bombers increased to 1360.

The formidable French army air force, second in strength only to the British at the end of the war of 1914–18, was substantially reduced, but up to 1932 it was still regarded as the largest in the world. Neglect of technical development rendered this strength more apparent than real. The French aircraft industry was nationalised in 1933. A decree giving legal status to a separate *Armée de l'air* was passed into law in July 1934, but first-line aircraft numbered less than 1000 by 1936.

The Italian *Regia Aeronautica* in the Abyssinian campaign of 1935 and 1936 contributed to the rapid defeat of an enemy possessing no air force, few modern weapons and using primitive methods of warfare. No fresh examples of the use of air power emerged except in one respect: Italian aircraft dropped mustard-gas bombs on their foes. It was the first example on record of this form of warfare from the air.

The Spanish civil war (1936–9) provided valuable training and a test for the equipment of the German and Italian air arms. The German air contingent, before their final withdrawal, had all their modern types in action including the Stuka dive-bomber. The concentrated devastating attack by German aircraft on the Spanish town of Guernica in 1937 provided a dress rehearsal on a small scale for the air offensive against Poland which opened the second world war two years later.

During the Russian manœuvres in 1936 parachute troops made their first appearance, when some 1200 were dropped in the course of operations. The German manœuvres of 1937 in Mecklenburg were attended by a British delegation. The final mass attack took place in view of Hitler and Mussolini, and was obviously staged to impress the members of the several nations who were present. Waves of Dornier 17 and Heinkel 111 formations passed over to the attack and it was rumoured that elsewhere parachute troops had been dropped. This new use of air power was later to play an important part in operations of the second world war.

In Britain hopes of averting war gradually faded after Munich (1938) and the tempo of preparations increased. Modern aircraft were coming from the factories but not at a rate comparable with German production. Once again history was to repeat itself and the initial advantage was to lie with the aggressor nation able to choose the moment of attack to co-incide with his estimated maximum superiority in trained men and in modern weapons. The strength and striking power of the *Luftwaffe*, hitherto impossible to assess with accuracy, was revealed immediately Germany attacked Poland on 1 September 1939. The Polish Air Force, composed of some 400 first-line machines, practically ceased to exist within forty-eight hours. The German squadrons then switched to the direct support of the invading army, the bombing of communications to dislocate traffic, and finally to an intense bombardment of Warsaw. It was an example of the contribution which air power could make when co-ordinated with the army plan.

With certain variations these '*Blitzkrieg*' methods were employed in the occupation of Denmark and Norway in April and May 1940. The rapid occupation of Denmark coincided with the capture of air bases in southern Norway. In these operations airborne troops were dropped on airfields to neutralise the ground defence. Reinforcements landing from transport planes followed. Thus the airfields were captured and held for the operation of fighters, bombers and reconnaissance planes in support of the land forces. Nearly all Norwegian airfields were in German hands within two or three days. Some 800 operational aircraft and between 250 and 300 transport planes were employed to support and supply the German forces. British and French contingents landing at various points on the Norwegian coast were under constant attack by Stuka dive-bombers and fighters. The few British fighters, transported by an aircraft carrier, operated from improvised airfields and were overwhelmed by the weight of the German air attack. This short-lived and unsuccessful campaign in Norway provided striking evidence to Britain of the strength of German air-power, and of the futility of embarking on land operations which could not be adequately supported by air cover. It also demonstrated, as it had done in the first world war, the advantage to Germany of shorter lines of air communications from home bases. Short-range fighter aircraft were able to fly direct to the scene of operations. Transport planes were available to the Germans in large numbers thanks to the very elaborate network of airlines which had been operated in peace-time.

The German offensive of May 1940 followed much the same pattern as on the two previous occasions except that, because of intensive aircraft production during the eight months' interlude, the *Luftwaffe* had increased in strength and was able to muster over 3800 aircraft. Attacks on the air forces of Holland and Belgium, and on British airfields in northern France, co-ordinated with a break-through in the Sedan area, forced the heavily out-numbered Allied squadrons to withdraw to bases farther west.

The swift advance through Belgium and France by mechanised forces was supported by continuous air attack. Dive-bombing by Stukas on unseasoned troops, and civilian refugees crowding the roads, lowered morale and generally added to the confusion. The alarming effect of this particularly noisy form of attack from the air lessened as the war progressed until it was finally abandoned by the Germans when the Ju 87 became an easy victim to British Hurricanes or Spitfires.

Throughout the period of the German offensive which overran Holland and Belgium, and finally led to the capitulation of France, one of the main problems which faced the British High Command was to decide how many fighter aircraft could be spared as reinforcements to France while retaining the necessary force in England for home defence against the German air attack which seemed certain to follow a French collapse. Twenty-five squadrons of Hurricanes and Spitfires was the figure decided upon as the minimum necessary for the purpose. Deliveries from production factories of the eight-gun Spitfires, superior in performance to the Hurricanes, were increasing. These fighters, operating from airfields in south-east England, played a most important part in covering the evacuation of the B.E.F. from the exposed beaches of Dunkirk, and 137 German aircraft were destroyed for the loss of 130 British planes.

During the few remaining days before the capitulation of France, R.A.F. squadrons were still on the Continent operating in support of the French, but the impetus of the German advance was so overwhelming that whatever air force had been available, on the 1940 pattern, it could not have saved France. The pressure from all quarters to use every available aircraft in a desperate effort to restore a rapidly deteriorating situation in a land battle is naturally very great. To yield to such pressure could lead to the useless sacrifice of an air force shortly to be urgently needed for the next, and perhaps even more vital, phase of the war. The High Command in Britain did not make this mistake. Eight months of war on the Continent, most of it inactive so far as the land campaign was concerned, had cost the R.A.F. nearly 1000 aircraft. War in the air had continued throughout the period, though losses had been particularly heavy in the vain endeavour, by low-level bomb attack, to stem the German advance in its early stages. In a rapid retreat heavy loss of material is inevitable but particularly so with aircraft. Apart from those destroyed by direct air attack, machines under repair or awaiting some minor spare part and therefore unable to fly must be abandoned on the airfields as they are overrun. In nearly all theatres of war at some period either one side or the other suffered considerable losses under these conditions.

The German plan for the invasion of Britain depended for its possible success on gaining air supremacy over the R.A.F. as a necessary preliminary to the landing of troops at selected points on the south-east coast. By August 1940 three *Luftflotten*, totalling over 3000 first-line aircraft, were concentrated at bases in France, Belgium, Holland and Norway. This force included bombers, dive bombers, fighters, seaplanes and transport aircraft. British fighter strength amounted to some 700 Spitfires and Hurricanes in about equal proportions, in addition to some Blenheims and Defiants of less performance. Anti-aircraft gun and searchlight defences were linked with the Fighter Command organisation, and a very complete system of raid warning by Observer Corps and radar stations provided the necessary information of the movements of German air formations. Though British day and night bombers did most valuable work in attacking German airfields and in bombing concentrations of barges and invasion craft at French and Belgian ports, it was the fighters of Fighter Command which won the air battle, later to be known as the Battle of Britain. In the opening phases of the battle attacks on south-east coast ports and on British shipping convoys in the Channel by German bombers, heavily escorted by fighters, seemed to have the intention of measuring the strength of Britain's air defences.

The period of the second phase of the German attacks can be taken as from 24 August to the end of September when the *Luftwaffe* at first concentrated its efforts against R.A.F. airfields in south-east England and later on London itself. In spite of diversionary raids on Tyneside to draw British fighters away from the vital area of possible invasion, it became clear by 1 September that the R.A.F. had not been defeated and that conditions necessary for invasion had not been achieved. However, to the German High Command, or more probably to Marshal Goering himself, it seemed just possible that Britain might sue for peace if the machinery of government could be paralysed and life to the community made unbearable by an intense bombing of London. Unlike the German air raids on London in the first world war these air attacks did not take the British public entirely by surprise. In fact they had been expected to occur from the day war was declared. Evacuation of children from London to less vulnerable areas had already taken place. Various branches and sections of ministries and business organisations had been dispersed to western towns or districts. Underground railway stations were made available as shelters. These and other measures were amplified as the air-raids spread to other cities and towns. The civil air-raid defence organisa-tion with its warning systems, fire and ambulance services, etc., not only became effective in action but helped to establish the confidence of the public in the counter-measures being taken and in their ability to withstand the onslaught. By the end of October London had survived some thirty-eight serious attacks, mostly on the city and dock areas, the *Luftwaffe* had lost 1733 planes[1] since 10 July, and the R.A.F., though strained to the utmost, still operated.

The high calibre of the fighter pilots, the technical ability of the ground crews, the efficiency of the whole operation systems from Command to Group to Section controls, and above all the remarkable results of the radar warning system, share the honours of victory in this Battle of Britain. Neither side possessed outstanding technical advantage in the matter of equipment or of performance of its latest fighters.

Following this failure to gain complete air supremacy over Britain Germany began systematic night attacks on industrial centres. Counter-measures by Fighter Command grew in effectiveness as the German offen-sive continued. Scientists evolved a means of bending the radio beams along which the *Luftwaffe* night bombers were guided to their targets. Decoy objectives, suitably illuminated, helped to deceive the attackers, and many bombs were dropped on waste land. R.A.F. night fighters were controlled from ground stations to positions from which, by means of their own radar apparatus, they could gain visual contact with hostile bombers. Intruder patrols by fighters over German airfields in occupied territory intercepted some of the returning raiders. British anti-aircraft fire became more effective. German losses increased and after a major

[1] Post-war figures confirmed from official German sources.

attack on London on 10 May 1941, Germany withdrew many of her bombers in preparation for the pending attack on the Soviet Union.

In the months which followed, mine-laying and attacks on ports remained Germany's chief activities, though on a reduced scale. The attacks were renewed on London for a short period early in 1944, after which the dwindling German bomber force played very little part in the air war. Her production effort was directed to building fighters in the endeavour to reduce the ever-increasing scale of the Allied bombing offensive on Germany. Unlike surface warfare with its alternating periods of preparation and actual battle, the air war was waged without respite by Britain and Germany. Only during the struggle for air supremacy over south-east England were British squadrons confined to a defensive role. In measuring the relative advantages of offence and defence it can be claimed that air power is most effective in attack. The normal life of an aircraft and its engine is measured in flying hours. To employ it in large numbers and for long periods on defensive patrols or on escort duty to convoys at sea may at times be very necessary, but it is the use of air power on missions causing damage to the enemy's war effort in his own territory that gives the most effective results. Between the extremes of defence and offence in air war the 'offensive-defensive' played a great part in Britain's air strategy. Submarines were bombed at their bases, German raiding aircraft were attacked on their airfields in occupied territory and V-weapon launching sites were constant objectives.

For Britain, in the early stages of the war, it was a question of staving off defeat whilst adequate air-striking power was built up. In the later phase Germany had expended her bombing effort and had concentrated on fighter defence in an endeavour to avoid capitulation before her V-weapon campaign had reached its full effect. In the following paragraphs can be traced the stages through which Britain, U.S.A., Germany, Italy, Japan and, to a lesser extent, the Soviet Union, passed in the air war. It will be seen how great was the part played not only by the relative strengths of the opposing air forces but by the rapid technical development of the aircraft itself in range and offensive power.

When Mussolini declared war at midnight on 10 June 1940 it almost seemed as if events had overtaken Italian preparations. No Italian 'Blitzkrieg' on the German pattern happened. There was no overwhelming attack on Malta by some of the 1500 first-line aircraft available to the Regia Aeronautica. Instead, the small force of R.A.F. bombers—200 strong—in the Middle East struck first from their advanced bases in the Western Desert, the Sudan and Aden. The Italian airfields and supply dumps seemed unprepared, some not even dispersed. Damage was done to aircraft on the ground and, most important, to the petrol dumps in Eritrea and Abyssinia. Insignificant though these initial attacks may have been in material damage, this modest but prompt British air offensive put the Italian air force on the defensive, as it was designed to do. It also helped to gain the respect of the Egyptians from whose territory operations were to be conducted for nearly three more years while Egypt remained a non-belligerent.

By February 1941, after the successful Wavell offensive on land, the Italian air force in North Africa had been defeated but the effort had left the R.A.F. in the Middle East depleted and in need of aircraft replacements and reinforcements which were slow to arrive from England. The air route for short-range fighters via France and North Africa was no longer available. In the German counter-offensive in March and April of 1941 the few air squadrons which could be spared from the Greek campaign were back to their original airfields: too far east to provide adequate and continuous air cover to isolated Tobruk or to the ships which supplied the garrison.

When the Germans invaded Yugoslavia and Greece on 6 April 1941 they met relatively small resistance on the ground or in the air from Yugoslavia. The *Luftwaffe* were in strength, over 800 aircraft supported by some 300 Italian planes. The small Greek air force had practically spent itself against the Italians. The R.A.F. mustered some eighty serviceable aircraft. Losses from German air attacks on forward airfields, in addition to those in the air, reduced this force to less than fifty serviceable aircraft. No reinforcements could be spared from the hard-pressed front in Cyrenaica. As in Poland, Holland, Belgium and France the impetus of the German advance was overwhelming. As in the case of all rapid withdrawals and evacuations, much R.A.F. aircraft material was lost in Greece. A notable feature in the employment of the German squadrons was the rapidity with which the preparations of airfields for short range fighters and dive bombers seemed to keep pace with the advance of their army. The ruthless employment of civilians contributed largely to their efficiency in this direction.

Crete lay only 120 miles from airfields in Greece and even less from Italian air bases in the Dodecanese. The *Luftwaffe* plan was first to eliminate any air resistance from British fighters which could operate from the three landing grounds in Crete, and then to isolate the island by attacks on shipping preparatory to invasion by sea and air. The force allotted for the purpose consisted of 180 fighters, 330 bombers and some 600 planes for towing gliders, dropping parachutists or carrying troops. Over 15,000 men were to be transported by air to Crete in addition to some 7000 to invade by sea. Less than forty British fighters could be mustered in Crete for defence against the attack. After six days of air fighting the surviving half-dozen fighters were withdrawn to Egypt. From then until the final evacuation at the end of May such action as was possible by bombers and fighters came from bases in North Africa over 250 miles away. By overwhelming superiority in the air the *Luftwaffe* had achieved its task. Sea power in narrow waters without air superiority was not enough to defend an island within short range of a strong force of shore-based aircraft, resolutely employed in conjunction with high-calibre airborne troops.

The German campaign against the Soviet Union opened on 22 June 1941. The tasks allotted to the *Luftwaffe* were: destruction of the Red Air Force, support for the army by attacks on rail and road communications, and close support on the battlefield. Out of an average of 3700 available aircraft, nearly 600 represented reconnaissance aircraft, with over 1000 bombers, 300 Stuka dive-bombers, some 400 fighters, 230 transport planes and nearly 150 seaplanes. The Red Air Force was numerically superior but its losses in the first two days went some way to reducing this superiority. The German air offensive was particularly successful against the rail and road communications in the early stages of the war, but the Red Air Force could not be entirely mastered in spite of its losses.

The *Luftwaffe* were therefore left with the task of fighting for supremacy in the air and at the same time of supporting the German army in a long and difficult campaign. To meet these commitments the strength of the *Luftwaffe* on the eastern front was still further increased, and by July 1942 averaged over 4000 serviceable aircraft. This was the first occasion on which the Germans were faced with an air war over more than one main front. Neither Germans nor Russians used their air forces for strategic bombing. Their operations were confined to the direct support of the land campaign.

Before the war no great value was placed on Malta as an air base. Italian airfields were only sixty miles from the island. With France as an ally there would be less-vulnerable landing grounds available in French North Africa. As events developed in June 1940, when France made an armistice, the spotlight immediately focused on Malta as the key staging-post in the air reinforcement route to the Middle East, and as a potential base for operations by air and by light naval forces or submarines against the air- and sea-routes from Italy to Tripoli and Cyrenaica. It had an integral part to play in Mediterranean strategy.

From 11 June 1940, when the first Italian bombs fell on Malta, until the end of 1942, this unsinkable aircraft carrier, as it was rightly called, survived its ordeal and remained a valuable British air base for reconnaissance of Italian and North African ports and sea communications as well as for attacks on supply routes. It was on account of its value for these purposes and for the British navy that the Germans, in 1942, made such determined efforts to neutralise it by persistent and heavy bombing of the island itself and of the convoys from east and west maintaining supplies. Starvation threatened on more than one occasion; petrol, bombs and ammunition ran short; but the Royal Navy's efforts and resolute merchant-navy captains and crews ensured that supply ships got through and the island sustained its defence.

The tide of the air battle of Malta was turned by the defenders in the summer of 1942. In August and September the R.A.F. air offensive on enemy ships of south-bound convoys to North Africa was stepped up. Beaufort torpedo planes and Wellington bombers from Malta seriously dislocated Rommel's build-up of supplies prior to the battle of El Alamein. Long-range Beaufighters took heavy toll of German and Italian transport planes. A valuable contribution was thus made to the famous victory of October 1942, the success of which shortly led to the relief of the island from air attack. The retention of such strategic bases is vital to the effective use of air power.

From a modest beginning in 1939 with the dropping of leaflets till the later stages of the European war with 12,000 lb. 'block-busters', the R.A.F. bomber offensive against Germany continued for five-and-a-half years with varying degrees of intensity. Because of French fears of reprisal during the first nine months of hostilities, only strictly military targets, where civilians would not be injured, could be attacked. As already recorded, during the Battle of France railway systems behind the German advance and airfields being used by German squadrons were attacked. Later, invasion barges being assembled at the Channel ports were the objectives. For the next two years industrial centres became the targets for British night bombers. Though the material damage and interruption to war production were slight, and bombing not very intense or accurate, this offensive was the one means available of attacking Germany. The experience gained by the air crews and in the methods of operating bombers proved of value during the years which followed. Moreover, it was some consolation to the British people to read or hear in the *communiqués* that Germany was being attacked. Public confidence was an important factor.

In 1942 deliveries of the large four-engined night bombers increased the striking power of Bomber Command. Sound training at operational training units added to its efficiency while the introduction of radio navigational aids improved the accuracy of aim. The small fast twin-engined Mosquito bombers with specially trained navigators were introduced as Pathfinders. They dropped marker bombs or target indicators on the objective ahead of the main striking force.

The Casablanca Conference gave a directive to the British and U.S. Bomber Commanders. It was dated 21 January 1943, and it laid down that: 'Your primary object will be the progressive destruction and dislocation of the German military, industrial and economic system and the undermining of the morale of the German people to a point where their capacity for armed resistance is fatally weakened.' The directive went on to emphasise the value of drawing German fighter strength away from the Russian and Mediterranean theatres of war. An intensive bomber offensive on Germany continued by day and by night. The American

8th and 15th Air Forces, now operating from British bases, could escort their heavy planes with long-range fighters right into Germany during the day raids. The targets varied from time to time. The Ruhr was devastated. The breaching of the Mohne dam in May 1943 led to much dislocation. The V-weapon experimental station at Peenemunde was heavily damaged and the German programme delayed. Before the end of the war the German battleship *Tirpitz* was sunk at Tromso by 12,000 lb. bombs. At Kiel, the *Admiral Scheer* was hit and capsized at the quayside and the *Lützow* was also sunk. Ever-changing tactics by both British and American formations kept their casualties within limits.

From April 1944 all strategic bomber forces were placed under the direction of the Supreme Allied Commander and preparations for the invasion were given priority. Railway centres in the back areas of northern France became the first objective. At the Battle of Caen heavy bombers participated directly, dislocating communications in the immediate rear of the enemy by 'carpet bombing', best described as an area barrage. That such action was possible in daylight by heavy bombers gives some idea of the measure of Allied air superiority achieved at this period. The V I weapons launched against Britain from sites on the French coast were continually attacked during the period.

From D-Day, 6 June 1944, to mid-August, over 17,000 tons of bombs were dropped. As the advance proceeded the strategic bomber forces were released from direct support of the armies and their attacks were concentrated on German oil supplies to such effect that gradually more and more German aircraft and armoured vehicles became immobilised. The intention of the Casablanca directive had been fully implemented. Air power had demonstrated its flexibility and made its great contribution to the final defeat of Germany. Whatever may have been the personal reaction of the German population to their severe ordeal under air bombardment, the disciplined Nazi regime ensured that no weakening of morale affected the fighting forces right up to the time of its final surrender.

The air/sea war in the Atlantic and home waters continued relentlessly from the first day of the war till its end. As in the first world war, Britain was faced with the problem of countering the German submarine campaign. In spite of the development of naval anti-submarine devices German U-boat commanders and crews continued to operate with efficiency and courage, changing tactics and technique in their endeavour to counter any effective measures of defence. Combined naval and air headquarters in Britain, and later on the other side of the Atlantic, co-ordinated defence measures by surface vessels and aircraft. Sunderland and Catalina flying boats reinforced by long-range bomber land-planes patrolled the ocean routes and shipping lanes through which the convoys passed. From bases in Britain, Iceland and later from North America, aircraft were directly responsible for the destruction of over 200 German submarines. The air effort involved was considerable. At times it led to the diversion of bombers from their normal offensive role. In absorbing a high percentage of Britain's war effort on the defensive as well as in jeopardising vital food and material supplies the German submarine campaign must be regarded as having been most effective. The long-range Focke-Wulf aeroplanes, too, were frequently operating, sometimes in co-operation with U-boats. Their activities over a wide sea area led to the carrying of fighters on specially fitted merchant vessels. These German aircraft using torpedoes or bombs were responsible for 13 per cent of British shipping losses.

Both British and German aircraft were frequently in action against coastal traffic. R.A.F. attacks with rocket-firing aircraft in the later phase of the war sank many ships and early in 1945 practically put a stop to movements of German troops from Norway to Denmark. Both sides employed aircraft for mine-laying on shipping lanes and approaches to ports. The Suez Canal was out of action for a short period as a result of German parachute mines. Air power proved its flexibility and its effectiveness in co-operation with sea power.

When the Japanese opened hostilities in central China in 1937 no reliable estimate of their air strength had been formed. The navy and army each had their own air arms and no independent air force existed. This organisation was not changed during the subsequent eight years. It became evident at an early stage that Japanese air strength was too great to be countered by the Chinese airmen. For the next four years valuable war experience was gained by the Japanese which influenced the technical development of their aircraft and the methods of operating them. Production of modern planes, bearing strong resemblance to American or German types, was greatly increased. Information as to performances and output figures was kept a close secret.

The plan to attack the American Pacific Fleet in Pearl Harbor was decided by the Japanese Supreme War Council at a meeting in September 1941. The object was to eliminate the American fleet prior to conquest and occupation of the Philippines, Malaya and the Netherlands East Indies. Of the ten 30,000-ton, 30-knot aircraft carriers available, six were allotted to the Naval Task Force. A total of 450 planes were carried including torpedo carriers, high-level bombers, dive-bombers and fighters. From a position 300 miles to the north-west of Oahu the air attack was launched at daylight on Sunday, 7 December 1941.

The result was devastating. The United States lost five battleships put out of action for one year or more, and three light cruisers put out of action for more than three months, besides other smaller vessels. The U.S. aircraft of both navy and army were parked close together on the airfields for protection against ground sabotage, and 200 out of a total of over 400 were destroyed or damaged. Enemy losses were approximately thirty aircraft either from anti-aircraft fire or as a result of interception by the few defending fighters which could take off. The element of complete surprise without a declaration of war and the efficiency of the Japanese air arm, particularly in their attacks with shallow-run torpedoes, resulted in a crippling blow to American naval strength in the Pacific. The American personnel casualties amounted to over 2400 killed or missing. At Manila the Japanese air attack on U.S. air bases in December 1941 also caught the aircraft on the ground and a high percentage of American planes was destroyed. Japan soon dominated the air and the Philippine Islands were finally lost when Corregidor fell to the Japanese in May 1942. Certain fleet actions between American and Japanese naval forces, in the Coral Sea, Midway and eastern Solomons, were fought at long range. The naval surface units never made contact and the battles were decided entirely by air action from carriers or from shore bases.

In December 1941 the British capital ships *Prince of Wales* and *Repulse* were sunk by Japanese air attack in the Gulf of Siam whilst attempting to prevent Japanese amphibious reinforcements of their air-ground forces moving down the Malay Peninsula. No air cover by British fighters from Singapore was available at the time of the attack. A combination of high-level bombing and low-level torpedo attacks accounted for the sinking of these two ships with the loss of nearly 850 officers and men.

After the tide of victory had turned in the Pacific, Allied strategy in the reconquest of territory was influenced by the need for advanced airfields. From these or from carriers, air power maintained superiority over the area of the new objective. It isolated Japanese forces from reinforcements from sea, provided close support to assault troops and when required provided by air the supplies necessary to maintain them. As American aircraft production reached new records and as the range of bombers increased, the Pacific air plan became more and more effective. Stage by stage the Allied advance along the north coast of New Guinea continued. Island after island was recaptured and became an air base. Kamikaze tactics in which Japanese pilots committed suicide by diving their bomb-loaded planes direct on to the decks of aircraft carriers and other unarmoured vessels caused American losses at Leyte and Okinawa.

In the final phase of the Pacific war, between April and August 1945, a period of intense direct air attack on Japan developed in preparation for the intended Allied invasion. From Okinawa attacks were concentrated on the Nagasaki area, destroying the docks and aircraft factory. From bases in China and from the Mariana Islands B.29 (Superfortress) planes continued strategic bombing of industrial centres. Night incendiary attacks were supplemented by daylight precision bombing. Oil refineries and oil installations were destroyed. Tokyo and Osaka suffered immense devastation and finally in August came the two atomic-bomb attacks on

Hiroshima and Nagasaki after which Japan surrendered. So ended this co-ordinated sea-air-land campaign in the Far East.

In 1942 after the loss of Malaya and Burma, as a result of Japanese preponderance on sea, land and in the air, the most outstanding feature of the South-East Asia air campaign, apart from the normal air operations in support of the army and in neutralising enemy air activity, was the development of air transport by both British and American air arms. By May 1942 China's only remaining line of communication with the outside world, the Burma road, was lost after the Japanese occupation of Burma. If China were to remain an active belligerent in the war against Japan some form of active support from her allies was essential.

To maintain supplies to Kunming in China a U.S. air transport service 'Over the Hump' was developed operating from bases in Assam and India. The route was particularly difficult because of the mountains to be crossed and of the danger of interception by enemy fighters. By November 1943 deliveries of supplies had been built up to 6490 tons a month. This service continued into 1945, and in July of that year the record airlift of 69,365 tons was achieved.

Early in 1944 Japanese land offensives in the Arakan and Imphal areas encircled and isolated the defending forces. In both cases large-scale air transport services by R.A.F. and American planes reinforced and maintained them until relieved. During the same period in north central Burma, Wingate's airborne long-range penetration group was flown more than 100 miles into the interior of Burma and commenced operations on the Japanese lines of communication. Guerrillas and other resistance movements in Burma and Malaya were regularly supplied by the same method. Airborne aviation engineer battalions with bull-dozers and all necessary equipment were organised for the rapid construction of air-strips. Their parachutists were dropped to prepare a space for the gliders carrying equipment and technicians. Once the Japanese army air force had been mastered in South-East Asia, air transport became a major function in the strategy of the land campaign. Supply problems to isolated groups were no longer so great an anxiety to an army commander.

Probably the most outstanding contribution to British air power was the Empire Air Training Scheme in Canada. From Vancouver Island to Nova Scotia stretched a chain of flying training schools operating under ideal conditions, unrestricted by blackouts or enemy air interference. Though aircrew training continued in Britain, Australia, New Zealand, South Africa and Rhodesia, the majority of those selected from the first three of these countries went to Canada. Germany had no such training area outside the war zone: the morale and efficiency of her pilots and aircrews diminished as the war progressed.

Since the days of the Royal Naval Air Service and the Royal Flying Corps during the first world war many young men from the Dominions and colonies travelled to Britain to join either one or the other service. This steady flow of volunteers continued after the formation of the Royal Air Force and during the whole of the peace interval. Thus in the R.A.F. squadrons of the second world war there were many Commonwealth members. In addition each dominion possessed its own air force, some with distinctive uniforms or badges but with organisation, administration and operation training similar to the R.A.F. These squadrons which served in the war in Europe and the Middle East formed an integral part of the R.A.F.

Throughout the war photographic reconnaissance at high altitude by the fastest type of aeroplane of the period, stripped of its armament, was regularly carried out to the limit of fuel endurance. Amongst many other important items of information obtained by interpretation of the photographs, sometimes in confirmation of intelligence reports from other sources, two were of particular interest to Britain. The first was the identification early in 1944 of unusual objects and apparatus at Peenemunde on the Baltic coast; and the other was the discovery of digging activities at various points near the coast in France. It soon became apparent that some new form of weapon was to be used against England. The discovery was kept a secret. It became a question of whether air attacks could delay the launching of the new campaign until the invading Allied armies overran the sites.

Though bombing did materially retard the German programme the first of these new weapons fell on London on 12 June 1944. Known officially as the V 1, and colloquially as the 'Doodle-Bug', on account of its shape and sinister noise, this flying bomb took the form of a small pilotless aircraft with jet propulsion. It contained an explosive charge of one ton. At the end of its timed run the motive power stopped and the missile dived to the ground, exploding on impact. Counter-measures by Fighter Command were immediately introduced. Kite balloons were concentrated in south-east England to form a barrage against these low-flying missiles, many of which were brought down by colliding with the mooring cables. Anti-aircraft fire and fast interception fighters shot down a considerable number. In August 1944 Meteor jet fighters made their first appearance and joined these interception operations.

Though occasional flying bombs continued to reach England up to March 1945 from the sites in Holland or after being released from aircraft, the scale of attack diminished in the autumn of 1944. Out of some 8000 V 1 flying bombs estimated to have been launched, only about 2300 reached the London area. This weapon, however, was used against Antwerp during the Allied advance.

After the V 1 came the German V 2 rocket, also launched from sites on the European coast. This weapon was some 50 feet long, tapering to a warhead point and carrying a ton of explosive. Though radar could give warning of its approach it could not be intercepted, and though its aim could not be precise it could cause severe damage to densely populated areas. Over 1000 of these rockets crossed the Channel and over half of them exploded in the London area, before the Allied invading armies in Europe put a stop to this form of attack.

The occupation of conquered territory from Norway to the Spanish frontier had been of enormous advantage to Germany. It provided depth for the air defence of Germany as well as bases for submarines, air forces and launching sites for V weapons. British or American bombs falling wide of the targets in these areas could harm only the people and towns in the occupied countries. British people in the target areas had stood up remarkably well to the normal bombing from aeroplanes which they had experienced, particularly in the first half of the war. Had Germany been able to develop to the full extent her V weapon campaign there is little doubt that the dislocation to normal life and the damage to cities and towns within range would have been an even more formidable problem. It would have necessitated widespread dispersal and consequent dislocation of the production of war material and of the conduct of the war effort. It is improbable, however, that it would have been decisive.

German air attacks, including those by V weapons, caused British civilian casualties to the number of 60,595 killed and missing, and 86,182 injured and needing hospital treatment. Comparable figures for the first world war were 1260 and 3490 respectively. No less than half a million people, excluding Fighter Command and anti-aircraft personnel, were employed on full-time defence measures in Britain against German air attacks.

Air power in direct support of an army taking the offensive had already proved its value to Germany in the early campaigns in Europe. The aircraft supply position in Britain had so far improved by 1942 as to enable a really effective air force to be allocated for close co-operation with the Eighth Army in North Africa. Thus the existing small but efficient Desert Air Force was expanded to become the First Tactical Air Force. As the African campaign progressed after victory at El Alamein, to be followed by the invasion of Sicily and later of Italy, this T.A.F. grew in strength and scope. Its commander worked alongside the army commander, using his squadrons for the maximum support of the land battle. He had at his disposal fighter squadrons in sufficient strength to gain air superiority over the battle area. His force also included fighter-bombers, some fitted to carry rockets, light bombers for attacks on enemy rear areas, photographic, reconnaissance, and artillery observation planes.

Airfield construction units and other necessary ancillary services completed a mobile force designed to enable squadrons, during rapid movement by armoured formations, to operate from new forward airfields with the least possible delay. In conjunction with the American air force the First T.A.F. maintained air superiority in the landings in Sicily and Italy and continued to support the invading armies in their long and arduous advance to the north.

It was on this pattern, though on a larger scale, that the Second Tactical Air Force was organised in preparation for the invasion of Europe to support the Twenty-First Army Group. The American organisation was generally similar. In both cases a number of transport planes were allotted for airborne operations. These Allied tactical air forces, supported for the occasion by Fighter, Bomber and Coastal Commands, dominated the air during the sea crossings and Normandy landings. That they were able to do this so completely was due, in no small measure, to the effect of the strategic bomber offensive which compelled the Germans to concentrate their fighters on the defence of the Reich.

During this European campaign little enemy air interference was experienced by the advancing Allied armies. The Allied Supreme Commander paid high tribute to the effectiveness of the British and U.S. air support, particularly in the defeat of the German counter-attack towards Avranches on 7 August 1944 when hundreds of enemy tanks and vehicles were destroyed, and at Falaise where the combined effect of air and artillery bombardment on the closing pocket of resistance was decisive. The rocket-firing Typhoon fighters were most effective in these operations. During the autumn of 1944 the Supreme Commander of the campaign had at his disposal or at call a British and American air strength, in round figures, of 4700 fighters, 6000 light, medium and heavy bombers and 4000 reconnaissance, transport and other types. Allied victory in north-west Europe owed much to the Allied tactical air forces.

The great development in the use of air power during nearly six years of war was largely due to rapid scientific and technical progress. Apart from the ordinary transport plane, employed in its original form throughout the various campaigns for many purposes, the performance of actual fighting aircraft increased to an extent and at a rate only possible when given high priority in a major emergency. The speed of fighter aircraft rose by over 200 miles an hour: with extra tanks their reinforcing range exceeded 1000 miles, and they could carry bombs or rockets. Bombers doubled their load capacity and their range. Radar emerged from the experimental stage and was adapted for a variety of purposes to aid either the offensive or the defensive. Each fresh development in aircraft, their weapons or accessories, opened up new avenues for employment or extended existing uses.

To sum up: during the second world war there were nine outstanding instances of the effective employment of air power. It was first used by the Germans as the spearhead of their attack, at the outset to neutralise completely their opponents' air forces and subsequently to give direct support to mechanised armies. Against Poland, Norway, Holland,

France, and later Greece this method was decisive. Overwhelming strength in the air gave advantage to the aggressor and largely accounted for the speed at which his invading forces advanced.

Secondly, the Germans effectively used air power in their invasion of Crete. Some 15,000 troops were transported by air from occupied Greece in spite of British naval forces remaining unchallenged by enemy warships in that area.

Thirdly, the flexibility of air power enabled British bomber policy to be changed in a matter of hours. Bombers could be switched to anti-submarine patrols, to mine laying, to the direct support of armies in a land campaign. Targets could be selected over a wide range of enemy territory. Oil plants, railway systems, industrial areas, submarine bases, shipyards, battleships and V-weapon factories or launching sites, each received priority at one time or another from Bomber Command.

Fourthly, the Japanese used it effectively in their surprise attack on the United States Pacific Fleet in Pearl Harbour without a declaration of war. It was a devastating act of aggression made possible by use of air power, reinforced three days later by the sinking of two British capital ships lacking air cover.

Fifthly, air power was used for the entire supply and maintenance of isolated forces for extended periods, as at Imphal and into China.

Sixthly, the British-American bombing campaign of 1944 and 1945 on railway systems and back areas in support of the Allied invading armies, on the enemy aircraft production industry and on oil plants, led to the immobilisation of a high proportion of German aircraft and armoured vehicles.

Seventhly, the United States used air power in the Pacific war for intense bombardment of each successive objective in the island-by-island strategy of that campaign.

Eighthly, air power made possible rapid reinforcement from one campaign area to another, as in the reinforcing route to the Far East.

Finally, the United States' use of two atom bombs against Japan produced effects sufficiently devastating to turn the scale against an enemy already on the verge of defeat.

In less than forty-five years air power developed from zero to a stage when it could be used as an instrument of attack more destructive in its effect than any other weapon hitherto designed by man.

CHAPTER XI

INTERNATIONAL RELATIONS, 1900–12

B Y 1900 the two dynamic forces of nationalism and industrialism had radically altered the balance of power throughout the world. Accompanied by increasing state control, they had extended European sovereignty to nearly the whole of Africa, led to new rivalries in Asia, and contributed to the spectacular development in wealth and strength of two non-European states, the U.S.A. and Japan. A further result was that the great powers in Europe were becoming greater, the small powers relatively weaker. Although the principal 'great powers' were still European, their relations with the peoples of other continents were of growing importance and the issues that divided them often concerned regions far beyond the confines of Europe. As the means of communication had multiplied in number and celerity, so the area and sensitivity of political repercussion had strikingly increased. By 1900 international relations were world relations in a sense unknown in 1800 or at the dawn of any previous century.

During the 1890's these relations underwent notable changes. With Prussia's victory in the war of 1870 the hegemony of the Continent had passed to the new German empire, which had made a grievous psychological blunder in annexing Alsace and Lorraine. Henceforward Germany, with a population second only to Russia in Europe, an army second to none, and a great industrial potential, was inherently the strongest single state on the European mainland. Bismarck, the founder of this empire and its Chancellor until 1890, therefore played a leading role in shaping international relations, and his primary concern had been to ensure that France should never be able to embark upon a war of *revanche*. Haunted by the 'nightmare' that she would form an anti-German coalition, he framed his policy so as to keep France in isolation. After co-operation with Austria and Russia in the Three Emperors' League had broken down owing to Austro-Russian rivalry in the Balkans he had constructed a system of alliances of which the corner-stone was the secret defensive Dual Alliance of 1879 with Austria-Hungary, supplemented by the Triple Alliance with Austria-Hungary and Italy concluded in 1882. The renewal of the Three Emperors' League in 1881, the accession of Roumania to the Triple Alliance in 1883, the Austro-Serbian alliance of 1881 renewed in 1889, the consent of England and Spain to agreements with Italy in 1887 designed to preserve the *status quo* in the Mediterranean area, and the conclusion in the same year of Germany's so-called

Reinsurance Treaty with Russia, secured that the remaining great powers, as well as a number of lesser ones, should move more or less closely within the German orbit. As a result, Bismarck had kept the peace of Europe, excluding the Balkan peninsula, for the best part of twenty years and the pattern of European relations had appeared relatively stable. But his fall in 1890, the uncertain temper of the brilliant, impulsive and indiscreet young emperor, William II, who dismissed him, and the uncertain policy of the lesser men who succeeded him and who, partly out of consideration for England, failed to renew the Reinsurance Treaty with Russia, but did renew the Triple Alliance (6 May 1891), inaugurated a period of fundamental change.

Bismarck had, on the whole, pursued a deliberate policy of limited liability. The aims of William II and his advisers were more ambitious but less clearly defined: hence Germany became a disquieting instead of a stabilising factor in European politics, all the more so because she was essentially a military monarchy in which the army was largely free from parliamentary control and responsible directly to the emperor. Alarmed by the renewal of the Triple Alliance and by Anglo-German friendliness, Russia, whose relations with Germany had been cool even while the Reinsurance Treaty was in force, began to look elsewhere. The natural ally, dictated by strategical and economic, though not by ideological, considerations, was Republican France, whose statesmen were eager for Russian friendship, and the Franco-Russian Alliance (an exchange of letters agreeing to joint action for the maintenance of peace dated 27 August 1891 and a secret military convention of 18 August 1892 ratified by the two governments in the winter of 1893-4) brought about just that conjunction which Bismarck had striven to prevent. In the military convention Russia undertook to use all available forces against Germany should France be attacked by Germany or by Italy and Germany together, while France promised to use all her available force against Germany should Russia be attacked by Germany alone or by Austria-Hungary supported by Germany. Although these agreements were wholly defensive and contained no 'suggestion of mutual support for the realization of any positive ambitions', they gave France a feeling of security unknown to her since 1871 and caused misgivings in England as well as in Germany, since it was with France and Russia that British interests chiefly conflicted. Above all, France's emergence from isolation meant that the great powers of continental Europe were now divided into two armed camps. The balance of power was likely once again to become a European issue. This was a new factor in international relations and one which remained fundamental until the outbreak of the first world war. As yet, however, not all the eventual partners had taken sides, and the permanence of the new grouping had still to be tested. Although there were now two alliance systems, the 'nineties were characterised by such a complex fluidity of policies that they have been called the period of the 'interpenetration of alliances'.[1]

Outside Europe there were also changes of fundamental importance. The extension of European dominion continued apace and brought fresh menaces of conflict, while a new phase of expansion began for the non-European states, the U.S.A. and Japan.

In the Far East the ancient empire of China was the chief bone of contention. There, first in the field, England had by 1890 established a commercial and diplomatic pre-eminence based upon sea power. In the north, Russia aimed at securing an ice-free port to serve as the terminus of the great Trans-Siberian Railway, which she had begun to build in 1891 with the aid of French capital, and which was to transform the strategic position in North-East Asia. In the south, France's acquisition of Indo-China had been indirectly at Chinese expense, as had the British annexation of Upper Burma in 1885, and both powers were now able to penetrate into south China. Foreign concessions and commercial establishments in Shanghai and other great Chinese cities were eloquent witness to the economic stakes at issue. Indisputably China was the 'sick man' of the Far East, but, as in the Near East with Turkey, the European powers disagreed upon his treatment. Thus, whereas Russia favoured the amputation of outlying areas and opposed the open door for commerce, Britain championed integrity and the policy of free trade which had brought her two-thirds of China's modest foreign trade.

It was, however, the intervention of Japan in 1894 which made the Far Eastern question a major factor in international relations. Japan, who had so recently emerged from feudal isolation and astounded the world by her ability to assimilate western ideas and techniques, was in dispute with China over the Ryukyu Islands and Korea and determined to prevent their falling under European, especially Russian, control. After a brief and successful war, by the Treaty of Shimonoseki (17 April 1895) she obliged China to cede the island of Formosa and on the mainland the Liaotung Peninsula with its valuable ice-free harbour, Port Arthur, to grant her most-favoured-nation status in China, and to recognise the independence of Korea. This outcome was extremely unwelcome both to Russia, whose rulers were beginning to envisage the seizure of Manchuria and the eventual reduction of China to the position of a client state, and to Germany, who, with Russia's reluctant acquiescence, was planning herself to seize a Chinese port; and these two powers together with France, who felt bound to support Russia, demanded that Japan should hand back the Liaotung Peninsula. Japan complied, accepting an indemnity instead, but harboured a deep resentment against Russia and Germany, against whom she would one day take her revenge. Thus Far

[1] For example, by G. Salvemini and W. L. Langer. See the latter's *The Diplomacy of Imperialism, 1890–1902* (New York and London, 1935), vol. I, p. 297.

Eastern affairs had led to a loose coalition in Asia of those European powers who were on opposite sides in Europe. In effect their co-operation, which continued intermittently for another ten years, was a local manifestation of the sort of continental alliance against England so often urged by anti-British statesmen in Europe. China's self-appointed champions did not go unrequited. Russia soon received her reward, notably in a concession for the construction of the Chinese Eastern Railway, which facilitated her penetration into Manchuria, while France obtained railway concessions in the Yunnan area. Two years later the spoliation of China went a stage farther when Germany seized a base in Kiao-Chow Bay on 14 November 1897, and when, in March 1898, Russia, having declined English overtures for a 'partition of preponderance',[1] occupied the coveted Port Arthur which she converted into a naval base. In both instances the European powers gained economic advantages in the adjacent territories and preferred to extort leasehold concessions instead of proclaiming outright annexation. This was a convenient new device 'whereby Foreign Powers might acquire the substance of colonial authority without a complete transfer of title'.[2] Inevitably the other powers felt obliged to seek some semblance of compensation, and accordingly England occupied Wei-hai-wei and France Kwang Chow Wan. The open-door policy had largely broken down, in spite of British and, subsequently (1899), American gestures to maintain it, and the struggle for 'spheres of influence' in China became the dominant concern.

These events had significant consequences. Chinese nationalist resentment manifested itself in the Boxer risings of 1900 in which the foreign Legations in Peking were besieged and many 'foreign devils', including the German Minister, met their death. At the same time Japan's feeling against Russia was embittered by the seizure of Port Arthur and she began to contemplate the possibility of war to prevent further Russian expansion. Her suspicions and those of England, throughout opposed to Russia's Chinese policy, were intensified when the Boxer risings enabled Russian troops to enter Manchuria in force. Thus, although the principal European powers combined to send an international force against the Boxers, the Chinese question at the beginning of the twentieth century threatened to multiply the occasions of friction between the white nations. In particular, it had added a vast new area to the wide field in which British and Russian interests already conflicted.

In the Near East, however, Russia's preoccupation with Chinese questions resulted in an interlude in her traditional Balkan rivalry with Austria, and this happier state of affairs was confirmed by an agreement of May

[1] Lord Salisbury to Sir N. O'Conor, 25 January 1898. G. P. Gooch and H. W. V. Temperley (eds.), *British Documents on the Origins of the War, 1898–1914*, vol. I (London, 1927), no. 9.
[2] G. F. Hudson, *The Far East in World Politics, A Study in Recent History* (2nd ed., 1939), p. 100.

1897 whereby the two powers renounced any conquests for themselves should the *status quo* in the Balkans be disturbed, and by the Muerzsteg Programme of 1903 in which they combined in efforts to settle the affairs of Macedonia. But this temporary improvement in Austro-Russian relations did not mean that Turkish affairs had ceased to be vexatious or significant. That shaky power had been shaken again by fresh stirrings of her subject nationalities, by risings in Armenia (1894), Crete (May 1896), and Macedonia. In 1895 England had threatened a naval demonstration to induce her to desist from solving the Armenian question by massacring the Armenians, and only the menace of Russian counter-measures had prevented the threat from being implemented. In Crete revolt had excited Greece to launch a hopeless attack upon Turkey, with the result that the great powers had intervened in order to prevent the conflict from spreading to the Balkans and had obliged the Turks to grant the Cretans autonomy under a Greek High Commissioner.

That Turkey had weathered these storms was, as so often before, largely due to the conflicting interests of the great powers. Traditionally England was the principal champion of Turkish integrity. Yet in 1895 Salisbury, convinced of the hopelessness of Turkish reform, had hinted at the desirability of something like partition, and it was Russia and Germany who had poured cold water on his suggestions. Again, in 1897, when Austria and Russia were considering the Macedonian situation, it was Russia who had rejected the Austrian proposal for the creation of an independent Albania and for the division of the remainder of European Turkey between the existing Balkan states. Preoccupied in the Far East, Russia preferred that there should be no Balkan upheaval. Within Turkey, however, the most significant development was the growth of German influence. Already in 1881 a German military mission had undertaken the training of the Turkish army and in 1888 a German syndicate had obtained a concession to build a railway from Ismid to Ankara. In 1889 the German emperor had paid a first visit to Constantinople and in 1898 at Damascus he demonstratively proclaimed his friendship for the Muslim world. The 1888 concession marked the beginning of a rapid extension of German economic influence. Naturally the German government favoured these developments which received powerful backing from the able ambassador sent to Constantinople in 1897, Baron Marschall von Bieberstein. Within a few years he had acquired a dominant situation in the Turkish capital, while the efficiency of German 'promoters, bankers, traders, engineers, manufacturers, ship-owners and railway builders'[1] soon undermined French and British interests and created something like a German economic empire in the Near East. Most significant of all were the grant obtained by the German-controlled Anatolian Railway Company in 1899 to build a commercial port at Haidar

[1] E. M. Earle, *Turkey, the Great Powers and the Bagdad Railway* (London, 1923), p. 37.

Pasha on the Asiatic side of the Bosporus and the concession in principle of an extension of their railway from Konieh to Baghdad and the Persian Gulf.

To Turkey herself these developments seemed eminently desirable: railways would bring prosperity to backward districts of the empire and enable the government to move troops more rapidly to defend the frontiers or deal with internal disturbances, while the economic and diplomatic support of distant and seemingly disinterested Germany appeared the best guarantee of Turkish integrity. But so far as international relations were concerned this economic penetration could not but have a political significance. What alarmed other nations was the new projection of German power diagonally overland in an axis from Berlin to Constantinople which threatened to divide Europe in two. Such an axis cut across Russia's possible line of expansion to the Mediterranean through the Balkans, while the revival of Turkish power under German influence promised to frustrate Russia's age-long aspiration to control the Straits. Furthermore, the prolongation of the axis through Asia Minor to the Persian Gulf could be seen as a menace to British interests in Egypt and Persia. Thus, although the Deutsche Bank sought to enlist the aid of British, French and Russian capital to finance the construction of the Baghdad Railway it was impossible for governments to regard this as a purely business undertaking. Russia had shown her alarm at the concession of Haidar Pasha; by the Black Sea Agreement of 1900 she forced the Turks to admit that any railway concessions in northern Anatolia and Armenia should be granted only to Russian citizens or to syndicates approved by the tsar; and she eventually withdrew her consent to the participation of Russian capital in the development of the Baghdad Railway. The British government on the other hand had been in favour of giving the railway an international character, but public opinion in England, already highly distrustful of Germany, made such an outcry against the participation of a British financial syndicate that they withdrew their support. This was a notable instance of the way in which diplomacy had sometimes to retreat in face of the new forces of publicity. The French government, impelled to follow Russia, likewise refused official backing, so that the Germans began the construction of the first section of the railway in 1904 without the financial aid of foreign governments. The intrusion of Germany into spheres long earmarked by other powers for themselves had introduced a new disturbing factor into international relations. In particular it imposed a new strain on the relations of Germany with Russia, France and England.

The third great area in which the European powers pursued their partitioning projects was Africa. Here the scene was dominated by the traditional colonial rivalry of France and England, the determination of Germany to make her influence felt, and the failure of the Italian attempt to conquer a new dominion.

English and French interests collided at many points but, whereas frontier disputes in the west were settled by an Anglo-French Convention of 14 June 1898, differences farther east were less easily composed. The main tension came with the struggle for control of the Upper Nile. For England, virtual mistress of Egypt since 1882, this was of vital concern, since the prosperity of Egypt depended upon the Nile waters. An attempt in 1894–5 to agree with France upon a definition of spheres of influence came to nothing. The French had never ceased to resent the fact that, argely through French timidity, the British had gained sole control of Egypt. Furthermore, some French colonial expansionists hoped to secure a continuous block of territory from the Atlantic to the Red Sea or Indian Ocean. For such a plan, as well as for applying pressure to Britain in Egypt, the Upper Nile region was of great importance, and in 1896 an expedition was sent to plant the French flag at Fashoda. In the same year Kitchener had been dispatched by the British government to reconquer the Egyptian Sudan, which had been evacuated in 1884, and in 1898 he captured Khartoum. On 25 September 1898, when he found Marchand's French troops at Fashoda and summoned them to withdraw, there occurred one of the gravest crises in Anglo-French relations since 1815. The British government mobilised the English press in support of its stand, Fleet Street being taken quite unusually into the direct confidence of the Foreign Office, and refused to negotiate until Marchand's force had been ordered to retire. For the second time in the 'nineties (there had been acute tension over Siam in 1893) England and France were on the brink of war. But the new French Foreign Minister, Delcassé, and his colleagues wisely recognised that France was in no condition to undertake a colonial war against the greatest naval power, and on 3 November they ordered the evacuation of the disputed territory. An Anglo-French Convention of 21 March 1899 demarcated the British and French spheres of interest in the region of the watershed between the Nile and the Congo and the problem of control of the Upper Nile was solved in favour of Britain. Yet the memory of Fashoda rankled and many observers at the turn of the century would have agreed that England had replaced Germany as France's chief enemy and would have regarded Anglo-French hostility as one of the most abiding features of international relations. Nevertheless, Fashoda taught Delcassé a lesson out of which eventual understanding was born: it was folly for France to risk enmity at one and the same time with the greatest naval and the greatest military power. She must choose, and, once it was clear that the obstacles to genuine friendship with Germany were insuperable, Delcassé shaped his policy accordingly.

Developments in South Africa indirectly contributed to this eventual understanding. Here the main conflicting interests were those of England and Germany, who had established herself in South-West Africa in 1884;

and the main cause of trouble was the economic development of the Boer Republic of the Transvaal. The gold rush of the 'eighties had led to the unwelcome influx into the Boer states of a large new white population which soon equalled and possibly outnumbered the original Boer stock. To these Uitlanders or foreigners the restrictive policies of the Boer President of the Transvaal became so irksome that revolt was openly plotted with the connivance of certain people in the adjoining British territories. But the Jameson raid of 1895, which attempted to precipitate such a rising, was a fiasco. Its most dramatic outcome was the intervention of the German emperor, whose congratulatory telegram to President Kruger on 3 January 1896 roused passionate resentment in England. Furthermore, the belief it encouraged in Kruger that he might rely on foreign support strengthened him in the intransigent attitude which led finally to the outbreak of the Boer War in October 1899.

For the moment, however, Russian and French reluctance to support Germany, and Germany's own realisation that she was helpless to intervene effectively without a powerful fleet, facilitated a *détente*. On 30 August 1898 the temporary improvement in Anglo-German relations was marked by the secret Angola agreement in which the two powers defined their spheres of interest and the areas which they would occupy in the event of Portugal abandoning her colonies. But the good effect upon Germany of this dubious arrangement was undone by the colonial guarantee reaffirmed by England to Portugal in the following year when it was clear that the Portuguese meant to retain them. The Germans felt that they had been tricked and the memory of this English 'perfidy' was undoubtedly a stumbling-block in the way of future Anglo-German arrangements. 'With these people', exclaimed the powerful director of the German Foreign Office, Baron von Holstein, 'it is impossible to enter into any engagement.'[1] So, although Germany abstained from exploiting British isolation during the Boer War and resisted Russian suggestions for some sort of intervention in an anti-British sense, events in South Africa during these years had sown seeds of distrust between Britain and Germany which would not easily be eradicated. Above all they taught the kaiser that sea power was a condition of the world power of which he and a great many Germans dreamed.

Colonial questions in Africa had thus led to grave friction between England and France on the one hand and England and Germany on the other; but they had generally been subordinated to European interests, and in neither case had they resulted in war or materially hindered the process of bringing ever-larger areas of the African continent under more effective European control. Another European power, Italy, however, was less successful, and her defeat at Adowa in 1896 by the Ethiopians,

---

[1] Quoted in H. Nicolson, *Sir Arthur Nicolson, Bart, First Lord Carnock, A Study in the Old Diplomacy* (London, 1930), p. 128.

whom she had hoped to reduce to vassalage, dealt a blow to white prestige, changed the direction of her imperialist ambitions and had important repercussions upon Italian policy in Europe.

Meanwhile the 'nineties were no less significant for the new advances made by the U.S.A. There, nationalism of an expansionist character was once again in the ascendant. Its belligerent tone, manifested by President Cleveland in the British–Venezuelan boundary dispute of 1895, gave a new extension to the Monroe Doctrine and obliged an England preoccupied by South African affairs to have recourse to arbitration. Still more important was the American war with Spain (April–August 1898) which led not only to the establishment of a United States' protectorate over Cuba and the annexation of the Hawaiian Islands and Puerto Rico, but also to American assumption of direct rule over Guam and the Philippines. The annexation of the Philippines—'the great aberration', as one historian has called it[1]—was a striking departure from the traditional policy of confining American political responsibilities to the western hemisphere. Although it did not of itself involve the U.S.A. in Far Eastern politics, it meant that in the long run, territorially and strategically as well as commercially, she was much more likely to become so involved. However reluctantly and hesitantly, the Americans were beginning to assume the cares and ambitions of a world power to which their wealth and population already committed them.

Although these extra-European developments did not seriously affect the systems of alliance within Europe they showed up the weak links in those systems, and the tension and danger of war created by such incidents as the Kruger Telegram and Fashoda gave rise to a sense of insecurity which impelled the major powers to seek to reinforce their positions. This reinforcement, which led to the completion of the alliance system, is a main theme of the next decade.

The sense of insecurity was increased by the growth of defensive armaments. The military budget of the German empire had nearly trebled since 1878 and those of England and France more than or nearly doubled. One way of relieving tension would have been by an agreed reduction of armaments and this was actually proposed by the tsar in 1898. The Russian note of 24 August suggesting an international conference urged that if armaments continued to grow there would be 'a cataclysm too horrible for the human mind to contemplate'. But the tsar's gesture, coming as it did shortly after Russia's seizure of Port Arthur, was met with incredulity and suspicion. Germany above all had 'no intention of binding herself in the question of military armaments',[2] and the only

---

[1] S. F. Bemis, who gives this as the title of one of the chapters of his *A Diplomatic History of the United States* (London, 1937).

[2] 'Dass wir nicht gesonnen sind, uns in der Frage der militärischen Rüstungen nach irgendeiner Richtung hin zu binden, brauche ich hier kaum zu erwähnen', Bülow's instruc-

positive results of the first Hague Peace Conference (May–July 1899) were the establishment of a permanent court of arbitration and the adoption of two conventions relating to the rules of war. In the long run the Hague tribunal was to prove an enduring and important piece of machinery for the adjustment of international relations; but immediately the discouraging effect of the conference was to make clear that the armaments race would continue. Soon this would be a danger at sea as well as on land.

While the Hague Conference was still sitting, France renewed and extended her ties with Russia, which to many Frenchmen at the time of the Fashoda crisis had seemed all too loose. On 9 August 1899 an exchange of letters took place in which 'the maintenance of the balance of power' was substituted for 'the maintenance of peace' as the prime object of the Franco-Russian alliance. This widened the scope of the alliance and implied that France would be readier to support Russia's Balkan ambitions. At the same time the military convention, hitherto to last as long only as the Triple Alliance, was prolonged indefinitely. The Franco-Russian alliance would now, in Delcassé's view, survive any break-up of Austria-Hungary (which more than one European statesman now envisaged as a possibility) and be ready to meet the consequences of such a momentous event. Nor was this all: in 1900 the military arrangements between the two powers were adapted to cover the risk of war with England, and an agreement to this end was ratified in 1901. In the dawn of the new century both powers could consider war with England a danger which they must take into account. This did not mean that Delcassé had abandoned the objective of an understanding with England, but indicates that he still doubted its possibility.

At the same time a *rapprochement* between France and Italy ended a period of tension dating from the French occupation of Tunis in 1881. France naturally welcomed any opportunity to make the third partner in the Triple Alliance sit more loosely to her obligations, while Italy, baulked of Ethiopia, cast all the more longing eyes across the Mediterranean on the undeveloped Ottoman dependency of Tripoli. For any attempt on Tripoli to succeed, the goodwill of France, who held the adjoining Tunisia, was essential. New men, in Italy the Prime Minister, Rudini, and the Foreign Ministers, Visconti Venosta and Prinetti, in France Delcassé and Camille Barrère, sent to the Rome Embassy in 1898, helped to bring about the change. In 1898 a commercial treaty ended the customs war begun in 1888 which had damaged Italy more than France. On 14 December 1900 a secret agreement followed, whereby France promised Italy a free hand in Tripoli in return for recognition of France's

tions to Münster, the chief German delegate to the conference. *Die Grosse Politik der Europäischen Kabinette 1871–1914*, vol. xv (Berlin, 1927), p. 190. Cf. G. P. Gooch, *Before the War, Studies in Diplomacy*, vol. i (London, 1936), p. 196.

interests in Morocco. The final triumph of French policy came in 1902 when Italy, who had just renewed the Triple Alliance for the fourth time and in doing so extorted an Austrian recognition of her interests in Tripoli, gave France a secret assurance that if France were attacked or obliged to declare war as a result of 'direct provocation' Italy would remain neutral. Her Mediterranean interests and skilful French diplomacy had thus led Italy to give an undertaking which, if it did not formally conflict with her obligations under the Triple Alliance, was certainly not in accordance with its spirit. Although the text was kept secret until 1920, a statement by Delcassé in the French Chamber made clear that France now had nothing to fear from Italy, and the improvement in Franco-Italian relations, already manifested in 1901 by the visit of an Italian naval squadron to Toulon, received further demonstration in an exchange of visits between the heads of the two states. Germany was naturally irritated at these developments, although in the Reichstag the Chancellor affected to treat the *rapprochement* as an innocent flirtation. Unfortunately for the Triple Alliance, the flirtation was, as a French historian has remarked, 'to develop into a liaison'.[1]

It was natural for France to seek to extend the circle of her friends. For her, isolation had been a painful punishment. But for England isolation had been splendid and deliberate, and the abandonment of that aloofness because of a new sense of the need for security was a pregnant event. Whether or not Bismarck in November 1887 made a veiled overture to England for a defensive alliance against France, there is no doubt that for British statesmen and a considerable section of British public opinion down to the Russo-Japanese War of 1904–5 Russia, not France, was the most formidable menace to British imperial interests. An alliance that did not bind Germany against Russia would be of doubtful value. So, while England had temporarily inclined her weight on the side of the Triple Alliance by the Mediterranean Agreement of 1887, she had not bound herself to it.

Bismarck's successors at first continued his friendly attitude. In 1890 there was an Anglo-German agreement whereby England exchanged Heligoland for considerable territories in Africa; and in 1891 the Germans made fresh soundings about an alliance. But as the fundamental attitude of both powers towards Russia remained unchanged these talks came to nothing. Thereafter relations between the two countries had tended to deteriorate. When the Franco-Russian alliance was concluded England's isolation was evident and the German rulers believed that England would soon come to them cap in hand and enable them to extract a high price for their friendship. Although at times they indulged in frankly hostile dreams of a continental alliance for the destruction of the British empire,

[1] M. Baumont, *L'Essor industriel et l'impérialisme colonial (1878–1904)* (Paris, 1937), p. 323.

their general policy was to keep a free hand as between Russia and England but to show that the hand was mailed and held a sharp sword. Thereby the kaiser was encouraged by Bülow to believe that he could play the role of *arbiter mundi*. So Germany entered upon a disconcerting course in which, in order to break the Franco-Russian alliance and to bring England to heel, she aggressively demonstrated her growing strength.

The first conspicuous example of this policy, the Kruger Telegram, was the first incident which made England feel that it would be wise to settle some of her differences and win a friend in Europe; but it was to Russia, not to Germany that she turned, and Salisbury's proposal for the mutual recognition of spheres of interest in Turkey, already alluded to (p. 304), was suggested as part of a wider settlement. This was the first of several such overtures, but, until her defeat by Japan, Russia saw in agreement with England a hindrance not an aid to her expansionist policy and turned a deaf ear.

It was above all the Far Eastern question which convinced an important section of British opinion, headed by the Colonial Secretary, Joseph Chamberlain, that the time had come to abandon isolation. Failing the U.S.A., and Japan, who was not yet disposed for an alliance that might provoke an armed clash with Russia for which she was still unprepared, Chamberlain gladly listened to the suggestion of the pro-British First Secretary of the German Embassy in London, Eckardstein, that the time had come to strengthen Anglo-German relations. In 1898 he suggested a defensive alliance based upon 'a mutual understanding as to policy in China and elsewhere'. But Eckardstein was too forward: China was not a vital German interest and his chiefs had no wish to side against Russia or to pull England's chestnuts out of the Far Eastern fire for her. By keeping a free hand they hoped rather to profit from the conflict between England and Russia which seemed so probable. The negotiations petered out and Chamberlain's subsequent public affirmation of England's need for an alliance with some 'great military power' aroused no enthusiasm in Germany or England. Indeed, an important factor in Anglo-German relations before 1914 was the lukewarmness or antagonism of British popular feelings towards Germany and the positive and increasing hostility of the great mass of German opinion towards Britain. This mutual antipathy, which dates mainly from the Boer War, was all the more widespread since the development of a cheap popular press in both countries in the 'nineties, for neither country properly understood the workings of the press in the other and neither government was fully able to restrain the hostile outpourings of its own newspapers. In such circumstances a genuine alliance would have been very difficult to accomplish.

In spite of his failure, Chamberlain was loth to relinquish his dream of partnership between the big army and the big navy, so alien to the main tradition of British foreign policy, and, when the kaiser visited England in November 1899, he reverted to the theme of an alliance, this time between England, Germany and the U.S.A. But when in a public speech at Leicester he referred to 'the natural alliance between ourselves and the great German empire' he met with strikingly little support in England, criticism in the U.S.A. and a storm of hostile comment in Germany. Moreover, in the Reichstag Bülow poured cold water on Chamberlain's overtures and spoke of the need for a strong German fleet. The second German Navy Bill, introduced in January 1900, with its principle that 'Germany must have a battle fleet so strong that even the adversary possessed of the greatest sea power will attack it only with grave risk to herself', continued the potentially challenging policy inaugurated by Admiral von Tirpitz, who had become Minister of Marine in 1897. England was rebuffed and when, by the Yangtse Agreement of 16 October 1900, 'the only formal agreement for diplomatic co-operation ever made between Great Britain and Germany',[1] the two powers undertook to maintain Chinese integrity and the open door for trade 'wherever both Powers can exert influence', they soon fell out because they differed sharply over its interpretation.

The last attempt to bring about an alliance occurred in 1901. Originating probably with a personal initiative of Eckardstein and favoured again by Chamberlain and his friends, it developed on the German side into a proposal that England should join the Triple Alliance. But Salisbury saw no advantage—'the liability of having to defend the German and Austrian frontiers against Russia is heavier than that of having to defend the British Isles against France'[2]—and as the Germans would be content with nothing less and were no longer interested in local co-operation, such as an agreement concerning Morocco proposed by the British, these negotiations, too, were fruitless. If the Germans genuinely wished for an alliance their insistence on a formal treaty sanctioned by Parliament showed a lack of psychological insight, for, as the Anglo-French *entente* was to show, a close working association with Britain was possible without any formal ties. Holstein and his colleagues still believed that they had only to wait a while longer for England to renew her suit and pay the price. In spite of a plain hint by Chamberlain in April 1898 they could not think it possible that she would turn elsewhere. Their miscalculation was grievous.

In the same year, 1901, the Far Eastern situation caused fresh preoccupation. Fear of Russian encroachments in Persia and Manchuria led to another unsuccessful British effort to settle Anglo-Russian differences, while Japan, who had vainly attempted to reach agreement with Russia on the basis of recognising Russia's predominance in Manchuria in return for Russia's recognition of Japan's supremacy in Korea, decided

---

[1] A. J. P. Taylor, *The Struggle for Mastery in Europe, 1848–1918* (Oxford, 1954), p. 393.
[2] *British Documents on the Origins of the War, 1898–1914*, vol. III, no. 86. Salisbury uses the words 'British Isles', although 'British Empire' would have been more appropriate.

that the time had come to choose between Russia and England. Preliminary talks indicated that Lansdowne, who had succeeded Salisbury as Foreign Secretary in November 1900, was disposed to negotiate, and in October 1901 the Japanese Ambassador in London, Baron Hayashi, was formally authorised to broach the subject of an alliance. At the same time Prince Ito was empowered to visit St Petersburg to explore the chances of an agreement with Russia. In view of their past experience the Japanese were by no means sure that either aim could be achieved. But after the failure of their own overtures to Russia, the British government, who valued the Japanese armed forces more highly and accurately than the continental powers, responded so promptly that the Japanese had already committed themselves in principle to the English alliance when Ito reported that a Russo-Japanese agreement was also within the bounds of possibility. They could not have both and could hardly afford to alienate England, who had abstained from interfering with their victory at Shimonoseki and had been the first to renounce extra-territoriality in Japan, by withdrawing when negotiations were so advanced. The die was therefore cast and on 30 January 1902 there was signed the treaty which marked England's abandonment of isolation (but not of her aloofness from Europe) and strikingly emphasised the status Japan had won for herself among the nations.

By the terms of the treaty, which was to last for five years, Japan appeared to gain more than England. By the first article each power recognised the other's special interests in China, but England also recognised those of Japan in Korea, whereas the Japanese had refused to extend their obligations to cover India, Siam and the Straits Settlements. By the second, if either power was involved in hostilities with another in defence of those interests the other was to preserve strict neutrality. By the third, if one of the signatories was at war with two powers in defence of those interests the other must come to its aid. In other words, England would be neutral if there was war between Russia and Japan, but would be bound to help Japan if France joined Russia. The treaty probably made war between Russia and Japan more likely but French participation more remote; for if 'France would not fight for the valley of the Nile, it was highly improbable that she would draw the sword for Korea'.[1] For England the important thing, as an American historian has pointed out, 'was not what was in *the* Alliance, but the fact that there was *an* Alliance';[2] for, were Russia and Japan to agree upon a common policy against other powers, British interests in the Far East generally would have been gravely menaced.

Although the treaty made war between Russia and Japan more likely,

[1] G. P. Gooch, *Before the War*, vol. I, p. 22.
[2] W. L. Langer, *The Diplomacy of Imperialism, 1890–1902*, vol. II (New York and London, 1935), p. 783.

it did not render it inevitable or preclude further attempts by Japan to settle her differences by negotiation. The deciding factor which led to conflict was the seizure of control over Russia's Far Eastern policy by an irresponsible militarist group.

In a military autocracy like Russia, when the autocrat himself was a man of weak will, as was Nicholas II, policy might be subject to violent oscillations as a result of the struggle of different interests to influence the tsar. Most of the ministers and established departments favoured a policy of peaceful penetration in China, but the appointment of Admiral Alexeiev as viceroy in the Far East responsible directly to the tsar marked the ascendancy of a sinister camarilla, headed by an adventurer named Bezobrazoff, who did not hesitate to envisage war to gain their ends. In consequence Russia failed to carry out her undertaking of April 1902 to evacuate Manchuria, and after several months of negotiation in 1903 Japanese requirements for a peaceful settlement remained unsatisfied. At last, convinced of Russian bad faith, the Japanese determined upon the event for which they had long prepared. If there was to be war it should come at the moment of their choosing, when their naval armaments had been completed and before the Trans-Siberian Railway was finished. On 8 February 1904, without declaration of war, they opened hostilities by an attack on the Russian fleet at Port Arthur. The Russians were taken by surprise, lost command of the sea, and quickly suffered a series of reverses. Port Arthur fell on 2 January 1905, after a seven months' siege; Mukden was captured in March 1905; and the Russian Baltic fleet, which had sailed half way round the world in an endeavour to regain mastery of the China Sea, was annihilated on 27 May at Tsushima. Contrary to the expectation of most European military experts, Japan had defeated the Russian giant unaided, and once again, as in the Crimean War, but still more dramatically, the tsardom was shown to be a colossus with feet of clay. Grave disturbances broke out in various parts of European Russia and, no longer in any condition to fight, the tsar's government gladly accepted the American President Roosevelt's offer of mediation. By the ensuing Treaty of Portsmouth of 5 September 1905, signed a month after the revision and renewal of the Anglo-Japanese Alliance for a further period of five years, they ceded Port Arthur and the southern half of the island of Sakhalin together with the southern half of the railway they had built in Manchuria. They also recognised Japanese supremacy over Korea, which Japan formally annexed in 1910. In spite of the disappointment of her public opinion, Japan could afford to waive her claim to any indemnity beyond the cost of maintenance of prisoners of war: she had attained her objectives and her moderation paved the way for an improvement in her relations with Russia and an eventual second agreement (1907) for the division of Manchuria into Russian and Japanese spheres of influence. It was the first time that an

Asiatic power had proved more than a match for a great European state in a major war. As Paul Cambon foresaw, although the war was confined to the Far East and involved neither France nor England, it was to alter the course of history and 'weigh upon the whole century'.[1]

In the meantime a most important change had been effected in the relations of the allies of Russia and Japan, namely France and England.

The keys which opened the door to understanding and which explain French policy lay in Morocco, which was virtually an enclave in France's North African dominions and had a long and ill-defined frontier with Algeria. During the reign of an energetic sultan, Muley Hassan, foreign influences had been kept at bay; but after his death in 1894 the Moroccan realm showed signs of disintegration. Afraid that some other great power would seek to profit by its weakness to establish its own influence there and jeopardise the security of Algeria, Delcassé decided that it was urgent for France to obtain recognition of her special interests. Accordingly, having in 1900 secured Italy's blessing, in 1902 he began negotiations with Spain, the other Mediterranean state which by reason of its geographical position was particularly concerned with Moroccan affairs. They failed, however, because Spain was reluctant to act without the consent of the power which held Gibraltar. It thus became clear that the way to agreement with Madrid lay through London and that Delcassé must try and obtain from England the same sort of recognition of France's position in Morocco that he had won from Italy. Meanwhile the desirability of a settlement with England had been emphasised by the Anglo-Japanese Alliance and the consequent risks to France of a collision in the Far East between her ally, Russia, and England's new partner, Japan.

In the negotiations which opened in August 1902 he was ably seconded by Paul Cambon, French Ambassador in London since December 1898, and his task was made easier by the Francophil disposition of Edward VII, who had ascended the throne in January 1901. Furthermore, an exchange of visits by King Edward and President Loubet in 1903 helped to create better feeling between the two countries. But it was not until 8 April 1904 that the comprehensive agreement which was the basis of the subsequent Anglo-French Entente was signed. In the interim there had been much hard bargaining, since the discussions had broadened out to cover the whole range of colonial interests. For England, France's eagerness to secure herself in Morocco afforded an obvious opportunity to obtain France's formal recognition of England's position in Egypt: but both the Moroccan and Egyptian questions had their complexities and the hoary question of the Newfoundland fisheries caused unexpected difficulties, for, in return for the abandonment of their rights on the Treaty Shore, the French demanded territorial as well as financial compensation,

[1] 'Tu es donc sur le théâtre d'événements qui peuvent changer le cours de l'histoire et qui vont peser sur le siècle entier.' *Correspondance, 1870–1924*, vol. II (Paris, 1940), p. 111.

and their request first for Gambia and then for an extensive area on the right bank of the Niger prolonged the negotiations for several weeks.

The final agreement took the form of three conventions. By the first France gave up her Newfoundland fishery rights, acquired at the Treaty of Utrecht, in return for the Iles de Los opposite Konakry and a rectification of the frontier between Gambia and Senegambia. The second regulated the condominium exercised by the two powers in the New Hebrides and delimited spheres of influence in Siam. By the third and most important, Britain recognised France's special position in Morocco in return for French recognition of the British position in Egypt. In addition there were certain secret articles, not disclosed until 1911, which provided for the eventuality of an alteration of the status of Egypt or Morocco, and in particular one which secured the interests of Spain should the sultan of Morocco at any time cease to exercise authority. The corollary of this was a fresh Franco-Spanish negotiation resulting in the secret Franco-Spanish convention of 3 October 1904, which defined Spain's sphere of influence and provided for her immediate right of action within it should both parties agree that the *status quo* could no longer be preserved. Thus Delcassé had gained the consent of three powers, Italy, England and Spain, to France's obtaining the lion's share of Morocco when the time proved ripe. But he had omitted to consult Germany, with the consequence that the Anglo-French Agreement, the crowning triumph of his career, was also to prove his downfall, although not the downfall of his policy.

This Agreement of 1904 was simply a common-sense settlement of outstanding disputes terminating a long period of friction. It envisaged no alliance: except in the case of Morocco, it made no provision for future diplomatic co-operation; and the very fact that its aims were limited whereas those of the earlier Anglo-German negotiations were wide and ill-defined probably helped towards its success. It was, moreover, a concrete proof of the improvement in Anglo-French relations to which the altered tone of the British and French press already bore witness. The reality of this improvement was soon to be put to the test and to survive triumphant. Out of the trial came genuine *entente*.

Meanwhile other events disposed the two governments to co-operate. The growth of the German fleet led the British authorities in March 1903 to decide upon the creation of a new naval base at Rosyth and to transfer the greater part of their naval forces to home waters. French friendship was therefore all the more desirable because of France's naval power in the Mediterranean. Both governments, too, were caused anxiety by the Russo-Japanese War and concerned to prevent it from spreading. Thus in October 1904, when the Russian Baltic fleet on its way to the Far East inadvertently fired by night on some Hull fishing vessels causing several casualties, French diplomacy played an important part in inducing the

Russians to make prompt reparation. Henceforward the French, acutely aware of the perils of Anglo-Russian friction, were tireless in urging Britain to settle her differences with Russia even as she had settled them with France.

It was Germany who put Anglo-French friendship to its first serious proof. Germany's first reactions to the Anglo-French Agreement had been conciliatory and there had been no special emphasis on German interests in Morocco, but in reality the German Foreign Office was profoundly vexed. In fact Germany's diplomatic position had seriously deteriorated: Italy was no longer a reliable ally, Austria-Hungary was a prey to increasing internal difficulties, and the Franco-Russian Alliance and Anglo-French Agreement now seemed to threaten her with encirclement. The kaiser and his advisers were soon to develop a nightmare of *Einkreisung*. Moreover, they were irritated at not having been consulted. 'Not for material reasons alone', wrote Holstein, 'but even more for the sake of prestige must Germany protest against the intended appropriation of Morocco by France....If we let ourselves be trampled upon in Morocco, we invite similar treatment elsewhere.'[1] The timing of the protest required careful thought, and for some months after the first conciliatory declarations Germany maintained a sphinx-like reserve. It was not until March 1905 that the world was startled by the kaiser's reluctant visit to Tangier and his resounding references to Germany's determination to protect her 'great and growing interests in Morocco'. The speech was the prelude to a powerful diplomatic offensive against France and the Anglo-French Agreement, accompanied by a violent press campaign.

There is little doubt that the timing and vigour of this apparent *volte-face* in German policy were affected by the Russo-Japanese War. Now that Russia was incapacitated Germany saw a striking opportunity to break the incipient Entente and get rid of Delcassé as Bismarck had got rid of Boulanger. There is evidence that the German Chief of General Staff favoured a preventive war against France, but, although Bülow was ready to use the threat of war and his conduct was a vivid example of the way in which war remained an instrument of national policy, it is not clear that he wished to go farther. Delcassé's offer to negotiate was rejected and Germany demanded an international conference to discuss the Moroccan situation. If the French stood firm there was risk of war; if they yielded, they would also be humiliated. Delcassé urged firmness on the ground that Germany was bluffing and that English support was assured. This was going too far; although England was stirred by the challenge to Anglo-French relations implied by Germany's conduct, all Lansdowne had suggested was 'full and confidential discussion between,

---

[1] *Grosse Politik*, vol. xx, pp. 208–9. Cf. G. P. Gooch, *Before the War*, vol. I, p. 247. '...Lassen wir uns aber jetzt in Marokko stillschweigend auf die Füsse treten, so ermutigen wir zur Wiederholung anderswo.'

the two Gov[ernmen]ts...in anticipation of any complications to be apprehended during the somewhat anxious period through which we are at present passing',[1] and there is no evidence for Delcassé's subsequent assertion that in case of war England had undertaken to land 100,000 men in Schleswig. But his colleagues placed less reliance on England, knowing that the British navy, her main strength, could not 'run on wheels',[2] and were painfully aware of Germany's military superiority. They rejected Delcassé's risky policy and he resigned on 6 June. Rouvier's offer of a Franco-German agreement was turned down by Bülow, and France was obliged to accept the proposal for a conference. It might now be hoped that France would realise that English support was worthless. When in the next month the kaiser secured a treaty with Russia which seemed to take the sting out of the Franco-Russian Alliance his elation was unbounded, for it looked as though the whole grouping of the European powers was about to be transformed to Germany's advantage. But what he beheld was a mirage.

The kaiser had encouraged the tsar to go to war with Japan, and in 1904, when war broke out, Germany, seeing an opportunity to try and 'mend the wire to St Petersburg', sent a draft treaty of defensive alliance to the Russian capital. Nothing came of it because the tsar felt that he would be bound to consult France if it were proceeded with; but Germany continued her courtship and strained her neutrality by coaling Russian ships, and in the following year in a *tête-à-tête* at Björkö in Finland, the kaiser persuaded the tsar to sign a treaty whereby, if one of the signatories was attacked by a European power, the other would support it in Europe. But the handiwork of the sovereigns was not found to be good in the sight of their absent ministers. Bülow, who thought that the words 'in Europe' made the treaty a liability when England with her vulnerable Indian empire was the enemy in view, actually went so far as to telegraph his resignation (which, however, he was persuaded to withdraw); while Lamsdorff at once declared such an arrangement impossible without reference to Russia's ally France, whom the Germans wanted to bring in only after the *fait accompli*. When the Russians sounded France about the possibility of extending the Franco-Russian Alliance to include Germany, they obtained the expected answer that French opinion would not tolerate a closer relationship. The tsar's consequent letter proposing an additional provision that the treaty should not apply in case of war between France and Germany ended the matter. In an alliance so emasculated Germany could have no interest and so, although never formally abrogated, the Treaty of Björkö was virtually stillborn.

These negotiations affected the development of the Moroccan question.

---

[1] *British Documents*, vol. III, no. 95.
[2] An expression used by the French Président du Conseil, M. Rouvier.

So long as there was a chance of forming the grand continental alliance with France and Russia the Germans had been conciliatory in their demeanour towards the French after Delcassé's resignation. But, once that project failed, the Moroccan question remained the chief card to play against the Anglo-French Entente. The return of a Liberal government in England encouraged Germany to resume an uncompromising tone, and she looked to the international conference she had demanded to give her satisfaction.

Once again, however, she was doomed to disappointment. At the conference which opened at Algeciras on 16 January 1906 she gained only Austrian support on the most contentious issue, namely the organisation of police in the Moroccan ports. Italy failed to back her, while Russia, urgently in need of a large French loan, stood firmly by France and England. The majority accepted the French view that the police organisation should be entrusted to French and Spanish officers; and the eventual compromise, incorporated in the Algeciras Act of 7 April 1906, whereby, while the sultan was to confide the organisation to French and Spanish officers, a Swiss inspector-general was to be superimposed who would make periodic reports to the Diplomatic Body on the functioning of the new police regime, was but poor consolation. The only advantage Germany had derived was the recognition that Moroccan affairs were a matter of international interest. To this extent France's desired freedom of action was restricted and the recognition meant that Germany could legitimately bring up the Moroccan question again should occasion arise. Apart from this, however, Algeciras was a serious check: Germany's diplomacy had overreached itself and her relative isolation had been publicly exposed; she had failed to obtain any tangible advantage for herself; and, last but not least, she had failed to break the Entente, which emerged the stronger for the test. The new British government had continued the policy of their predecessors. Not only had they, as they were bound, given France their diplomatic support, but they had hinted that, in the event of a German attack upon France, England could not remain neutral. Furthermore, although he had refused to give France a written undertaking of armed support, Grey agreed (31 January 1906) that military and naval staff conversations should take place as a precautionary measure. It was expressly stipulated that these talks should be in no way binding on either government, but the fact that they could occur in time of peace was of the highest significance and committed the British authorities more than they knew. England had returned unmistakably to her traditional policy of maintaining the balance of power.

Although the Treaty of Björkö was secret, an indication that something was stirring the waters was conveyed by the Russian soundings in Paris and made a settlement of Anglo-Russian differences all the more desirable. The failure of Germany's schemes for an anti-British continental alliance,

Russia's defeat and the end of the war with Japan, her co-operation with the Entente powers at Algeciras and the change of policy favoured by Iswolsky, who became Russian Foreign Minister on 10 May 1906, all facilitated matters, and negotiations were formally opened on 6 June. Their progress was rendered slow by the internal instability of Russia and by public criticism in England of the measures taken to cope with it, by Iswolsky's understandable desire not to offend Germany and suffer the fate of Delcassé, and by the objections of the Russian General Staff; but eventually a convention was signed on 31 August 1907. From the British point of view the agreement, which related to three points of friction, Persia, Afghanistan and Tibet, was satisfactory since the main objectives were secured. Russia's recognition of the principle of Persian independence and integrity and the delimitation of spheres of influence within that country, her acknowledgement that Afghanistan was of special interest to England, and agreement to maintain Tibet as a buffer state under Chinese suzerainty, all appeared to check any further expansion menacing to the safety of India, which was England's paramount concern. Although the Persian problem would still cause the British Foreign Office many headaches, the great Anglo-Russian conflict of interests was virtually liquidated by the agreements.

The Anglo-Russian convention was negative in character: it contained no special assurances of friendship or co-operation and it was not welcomed in either country as the Anglo-French Agreement had been welcomed in England and France. Although it swung Russia slightly nearer to the Entente there could not be said as yet to be an Anglo-Russian or Triple Entente and it did not preclude Russia from maintaining good relations with Germany; indeed Iswolsky was most anxious to do so and went out of his way to be co-operative, for instance at the ineffective second Hague conference in 1907. Nor was it part of a deliberate English design to encircle Germany. As has been well said, the two groups stood side by side rather than face to face and it was 'not a question of getting Russia to join England against Germany: it was solely a question of preventing Russia from joining Germany against England'.[1] Unfortunately, however, Germany saw in it an anti-German move, and this impression was strengthened when the tsar and King Edward VII met at Reval in June 1908. Unfortunately, too, the convention had the effect of shifting the main direction of Russia's foreign policy to still more dangerous waters. Checked by Japan in the Far East, prevented from further expansion in the direction of India, she turned once more to the Balkans.

But it was Austrian initiative which led to the first major Balkan crisis of the twentieth century. The Magyarising policy of the Hungarian government and the resentment it caused among their Serb and Croat

[1] H. Nicolson, *op. cit.* pp. 234–5.

populations intensified the racial problems of the dual monarchy. The deterioration of Austria's relations with Serbia since the sanguinary overthrow of the Obrenovich dynasty in 1903 and the tendency of the new Serbian rulers to look to France for money and munitions and to Russia for political support and to allow Belgrade to become a centre of Pan-Serb aspirations confronted the rulers of Austria with a foreign problem which was likely to be all the more difficult once Russia resumed an active interest in Balkan politics. So long as the Pole, Goluchowski, remained in charge, Austrian policy was cautious. But his replacement in 1906 by Aehrenthal and the appointment of Conrad von Hötzendorff as Chief of Staff brought to the fore men of more masterful and adventurous stamp. Aehrenthal, who had been Ambassador at St Petersburg, was, like Iswolsky, Bülow and others, an example of the typical continental Foreign Minister trained in the narrow school of diplomacy instead of in politics. As he was reputed to be on excellent terms with the Russians and anxious to reconstitute the Three Emperors' League his appointment was regarded as an earnest of Austria's desire to maintain friendly relations with Russia. But when his initial attempts at economic conciliation with Serbia broke down, largely owing to opposition at home, he embarked upon a coercive policy which quickly led to complications. His announcement early in 1908 of Austria's intention to build a railway to Mitrovitza in Turkey through the Sanjak of Novibazar, which separated Serbia from Montenegro, was intended as a warning to Serbia. But, made regardless of Russia's friendly intimation that complications might ensue, it virtually ended the Austro-Russian co-operation in the Balkans begun in 1897, and inaugurated a period in which the growing personal enmity of Aehrenthal and Iswolsky had the gravest consequences for European relations.

At first Russia made a counter-proposal for a railway from the Danube to the Albanian coast, and the next months might have witnessed no more than a competition in railway projects had not the general situation been transformed by the Young Turk revolution at Constantinople in July. By the Berlin Treaty of 1878 Austria had been accorded the right to administer the Turkish provinces of Bosnia and Herzegovina indefinitely and to garrison the Sanjak of Novibazar. The Young Turk revolution confronted Austria with the probability that the predominantly Serb populations of Bosnia and Herzegovina would demand the right to send representatives to the Turkish Parliament, now proposed, and that Turkey, infused with a new nationalism, would reassert her claim to full sovereignty over two provinces which Austria had in fact governed for thirty years. The grant of such demands was inconceivable for the Austrian rulers and Aehrenthal's remedy, approved by his government in August, was the annexation of the two provinces at a suitable moment, accompanied as a conciliatory gesture to Turkey by the withdrawal of Austrian troops from the Sanjak. 'Annexation', as has been said, 'would both solve the confused relations with Turkey and create an insuperable barrier against the seditious dream of a great South Slav kingdom; Serbo-Croat unrest, with nothing to hope for from Serbia, would be silenced, and the monarchy would now be free to accomplish the mission of economic betterment which thirty years of occupation had left unfulfilled.'[1] For the success of the scheme Russian support was essential, and negotiations to this end culminated in a secret interview between Aehrenthal and Iswolsky at Buchlau on 16 September. As a result Aehrenthal believed that he had secured Russian approval for the projected annexation, in return for Austrian support of a Russian proposal to modify the Straits regime so as to give the warships of the Black Sea powers free access to the Mediterranean.

But the plan miscarried. When Iswolsky went on to Paris and London he encountered difficulties. France was non-committal and England would not agree to his Straits proposals: the cabinet felt no obligation to support Russia because of the recent Anglo-Russian agreements and was unmoved by Iswolsky's talk of the consequences for Anglo-Russian relations if his demands were not met. Meanwhile Aehrenthal, eager to secure Austria's share of the bargain, had declared the annexation of Bosnia and Herzegovina on 6 October, the day after the prince of Bulgaria, acting in collusion with him, had proclaimed his country's complete independence of Turkey and assumed the title of king. Thus Iswolsky's policy had broken down while Aehrenthal's had triumphed. Iswolsky had aimed at a *coup* in the Straits, a misdirected aim since the Russian people were more easily roused on behalf of the Balkan Slavs than by the old Straits question, but he had to return without this *quid pro quo* of the Buchlau bargain. Much mortified, he sought escape by asserting that he had been duped by Aehrenthal, demanding a European conference to discuss the Bosnian question, and encouraging the Balkan Slav agitation which followed upon the annexation.

Aehrenthal's attempt to solve the Serb problem thus led to a grave crisis which lasted for six months. To most European powers his action came as a shock. Although it made no practical difference to the two provinces, it was, as Grey wrote, the 'arbitrary alteration of a European Treaty by one Power without the consent of the others' and as such 'struck at the roots of all good international order'.[2] In consequence, England condemned the annexation just as she had condemned Russia's denunciation of the Black Sea clauses of the Treaty of Paris in 1870. To Germany the Austrian *fait accompli* was equally unwelcome. Bülow was indignant at not having been consulted beforehand by his ally and the kaiser saw his cherished Turkish policy in jeopardy. Yet Germany could not afford to see Austria weakened, and therefore supported Austria in her refusal of any conference which did not meet merely to confirm the annexation.

[1] A. J. P. Taylor, *The Habsburg Monarchy, 1815–1918* (London, 1941), p. 260.
[2] Viscount Grey, *Twenty-five Years, 1892–1916* (London, 1925), vol. I, p. 175.

Since the failure of the Björkö policy and the signature of the Anglo-Russian agreement Germany was all the readier to bolster up Austria by winning a diplomatic victory against Russia.

In the Balkans Austria's action had provoked a ferment: 'Turkey formally protested, and a boycott of Austrian goods began; Montenegro begged for frontier modifications and abolition of the fetters of the Berlin Treaty; in Serbia there was talk of war.'[1] As the rift between Austria and Russia became apparent so the bellicosity of the Serbs, who hoped for Russian aid, increased and Austro-Russian relations drifted into a state of dangerous tension. The decisive factor was the firm support given to Austria by Germany. After Bülow had rejected an offer of mediation by the western powers, Austria felt strong enough to demand Serbia's withdrawal of her opposition to the annexation, and when the Serbs complied but refused to give a written promise of future good behaviour she prepared for coercion. All in fact depended on Russia and Germany, for Serbia could not risk war without Russian assistance and Germany was determined to prevent that assistance from being forthcoming. On 22 March 1909 the German Ambassador in St Petersburg was instructed to obtain a definite reply to the question whether Russia accepted the Austrian note and the abrogation of the article of the Treaty of Berlin relating to Bosnia-Herzegovina. 'We should regard an evasive, conditional or ambiguous reply as a refusal. We should then withdraw and let things take their course.'[2] Unready to face another major war so soon after her defeat by Japan, Russia could only submit, whereupon Serbia, too, climbed down and gave the required guarantee. Turkey had already on 26 February acknowledged the annexation in return for an indemnity of some £2,400,000. Aehrenthal's triumph was complete.

But it boded ill for the future. So far from cowing the Serbs it antagonised them further and made Austria's Slav problem still more difficult. It was a blow to what international morality remained and, above all, a bitter humiliation for Russia who had been helpless while Serbia was browbeaten and had to accept Austria's annexation of Bosnia and Herzegovina without compensation either in the Straits or elsewhere. In consequence, Germany's dreams of a continental alliance and Austria's visions of a new Three Emperors' League were farther than ever from fulfilment: still more so after the German emperor had rubbed salt into Russia's wounds by declaring that he had supported Austria 'in shining armour'. The Bosnian crisis did what neither the Anglo-Russian convention nor the meeting of sovereigns at Reval had been able to achieve, it created the Triple Entente. Although Russia was disappointed by lack of

---

[1] G. P. Gooch, *Before the War*, vol. I, p. 403.

[2] '…Jede ausweichende verklausulierte oder unklare Antwort würden wir als eine Ablehnung betrachten müssen. Wir würden uns dann zurückziehen und den Dingen ihren Lauf lassen….' *Grosse Politik*, vol. XXVI, p. 694.

support from France and England and some British diplomats, aware of this, vainly urged Grey to convert England's *ententes* into alliances, she could not afford to retire into isolation, and co-operation with the western powers was the only alternative. Germany's attempt to mend the wire by an offer in 1910 to abandon support of Austria in the Balkans in return for a Russian promise not to help England against Germany came to nothing. Austro-Russian rivalry in the Balkans was again a dominating and dangerous factor in European politics. Moreover, the change in the Balkan balance of power had alarmed Italy, causing her to move still farther away from Austria, against whom Italian irredentist feeling was always strong, and to conclude the secret Treaty of Racconigi (24 October 1909) with Russia, whereby she undertook to support the Balkan *status quo*, should it again be threatened by Austria, in return for Russian recognition of her interests in Tripoli. In reply Austria tried to safeguard her position by promising not to make any new annexation without prior agreement with Rome to give Italy compensation. Bülow had grievously miscalculated. By his unconditional aid to Austria he had committed himself to the support of methods and aims of which he disapproved and about which he had not been fully consulted. Furthermore, and still more ominous for the future, he had encouraged Austria to continue her risky policies, firm in the conviction that Germany would be obliged to stand by her. The roles had been reversed and it had been Germany's turn to play the part of 'brilliant second' to Austria. As in the Moroccan affair Bülow had hoped to break the Anglo-French Entente, so now his policy was explicable partly by his avowed desire to break 'the encircling ring'; and, as in 1905-6, it had precisely the opposite effect. The 'ring', hitherto mainly a figment of German imagination, began to assume reality. It was unlikely to dissolve so long as the thunder-clouds hung over the Balkans and the North Sea. Even as Austria's Balkan policy seemed a threat to Russia, so Germany's naval programme seemed an unprovoked menace to England.

Although the early German Naval Bills and jingoistic propaganda of the German Navy League had attracted much attention, the German naval programme did not become a diplomatic issue and a leading factor in Anglo-German relations until 1906. By this time the Moroccan crisis with its risk of war had made the British government aware that friction with Germany would inevitably increase the pace and burden of highly unwelcome competition in naval armaments. The Liberals who assumed office in 1905 were eager to reduce expenditure, and accordingly in 1906, welcoming the Russian invitation to a second Hague conference, they proposed a limitation of armaments. Such a proposal was hardly likely to be acceptable in Germany. By now, as a result of constant propaganda, the majority of the German people had come to believe that a big navy was essential for the maintenance of Germany's interests and prestige as a great power or, as Bethmann-Hollweg put it in 1912, 'for the general purposes of her greatness'. The implementation of the naval programmes was regarded as a fundamental point of policy. It was one of the few aims to which the volatile German emperor remained unflinchingly constant and its modification would probably have required a radical change of men and outlook. Moreover, England's proposals were necessarily suspect, for she now appeared to demand recognition of her naval superiority for all time. The result of the Hague conference of 1907 therefore was merely to increase distrust. With no hope of international agreement to limit armaments, the only course left was that of direct discussions. Meanwhile the armaments race must continue, since for Britain naval superiority was a matter of life and death and the pretension of Germany, the strongest military state, to bid for equality at sea a grave risk to the balance of power.

At first the Germans were unwilling to negotiate, but eventually Bülow, constantly warned by Metternich, the German Ambassador in London, of the strength of English feeling (intensified by the belief, justifiably shared by the British government in the winter of 1908–9, that Germany had been accelerating the building of her ships), considered the possibility of slowing down Germany's naval construction in return for a promise of British neutrality. But Tirpitz's reply to such a suggestion in the spring of 1909 was unpromising—his suggested ratio of 3:4 was hardly likely to be acceptable—and before any overture was made to England Bülow had resigned and was succeeded, in June 1909, by Bethmann-Hollweg. Bethmann-Hollweg, a not very forceful civilian and a newcomer to foreign affairs, was unlikely to make a radical change in policy. He did, however, accept Bülow's notion of securing a political bargain, and negotiations begun in 1909 continued intermittently but fruitlessly until 1912. Bethmann's offer was to retard the German naval programme, not to reduce it, in exchange for British neutrality in case of an attack upon Germany. Such an undertaking would have been difficult for England in view of her commitments to other powers, even if the naval concessions offered had been greater; but her repeated assurance that the treaties and *ententes* she had concluded were not directed against Germany, and her offers to make an agreement on outstanding questions such as the Baghdad Railway were not considered enough. Grey's proposals for exchanges of naval information also came to nothing and in 1911 negotiations seemed near a deadlock when a fresh Moroccan crisis blew up to imperil European peace and increase Anglo-German mistrust.

The Algeciras Act had not restored order to the Shereefian empire. In 1907 the sultan had been driven from his capital and a state of anarchy ensued which encouraged French penetration. However, in 1909, while she was still preoccupied by the Bosnian crisis, Germany had come to an agreement with France which seemed to foreshadow a new period of co-operation. While France undertook that the nationals of both countries should be 'associated in the enterprises for which they obtained concessions' Germany recognised France's special political interests. Unfortunately the economic side of the agreement gave rise to misunderstandings, especially when France proposed to build railways and refused to admit German personnel to run them on the grounds that this trenched upon her political interests. By 1911 relations had deteriorated, and when fresh disorders impelled the French to send troops to Fez to protect the sultan and European life and property the Germans reopened the Moroccan question with a startling gesture reminiscent of the Tangier incident of 1905. On 1 July a gunboat, the *Panther*, was sent to the closed Moroccan port of Agadir to protect alleged German commercial interests and the world was informed that, since, in the German view, the occupation of Fez nullified the Algeciras Act, the time had come for a fresh 'friendly exchange of views'.

There was much to be said for the German argument that a military expedition like the French one to Fez was only too likely to turn into a permanent occupation and that France and Germany must reconsider their Moroccan arrangements; but Germany's manner of proceeding was again open to serious criticism. Ignoring a French offer to smooth out differences in a general negotiation she preferred to seize a pledge first and talk afterwards: this, Zimmermann, the Under-Secretary of State for Foreign Affairs, had argued, was the only way to induce France to offer satisfactory compensation. For some days after the *Panther's* arrival at Agadir, Kiderlen, now Secretary of State, imitated the sphinx-like silence of Bülow in the first Moroccan crisis and tension was acute. There was much uncertainty as to Germany's ultimate intentions: for instance, as there were no commercial interests in the Agadir region it was believed by many that she intended to demand or seize an Atlantic port. The French Foreign Minister had at first asked the British government to make a counter-demonstration; they refused this but warned Germany that they could not recognise any new arrangement which was come to in Morocco without them. Meanwhile Caillaux, the new Germanophil French Prime Minister, accepted the German suggestion of an 'exchange of views'. The Germans then revealed their hand. In return for recognition of France's complete freedom of action in Morocco they demanded practically the whole French Congo. When the French Cabinet on 17 July rejected their terms it seems that Kiderlen was ready to envisage war or at least to use the threat of it in order to intimidate the French into compliance. In these circumstances England's attitude was of decisive importance. On 21 July Grey told the German Ambassador in London that Germany's demands were excessive and that her action at Agadir still required explanation, and Lloyd George, the Chancellor of the Exchequer, who was believed in Berlin to be the leader of the pro-German section in the Cabinet, declared in a resounding speech at the Mansion House that if Britain were 'to be treated where her interests were vitally affected as of no account…peace at that price would be a humiliation intolerable for a great country to endure'. There was no mention of Germany or the Moroccan question, but the warning was clear, and the indignation of the German government and people showed that they knew that their bluff had been called—courteous assurances about Germany's intentions were speedily sent to London. Peace was preserved, but German prestige had suffered and there followed several weeks of hard bargaining between France and Germany during which there were twice threats of rupture and renewed rumours of war. Finally, a financial panic in Germany in September accelerated a settlement and on 4 November 1911 a fresh Franco-German agreement was signed. While Germany undertook not to impede French activity in Morocco and recognised France's right eventually to establish a protectorate there, France ceded part of the interior of the French Congo pointing towards the Belgian Congo (on which the Germans hoped to obtain a pre-emption) together with a strip of territory giving this new German acquisition access to the sea.

Although Delcassé's policy had triumphed in the end and France was now potentially mistress of Morocco, and although Germany had extended her colonial dominion at small cost to herself, the Agadir crisis left neither side content. In Germany Kiderlen, who had countenanced if not encouraged the public clamour for territorial compensation in Morocco, was strongly criticised and the Colonial Secretary resigned in protest at the weakness of his policy; while in France the settlement was also attacked by colonial interests, and the discovery that Caillaux had conducted part of the negotiations independently of his Foreign Minister led in January 1912 to the fall of his cabinet. He had indeed hoped to make the Moroccan question the basis of a general settlement of differences with Germany on the lines of the Anglo-French Agreement of 1904; but the hope was vain, for the methods of German diplomacy and the strong feeling roused in both countries made its realisation impracticable. Instead of bettering relations with Germany Agadir had demonstrated once again the solidity of France's *entente* with England. In view of the risk of war, staff conversations had been resumed. England had already been making plans for the dispatch of an expeditionary force to France in case of emergency and now discussion of the technical details was pressed on apace. Still more conspicuous was the deterioration of Germany's relations with England, who now knew that for her the dominant questions of international relations were whether she intended to maintain the Triple Entente and whether she 'ought to submit to any dictation by Germany whenever she considers it necessary to raise her voice'.[1]

[1] Sir A. Nicolson to Sir Edward Goschen 24 July 1911 and to Lord Hardinge 14 September 1911. Quoted in H. Nicolson, *op. cit.* pp. 347, 350.

One further consequence of Agadir remains to be noticed. By opening the way to the French protectorate of Morocco, which was actually established early in 1912, it impelled Italy to move upon Tripoli. Already alarmed by Young Turk nationalism and fearing German competition, Italy believed she must act 'now or never'. On 25 September 1911, without warning, she published a statement of grievances against Turkey, and four days later, having rejected Turkish offers to negotiate, she declared war. The Treaty of Paris of 1856 guaranteeing the independence and territorial integrity of the Ottoman empire, the Treaty of Berlin of 1878 which had reaffirmed that guarantee, and the Hague conventions to which Italy was a party were flung to the winds. She was determined to leave no time for outside intervention and had not even consulted her allies beforehand. She found her justification in the fact that three great powers, France, Austria and Russia, had all signed agreements giving her a free hand. A further blow had been dealt at international morality, and Italy's conquest and annexation of Tripolitania and Cyrenaica was the signal for the Balkan states to make a concerted attack upon Turkey. The new complications caused by the Balkan wars are part of the immediate prelude to world war.

CHAPTER XII

THE APPROACH OF THE WAR OF 1914[1]

THE 'first world war' is a misnomer. Its causes were no more world-wide than its battlefields. The national antagonisms which exploded in it were European, and the alignment of the belligerent powers inside and outside Europe did not correspond to the lines of real cleavage between either the imperial interests of European powers or extra-European national ambitions. As world-wide causes have been assigned to the war, so also have causes comparatively remote in time. In each case the enlargement in retrospect of its true limits above all reflects the magnitude of the experience for contemporaries. But it accords as well with the preoccupations of various doctrinaire schools of international and national politics and history which have helped form popular interpretations of the war. The dogma, for instance, that war at this stage of history must express 'imperialist contradictions'—one not confined to Marxists—required that the war should be treated as global, while the doctrine current in post-war Europe that it was the necessary result of German authoritarian militarism required that the origins of the war should be traced back to the foundation of the second German empire.

Most schools of interpretation accept a distinction between remote and immediate origins of the war of 1914 and to most a dividing line in 1912 makes sense, if not for all the same reasons. Then began the crucial developments in two of the three main causes of the crisis of July 1914, or at least of the final order of battle, the alliance system and Balkan nationalism—the third being Anglo-German naval rivalry. Then, too, as distinct from those European issues, the last cause of conflict overseas had just been extinguished by a Franco-German agreement over Morocco.

The Moroccan convention of November 1911 licensed a French protectorate in exchange for territorial cessions in central Africa, and its critical reception by both French and German nationalists is one measure of its merits. In France, Caillaux's government which made it was replaced by the so-called 'great ministry' of Poincaré which accepted the settlement while appearing less disposed to further appeasement. It was one of Poincaré's first preoccupations to overhaul the Russian alliance, which the Moroccan crisis had shown to be as inadequate a moral support for France as the Bosnian crisis four years earlier had shown it to be for Russia. But the crucial fact was that the Russians met Poincaré more

[1] The editor and author are greatly indebted to Dr A. E. Campbell for abridging the text of this contribution.

than half way, for it was apparent that the next international crisis would be a Balkan one in which Russia had more to gain than France. The Russians thus took the diplomatic initiative; the Balkan League developed early in 1912 under Russian patronage, and without French co-operation or indeed full awareness.

Meanwhile it was in Germany that the Moroccan agreement was producing the most far-reaching repercussions. In the settlement with France Germany had, said Admiral Tirpitz, 'suffered a diplomatic check, and we must salve it by a supplementary naval bill'.[1] As naval secretary he gained the support of the Kaiser Wilhelm for this bill, usually known as the *novelle* of 1912, against the opposition of the chancellor, Bethmann-Hollweg. Though loyal to it in negotiation, Bethmann was unsympathetic to the political strategy behind the German battle-fleet—that it would serve as a deterrent to British intervention in a continental war. Under Tirpitz's original 'risk theory', the German fleet had only to make victory so costly to the British fleet that it would be vulnerable to third powers, but this had become inadequate as the other naval powers, except isolationist America, had become British associates rather than potential enemies. The German fleet had therefore to aim higher—it needed at least a hope of victory—and Tirpitz, with a reasonable confidence in the superiority of German design, was thinking in terms of parity by 1920.[2] The competition in oceanic cruisers was secondary, but it kept for the navy the support of influential colonial and commercial pressure-groups.

British numerical superiority in up-to-date battleships had been sacrificed by the completion of the revolutionary *Dreadnought* in 1908. It was being regained, particularly since the slogan of 'two keels for one' had been accepted by the public and the Admiralty. But this naval competition strained the Liberal government's principles as well as their budgets, and when a forecast of the *novelle* reached London it found them ready to negotiate once more. The visit to Berlin of the supposedly Germanophil secretary of state for war, Haldane, followed in February 1912. But the Germans asked for concessions over German colonial expansion, and over the continuation of the German Baghdad railway to the British-dominated Persian Gulf; they even asked for a declaration of neutrality. And when the text of the *novelle* was examined in London it was found to involve large increases in personnel, as well as the raising of a fresh battle squadron from some old and some new ships, while all that had been offered was postponement of these last. That was not worth colonial concessions, still less what amounted to the abandonment of the *entente* with France.

The kaiser may have gained a genuine impression that agreement had been reached during his talks with Haldane, although the latter had

[1] Tirpitz, *My Memoirs*, vol. 1, p. 211 (English edition, London, 1919).
[2] E. L. Woodward, *Great Britain and the German Navy* (Oxford, 1935), p. 316.

neither full powers nor full information. He affected indignation at being let down, but negotiations were allowed to drag on in London. The offer of a British declaration of non-aggression proved unacceptable, and Bethmann instructed the German ambassador in London that an agreement 'pledging England's neutrality and nearly amounting to a defensive alliance with us' was the sole condition which would justify the amendment of the *novelle*.[1] This fully endorsed Tirpitz's doctrine of the deterrent function of the German battle-fleet. Moreover, the deterrent had to be recognised by the British; the official tendency in London to treat the German fleet as merely a prestige symbol was resented as insulting.

The British answer to the *novelle* appeared in the Admiralty estimates of 18 July. British additional construction would be nearly double the new German increases, and these rates of building to maintain a ratio of 8:5 in battleships were maintained until the outbreak of war. But Tirpitz, in an inconsistent decision, slowed down building under the *novelle*. The British estimates were adjusted proportionately, and so the impulse was supplied for Churchill's proposal, repeated in 1913, for a 'naval holiday' with no new building for one year on either side. That was the last plan for naval limitation and it was ill-received in Germany as being, for technical reasons, favourable to Britain.

The naval stalemate, however, did not exacerbate relations. The German government still did not recognise that instead of imposing neutrality the uncompromising character of the naval challenge was making neutrality more obviously impossible. The idea of a 'political agreement' with Britain was to persist in German diplomatic strategy until the end. It did so without encouragement from London, but the two remaining themes in the Haldane negotiations, a colonial bargain and a Mesopotamian railway settlement, were more profitably taken up and developed slowly during the next two years into agreements stillborn on the outbreak of war.

The Anglo-German negotiations were alarming to the French and to the committed friends of France.[2] The French therefore exploited the refusal of a neutrality declaration to the Germans with a request for declarations about the Entente. They were helped by the simultaneous development of naval strategy. A reinforcement of the British battle-fleet in home waters from the Mediterranean was carried through, and although it was formally declared to be uncoordinated with French naval movements, French battleships were transferred in the reverse direction so that a naval obligation to defend the Channel coast of France began to build up. It was rather to check than to establish this developing strategic link,

---

[1] Bethmann to Metternich, 18 March 1912. *Die Grosse Politik der Europäischen Kabinette, 1871–1914* (Berlin, 1922–27), vol. xxxi, no. 11406.

[2] The British ambassador in Paris, Bertie, even incited Poincaré against his own government. Poincaré, *Au Service de la France* (Paris, 1927–33), vol. i, p. 170.

that Grey decided to give it formal but secret definition in an exchange of letters with the French ambassador on 16 and 17 November 1912. These expressly stated that the redisposition of the fleets involved no engagement, any more than the military and staff talks—which went back to 1906. But Grey's letter continued by promising consultation in case of an apprehended attack or a general threat to peace from a third power, and then recourse to the joint staff plans if action were decided upon.

This fundamental text of the 'Entente cordiale' was not disclosed outside the British cabinet until the outbreak of war, except to the Russians earlier in 1914 as a concession to the French wish to formalise the Triple Entente. It was then, too, that British naval staff talks were secretly arranged with the Russians for the same diplomatic reason, though their strategic significance was negligible. Indeed, the independent bond between Russia and Britain was tenuous—the security that it gave to Russia came solely through British obligations or intentions towards France. Direct Anglo-Russian relations were still troubled by Russian political intervention in Persia. The Russians, Sazonov believed, could presume on ultimate British complaisance in Asia for the sake of 'political aims in Europe of vital importance'.[1] But the reverse process was also effective, and friction continued until July 1914.

While the Entente owed its 'triple' character to the two-way relationship of France within it, the rigour of the Franco-Russian alliance attenuated the British obligation to France. As Grey was to insist at the last moment in 1914, Britain was not morally bound to follow France in action imposed on the latter by a treaty such as Britain had deliberately refrained from concluding even with France, much less Russia. All the more was this the case when the French commitment to Russia became extended by the entanglement of Russian policy and prestige with the so-called Balkan League. The basis of the league was the treaty of alliance between Serbia and Bulgaria, signed on 13 March 1912.[2] Its ostensible purpose was to resist Austro-Hungarian expansion, but a secret annexe provided for the partition of Macedonia, the remaining Slav-speaking territories under Turkish rule. The Russians were accessory to the negotiations from the start; they were not merely implicated by the important provision that the tsar should arbitrate between the parties. Their motives were not solely adventurous, nor those of revenge for the diplomatic defeat over Bosnia in 1908-9. Fear of Austria-Hungary re-occupying the *sanjak* of Novibazar to keep Montenegro and Serbia apart and to push a projected railway through it all the way to Salonika was a genuine and early motive. Later the temptation of opportunities for Russia in the partition of Tur-

[1] B. von Siebert, *Diplomatische Aktenstücke zur Geschichte der Ententepolitik der Vorkriegsjahre* (Berlin, 1921), pp. 205-6.
[2] 29 February, o.s. The texts of all the Balkan League treaties are to be found in the appendices to J. E. Guéchoff, *La Genèse de la guerre mondiale* (Berne, 1919).

key came to the fore, although how the leadership of Balkan national ambitions was to bring Russia to the coveted control of Constantinople and the straits had not been thought out.

The facts of the alliance between the Balkan states were incompletely revealed to their French allies by the Russians, in spite of pressing French enquiries, until Poincaré's visit to Russia in August 1912. When Poincaré did see the text of the secret Serbo-Bulgarian treaty he told Sazonov that 'France would not give Russia military aid over Balkan issues if Germany did not provoke the *casus foederis* of her own initiative, that is if she did not attack Russia'. The reference was to the military convention of 1892, which provided that 'if Russia is attacked by Germany or by Austria supported by Germany, France will employ all the forces at her disposal to fight Germany'. This was the basis of the Dual Alliance ratified in treaty form in 1894. But it had become increasingly obvious since 1908 that the emergency causing Russia to call upon the alliance would be an Austrian attack on a Balkan Slav state, followed by Russian intervention against Austria and in turn German intervention against Russia. Poincaré was in fact implying support in the new circumstances, otherwise the necessary reservation would have been that Russia should not attack Austria first. Reaffirming the alliance obligation without this caution, as Poincaré did in 1912,[1] meant that the defensive character of the alliance had been changed, or alternatively that Austria's Slav neighbours were henceforth included in it. There is little doubt that Poincaré yielded to Russian importunities for fear of losing the whole alliance which he considered precious to France in its defensive form. That he does not make the point in his memoirs follows from his refusal to admit that the alliance was in fact transformed in Russian interests.

When Poincaré was in St Petersburg a conflict in the Balkans was imminent. Greece had joined Serbia and Bulgaria in a treaty concluded on 29 May, to which Montenegro had committed herself orally, and the whole Balkan League meant to take advantage of the continuing war between Turkey and Italy which had been one of the incentives to its formation and was now stimulating insurrection in Albania and Macedonia.

The Balkan crises tested Austro-German solidarity over the same strategic issues, if not in such a dramatic situation as that of 1914, and the question arises why they did not produce the same fatal result. The common supposition that Germany simply refused support to Austria-Hungary in 1912–13 and accorded it in 1914 misrepresents the course of events. Both Austrian policy and the German response to it were uncertain. Far from seeking to chastise the Serbs, the Austrian foreign minister Berchtold at first took the lead in diplomacy to ward off the crisis. He proposed joint admonitions to the Turkish government in

---

[1] *Un Livre noir* (Paris, 1922–34), vol. I, p. 323; R. Poincaré, *op. cit.*, vol. II, pp. 200 ff., 340 ff.

favour of provincial decentralisation and warnings to the Balkan governments to keep the peace. German anxiety at this unilateral action was
more an affirmation of the exclusiveness and solidarity of the alliance than
the reverse.[1] And ultimately Berchtold's plan, with the added warning
that the powers would not license changes in the territorial *status quo*,
was accepted, the two most interested powers, Austria and Russia, being
charged with acting on behalf of all. This promising concert of Europe
had depended above all on Sazonov's revulsion at the apparition of
Balkan nationalism which he had so casually invoked. It was both temporary and futile. The powers' joint action coincided with Montenegro's
declaration of war on Turkey on 8 October and this was followed by
Serbian, Bulgarian and Greek intervention ten days later, all without the
Russian licence which the Slav states' mutual engagements contemplated.

The first crucial question which the war brought up was that of the
sanjak of Novibazar, which Austria had occupied until 1909, which was
weakly held by the Turks and which the Serbs had to invade in order to
join up with the Montenegrins. This challenge to Austrian prestige and
strategic control Berchtold declined in advance, counting on the re-
establishment of the *status quo*[2] but against the general staff's advice.
No guarantee from Germany against Russian intervention if the Serbs
were to be ejected was asked for, and that in spite of some evidence that
it would have been given if asked.[3]

The main reason for the attachment of all the great powers to the *status
quo* in the first diplomatic phase of the Balkan crisis was uncertainty as to
who would win in a shooting war. The first few days of hostilities removed
all doubts. The Bulgars drove through Thrace towards the straits, and were
just forestalled in Salonika by the Greeks. Meanwhile the Serbs reached
the Adriatic. The Bulgars were stopped by Turkish resistance outside
Constantinople, but their advance was unwelcome to the Russians. The
Serbian successes threatened only the Austrians. At this point, therefore,
Russian official policy and Pan-Slav sentiment began to coalesce in sponsorship of the Serbs, while in Vienna an old idea was revived of building
up Bulgaria as the rival Balkan nation in disgrace with St Petersburg.

Recent historians have entertained perhaps too easily the possibility
for Austria of a reconciliation with the Serbs.[4] There was indeed a
'trialist' school of thought which favoured equalising the status of the
Slavs inside the empire with that of the Germans and Magyars. Such a
move the Serbian government were believed to be ready to welcome if

[1] Kiderlen to Bethmann-Hollweg, 2 September 1912. *Die Grosse Politik*, vol. xxxiii,
no. 12,135.
[2] L. Albertini, *The Origins of the War of 1914* (Eng. ed. I. M. Massey, London, 1952–7),
vol. i, p. 387.
[3] *Oesterreich-Ungarns Aussenpolitik, 1908–1914* (Vienna, 1930), vol. iv, no. 4022.
[4] For example, E. Eyck, *Das persönliche Regiment Wilhelms II* (Zürich, 1948), p. 643;
Albertini, *op. cit.* i, pp. 394–5; A. J. P. Taylor, *The Struggle for Mastery in Europe*, p. 491.

only Austria would tolerate their acquisition of an Adriatic port.[1] But although overtures were made in the autumn of 1912 and again a year later, their sincerity must be suspect considering the secret influence in Serbia of nationalist extremists who had no use for compromise.

In their determination to keep the Serbs away from the Adriatic, the Austrians used the principle of nationality in persuading the powers to create the state of Albania. This block of non-Slav people, formerly under Turkish rule, covered the whole coastline from Montenegro to Greece but the Russian government pressed the Serb case for a free port on the coast, in particular Durazzo, if not a corridor to it as well. Tension between the two great powers rose to the pitch of reinforcing covering troops on both sides of the Galician frontier, a mutual demonstration which was to last for months. There was no demand from Vienna nor refusal from Berlin of support for intervention against the Serbs who had overrun part of Albania; sufficient German encouragement to maintain the war of nerves was gratuitous. The kaiser's utterances were, as usual, both inconsistent and emphatic. But Bethmann declared in a Reichstag speech on 2 December that 'if Austria in the course of securing her vital interests …is attacked by Russia' Germany would fight.[2]

The Russian sponsorship of Serbian claims, however, was largely bluff. As early as 9 November the Serbs had been warned not to count on Russian support.[3] But Pan-Slav feeling was running high in Russia, with militant devotees among the grand dukes and the general staff, so the Serb cause could not be brusquely abandoned. As it was, the suspicion of Russian apathy disconcerted Poincaré, and he complained to Izvolsky that Austrian military preparations were not being adequately countered.[4] Behind this seems to have been a conviction that Europe was near war, and that if Russia was not ready to draw off German as well as Austrian forces France would have to bear the brunt. Implicit, surely, was the new interpretation of the *casus foederis* for France which Poincaré had given in St Petersburg and Izvolsky maintained that he had since confirmed.[5]

The victorious Balkan allies and the defeated Turks concluded an armistice on 3 December and a peace conference opened in London. At the same time a conference of ambassadors of the great powers was formed there to supervise a Balkan and Aegean settlement. It immediately agreed on the status of Albania and the exclusion of the Serbs from the Adriatic—a decision followed by the Austrian resignation of Novibazar. The conference reflected the disposition of the great powers to agree, and the issues between them were not directly affected by the break-up

---

[1] *Oesterreich-Ungarns Aussenpolitik*, vol. v, no. 5005.
[2] Eyck, *Das persönliche Regiment Wilhelms II*, p. 639.
[3] Siebert, *Diplomatische Aktenstücke zur Geschichte der Ententepolitik*, p. 577.
[4] *Un Livre noir*, vol. I, p. 369.
[5] *Ibid.* p. 326.

of the Balkan peace conference or by the resumption of the conflict as the so-called 'Second Balkan War'. What mattered was the incompatibility of Serbian victory and expansion with the prestige and therefore security of the Habsburg empire, and so, after the creation of Albania, the question of its future frontiers now overrun by the Serbs and Montenegrins became crucial between the Austrian and Russian governments. Where Austria-Hungary must stand and risk a general war Berchtold had certainly not decided in advance but the German Chancellor complained on 10 February that he was being kept in the dark. Indeed, at this time both Bethmann and Moltke were working to moderate Austrian policy.[1] Bethmann observed prophetically that it was 'almost impossible for Russia to look on inactive in case of a military operation by Austria-Hungary against Serbia'. It was not until six weeks later that the ambassadors' conference registered an Austrian concession over the disputed frontier villages of Dibra and Djakova, but relaxation of tension meanwhile between Vienna and St Petersburg and the stand-down of troops in Galicia are attributable to the German attitude.

That the Germans were blowing hot and cold was, however, shown in the Scutari crisis which followed in April 1913. That town, still held by the Turks and allotted by the powers to the new Albania, was invested in turn by the Serbs, who retired on Russian instructions, and by the Montenegrins under their king Nikita, who did not. A warning from Austria that if the London powers did not jointly secure Nikita's withdrawal she would take independent military action was not discouraged in Berlin, and the Germans warned the French explicitly that if Russia intervened Germany would fight. Meanwhile Sazonov's actions had been at least as pacific as were Bethmann's in the preceding crisis, and he had admonished the Montenegrins for their 'passionate and foolish attitude', in opposition to the 'supreme interests of European peace'.[2] But no one believed that Pan-Slav sentiment would allow Russia to abandon the Montenegrins, and the apparent danger of war was only averted by King Nikita's sudden submission. He is said to have gambled on the Vienna bourse over the crisis so that he could take his profit on ending it.

The Scutari episode held lessons. By the vicious conventions of twentieth-century politics and publicity the evacuation of Scutari without Austrian military action was to be regarded as a humiliation for the empire. So domestic criticism of Berchtold as a weak Russophil disposed him to more desperate courses, even if this was not immediately apparent. After the settlement of the Scutari problem the Balkan belligerents were brought back to London to negotiate, and their delegates finally signed the Treaty of London on 30 May. This reduced European Turkey to a bare hinterland of Constantinople and the Straits, the exact demarcation

---

[1] *Die Grosse Politik*, vol. xxxiv (i), nos. 12,818, 12,824.
[2] Albertini, *The Origins of the War of 1914*, vol. i, p. 446.

of the Greek and Bulgarian shores of the Aegean coast being entrusted to the great powers as was the disposition of the Aegean islands, while the partition of Macedonia was left to Serbia and Bulgaria to negotiate.

It was when these two states fell out that Berchtold returned to the plan of building up Bulgaria so as to encircle Serbia. Such an idea was unpopular in Berlin, above all because Roumania, the nominal satellite of the Triple Alliance, was also a rival of Bulgaria. Yet in spite of her Hohenzollern King Carol, Roumania could not in the long run be held to the alliance. The intelligentsia were Francophil and the nationalist public of all classes saw their enemy in Hungary with its minority of a million or more Roumanians in the province of Transylvania. This the Germans failed to realise. After the ill-judged Bulgarian surprise attack on the Serbs and Greeks they maintained their objections to Austrian intervention to save the aggressor. It was expected, even by the bellicose Austrian chief of staff, General Conrad von Hoetzendorff, that Austrian action would bring in Russia, and it is doubtful how far Berchtold's warlike plans represented serious intentions. But when Greece, Turkey and finally Roumania joined Serbia, the Germans disavowed their ally's policy by publicly approving the Treaty of Bucharest of 11 August 1913 and trying to incite the press to work for Berchtold's removal.[1] Nor was this all. This treaty and the Treaty of London left over certain questions for decision by the powers, and when the aspirations of Bulgaria and Greece conflicted the kaiser placed Germany in the opposite camp to the Austrians. The latter found themselves on the same side as the Russians, whose temporary concern was to stop the Greeks from creeping up the coast towards Constantinople.

It was not until the autumn of 1913 that Berchtold won his first clear-cut diplomatic victory over the Serbs with German support. The Serbs were slow in withdrawing troops from northern Albania and indiscreetly avowed their hope of obtaining a frontier rectification. Cumulative warnings from Vienna were inadequate and were disregarded before the ultimatum of 18 October, which gave the Serbs a week to retire. The Germans were only informed of the note at the last moment (and the Italians after its dispatch). But the kaiser was enthusiastic. He deprecated a peaceful solution even, pointing out to General Conrad, 'The other [powers] are not prepared'.[2] This was true, since the last Austrian warning before the ultimatum had caused both Sazonov and the French to tell the Serbs to back down. The Serbs did back down at once, but what was most striking about the success of Berchtold's undertaking was the appeal of the virtual *fait accompli* to the German government, in particular to the kaiser. It was as if consultation was really unwelcome, as if the principle was being established that Austria was responsible, morally

---

[1] *Die Grosse Politik*, vol. xxxvi (i), no. 13,781, where the kaiser declared this aim.
[2] Conrad von Hoetzendorff, *Aus meiner Dienstzeit* (Vienna, 1922–5), vol. iii, p. 470.

and strategically, for her own Balkan policy and Germany only for its consequences.

The truth was that apart from such an opportunist support of Austria-Hungary in a preventive war against 'Slavdom and Gaul', which the kaiser regarded as inevitable, no official German strategy and certainly no clear war aims existed. The kaiser was too volatile and yet fundamentally too conservative a European. Characteristic was his dictum that 'the true interests of Europe can be defended by the two main powers in the [two] groups, standing shoulder to shoulder, namely Germany and England'.[1] In world politics the 'yellow peril' interested him more than competition with Britain and he scoffed at what he called the 'crazy vision of an African colonial empire'.[2] Nor was the *Drang nach Osten*, the 'urge to the East', supposedly revealed in the Baghdad railway, by any means a leading official preoccupation. German policy during the Balkan wars had not been appreciably affected by the German association with the equipment and training of the Turkish army since the 1880's, nor by the exploitation of this for diplomatic prestige in Turkey by Marschall von Bieberstein.

Not only Germany's but the other great powers' commitments in the decrepit Turkish empire were tested at the end of 1913. A new and large German military mission was invited to Turkey to rehabilitate the army once again. The news that a German general, Liman von Sanders, was to command the Constantinople army corps, as well as lead the mission, came in November as a shock to the Russians—perhaps a calculated one. In St Petersburg it seemed time to consider again the ultimate issues of war and peace in the question of the straits. By January Sazonov was prepared to face general European complications in order to induce the Turks to drop Liman, and he proposed the occupation by all three *entente* powers of selected points in Asia Minor.[3] But it was already obvious that he could not count on such co-operation. The French had been prepared to protest to the Turkish government against 'handing the keys of the Straits' to the Germans,[4] but the British could not even go so far as that when they realised that their own adviser to the Turkish navy, Admiral Limpus, held an equivalent naval command to Liman's military one. In any case they feared an accommodation at their expense between St Petersburg and Berlin as more likely than a war.[5] But the immediate interest of Germany in a partition was overestimated in London. The

[1] *Die Grosse Politik*, vol. XXXVI (i), no. 13,781.   [2] *Ibid.* vol. XXXI, no. 11,422.
[3] Memorandum of 6 January summarised in *Der grossen Katastrophe entgegen* (Berlin, 1929) by Baron M. Taube (who was Sazonov's assistant), p. 291.
[4] *Documents diplomatiques français, 1871–1914*, 3ème série, vol. VIII, no. 544. The French documents do not support the contention of E. Brandenburg (*From Bismarck to the World War*, Oxford, 1927, p. 461) and other German apologists that France was encouraging Russian belligerency. *Ibid.* vol. VIII, nos. 598, 689, 694.
[5] *British Documents on the Origin of the War, 1898–1914* (London, 1926–38), vol. X (i), no. 180.

Germans had designs on Turkish territory but were not ready for annexation. They wished, more than the Russians, to postpone the moment of partition as long as possible.[1]

In the event a conciliatory solution was found in Berlin by promoting Liman to a rank which put him above a corps commander in Turkey and thus left him as adviser only. This concession overtook a ministerial conference at St Petersburg in January which was devoted to the emergency. There the minister for war Sukhomlinov claimed that Russia was 'perfectly ready for a duel with Germany' if necessary, although the general staff was counting, with Sazonov, on French and possibly even on British support. The conclusion of the conference against risking war without *both* 'entente' partners deferred to the opposition of the premier, Kokovtsov—but Kokovtsov was about to leave office because of his incompatibility with the court regime.

The Liman episode had two serious consequences affecting the balance of war and peace six months later. There was a re-appraisal of Russian strategy and armaments, and there was the emergence of a new and ominous ill-feeling in Russo-German public relations. Second thoughts made the Russian general staff conclude that an offensive in the Straits would have been impracticable, and led to fresh appropriations for the Black Sea fleet, the retention of conscripts with the colours and vigorous publicity for rearmament.[2] This was taken as provocation by German official and public opinion and set off a newspaper war probably stimulated by both governments. Soon the Allies, Austria-Hungary, and to a lesser degree France, were drawn into a 'controversy which could hardly be more embittered', as the British ambassador wrote from Vienna, 'if a war were on the point of breaking out'.[3]

The newspaper campaign in Russia linked Russian preparedness with admonitions to France. Russian public and official opinion was particularly anxious for the maintenance in France of the new law for three years' military service. The law had been passed in the spring of 1913, virtually simultaneously with the last great army expansion in Germany. Neither measure seems to have been definitely provoked by the other, but in each case the opportune competition reduced domestic criticism. Three years' service in France was the only way of making up for Germany's fifty per cent advantage in population and its higher birth rate. The parties of the left were against it, but the premier in 1914, Viviani, had promised Poincaré to leave the law intact. Such a party compromise reflected the deeper tension in French than in Russian relations with Germany, even if the French press was more discreet. Exhibitions of German militarism, especially in Alsace or Lorraine, were given ominous importance. In

---

[1] Jagow to the German Ambassador in Constantinople in July 1913. Brandenburg, p. 459.
[2] M. N. Pokrovskii, *Drei Konferenzen zur Vorgeschichte des Krieges* (Berlin, 1920), pp. 66–7.
[3] *British Documents on the Origins of the War, 1898–1914*, vol. x (ii), no. 526.

both France and Germany parties of the left deplored the tension and an inter-parliamentary conference met at Berne in 1913 as a demonstration against nationalist alignments. Events proved its superficiality as well as frustrating its second annual meeting.

Britain was not remote from these agitations. The alarms in Russia led to pressure on Britain to tighten its links in the Triple Entente. The British royal visit to Paris in April stimulated French advocacy of the Russian plea and Grey gave way to the extent of linking the communication to the Russian ambassador of the Anglo-French agreement of 1912 with a move towards Anglo-Russian naval staff talks. The Germans got wind of this and were barely placated by Grey's prevaricatory answer to a parliamentary question to the effect that no agreements existed which would hamper Britain's free choice whether to wage war or not.[1] Meanwhile the direct Anglo-German negotiations on extra-European issues, to which Berlin had probably attached too general a political significance, approached their conclusion. By the end of July no obstacle remained to the signature of the agreement for the hypothetical partition of the colonies of Britain's Portuguese ally. On 27 July the kaiser authorised the signature of the Baghdad railway treaty which exchanged British control of the Persian-gulf shipping for German control of the line to the Basra railhead. Linked with this treaty, and at least equally significant, had been a series of semi-private, semi-governmental tripartite negotiations in which the Turks shared, over oil and shipping interests—which were producing the incongruous result of the two rival imperial navies relying on the same source of fuel.

The diplomatic stabilisation in the Near East and Africa—with its Far Eastern parallel in the partition between Russia and Japan of claims on China beyond the wall—had no bearing on European antagonisms unless to free the protagonists entirely from other preoccupations. Contemporaries were in little doubt about the two crucial European factors: first the ripeness of the Habsburg empire for dissolution—or its converse the expansive force of Yugoslavism—and second the preponderance of the German army for good or ill. Jagow, the German Secretary of State, compared the prospects of Austria and Turkey in terms of 'a race between the two empires, which goes to pieces first' and deplored the lack of imperial sense among German Austrians.[2] Tschirschky, in Vienna, foresaw the latter joining Germany as the result of an eventual partition, and asked 'whether it really pays us to bind ourselves so tightly to this phantom of a state'.[3] Yet the Germans had little patience for the symptoms or the fancy remedies of the dying empire. They regarded the coming threat of the union of Serbia and Montenegro as irresistible, they deprecated a connection with Bulgaria and continued to urge the conciliation of

---

[1] *British Documents on the Origins of the War, 1898–1914*, vol. x (ii), no. 548.
[2] *Ibid.* no. 532.   [3] *Die Grosse Politik*, vol. xxxix, no. 15,734.

Roumania until that country's final defection was manifested by a Russian imperial visit in June 1914.[1]

That German military dominance obstructed the natural course of Slav liberation was not the sole grudge against it even of Russia. It was intolerable in itself. Sazonov's words are revealing. 'To feel the stronger and yet to give way to an opponent whose superiority consists solely in his organisation and discipline' was 'humiliating' and led to 'demoralisation'.[2] It was not known how unsystematic and—to give it its due—negative German foreign policy was behind its weapons. Alarmists could point to the domestic and foreign best-seller, *Germany and the Next War*, by the military publicist General Bernhardi, which demanded a final subjugation of France and revived Treitschke's aspersions on the 'unseemliness' (*Unsittlichkeit*) of world peace, And in fact, though not to public knowledge, these views sometimes echoed in the kaiser's mind, with a possible influence in official quarters, as when he wrote in 1912 of the 'eunuch-like' tendency to 'emphasise world peace'.[3] The temper of Europe was described in famous words by Colonel House, the American president's personal envoy on a peace-making mission whose very existence was significant enough. 'The situation is extraordinary. It is militarism run stark mad. Unless someone acting for you can bring about a different understanding there is some day to be an awful cataclysm. There is too much hatred, too many jealousies.' There was also, in spite of the German army, too much incompatible confidence among the general staffs—that built-in error of generals promoted for their leadership, not in counsel but in battle where euphoria is an indispensable virtue. They were not interested in deterrents but in victories.

While the tsar was driving in an outpost of the Triple Alliance on his visit to the king of Roumania, the kaiser was conferring with the Archduke Francis Ferdinand on Austro-Hungarian and Balkan problems at the latter's residence in Bohemia. Barely a fortnight later these issues were given a tragic twist by the assassination on 28 June of the archduke and his morganatic wife by a Bosnian Serb of Austro-Hungarian nationality, Gavrilo Princip. The murder was planned from Belgrade by the Serbian secret society *Crna Ruka* (the Black Hand) because Francis Ferdinand stood for Habsburg federalism and this threatened the establishment of a greater Yugoslavia. The young assassins declared this motive at their trial as a private one,[4] and the Austro-Hungarian government did not realise the scope of the organisation behind them. Still less did they know that its leader was Dimitrievič, *alias* Apis, and that he was simul-

---

[1] *Oesterreich-Ungarns Aussenpolitik*, vol. VIII, 9902.
[2] *Mezhdunarodnye Otnosheniya v Epokhu Imperializma*, series iii (1931), vol. I, no. 289.
[3] *Die Grosse Politik*, vol. XXXIII, no. 12,225.
[4] A. Mousset, *Un Drame historique, l'attentat de Sarajevo* (Paris, 1930) (text of interrogations), p. 151.

taneously head of the Black Hand and of military intelligence at the Serbian war office. The case against the Serbian government rested upon the general licence, indeed encouragement, given to irredentist nationalism and the alleged supply of arms to terrorists by Serbian officials in the *Narodna odbrana* (National Defence), an open patriotic association which the Austrians confused with the secret Black Hand. Austrian police intelligence was in fact as poor as their police precautions and the failure of these must be held to weaken their case against the Serbs. What remains uncertain is how much the Pašić government in Serbia knew of the Black Hand's plans and, if complicit, whether they were acquiescent or intimidated.

The problem of war and peace set by the Sarajevo murder did not differ essentially from the emergencies in previous years when the Austro-Hungarian government had forgone the temptation of a *casus belli* against the South Slavs because of the risk of Russian intervention and the un-certainty of German counter-support. General Conrad thought the oppor-tunity less favourable than earlier ones, while resolving that it must not be missed.[1] The gamble appealed to the court's and the bureaucracy's mood of studied desperation. By 1 July official opinion in favour of war was general enough for Tisza to protest to the emperor, after a ministerial council at which he was the sole dissentient, against the 'fatal blunder',[2] as he saw it, of using Berchtold's inadequate *casus belli*. But this time there was to be no mistake about German co-operation. A special mission was sent off to Berlin to sound out the senior partner in the Triple Alliance.

The message to the German kaiser which Count Hoyos presented on 5 July consisted of a letter from Francis Joseph covering a general memo-randum on Austrian Balkan policy. This re-stated the Austrian plan of winning over Bulgaria as an ally against Serbia and a check upon the defection of Roumania, and warned that it was against Germany that Russian intrusion in the Balkans was really aimed. Neither document explicitly proposed immediate action, still less did they contain a plan for this, but the letter declared that future policy must be based on the 'isolation and reduction of Serbia'[3] and counted on the kaiser agreeing that the 'focus of criminal agitation in Belgrade must not survive unpunished'.

Hoyos and the Austro-Hungarian Ambassador Szögyény found the kaiser in a receptive frame of mind, indignant at an act of regicide whose victim was a personal friend, yet impatient to dispose of urgent business so that he could leave the next day for his annual cruise with the German fleet. He hastened to give his concurrence in Austrian intentions subject to the formality of consultation with the imperial chancellor. Szögyény was able to telegraph at once that German support was promised even if it should come to war with Russia and that if the Ballplatz saw the

---

[1] Conrad, *Aus meiner Dienstzeit*, vol. IV, p. 72.
[2] *Oesterreich-Ungarns Aussenpolitik*, vol. VIII, no. 9978.   [3] *Ibid.* no. 9984.

'necessity of military action against Serbia' the kaiser would regret to see them miss 'the present favourable moment'.[1] Before joining his yacht on 6 July the kaiser conferred briefly with representatives of the army and navy staffs—Moltke and Tirpitz were away. He warned them of the possible contingency of war with Russia and consequently with France as well, but he did not think Russia was 'ready to fight' and he did not apparently discuss Great Britain's position at all.

Meanwhile consultation between the kaiser and the imperial chancellor, who arrived in Potsdam after the Austrians, was equally perfunctory; historians have long ago dissolved the myth of a full dress 'crown council' approving a war plan.[2] The result, according to Szögyény, was a confirmation by the chancellor of his master's undertakings. The difference between his report of the chancellor's assurances and Bethmann-Hollweg's own account in telegraphing to Tschirschky does not lead very far. Bethmann-Hollweg's telegram recorded the kaiser's agreement with the general Balkan policy proposed by Vienna—in which, as regards Bulgaria and Roumania, the Germans proceeded to co-operate—and added that as regards the 'questions at issue with Serbia' the kaiser 'would take up no position since they extended outside his competence'.[3] But he would 'stand loyally on the side of Austria-Hungary'.

The claim on behalf of Bethmann that this lack of explicitness implied reservations has to contend with the fact that no positive hint, even in favour of moderation, was given to Vienna until nearly three weeks later, when the scope of diplomacy to prevent the outbreak of war was being narrowed by military policy solely concerned with its most advantageous timing. Meanwhile Tschirschky's interpretation of his instructions, pressing upon Germany's ally both a free hand and an unconditional guarantee, was continuously encouraged. In this neither the chancellor nor the kaiser was deliberately picking a quarrel among the great powers; rather they were approving a supposedly unequal contest between one great and one minor power which they calculated could be localised. As to the consequences of miscalculation they showed themselves recklessly indifferent. The alignment of their potential enemies received no serious political and strategic appreciation whatever. The charge of 'imposing' war, attributed to Germany in the Versailles treaty, was therefore misconceived. It was levity rather than a grand design which produced the fatal commitment. Where deliberation entered was in treating the commitment to Austria as more rigid than it necessarily was, and in making a virtue of preventive war against Russia and France out of the arguable necessity of ensuring an Austrian political victory over Serbia.

Armed with the encouraging German response Berchtold obtained from

---

[1] *Ibid.* no. 10058.
[2] S. B. Fay, *The Coming of the World War* (1936 ed.), vol. II, p. 181.
[3] *Die deutschen Dokumente zum Kriegsausbruch* (Charlottenburg, 1919), vol. I, no. 15.

a ministerial council on 7 July a decision in favour of provoking the Serbs to war in preference to exacting their diplomatic humiliation.[1] He argued that the Germans would see any sort of bargain as a 'confession of weakness which could not fail to react on our position in the Triple Alliance and the future policy of Germany'. This view was strengthened by Szögyény's reports of Berlin's impatience and of the opinion prevailing there that Russia was preparing for a future aggressive war, but was not yet ready for a defensive one.

Meanwhile a plan of action was taking shape. Tschirschky could report to Berlin on 10 July that a 48-hour ultimatum was to be delivered in Belgrade and that it would be for Berchtold a 'very disagreeable' solution if it were accepted.[2] But the Germans refused to help formulate the demands. They rejected responsibility for the form of the diplomatic operation while accepting its consequences. What the Germans did want was to speed up Austrian preparations, while foreign apprehensions were lulled by such deceptions as keeping both countries' chiefs of staff on leave. The Austrian timing of the ultimatum for 23 July was explained to Berlin as necessitated by the state visit to St Petersburg of Poincaré and Viviani between the 16th and 22nd of the month. It was better to wait till the French had gone home. But to Conrad Berchtold explained the delay by the need of getting in the harvest before mobilising, and by the process of investigation into the murder, as well as by the diplomatic problem.[3]

The preparation of the case against Serbia was not plain sailing; its own investigator sent to Sarajevo by the Ministry of Foreign Affairs could report no proof of even indirect responsibility, still less official complicity.[4] Nevertheless the terms of an ultimatum were drafted by 19 July and approved by a ministerial council and by the emperor, so that the text could be sent off on the following day, for communication to the powers after delivery of the note in Belgrade in the evening of 23 July. Its tenor had, of course, been known in Berlin for several days, but the Germans' interest in foreknowledge of the actual text seems to have been only in order to prepare the press.[5] The Secretary of State, Jagow, claimed that he criticised its severity to the Austrian ambassador, but twenty-four hours after its receipt he was telegraphing to the major German embassies that he had no knowledge of its contents.[6] It was the predetermined German policy to turn a blind eye to the terms of the ultimatum.

The degree of collusion up to this stage between the two central powers is registered by a report from Schoen, the Bavarian representative in

<hr>

[1] *Oesterreich-Ungarns Aussenpolitik*, vol. VIII, no. 10,118.
[2] *Die deutschen Dokumente zum Kriegsausbruch*, vol. I, no. 29.
[3] Conrad, *Aus meiner Dienstzeit*, vol. IV, p. 72.
[4] *Oesterreich-Ungarns Aussenpolitik*, vol. VIII, no. 10,252.
[5] *Die deutschen Dokumente zum Kriegsausbruch*, vol. I, no. 83.
[6] Jagow, *Ursachen des Weltkriegs*, p. 110. Bethmann-Hollweg also recollected his and Jagow's misgivings (*Betrachtungen zum Weltkriege*, vol. I, p. 139).

Berlin, on an interview with the Undersecretary of State, Zimmermann, which he sent to Munich on 18 July. Schoen predicted the terms of the Austrian ultimatum, recorded the complete full powers (*Blankovollmacht*) given to Austria, and explained how the Germans, when giving immediate diplomatic support to the Austrian case, 'will claim to be as much surprised by the Austrian action as the other powers'.[1] Germany wanted the conflict localised, hoped that Russian opposition might be no more than bluff, and that France and Britain might urge prudence in St Petersburg, but Schoen's information showed that even British neutrality was not expected if the balance of power appeared to be jeopardised by a threat to the existence of France. A still more authoritative explanation of the motives of German policy was given in a private letter from Jagow to Lichnowsky who had been criticising from London the submission of German policy to Austrian interests. Arguing that Austria, Germany's only available ally, needed to chasten Serbia if she was to achieve 'political rehabilitation' and if 'the stabilisation of Russian hegemony in the Balkans', which he described as 'inadmissible', was to be averted, Jagow expressed hopes of localising the conflict. But although he did not want a 'preventive war', it was a better moment for a show-down with Russia than it would be a few years hence. 'Then she [Russia] will overwhelm us with the number of her soldiers, then she will have built her Baltic fleet and her strategic railways. Meanwhile our group will become weaker all the time.'[2]

This was the Austro-German commitment at the beginning of the fourth week of July. Was it to any degree induced or confirmed by faults of commission or omission on what became the other side? Apologists for the central powers, while shuffling direct responsibility between Berlin and Vienna, have found it extenuated by a provocative attitude on the part of Belgrade, by the challenging consolidation of their front by the French and Russians, and by a misleading posture of neutrality on the part of Great Britain. There is some historical significance in all these charges, whatever their polemical bearing. Contemporary reporting from Serbia was partisan, but leaves no doubt that public opinion was excited and that an exchange of abuse with Austria had started in the press directly after the Sarajevo crime. The government's behaviour was, on the whole, correct; their offence was failure to initiate a Serbian investigation into the background of the assassination. Coercion by the Black Hand or fear of damaging disclosures, rather than deference to public opinion, may account for their tactless passivity. Pašić and his colleagues were showing no ardour for a sacrificial war of national liberation, and their fear of its imminence culminated in circular representations to the powers, protesting Serbian innocence and willingness to give Austria reasonable satisfaction, although this step did not effectively anticipate the Austrian ultimatum.

[1] *Die deutschen Dokumente zum Kriegsausbruch*, vol. IV, Anhang IV.
[2] *Ibid.* vol. I, no. 72.

There is no evidence of Serbia having received any significant reassurance or suasion from the Russians from the beginning of the crisis until after the Austrian terms were announced. What mattered, however, was not the independent Russian reaction to signs of Austrian preparations— for these as we know were to be discounted as bluff in Vienna and Berlin —but the development of Franco-Russian solidarity, and the arrival of Poincaré and Viviani in St Petersburg unquestionably coincided with an increase in tension.

The French government had shown no more initiative in the Austro-Serbian question during the first fortnight of July than the other Entente powers, and on 15 July its leaders embarked on their planned visit to Russia with an agenda for consultation in which Serbia had a low priority compared, for instance, with the improvement of Anglo-Russian relations.[1] They were due to arrive on 20 July, to leave again on the 23rd and to be back in Paris on 28 July. These dates were kept, and during all that crucial period policy at the Quai d'Orsay was paralysed. So much is apparent from the positive and negative evidence of the French documentary material, including Poincaré's own memoirs. But the paucity of information about the Russian visit—which the published Russian documents barely supplement—is hardly to be explained by a lack of activity.[2] There can be no doubt that some immediate assurances were exchanged between the allied leaders. On 21 July Sazonov for the first time told the German ambassador that Russia would not tolerate threats let alone military action against Serbia, her policy being, so he said, '*pacifique mais pas passive*'.[3] This attitude was endorsed by Poincaré himself on the same day in lecturing the Austrian ambassador on the fact that 'Serbia has friends and thereby a situation dangerous to peace may arise'.[4] Yet the only ostensibly factual record of Franco-Russian agreement on joint policy during the visit is provided by a telegram of 24 July from the British ambassador. Buchanan reported 'a perfect community of views' between France and Russia on European problems, and 'a decision to take action at Vienna with a view to the prevention of a demand for explanations or any summons equivalent to an intervention in the internal affairs of Serbia'.[5] No Franco-Russian counter-ultimatum in Vienna ensued, but the context suggests the recognition by the French government of the defence of Serbia's independence as a *casus foederis* for France. Poincaré's personal critics and revisionist historians have seized on the Russian visit as the culmination of a conspiracy between the two military allies.

---

[1] Albertini, *The Origins of the War of 1914*, vol. II, p. 188.
[2] *Documents diplomatiques français, 1871–1914*, 3ème série, vol. X, p. vi. P. Renouvin, 'La Politique française en juillet 1914' (*Revue de l'histoire de la guerre*, janvier 1937 (pp. 1–21)).
[3] *Die deutschen Dokumente zum Kriegsausbruch*, vol. I, no. 120.
[4] *Oesterreich-Ungarns Aussenpolitik*, vol. VIII, no. 10,461.
[5] *British Documents on the Origins of the War, 1898–1914*, vol. XI, no. 101.

In contrast, the diplomacy of Great Britain has been blamed even at this stage for an obtuse impartiality.[1] It is true that the German ambassador told Grey as early as 6 July of the probable Austrian action and even of the possibility of German support. Lichnowsky's warning was confirmed as regards Austria by the British ambassador in Vienna and even the 'egging on' of Austria by Germany was detected by Crowe, the most acute of Grey's Foreign Office advisers, on 22 July. Yet on the same day Grey could tell the French ambassador: 'Probably Berlin was trying to moderate Vienna.'[2] Although Grey impressed on both the Austrian and German ambassadors his mounting anxiety, he made no imputations. And as late as 23 July he was speaking of a war between the other 'four great Powers' with British neutrality consequently implied.[3]

The hint of British neutrality was no doubt an avoidable mistake, and Grey's tendency to treat the German government as an uncommitted power, only less impartial than Britain, may have been due to intellectual error rather than to a judgment of tactical expediency which subsequent evidence of second thoughts in Berlin to some extent justified. But the tendency has been to exaggerate and to antedate Grey's opportunity of influencing events. Whatever the defects of Grey's analysis before Austria-Hungary's commitment was complete it was unthinkable to counter the latter by virtually guaranteeing Russia through France against Germany. Such an improvisation on the consultative pact with France—which was all the 1912 exchange of letters amounted to—would have required his colleagues' deliberate sanction. But there could be no question of seeking this yet in a cabinet divided already over the Ulster crisis. On the other hand, a private warning to Germany, without encouraging France and Russia, would have been a doubtfully practicable bluff and alien to Grey's straightforward methods. And to encourage Britain's Entente partners on his own responsibility would have involved the risk of leading them to 'face the ordeal of war relying on our support' only to find that this was not in the event forthcoming.[4] That risk could not be taken. If Grey did not regard British intervention as a means of averting war it was because his thinking was limited automatically by the realities of British politics.[5]

[1] See, for example, Albertini *op. cit.* vol. II, pp. 214–16.
[2] *British Documents*, vol. XI, no. 72.
[3] Lichnowsky had been warned of much stronger language to Mensdorff though it was to include an offer to support 'moderate' (*gemässigt*) demands in Belgrade. In reporting this he added that Germany was counted on not to support the exploitation of the Sarajevo murder for Austria's Balkan ambitions—a caution which drew the kaiser's comment: 'An enormity of British shamelessness.' *Die deutschen Dokumente zum Kriegsausbruch*, vol. I, no. 121.
[4] Grey, *Twenty-Five Years* (1935 ed.), vol II, p. 158.
[5] It is a debating point rather than a historical one, since it did not enter into Grey's calculations, that an earlier British commitment, if it had not averted war, might well have placed Grey among the principal accused in the war-guilt controversy. He might not have been blamed for using war as an instrument of national policy but he would doubtless have been blamed for encouraging the French and Russians to do so.

But this was not the only element in Grey's calculation. Before Austria had virtually ruled out a diplomatic solution he might well doubt the wisdom of increasing Russian confidence, and therefore Serbian intransigence. He continued to believe in Sazonov's good faith, though less in his good sense, but he also believed in Bethmann's and, convinced that Austrian policy could be ultimately controlled by the Germans, he meant to avoid an antagonism to Germany which would reduce the effectiveness of his influence in Berlin.

The fact remains that German policy did not hang upon British non-intervention. The German Foreign Office, as Schoen's report shows, expected British intervention if it was required to save France, while of the two strategic doctrines in vogue in Germany one disbelieved in British neutrality and the other disregarded the question. For the first of these, Tirpitz's blue water school, the world rivalry of the two naval, commercial and imperial powers must be the primary motive in German policy. Far from accepting war with Russia, Tirpitz would have had Germany seek a *rapprochement* at Britain's expense, for '*coûte que coûte* we must set the Whale against the Bear'.[1] Such a diplomatic revolution was also favoured by German conservatives of a very different stamp and supported by a strong pro-German faction at the court of St Petersburg.[2] The other school of strategy, without predilections for Britain or Russia, was that of the Grand General Staff, which believed that the supremacy of Europe would be settled in battle on the plains of Flanders and Poland. Their time-table for the successive defeats of France and Russia did not leave room for the unimaginable introduction of a full-sized British army, nor for the long-term influence of sea power. Between these two schools the kaiser had blundered for years, not fully aware of their contradictions; but the policy of 5 July was that of the general staff.

The Austro-Hungarian ultimatum to Serbia was delivered in Belgrade at 6.00 p.m. on 23 July and its acceptance was required within 48 hours. The demands were formidable, but they were not disproportionate to the allegations which introduced them—nor indeed to the unknown truth of Serbian intrigue. They included public repudiation of irredentist ambitions and the dissolution of the *Narodna Odbrana* among other concessions humiliating to pan-Slavism.[3] Russian susceptibilities were not acknowledged but acceptance of the risk of war was confirmed in a telegram to St Petersburg supplying the Austrian ambassador Szápáry with a brief in support of the ultimatum. 'If', it began, 'Russia judges the time ripe for a final reckoning with the Central Powers the following instructions

---

[1] Von Tirpitz, *My Memoirs* (English ed.), vol. I, p. 174.

[2] This was a far less fanciful switch of policy than a tendency for France to combine with Germany and Britain against Russia, which some historians have managed to discern: for example, A. J. P. Taylor, *The Struggle for Mastery in Europe*, p. 514.

[3] *Oesterreich-Ungarns Aussenpolitik*, vol. VIII, no. 10,395; vol. XI, Appendix A.

will be superfluous.'[1] This imputation ignored, of course, the common assumption in both camps that Russia would not be ready until 1917.[2] But it owed nothing to the theory—since so popular—that war offered tsarist Russia the last chance of national unity. Whether the revolutionary movement in Russia and the big political strikes of the summer of 1914 influenced the tsar and his advisers, is unknown. But on the evidence pan-Slavism—the only vital political force favourable to the dynasty—was not exploited.

When the Austrian terms reached Sazonov he is said to have exclaimed: 'This means a European war.'[3] But in his interviews with the Austrian and German ambassadors there was no sign of satisfaction, only indignation. To the German ambassador Pourtalès he gave the warning that 'if Austria swallows Serbia we will make war on her'.[4] This produced a deceptive reassurance, that Austria intended no annexation, which concealed a plan to feed Serbia to the other Balkan nations. The headless French government responded non-committally, but the Italians objected to 'such far-reaching aggressive action' without consultation.[5] It already looked as if Italy would join the highest bidder or the most likely winner after the first battles; in Italy, as in Roumania, public opinion was favourable not to her allies but to the Entente. Even Grey's impartiality did not flatter Austro-German hopes of 'localising the dispute'. The provocation given to Russia seemed to him too strong, and he appealed for German action in Vienna as a part of four-power mediation.[6] In any case, however, his limited control over British policy did not justify his making representations in St Petersburg.

The Russian reaction was not merely verbal. The council of ministers approved a plan of partial mobilisation against Austria to be applied at the appropriate moment. They also approved advice to the Serbs to withdraw from Belgrade and throw themselves on the mercy of the great powers. This has been interpreted as incitement to reject the Austrian ultimatum, but the full argument depends on an arbitrary reconstruction of missing correspondence.[7] And as late as 27 July the reply sent by the tsar to a Serbian appeal was distinctly equivocal. Meanwhile Sazonov's indignation did not prevent him from asking the Austrians for an extension of the time-limit. But the chief aim of Russian diplomacy at this point was a British demonstration of solidarity with Russia and France. When Buchanan reported Sazonov's appeal for this, Crowe gave his

[1] *Ibid.* no. 10,685.
[2] The date set for a 'general settlement' according to the Serbian minister Jovanović. Albertini, *op. cit.* (Italian edition), vol. I, facsimile letter facing p. 400.
[3] Schilling, *How the War Began in 1914* (*Diary of the Russian Ministry of Foreign Affairs*) (London, 1925), p. 29.
[4] *Die deutschen Dokumente zum Kriegsausbruch*, vol. I, nos. 160, 205.
[5] *Ibid.* no. 156.
[6] *British Documents on the Origin of the War, 1898–1914*, vol. XI, nos. 99, 116.
[7] For example, in Albertini, *op. cit.* vol. II, pp. 353 *et seq.*

opinion that France and Russia had already decided to accept the Austrian challenge so that the only question was whether Germany had determined on war. He suggested a warning to Berlin if France or Russia began to mobilise. But he failed to shake Grey's conviction that the British public would not sanction war over a Serbian quarrel.[1]

Since the Serbian reply did not amount to unconditional acceptance of the Austrian terms the Austrian ambassador left Belgrade and the predetermined Austrian partial mobilisation—against Serbia only, not Russia—thereupon ensued. Actually the Serbs' own mobilisation had just preceded not only this but the delivery of their reply to the ultimatum which they thus took at its word. Yet the Serbian note was highly conciliatory. About half the demands had been accepted outright, others had been evasively but deferentially answered. Moreover, an offer to submit the points left at issue to the international court at the Hague was added. The kaiser rightly called this a 'brilliant achievement for a time limit of only 48 hours', but the Austrians, he thought, had scored 'a great moral success' and 'all grounds for war disappear'. This was the common opinion in Europe, as the Austrians realised, but the powers were so strategically divided that the prospects of conciliation were seen to be poor. Pessimism aided the forces which were to justify it.

One proposal for conciliation had emerged already in the British plan for a conference, accompanied by a standstill in operations. Grey was influenced by gratifying recollections of the London conference of 1913, but the situations were profoundly dissimilar. In the earlier Balkan crises no great power had been an immediate party to the quarrel, nor had the Austro-Hungarian government been either single-minded or fully supported by Germany. The value of a conference in 1914 would have been to gain time for compromise. But the desire for compromise was not general and each nation's military planners were known to believe—incompatibly with one another—that time was on the side of their adversary.

Although the German government agreed to four-power mediation in principle, they rejected the conference proposal on the ground that for Austria it would amount to a 'court of arbitration'.[2] The French and Italians accepted, but Sazonov announced his preference for direct talks with the Austrians, to be met a day later by Berchtold's refusal to discuss Austrian relations with Serbia on the basis of the ultimatum and the reply.[3] Next the British were told in Vienna that it was too late for mediation; in fact, the declaration of war on 28 July was deliberately intended to frustrate mediation. Berchtold said as much when asking the Emperor Francis Joseph's sanction two days earlier; it seems that the urging towards

---

[1] *British Documents on the Origins of the War, 1898–1914*, vol. XI, no. 101.

[2] *Ibid.* vol. XI, no. 185.

[3] *Ibid.* vol. 179, no. 198. *Mezhdunarodnye Otnosheniya v epokhu imperializma*, series iii, vol. 5 (1934), nos. 116, 188.

a *fait accompli* came from the German general staff.[1] In fact Austrian military planners did not want active operations before 12 August, and their bombardment of Belgrade was staged to end political measures rather than to open their offensive.

This first declaration of war was not decisive. Russian-Austrian talks continued, although Sazonov declared that they were manifestly futile.[2] German representations in Vienna were actually stimulated, but by this time the unity of command over German policy was questionable. Most serious was the effect on Russian preparations for war and hence on German relations with Russia. So-called 'premobilisation', involving some preliminary measures, had begun on 25 July both in Russia and in Germany. This phase, by custom not regarded as hostile, played a relatively small part in the rapid German mobilisation so that the far slower Russians were greatly the gainers. News of the declaration of war on Serbia raised, however, the question of Russian mobilisation, partial or total. The military arguments for the more radical course were considered strong, and it could be held that the chance of avoiding war was so slight that to prepare in time was the first consideration. Developments during 29 July favoured these arguments. Evidence that there was some prospect of Austrian concessions was outweighed by news of the bombardment of Belgrade and a separate German threat to mobilise if Russia did not cease her minor military preparations.[3] There had been the usual muddle in Berlin; the quasi-ultimatum which Sazonov received from Pourtalès did not correspond to what Bethmann and Jagow were saying elsewhere.[4] But Sazonov was now convinced that the attack on Belgrade showed that the Austrians had only been negotiating to gain time.[5] He was converted to general mobilisation and agreed to persuade the reluctant tsar to sanction it. Recent reassurance of French support may have aided the Russian government's decision, but their ally was in fact far from approving such impatience.[6]

Hardly had the instructions for general mobilisation been approved than they were cancelled at the tsar's order and the partial mobilisation, of which the powers had already been notified, substituted. This was the result of a direct message from the kaiser to the tsar. The telegraphic correspondence between the two imperial cousins belongs to the period

[1] *Oesterreich-Ungarns Aussenpolitik*, vol. VIII, nos. 10,855, 10,656; *Die deutschen Dokumente zum Kriegsausbruch*, vol. I, nos. 213, 257.

[2] *British Documents*, vol. XI, no. 258.

[3] *Mezhdunarodnye Otnosheniya v Epokhu Imperializma*, series iii, vol. 5, no. 224.

[4] For example in *British Documents*, vol. XI, no. 263 and *Die deutschen Dokumente zum Kriegsausbruch*, vol. II, no. 385.

[5] *Oesterreich-Ungarns Aussenpolitik*, vol. VIII, no. 11,003.

[6] Poincaré, *Au Service de la France*, vol. IV, p. 385. The timing and meaning of assurances from the dispersed French ministers before the warning on 30 July from Viviani in Paris not to provoke German mobilisation is highly controversial. It is discussed exhaustively in Albertini, vol. II, ch. XIII.

of second thoughts in Germany. Unfortunately the kaiser was too frantic and inconsequent and the tsar too weak and uncomprehending to control the situation for good or evil. Until after he returned from his cruise the kaiser's influence had been wholly bellicose. But from the time he saw the Serbian reply the affectation of martial trenchancy and political infallibility in his comments and instructions began to alternate with self-pity, even common sense. It occurred to him at once that Austrian 'honour' might be satisfied by the seizure of Belgrade. This harmonised with the support which Bethmann-Hollweg had already begun to give the British move for mediation—stimulated without doubt by the diminishing prospect of British neutrality unless Germany could earn it. On the 27th Grey's guarded words to the German ambassador about the scope of a European war caused Lichnowsky to warn Bethmann explicitly that 'in case of war we would have England against us',[1] so that the British offer of pacification in St Petersburg in exchange for similar action in Vienna should be followed up.

Bethmann sent on Lichnowsky's telegram to Vienna with his blessing. His object was probably to lessen German responsibility in the eyes of the world, but domestic politics also required that Germany should appear 'forced into war', as he explicitly stated.[2] Some saving clauses in his instructions to Tschirschky, in particular that the ambassador should 'carefully avoid giving the impression that we want to hold Austria back',[3] also suggest that he was less preoccupied with averting war than with improving the grounds for waging it. Whatever Bethmann's own position, the increasingly strong remonstrances which he ordered in Vienna were almost certainly rendered ineffective by the Secretary of State, Jagow, as well as by Moltke. The Austro-Hungarian ambassador in Berlin, Szögyény, reported on 28 July that the apparent German support for British proposals for mediation was only formal and that the German government were really 'decisively against heeding them'.[4] Whether or not Szögyény overdid Jagow's gloss on the Chancellor's views, Berchtold took him at his word and proceeded to treat the official German representations with calculated indifference. It is not known how faithfully Tschirschky interpreted the Chancellor's instructions, let alone his mood, but Bethmann's arguments and reproaches got merely evasive answers. The Austrians had concluded that a prestige victory would be valueless and that operations must go on.

Meanwhile the situation in Berlin had changed. Bethmann's last and most indignant telegram to Vienna was cancelled[5] and the kaiser's support

[1] *Die deutschen Dokumente zum Kriegsausbruch*, vol. I, no. 265.
[2] *Ibid.* vol. I, no. 277. [3] *Ibid.* vol. II, no. 323.
[4] *Oesterreich-Ungarns Aussenpolitik*, vol. VIII, no. 10,793.
[5] *Die deutschen Dokumente zum Kriegsausbruch*, vol. II, nos. 441 and 450. It had included the words: 'If...Vienna rejects everything it will prove that it absolutely wants war...and Russia will remain guiltless.'

in recommending the 'halt in Belgrade' to the Emperor Francis Joseph was too feeble and came too late.[1] The Austrians had successfully temporised long enough to let the mounting anxieties of the German general staff at Russia's military preparations gain the ascendancy in German policy. On 29 July that body had formally warned the Chancellor of the decreasing lead in mobilisation which Germany would retain if Russian and French preparations went on. Military intelligence about these preparations overwhelmed Bethmann, late on 30 July, but Moltke had already been working against him in messages to Conrad in Vienna. 'Mobilise at once against Russia', he urged, 'Germany will mobilise.'[2] This injunction caused Berchtold to remark: 'Who gives the orders, Moltke or Bethmann?' It was a pertinent observation. Only the lack of co-ordination, indeed the division of power in Berlin, made it possible for the dependent ally to rebuff formal representations in favour of compromise from the superior power. It says more for Bethmann's loyalty than his trustworthiness as a historical source that he did not use this defence in his memoirs.

The impatience of the German generals on 30 July and the pressure they exerted on Bethmann and Conrad is sufficiently explained by the Russian measures of partial mobilisation; there is no need to assume a premonition of the general mobilisation on the following day. Thus the simultaneous Austrian and Russian general mobilisations were independent developments in the disastrous Russo-German race, and of the two the Russian action was the provocative and fatal one. Indeed, the extension of Austrian mobilisation against Serbia to other districts was simply the orthodox move in reply to the Russian partial mobilisation specifically directed against Austria-Hungary.

The Russian decision on 30 July, made public the next morning, was taken on purely military grounds, the impracticability of partial mobilisation, and the belief that German general mobilisation was imminent. The generals had pressed for the reversal of the tsar's last order of the previous day, and the weak and sanctimonious autocrat was driven against his pacific and Germanophil inclinations by Sazonov's advocacy into his habitual refuge of fatalism. The French made a last-minute plea for caution, but it is still not clear what bearing, if any, it had on the Russian decision. The relevant telegram of 30 July, while confirming the alliance obligations of France, suggested that Russia '...should not immediately proceed to any measure which might offer Germany a pretext for a total or partial mobilisation of her forces'.[3] This must be accepted as sent in good faith, but there are grounds for supposing that the warning was passed on late, imperfectly or not at all by the French ambassador

---

[1] *Ibid.* no. 437.

[2] *Oesterreich-Ungarns Aussenpolitik*, vol. VIII, no. 11033; Conrad, *op. cit.* vol. IV, pp. 152–3. Conrad's quotation of his own correspondence does not of course possess complete authenticity.

[3] *Documents diplomatiques français, 1871–1914*, 3ème série, vol. XI, no. 305.

Paléologue, whose conduct throughout the crisis is suspect.[1] No such cautionary advice came from London. Rightly or wrongly it remained Grey's conviction that he must not exert influence when he could not accept responsibility for its indirect consequences.

The Russian general mobilisation was the decisive calamity. This is true even given the excuse that it was merely forestalling German action of the same kind. It is not certain that the Russian partial mobilisation was in fact inducing a German counter move in spite of Moltke's telegrams to Conrad. Moreover, Russian mobilisation was necessarily ineffective, for any attempt to reduce the German lead in the ultimate phase could be swiftly neutralised by Germany. Historians should not tolerate the illusion of the contemporary strategists that rapid mobilisation was all-important. Never has the dogma of the offensive been more prevalent; never, because of the lead of firepower over tactical mobility, has that dogma been less applicable.

There was no question in 1914 but that general mobilisation by a great power must be followed by hostilities. The position was too competitive for the professionals to entertain the politicians' pretence that the Russian army could stay inactive on a war footing indefinitely. The German government's immediate declaration of a state of war emergency (*Kriegsgefahrzustand*) on 31 July, followed by their ultimatum demanding the cessation of Russian military preparations, constituted only technically the initiative in aggression. But simultaneously they proceeded to extend their strategic initiative to the extremes demanded by the so-called Schlieffen plan.

That was a different matter. The famous plan, on which training and mobilisation had been based through twenty years of its evolution, from Schlieffen to Moltke, envisaged a 'lightning' (*blitzschnell*) offensive to knock out France before turning on Russia—which would be meanwhile held by a German defensive campaign. Tactically, that involved an approach march through Belgium to envelop the French left flank.[2] In this war on two fronts the west had priority, so a collision with France had to be brought on. Simultaneously therefore with the 12-hour ultimatum to Russia an 18-hour ultimatum went off for delivery in Paris demanding an assurance of neutrality. A request for free passage through Belgium had already been sent off for delivery in Brussels as soon as operations against France were due to start. But operations were delayed, for the French did not accept the initiative in declaring war. Had they acceded to the demand for neutrality the German ambassador was to require further—so set was his government on the inevitability of a two-

[1] This is the result of criticism of his evidence as much as the notoriety of his warlike views. See Albertini, *The Origins of the War of 1914*, vol. II, pp. 618–19.

[2] The incursion of the German armies into Holland as well had been dropped from the original plan; it was to be restored in the most thorough, though differently phased, use of the whole plan in 1940 (see above, ch. x).

front war—the temporary surrender of two frontier fortresses as a guarantee. But when they neither promised neutrality nor declared war it was
considered in Berlin that a short postponement of the onslaught would be
just worth while in the hope of some French initiative or provocation
which might affect the British attitude. The Germans were not going to
compromise the Schlieffen plan for the sake of Great Britain; they had
no alternative war plan and the challenge to Britain as a guarantor of
Belgian neutrality must ensue. But whereas general war on the Continent
was seen in virtually all quarters to be inevitable within a few days once
Russia and Austria had begun to mobilise, immediate British intervention
was not. It was not appreciated in France or Germany—perhaps not in
Britain itself—that Belgian neutrality rather than the fate and conduct of
France would be the crucial issue.

Since Grey's admonitions on 27 July which had produced second
thoughts in Berlin, the development of British parliamentary and public
opinion had not kept pace with the requirements of effective diplomacy.
Nor had the views of the cabinet. Though the Liberal press was conspicuously divided, the bulk of the Liberal party's supporters were unprepared for war. Pacifist and isolationist, they inclined to believe that war
was financially impossible in the modern world as well as immoral, and
that Germany as a great commercial power must be predisposed to peace.
Did not Germany, furthermore, possess a powerful and internationally
minded socialist movement, and great trade unions opposed to militarism?
Many conservatives and most socialists also held one or other of these
illusions. Moreover, of the putative allies, Russia was the classic enemy
at once of the British empire in Asia and of international socialism and
democracy, while sympathy for France was counteracted by suspicion
of her interest in a war of revenge.

These political inhibitions produced a schism in the cabinet in the last
week of peace. In Churchill's opinion the cabinet would have 'broken up'
if Grey had pushed ahead of events and sought authority for threats to
influence them.[1] Public opinion was to unite on the issue of Belgian
neutrality when it was nakedly presented by the Germans, but the cabinet
would not have united upon it as a hypothetical *casus belli* a few days
earlier. How full and how early a commitment to intervention Grey
wanted to make is not known. Two things are however certain. First,
until the Russian general mobilisation order it was not 'too late' for the
Germans to have insisted upon compromise in Vienna. This could have
been achieved with no more loss of face to Austria—indeed on more
favourable terms—than at an earlier stage. Secondly, there was sufficient
evidence, well before the Russian general mobilisation and without an
explicit warning, for the Germans to reach the conclusion that Britain
would intervene. That evidence of British intentions had no effect on the

[1] *World Crisis* (London, 1929), p. 204.

diplomatic situation was due to the fact that there was no more unity of command in Berlin than in London.

Grey did not press the cabinet on the Belgian question; his limited objective was a guarantee to protect the northern coasts of France against the German fleet in view of the linked redistribution of French and British naval units which had left the Channel ports undefended. Meanwhile, confronted with the importunity of the French and German ambassadors, seeking respectively intervention and neutrality, his method was to promise the former less than he was threatening the latter. On 29 July the ambassador in Berlin, Goschen, reported Bethmann's unwise plea for British neutrality on condition that France was not deprived of European territory; the answer made it clear that Britain could not afford to see France crushed.[1] On 31 July the mobilisation of Russia and Germany, the German declaration of war emergency and the German ultimata to Russia and France led Grey to require assurances from Paris and Berlin that Belgian neutrality would be respected, but he refused to offer Lichnowsky an assurance of British neutrality in return.[2] On the other hand, he was still refusing any commitment to France on 1 August, pointing out that French commitments to Russia were unknown to Britain. Formally speaking the French government showed no resentment at the British attitude.

It was not until 2 August that the British cabinet was prepared to concede a guarantee of the French northern coasts. By then a formal assurance of support for intervention had come from the Conservative party, Luxemburg had been invaded, France and Belgium had begun to mobilise and the Belgians had made it clear that they would resist if their turn came.[3] The movement of the German army into Luxemburg had been accompanied by perfunctory allegations of imminent French incursions; the invasion of Belgium was being similarly prepared by a grotesque charge of unneutral conduct, and attempts began to create or invent incidents on Germany's frontier with France.

This propaganda made little impression. In contrast, the facts of French conduct eased the way for British intervention. Not only were French forward defences evacuated to avoid provocation but mobilisation was delayed until the commander-in-chief was threatening his resignation.[4] And the German ultimatum was met with the suggestion that news of promising developments in Austro-Russian relations made it premature.[5] In fact, these marked no advance. Sazonov had produced a new formula,

[1] *British Documents*, vol. XI, nos. 293, 303.
[2] *Ibid.* no. 448.
[3] The international guarantee of Luxemburg differed from that of Belgium in being 'joint' only and not 'several' as well, thus involving a lesser obligation upon an individual guarantor.
[4] Albertini, *op. cit.* (Italian edition), vol. III, p. 97.
[5] *British Documents*, vol. XI, no. 428.

but it did not offer a standstill in mobilisation or the 'halt in Belgrade'.[1] Berchtold, for his part, was merely repeating earlier prevarications. Meanwhile, German support for mediation had collapsed. Bethmann had become the advocate—for military reasons—of an early declaration of war on France, in spite of the obloquy; the opposition came from Tirpitz, not yet ready for a naval challenge to Great Britain. Once committed to a strong policy Bethmann was not strong enough to face modifying it in response to new developments. It was the kaiser who took most interest in a supposed British offer on 1 August to guarantee the neutrality of France if the German armies did not attack her.[2] What was actually said is still obscure; there was almost certainly confusion of thought, if not irresolution, in London. In contrast the fatal rigidity of German military and political thinking is shown by Moltke's embarrassment and the harsh terms of the chancellor's proposed acceptance. He would require Britain to 'engage herself with her entire armed forces for the unconditional neutrality of France during a Russo-German conflict', the scope and duration of which was 'for Germany alone to decide'.[3]

In the event, the declaration of war upon France and the final ultimatum to Belgium followed according to plan on 3 August, providing Grey with the ripe case for intervention which he made in his famous speech on that day. The speech systematically mingled national interest and duty, first setting out each moral obligation and then appealing for a judgment on the basis of political interest. Grey won almost unanimous support but he did not ask for a vote for war. That followed an unheeded summons to Germany to stop the invasion of Belgium.

Like the chance of British neutrality—if it existed—the chance of support from their nominal allies, Italy and Roumania, was discarded equally deliberately by the central powers. The race for the operational offensive had prevented the sequence of declarations of war taking the logical form of Russia against Austria, followed by Germany against Russia, and France against Germany. Hence technical aggression by Germany released the satellite allies, whose public opinion would not, in any event, have allowed them to fight.[4] Berchtold, who had ignored the German plea that Italy should be bribed with 'compensations', thought her neutrality was good enough.[5] Instead of their defecting allies, those allies' recent victims, Turkey and Bulgaria, were to join the central powers, though not at once.

In his last interview with the British ambassador, Goschen, Bethmann uttered the famous reproach that Britain was—in contrast to the other powers—going to war for the sake of a 'scrap of paper'. It was an error in political analysis as well as in public relations. The issue of Belgian

---

[1] *Die deutschen Dokumente zum Kriegsausbruch*, vol. II, no. 421.
[2] *Ibid.* vol. III, nos. 562, 575.   [3] *Ibid.* no. 578.
[4] *Documenti Diplomatichi italiani*, quinta serie, vol. I, no. 101.
[5] *Diplomatische Aktenstücke zur Vorgeschichte des Krieges 1914* (Vienna, 1919), vol. III, no. 117.

neutrality indeed dissolved isolationism and pacifism in Great Britain as only a moral factor could do. But in taking the guilt out of distrust and jealousy of Germany it put these forces in the service of what was fundamentally balance-of-power politics. Elsewhere, without this sanction, the final challenges of the crisis fired nationalism equally beyond expectations. In countries where great political parties of the left professed adherence to an international socialist cause, in France and Germany, parliamentary solidarity with the government was virtually unanimous. Grey's appeal in the House of Commons for intervention on the side of law and order stirred no more conscientious enthusiasm than did Bethmann's declaration in the Reichstag that 'necessity knows no law', his promise that 'the wrong we do we shall try to make good' and his plea that 'whoever is threatened as we are can only think how to hew his way through'. The peoples did not ask for positive war aims and there were none fit to give them besides the will of France to recover Alsace and Lorraine. Neither the Germans nor the British had a ready-made imperial plan in stock; even the Austrians had no acquisitive purpose in the partition of Serbia, while the Russian territorial ambitions were at least as repugnant to their allies as to their enemies. Each belligerent government was prepared to claim that the war was at the worst preventive, and each hastened to compile and publish a collection of its recent diplomatic correspondence, with exculpatory omissions and paraphrases, in order to prove more than this. These publications, distinguished in macabre cooperation by a different colour for each of the first six combatants, on the whole satisfied the intelligentsia of each country—in spite of the rival publications, soon available in translation—that the war was not merely a preventive but a defensive one.

CHAPTER XIII

THE WAR OF 1914–18

W HATEVER the verdict on Germany's responsibility for the war its outbreak found her well prepared. On land she could reckon on some 5,000,000 trained men where France could produce only 4,000,000. If, on paper, Russia had far larger numbers, in organisation, training, equipment and administration the German army was far ahead of the Russian and, except in the quality of its field artillery, could compare favourably with the French, especially in machine-guns and heavy artillery. The 2,500,000 men whom Austria-Hungary could produce included heterogeneous and far from harmonious elements, half of them Slavs, mostly but luke-warm as opponents of Russia and not to be relied on against Serbia, though readier to fight the Italians. Better trained and equipped than the Russians, the Austrian army was to have a chequered record and, when successful, usually owed much to German co-operation and even direction.

Compared with these countries Great Britain could make only a numerically insignificant original contribution on land. Half her 250,000 men 'with the colours' were overseas, and as her shores could not be entirely denuded of trained formations, barely 100,000 men were available for the first encounter; these were more highly trained than either their allies or their enemies and were to give the Germans a surprising lesson in musketry. The best-trained, best-organised and best-equipped force with which Great Britain has ever started a war, it grievously lacked numbers: more than once in 1914 a small additional British force might have turned the scale in a tense and fluctuating situation. Even Belgium, caught with her army undergoing reorganisation, could mobilise more men in August 1914 than Great Britain.

All the belligerents were in process of developing air forces but, vitally important as the air-arm was to become, it was in all cases in its infancy and as yet confined to reconnaissance work; although air-fighting and close co-operation with the other arms, especially the artillery, were soon to develop (see above, ch. x).

At sea the British navy was superior to the German in modern battleships and battle-cruisers, much stronger in older battleships whose value the development of the *Dreadnought* type had substantially diminished, and in armoured cruisers. It had a quite insufficient lead in the lighter cruisers and destroyers, of which it needed many more, while in submarines Britain's advantage was small. But the British navy was greatly handicapped by having so infinitely more to defend than to attack;

359

whereas Germany stood to lose little more than ships and men, to Britain a major naval defeat would bring disaster. The German merchant marine could disappear from the high seas without appreciably reducing Germany's ability to wage war, whereas to Britain the maintenance and security of sea-borne trade was vital. The British navy has never had a more difficult hand to play, or its opponents a more promising one. If in seamanship and sea experience the British navy had great assets, in training for war and in some technical respects its opponents were far more nearly its equals. The French fleet, if definitely weaker than the German, could do useful work in the Mediterranean where the small Austrian navy was hardly a serious menace. The Russian fleet was unlikely to cause Germany enough anxiety in the Baltic to distract capital ships from the High Seas Fleet.

Confronted by enemies between whom she and her neutral neighbours virtually prohibited effective communication, Germany could hardly hesitate about the strategy to adopt. Her readiness for war, the superior speed of her mobilisation and her splendid railways enhanced the advantages of her interior lines. The weaknesses of Russia's railways, the vast distances to be covered and the interval that must elapse before she could develop her strength, even had her staff work and administration been more efficient, enabled Germany to leave her eastern frontier but lightly guarded and to concentrate her strength against France, the most dangerous enemy. For reaping full advantage of her superior numbers German strategists had long ago determined upon a large-scale enveloping movement for which the short Franco-German frontier, largely mountainous or strongly fortified, offered insufficient room. The plan devised by von Schlieffen, Chief of the German General Staff from 1890 to 1905, and adopted with modifications by his successor, von Moltke, involved the passage through neutral Luxemburg and Belgium of a strong right wing. This would penetrate deep into France and, sweeping round the French left, roll their armies eastward; the German left, meanwhile, would either hold up any advance into Lorraine or, should the French abstain from attacking, would itself attack to detain troops who might otherwise reinforce their imperilled left.

Of Germany's 1,500,000 men immediately available in the west, half were allotted to the three armies forming the right wing, nearly 400,000 to two in the centre, who were to advance through the Ardennes and connect the right with two more in Lorraine, 350,000 strong. The Germans calculated on rapidly overcoming any resistance Belgium might offer and were prepared to risk encountering any force with which Britain might honour the 'scrap of paper' they themselves proposed to ignore.

French military thought had undergone various changes since 1870 and now advocated a vigorous offensive. Anticipating a movement through Belgium but underestimating its strength and extent, the French meant to attack on both sides of Metz, with two armies east of it and two advancing into the Ardennes, hoping by striking at the German communications to paralyse their offensive before it could overcome the resistance the French left might offer with Belgian or British aid. This was no true counter-attack, delivered against an enemy placed at a disadvantage by having attacked. To meet attack by attacking elsewhere required a greater numerical superiority than was enjoyed by the 450,000 men who attacked east of Metz or by the 360,000 engaged in the Ardennes; and meanwhile General Lanrezac's 250,000 on the Belgian border were exposed to more than twice their numbers.

The French offensive was soon defeated: on 20 August 1914 east of Metz they were repulsed at Sarrebourg and Morhange; in the wooded defiles of the Ardennes the superiority of their '75's' over the German field-gun availed them little, and they were worsted in heavy fighting at Virton and on the Semois on 24 August. Both wings had to retire behind the frontier and adopt defensive positions. But if repulsed they had not been broken and the Germans had done little to exploit their success. The French reverses accentuated the danger which already menaced their left. Invading Belgium on 4 August 1914 the Germans, though stubborn resistance at Liége and on the Gette delayed them for fully four days, had by 18 August forced the Belgian field army back upon Antwerp and could fall in force on Lanrezac's Fifth Army from north and east and swing round through Brussels (10 August) to envelop its uncovered left. Fortunately for the Allies Lanrezac had halted on the Sambre: he was awaiting reinforcements and expecting the British Expeditionary Force, one cavalry and four infantry divisions under Sir John French, to come up on his left. This 'B.E.F.' had begun crossing to Havre, Rouen and Boulogne on 9 August in great secrecy, and by 19 August it was concentrated behind Maubeuge. Advancing to join Lanrezac in a wheel northeast, it came into contact on 21 August with Germans near Mons, just as overwhelming forces pressing in upon Lanrezac's front and right were thrusting him back. At Lanrezac's urgent request Sir John French agreed to stand and fight and by fulfilling his promise most successfully (23 August) did much to extricate Lanrezac's imperilled army.

Mons not only checked the wheel of von Kluck's First Army, but, like the Belgian resistance, this British intervention appreciably upset the German calculations. They were surprised to meet the British at Mons, astonished to be so effectively resisted: they had also imagined that if the B.E.F. landed it would be at Ostend or Calais, and therefore failed to realise how its communications really ran. Command of the sea had played its part in perplexing and misleading them.

All now turned on the Allies' gaining enough time to transfer to their endangered left the forces available through their adopting the defensive in Lorraine, where the Germans lacked the numbers needed to overcome the strong French defences. Meanwhile, to avoid being brought to decisive action before reinforcements could redress the balance, the B.E.F. and Lanrezac had to retreat, and much valuable territory was sacrificed before the Germans were eventually halted on the outskirts of Paris. But General Joffre, the French C.-in-C., had been prompt to order the measures needed. The essential object was achieved, largely through the stubborn defence of the British left wing at Le Cateau (26 August) and Lanrezac's check to Bülow's Second Army at Guise (29 August); both slowed down the German advance, while Kluck's misdirected pursuit after Le Cateau failed to press the British closely. Moreover, for the full Schlieffen plan of including Paris in the encircling move, even their numbers were insufficient, and on 30 August Kluck changed direction south-east in hopes of intercepting Lanrezac, only to be delayed by encountering the B.E.F. again and to miss Lanrezac and eventually to make a flank march across the front of the Paris defences. This produced the opportunity for a counter-stroke for which Joffre had been preparing.

A fresh French army under Maunoury moved north-east from Paris against the weak flank-guard covering Kluck's right, thereby forcing him to suspend his advance (5 September) and retrace his steps north-west. This created a gap between his army and Bülow's, into which the B.E.F. penetrated, crossing the Marne on 9 September and advancing against Kluck's left rear while he was closely engaged against Maunoury on the Ourcq. His position was untenable, but a skilful and timely retreat across the Aisne extricated him, though, with his right uncovered, Bülow also had to retire. Strategically, the Marne was of critical importance, throwing the advancing Germans back on the defensive just in time. But the Allies could not clinch strategical success by tactical victory. Behind the Aisne Kluck succeeded in checking them (14–15 September), while the timely arrival of a corps released by the fall of Maubeuge (8 September) filled the dangerous gap between him and Bülow. To the eastward French and Germans were holding each other, the French having successfully repulsed vigorous attacks on and near Nancy, and all now depended on the efforts of both combatants to turn their enemy's still open western flank with troops brought across from farther east. In this race to the sea both sides extended their line northward from the Aisne, past Amiens and Arras to Flanders, each, in turn, checking and being checked. Meanwhile to eliminate any danger from the Belgians and to complete the conquest of Belgium, the Germans turned upon Antwerp and took it (9 October), though the Belgian army succeeded in escaping behind the Yser.

Too late to save Antwerp, fresh British forces drawn from garrisons overseas had been sent to Flanders, whither the B.E.F. was now transferred, partly for the administrative advantage of being near its ports. This transfer, completed by 18 October, placed the B.E.F., now reinforced by two Indian Divisions, in position to resist a great effort to reach the Channel ports and roll up the Allied line from the left. In 'First Ypres' British, Belgians and French stubbornly and successfully withstood violent and repeated attacks by much superior numbers, although the Germans threw into the battle substantial reinforcements, including most of the five new corps which they had already succeeded in mobilising. Before the end of November the Germans had been checked; they had failed to give France the 'knock-out' blow on which they had reckoned, and they had not taken Ypres or reached the Channel ports. But France and Britain had lost heavily in thwarting them and they were consolidating a strong position in French territory from which they must be dislodged before peace negotiations could be contemplated. The German assumption of the initiative in greatly superior strength had gained them great advantages, military and political, even if they had failed to achieve all they had hoped for. They had been thwarted, they were far from having been defeated, and their front, continuous from the sea to Switzerland, presented no flanks to be turned.

To this German lack of more complete success events in the east had contributed. Russia, taking advantage of the weakness of the German holding forces facing her, had, somewhat unexpectedly, invaded East Prussia in August, causing troops to be hurried from the west to the rescue. After initial successes the Russians had suffered disaster at Tannenberg and the Masurian Lakes. This success the Germans could not exploit, as substantial forces had to be diverted to assist the Austrians and prevent an invasion of Silesia. An Austrian advance had ended in disaster and retreat (11 September), and the Russians had profited by their success to overrun Galicia, to be checked in turn by Hindenburg's invasion of Poland. Here fierce and fluctuating fighting, particularly severe round Lodz (November), went mainly in favour of the Germans, though the Grand Duke Nicholas thwarted their attempts to capture Warsaw. But the Russian losses were colossal and the enormous inroads into their inadequate reserves of munitions were not easy to replace from Allied sources, for Turkey had joined the Central Powers (20 October), and the Black Sea route was barred to Russia's allies.

It was some set-off that two Austrian attempts to crush Serbia had been defeated, but troops from India had had to be sent to safeguard not only the Suez Canal but also the Persian oil-fields on which the British navy largely depended for fuel, this last move starting a minor campaign soon to expand considerably and disadvantageously.

At sea nothing very conclusive had happened. After causing considerable trouble the *Emden* and other German cruisers had been rounded up and the German merchant marine had vanished from the oceans; von Spee's China squadron, after destroying two armoured cruisers at Coronel (1 November), a great blow to British prestige, had been wiped out off the Falkland Islands (8 December) mainly by two battle-cruisers detached from home waters; while the submarine had achieved disquieting but not extensive successes. The High Seas Fleet meanwhile was maintaining that defensive 'masterly inactivity' which had before this been forced upon superior British fleets desirous of decisive action; but the British Expeditionary Force had reached France unimpeded, nor had any diversionary landing on British shores been ventured, although the threat could not be neglected.

By December 1914 major operations had been suspended on the western front. Both sides were for the moment exhausted, both had drawn very heavily on their trained men and on their reserves of munitions, and both needed a pause in which to develop their resources, human and material. To Great Britain pre-eminently this pause was vital. Great as was the latent strength of the king's dominions, machinery for developing it hardly existed, and to raise, equip and train forces commensurate with what was at stake seemed insuperably difficult. Great Britain had rallied to the war with virtual unanimity, but it threatened to be decided before she could bear an adequate share. Fortunately for her Lord Kitchener, who had become Secretary of State for War, had the vision to foresee a prolonged struggle and the imagination and courage to attempt the creation of a British army of millions. The task was gigantic but the response was magnificent: volunteers flocked forward, far faster than they could be armed or equipped, while their training was terribly impeded by lack of instructors. Improvisation presented enormous difficulties, which enhance the credit for what was eventually achieved. What basis there was to build on was sound: the 'old army's' share in creating the 'new armies' should not be overlooked (see also p. 262).

It was even harder to surmount the manifold obstacles to diverting the country's industries to producing the masses of munitions which modern war required. Factories had to be built to make the machines to make the munitions, labour had to be found and properly utilised, a task not made easier by trade union practices even if these were soon waived or suspended. Problems of most varied intricacy presented themselves: new organisations had to be devised and new laws passed, culminating in a National Registration Act (July 1915) which, while largely concerned with recruiting, was indispensable for the direction of labour. Meanwhile, after much valuable preliminary work had been done at the War Office, a Ministry of Munitions had been created (June 1915), which by 1918 was to make the British the best supplied of all the combatants. Until well into 1916 lack of arms, especially heavy guns, and of munitions of every sort, handicapped and even imperilled the British, while even in 1917 this handicap was still felt; if by then the Germans had largely lost the lead which their quickly reorganised industries had at first secured them.

Other results of British unreadiness for war were equally serious: the

consequences of the heavy burden it had imposed on the French throughout 1915 were to react acutely on the British in 1917 and to bring disaster
near in 1918, for France was approaching exhaustion before Britain could
develop her full effort. Moreover, the handling of Britain's war effort
was never too happy. The Cabinet, with which lay the decisions as to
policy, lacked the knowledge of war and its problems needed for estimat-
ing correctly how that policy should be executed. The General Staff having
been virtually set aside, projects were often adopted without proper expert
examination of the technical and practical factors involved; nor did
unfamiliarity with these problems deter some politicians from even planning campaigns. Even when the 'Dardanelles Committee', virtually an
'inner Cabinet', took over from the whole Cabinet, its members still
lacked the necessary qualifications and failed to co-ordinate policy effectively. France and Germany were better off.

The strategical deadlock on the western front during the winter of
1914-15 did not involve tactical inactivity. Trench warfare was vigorously
pursued, both sides harassing their opponents so far as their ammunition
supply and other difficulties allowed, while several substantial operations
were undertaken, notably by the French in Champagne, but without
altering the general situation. Still, nothing had happened to dispel
the belief that the offensives Joffre was planning for the spring would expel
the Germans from France. The great tactical advantages which barbed
wire and the machine-gun had bestowed on the defence had not yet made
themselves fully apparent, nor was it realised how much artillery and
ammunition would be required to master the formidable field-fortifica-
tions the Germans had constructed. The initial success of a British attack
at Neuve Chapelle (10 March) was encouraging: that it was not exploited
could be attributed to unforeseen difficulties that another attack might
avoid.

The French, however, were hardly expecting substantial assistance
from the British, for although three more regular divisions, relieved by
Territorials at overseas stations, several Territorial Divisions and one
from Canada had reinforced the B.E.F., the British, even in April, were
holding only 30 miles of front to the French 400; the Territorials and
the recruits who had replaced the casualties of 1914 lacked training and
experience, while the shortage of guns and ammunition remained acute.
However, with the Germans on French soil no Frenchman would have
contemplated anything but an offensive in France for 1915, despite all
its difficulties, not the least being that the flankless German line offered
no alternatives to frontal attacks.

To that offensive various alternatives were being suggested, though not
by those qualified to appreciate the great practical difficulties, especially
administrative and geographical, of campaigning in the Balkans, while
no decision was likely to be reached by the defeat of Germany's dependants

as long as the main German army remained unbeaten. Indeed, the diversion of Allied resources to the Balkans would merely have played the German game by removing them from what all Germans realised was the vital front, in France, and more effectively early in 1915 even than later on. The Central Powers would have been appreciably assisted in meeting an attack from another quarter by their 'interior' position and superior railway communications. To meet the Germans in strength in Hungary would have helped little.

Falkenhayn, who had in September replaced Moltke, the scapegoat of the Marne, as Chief of Staff, was in no doubt about the vital front. He would have utilised the large reserves Germany had now accumulated to renew the offensive in France. Fortunately for the Allies he was overruled, for the B.E.F. was no longer the B.E.F. of August 1914: short of guns and shells, it found it hard enough to withstand an attack at 'Second Ypres', while it certainly could not have provided the help it gave in 1916 to the defenders of Verdun by substantially extending its front, still less by attacking effectively, as on the Somme.

Falkenhayn had reluctantly to relinquish his projected offensive in France and to divert his reserves eastward largely to keep Germany's weaker partner, Austria, in the war. If the winter had seen the Russians cleared out of East Prussia (February) and badly mauled, little progress had been made in exploiting this success, while with the Russians threatening to cross the Carpathians and invade Hungary, Austria seemed likely to collapse unless she received substantial German assistance. Moreover, it could be argued that once Russia had been decisively beaten, the western allies could be tackled to more advantage.

Russia's situation was hardly satisfactory: whatever she might achieve against an unsupported Austria, her shortage of arms and ammunition, the inadequate training and equipment of her reserves, her heavy losses in trained officers and men and her grave defects in staff-work and administration, seemed to offer German efficiency an easy success. Meanwhile, Turkey was pressing Russia in the Caucasus, and if Germany could not ignore Austria's needs, it was equally urgent for the Allies to open up direct communications with Russia so as to provide her with arms and equipment to enable her more effectively to withstand the Germans, even perhaps to attack in sufficient force to distract substantial German forces from the west.

One possible means to this end lay in overcoming Turkish resistance and reopening the Black Sea route. This purpose entirely differentiated the attempt to reach Russia by forcing the passage of the Dardanelles from projects for an Allied offensive in the Balkans and from the later policy of 'knocking away the props', the satellites on which Germany did not in fact depend. A properly planned and prepared 'conjoint' expedition might well have succeeded and with far-reaching results. To eliminate

Turkey would in itself avail little, but if thereby Russian resistance could have been made really effective it might have been of paramount importance.

However, a promising project was grievously mishandled. The amazing order to the navy to 'bombard and take' the Gallipoli peninsula without troops for the work ashore, which no navy could accomplish, ignored completely the teaching of experience and invited failure. It shows that the project was adopted by the British Cabinet without proper consultation of expert advisers and with little idea of the essential requirements of success. It asked the impossible from the navy. To persevere with the enterprise after the naval attack had failed (18 March) meant that when troops eventually arrived the priceless advantage of surprise had been thrown away, while Turkish industry and German skill had prepared adequate defences and reduced to a minimum any chance of success. The army also was being asked far too much. That lodgements were effected on the Gallipoli peninsula (25 April) was a notable achievement, but so many men were absorbed in forcing the landing that insufficient reserves were left fresh to exploit it. Subsequently, repeated efforts by inadequate forces all fell short of success, sometimes by a narrow margin: reinforcements always arrived too late to accomplish what they might have achieved a month earlier.

Wisdom after the event may suggest that the principal British effort in 1915 should have been made at Gallipoli, that fewer men and shells than were expended with scanty success in France in May might have turned the scale at Cape Helles and opened up the road to Russia. Still the Allies could not risk reducing their forces on the vital western front; should the Germans attack there in force, as well they might, the Allies might be very hard pressed to withstand them. Indeed, three days before the landings at Gallipoli (22 April) the Germans had struck at a weak spot in the Allied line, at Ypres, and most effectively, thanks to using the poison gas they were pledged not to employ. Its effectiveness apparently surprised them and they failed to exploit the opening sufficiently to overcome the stubborn resistance of the British Second Army, though much of the Ypres salient was wrested from the Allies. 'Second Ypres' showed that in the west, where the Allies could not risk defeat, their position was not so secure as to justify taking any chances.

The foothold secured at Gallipoli warranted further efforts, but the fresh landing at Suvla Bay (6 August), which was accompanied by a break-out from 'Anzac', the lodgement effected in April by the Australians and New Zealanders, merely achieved another stalemate at a heavy cost. The staleness of the experienced troops, the rawness of the unacclimatised reinforcements and a conspicuous lack of energy and dash in those in actual command at Suvla marred a promising opening; after that evacuation soon became inevitable, especially after a renewed attack on Serbia, backed by Bulgaria's full force, had established a new drain on the Allied resources by diverting French and British troops to Salonica. That the evacuation was so successfully accomplished at Suvla and Anzac in December and repeated at Cape Helles in January speaks volumes for those who organised it so skilfully and carried it out so steadily. Where the loss of half the force had been feared, hardly a man was lost. Still if this was some mitigation of the failure and if, as appeared later, Turkish casualties had so substantially exceeded the Allies' that the Turks were left incapable of attacking in force anywhere, the expedition had not achieved its essential object and its cost had been heavy.

For this disappointment the western front had afforded little compensation. After vigorous French attempts to break through in Artois in May and June had been thwarted, to renew them in September on a larger scale there and in Champagne may have been unwise; but to abstain from attack was not to be contemplated by French opinion, military or civilian, nor could the Germans be left unhindered to consolidate their hold on French territory or to release troops to exploit success in Russia. If France was going to attack, the British, despite their almost negligible success at Festubert in May, could hardly remain inactive, even if their still inadequate ammunition supply made another offensive premature. Attacking at Loos (25 September) (at a point chosen by the French), the British First Army started well, but Sir John French's unfortunate holding back of his reserves sacrificed all chances of developing the opening, though some ground was gained and held. The French achieved more, especially in Champagne; and if no break-through was effected ground was gained, German troops were diverted to the west from Russia and, though their hold on France was substantially unaltered, the Germans had been quite hard pressed and had had serious losses; while, heavily as France had lost, help was at hand, for by the new year the B.E.F. had been raised to nearly 1,000,000 men and its frontage now extended to sixty miles, including a stretch astride the Somme.

On the Russian front a summer of almost incessant fighting had resulted in great gains of ground by the Central Powers, thanks to the employment of substantial German forces. Starting with Mackensen's dramatic breakthrough near Gorlice in Galicia (May), the Germans had gained success after success, making vast captures of men and guns, completely clearing Poland (where Warsaw fell on 4 August) and most of Lithuania. Still, even this fell short of decisive victory: if the Central Powers could feel secure on their eastern front, Russia had not been put out of the war and the retreat from the Polish salient actually left her front shorter and straighter, without vulnerable flanks; moreover, Russia could better afford heavy casualties than any other belligerent and her output of munitions was slowly improving. Italy's entry into the war in May had distracted considerable Austrian forces to their common frontier, where, however, the great advantages, tactical and strategical, which its topography conferred on the Austrian defender, had thwarted several Italian attacks, repeated without variety and at a heavy cost.

Meanwhile the overthrow of Serbia, taken in flank from Bulgaria and by Germans as well as Austrians from across the Danube, had culminated in the terrible retreat of the survivors to the Adriatic and their rescue by Allied ships. This left stranded at Salonica the substantial Allied force which had arrived too late to help effectively. As their retention in Macedonia was not causing any equivalent German detachment, it was hard to justify on military grounds, while it was complicating Allied relations with Greece. Greece, after M. Venizelos had been dismissed from office, had repudiated its treaty obligations to Serbia and had adopted an ambiguous position of doubtful neutrality. However, the French were insistent on continuing the venture in Macedonia, but would not agree to its being left solely to them, which apart from political considerations the British General Staff would have welcomed. Britain had quite enough minor campaigns to conduct without Macedonia, especially as the Mesopotamian campaign had miscarried.

Here, after the Basra vilayet had been occupied, the War Cabinet, seeking a spectacular success somewhere, had over-optimistically sanctioned an advance on Baghdad. This rash venture, attempted without adequate forces or properly organised communications, had been checked at Ctesiphon (22 November) and British troops were besieged in Kut al Amara, whose relief, attempted by an improvised force hurried forward despite a grave shortage of transport, was proving costly and unsuccessful.

At sea the situation was virtually unchanged; after their battle-cruisers had narrowly escaped from superior forces off the Dogger Bank (28 January 1915) German raids and excursions into the North Sea had almost ceased. The submarine had scored ominous successes, notably against the older vessels supporting the troops at Gallipoli; but the campaign against commerce, though sufficiently successful to cause serious anxiety, had not been fully developed, largely because Germany could not ignore the protests caused by the loss of American lives in the *Lusitania* (May). However, the U.S.A. had not abandoned a profitable neutrality, and the need for considering American susceptibilities was still seriously limiting the efficiency of the blockade of Germany. Altogether Allied prospects for 1916 were hardly encouraging, though Sir William Robertson's appointment as C.I.G.S. (December 1915) promised better direction of British efforts.

Germany's action in 1916 in directing her main effort against the western front virtually condemned her policy in 1915. She had exploited her success beyond what was needed to render Russia incapable of assisting France, and had thereby given her western enemies a respite. Attacking in force at Verdun (21 February), Falkenhayn not only anticipated the combined Allied offensive planned for all fronts, but achieved formidable success and taxed French resources to the utmost. The attack, vigorously maintained well into June, made threatening advances on both banks of the Meuse, besides costing the defence even heavier casualties than the attackers suffered. Only with the greatest difficulty were the Germans withstood. Fortunately for the Allies the British could now help on a scale impossible in 1915, and Sir Douglas Haig, who in December had replaced Sir John French as commander-in-chief, could release an army to reinforce Verdun by taking over twenty miles of front between Arras and Lens. For a major offensive the British were still hardly ready: their new troops, fine fighting material but still only partially trained, needed more experience of active service: the munitions situation, if improving, was far from satisfactory especially in quality, when, to relieve the increasing pressure on Verdun, Sir Douglas Haig had to start his offensive (1 July) too soon for him.

British interests would also, as at Loos, have chosen another battleground, for French insistence on attacking astride the Somme greatly increased administrative difficulties in preparing the attack, advertised the Allied intentions and entailed grave tactical disadvantages. The German front, presenting no flanks, left no scope for anything except a frontal attack, nor did the artillery and ammunition available allow the type of simultaneous bombardments at several points which in 1918 were to conceal the real intention, distract attention and restore the element of surprise, normally the main asset of the initiative. Fortunately for the Allies, they now enjoyed that supremacy in the air already established as urgently necessary. From reconnaissance the air arm had quickly passed to observation and direction of artillery fire, and direct support of troops. To control the air for these purposes and to deny it to the enemy, air supremacy had to be fought for with increasing vigour, and its possession fluctuated with new machines and new tactics. From now onwards the side with air ascendancy enjoyed increasingly great advantage.

The first day's attack, disappointing and costly on the British left and centre, achieved more where it was less expected, on the British right and on the French front beyond the Somme. This opening, British persistence and determination ultimately succeeded in developing; though after a well-planned and executed dawn attack (14 July) had broken into the German second position but could not be adequately exploited, two months had followed of desperate, costly and apparently inconclusive struggles, for Ginchy and Guillemont, for Delville Wood and Longueval, for High Wood and Pozières. With little to be risked by thinning the inactive parts of the front, the defenders could always produce reserves to patch a hole before it could be widened, and those who carried a line were faced by prepared positions behind which the reserves had massed. Still, if progress was slow and painful, all available German reserves had to be employed to hold the attack, and on 16 July the Verdun offensive was definitely abandoned, a great relief for France.

In a fresh thrust on 15 September the British experimented with their 'secret weapon', the 'armoured fighting vehicle' or 'tank', for whose construction the main credit belongs to Colonel Swinton, R.E., and to Winston Churchill. The employment of tanks has been criticised as premature, but their actual performances in their first action suggest that, without this experience of their defects in design and of the problems involved in their co-operation with other arms, to have held back till larger numbers of the same pattern were available must have had even more disappointing results. Further attacks, on 25 September and ten days later, achieved more, the stronghold at Thiepval being at last taken (26 September), with a substantial advance on the Allied right; tactically, the Germans, pressed back to improvised defences far inferior to those already penetrated, were badly placed when, early in October, heavy rains came to their rescue and prevented the handicapped attackers from reaping the full fruits of their costly efforts. Mud stopped the offensive in November, much to the defenders' relief, though even then Joffre urged its continuation.

The failure to break through in July had inevitably resulted in the battle of attrition Foch and Joffre had all along regarded as the only means of wearing down the German power to resist: it had been very costly and the little ground gained seemed dearly purchased. But, by their own admissions, the Somme had cost the Germans even more than it had cost the Allies; they had been fought to a standstill (Ludendorff) and viewed the renewal of the offensive with apprehension, especially as they had lost much of the notable advantage they had till then enjoyed in the survival of so many irreplaceable trained officers and men. On this account and because of their consequent decline in efficiency and fighting power, they recognised the Somme as the real turning-point in the war, morally and materially; even if they had prevented a break-through the margin had been slender. Moreover, the French had regained important ground at Verdun (19 October and 25 December) and the end of 1916 found the German position on the vital western front definitely changed for the worse. Verdun, moreover, had inspired the French with fresh confidence.

Elsewhere events had followed a more chequered course. Russia's vast reserves had replenished her ranks and in June her armies, better supplied and armed than hitherto, had developed an offensive in which General Brusilov achieved dramatic success against the Austrians, who lost heavily, including 500,000 prisoners, and were pressed right back; while if against the Germans little progress was made they had to divert to Russia resources they could ill afford from France. The Austrians moreover had to suspend a promising offensive in the Trentino (May–June). Falkenhayn's fall, which now followed (28 August), transferred control of the

Central Powers' operations to Hindenburg, with Ludendorff as colleague, to win a prompt triumph over Roumania, which might have joined the Allies to better effect when Brusilov was advancing but now merely incurred disaster and lost two-thirds of her territory. Partly for want of ammunition, later efforts by Brusilov achieved little. An attack from Salonica under the French general, Sarrail, gained some ground without assisting Roumania. It left unchanged the Allies' position in Macedonia, where the enemy included only a handful of Germans, while the maintenance of large forces in a malarious climate greatly increased the strain on the over-taxed and dwindling Allied shipping.

In Egypt the threatened Turkish attack had only amounted to a small advance in August, easily repulsed, and before the year ended British troops were across the Sinai desert, thereby securing a better defensive position than the Canal line, and were menacing Palestine. In Mesopotamia Kut had fallen (25 April), despite gallant efforts by the relievers, handicapped by transport troubles and great tactical difficulties; but the Turks had not tried to exploit their success and the British had maintained undisturbed an advanced position up the Tigris, while their forces were being reorganised and their transport and rearward services made capable of supporting the renewed offensive in which General Maude was to recover Kut (February 1917) and capture and secure Baghdad (March 1917).

In another main theatre of war the year 1916 had seen a change in the Allies' favour. In East Africa an initial reverse at Tanga (November 1914) had left the British on the defensive, until early in 1916 large reinforcements from South Africa under General Smuts renewed the attack. An unhealthy and undeveloped country caused them serious transport difficulties and assisted the German commander, Lettow-Vorbeck, again and again in skilfully evading very stereotyped efforts to corner him and his men. However, he had continually to yield ground, and by the end of 1916 nearly all German East Africa was in Allied hands. If to the end Lettow-Vorbeck remained at large, by 1917 serious fighting was over. In the closing stages African troops better suited to the climate largely replaced Europeans and Indians.

At sea 1916 had seen the one fleet action of the war, the battle of Jutland (31 May). The heavier losses the British battle-cruisers suffered in the opening stages, and the British failure to win the 'Trafalgar' the country was expecting, gave Germany some cause for satisfaction but no claim to anything more. If von Scheer was reckoning on drawing Jellicoe's battleships within effective torpedo range without engaging in the gun duel which he wished to avoid, his prompt breaking off action to profit by the mist to get away from the deployed Grand Fleet speaks for itself. He may have skilfully evaded what he clearly feared to incur, and had perhaps rather optimistically risked. Jutland left the strategical situation unaltered. Such 'command of the sea' as the British could already claim remained unshaken. That the High Seas Fleet never seriously repeated its challenge is the best commentary on the battle. Admittedly a Trafalgar would have freed many much-needed lighter craft for the anti-submarine warfare in which the Allies were doing none too well; but Admiral Jellicoe was 'the one man who could have lost the war in an afternoon' and this he had avoided.

A week after Jutland Lord Kitchener, travelling to Russia to arrange for the better co-ordination of the Allied efforts, was drowned when H.M.S. *Hampshire* struck a mine. His vision and courage in creating the new armies had been of inestimable value: no other man could have had the prestige and determination for a task of such outstanding difficulty. His death appreciably weakened Asquith's position. Lloyd George, who succeeded Lord Kitchener at the War Office, now urged the creation of a small War Cabinet under his own chairmanship to secure a more vigorous conduct of affairs, and Asquith's rejection of the project led to a ministerial crisis and his replacement by Lloyd George (December 1916). The new prime minister's energy and driving power were largely off-set by his lack of familiarity with military problems. In his impatient anxiety to get quicker results cheaply he was too ready to put forward proposals based on an inability to appreciate the strategical, geographical and administrative factors involved; he could not realise why his projects were unwise and impracticable, while he was too self-confident to listen readily to argument or to relinquish his short-cuts to victory. His interference often hampered rather than helped, while the question of manpower, where his energy might have been applied to better purpose, was never properly handled. The National Service Acts were never well applied: far too many fit men were left in inessential civilian occupations when the army was short of recruits, for lack of whom it was to be worn to the bone in 1917, while in 1918 disaster was all but incurred.

December 1916 also saw a measure more advantageous to Germany than to the Allies: the ill-advised supersession of General Joffre, as the result of political intrigues, and his replacement by General Nivelle, the junior of the French army commanders, whose recent local successes at Verdun had inspired confidence in the French Premier, M. Briand. Just before this the death (21 November) of the aged emperor, Francis Joseph, had placed on the Habsburg throne Charles VIII, who would have gladly concluded a separate peace for Austria, if an Entente which included Italy would have accepted his overtures or if his German ally would conceivably have let him carry out his project. The Central Powers did indeed put forward vague proposals for negotiation in December, but the Allies' uncompromising reply (10 January 1917) ended the matter.

General Nivelle promptly discarded the plan devised by Joffre and Sir Douglas Haig for exploiting the unfavourable tactical and strategical situation in which 1916 had left the Germans on the Somme. This in-cluded a British attack astride the Scarpe in conjunction with a French attack between the Somme and the Oise, to be followed by a French attack on the Aisne and by the main British attack in Flanders, where the capture of the Belgian coast was urgently needed to deprive the dangerous submarines of bases. Left to himself Haig would have started by attacking in force here, where a big success promised more, but, as usual, he was ready to meet Joffre's wishes.

This plan would have involved successive attacks with limited objec-tives aimed at continuing to wear down the enemy; General Nivelle pro-posed to break through by one smashing blow, to be delivered in great force between Rheims and Soissons. To concentrate all possible French forces for this, he expected the British to take over yet another twenty-five miles of front and to confine themselves to distracting and detaining Ger-man reserves. His successes at Verdun had led him to underestimate the difficulties of applying his methods on a much larger scale. His optimistic confidence was hardly shared by the more experienced French Army Com-manders, who saw in his project a reversion to methods discredited by failure in 1914 and 1915. While their misgivings were to be justified, the great risk was that France, though ready to rally for a supreme effort, was nearing exhaustion and was ill-prepared for disappointment should Nivelle's optimistic anticipations not be fulfilled.

Unfortunately this short-cut to victory captivated Lloyd George, who contemplated placing the British Armies in France unreservedly at the disposal of this almost untried foreign commander-in-chief. This dan-gerous proposal was, however, modified, and while in the coming opera-tions the British were to conform to Nivelle's plans, Haig retained complete control of them with a right to appeal to the War Cabinet against unreasonable French demands.

The change of commander and plan naturally affected the exploitation of the situation on the Somme. An unusually severe and prolonged winter, which had accentuated the hardships of trench warfare and im-peded the local operations, undertaken with considerable success, for harassing the Germans and advancing the front, had also reduced the roads and railways behind the British lines to a state which in any case must have seriously delayed the resumption of the attack. Still, had Joffre's plan remained unchanged, it should have been easier to interfere with the German withdrawal in March to their new rearward position, the 'Hindenburg line', which ran from near Arras to Missy sur Aisne. Its construction, begun by Hindenburg's orders in September, was an unequivocal admission of Germany's defeat on the Somme, though its shorter line promised to economise force and allow of collecting reserves. The chances of preventing a retirement being carried out according to plan were much reduced by the adoption of Nivelle's project, though on the Ancre front British pressure forced the Germans to withdraw earlier than they had intended. Pursuit was much impeded by the belt of devastation they left behind them, and when the Allies eventually crossed it the defences which confronted them, carefully sited and constructed, proved formidable in the extreme: only after sharp fighting were the Germans ousted from their outpost positions covering the new line. However, while the retirement had evaded the blow the French should have delivered between the Somme and Oise, it left almost unchanged the positions opposite Arras and on the Aisne and so far did little to affect Nivelle's plans.

Meanwhile a vital decision had been taken by Germany—to resort to unrestricted submarine warfare (1 February 1917), a plan not yet adopted for fear of bringing the U.S.A. into the war. This was now risked, as it was hoped to strike so effectively at Great Britain's most vulnerable spot that, if the German defences in the west could hold, victory might be secured at sea before the U.S.A., much less prepared for war than Great Britain in 1914, could intervene effectively. America's reply to this challenge was to declare war (2 April), and before April was out U.S. warships had arrived to assist in the anti-submarine campaign. At first, however, German expectations of victory at sea seemed likely to be justified: the submarine, whose effectiveness reached its peak in the summer of 1917, brought Germany to the verge of success and only the adoption, despite all doubts and difficulties, of the convoy system for Allied merchantmen averted the danger. For this much credit belongs to Lloyd George's insistence that the experiment should be tried, if far more to those who had the knowledge and skill required for the solution of the practical difficulties involved, who worked out the details and so ensured successful working, notably Rear-Admiral Duff and Paymaster-Captain Manisty. Thanks largely to them and to the merchant navy's fine response to what was required of it, before the end of 1917 the submarine attack was being mastered.

The British attack (9 April 1917) on a 12-mile front astride the Scarpe was a surprise and highly successful, gaining valuable ground, including the Vimy ridge, and inflicting heavy casualties cheaply. However, the disappointing results of General Nivelle's offensive (16 April–7 May) largely discounted this success. Actually considerable captures were made and some ground was gained, but the Germans, forewarned, were fully prepared and easily prevented the complete break-through Nivelle had expected; and with France looking for decisive victory, anything short of this was almost equivalent to failure. To assist the French and to distract German attention and reserves, the British had to continue attacking on the Arras front into May, when the French offensive was finally suspended and Nivelle was replaced by the more cautious General Pétain. These later British attacks, improvised and expected, met ever stiffer resistance and achieved much less at an increasing cost. This adversely affected the Flanders offensive by weakening the force available, and meanwhile the disappointment was affecting the French army and nation most disastrously. The heavy casualties and the indifferent and over-taxed arrangements for the wounded, exaggerated and over-emphasised in some political quarters, left the French army depressed and dejected, quite unable to continue attacking and on the verge of collapse. Some units actually mutinied, some refused to attack, others to go into the trenches, serious disorders disturbed the rearward areas and for weeks disaster seemed imminent. Had the Germans discovered the true situation and attacked in force, decisive success might well have been theirs.

Fortunately for the Allies their enemy seemed never to realise this and therefore failed to utilise the opportunity; while by their attacks at Arras and then in Flanders the British maintained the initiative, distracted German attention and prevented any counter-offensive against the shaken French front: moreover, 1916 had greatly reduced Germany's available reserves, and only after hostilities in Russia had been suspended could large enough forces be transferred to the west to allow of their resuming the offensive. Meanwhile Pétain was carefully nursing the French army back to efficiency by leaving the fighting to his ally.

On 7 June the British Second Army began the Flanders attack most successfully, recapturing the Messines–Wytschaete ridge, an indispensable preliminary to any advance from the Ypres salient. The next stage was, however, delayed, mainly to transfer guns from the Arras front, and its start (31 July) coincided with unusually heavy rain, particularly detrimental in this area. Fair success was nevertheless achieved both on this day and in subsequent attacks during August, but the great strength of the German defences across the ridge leading directly eastward towards Menin made it necessary to revise the plan of attack, and this rather than the weather or the state of the ground delayed its resumption until 20 September. Then and on 26 September and 4 October limited attacks were most successful and, by the Germans' own accounts, they had lost heavily and were very hard pressed indeed, when, as in 1916, really bad weather made the maintenance of the attacks extremely difficult and gave the defenders urgently needed relief.

Pétain, however, was so insistent on the British continuing their attacks until the French recovery was more assured that, despite its heavy demands on his troops, Sir Douglas Haig could only comply. 'Third Ypres' may have been costly and have failed to reach the Belgian coast or thereby influenced the submarine campaign, but German accounts, official and independent, are emphatic that it inflicted heavier casualties than the Allies suffered, while by procuring the French 'time to reinvigorate their badly shattered troops' it had protected them from attacks which they would have been ill-prepared to withstand. In 1917 the initiative in the west was never with the Germans; they had to play the tune which the Allies called and could not take their opportunity.

This was the more important because with the revolution affairs in Russia had turned disastrously against the Allies. Immediately after the tsar's abdication (15 March) it had been hoped that the revolution would mean greater vigour in prosecuting the war, but these expectations were over-optimistic. A Russian offensive (July) soon collapsed after some initial success; by October hostilities had been virtually suspended and it became clear that Russia would soon be out of the war and that, too, before the U.S.A. could give effective assistance on land. The U.S. navy was giving substantial help, especially with the convoy system, while with the chief neutral now a belligerent, American views on neutral rights naturally underwent some modification; but the very extent and thoroughness of their preparations for raising and training an enormous army seemed likely to defeat their own ends. The war threatened to be decided against the Allies before America's millions could intervene, should the German reinforcements which had become available from the eastern front snatch an eleventh-hour victory in the west.

The first indication of this possibility was given in Italy where, despite some costly gains from their repeated attacks on the Isonzo (August and September), the Italians were no nearer victory, and were near to exhaustion as Austria was sinking. Italy too was feeling the strain of so many efforts with so little to show for their cost. In October German reinforcements headed a great counter-stroke which broke clean through at Caporetto (24 October) and sent the Italians rolling back in disorder. Disaster threatened and a dozen French and British divisions had to be hurried to Venetia to stem the rout. The Austrian administration proved unequal to maintaining the pressure of the offensive and the Italians rallied behind the Piave. But without the divisions diverted to Italy, the British Third Army was unable to exploit the promising opening its surprise attack had made at Cambrai (20 November), when tanks, now much improved, first proved really effective. Indeed the Germans, reinforced from Russia, struck back successfully (30 November) at a line thinly held by tired troops and, though eventually checked, recovered much ground, thereby almost reversing the original verdict.

In Palestine a British advance, attempted in inadequate force on an unduly optimistic appreciation of the situation, was defeated at Gaza in April, and the Egyptian Expeditionary Force had to be reinforced from India and Salonica and reorganised under General Allenby before it could tackle effectively the strong defences between Beersheba and Gaza. These it eventually pierced (31 October–5 November) and capped this success by advancing up the coast-plain past Jaffa to turn eastward into the Judaean hills and take Jerusalem (9 December), which it held despite vigorous counter-attacks. It was a triumph over great tactical and administrative difficulties, but the 120,000 British in Palestine were fighting Turks, not Germans, and were hardly contributing much to defeat the main enemy; in Mesopotamia, also, British successes failed to distract German troops eastward, but the troops employed there were mainly Indians. Here, despite the death of General Maude (November), the chief architect of success in that theatre of war, the position round Baghdad had been successfully consolidated and extended. In Macedonia scanty success had attended an ill-coordinated Allied offensive (April–May), and the stalemate which had followed merely emphasised the futility of employing substantial Allied forces against Bulgarians formidable on their own ground but most unlikely to be used elsewhere.

The immediate Allied prospects at the end of 1917 were therefore hardly propitious; with peace about to be dictated to Russia at Brest Litovsk (2 March 1918) and Roumania bound to collapse, large reserves would now be at Hindenburg's disposal. The French army had hardly yet recovered from 1917, and the British, having had since April to bear the brunt of the fighting, had lost heavily and, being much below establishment, needed very large drafts. Over 100,000 Americans had reached France, but they were hardly ready yet for a leading part and their determination to keep their forces separate and not let units be temporarily incorporated in Allied formations, though natural enough, involved some risk that the separate American army might find the opportunity for effective intervention seriously jeopardised. The creation in November of a Supreme War Council at Versailles to co-ordinate operations availed little; neither British nor French could spare troops for the General Reserve it should have controlled. That in that month M. Clemenceau became Premier of France was far more helpful to the Allied cause: his energy and will to win were coupled with some appreciation of strategical principles and needs.

With all indications pointing to an early German onslaught in France, the British Cabinet would have done well to attend to the grave warnings of its qualified professional advisers and to have recalled sooner to France, from fronts on which the war could not be won, some of the troops whom indeed it had to hurry back after grave damage had been done. However, not only was Sir William Robertson superseded as C.I.G.S. and replaced by the more supple Sir Henry Wilson, but in addition the Cabinet refused to enforce the National Service Acts with sufficient vigour to provide adequate drafts for France and favoured a policy of 'knocking out the props', not realising that the defeat of Germany's dependants, even if accomplished, would not diminish German strength in the vital theatre but would follow on Germany's defeat there. In seeking victory in Palestine they nearly lost the war in Picardy. Denied the drafts so urgently needed, Sir Douglas Haig was ordered by the Cabinet to disband one battalion in each infantry brigade, a step which entailed grave disadvantages, tactical and moral. Moreover, he was also required to take over thirty miles more of front, extending his right past St Quentin to the Oise, a measure which depleted still further his scanty reserves.

But the French authorities, civil and military, were far from satisfied with the contribution that British manpower was making, or that so many troops needed to be detained in England or employed in lesser theatres of war. The danger was further aggravated because, after two years of offensive warfare, the British lines naturally needed much re-adjustment and repair before meeting an attack. Not only was their long new front very far from satisfying British standards, but the labour to improve it and adequate reserves behind it were both lacking. However, if risks had to be run they could but be on the British right, rather than on the fronts covering Arras and the Channel ports. Here, with the gains made on the Somme behind their line, ground could be yielded less disadvantageously, and the dangers incurred by holding this front lightly would be less acute than farther north.

If the Allies started 1918 indifferently placed, for the Germans the immediate situation was more favourable than their more distant prospects. Although the counter-measures against the submarine were proving sufficiently effective to discount the probability of its achieving decisive success against Allied shipping or preventing American troops from reaching Europe, with Russia out of the war Germany had regained numerical superiority in the west: and with that she recovered also the initiative lost in 1916. By throwing in all available reserves victory might yet be snatched if her own dwindling resources, human and material, would suffice. The blockade, however, far more effective since the U.S.A. had joined the Allies, was beginning to tell, and the German losses during 1917, especially at Ypres, repeating those of 1916, had involved a deterioration in the quality and training of their troops: moreover, like Nivelle in 1917, they were risking grave consequences in banking on complete success. Nothing but decisive victory would meet their needs. If the Allies could weather the coming storm their chances would improve appreciably.

The Germans were so massed that they might be hurled against either the British right or the French left. In attacking the British they were striking at a thinly-held line, recently taken over from the French, with half-prepared rear defences and inadequate reserves, while they reckoned correctly that Pétain, none too confident of defeating the attack he anticipated against his own front, would hardly hurry to denude it of reserves to assist his ally. Delivered in overwhelming force on 21 March on the St Quentin–Arras front, their attack profited much from fog, which virtually neutralised the machine-guns on which the British defensive system largely depended. In five days of desperate fighting and heavy losses for both sides, the British Third and Fifth Armies were driven back, over-matched and outnumbered but resisting so stubbornly that Luden-dorff's expectations were not realised and an actual break-through was averted. But the British situation was critical; losses of men and guns were crippling. Bapaume and Peronne and the line of the Upper Somme were lost. French help, doled out sparingly, did little to check German progress and, with Pétain contemplating a retirement upon Paris and prepared to sacrifice connection with the British, disaster seemed immi-nent when, at a conference at Doullens (26 March), virtual unity of com-mand was achieved. Ferdinand Foch was appointed, largely at Sir Douglas Haig's instance, to co-ordinate the Allied operations.

This brought a turn in the Allies' favour. More ground had still to be yielded, but from Foch French help was more liberal and more effective: an extension northward of the attack to Arras, unassisted by fog, failed to penetrate the line (28 March), and the momentum of the advance died down, supplies and heavy guns being delayed in crossing the devastated battle-ground of 1916 and 1917. Moreover, Ludendorff let himself be distracted into seeking to exploit his successes southward against the French, instead of concentrating on thrusting the British westward, thereby extending his front unduly, and hardly improving his chances. By 5 April the offensive had shot its bolt: heavily as the Allies had lost in men and ground, the Germans, like Nivelle, had not attained all they expected and needed, while their losses had exceeded what they could afford for anything short of that.

Thwarted in Picardy, Ludendorff shifted his attack to Flanders and, striking at a weak spot, broke through the Portuguese (9 April). Opposed mainly by tired divisions, which had lost heavily in March, the Germans, mostly fresh troops, made great advances, though once again their expec-tations were not fully realised. Before the advance was checked, at the end of April, the British had lost much ground, including all the gains of 1917, though Ypres still held out. British casualties again had been heavy, but a determined resistance, assisted eventually by French reserves, again had halted the Germans short of their objectives. Moreover, in so far as Ludendorff was aiming at attrition, he had hardly scored; his troops, markedly inferior to those who had fought on the Somme, had achieved much by weight of numbers, but had given good targets and lost heavily. The Allies had again averted defeat and gained vital time for American help to become effective.

If Ludendorff now changed his immediate objective and developed a series of attacks upon the French, it was because, far from having relin-quished his determination to crush the British, he hoped thereby to leave the French exhausted and incapable of intervening effectively, when he could turn again upon the British, in whose defeat he saw the surest road to decisive success. But the blockade was now making itself felt and the Germans had to pause between their attacks. Delivered between

Soissons and Rheims (28 May) their next attack, which fell largely on shattered British divisions withdrawn to a sector reported 'quiet', completely surprised the French and made alarming and rapid progress. The ground lost to the Nivelle attack was regained, and the Germans were over the Marne before they were with difficulty checked (2 June). Another attack enlarged these gains (9-14 June), but their successes placed them in a deep salient with poor communications, which invited attack and proved their undoing when, after another thrust (15 July) had been held both east and west of Rheims, counter-attacks in which British and American troops shared were started on both flanks and soon won back nearly all that had been lost. The French could claim a positive success, something more than thwarting an offensive.

The Allied situation had been anxious and critical but the worst was over. The British Cabinet had been startled into taking the measures which might, if taken earlier, have much reduced the losses they now sought to replace; the drafts unwisely withheld earlier in the year were now dispatched; fit men were routed out of civil employments, many exemptions were cancelled and the age for military service raised. Moreover, substantial forces had been withdrawn from Italy, Macedonia and Palestine, losses in guns and material had now been made good; and with large Comonwealth and American forces ready to co-operate, the Allies could pass to the offensive and deprive Ludendorff of the initiative before he could start another big attack in Flanders, for which his decreasing reserves were now hardly sufficient. He had spent more than he could afford without achieving victory.

On 8 August General Rawlinson's Fourth Army, with the French First on its right, struck east of Amiens with dramatic success. 'The black day of the war', by German admission, was followed at short intervals by successive attacks at other points. With sufficient artillery and ammunition for several simultaneous attacks the British had no longer to wait, like Ludendorff after his March offensive, till the heavy guns could be shifted to a new front. Surprise was now possible, blow could follow blow in rapid succession; attacks were not pressed unprofitably but were broken off, to be resumed as soon as the enemy had been distracted by a fresh attack elsewhere. Kept wondering where the next blow would fall, the Germans were given no time to rest or to readjust their dispositions: they lost heavily in men and guns and were driven from stronghold after stronghold, their reserves being thrown in to little effect. Depressed by repeated reverses and retirements, they were losing hope as well as ground. Their resistance, though often stubborn, was weakening; while the Allies, encouraged by success and the pace at which they found themselves advancing, attacked again and again. On the Aisne and to the eastward the French joined in effectively and an American attack (12 September) wiped out the St Mihiel salient near Verdun. By the middle of September the British Third and Fourth Armies were again confronting the Hindenburg Line.

To attack this formidable barrier without a substantial numerical superiority required confidence and determination. Even Marshal Foch was doubtful of success, but, undeterred by receiving no encouragement or support from the War Cabinet, Sir Douglas Haig had the vision to see that success was possible, and the courage and resolution to venture the attempt to finish the war without subjecting the troops to the test of another winter of endurance. Between 27 September and 8 October the British broke through the Hindenburg defences between St Quentin and Cambrai, an outstanding and decisive success which was effectively exploited. Simultaneously in Champagne the French were pressing forward, and as their front shortened with their advance, troops were freed for a projected attack in Lorraine, while Belgians, French and British had started advancing most successfully. With the whole front from Ypres to Verdun in movement the Germans had no chance to rally. Their failure to hold defences as strong and elaborate as the Hindenburg Line convinced their military leaders that the war was lost, and on 4 October a request for an armistice was addressed to the President of the U.S.A. During the next month Allied pressure was not relaxed, the troops responded to repeated calls, and the Germans were driven from position after position, suffering heavily. By 11 November, when they had to accept the Allied terms, they had been ousted from western Belgium and only a fringe of French territory remained in their possession; although their surrender adroitly anticipated the attack in Lorraine which should have given Marshal Foch and France a conclusive victory on German soil.

The German defeat in the west had already made itself felt elsewhere. If Germany could not avert her own overthrow, her satellites could expect no help. Bulgaria had capitulated on 30 September after the Allies had broken through west of the Vardar and were advancing towards the Danube. In Palestine the weakened and war-weary Turks, incapable of offering the resistence of a year earlier, had collapsed beneath Allenby's sledge-hammer blow (18 September). A great cavalry pursuit, in which the air-arm co-operated notably, had swept well beyond Damascus before Turkey also capitulated (31 October), by which time another advance up the Tigris had brought the British almost to Mosul. In Italy the offensive had been resumed, both in Venetia and in the Trentino (27 October), whereupon the ill-assorted fabric of the Habsburg monarchy had revealed its weaknesses by the promptness and completeness of its military collapse. Once Germany's defeat was assured her satellites had not waited: that their surrender accelerated her collapse in the west has merely been alleged to buttress the baseless legend that the German army was never defeated.

In the final stage of that defeat the hardest fighting and the heaviest losses had inevitably fallen to the British: the French had attacked repeatedly with success, but Foch and Pétain had not asked too much of them or given them the leading role, as the casualties and captures of the last four months indicate. The Americans, full of dash and energy, had suffered from the valour of inexperience, but, like the British New Armies in their baptism of fire, they had shown great promise, and the taste they had given of the wrath to come helped to discourage the Germans from seeking to prolong the war into 1919.

Of the many inventions, new devices or methods and surprises which the war brought, some few soldiers had to some extent anticipated 'trench warfare', the inevitable outcome of the continuous front established in the west in 1914, with the increased importance it gave to the machine-gun. Poison gas and the 'armoured fighting vehicle' were greater surprises. As the Germans failed to exploit the opportunity offered them by their initial success, they may perhaps have had cause to regret starting gas warfare, once the Allies had devised protective devices and were retaliating effectively. The 'armoured fighting vehicle', so defective and disappointing when first used that the Germans failed to appreciate its possibilities, played an increasingly important part once its original defects had been remedied and experience gained of its co-operation with guns and infantry. But the extension of warfare to the air surpassed all other innovations, if the submarine ran it close. In the last years of the war to secure air supremacy had become of paramount importance, and the co-operation of the air-arm with the troops contributed greatly to the success of the final Allied offensive (see also ch. x).

Britain's unpreparedness for war and her politicians' unfamiliarity with its problems had been largely responsible for the prolongation of the war into 1918, since until 1916 France had had so unequal a burden to bear that, when the British were ready for a decisive effort, the French were hardly equal to supporting it fully; while Russia's tremendous sacrifices and effort in the early stages of the war had been instrumental in thwarting the German attempt to secure a quick decision, they had also helped to bring about revolution in 1917. For the surmounting of the peril which faced the Allies between 1914 and 1916 much credit must go to Marshal Joffre, whose steadfastness and resource have given him a secure place among the great soldiers of France, along with Marshal Foch, who was so largely instrumental in saving the situation in the crisis of 1918 and in successfully co-ordinating the subsequent operations of that year. Sir Douglas Haig also ranks high among the great figures of the war. Resolute and calm, vigorous and tenacious, not easily depressed, a loyal colleague of Joffre and Foch, he showed vision and insight, not least in realising that an end could and therefore should be reached in 1918, and his drive and determination went far to ensure that the end was reached, limited though his resources were. Too reserved to win affection or acquire a personal influence over masses, he inspired the essential trust and confidence. With him another British soldier, Robertson, is naturally coupled; straightforward, hard-headed, with a wonderful capacity for reaching the root of a problem without overlooking difficulties of detail, ready to face unpleasant facts, never seeking success through evasion, he did invaluable work in co-ordinating the multifarious operations and in seeking to concentrate on essentials. Unfortunately he could not credit how able men could talk so freely on military matters and propose plans of campaigns without any real understanding of elementary things. At sea, if he did not win a Trafalgar at Jutland, Admiral Jellicoe handled a most difficult task with steadfastness and judgment and achieved what was essential.

Germany made Falkenhayn the scapegoat for failures largely resulting from the overruling of his advice. If the decision not to attack in France in 1915 was mainly Hindenburg's and Ludendorff's, they had themselves to thank for taking the wrong road and thereby missing their best chance to defeat their main enemies. In the war of attrition, inevitable once the continuous front was established in the west, Germany was largely worn down by superior resources. She had reckoned on rapid victory, on a 'Blitzkrieg' success such as brought her in 1940 to a position she never reached in 1914-18: she had narrowly missed it in 1914, she might have reached it in 1915, and it is ironical that the weakness of Austria, whose responsibility for provoking the war was not inconsiderable, hung a millstone round her partner's neck. Turkey, indeed, proved a more useful satellite by diverting Allied efforts to ventures of minor importance and doubtful value.

To that war of attrition, costly and difficult as a means to victory, no practical alternative has been suggested. The German army was the hard core of the Central Powers' resistance, their military centre of gravity, and while it remained unbroken they held together firmly enough. The initial advantage secured in August 1914 established Germany in a position, military and political, from which she had to be dislodged. As she had had time to consolidate her military position, the additional strength which the conditions of 1914-16 gave to the prepared tactical defensive increased the cost and difficulty of evicting her from France. Even when the attack had so greatly improved its equipment and its methods, without 'hard pounding' the attack could not have prevailed. There was no easy road to victory.

If the heaviest fighting and the chief losses fell on the armies, and if in no previous great war in which Great Britain had fought were great naval battles so few, the British navy's part was nevertheless of fundamental importance. The war was fought out on land but largely by forces which the Allied navies had landed and which they maintained after landing. The submarine, Germany's greatest asset against an enemy who depended on the use of the ocean waterways not only for military movements and for commerce but for mere existence, was the most prominent factor in the naval war and very nearly turned the scale against the Entente. In the end the submarine was thwarted, mainly by the skill, devotion and endurance of British sailors, among whom the Merchant Marine vied with the Royal Navy in its courageous facing of danger; while it was at sea that the United States made their chief contribution to the Allied success, potent as was the threat of what America might do on land in inducing the German surrender. Russia's contribution to the final success was large. Before their 'home front' collapsed, the Russian armies, fighting at crippling disadvantages, had distracted German efforts from their true goal and had taken a heavy toll of the common enemy, although the revolution of 1917 gave Germany a much needed respite and nearly turned the tide against the Allies. Nothing, however, outweighed the steadfastness of France in standing up with but slender aid to the original German onslaught, a successful resistance which laid the foundation of ultimate victory.

CHAPTER XIV

THE RUSSIAN REVOLUTION

THE revolution of 1917 broke out in the middle of the first world war, in which Russia, although belonging to an eventually victorious coalition of powers, suffered the heaviest defeats. The revolution may therefore appear to have been merely the consequence of military collapse. Yet the war only accelerated a process which had for decades been sapping the old order and which had more than once been intensified by military defeat. Tsardom tried to overcome the consequences of its failure in the Crimean War by the emancipation of the serfs in 1861. Defeat in the Russo-Japanese War of 1904–5 was immediately followed by an *annus mirabilis* of revolution. After the military disasters of 1915–16 the movement started again from the points at which it had come to a standstill in 1905: the December rising of the workers of Moscow had been the last word of the revolution in 1905; its first word in 1917 was the armed rising in St Petersburg. The most significant institution created by the revolution of 1905 had been the 'council of workers' deputies' or the soviet of St Petersburg. After an interval of twelve years, in the first days of the new upheaval, the same institution sprang into life again to become the main focus of the drama that was now to unfold.

When the events of 1917 are compared with the great French revolution or the English puritan revolution, one is struck by the fact that conflicts and controversies which, in those earlier revolutions, it took years to resolve were all compressed and settled within the first week of the upheaval in Russia. The classical prelude to other revolutions, consisting in disputes between the monarch and some sort of a parliamentary body, was lacking in 1917. The defenders of the old absolutism of the Romanovs had almost no say; they disappeared from the stage, as it were, as soon as the curtain was raised. The constitutionalists, who had wished to preserve the monarchy but to subject it to a degree of parliamentary control, had almost no chance openly to state their programme; in the first days of the revolution the strength of the republican feeling compelled them to fold up their monarchical banners and to pursue their objectives as constitutionalists *tout court*. No counterpart of the French states general or the English parliament existed. The main content of the events of 1917 was the struggle between groups that until recently formed the extreme wing of a clandestine opposition, the Russian Gironde (the moderate Socialists) and the Russian Mountain (the Bolsheviks).

The 'constitutionalist' phase of the revolution had actually been played out before 1917. In his October Manifesto of 1905, the tsar had promised to convene a representative parliament. But whereas Charles I or Louis XVI, before they were dethroned, had made to their national parliamentary institutions concession after concession, Tsar Nicholas II quickly recovered from the 'panic' of 1905 and reasserted himself as the autocrat of All the Russias. The political history of the years 1906–16 was marked by the continuous degradation of Russia's quasi-parliaments, the dumas. These were mere consultative bodies, without right to control the government; they were suspended or disbanded by the tsar's arbitrary edicts; and their members were not infrequently imprisoned or deported. In March 1917 there was thus no real parliamentary institution to serve as a platform for the contending parties or to provide a framework for their controversies. The soviet was destined to become the spectacular and powerful centre of the whole movement.

The warning of 1905 was wasted on tsardom. Not only did the autocratic government continue—it did so in an atmosphere of growing corruption and decadence, in which the bizarre Rasputin scandal was possible. The economic and social structure of the country remained unchanged, in all essentials. About 30,000 landlords were still in possession of nearly 70 million *dessyatin* of land.[1] On the other hand, 10·5 million peasants owned only 75 million *dessyatin*. One-third of the peasantry was completely landless. The technical level of agriculture was barbarously low: according to the census of 1910, 10 million wooden ploughs and *sokhas* and 25 million wooden harrows were in use and only 4·2 million iron ploughs and less than half a million iron harrows. Mechanical traction was almost unknown. More than one-third of the farmsteads possessed no implements at all, and 30 per cent had no cattle. No wonder that in the last years before the war the average yield of grain per acre was only one-third of that harvested by the German farmer and one-half of that harvested by the French peasant.

This stupendous burden of poverty was made even heavier by the annual tributes which the peasantry paid to the landlords—their value was estimated at 400–500 million gold roubles per year. More than half of the estates mortgaged at the 'Gentry's bank' were rented to the peasants for sharecropping or other feudal forms of rent. The landlord's share was often 50 per cent of the crop. More than half a century after the emancipation of the serfs the survivals of serfdom were numerous and strong, and in some parts, as in the Caucasus, 'temporary serfdom' openly existed until 1912. The demand for lower rents and for the reduction and abolition of 'servitudes' grew more and more insistent, until it was superseded by the clamour for the total expropriation of the landlords and the distribution of their estates among the peasants.

Such conditions made a gigantic *jacquerie* inevitable, sooner or later. The disorganising effects of the war heightened the explosive mood of

[1] 1 *dessyatin* equals 2·7 acres.

the peasantry. The successive mobilisations of 1914–16 deprived farming of nearly half its fit manpower; cattle were slaughtered *en masse* for the needs of the army; and the output of agricultural implements fell to 25 per cent of normal, while their import from abroad, on which agriculture had heavily depended in peace-time, stopped altogether. With the decline in production the burden of the rents became unbearable, and the peasants' hunger for land irresistible. In the interval between 1905 and 1917 only one major agrarian reform had been attempted: the Stolypin reform of November 1906 had intended to facilitate the growth of a layer of wealthy farmers, upon whose conservatism the regime could rely. But the effects of the belated reform were relatively insignificant, and they were largely undone by the war.

Agricultural poverty was matched by industrial backwardness. On the eve of the war, Russian industry produced 30 kilograms of iron per head of population, compared with 203 in Germany, 228 in Great Britain and 326 in the United States. The output of coal per head of population was 0·2 tons in Russia, 2·8 in Germany, 6·3 in Great Britain and 5·3 in the United States. The consumption of cotton was 3·1 kilograms per person, compared with 19·0 in Great Britain and 14·0 in the United States. Russia possessed only the beginnings of electrical and machine-building industries, no machine-tool industry, no chemical plants, no motor-car factories. In war the production of armaments was forced up, but output in the basic industries declined. In 1914–17 no more than 3·3 million rifles were manufactured for the 15 million men who had been called up. Industrial backwardness was inevitably translated into military weakness, despite the delivery of arms and munitions by Russia's western allies. Yet, by a strange paradox, Russian industry was in one respect the most modern in the world: it was highly concentrated, and the coefficient of concentration was higher than even in American industry at that time. More than half the Russian industrial proletariat worked in big factories employing more than 500 persons. This was to have its political consequences, for this unparalleled concentration gave the industrial proletariat a very high degree of organisation and political striking power, qualities to which it owed, at least in part, its dominant position in the revolution. But before the leading class of the revolution was to display its strength, the weakness of the old regime was further aggravated by its financial bankruptcy. Russia's total war expenditure amounted to 47,000 million roubles, of which less than one-tenth was covered by ordinary revenue—foreign and domestic war loans amounted to 42,000 million roubles. Monetary inflation was rampant: ten times as much money as in 1914 circulated in the summer of 1917. When the year of revolution opened, the cost of living had risen to 700 per cent of pre-war. Strikes and bread riots frequently broke out in Petrograd,[1] Moscow and other industrial centres throughout 1916.

[1] During the war St Petersburg was renamed Petrograd.

'If posterity curses this revolution, they will curse us for having been unable to prevent it in time by a revolution from above'—thus Maklakov, one of the leaders of the Liberal bourgeoisie, summed up the attitude of the court, the government and also of the Liberal middle class on the eve of the upheaval. True enough, the Liberal and semi-Liberal opposition in the duma had a premonition of the gathering storm. In August 1915, after military defeats which cost Russia 3·5 million men and entailed the loss of Galicia and Poland, a progressive bloc was formed in the duma. It embraced the Constitutional Democrats (Cadets), led by P. N. Miliukov and Prince G. E. Lvov; the Octobrists (led by A. I. Guchkov), that is conservatives who had given up the demand for a constitutional government and had reconciled themselves to autocracy; and a group of extreme right nationalists, whose spokesman was V. V. Shulgin. The progressive bloc confronted the tsar, rather timidly, with the request for a government 'enjoying the confidence of the country'. This formula did not even imply that the new government should be responsible to the duma—the bloc did not ask the tsar to limit his autocracy, but merely to make it more palatable. The main preoccupation of the progressive bloc was with the conduct of the war. The leaders of the bloc were alarmed by defeatist influences at the court. It was widely believed that various coteries counselled the tsar to seek separate peace with Germany. The clique around Rasputin, made powerful by the tsarina's mystical admiration for the illiterate and licentious Siberian monk, was especially suspect of defeatism. The leaders of the progressive bloc were united in the determination to pursue the war and were encouraged by the envoys of the western powers in the Russian capital. There were stirrings of opposition in the supreme command. General Brussilov, the commander-in-chief, viewed with cautious, non-committal sympathy the moves of the civilian politicians. A plan of a conspiracy against the tsar was later attributed to another officer, General Krymov. If any such plans were hatched, none of them materialised. The tsar was strangely obstinate in his refusal to make concessions. The courtiers did their best to stiffen his attitude and to prevent him from calling in a Russian Necker or Turgot and from thus opening the sluices for revolution. On 3/16 September 1915 the tsar decreed a 'temporary dispersal' of the duma. He changed the government, but he did so in a way calculated to insult the progressive bloc and the opposition at large. Every reshuffling brought into the administration more and more odious figures and thickened the fog of defeatist intrigue. In two years of war, Russia had four prime ministers, six ministers of home affairs, three foreign ministers and three defence ministers. 'They came one after another...[wrote Miliukov, the Cadet historian of the revolution] and passed like shadows, giving place to people who, like themselves, were only...protégés of the Court clique.' Late in 1916 the duma reassembled, and the leaders of the progressive bloc openly expressed their alarm. In a philippic, in which for the first time he openly denounced the tsarina herself, Miliukov repeatedly flung at the government the question: 'Is this stupidity or treason?' Once again the tsar replied in his customary manner: the speeches of the critics were confiscated, the duma itself was dispersed. The sluices were tightly locked against the tide of revolution, with the result that the flood was mounting ever higher until it would sweep away all barriers at once, and with them the age-old throne of the Romanovs.

The futility of all attempts to induce the tsar to change his attitude was for the last time underlined by the assassination of Rasputin, the court's 'evil genius', on the night of 17/30 to 18/31 December 1916. The 'Holy Monk' was assassinated by Prince Yussupov, a relative of the tsar, in the presence of other courtiers. The event demonstrated to the whole country the divisions in the ruling class—the assassins in fact aimed at destroying the pro-German influence at the court. For a while the hopes for a change in the method of government rose, but they were quickly disappointed. The tsar and the tsarina, resentful at the assassination of their 'Holy Friend', clung even more obstinately to their customary ways. Their behaviour was an object lesson—one that was thoroughly assimilated by the people—that the removal of one clique of courtiers would not bring about the universally desired change, that the resented state of affairs was bound up with the tsar himself, or, more broadly, with the entire monarchical order. Meanwhile the country was sinking into ever-deeper chaos: defeats in the field, starvation, orgies of profiteering and endless mobilisations continued; and the temper of the people was growing more and more restive.

Grey staff nonentities [wrote Trotsky]...would stop up all cracks with new mobilisations, and comfort themselves and the allies with columns of figures when columns of fighters were wanted. About 15 million men were mobilised, and they brimmed the depots, barracks, points of transit, crowded, stamped, stepped on each other's feet, getting harsh and cursing. If these human masses were an imaginary magnitude for the front, inside the country they were a very real factor of destruction. About five-and-a-half million were counted as killed, wounded and captured. The number of deserters kept growing. Already in July 1915 the ministers chanted: 'Poor Russia, even her army, which in past ages filled the world with the thunder of its victories...turns out to consist only of cowards and deserters.'

Yet when at last the revolution came, almost nobody recognised it or gauged its elemental power. Like its great French predecessor, it was at first mistaken for a riot, and not only by the tsar, the court and the Liberal opposition, but by the revolutionaries. All were overtaken by the avalanche of events. The tsar continued to issue menacing orders up to the moment of his abdication. The Octobrist and Cadet leaders pressed for a change of the tsar's ministers after the tsar himself had become unacceptable to the country. Then they urged the tsar to abdicate in favour of his son or his brother after the insurgent people had rejected the dynasty as a whole and the republic had become a fact. On the other hand, the clandestine groups of socialists—Mensheviks, Bolsheviks, Social-Revolutionaries—thought that they were witnessing one of the successive bread riots when the riots turned out to be strikes and demonstrations culminating in a general strike; they were still deeply worried that the strike would be broken by armed force when the garrison of the capital joined in the revolt; and they were still wondering about the outcome of the whole struggle when they suddenly awakened to the fact that power lay in their hands. And then they began to look round, in deep embarrassment, to whom to hand it over. The revolutionaries themselves seemed hypnotised by the power of the old order after that order had disintegrated and collapsed.

This was, briefly, the sequence of events. On 23 February/8 March there were widespread strikes in Petrograd. Housewives marched in street demonstrations—this was the International Women's Day. A few bakers' shops were attacked by crowds, but, on the whole, the day ran its course peacefully. On the next day the strikes continued. Demonstrators, breaking through police cordons, penetrated into the centre of the city to protest against hunger and demand bread. Before they were dispersed, shouts of 'down with autocracy!' came from their ranks.

On 25 February/10 March all factories and industrial establishments in the capital were at a standstill. In the suburbs workers disarmed policemen. Military detachments were called out to break up demonstrations. A few clashes occurred, but more often than not the soldiers avoided firing at the workers. The Cossacks, who had been so prominent in suppressing the revolution of 1905, even supported the demonstrators against the police. On the following day the tsar, from his military headquarters, issued an edict disbanding the duma. The leaders of the duma were still afraid of defying the tsar's authority and decided not to convene the duma but to call upon deputies to remain in the capital. A committee of the duma was formed to keep in touch with events. On the same day the tsar ordered the general commanding the Petrograd garrison to suppress the movement immediately. In several places the military fired at crowds. In the evening the entire garrison was in a state of ferment, with soldiers holding meetings in barracks to consider whether they should obey orders to fire at workers' demonstrations.

27 February/12 March was the decisive day. New sections of the garrison joined in the revolution. Soldiers shared their weapons and ammunition with the workers. The police disappeared from the streets. The movement assumed such impetus that in the afternoon the government was completely isolated—its writ ran only within the Winter Palace and the offices of the Admiralty. The ministers still hoped to crush the revolution with the help of troops which the tsar had ordered to be moved

from the front to Petrograd. Late in the afternoon leaders of strike committees, elected delegates of factories and representatives of the socialist parties met to form the Council of Workers' Deputies (the soviet). On the morning of the following day it became clear that no troops from the front would rescue the government—the transport of those troops had been stopped under way by railwaymen. The garrison in the capital was completely revolutionised. Regiments elected their delegates who were soon admitted as members to the soviet, the latter changing its name into Council of Workers' and *Soldiers'* Deputies. The soviet, commanding the complete obedience of workers and soldiers, was now the only *de facto* power in existence. It resolved to form a workers' militia; it took care of the provisioning of the capital; and it ordered the resumption of civilian railway traffic. Crowds stormed the Schlüsselburg Fortress, Russia's Bastille, and freed political prisoners. The tsarist ministers were placed under arrest.

Confronted with the accomplished fact of revolution and with the dominant position of the soviet, the duma committee, hitherto reluctant to challenge the tsar's authority, at last made up its mind to form a government. On 1/14 March the composition of a provisional government, presided over by Prince Lvov and including the Octobrists and Cadets, but not the socialists, was agreed upon. (Only the name of the *Trudovik* Kerensky was placed on the list of ministers, as minister of justice, but Kerensky was to assume office as an individual not representing his own party.) On the day of its formation, the provisional government sent Guchkov and Shulgin to the tsar in order to persuade him to abdicate in favour of Tsarevich Alexei. The tsar put up no resistance, but he resolved to resign in favour of his brother, the Grand Duke Mikhail, not in favour of the tsarevich. On 2/15 March he signed the act of abdication. Meanwhile Miliukov, foreign minister in the provisional government, publicly announced the abdication before he had learned about its details. He told a meeting of army officers that the tsar would be succeeded by his son and that until the new tsar came of age Grand Duke Mikhail would act as regent. The assembled officers protested that they could not return to their detachments unless the announcement about the regency was withdrawn. At the soviet Kerensky had already spoken in favour of a republic and had met with enthusiastic applause. The provisional government was divided, and the monarchist and republican ministers put their case before the Grand Duke Mikhail. Miliukov urged the duke to accept the succession, while Rodzianko, president of the duma, and Kerensky counselled abdication. The Grand Duke resigned; but the provisional government was incapable of pronouncing itself in favour of either monarchy or republic and decided to leave the issue open until the convocation of a constituent assembly.

From the first hours of their existence, the provisional government and the soviet of Petrograd confronted each other as virtual rivals. The soviet had no legal title with which to support its authority; it represented the forces that actually made the revolution, the workers and the soldiers. The provisional government had behind it the upper and the middle classes. Its legal titles were dubious. True enough, the tsar put his signature to the act appointing Prince Lvov to be the prime minister, but historians still argue whether he did so before or after the abdication. In the confusion of the eventful days the leaders of the new government, in all probability, forgot the niceties of constitutional form; and the tsar seems to have sanctioned the formation of Prince Lvov's government at a time when, in strict law, his sanction had no validity. Whatever the truth, the revolution had anyhow discarded the tsar as the legal source of power. The provisional government represented the last duma, which we know had been disbanded by the tsar before he abdicated. The duma had been elected on the basis of an electoral law, the product of Stolypin's *coup d'état* of 3/16 July 1907, which made it utterly unrepresentative. This circumstance accounts for the duma's unpopularity in 1917 and for its subsequent quiet and complete eclipse. But the chief weakness of the provisional government was that it was incapable of exercising real power. The middle classes which it represented were panic-stricken and politically disorganised—they could not pit their strength against that of the armed workers united with a rebellious army. The provisional government could therefore exercise its functions only if the soviets in Petrograd and in the provinces were ready to take their cue from it. But its social and political objectives were so strongly at variance with the prevailing radical mood that it could pursue those objectives only by devious and equivocal ways. The most influential ministers—Lvov, Miliukov, Guchkov—hoped for the restoration of a constitutional monarchy; they looked forward to the ebb of the revolution and were prepared to speed up that ebb, if possible; they were anxious to re-impose industrial discipline upon the workers and to avert agrarian revolution. Finally, they were determined to continue the war in the hope that victory would give Russia that control over the Turkish Straits and the Balkans which the secret London Treaty (1915) had promised her. None of these objectives could be disclosed without provoking dangerous bursts of popular indignation.

The soviets, on the other hand, were not only based on the working class (and, in Petrograd, on the garrison as well). Thanks to the mode of their election they were in the closest touch with the fluctuating popular moods and in the best position to rally the masses for any action. The deputies to any soviet were elected at the factories by the total mass of workers, and at the barracks by entire regiments. But the deputies were not elected for a definite term. The electorate at any time could recall any deputy, if it did not approve of his attitude, and elect a new one in his place. This was the original feature of the soviets, a feature which in later years they were to shed in practice, although not in precept. As representative bodies, the soviets were more narrowly based than parliaments elected by universal suffrage. They were a class organisation *par excellence*, and the mode of their election precluded any representation of the upper and middle classes. On the other hand, the soviets of 1917 represented their electorates much more directly and sensitively than could any normal parliamentary institution. The deputies remained under the constant and vigilant control of the electorate, and they were in fact frequently revoked. Through an almost ceaseless succession of by-elections the composition of the soviets changed with the moods in factories, barracks and on the land. Moreover, as the votes were cast not in territorial constituencies but in productive or military units, the capacity of the soviets for revolutionary action was enormous. Like gigantic strike committees, they issued orders to men in factories, railway depots, municipal services and elsewhere. The deputies were *sui generis* legislators, executive agents and commissars: the division between legislative and executive functions was extinguished. Towards the end of the February/ March revolution the Petrograd soviet became the leading body of the insurrection. It was to play that part once again after an interval of eight months.

Yet, after the events of February/March, the soviet did not so much ride the wave of revolution as it was carried by it. Its leaders were torn between the sense of their own power and the fear of using that power. On 2/15 March the Petrograd soviet issued its famous Order No. 1. This admitted soldiers' deputies to the soviet, called upon the soldiers to elect their committees, to take political orders from the soviet, and to carry out no directives that might contradict those of the soviet. Above all, the order warned the soldiers to keep watch on arms depots and to resist any attempt that might be made by the officers to disarm the rank and file. This was the first apple of discord between the provisional government and the soviet after the soviet had acknowledged the government's authority. The provisional government charged the soviet with undermining military discipline. On its part, the soviet, afraid of a counterrevolutionary attempt by the officers' corps, held that it could secure its own existence only through the allegiance of the army's rank and file. It was in its own interest therefore that it warned the revolutionised troops against attempts at disarming them. Order No. 1 aroused anew the soldiers against the officers; it also aroused the officers against the soviet. It raised the issue of the mutual relationship between the provisional government and the Petrograd soviet or the soviets at large. From the beginning that relationship bore all the characteristics of a dual power. The whole period from February/March till October/November can be viewed as a series of desperate attempts to solve that problem. All the time the two bodies were overlapping, stepping on each others' feet, trying to patch up their differences and to disentangle their responsibilities. The dual power was by its nature transitional. In the end either the provisional government or the soviets had to assert themselves and to eliminate their rival. The Cadet party and the officers' corps aimed at the elimination of the soviets; the Bolsheviks aimed at the elimination of the provisional government. Only the parties of moderate socialism hoped to consolidate the dual regime, that is to transform the transitional constellation into something permanent.

The trend of events from the abdication of the tsar to the seizure of power by the Bolsheviks can be divided broadly into four phases:

In the first phase, lasting from 2/15 March to 3/16 May, the conservative and Liberal leaders of the landlords and the bourgeoisie alone held the reins of government and tried to mould the *de facto* republic in their own image and likeness. At the beginning of this phase, the leaders of the soviet[1] accepted the authority of the provisional government. Towards its end the representatives of the Liberal landlords and bourgeoisie were no longer capable of ruling by themselves. The first provisional government had been used up in the process of revolution.

In the next phase, from 3/16 May to 2/15 July, the first coalition of Liberals and moderate socialists endeavoured to save the bourgeois democratic regime. In this coalition, still presided over by Prince Lvov, the Liberals (Cadets) were the senior partners; but they stayed in office through the support of their junior partners, who at this time commanded a strong majority in the soviets. The need for a coalition government revealed that the bourgeois-liberal regime was at the mercy of moderate socialism, while moderate socialism was at the mercy of the soviets. By lending their support to the Liberal bourgeoisie, the leaders of moderate socialism appeared to their followers to be discarding their own principles. Towards the end of this phase they came to share the unpopularity of their Cadet partners. They might have saved themselves by breaking up the partnership and alone assuming power, but they could not bring themselves to make this step.

The third phase (3/16 July–30 August/12 September) was opened by an abortive revolution; it ended with an abortive counter-revolution. In the middle of this period the moderate socialists tried to salvage the coalition by assuming, at least in name, its leadership and forming a new government under Kerensky. But the bulk of the proletariat in Petrograd, although not yet quite ready to place the Bolsheviks in power, was already determined to break up the coalition. It menacingly confronted the moderate leaders with the demand that they alone (or they and the Bolsheviks) should assume office and openly exercise power in the name of the soviets. This was the essence of the semi-insurrection of the July

[1] 'Soviet' (in singular) refers to the Petrograd soviet throughout this chapter.

days, which was defeated by the moderate socialist leaders with the help of the army. It was during this crisis that Prince Lvov's government ceased to exist. Not only the workers and soldiers, but many of its middle-class supporters, had turned against it. The bourgeoisie was now divided: one section, whose influence was declining, still sought to preserve the alliance with moderate socialism; another and more powerful section had come to place its hopes on a counter-revolution capable of eliminating the soviets. That section of the bourgeoisie supported General Kornilov's counter-revolutionary *coup*. The *coup* was defeated by Kerensky but only with the help of the Bolsheviks. The defeat of the two abortive movements weakened, for a very short time, the uncompromising elements in both camps; it created a fleeting social equilibrium in which the attempt could be undertaken to galvanise the Cadet-Socialist coalition.

By the beginning of the fourth phase (30 August/12 September–24 October/6 November) both wings of the coalition had withdrawn from the government: the Liberal bourgeoisie because it sympathised with Kornilov, and the moderate socialists because they blamed Kerensky for having allowed Kornilov's plans to be hatched under the protective wings of his government. Kerensky was now able to form only a rump cabinet, the Directory, which was so much suspended in a vacuum that it took on the appearance of Kerensky's personal government. But having defeated Kornilov with the help of the Bolsheviks, Kerensky found that the Bolsheviks had in the meantime gained a majority in the soviet of Petrograd. The revolution deepened. As the Bolsheviks came to sway the soviets, the moderate socialists tried to assert themselves outside the soviets, once again finding some common ground with the Liberal bourgeoisie. Thus the third and the last coalition was formed, which was to survive for one month only, a month filled with feverish Bolshevik preparations for the overthrow of the February republic.

The parties that confronted one another had existed and argued over the objectives of the anticipated revolution long before its outbreak. They had agreed that the upheaval would be anti-feudal and bourgeois in its objectives, a repetition in many ways of the great French revolution. Roughly up to the first world war it had been an axiom for all of them that Russia was not 'ripe for socialist revolution'—only Trotsky had denied that axiom as early as 1906. But in spite of this agreement on the broad historical perspective the cleavages between the parties had been deep. Unlike France in 1789, Russia had entered the era of bourgeois revolution at a time when she already possessed a very active and politically minded, though numerically weak, industrial proletariat, which was strongly imbued with socialism. In 1905 already that proletariat was the chief driving force of the revolution, a circumstance which could not but frighten the Liberal bourgeoisie, no matter how much the socialist theorists dwelt on the 'bourgeois' character of the revolution. The Liberal bourgeoisie refused to lead the anti-tsarist movement and rallied to the defence of the throne. Its reconciliation with tsardom was half-hearted: the Cadets still hoped gradually to convert tsardom into a constitutional monarchy, while the Octobrists made peace with the dynasty, such as it was.

This attitude of the middle class gave rise to a significant controversy in the Russian Social Democratic Workers' Party. Its moderate wing, the Mensheviks, believed that since the revolution could only be anti-feudal or anti-absolutist, the leadership in it would naturally belong to the bourgeoisie and not to the working class. For all its equivocal attitude, it was said, the bourgeoisie would eventually be driven by events to assume a directing role in the establishment of a parliamentary democracy on the western European model. The Bolsheviks, and especially Lenin, argued that as the bourgeoisie had passed or was passing into the camp of counter-revolution, only the industrial working class could lead the nation, or at least its majority, the peasants, in the struggle against the absolutist order. But, the Bolsheviks added, even though the revolution would be led by a class with socialist aspirations, it could not aim at establishing socialism in Russia before a socialist revolution had triumphed in western Europe. The revolutionary government would share out the landlords' estates among the peasants, set up a democratic republic and separate church from state; it would, in addition, introduce the eight-hour day and progressive social legislation; but it would not establish public ownership over industry or abolish private property at large—it would only substitute bourgeois forms of property for feudal and semi-feudal ones. Only after a period of intensive bourgeois development, the duration of which could only be a matter for conjecture, would the time come for socialist transformation. What was of immediate importance was that the working class should not shrink from leadership in the 'bourgeois' revolution and not wait, as the Mensheviks counselled, until the bourgeoisie took the initiative. It was with this perspective still in their minds that the Bolsheviks in Petrograd participated in the movement of February/March 1917.

Another significant difference between Mensheviks and Bolsheviks, one over which they had first split in 1903, concerned their methods of organisation. The Bolsheviks possessed a closely knit organisation with a distinct doctrine of its own, with carefully worked-out tactics and strict internal discipline, which allowed their central committee to plan its moves in the sure knowledge that its orders and instructions would unfailingly be carried out by the rank and file. The party had its recognised leader in Vladimir Ulyanov Lenin, in whose personality were blended such diverse qualities as enormous scholarship, the passionate temperament of the revolutionary, tactical genius and great administrative abilities. Lenin swayed his party by means of his powers of persuasion and through his moral authority rather than by means of that mechanical discipline which later became the characteristic trait of Bolshevism. Menshevism, on the other hand, was more or less shapeless in organisation and vague in matters of doctrine. One of its wings bordered on bourgeois liberalism, another on Bolshevism; in between these wings there was a wide gamut of intermediate shades. The Mensheviks had many gifted politicians, great orators and brilliant writers, but no national leadership capable of conducting a clear-cut policy. The February/March revolution found the party split into fragments. Tseretelli and Chkheidze, two Georgians, were its most authoritative spokesmen in the heyday of the February republic. Tseretelli had been a hard-labour convict under tsardom, and his martyrdom gave him considerable influence in the councils of the soviet and then in the coalition. Chkheidze had been the chief socialist spokesman in the duma. Tseretelli led the right wing of the party, Chkheidze spoke for its centre. On the extreme right stood Plekhanov, the founder of Russian social democracy, to whom Lenin, in his youth, had looked up as to his teacher and guide. On the left, Martov, the originator of Menshevism, headed the group of Menshevik internationalists. The *Mezhrayontsy* (Inter-borough Organisation) were former Mensheviks and former Bolsheviks who, for one reason or another, had stood outside their original organisations. Headed by Trotsky, this group was to join the Bolsheviks in July 1917. In the no-man's-land between Menshevism and Bolshevism there was Maxim Gorky's *Novaya Zhizn* (New Life), where freelance socialists expounded their views.

The Social Revolutionaries formed, like the Mensheviks, a loose federation of groups and individuals lacking coherent leadership. The party's traditions went back to the *Narodnik* movement, with its pro-muzhik attitude, its advocacy of a peasant socialism and its terroristic methods of struggle against tsardom. On the right wing of the Social Revolutionary party there were men who, like Kerensky, would have been at home in, say, the French radical party and who tried in vain to hypnotise the revolution with fireworks of parliamentary oratory. By Kerensky's side stood Savinkov, the ruthless romantic terrorist now converted into a good patriot and into an advocate of 'law and order'. The centre of the party had its most gifted spokesman in Chernov, minister of agriculture in the second coalition government who had only recently, together with Lenin, taken part in the anti-militarist conference of socialists at Zimmerwald (Switzerland). The left wing of the party, most authentically identified with the old revolutionary strand of the *Narodnik* movement, was represented by the veterans Spiridonova and Natanson who were to join hands with the Bolsheviks in October/November. While the following of the Bolsheviks and Mensheviks was predominantly urban, the Social Revolutionary leaders, though they belonged to the intelligentsia, were the mouth-pieces of the peasantry. The right wing spoke with the conservative voice of the wealthy farmers, the left was inspired by the peculiar peasant anarchism that had deep roots in Bakunin's country. But, on the whole, the Social Revolutionaries were inclined to look for guidance to the Mensheviks, especially in the first months of the revolution.

The belief in the 'bourgeois' character of the revolution, general in February and March, accounted, up to a point, for the puzzling behaviour of the leaders of the Petrograd soviet and for their readiness to acknowledge the government of Prince Lvov. This act seemed in perfect harmony with the Menshevik conception, according to which the bourgeoisie should form the provisional government in a 'bourgeois' revolution. It was not the socialists' job to participate in such a government; they could only support it from outside against attempts at counter-revolution, and at the same time they had to defend, from outside, too, the claims of the workers against the bourgeoisie. To these principles the moderate socialists remained faithful in the first phase of the revolution, before they joined the Cadets in the coalition government. The attitude of the Bolsheviks was confused at first. They had been accustomed to think of the bourgeoisie as a counter-revolutionary force, and now they saw its leaders at the head of the first *de facto* republican government. What was to be the leading role of the proletariat in this revolution? Nurtured in a spirit of uncompromising opposition to the upper classes, Lenin's followers could not reconcile themselves with Prince Lvov, Guchkov, Miliukov, the leaders of the landlords and the industrialists. But on the other hand, the belief that the revolution should stimulate the development of modern capitalism in Russia rather than attempt to introduce socialism pointed to the need for some conciliation. In his Swiss exile Lenin himself had already solved the dilemma: he had become convinced that the 'bourgeois' revolution was only a prelude to the socialist one, that the Russian working class should, with the support of the peasantry, overthrow the bourgeoisie and establish its own dictatorship. This was an important departure from his own previous prognostications, one that his followers in Russia had not yet made. Without Lenin's guidance, they vacillated between unreserved opposition to the provisional government and conditional support for it. In the days of the February/March revolution they were led by a few young radical men, of whom only Molotov was later to attain international fame. On 12/25 March, two of their more important leaders, Stalin and Kamenev, returned from Siberian exile and found the views voiced by Molotov and his friends to be imprudently hostile to the provisional government. Kamenev in particular counselled the Bolsheviks to adopt a more conciliatory attitude. Lenin, in his letters from Switzerland, was already expounding the ideas that were to underlie the October/November revolution, but from afar he could not induce the party to accept them. Thus in Petrograd, during the honeymoon of the February republic, Bolsheviks, Mensheviks and Social Revolutionaries, although differing from one another in traditions and outlook, still agreed on the 'bourgeois-democratic' limits of the revolution. Hence the idyllic mood of unity in the ranks of 'revolutionary democracy', a mood in which Bolsheviks and Mensheviks seriously considered their merger into one party.

The basic questions concerning the tasks of the revolution were complicated by the attitude of the parties towards the war. The Cadets and Octobrists hoped that the revolution would not prevent their government from waging war and preserving the continuity of Russian foreign policy. Under the secret London Treaty of 1915, we know, Russia had been promised control over the Dardanelles and territorial acquisitions in the Balkans. Miliukov, as foreign minister of the first provisional government, tried to reaffirm these objectives as the war aims of revolutionary Russia. But in order to attain them, the army had to fight; in order that the army should fight, discipline had to be re-established in its ranks and the authority of the officers' corps had to be restored. The Liberal foreign minister became a consistent advocate of 'strong government'. But the restoration of discipline was possible only if the soviets willingly co-operated in this endeavour. Yet, even under the leadership of the most moderate socialists, the soviets could at best make only half-hearted attempts at exorcising the spirit of the revolution from the armed forces. For one thing, nearly all socialist groups and parties had been vaguely committed to anti-militarism. Most of them had denounced the war as a reactionary and imperialist adventure, as long as it had been conducted 'for the Tsar and the Fatherland'. The overthrow of tsardom made a big difference. It was now possible to claim that the character of the war had been altered and that Russia's revolutionary democracy, allied to the parliamentary democracies of France and Britain, was engaged in a life-and-death struggle against the reactionary monarchies of the Hohenzollerns and Habsburgs. This was what nearly all socialists (including some Bolsheviks) claimed in February and March—to this extent they became patriots or 'social-patriots'. But precisely because they had come to accept the war for the reason just given, they could not openly embrace the war aims of the old regime. 'A democratic peace, without annexations and indemnities' was the slogan of the day. This and promises of a quick end to the war were believed in with deep earnestness by millions of hungry and unarmed soldiers in the trenches. It was enough for Miliukov to intimate in a note to the western allies (18 April/1 May) that his government would honour the diplomatic and military obligations of the tsarist government and pursue its war aims to provoke a storm of protest all over Russia. It was over this issue that the first coalition broke down, after Miliukov had resigned from the ministry of foreign affairs and Guchkov from the ministry of war. The suspicion of the soldiers in the trenches and of the workers in the cities was for the time being allayed by the appointment of Kerensky to be the minister of war. Yet, in the honey-moon of revolution, the socialist parties were not yet very seriously divided even in their views on the war; they still spoke and acted in a spirit of sentimental pacifism, which did not prevent them from half-supporting the war effort. The real cleavage was still to come.

From its first to its last day, the revolution was centred on Petrograd, and to a lesser extent on Moscow and other industrial towns. To the cities belonged the political initiative. But the revolution was by no means a purely urban affair. To paraphrase Marx's saying, the proletarian solo was powerfully supported, all over the country, by the chorus of an insurgent peasantry. From month to month and then from week to week the clamour rose for a root and branch reform in the countryside. By the middle of the year impatient peasants began to attack their landlords, burn their mansions and share out their land, until the whole movement acquired the impetus of a genuine peasant war. The disintegration of the army may be regarded as just one facet of this agrarian revolution. The army consisted largely of peasants, who expected the new regime to satisfy their demand for land and who then ascribed the government's procrastination to the fact that the landlords were so strongly represented in it. In truth, the Cadets and the Octobrists wished to avoid radical changes in the structure of agriculture. The moderate socialists had for a long time advocated agrarian revolution; but now they hesitated: should this revolution be carried out in the middle of war? Was not the abolition of landlordism so fundamental a matter that only a constituent assembly could deal with it? It might have seemed that in these circumstances the convocation of the constituent assembly should have been the govern-ment's most urgent business. Yet, each successive government kept post-poning the assembly on the ground that political passions would be let loose in the elections, to the detriment of the war effort. The truth was that the 'political passions' had been let loose anyhow, and that every post-ponement of the assembly added fuel to them. The bourgeois ministers insisted on delay, fearing that an assembly convened at the height of the revolution would be too radical; and the socialist ministers sacrificed the assembly to save the coalition. Through their behaviour in this matter both Cadets and socialists unwillingly contributed to the eventual ascen-dancy of the soviets, which, apart from municipal councils, were the only elected representative bodies in existence. A constituent assembly con-vened early enough might have overshadowed the soviets and reduced them, in the eyes of the people, to sectional bodies trying to usurp power. In the constitutional vacuum of 1917 the opposite happened; something like a soviet constitutionalism took hold of the minds of the masses; and *vis-à-vis* the soviets it was the successive provisional governments, backed by no popular representation, who appeared more and more in the role of usurpers. The Bolsheviks were most insistent in calling for an immediate constituent assembly. They had not yet clearly thought out in what relationship the assembly and the soviets would stand towards one another, and it had hardly entered their mind that they themselves, the Bolsheviks, would convene the constituent assembly in a few months' time only to disperse it straightway. But, paradoxically enough, in advocating the rights of the assembly between February/March and October/November, this extreme party of the revolution also appeared to be more devoted to constitutional form than were the other parties. As to the great underlying issue of land reform, the Bolsheviks held no clear views at first. In the past Lenin had on many occasions spoken in favour of the nationalisation of land, which was in line with the collectivist outlook of his party. The idea that the large estates be shared out among the peasants, which the Bolsheviks were to do after their seizure of power, had been part and parcel of the programme of the Social Revolutionaries, not of the Bolsheviks; and the author of that programme, Chernov, was the minister of agriculture in the second coalition. Only one group of Bolsheviks, to which Stalin had belonged, had, in the previous decade, advocated the 'distribution' of land.

Thus on all major issues—the character of the revolution, the war and the land—the differences between the rival socialist groups seemed at first vague or superficial. The sharp line of demarcation that was to separate Bolsheviks from all other parties was drawn by Lenin only after his return from Switzerland in April 1917. His journey through Germany and Sweden had been arranged by Swiss socialists, after the British government had refused revolutionary emigrés permission to return through Britain. The German government was aware of Lenin's anti-war activities, and it hoped that his propaganda would sap Russia's military strength; but it did not expect that in a few months it would have to parley with Lenin as head of the Russian government. Nor did it expect the boomerang effect of Lenin's propaganda upon the German forces, one of the important factors in the disintegration of Germany's military power in 1918. Lenin, as it is clear from documentary evidence, himself conducted no negotiations with the German authorities and took no obligation upon himself except to promise through the Swiss inter-mediaries that he would use his influence in Russia to secure, by way of compensation, the exit of some Germans from Russia. His unusual journey evidenced his anxiety to find himself as soon as possible in the centre of the revolution and there to assume the leadership of his party. He arrived with a clear idea of the course that Bolshevism was to steer. In his famous April Theses, and in a number of speeches, he forecast that the revolution would soon pass from its 'bourgeois-democratic' to its socialist phase and find its consummation in a proletarian dictator-ship. This should take the form of government by the soviets, a 'new type of state' best suited for the building of socialism. But if all power was to go to the soviets, the workers ought to confront Prince Lvov's government with irreconcilable hostility. That government was the dictatorship of the bourgeoisie veiled only by the complicity of the moderate socialists. The Bolsheviks ought to do away with the ambiguity of their own attitude and to explain their position frankly to workers, soldiers and peasants until they, the Bolsheviks, obtained a majority in the soviets and were thereby entitled to wrest power from the bourgeoisie. Ambiguity was likewise inadmissible in matters of war and peace— the party must lend no support to the war which, despite the change of the regime, was still 'imperialist through and through'. It was the task of the proletariat 'to transform imperialist war into civil war'. The land of the big landlords must be shared out among the peasants, this being the chief task in the 'bourgeois' phase of the revolution. The transition to the socialist phase would be speeded up by the outbreak of revolution in western Europe, which Lenin believed to be imminent. Meanwhile 'workers' control', or rather control exercised jointly by workers and capitalists, over industry would be a step towards socialisation. The new state would give the people incomparably more freedom than they could obtain under bourgeois democracy.

Having begun the revolution it is necessary to strengthen and continue it [thus Lenin addressed a meeting of soldiers shortly after his return]. All power in the state, from top to bottom, from the remotest village to the last street in the city of Petrograd, must belong to the Soviets of Workers', Soldiers' and Peasants' Deputies....There must be no police, no bureaucrats who have no responsibility to the people, who stand above the people; no standing army, only the people universally armed, united in the Soviets—it is they who must run the state. Only this power, only the Soviets, can solve the great question of land. The land must not belong to the feudal owners....Unite, organise yourselves, trusting no one, depending only on your own intelligence and experience; and Russia will be able to move with firm, measured, unerring steps towards the liberation both of our country and of all humanity from the yoke of capitalism as well as from the horrors of war!

This vision of the proletarian dictatorship, a state without police, bureaucrats and standing army, had an overwhelming appeal. Retrospectively, it may seem to have been a piece of sheer demagogy designed to wreck the remainder of any existing governmental authority. But such an interpretation of Lenin's attitude is disproved by his study *State and Revolution*, in which he developed the same ideas in a theoretical and scholarly manner, a study which could not have been written with an eye to the rewards of popularity but which reflected Lenin's profound conviction. In view of the subsequent evolution of the soviet regime, it is all the more important to remember how widely Lenin's vision of the proletarian dictatorship differed in 1917 from its materialisation in later years. Still another pronouncement of great significance, which Lenin made soon after his return, concerned the future of the labour movement in the world as well as in Russia. He advanced the idea of the third, the

Communist International, made necessary, in his view, by the abandonment of class struggle and of socialist internationalism by the leaders of the Second International.

This set of ideas was at first received with stupefaction by many or most of Lenin's own followers. But, using all his powers of persuasion and helped by currents of radicalism in his party, Lenin soon converted most Bolsheviks to his views. On 14/27 April the Petrograd conference of the party passed Lenin's April Theses and shortly afterwards a national conference of Bolsheviks also endorsed them. This was in many ways the most momentous event since the tsar's abdication: the honeymoon of the first revolution, with its pretence of 'unity in the ranks of revolutionary democracy', was over; and the programme of the next revolution was now accepted by the party that was to accomplish it. In the national conference of Bolsheviks which passed Lenin's motions only 133 delegates took part, representing 76,000 members. In February the membership had amounted to less than 30,000. But the strength of Bolshevism consisted in the quality, not the quantity, of its membership. The average Bolshevik was an influential leader and organiser in his factory or work-shop, increasingly capable of swaying the vast mass of workers who adhered to no party and even those who at first followed the Mensheviks.

After the collapse of the first coalition, in May and June, there was increasing evidence of popular disillusionment with the February regime. Municipal elections in the capital exposed the weakness of the Cadets, the party that predominated in the government; half the vote went to the Mensheviks; and some of the radical working-class suburbs voted solidly for Lenin's party. As a minority, the Bolsheviks displayed great tactical shrewdness and elasticity. Lenin made his party use every opportunity of putting its views before the masses, but he did not call for immediate revolution. For the time being, as long as the moderate socialists swayed the soviets, he ruled out any attempt on the part of the Bolsheviks to seize power. He urged the soviet majority, Mensheviks and Social Revolutionaries, that they themselves, without the Cadets, should form the government and thus justify the confidence which the working class placed in them. He advanced this policy at the first All Russian Congress of Soviets opened in Petrograd on 3/16 June, and it carried much conviction with the workers and soldiers who had followed the moderate socialists. The latter had just joined the second coalition government constituted by ten bourgeois and six socialist ministers. The Bolshevik agitators now raised the slogan 'down with the ten capitalist ministers', a slogan which stirred the suspicion, shared by the Menshevik and Bol-shevik rank and file, of the bourgeois ministers. The more the Menshevik leaders clung to the coalition, the wider grew the gulf between themselves and their own followers. While the congress of the soviets was in session, its Menshevik-dominated executive committee called a demonstration for 18 June/1 July, hoping that the working class would on this occasion come out in favour of the coalition. But to the surprise and dismay of the moderate leaders, about half-a-million workers and soldiers passed before them with banners and posters carrying the inscriptions: 'down with the war', 'down with the ten capitalist ministers', and 'all power to the soviets'. Lenin had evidently gained for his tactics the support of the proletariat in the capital.

In the next few weeks the revolution reached a strange turn. The Bolsheviks had already behind them the workers and much of the garrison in the capital, but in the provinces the moderate socialists still wielded the greater influence. Lenin and Trotsky hoped that this 'lag' between the capital and the provinces would soon disappear. In the meantime they were anxious to avoid any decisive test of strength; they wished to postpone such test until they could be reasonably sure that they could win it and that a Bolshevik government established in the capital would not be crushed by forces drawn from the provinces. Yet the impatience of their own followers in Petrograd led to the abortive rising of the July days. On 3/16 July the first regiment of machine-gunners, joined by sailors of the Baltic fleet and masses of workers, staged an armed demonstration, besieged the seat of the Petrograd soviet and menacingly urged the moderate socialists to transfer power to the soviets, in which they themselves had the majority. The Bolshevik Central Committee tried to curb the movement and to prevent it from becoming a real insurrection. The government brought front troops to the capital and suppressed the demonstrations. In the middle of these disturbances the news reached Petrograd of the collapse of the Russian offensive on the south-western front—the operation had been in progress since 18 June/1 July. The defeat, which was to lead to the final disintegration of the army, gave rise to violent recrimination. The Bolsheviks made themselves the champions of the ill-armed, ill-fed and ill-clad soldiers and charged the government with inability to put an end to orgies of profiteering by which food and clothing were withheld from the troops; they accused Kerensky, the minister of war, of having undertaken the offensive under pressure from the western powers, and they used the position at the front as an argument for peace. The government in its turn attributed the defeat to the subversive influence of the Bolshevik agitators in the trenches. As the demonstrations of the July days were being suppressed, the Bolshevik leaders were accused of being in the service of the German General Staff. The accusation, launched in a popular paper and supported with faked documents, released a storm of indignation in which it was easy for the government to inflict telling blows on Lenin's party. Officers' Leagues and other right-wing associations attacked Bolshevik headquarters, demolished the editorial offices of *Pravda*, and went out on punitive expeditions to the Bolshevik suburbs. On 6/19 July the government ordered the arrest of Lenin, Zinoviev, Kamenev, Kollontai and other Bolshevik leaders. Lenin and Zinoviev went into hiding from which they were to come out only on the day of the October/November revolution. Trotsky, Kamenev and others were arrested. On 12/25 July the government reintroduced the death penalty for offences against military discipline committed at the front. On 18/31 July General L. G. Kornilov was appointed commander-in-chief in place of General Brussilov.

These events resulted in a 'shift to the right', the strength of which, however, was exaggerated at the time. Lenin, assuming that the soviets had played out their revolutionary role, advised his followers, as they assembled for their semi-clandestine sixth congress, no longer to advocate the transfer of power to the soviets. The leaders of the Officers' Leagues and other right-wing organisations considered the moment to be propitious for the final suppression of the soviets and all they stood for. In fact the strength of the soviets was still great, and the threat from the right provoked the moderate socialists to action. On 24 July/6 August the executive committee of the soviets confronted Prince Lvov with an ultimatum, in which it demanded the immediate and formal proclamation of the republic, the disbandment of the duma, and the prohibition of the sale of land until the passing of a land reform by the constituent assembly. Prince Lvov refused to accept these demands, and his government ceased to exist. The second coalition was formed under Kerensky as premier and minister of war. It inherited from its predecessor its internal divisions and its indecision. It satisfied neither of the parties who joined it. But now it was the turn of the right wing to strike.

For 12/25 August, Kerensky convened a 'State Conference' to Moscow, in which all parties and social and economic organisations were represented. The state conference was intended to enhance the prestige of the government; and it was convened at Moscow, where the Bolshevik influence seemed weaker than in Petrograd. The opening of the assembly, however, was marked by a general strike in Moscow, a meaningful reminder of the growing strength of Bolshevism in Russia's second capital. The conference itself revealed the widening gulf between left and right; that is, between the moderate socialists on the one hand, and the Cadets and military leagues on the other. The Conference also witnessed the incipient antagonism between Kerensky and Kornilov, the newly appointed commander-in-chief. Its debates were repeatedly interrupted by stormy ovations and counter-ovations staged now by the left and now by the right, now for Kerensky against Kornilov and then for Kornilov against Kerensky. The right wing hailed the commander-in-chief as the saviour of Russia, the man destined to re-impose discipline upon a disintegrating nation. The left acclaimed the premier as the defender of the revolution from both the extreme left and the extreme right. Outside the conference hall, the prime minister and the commander-in-chief reviewed rival military parades. In this antagonism, which was in part personal, major political differences were involved. Both Kerensky and Kornilov agreed on the need for a strong government vested with plenary powers. But Kornilov regarded the officers' corps as the chief prop of such a government and himself as the candidate for the dictator's post. Kerensky wished to free his government from the pressure of the soviets, but willy-nilly he had to rely on the soviets' support—he himself was still a member of the soviet executive committee. He had issued the order re-introducing the death penalty at the front. Kornilov wished capital punishment to be re-introduced all over the country, for offences against 'law and order'. Kerensky hoped to curb the aspirations of the soviets by using the army as a counterweight to them, while Kornilov's aim was the total dispersal of the soviets.

On 21 August/3 September Russia suffered another major defeat: Riga was captured by the Germans. The circumstances of that defeat were obscure. From the left came the charge that the supreme command deliberately ceded 'Red Riga' to the enemy. As to Kornilov, he used the fall of Riga as an excuse for his revolt against the government. On 25 August/7 September he ordered strong Cossack detachments to march on Petrograd and he openly withdrew his allegiance from the government. Kerensky denounced the commander-in-chief as a rebel and resolved to suppress the mutiny with the help of the Bolsheviks. He armed the Red Guards, appealed to the Baltic sailors and encouraged Bolshevik agitators to go out and meet Kornilov's troops. The Bolshevik propaganda among the latter was so effective that Kornilov's soldiers refused to obey his orders and to fight against red Petrograd. On 30 August/12 September Kornilov was deposed from his post and arrested, and Kerensky became commander-in-chief in his place.

The abortive revolution of the July days had resulted in a temporary and superficial shift to the right; Kornilov's abortive counter-revolution was now followed by a momentous shift to the left. Its first, indirect, manifestation was the collapse of the second coalition. No sooner had Kornilov moved against the government than the Cadets withdrew from it, either because they were in sympathy with the mutiny or because they refused to share responsibility for Kerensky's action. Simultaneously, however, the Menshevik and Social Revolutionary ministers, too, resigned. Their parties were inclined to blame Kerensky himself for a degree of complicity or negligence in the early stages of Kornilov's conspiracy. For nearly a month no regular government could be constituted. On 1/14 September Kerensky formed a Directory, composed of five ministers among whom he was the only personality of recognised political standing. His personal rule, or rather his personal incapacity to rule, which his Bolshevik critics exaggeratedly labelled as Bonapartism, was to bridge the gulf between the opposed political camps.

The shift to the left was more directly felt when on 31 August/13 September the Bolsheviks for the first time obtained a clear-cut majority in the Petrograd soviet. Trotsky, released from prison on bail, was elected president of the soviet, a post he had held in the soviet of 1905. Five days later the Bolsheviks were in a majority in the soviet of Moscow, and soon afterwards in most provincial soviets.

From this swing of opinion, Lenin concluded that the time had come for his party to seize power. From his hiding-place in Finland, early in September, he urged the Central Committee of his party to prepare for armed insurrection. This was the natural conclusion of Bolshevik policy as it had developed since April. The February/March regime, according to Lenin, had been made possible by the abdication of the soviets in favour of the provisional government, and this abdication had been effective because the moderate socialists had swayed the soviets. With the Bolsheviks on the ascendant, the soviets must regain full power. Since the government was not likely to bow to the will of the soviets, it must be overthrown by armed insurrection. The government, too, and its Menshevik and Social Revolutionary supporters felt that this was the logic of the situation, but they refused to believe that the Bolsheviks would act on it. Altogether apart from this, they were helpless in face of the overwhelming forces arrayed against the 'bourgeois democratic' republic. It was very difficult, if not impossible, for the moderate socialists openly to defy the authority of the soviets, an authority which they themselves had upheld on many occasions, merely because the soviets were now under Bolshevik influence. At this late hour Kerensky still refused to convene the constituent assembly. Instead, he convened a substitute for it, the so-called Democratic Conference, which was in session in Petrograd from 14/27 September to 22 September/5 October. Its main outcome was the formation of the so-called 'pre-parliament', an advisory body whose authority, since it lacked any mandate from the electorate and had no power to control the government, was very feeble. It was further weakened when the Bolsheviks, after some hesitation, decided to boycott the pre-parliament. The main task of the democratic conference had been to find ways and means for the reconstitution of a normal government in place of the rump Directory. But even after the Bolsheviks had seceded, a majority of the conference voted against the renewal of the Cadet–socialist coalition. When Kerensky, three days after the end of the conference which he himself had exalted as the only representative assembly, defied its resolutions and replaced his Directory by the third and last coalition government, that government commanded even less authority than its predecessors. In theory it might have reasserted itself by appealing once again to the elements that had stood behind Kornilov. Lenin was firmly resolved not to give the third coalition enough time for that.

On 10/23 October the Bolshevik Central Committee met to discuss Lenin's scheme of insurrection. Lenin arrived from his hiding-place to urge that 'much time has been lost.... The question is very urgent and the decisive moment is near.... The majority is now with us.... The situation has become entirely ripe for the transfer of power.' Two members of the Central Committee, Zinoviev and Kamenev, Lenin's close disciples and friends, were opposed to insurrection. A day after this session of the Central Committee they thus formulated their warning: 'Before history, before the international proletariat, before the Russian revolution and the Russian working class, we have no right to stake the whole future on the card of an armed uprising.' They urged the Central Committee to wait for the constituent assembly, which the government promised to convene and which would be swayed by a radical majority; they conceived the new state as a combination of a Soviet republic with a parliamentary democracy and held that Lenin's policy would lead to debacle. Lenin, they alleged, overrated the strength of the Bolsheviks and underrated that of the provisional government; he also believed that the Russian revolution would be saved by a socialist upheaval in Europe, whereas they denied the proximity of proletarian revolution in the west. Against these arguments Lenin repeated that it was no use waiting for the constituent assembly, for the government had so many times postponed its convocation and it would do so again; meanwhile the Officers' Leagues would have enough time to prepare a counter-revolution and establish their dictatorship. Lenin confidently predicted that, if the insurrection was speeded up, its opponents could muster only insignificant strength against it and that 'all proletarian Europe' would rise. His attitude was shared by ten members of the Central Committee: Trotsky, Stalin, Dzerzhinsky and others. Only Zinoviev and Kamenev cast their votes against his motion. The dramatic debate went on almost till the day of the rising; but to the end Zinoviev and Kamenev were outvoted; the majority of the party accepted Lenin's guidance.

While Lenin was the moving spirit of the insurrection and, from his hiding-place, prepared his followers for it, Trotsky was its actual leader and organiser on the spot. Lenin had urged his party to stage the rising in its own name, without paying attention to constitutional niceties, and to start it as an openly offensive operation against the government. Trotsky, however, was careful to place the insurrection in a wider political context, to conduct it under the auspices of the soviets and not only of the Bolshevik party, and to give to it the appearance of a defensive action designed to protect the revolution from a counter-revolutionary *coup*. His artful tactics greatly facilitated the Bolshevik victory: many of those who would have hesitated to support a rising staged, as it were, as the private affair of one party only, favoured the enterprise when it was backed by the authority of the Petrograd soviet or of the soviets at large;

and many who might have shrunk from an openly offensive action supported that action when it was justified on defensive grounds. In fact the rising had its defensive elements: the Bolshevik leaders, at any rate, were convinced that if they themselves delayed action they would be forestalled by another, and this time successful, counter-revolutionary *coup, à la Kornilov.*

But in what way could the 'transfer of power' to the soviets be accomplished? In June the first All Russian Congress of the soviets had taken place and had elected a central executive committee which was to convene the next congress in September. That central executive committee (*TsIK*) was still dominated by the Mensheviks and Social Revolutionaries even after the soviets on the spot had come under Bolshevik influence. The leaders of *TsIK* repeatedly postponed the second congress of the soviets, at which, it was clear, the Bolshevik party was certain to have a solid majority. In the end they yielded to pressure from the Petrograd soviet and convened the congress for the latter part of October, or for the beginning of November, according to the new calendar. The Bolsheviks linked the date of the insurrection to the forthcoming congress. After a last and final postponement, the congress was to be opened on 25 October/7 November. The insurrection was prepared to take place one day earlier so that the congress should be able at once to sanction its expected outcome, the formation of a Bolshevik government. The insurrection itself was carried out, on behalf of the Petrograd soviet, by the Revolutionary Military Committee which had been elected by that soviet. It was one of history's ironies that the setting-up of this revolutionary military committee had not been proposed by Bolshevik members of the soviet. In the first half of October Petrograd was astir with rumours, for which there appeared to be some basis in governmental statements, that with the advance of the Germans the city would be evacuated and the government would move to Moscow. The rumours were later officially denied but in the meantime, amid the panic and indignation to which they gave rise, the Mensheviks proposed that the Petrograd soviet should assume responsibility for the defence of the capital. To this the Bolsheviks readily agreed. The revolutionary military committee was to keep in touch with the city's garrison, to acquaint itself with its disposition and to assess its strength. Ostensibly these activities served to prepare the defence against the Germans, but at the same time they formed the preliminaries to insurrection. Somewhat later Kerensky ordered a re-distribution of military forces which again was ostensibly designed merely to strengthen the front, but which was meant to enhance the position of the government in the capital by sending the most revolutionary regiments to the front. The revolutionary military committee vetoed this reshuffling of armed forces. Under Trotsky's guidance it sent its commissars to all the detachments stationed in and around

Petrograd in order to control the movement of troops. This was a challenge to the government and to the regular command, one which Kerensky could not leave unanswered. On 23 October/5 November he ordered the suppression of Bolshevik newspapers and issued writs for the arrest of the Bolshevik leaders who had been released on bail. The next day he indicted the revolutionary military committee before the pre-parliament and ordered an inquiry into its activities.

While Kerensky was addressing the pre-parliament and indulging in belated threats against the Bolsheviks, the revolution had actually begun. His threats merely provided the Bolsheviks with a defensive pretext for the insurrection. The revolutionary military committee had started it with its famous Order No. 1: 'The Petrograd Soviet is in imminent danger. Last night the counter-revolutionary conspirators tried to call the cadets and the shock-battalions into Petrograd. You are hereby ordered to prepare your regiment for action. Await further orders. All procrastination and hesitation will be regarded as treason to the revolution.' The plan of the military operations had been laid down with great precision by Trotsky, Podvoisky, Antonov-Ovseenko and Lashevich, members of the revolutionary military committee. During the night from 24 to 25 October (6–7 November), Red Guards and regular regiments occupied with lightning speed the Tauride Palace, the seat of the pre-parliament, the post offices and the railway stations, the National Bank, the telephone exchanges, the power stations and other strategic points. While the movement which overthrew tsardom in February/March lasted about a week, the overthrow of Kerensky's last government took a few hours. On the morning of 25 October/7 November Kerensky had already escaped from the capital, hoping to rally front troops for the fight. At noon his government was besieged in the Winter Palace just as the tsarist government had been in the final phase of the February/March revolution. Within one night, almost without bloodshed, the Bolsheviks had become masters of the capital. The astonished population awakened in the morning to read posters announcing:

The Provisional Government has been overthrown. Governmental authority has passed into the hands of the... Revolutionary Military Committee which leads the proletariat and the garrison of Petrograd. The cause for which the people has struggled: the immediate offer of a democratic peace, the abolition of the landlords' property of the land, workers' control over production and the formation of a Soviet Government—this cause is now secure. Long live the revolution of soldiers, workers and peasants!

In the evening the second congress of the soviets was opened. The majority of its delegates (390 out of 649) were Bolsheviks. For the first time since July Lenin appeared in public to address the congress and to table two momentous motions on peace and on the land. His Decree on Peace called 'upon all belligerent nations and their governments to start immediate negotiations for a just, democratic peace...without annexations...without the seizure of foreign lands and without indemnities.' The Decree on Land stated simply that 'landlord property is abolished forthwith without compensation'. While the congress applauded news of the arrest of the members of the provisional government, the first Council of People's Commissars was formed on 26 October/8 November with Lenin as its head, Trotsky as commissar for foreign affairs, Stalin as commissar for nationalities, Rykov (home affairs), Miliutin (agriculture), Shlyapnikov (labour), Lunacharsky (education), and Antonov-Ovseenko, Krylenko and Dybenko as the joint chiefs of the commissariat for military and naval affairs. The programme of this new government was still hazy in many respects. But its leaders were determined to establish a proletarian dictatorship and to gain for it the support of the vast mass of the peasantry which formed the bulk of Russia's population. They hoped to obtain that support by sharing out among the peasants 150 million *dessyatin* of land that belonged to the large estates. Their next immediate objective was to conclude peace. At the moment of the revolution they firmly believed that other European countries would so quickly follow Russia's example that the peace would be concluded between revolutionary proletarian governments of the main belligerent countries. The leaders of the new regime were less clear in their mind how far they should go in socialising industry—they nationalised the banks and transport but left most industries under the dual control of industrialists and workers. Finally, they set out to build up the soviets into 'a new type of state' superseding bourgeois democracy and representing workers and peasants on the basis of 'proletarian democracy'.

Frederick Engels once wrote that 'people who boast that they have made a revolution always find on the next day that they had no idea what they were doing, that the revolution made does not in the least resemble the one they intended to make'. Engels drew this generalisation mainly from the experience of the great French revolution, but its truth was up to a point confirmed by the fortunes of the Russian revolution and reflected in the deeds, beliefs and illusions of its actors. In April 1917 Prince Lvov boasted in a mood of elation: 'We can consider ourselves happy people. Our generation has been lucky to live in the happiest period of Russian history.' Only a few weeks later this 'happiest period' was in the eyes of the same man the blackest disgrace in Russian history. Kerensky in his heyday asked a meeting of soldiers: 'Is the Russian free state a state of mutinous slaves?...I regret that I did not die two months ago: I would have died dreaming the great dream that once for all a new life had begun for Russia, that we could live without the whip and the bludgeon, respect one another and administer our state not as did previous despots.' The disillusionment of men like Lvov and

Kerensky was growing as the revolution was using them up and throwing them overboard. They did not in any real sense *make* the revolution; they had no clear conception of its development; and in them the clash between illusion and reality was absolute.

The case of the Bolsheviks was different. They were the only party which in 1917 knew what they wanted and were capable of acting. They had a masterly understanding of all factors of the upheaval and they represented a profound historic urge of the Russian people. And yet they, too, were to find out that the revolution they made was different from the one they had intended to make. They, too, had yet to learn, in a long series of cruel lessons, that the assumptions on which they had acted had not been free from major and even tragic illusions.

On the eve of the October insurrection, in his controversy with Zinoviev and Kamenev, Lenin had stated his two main assumptions. He was confident that the revolution would justify itself *nationally*, that it would be supported by an overwhelming majority of the Russian people. He also believed that the revolution would justify itself *internationally*, that it was the prelude to imminent international revolution. His first assumption, that Bolshevism would be able to assert itself on the national, Russian scale, was soon vindicated to an extent of which he himself had not dreamt. For two-and-a-half years the Bolsheviks were to wage a savage civil war against White armies and foreign troops of intervention. If from this grim trial Bolshevism eventually emerged with flying colours this must have been due—in the last resort—to the deep popular appeal it had at the time. In one of its aspects the civil war was in fact a tense competition in which Bolshevism and the forces of the *ancien régime* tried to gain the support of the peasantry. This competition was won by Bolshevism. The 150 million *dessyatin* of land which the *muzhiks* obtained under the first decree issued by the Soviet government formed a wide and solid foundation for the new regime. In defending the Bolsheviks against the White generals and foreign interventions the Russian peasantry defended itself against the return of the landlords trailing behind the White armies. It may be argued that Lenin and Trotsky 'bribed' the peasantry; and in a sense this is true. But this does not alter the fact that the old system of land tenure was for the bulk of the Russian people an unbearable anachronism; that the peasantry's hunger for land had to be satisfied; that none of the old parties was willing or capable of satisfying it without delay; and that the agrarian revolution of 1917 gave the soviet system a stable foundation. So great indeed was the initial strength which the Bolsheviks acquired from it that it enabled them not only to outlast the civil war but to risk, about a decade later, a dangerous conflict with vast sections of the peasantry over the collectivisation of land and to outlast that conflict, too. Into its own national soil Bolshevism had struck firm, indestructible roots.

413

The second assumption, on which Lenin and Trotsky urged their followers to launch the revolution—the imminence of proletarian revolution in the west—was the half-illusory element in the beliefs and hopes of Bolshevism. It was only half and not altogether illusory, because the potentiality of revolution did exist in several European countries. But the potential did not become actual. When in November 1918 revolutions did break out in Germany and Austro-Hungary, they confined themselves to the substitution of bourgeois parliamentary republics for the old monarchies; they did not find their expected consummation in proletarian dictatorships. Moreover, these revolutions occurred later than the Bolsheviks had expected; and in the meantime the soviets had been compelled, by their isolation and war-weariness, to sign the 'shameful' peace of Brest Litovsk. In 1918–20 the sympathy of the European working-classes for Soviet Russia was strong enough to hamper and eventually to bring to a standstill foreign intervention. To this extent Lenin was not wrong when he placed his hopes on 'proletarian Europe'. But his hopes had reached farther—he had looked forward to the revolutionary triumph of 'proletarian Europe'. He had always been acutely conscious of the 'backward, Asiatic' character of the Russian civilisation and he could not easily see how socialism could be achieved in Russia alone. In 1905–6 and for some years after he had expected only a 'bourgeois-democratic' revolution in Russia, precisely for this reason. In 1917 he persuaded his party that the revolution could pass from the 'bourgeois-democratic' to the socialist phase, but he was also convinced that it could do so because it would not stop at Russia's frontiers. Once the revolution won in the highly industrialised and civilised countries of the West, so he repeatedly argued, the construction of socialism would assume an international character and advanced Europe would help Russia with machines, technical advice, administrative experience and education. In the meantime Russia had the political initiative of revolution; and in order to speed up the process the Bolshevik party set up the Communist International in 1919. However, towards the end of the civil war, or at any rate by 1921, it became clear that the bourgeois parliamentary regimes of western Europe had withstood the onslaughts of communism, for the time being at least. Soviet Russia stood alone—a prodigy of devastation and poverty. A readjustment of the Bolshevik perspective was unavoidable, and not one but a series of readjustments followed. The first was the partial readmission of capitalism under the New Economic Policy (NEP) of 1921. The next was the enunciation by Stalin in 1924 of the doctrine of socialism in one country, the essence of which was the affirmation of the self-sufficiency of the Russian revolution. The vision of a joint advance of many nations towards socialism had faded for the time being, or become more remote. What replaced it or overshadowed it was the vision of Russia's lonely progress towards the remote socialist objective through all the harsh trials of a state-controlled industrial revolution and of a forcible collectivisation of agriculture.

In another and equally important respect, too, the outcome of the revolution was to differ greatly from the expectations of its makers. 'We never anticipated that we would have to resort to so much terror in the civil war and that our hands would become so bloodstained': thus in October 1920 Zinoviev publicly confessed to a congress of German Independent Socialists at Halle. In the grim ruthlessness of the civil war the whole character of the revolutionary state was transformed. In 1917 Lenin advocated the Soviet system as a higher type of democracy, as a new state 'without police, bureaucrats and a standing army'. True enough, the possessing classes were disfranchised, and the new state was a proletarian dictatorship. But the disfranchisement of the bourgeoisie was at first considered to be a more or less provisional measure, dictated by an emergency; and, at any rate, the proletarian dictatorship was to give to the workers and peasants, that is to the overwhelming majority of the nation, more political as well as economic freedom than they could obtain under a bourgeois democracy. By the end of the civil war the workers and the peasants, too, had been deprived of their political freedoms, and the foundations had been laid for the single-party system. In the light of later events it has often been assumed that Lenin's party had from the outset deliberately worked to achieve this result, but this view is not borne out by the facts. It was only in the civil war, when the Bolsheviks were often unable to tell foe from friend, that they actually suppressed the parties of the opposition and established their own political monopoly, gradually and gropingly, under the pressure of events. In later years the sense of Russia's isolation in a hostile world coupled with the inertia of government by coercion prompted the final abolition of 'proletarian democracy' and the transformation of the Soviet regime into a terroristic police state. History's irony took a bitter revenge upon the men who had set out to build a state 'without police, bureaucrats and a standing army'. Yet, despite some Bolshevik illusions, which time and events dispelled either gradually or in the most violent manner, it cannot be doubted that the Bolshevik revolution, like the great French revolution before it, opened a new epoch not only in Russian history. The day of 25 October/ 7 November 1917 stands like a huge and indestructible landmark in the annals of mankind; and although by no means all the implications of the upheaval then initiated have come to light by the middle of the century, the October Revolution can already be seen to have initiated Russia's extraordinary ascendancy as a world power, and also to have found a gigantic sequel in the Chinese revolution.

CHAPTER XV

THE PACIFIC IN THE FIRST WORLD WAR
AND IN THE SETTLEMENT

THE outbreak of war in Europe in August 1914 at once directly involved the Pacific. Three of the principal belligerents, Britain, France and Germany, had extensive interests in the Pacific area. In China, where the weakness of the central government made the policy of other powers towards her an especially important matter, all three countries (and also Russia) were vitally concerned, both politically and economically. In the island groups of the Pacific, political control was mainly in their hands. In addition, Britain had other special interests of her own. The Dominions of Australia, New Zealand, and Canada lay within the Pacific or on its fringes. And, beyond that, Britain had been joined with Japan in a formal alliance since 1902.

The declarations of war by the three powers immediately involved not only their dependent territories but, in the case of Britain, the three self-governing Dominions as well. And the entry of Japan into the war was not long delayed. The Anglo-Japanese Alliance was popular with the Japanese. By giving them added political prestige as well as naval security it had assisted their spectacular rise in world politics. Japan had built considerably, by 1914, on the foundations which had been laid in her victories over China in 1895 and Russia in 1905. Korea had been annexed in 1910; and, by agreement with Russia, Japanese influence had been built up in eastern Inner Mongolia and southern Manchuria. Japan thus had a sphere of influence in northern China comparable with those of Britain, Germany and France south of the Great Wall. The war seemed to provide an opportunity for still further extension of Japanese influence in the Far East, and, at the same time, to give the Japanese government an opportunity of demonstrating that the Anglo-Japanese Alliance was an agreement between equals, not the extension of patronage by a European power to an Asian one.

On the outbreak of war, therefore, Japan offered her services to Britain under the terms of the Anglo-Japanese Alliance. The British Foreign Secretary, Sir Edward Grey, was reluctant to bring Japan into the European conflict. On the other hand, Britain stood in clear need of naval assistance in the Pacific. The China Squadron based on Hong Kong was not strong enough both to undertake the reduction of the German base on the China coast, at Tsingtao, and to protect Allied shipping in the North Pacific; and the Royal Australian Navy was too fully employed in the South Pacific to be able to send any vessels to its aid. The British

Ambassador at Tokyo, therefore, presented a formal request 'that the Japanese fleet should, if possible, hunt out and destroy the armed German merchant cruisers who are now attacking our commerce'.[1] It was hoped that this would lead only to a limited participation in the war by Japan; and, a few days later, the Australian government was informed from London that it was expected 'that the action of Japan will not extend to the Pacific Ocean beyond (the) China seas'.[2] On 15 August, however, Japan sent an ultimatum to Germany—with none of the British limitations attached. When Germany failed to comply with its terms, Japan declared war.

In the South Pacific, military operations were both limited in scope and confined in time to the opening months of the war. They were concerned, on the part of the Germans, with the disruption of Allied shipping and communications and, on that of the Allies, with the protection of these services and the occupation of the German Pacific territories.

The German colonies were taken with little opposition. A New Zealand expeditionary force, supported by vessels of the Australian and French navies, reached German Samoa at the end of August. It was informed by the Governor that, though he would not surrender the territory to the Allied force, he would not order any resistance to it. When the cruisers *Scharnhorst* and *Gneisenau* arrived in Samoa a fortnight later they found the occupying force in possession and steamed away, without offering any opposition. Similarly, there was no large-scale resistance to the Australian expeditionary force which occupied Rabaul, the capital of German New Guinea, in September and the remaining ports of the territory later in the year.

The occupation of the Mariana, Caroline, and Marshall Islands presented no greater military hazards, but it raised important questions of Allied strategy. Naval concern with the German possessions in the Pacific was not with the fact that they were under German rule but with the more specific danger that resulted from the existence in them of powerful radio stations. Two of these were put out of operation by the occupation of Samoa and Rabaul; but there were others at Nauru and at Angaur and Yap in the Carolines. Coupled with the fact that, at the outbreak of war, most of the larger ships of the German East Asia Squadron were cruising in the Pacific, the continued operation of these stations presented a real threat to Allied security. From the first days of the war, the commanding officer of the Australian navy, Rear-Admiral Sir George Patey, had been concerned primarily with these two objectives—the discovery and destruction of the German warships; and the dismantling of German radio

[1] Quoted in A. Whitney Griswold, *The Far Eastern Policy of the United States* (New York, 1938), p. 181.
[2] Quoted in Arthur W. Jose, *The Royal Australian Navy, 1914–1918* (Sydney, 1937), p. 129.

417

stations. He had been engaged in a search of the coasts of the Bismarck Archipelago, where he thought German ships might be concentrating, when he was ordered to convoy the New Zealand force to Samoa. After that operation was satisfactorily completed, he hoped to resume his search; but he was ordered to convoy the Australian force to Rabaul. One of the cruisers under his command was sent to Nauru to destroy the radio station there on its way to New Britain. But the German possessions in the Marianas, Carolines, and Marshalls still remained beyond the sphere of Australian naval action.

Meanwhile, the British and Japanese governments had begun discussing the respective fields of operations of their naval forces. Agreement was finally reached that the Japanese should patrol the waters north of the equator and the Australians those south of it. At almost the same time as this decision was announced, the Japanese occupied Yap, which was within the area for which they had assumed patrolling responsibilities. They stated that their occupation was temporary and that they were willing to hand the island over to an Australian force. Preparations therefore continued in Australia for the dispatch of an expeditionary force to the German islands; but before it sailed rioting occurred in Tokyo in protest against the intended transfer. The Japanese government thereupon requested British agreement to her continued occupation. The request was accepted; and, on 3 December, the British government informed Australia that 'we consider it most convenient for strategic reasons to allow them to remain in occupation for the present leaving whole question of (the) future (of the islands) to be settled at the end of (the) war'.[1]

The same period which saw the completion of the Allied occupation of the German territories also saw the end of German naval activity in the Pacific. For several months the German ships had been able to inflict sporadic damage on Allied interests; but their activities had been circumscribed from the start by their lack of any adequate base other than their headquarters at Tsingtao, to which they could not return. The big cruisers *Scharnhorst* and *Gneisenau* had sailed eastward towards South America, where they succeeded in sinking two British cruisers before being chased to their destruction at the hands of a British squadron off the Falkland Islands early in December. By the end of the year, the remainder of the German forces were either destroyed or driven into neutral ports by lack of coal. Except for the visits of two German commerce raiders in 1917, the South Pacific remained securely under Allied control during the remainder of the war.

In its ultimatum to Germany, the Japanese government had made two demands: that all German warships should be moved out of Chinese waters; and that Germany should hand over to Japan her leasehold at Kiaochow Bay, in Shantung. The second of these was of crucial impor-

[1] S. S. Mackenzie, *The Australians at Rabaul* (Sydney, 1937), p. 160.

tance. In 1898 Germany had acquired from China an area of about 200 square miles on a 99-year lease. Here, the strongly fortified naval base of Tsingtao had been built; and, from Tsingtao, a railway had been built, with German capital, running inland to Tsinan. These developments, together with the acquisition of mining rights and other privileges in the country thus opened up, had turned Shantung province into a German sphere of influence.

The delivery of the ultimatum marked the failure of attempts by the governments of China and the United States to secure agreement to the maintenance of the *status quo* in the Far East. The Japanese were unwilling either to allow the Germans to retain the Kiaochow leasehold or to agree to its being handed over to China for the duration of the war. They were determined, if possible, to destroy the German position in the area permanently. They had accepted the British request for the inclusion in the ultimatum of the words 'with a view to eventual restoration of the same to China'; and the Premier, Count Okuma, issued a press statement assuring the world 'that Japan has no ulterior motive, no desire to secure more territory, no thought of depriving China or other peoples of anything which they now possess'.[1] But, in the Japanese view, whatever the future might hold, the present need was for the occupation by them of the German stronghold.

When the time allowed for a reply to the ultimatum had expired, a Japanese fleet was sent to invest Tsingtao, and Japanese troops supported by a small British force were landed in northern Shantung. The Chinese, after protesting at this action, proclaimed a war zone within which they disclaimed responsibility for the actions of the belligerents. Neither the Japanese nor the Germans, however, accepted the definition of the zone; and the former, in particular, insisted that control of the Tsingtao–Tsinan railway was essential to them for the success of their operations. Tsingtao itself fell on 10 November, and its garrison was sent to Japan as prisoners. The Japanese showed, at this stage, that they intended to maintain their occupation, and they set up a military administration to control both the leasehold and the railway.

The Chinese government protested against this action. On 7 January 1915 it abruptly cancelled the war zone and demanded withdrawal of the Japanese forces, return of the leased territory, and payment of damages for operations outside the leasehold area. The Japanese retorted by charging the Chinese of acting with 'want of confidence in international good faith and regardless of friendly relations'.[2] Firmly in control of Tsingtao, the Japanese government concluded that the time had come for the settlement of what it described as 'outstanding questions between

[1] H. W. V. Temperley (ed.), *A History of the Peace Conference of Paris* (London, 1924), vol. VI, p. 373.
[2] T. E. La Fargue, *China and the World War* (Stanford University, 1937), p. 27.

Japan and China'. On 18 January, it presented the Chinese premier, Yuan Shih-ka'i, with its Twenty-one Demands.

The dispute over the occupation of Kiaochow provided the occasion for, rather than the cause of, the Japanese *démarche*. The matters which Japan wanted to settle were of long standing. These included the permanent elimination of Germany from Shantung, a more explicit recognition by China of Japan's special position in southern Manchuria, and a strengthening of her position south of the Great Wall. During the ten years preceding the war the American government had begun to insist on the observance of the 'open-door' policy in Manchuria, as in the rest of China; and American capitalists had begun to interest themselves in southern Manchurian railways. The Chinese had shown that they welcomed this conflict between Japan and America, and they had played it up by showing a minimum regard for Japanese treaty rights in the area. Japan, on the other hand, was determined not only to maintain but to improve her position there, since she sought in Manchuria an increasing supply of raw materials for her industries and land on which to settle excess population from Korea. Farther south, Japan had been alarmed by rumours of American plans to finance the building of a naval dockyard on the Fukien coast, opposite Formosa, and by reports that the Chinese government was considering the nationalisation of the Han Yeh-ping coal and iron enterprise, on which her industries were dependent. The dispute over Kiaochow provided an admirable opportunity for bringing these matters to a head. Japan had been embittered in the past by the way in which the western powers had intervened at the end of her successful wars with China and with Russia to rob her of some of the fruits of victory. If she could reach a settlement with China on this occasion before the war ended, she would stand a chance of enforcing far more favourable terms than she was likely to obtain if she waited for the final peace settlement, when, once again, the other powers would be likely to exercise a restraining influence.

The demands were arranged in five groups.[1] Group One dealt with the position in Shantung. The Chinese government was required to 'give full assent' to any agreement Japan might eventually make with Germany regarding the Kiaochow leasehold and other German rights in Shantung. It was required not to alienate land in the province 'to any other Power'; but, on the other hand, it was to agree to the Japanese building an additional railway. And, finally, certain towns were to be thrown open to foreign residence and trade. In other words, Shantung was to be made a Japanese sphere of influence. The demands in Group Two were concerned with southern Manchuria and eastern Inner Mongolia. In a preamble, China was to recognise 'the predominant position of Japan' in the two

[1] Quotations from the text of the demands are from the Japanese translation. This is printed in full in T. E. La Fargue, *op. cit.* Appendix I, pp. 241–3.

regions. More specifically, she was to make a number of concessions, of which the most important were as follows: an extension for 'a further period of 99 years' of the Japanese lease of Port Arthur and Dairen and control of the South Manchuria and Antung–Mukden railways; the grant of complete freedom to Japanese subjects to reside, acquire land, and carry on business throughout the two areas; and the acceptance of an obligation to consult Japan about any proposal involving the use of foreign capital or foreign experts. In Group Three, Japan provided for the conversion of the Han Yeh-ping Company into a joint Sino-Japanese enterprise. Group Four comprised a single, brief article binding the Chinese 'not to cede or lease to any other Power any harbour or bay on or any island along the coast of China'. The real purpose of this provision was to turn the Fukien coast into a Japanese sphere of influence. In Group Five, the wider ambitions of the Japanese were revealed most clearly. The Chinese government was to employ Japanese as political, military, and financial advisers, to place the police, 'in localities...where such arrangements are necessary', under joint Sino-Japanese control, and either to purchase arms from Japan or to establish an arsenal under joint Sino-Japanese management. In addition, the Japanese were to be given the right to construct railways linking the middle Yang Tze with the South China coast and to be placed in a privileged position in regard to the development of Fukien province. Finally, Japanese subjects were to be given special rights relating to religious, educational, and medical work.

In presenting the demands, the Japanese minister at Peking had enjoined secrecy upon the Chinese government. The latter realised, however, that only by allowing their contents to leak out could opposition to them be stimulated. Negotiations between the Japanese and Chinese governments therefore took place against a background of critical comment—not only in China and among the western powers, but even in Japan itself. In addition, the British Foreign Secretary took advantage of a clause in the Anglo-Japanese Alliance to urge moderation. As a result, the Japanese substantially modified their demands. The whole subject-matter of Group Five was postponed 'for later negotiation'; the terms relating to railway concessions in South China and to Fukien province were dropped; the proposal for joint control of Han Yeh-ping iron and coal was given up; and the intention of returning the Shantung leasehold to China was explicitly recognised. On the other hand, Japan held to her demand for an extension of her leaseholds at Port Arthur and Dairen and of the South Manchuria and Antung–Mukden railways and for the final elimination of Germany from Shantung. Agreement between the two governments was virtually reached on these terms; but the Chinese continued to protract the negotiations as long as possible. Eventually, Japan sent an ultimatum requiring China to accept the terms within two days and took steps for a general mobilisation and evacuation of Japanese nationals from China. Faced with this threat, the Chinese signed the draft treaties. In this way, they were able to claim later that the terms did not bind them, as they had been signed under duress.

Meanwhile, the internal stability of China had been weakened by the war in other ways than through the diplomatic pressure of Japan. By 1914 the government of Yuan Shih-ka'i had established itself fairly firmly on the ruins of the former Manchu empire; but it depended for its strength more on foreign financial aid than on internal popularity. In 1912 banking houses of the six powers most closely interested in China—Britain, France, Germany, the United States, Russia, and Japan—had formed a 'consortium', through which they agreed to act jointly in financing the country's administrative reorganisation. Early in the following year, before the terms of the reorganisation loan had been announced, President Wilson ended American participation in the scheme because he considered it 'to touch very nearly the administrative independence of China itself'.[1] After the outbreak of war in 1914, the active participation of European bankers in the scheme was also virtually ended. European finance also ceased to be available for railway building and other developmental projects; and even American money found its way into Allied loans, rather than to China. Japan thus became the principal source of loan money available to the Chinese government or for investment in Chinese development. The Japanese used their position skilfully. Whereas the 1913 loan agreement had been criticised for strengthening Yuan Shih-ka'i, as President, at the expense of the parliament, later Japanese loans strengthened rival factions at the expense of Yuan.

To Yuan Shih-ka'i the fall of the Manchus had marked, not a revolution, but the ending of a dynasty. When he had assumed the presidency, his aim had been to prepare the way for his own accession as emperor. But by the middle of 1915 his chances had gone. His dealings with Japan over the 'Twenty-one Demands' had destroyed his prestige in China, while making the Japanese government his implacable enemy. His financial difficulties, coupled with Japanese aid to his rivals, brought his downfall nearer. In December the commander of the forces in Yunnan province rose in revolt and denounced Yuan's pretensions. Other garrisons followed the example. In March 1916 Yuan abandoned his plans. In June he died, overwhelmed by his failure.

With the death of Yuan Shih-ka'i, China relapsed again into a period of disorder. A weak government established itself at Peking, under the presidency of Li Yuan-hung, with Tuan Ch'i-jui, a northern military commander, as premier. In February 1917 this government found itself faced with an important problem of foreign relations. When Germany announced the resumption of unrestricted submarine warfare, President

[1] Quoted in A. Whitney Griswold, *op. cit.* p. 172.

Wilson determined to break off diplomatic relations with her and to urge all neutral powers to take similar action. It was widely assumed that the American action would lead shortly to her active participation in the war. In China, the American request was assessed by politicians in terms of its likely internal repercussions. Tuan Ch'i-jui was in favour of acting promptly upon it, in the hope that he could obtain financial support which would free the executive from dependence on parliament. In parliament, the Kuomintang majority was against it because of fear of Tuan's government and of the increase in the army which would probably result from it. The President, also, favoured continued neutrality.

The American approach to China caused the other powers to reconsider their own attitudes. Japan had up till this time firmly opposed all suggestions that China should join the Allies. Now, the Japanese began to fear that she would eventually enter the war as the *protégé* of America, whose attitude towards Japanese claims in China would almost certainly be unfavourable. It seemed better to encourage China to join the Allies as soon as possible. For other reasons, the British and French governments had reached the same conclusion. They wished to recruit Chinese coolies for work behind the lines on the western front, to obtain the use of German ships tied up in Chinese ports, and—as a long-term gain—to acquire the properties and business of German firms in China. In addition, they were anxious to put an end to the propaganda and espionage which were being organised from the German Legation in Peking.

Allied action in support of this policy consisted primarily of outlining in tempting terms the gains—in the form of loans and concessions—which China was likely to obtain by joining them. The Chinese parliament was impressed by these approaches. It was also shocked by the news which reached Peking during February 1917 of the heavy loss of Chinese lives when a French ship was sunk in the Mediterranean by German submarines. On 10 March it voted overwhelmingly in favour of breaking off diplomatic relations with Germany. Four days later, the Chinese government formally took that step.

To the Allies, the important question now was: how soon would the Chinese go farther and declare war? It soon became clear that the answer was, from their point of view, a disappointing one. In parliament, doubts as to the wisdom of associating with the Allies were again increasing. Members began to look sceptically for some sign that China would obtain the benefits that had been held out as inducements for breaking with Germany. They were made aware, too, by the merchants of the probable loss to Chinese commerce that would result from the abandonment of neutrality. Further, they had never overcome their fear that entry into the war would accentuate internal disorder and increase the power of the militarists. This fear was intensified when the provincial military governors, who met in conference in Peking in April, were converted by Tuan to support of the war policy by the expectation of foreign financial assistance. Finally, the success of the revolution in Russia seemed to place the victory of the Allies again in doubt. Parliament, therefore, delayed its decision.

At this point, the Chinese government lapsed into confusion. Parliament was mobbed by a crowd clamouring for war, obviously with the connivance of Tuan and the military governors. This action precipitated a demand for Tuan's resignation from the premiership; and he was dismissed by the President. The military governors thereupon declared themselves against the President who, in desperation, summoned one of their number, Chang Hsün, to his aid as mediator. Chang, however, would come to Peking only on one condition—that Parliament should first be dissolved. The demoralised President agreed to this, also. Two consequences quickly followed: a separate government was set up in Canton by a section of the dissolved parliament; and Chang Hsün, arriving in Peking, ignored his obligation to the President and proclaimed instead the restoration of the Manchu dynasty. In a little over a week, however, the 'restoration' was brought to an end by Tuan Ch'i-jui, who re-established himself as premier at the head of a military government.

Allied pressure for a declaration of war was again placed on the Peking government. Tuan responded sympathetically, unimpeded as he now was by either president or parliament and as anxious as ever for financial assistance. On 14 August the existence of a state of war between China and both Germany and Austria-Hungary was proclaimed. In the following month, the Canton government gave a semblance of unity to Chinese foreign policy by recognising the action that had been taken.

The Peking government obtained certain immediate gains from its entry into the war. It took possession of the German and Austrian concessions at Hankow and Tientsin and abolished the extra-territorial rights of citizens of those countries. It was granted by the Allies a five-year remission of the Boxer indemnity payments and agreement to an increase in the customs tariff. But in its main hope—of substantial financial assistance—it was again disappointed. The American government decided that its power of granting loans to nations at war with Germany could not be applied to China, as she had not entered the war at the time the Act was passed (in April 1917). Instead, it proposed the formation of a new consortium composed of Britain, America, France and Japan; but negotiations for its establishment became protracted, and the agreement did not, in fact, begin to operate till well after the end of the war.

For the Chinese, the main result of their entry into the war was, thus, a further increase in their dependence on Japan. In the absence of any alternative, the Peking government raised a series of loans in Tokyo, in return for the granting of railway and mining concessions and the pledging of national assets as security; a 'war participation board' was set up in Peking with a Japanese adviser; and secret military and naval agreements were made which brought Chinese military and naval establishments under Japanese control. For the Allies, the results were likewise disappointing. They were able to lease the German and Austrian ships which had taken refuge in Chinese ports. But the Chinese were not able to take any effective part in the military operations of the war, on account of the domestic conflict between the Peking and Canton governments. And, despite repeated Allied requests, German and Austrian residents in China were not deported till after the armistice.

During the latter half of 1917, the Japanese government was also attempting to strengthen its position in China in other ways. After the United States had joined the Allies in April, British and French war missions were sent to Washington to work out effective means of military and political co-operation. They were followed by a similar Japanese mission. The real interest of the Japanese, however, was far less in the immediate problems of the war than in the future attitude of America towards Japan's position in China. The leader of the mission, Viscount Ishii, sought to obtain the agreement of America that Japan had a 'paramount interest' in China similar to that which America claimed for herself in Mexico. The American Secretary of State, Robert Lansing, on the other hand, at first urged that there should be merely a joint Japanese-American declaration affirming their intention to respect the 'open-door' policy and the territorial integrity of China. From this initial conflict of view, the two negotiators advanced to a compromise solution—the somewhat ambiguously worded Lansing–Ishii Agreement, signed on 2 November. In this document, the United States accepted the argument 'that territorial propinquity creates special relations between countries, and, consequently, the Government of the United States recognises that Japan has special interests in China, particularly in the part to which her possessions are contiguous'. The Japanese government, on the other hand, reaffirmed that it would 'always adhere to the principle of the so-called "open door" or equal opportunity for commerce and industry in China' and denied that it had any intention 'to infringe in any way the independence or territorial integrity of China'.[1] The agreement was differently interpreted by its two signatories. To Ishii, it marked American recognition of Japan's position in southern Manchuria and acquiescence in the advancement of a type of Japanese 'Monroe Doctrine' in the Far East. To Lansing, on the contrary, Japan's 'special interests' had been recognised only in a geographical, and not a political, sense. In his explanation of the agreement, he laid stress on the undertakings Japan had given in return. On balance, Ishii had probably come the better out of the encounter: the words 'special interests' meant, in the ordinary

[1] The full text of the agreement is printed in *Papers Relating to the Foreign Relations of the United States, 1917* (Washington, D.C., 1926), pp. 264–5.

usage of diplomacy, what he said they did; the interpretation placed on them by Lansing appeared to be a piece of special pleading. Japan had gained an admission from America which could not fail to be useful in the arguments over China which both governments knew would follow the war. In the meantime, America turned to the problems of the western front; and Japan continued to enjoy her temporary supremacy in the Far East.

Within a few days of the signing of the Lansing–Ishii Agreement, another event occurred to complicate further the Far Eastern situation. The Bolsheviks seized power in Russia. For the Allies, this had one clear consequence: Russian co-operation with them, which had been continued since April by the Kerensky government, so far as its circumstances permitted, was at an end. If the new Russian government succeeded in maintaining itself, a separate peace seemed certain; and the disappearance of the eastern front would be accompanied by the German acquisition of large quantities of military stores and by the return of prisoners of war. To the British and French, in particular, this prospect was alarming, since it would cause increased pressure on their already heavily strained forces in the west. They therefore began to consider measures for rallying the White Russian forces and preventing Allied stores falling into the hands of the Bolsheviks by landing expeditionary forces in the Murmansk region of European Russia and at Vladivostok, in Siberia. In the Far Eastern part of this plan, they were enthusiastically supported by the Japanese, who saw in it another opportunity for extending their influence on the mainland of Asia.

While the Allied powers were still considering these broader implications of the changes in Russia, a situation had arisen in northern Manchuria which seemed to demand immediate action. By liberal interpretation of the Chinese Eastern Railway Agreement of 1893, the Russian imperial government had gradually assumed complete administrative control of the railway zone, so that centres like Harbin were ruled as though they were Russian colonies, not part of the territories of China. When news of the Bolshevik *coup* reached Manchuria, supporters of the new regime strove to bring the administrator of the zone and general manager of the railway, General Horvat, under their control. To protect Horvat's authority, the Allied representatives in Peking persuaded the Chinese government to send troops to the area. These forces quickly accomplished their task and then withdrew.

The railway zone thereupon became a centre for Russian anti-Bolshevik plotting. In the spring of 1918 a Russian irregular force, assisted by Allied arms, moved out into Siberia. In June it was defeated by the Red Army, which was reported to have the help of German and Austrian prisoners of war, and retired again into Manchuria. This event gave the Japanese an opportunity to claim that a Russian invasion was likely and, under this pretext, to bring into operation their military pact with China and send an occupying force into northern Manchuria.

Meanwhile, discussions had been proceeding between the Allies regarding the landing of forces at Vladivostok. To this project, the American government for some time remained inflexibly opposed. But, as the year 1918 advanced, opposition became more difficult to maintain. The desperate position on the western front lent weight to any project which might create even a minor diversion; the alleged plight of 50,000 Czech troops, who were marching east to Vladivostok to offer their services to the Allies, merited assistance; and the growing determination of the Japanese to take action, in any event, made it seem desirable for the other principal Allied powers to act with them. Further, the local situation in Siberia became increasingly propitious. Four anti-Bolshevik groups were active in the region; and the most important of them, that led by Admiral Kolchak, had established its authority over large areas. Japanese, American, British and French forces were thus landed in August and September.

By that time the reasons for the action—which had never been as strong as they had been made to appear—had already begun to recede. The hope that it would assist the war in the west, by releasing the Czechs for European service or by creating a diversion, had been abandoned. And the prospect of creating an effective anti-Bolshevik government was not a real one. Kolchak and, to a lesser extent, the other military leaders could maintain a temporary ascendancy in a demoralised country by force of arms and of Allied aid; but they lacked any basis of popular support on which to erect a stable government.

When the Allied powers signed an armistice with Germany on 11 November 1918, the world war came to an end; but, in the Far East, as on the other borders of Russia, Allied military activity, which had been undertaken as part of the over-all strategic plan for the defeat of the Central powers, was continued for other reasons. In Siberia, Allied forces remained till all prospect of successful Russian opposition to the Communist regime had disappeared and, on the part of Japan, till every expectation of using the venture as a means of further extending her influence on the mainland of Asia had been disappointed.

At the end of the war the situation in the Pacific differed from what it had been in 1914—very substantially in terms of the immediate military and political balance of forces, and far more fundamentally in terms of probable future developments. Japan had taken over the German leasehold and other concessions in Shantung and had occupied the German Pacific islands north of the equator; and she had also extended her influence in Manchuria. Australia and New Zealand had occupied the German islands in the South Pacific. Russia was fully pre-occupied, for the time being, in combating White Russian groups and foreign expeditionary forces. But these changes were over-shadowed, so far as the years ahead were concerned, by others of a more general kind. The war had so weakened France that she could no longer be a major participant in the politics of the Far East. Britain, also, was—at least relatively—in a much weaker position. With her world-wide commitments, she could no longer maintain her naval predominance. Japan and the United States, on the other hand, had emerged from the war in far stronger positions than they had had when it began. Both countries were in a period of rapid economic growth; and, in both, the war had produced a sharpened awareness of the implications for internal security and prosperity of securing a solution of international issues satisfactory to themselves. The position of China in world politics was also changing. By 1914 she had been reduced to a semi-colonial status by the powers and to a condition of internal disorder by the collapse of her ancient political institutions. At the end of the war, her position, overtly, was not very different, except in matters relatively of detail, such as the abolition of the extra-territorial rights of Germans and Austrians. But there were already operative economic, social, and political forces which were beginning to transform China into a modern state.

In the short run, that is, the actual changes brought about by the war and by the influence of the powers which had contributed most towards victory loomed largest; but, in the long run, international relations in the Pacific area would be most strongly affected by the growing power of the United States and Japan and, eventually, by the changed status of China. It was inevitable that the peacemakers should be influenced primarily by the first set of factors, but equally inevitable that their decisions should be tested by the second.

The Peace Conference opened in Paris in January 1919, just two months after the signing of the armistice, with a meeting of the Supreme War Council. This meeting determined the formal composition of the conference. Britain, France, Italy, Japan and the United States were designated 'major powers' and were each to be represented by five plenipotentiaries. Most of the lesser powers and the British Dominions (apart from New Zealand) and India were each to have two. New Zealand was to have one. An executive committee for the conference was constituted of two representatives of each of the major powers (the Council of Ten). This latter body was later found to be too large and was divided into two— a council of Presidents or Premiers (the Council of Four, Japan not being represented in Paris by her Premier) and a council of Foreign Ministers (the Council of Five) (see ch. XVI).

Of the matters discussed by the conference, three were of predominant concern to the Pacific—the disposition of the German Pacific islands, the settlement of the problem of Shantung, and a proposal by Japan for the inclusion in the Covenant of the League of Nations of a clause guaranteeing racial equality.

The question of the Pacific islands came up early on the agenda; but it became clear that the freedom of action of the conference in regard to it had been gravely compromised when the British delegation revealed the existence of secret treaties entered into during the course of the war. Early in 1917, when the resumption by Germany of unrestricted submarine warfare had placed a great strain on Allied shipping, the British government had asked the Japanese to send destroyers to the Mediterranean. The request had been accepted in return for an undertaking by Britain to support Japanese claims to the German islands north of the equator (the Marianas, Carolines, and Marshalls) and to the German concessions in Shantung. Japan, on her part, had agreed to support British claims to the German islands south of the equator (Samoa, New Guinea and Nauru).[1] The British promise to Japan had been reluctantly acquiesced in by the Australian and New Zealand governments; and, shortly afterwards, France and Italy had also entered into similar undertakings.

To the Japanese government, its claim to the Micronesian islands had always been one to complete political control unfettered by any continuing international obligations. The Australian and New Zealand governments had developed similar expectations in respect of Nauru, German New Guinea, and German Samoa. In this, they came squarely into conflict with President Wilson's policy of international trusteeship for ex-enemy territories unready for self-government and with the mandates provisions which were being incorporated in the Covenant of the League of Nations. Despite the sympathy for Wilson's policy in the British delegation, the Prime Ministers of Australia and New Zealand insisted on the full satisfaction of their countries' demands. Complete control of the former German territories in the South Pacific was necessary, they claimed, to the security and well-being of Australia and New Zealand. In particular, they demanded the power to impose restrictions on trade and immigration. In adopting this line, they had followed a very similar attitude to that of General Smuts in respect of South African claims to German South-west Africa. The conference was thus presented with a revolt by a considerable proportion of the prospective mandatories. To resolve this impasse, a new class of mandate—known as Class C—was provided for in the Covenant. 'There are territories, such as South-West Africa and certain of the South Pacific Islands', the Covenant declared, 'which, owing to the sparseness of their population, or their small size, or their remoteness from the centres of civilisation, or their geographical contiguity to the territory of the Mandatory, and other circumstances, can best be administered under the laws of the Mandatory as integral portions of its territory....' By this formula of allowing the territories to be administered under the laws of the mandatory, the claimants gained the right to impose the restrictions they desired—which were already part of their own law.

[1] H. W. V. Temperley (ed.), *op. cit.* vol. VI, pp. 634–7.

They were restricted only by a general ban on fortification of mandated territories and by an obligation to protect native interests. The compromise satisfied neither Wilson nor the prospective mandatories, but it was accepted by both with reluctance.

The decision on the terms of the Pacific mandates gave the Japanese cause for satisfaction. The islands which they were to administer would be of some value, though that value was limited by their small size and paucity of resources. Of greater moment to them was their proposal for a declaration in favour of racial equality. In the League of Nations Commission, which was drafting the Covenant, the Japanese representative moved for the insertion of a clause in these terms: 'The equality of nations being a basic principle of the League of Nations, the High Contracting Powers agree to accord, as soon as possible, to all alien nationals of States members of the League equal and just treatment in every respect, making no distinction, either in law or in fact, on account of their race or nationality.'[1] In the drafting of this clause, the Japanese had consulted President Wilson and Colonel House of the American delegation and gained a sympathetic response from them. The matter was of great significance to Japan and to other non-western nations from the standpoint of prestige. But it had a directly practical importance of even greater moment. As House remarked: 'The world said they (the Japanese) could not go to Africa; they could not go to any white country; they could not go to China, and they could not go to Siberia; and yet they were a growing nation, having a country, where all the land was tilled; but they had to go somewhere.'[2] These reasons were weighty ones, from the Japanese standpoint, in favour of the proposed clause. But they were regarded as equally weighty ones for opposing it by the representatives of countries which feared Japanese immigration. In the Commission, the British representative, Lord Robert Cecil, urged that its consideration be postponed as 'a matter of highly controversial character'.[3] Outside, the Australian Prime Minister, W. M. Hughes, protested that such a clause could be used to open his country to a flood of immigration from Asia. The Japanese later made a modified proposal that the Covenant should simply 'endorse the principle of equal and just treatment to be accorded to all aliens, nationals of states members of the League'.[4] To this proposal, Hughes renewed his opposition and demanded the express exclusion of immigration from the scope of the resolution. Finally, the Japanese asked only that the phrase 'by the endorsement of the principle of equality of nations and just treatment of their nationals' should be

[1] David Hunter Miller, *The Drafting of the Covenant* (New York, 1928), vol. I, p. 183.
[2] David Hunter Miller, *My Diary at the Conference of Paris* (privately printed, New York, 1924), vol. I, p. 116.
[3] R. S. Baker, *Woodrow Wilson and World Settlement* (New York, 1922), vol. II, p. 235.
[4] Ernest Scott, *Australia During the War* (Sydney, 1937), p. 791.

inserted in the preamble of the Covenant. In this form, it seemed, the Commission could be expected to support the Japanese proposal. But the indefatigable Hughes was neither satisfied nor defeated. He threatened to take his appeal beyond the conference halls of Paris—to the people of the British Dominions and the western states of America. Only recently, California had enacted more stringent alien land laws; and the British Dominions had all practised racial discrimination. In these circumstances, both President Wilson and Lord Robert Cecil refrained from voting when the Japanese motion was put. Even so, eleven out of seventeen votes were cast in its favour. At this point, Wilson declared that unanimity was necessary for it to be carried and avoided an immediate crisis at the price of engendering a bitter and lasting resentment in Japan and, in varying degrees, in other Asian countries.

After their defeat on the issue of racial equality, the Japanese became even more determined to secure recognition of their claims in Shantung. This subject had been raised in the opening weeks of the conference, along with Japanese claims to the Marianas, Carolines, and Marshalls; but, from the end of January till the middle of April, discussion of it was suspended, while the conference was occupied with other matters.

The Japanese case was, essentially, a straightforward one. In 1915, in the treaties which followed the presentation of the Twenty-one Demands, China had agreed to accept whatever agreement might be reached on Shantung between Japan and Germany. In September 1918 the Peking government had signed a further agreement with Japan. In this, the Chinese agreed that the former German railway should become a joint Sino-Japanese concern and that Japan should finance the building of two important branch lines. In return, the Chinese had received from Japan a loan of 20 million yen. Further, the Japanese had, of course, been in occupation of the German concessions in Shantung since the beginning of the war; their special interest in the area had been recognised by the United States in the Lansing–Ishii Agreement; and their contribution to the Allied cause as a whole entitled them, they considered, to sympathetic treatment by the conference. Fortified by these facts and arguments, and by the secret promises of support received from Britain, France, and Italy in 1917, the Japanese demanded that the German leasehold in Shantung should be handed over to them. They undertook that the leasehold would eventually be restored to China. Only the economic concessions would be retained, and these would be dealt with in accordance with the existing Sino-Japanese agreement.

On their face, these proposals were not unreasonable. Provided the Japanese honoured their undertaking to return the leasehold, China would obtain as much as she could hope to do, except in a general revision of her treaty relations with foreign powers. Further, relations between the Japanese and Peking governments were not uncordial, as had been shown

431

by the agreement between them on Shantung signed in September 1918 and by the visit of the Chinese premier's chief lieutenant, Hsü Shu-cheng, to Tokyo in November. Yet the proposals met with passionate opposition from the Chinese delegation at the conference.

Some of the principal reasons for this opposition are to be found in the composition of the delegation itself and in its relations with Peking. The senior member of the delegation was Lu Cheng-hsiang, Minister of Foreign Affairs in the Peking government, a former imperial official with the classical training that entry to the civil service had then involved. Associated with him were three men with a very different background and outlook—S. K. Alfred Sze, Minister to Britain; V. K. Wellington Koo, Minister to the United States; and C. T. Wang, representing the Canton government. These men were younger than Lu; but, more important, they had been exposed in youth to the influence of western education in China and had later all graduated from American universities. Like other Chinese leaders of the returned-student group, they sought to destroy the fetters placed upon Chinese sovereignty by the powers and to see their country take her place as an equal in the family of nations. At Paris they quickly assumed dominance in the Chinese delegation, and in this they appear to have been helped by two things. First, the sheer weakness and disorganisation of the Peking government gave the delegation a freedom from control from home which was quite exceptional. Secondly, during the critical months of the conference, the Peking government was conducting discussions with the Canton authorities on the conditions for the re-establishment of unity in China. From the point of view of internal order, these discussions were even more important and more critical than the decisions of the conference. The Peking government may, therefore, have not only acquiesced in the vigorous and independent line of its delegation in Paris but have positively welcomed it, since it distracted public attention from the discussions proceeding at home and allowed them to proceed more calmly.

The Chinese case was presented by Wellington Koo. He demanded the direct return to China of the leasehold and of all other rights in Shantung which had been possessed by Germany at the outbreak of war. He claimed that the German lease had been obtained from China by force and that the 1915 treaty with Japan had likewise been signed under duress. Moreover, the Chinese government had declared, when it entered the war, that all treaties between it and Germany were abrogated, so that there were no longer any rights in existence which could be ceded to Japan. But these legal considerations were complemented by matters of national interest and of moral right. Shantung was an integral part of China, with a population of 36 millions; it included, in the Kiaochow area, one of the principal gateways to Peking and to the whole of north China; and it was, further, 'the cradle of Chinese civilisation, the birthplace of Confucius and Mencius, and a Holy Land for the Chinese'.[1]

This argument, with its combination of logic and eloquence, was partly founded in a consciousness of American support. In its turn, it further increased the confidence of the Chinese delegation. In the world's press, it obtained widespread and favourable publicity. In China itself, it was hailed by students and intellectuals as the harbinger of a new age in their country's relations with foreign powers. As a result, the delegation increased its demands when the subject came up for final settlement. They asked for the abrogation not only of the 1915 treaty with Japan regarding Shantung but for that of all the treaties and agreements of 1915 and 1918 including those relating to Manchuria and Inner Mongolia.

The reaction of Japan was obvious. From the first, the Japanese had been determined to use the issue to assert their status as a great power. Now, they had also to oppose claims which would, if accepted, have destroyed the whole basis of their position in China. But they could do so in circumstances which were much more favourable to them. At the beginning of the conference, it was American support for the Chinese case which they had to fear. By its end, American influence had fallen away. The Japanese case was accepted *in toto*.

The decision on Shantung came to the Chinese delegation as a shock and a bitter disappointment. Their exclusion from the inner councils of the conference had left them with the illusion that American support would ensure their success. Instead, the only consolation which President Wilson could now offer them was to point to the fact that Japan had reaffirmed her intention of restoring the sovereignty of the leasehold to China and that the territorial integrity and political independence of their country would in future be guaranteed by the League of Nations. The delegation struggled, in vain, to have the whole question re-opened. Meanwhile, in China opposition to the decision and to the Peking government, which was held responsible for it because of its record of dealings with the Japanese, spread rapidly. Student demonstrations in Peking merged into rioting. They were followed by strikes and by boycotts on trade with Japan in many parts of China. In the middle of June, the cabinet resigned. When the time came, on 28 June, for the signing of the peace treaty with Germany at Versailles, the Chinese delegates absented themselves.

For the Chinese leaders in Paris and for the growing body of forward-looking opinion which they represented, the conference at Paris had been a failure. They had made one gain: the wartime abrogation of treaties between China and both Germany and Austria-Hungary was declared permanent. German and Austrian citizens would no longer possess extra-territorial rights or residential concessions in Chinese cities; the German

[1] The words are those of the official record of proceedings (quoted in La Fargue, *op. cit.* p. 198).

and Austrian governments would have no power over the Chinese customs tariff. But on the bigger issues, they had gained little. In Shantung, they had only the unilateral guarantees of the Japanese government regarding its future intentions. In regard to the main body of treaty restrictions upon Chinese freedom of action, they had been forced to accept the view that these were not matters for the Peace Conference but for the League of Nations. Only indirectly—in so far as they had created an awareness that the treaties were due for revision—had they improved China's position.

For Japan, the conference had been both a success and a failure. On the one hand, the Japanese had gained acceptance of their case regarding Shantung and recognition of their claims to the Micronesian islands. On the other, they had not only met defeat but encountered the bitter hostility of many of the powers during the discussion of their resolution on racial equality. Even more significantly, the antagonism of America, which was showing itself in the Siberian campaign and in the popular anti-Japanese agitation in California, had been revealed during many parts of the conference. The Japanese still had good reason to feel that their country was regarded as an interloper among the great powers.

The conference had produced a settlement of a number of specific issues in the Pacific area; but it had done little to reduce the basic international tensions which would determine whether the future was to be one of peace or of further war.

The survival into the post-war years of major areas of dispute, and of a general sense of insecurity, found its most costly expression in the naval building programmes of America, Britain and Japan. In the United States, the so-called '1916 Program', which had provided for the construction of ten battleships and six battle-cruisers, had been suspended on America's entry into the war; but it was reinstated, and even extended, when the war was over. In Japan, expenditure on the navy was almost tripled between 1917 and 1921; and approved plans of construction involved a further rapid increase during the ensuing six years. In Great Britain, it was impossible to aim at restoration of the pre-war naval supremacy; but, in March 1921, the government announced a programme of construction which would keep the Royal Navy at least equal in strength to any other. In their different ways, these three programmes all contained —and were clearly seen to contain—the seeds of disaster. By 1921 the Japanese navy was already absorbing about a third of total budgeted expenditure. In America, President Harding had been faced with demands, even before his inauguration, for a reduction in defence expenditure. In Britain, the restatement of policy gave little consolation in the circumstances of the national economy and of an international arms race. And there was no illusion that this expenditure would bring increased security.

Little could be done by any one power unilaterally, however, either to limit the growth of naval armaments or to reduce the sense of insecurity on which it was based and which it tended further to increase. One of the main sources of international tension was the situation in the Far East. The American and Japanese governments continued to regard one another's policies towards China with intense suspicion. From the American point of view, the position was complicated by the existence of the Anglo-Japanese Alliance. This had always tended, the American government considered, to lead Britain into toleration of Japanese claims. It was likely to do so still more in the circumstances of the post-war period, when Britain had lost her former naval predominance in the Pacific. The Alliance was due to expire in July 1921. Would it be renewed and, if so, on what terms? This problem was worrying not only the governments of the two signatory powers but also the United States, the British Dominions, and China.

During the early months of 1921, the British and American governments made their position on the two major issues—limitation of armaments and the future of the Anglo-Japanese Alliance—clearer to one another in a series of public statements and private discussions. By June, the British government knew that the United States favoured the calling of a disarmament conference and desired that the Anglo-Japanese Alliance should be renewed only with substantial modifications, if it were not wholly abandoned. The United States government, on its part, knew that Britain had accepted the principle of naval parity with America and was willing to revise, though not to abandon, the Anglo-Japanese Alliance. From the British and American points of view, it thus remained to resolve the differences which still existed and to find a way of giving effect to the resultant agreement.

The first stages in this process were taken during the Imperial Conference which assembled in London in the second half of June. The Canadian Prime Minister, Arthur Meighen, took the American view that renewal of the Alliance was undesirable: to Canada, the friendship of the United States was important above all else. But in holding this opinion he was alone. The British prime minister, David Lloyd George, and the foreign secretary, Lord Curzon, were concerned with the security of British territories and interests in Asia. They could not agree to the purchase of American friendship at the cost of the alienation of Japan. In this they were supported by the prime ministers of Australia and New Zealand. This difference of view was not ironed out. Meighen, however, regained the initiative with a further suggestion which won general support: that there should be a conference on Pacific and Far Eastern problems between Britain, the United States, Japan, and China.[1]

This proposal was placed by Curzon before the Japanese and American

[1] On this incident see J. Bartlet Brebner, 'Canada, the Anglo-Japanese Alliance and the Washington Conference', *Political Science Quarterly*, vol. L, no. 1, pp. 45–58 (March 1935).

28-2

ambassadors in London, and the latter was asked to suggest to his government that President Harding should issue the invitations to the conference. In Washington the time was ripe for the taking of such an initiative. Congress had severely reduced the appropriation for the navy and passed a resolution requesting the President to reach agreement with Britain and Japan for a curtailment of naval building. Rumours of the British proposal reached the secretary of state, Charles Evans Hughes, ahead of the formal notification. He acted quickly in order to retain the initiative for the United States. The American government sent cables to Great Britain, Japan, France and Italy inviting their governments to attend a conference at Washington on the limitation of armaments. When the British proposal for a conference was received, Hughes immediately suggested to Britain that the scope and, so far as necessary, the membership of the Washington conference should be widened, so as to include Pacific and Far Eastern questions. To this procedure the British government agreed.

From this point on, the initiative in organising the conference was taken almost entirely by the Americans. The British, French and Italian governments accepted the invitation promptly and without qualification. The government of China, which had been added to the list of prospective members when its scope was widened, also responded with enthusiasm. To China, it seemed to provide an opportunity for raising once again the vexed question of the restrictions placed on her sovereignty by the treaty rights of the powers. The attitude of Japan, however, presented Hughes with a more difficult problem. The Japanese government was not unwilling to enter into discussions on the limitation of armaments. The naval programme and the Siberian expedition were proving a severe tax on Japan's resources. Business interests were demanding a reduction in military and naval expenditure. Further, Japanese politics were passing through a liberal phase. In 1920, a commoner, Hara, had become Premier for the first time, and the responsibility of cabinet to the diet, rather than to the military leaders, seemed to be in process of establishing itself. On the other hand, the Japanese were suspicious of American motives in proposing discussion of Pacific and Far Eastern affairs. Was not this an attempt to force the abandonment of the valued Anglo-Japanese Alliance? Did not America hope to undermine the Japanese position in China in her own interests? The Japanese accepted the invitation but added the comment that they preferred 'to look forward to the future' rather than to engage in the re-examination of old grievances.[1] At a relatively late stage in the preparations, invitations were also extended to Belgium, the Netherlands and Portugal, on account of their interests in the Far East. Like China, they were to be excluded from the discussions on the limitation of armaments but to participate in the Far Eastern and Pacific section of the conference.

[1] Senate Documents, 67th Congress, 2nd session, no. 126, p. 755 (Washington, D.C., 1922).

The conference was opened, at Washington, by President Harding on 12 November. Hughes was elected chairman, on the nomination of A. J. Balfour, the leader of the British delegation. He plunged at once into the main business of the conference. 'The world looks to this conference', he said, 'to relieve humanity of the crushing burden created by competition in armament, and it is the view of the American Government that we should meet that expectation without any unnecessary delay.'[1] He went on to outline specific proposals. He suggested that the United States, Great Britain, and Japan should immediately halt their construction of capital ships, scrap all unfinished capital ships (together with a proportion of older ones in service), and agree to a ten-year naval holiday. On behalf of the United States, he offered to scrap fifteen battleships under construction and fifteen older ones, if Britain and Japan agreed to carry out reductions on the same scale. This would involve the loss of 40 per cent of existing capital-ship tonnage. For the future, he proposed that the relative strengths of the three fleets in capital ships should be held at the existing level. This would mean that, for the duration of the agreement, the maximum tonnage of capital ships would be: United States, 500,000 tons; Great Britain, 500,000 tons; Japan, 300,000 tons.

Hughes's proposal was at once accepted in principle by the British and Japanese delegations. Both, however, attached reservations. Most important were those of the Japanese. They demanded a ratio in capital-ship tonnage of 10:10:7, in place of the proposed one of 5:5:3. Also, they insisted on retaining a newly completed battleship, the *Mutsu*, and offered to scrap in its place a smaller vessel which, under Hughes's scheme, they would retain. After lengthy negotiation, they gave way on the major point but still insisted on keeping the *Mutsu*. To meet them, the permitted tonnages for the three powers were raised to 525,000 for Great Britain and the United States and to 315,000 for Japan. France and Italy, after much bargaining, each accepted a tonnage of 175,000. A similar ratio was agreed to in respect of aircraft carriers; but other classes of war vessels remained uncontrolled, at the insistence of the French. A further condition was imposed by the Japanese, as part of the price for their agreement to the limitation of capital ships. They insisted that a general halt should be called to the construction of naval bases and fortifications in the Pacific. This condition was eventually defined so as to exclude the metropolitan territories of the signatories (including the British Dominions, which were represented in the British delegation) and certain other areas (notably Hawaii); but it was to apply, most significantly, to the Philippines, Guam, and Hong Kong.[2] The effect thus was to insure the

---

[1] Quoted in M. J. Pusey, *Charles Evans Hughes* (New York, 1952), vol. II, p. 468.

[2] For the text of the treaties and agreements signed at Washington, and for a record of the proceedings of the conference, see *Papers Relating to the Foreign Relations of the United States, 1922* (Washington, D.C., 1938), vol. I, pp. 1–384.

Japanese mainland against naval attack from any possible base within convenient operational distance.

Concurrently with the negotiations on naval armament, the conference was considering the various Pacific and Far Eastern questions which were before it. Most intimately connected with the naval issue was the problem of the Anglo-Japanese Alliance. To Japan, the Alliance had been for twenty years the cornerstone of her diplomacy. To America, its continuance had come to seem intolerable—a standing challenge to the peace of the Far East. What, then was to be put in its place? Balfour at first proposed a three-power treaty between Great Britain, Japan and the United States. But this was unacceptable to Hughes, who feared that America might be outvoted by her two allies. At his suggestion, France was also included. He further insisted that the new Four-Power Treaty should be much weaker than the old Alliance. It therefore merely pledged the four powers to respect each other's rights in their 'insular possessions and insular dominions in the region of the Pacific Ocean' for a period of ten years. If a controversy should arise between any of them on 'any Pacific question', there would be a joint conference; and, if any of them should, in respect of similar questions, be 'threatened by the aggressive action of any other Power',[1] they would consult together. In the event, even these consultative provisions were never invoked. The Four-Power Treaty became, as the Americans intended and the Japanese feared, little more than a diplomatic device to end the Anglo-Japanese Alliance.

The negotiation of the Four-Power Treaty gave the Americans an opportunity to force a settlement of a problem which had worried the State Department ever since the Peace Conference—the status of Yap. The atoll of Yap, in the Carolines, had a special importance because of its use as a cable station. From Yap the cables of the German-Netherlands Telegraph Company ran to Shanghai, Menado (in the Netherlands East Indies), and Guam. From Guam, in turn, cables ran to the United States, Japan and the Philippines. At Paris, President Wilson had intended, according to his later statements,[2] to insist that Yap should be internationalised. But, in fact, it had been included in the mandate to Japan over the former German islands in the North Pacific. Subsequently, the American government contended that, as the disposition of German territories had lain in the hands of the Allied and Associated powers, some specific act of acquiescence by those powers—including America—was necessary to validate the mandate. On the part of America, there had been no such act. At Washington, Hughes used this argument of America's non-acquiescence as a reason for insisting that an understanding on the

---

[1] *Ibid.* p. 35. On the drafting of this treaty see J. Chal Vinson, 'The drafting of the Four-Power Treaty of the Washington Conference', *Journal of Modern History*, vol. xxv, no. 1 pp. 40–47 (March 1953).
[2] Quoted in Pusey, *op. cit.* p. 446.

subject of Yap should be reached before his country committed itself to the Four-Power Treaty. In response to this pressure, the Japanese agreed to grant to American citizens equal cable, radio, and residential rights and facilities with the Japanese; and these terms were later embodied in a treaty, in which American consent to the mandate was also affirmed.

The third major series of problems was that relating to the position of China. On matters of general principle, the nine powers at the conference signed a treaty closely in line with the requests of the Chinese spokesman. They bound themselves to respect 'the sovereignty, independence and integrity of China', to provide 'the fullest and most unembarrassed opportunity' to China to establish a stable government, to maintain the principle of equal opportunity for the commerce of all nations, and to refrain from taking advantage of conditions in China for the purpose of seeking special rights or privileges. A proposal to establish a board of reference to deal with questions arising out of the treaty was, however, turned down. Provision was made only for 'full and frank communication between the contracting powers' whenever, in the opinion of any one of them, 'a situation arose which involved the application of the Treaty'. In other words, the conference was happy to express liberal sentiments, in vague general terms, but cautious in committing itself to specific action in support of them.

This latter fact emerged clearly in the discussion of the Chinese government's specific points of grievance, such as the foreign control of customs tariffs, the existence of the foreign concession areas, and extra-territoriality. In respect of customs matters, the powers signed a treaty by which China was permitted to impose significantly higher, though still limited, rates of duty; and a commission was set up to reform the tariff administration. A similar commission was established to investigate the working of extra-territorial rights, with a view to their future abolition, if possible. And other minor concessions were granted in respect of postal and radio matters.

Among the most important of China's grievances were those relating to the position of Japan. These included the thorny problem of Shantung. The Japanese government had followed up its promise at the peace conference to return sovereignty over the leasehold by suggestions to the Chinese that the matter should be discussed between them. The latter had, however, declined the Japanese invitations. They were anxious to have the support, in any negotiations, of other powers. From the Chinese point of view, the Washington Conference provided an ideal opportunity for such negotiations. The Japanese, for similar reasons, refused to let the conference consider the matter: they considered that it had become a purely Sino-Japanese question; and they were unwilling to have their own bargaining position weakened by the intrusion of outsiders. As the subject was too important to be left, the parties eventually agreed to a compromise by which discussions took place, technically outside the conference, with Hughes and Balfour present as observers. Negotiations proved long and intricate, with the observers persuading and cajoling the principal parties till finally a settlement was reached. By its terms, Japan agreed to restore full sovereignty to China, together with the owner-ship of former German public properties. China, for her part, agreed to purchase the railways with money borrowed from Japanese bankers and to recognise certain Japanese interests in the mines. Japan further undertook to withdraw her troops and China to open the territory to foreign trade.[1] When this agreement was announced, Britain offered to surrender her lease of Wei-Hai-Wei, in order to restore to China full control over the whole of Shantung province.

The Chinese delegation also asked that the conference should review the 'Twenty-one Demands' and the so-called 'special interests' of Japan in China which were based upon them. They contended, once again, that the treaties based on the Demands were invalid. This the Japanese denied absolutely. They offered, however, in the interests of a satisfactory settle-ment, to make concessions. The contentious Group Five of the Demands, which in 1915 had been postponed for future negotiation,[2] they now offered to withdraw. Group One—comprising those relating to Shantung —had been superseded by the new agreement. The major matters remain-ing for discussion were, in fact, the sections in Group Two relating to Japanese interests in southern Manchuria and eastern Inner Mongolia. In regard to these, the Japanese made two purely nominal concessions. They agreed to throw open to the consortium their option over railway loans; and they disavowed their intention to insist on the appointment of Japanese as advisers in the administration of southern Manchuria—a disavowal which cost them nothing owing to the strength of their existing influence in the region. Beyond that they would not go; and they were confident that the other powers, which had made no major sacrifices themselves, would not, and could not, force them to. Japan insisted on retaining her full rights in the Kwantung leasehold, which included Port Arthur and Dairen, and in the South Manchuria Railway. These they regarded as essential to them. As southern Manchuria and Inner Mon-golia were becoming of ever growing importance to the economies of Japan and Korea, the retention of control over the communications system of the area had become a major object of policy.

During the three months over which it extended—November 1921–February 1922—the Washington Conference thus surveyed a vast range of problems; it analysed them in great detail; and it took firm decisions in respect of them. The principal naval powers adopted a plan for the limita-tion of armaments; the leading powers in the Pacific agreed on a procedure

[1] *Papers Relating to the Foreign Relations of the United States, 1922*, pp. 948–60.
[2] See above, p. 421.

of consultation to be adopted when disputes should arise; and the powers with interests in China, in a complex series of treaties and resolutions, redefined their relations with that important but ill-organised country. Several further decisions were to flow later from the formal acts of the conference, or from discussions which took place while it was in session: the Lansing–Ishii Agreement was finally abrogated in 1923; Japan withdrew from Siberia late in 1922 and from northern Sakhalin in 1925.

What, then, was the magnitude of the conference's achievement? How far had it destroyed the causes of tension which the Versailles settlement had left untouched? In what manner had it contributed to the maintenance of peace? Its chairman, Charles Evans Hughes, to whom its decisions on disarmament had always been the kernel of its work, was in no doubt. Speaking of the naval treaty, he said: 'This Treaty ends, absolutely ends, the race in competition in naval armament....In other words, we are taking perhaps the greatest forward step in history to establish the reign of peace.'[1] The members of other delegations and the leaders of their governments spoke of the conference in equally enthusiastic terms. The Japanese premier, Takahashi, for example, described the conference's achievement as a whole as 'a blessing to all mankind'.[2] The press similarly acclaimed it. And these enthusiastic judgments were not the result, merely, of a temporary intoxication: they continued to be re-asserted for many years.

The conference had, indeed, achieved solid results. It had brought clarity and precision into a wide range of international relationships in which doubt and uncertainty had ruled before. By doing so, it had increased the prospects of continued peace, since rivalries and antagonisms had thriven on the suspicions born of uncertainty. But this was the real core of its achievement. When the powers had appeared to be making concessions, or accepting restrictions, as in the naval treaty, they were, generally, committing themselves to little more than they believed they would be forced to accept by other circumstances. The American government, for example, considered it had scant chance of securing Congressional support for its full naval programme. Similarly, in agreeing not to fortify most of their Pacific territories, both America and Britain were fully aware of the financial difficulties which would almost certainly prevent their doing so on a useful scale. On the other hand, when a power had important interests at stake and was in a position to protect them— as in the case of Japan in Manchuria—the conference did little but accept the *status quo*. The Four-Power Treaty, in another way, revealed the same weakness. Its signatories were well aware that there would remain many 'Pacific questions' on which disagreement could arise, yet they were content to devise only a weak form of consultation as a means of dealing with them.

[1] Quoted in Pusey, *op. cit.* vol. II, pp. 488–90.   [2] *Ibid.* p. 508.

The Washington Conference thus enhanced the chances of peace in the Pacific in the short run, while contributing little towards a long-term solution. The reason for this was a simple one. As the world war had shown some years earlier, the balance of power in the Pacific was shifting. What was necessary, if war was to be avoided, was not merely a formalising of existing relationships, but the devising of means for the peaceful acceptance of change. That such a means had not been found, either at Paris or at Washington, was not, however, a reflection upon the statesmen who took part in these conferences but a consequence of the political and economic forces which had dominated the foreign policies of the powers during the first quarter of the twentieth century.

CHAPTER XVI

THE PEACE SETTLEMENT OF VERSAILLES
1918–33

AT eleven o'clock on the morning of 11 November 1918 the cease-fire sounded along the western front. It was the end of the first world war, which had killed not less than 10 million persons, had brought down four great empires and had impoverished the continent of Europe.

The defeat of Germany, so long invincible to more than half the world, had been registered at dawn that day in the Armistice of Compiègne (see ch. XIII). Its heavy terms were in the main those proposed by Marshal Foch, the allied generalissimo, and lay between the views of the British Field-Marshal Haig, who overestimated the German capacity for continued resistance and advocated more lenient conditions, and those of the American General Pershing, who had argued in favour of refusing an armistice and maintaining the allied advance. This matched the attitude of the former president Theodore Roosevelt and a popular American demand for unconditional surrender. As it was, one month after the armistice, Ebert, head of the first government of the new German republic, greeted returning German formations at the Brandenburger Tor with the words: 'No foe has overcome you.... You have protected the homeland from enemy invasion.'[1]

No less important in the long run than the terms of the armistice were the preconditions governing its signature. When the German government had applied to President Wilson on 4 October 1918 for an armistice it had adroitly proposed that peace negotiations, and not only those for an armistice, should be based upon the 'fourteen points' of his address of 8 January 1918, as amplified in his subsequent pronouncements (see ch. XIII). During the preparatory allied discussion of armistice terms in Paris and Versailles at the end of October, the European prime ministers, Lloyd George, Clemenceau and Orlando, along with Sonnino, Italian foreign minister, were chary of committing themselves contractually to the frequent imprecisions of the fourteen points. Lloyd George asked: 'Should we not make it clear to the German Government that we are not going in on the Fourteen Points of peace?'[2] But Wilson's harbinger and confidant, Colonel House, threatened that if they were refused as a basis, the United States might abandon her associates and conclude a separate peace with the enemy. By 5 November the American government was able to transmit to the German government in the Lansing Note

[1] Friedrich Ebert, *Schriften, Aufzeichnungen, Reden* (Dresden, 1926), vol. II, pp. 127–8.
[2] Charles Seymour, *The Intimate Papers of Colonel House* (London, 1926f.), vol. IV, p. 167.

a declaration by the allied powers of 'their willingness to make peace with the Government of Germany on the terms of peace laid down in the President's address to Congress of January, 1918, and the principles of settlement enunciated in his subsequent addresses',[1] subject to two qualifications: first, the Allies reserved complete discretion concerning the freedom of the seas (point II)—an important success for Lloyd George against standing American resentment of the British doctrine of blockade; secondly, by the stipulation that the invaded territories must be 'restored' (points VII, VIII and XI) the Allies 'understand that compensation will be made by Germany for all damage done to the civilian population of the Allies and their property by the aggression of Germany by land, by sea, and from the air'[2]—a category much narrower than the possible but unrealisable claim to the whole of the direct cost of the war to the Allies, then estimated at around £24,000 million. Such was the so-called Pre-armistice Agreement respecting the fourteen points entered into in connection with the armistice with Germany, but not with the earlier armistices with Bulgaria, Turkey and Austria-Hungary, to which territories the points were largely relevant.

The allied powers did not communicate to the German government the official American commentary on the fourteen points provided by House who, at the meeting of the Allied Supreme War Council on 29 October, pointed out that Wilson 'had insisted on Germany's accepting all his speeches, and from these you could establish almost any point that anyone wished against Germany'.[3] Certainly the commentary rendered the points rather more adaptable. For instance, the phrase 'open covenants of peace, openly arrived at' (point I) 'was not meant to exclude confidential diplomatic negotiations involving delicate matters'[4]—Wilson had explained this to the Senate. As regards the readjustment of Italian frontiers 'along clearly recognisable lines of nationality' (point IX) it was now suggested that 'Italy should have her claim in the Trentino, but that the northern part, inhabited by Germans, should be completely autonomous'.[5]

The American commentary likewise dealt gingerly with the 'open-minded, and absolutely impartial adjustment of all colonial claims' (point V) and subsequently, in initiating the discussion upon them in the first days of the peace conference, Wilson said that 'he thought all were agreed to oppose the restoration of the German Colonies'.[6] This principle,

[1] *British and Foreign State Papers* (H.M. Stationery Office, London), vol. CXI, p. 650.
[2] *Ibid.* p. 651.
[3] David Lloyd George, *The Truth about the Peace Treaties* (London, 1938), vol. I, p. 80.
[4] *Papers relating to the Foreign Relations of the United States, 1918: Supplement I* (State Department, Washington, 1933), vol. I, p. 405.
[5] *Ibid.* p. 410.
[6] *Papers relating to the Foreign Relations of the United States: the Paris Peace Conference 1919* (Washington, 1942f.), vol. III, p. 718. Henceforward cited as *The Paris Peace Conference 1919.*

welcome to the British empire, was adopted at once by the Supreme Council (24 January 1919) and later discussion turned upon its application, notably the form and attribution of mandates, the new instruments of trusteeship under the League of Nations (see ch. XVII), whereby allied powers took over the outlying territories of the German and Turkish empires. In this latter connection Lloyd George had already, at a brief allied conference in London at the beginning of December 1918, used the great preponderance of British forces in the Turkish theatre to obtain Clemenceau's verbal agreement, honourably kept, to modify to British advantage the secret Sykes–Picot Agreement of 1916 for the disposal of the Turkish empire (see ch. XIII); Palestine, which was to have been under international control, would now pass under British, and oil-bearing Mosul was to be transferred from the French to the British sphere of influence. The British prime minister also secured Allied recognition of the right of the battle-tested British Dominions to send delegates to the peace conference. Lloyd George was compelled, indeed, to concede what Castlereagh in like circumstance a century earlier had withheld, namely his agreement that the freedom of the seas might be discussed; but when the conference came Wilson tactfully avoided raising this vexed issue. Thus at the outset Lloyd George, reinforced by a fresh mandate from the British electorate in the Coupon Election of December 1918, had skilfully secured a strong position for Britain and had set her on the way towards obtaining much, if not most, of what she mainly aimed at on and across the seas as regards the suppression of the German fleet and colonies, the doctrine of blockade, her economic and strategic position in the Middle East on the route to India, and her constitutional evolution of empire.

If the initial position of Britain was stronger than that of the hard-tried continental allies, France and Italy, stronger again was that of America away across the Atlantic. It was, indeed, the strongest in the world. The United States, unlike the European allies, emerged from the war not poorer but much richer, with the others heavily indebted to her not only in gratitude for precious aid but also in hard cash to the extent of about £2000 million. At the same time many Americans tended to think of themselves, despite their participation in the war, as impartially aloof from the rapacious feuds of old Europe. This attitude found divergent expressions, on the one hand in the isolationism of Senator Borah of the Republican party, and on the other in the idealism of President Wilson, the leader of the Democrats. His aspiration towards a finer ordering of international society had sent a thrill of hope through the war-weary world. It seemed that here at last was the old ideal of the philosopher-prince new-made in a professorial president with the power as well as the purpose to lead mankind into a more generous future. America appeared the richest nation both in substance and spirit so that even the old Tiger, cynical Clemenceau, believed or said he believed that she 'had opened a new and more splendid ethical era'.[1]

International relations were now to take an exciting jump ahead into the League of Nations. This was largely, though not entirely, done under Wilson's influence and he was the focus of expectation when he landed in Europe on 13 December 1918, the only head of a state who was, unwisely as many thought, to be a delegate to the Peace Conference of Paris. Preliminary meetings of the conference began a month later and it was formally opened in plenary session on 18 January 1919. Twenty-five allied and associated nations from the five continents were represented at this inauguration of the first peace 'congress of the world' (Wilson).

The delay in starting the conference was scarcely excessive considering the unexpected suddenness with which the war had ended; but once begun the conference, and specifically the Council of Ten comprising two representatives each of the Principal Allied and Associated Powers (British Empire, France, Italy, Japan, United States), still delayed in getting to grips with the main issues. Not only were the negotiators reluctant to show their hands too early but, instead of being able to concentrate upon the chief problems, the delegates discovered that they constituted 'a cabinet of the nations' (Lloyd George) subject to the pressure of current events. On the agenda, questions of immediate urgency tended to displace those of ultimate importance at a time when the resurgent Poles were fighting Ukrainians in Galicia, Germans in Posnania and Czechs near Teschen, with other local conflicts proceeding or threatening in Transylvania and Carinthia and on the eastern shores of the Baltic and of the Adriatic. And the post-war ferment was not only national but also social. From the beginning the massive phenomenon of the Russian revolution loomed up behind the conference, as was indicated within its first week by the abortive Prinkipo Proposal (see ch. XIV). In Berlin the socialist government had indeed just crushed the Spartakist extremists by turning the militaristic free-corps against them, but soviet republics were shortly to arise in Bavaria and Hungary while a wave of strikes further diminished confidence and dislocated the enfeebled economy of Europe, especially in Italy and England. In France, with her northern coalfields wantonly devastated by the Germans, coal production in 1919 was reckoned to be about 40 per cent of that in 1913. Furthermore, throughout the world, an epidemic of virulent influenza killed about twice as many people as the war had done.

Sickly Europe was short not only of coal and other raw materials, but also of food. Much was done here by the American Relief Administration under the influential Hoover, who became head of the Food Section of the Supreme Economic Council, judiciously constituted on 8 February

[1] Conversation of 9 November 1918 with House, as reported by the latter: *op. cit.* vol. I, p. 344.

1919 by the Council of Ten in order to co-ordinate such organs as the short-lived Supreme Council for Supply and Relief, the Allied Blockade Council and the Allied Maritime Transport Council, and to correspond in some measure to the Supreme War Council on the military side. The Council of Ten was itself preoccupied about that time with executive matters of military and economic detail in connection with the renewal of the armistice with Germany and the relaxation of the blockade, which it had specifically maintained. The thirty-six-day Armistice of Compiègne, finally renewed at Trier on 16 February 1919, had been provisionally renewed on 13 December 1918 and again on 16 January 1919 when it was stipulated that 'in order to secure the provisioning of Germany and of the rest of Europe'[1] the German merchant fleet should be placed under Allied control for the duration of the armistice without prejudice to its final disposal, and under promise of 'suitable compensation' for its use. This was one of the additional demands which the Allies saw fit to make. These 'aggravations of the armistice' (Wilson) understandably incurred some moral criticism, but the demand for the German merchant fleet was, in view of the general shortage of tonnage caused by the German submarine campaign, a reasonable provision to facilitate the relaxation of the blockade in execution of the declaration in the original armistice convention that the Allies 'contemplate the provisioning of Germany during the armistice as shall be found necessary'.[2] The grim hunger in Germany was less severe than in some other parts of central Europe, but on 17 January the Allies declared their willingness to permit Germany to import a first instalment of 270,000 tons of food if the merchantmen were handed over forthwith. The German government, however, now refused to do this until it first received an Allied guarantee of specified deliveries. Complex negotiations ensued concerning terms of delivery and methods of payment. The French authorities, intent as ever upon German reparation for German devastation, were reluctant to allow Germany to pay in gold but were overborne by the forceful intervention of Lloyd George at a meeting of the Council of Ten on 8 March which led to the solution of the question six days later in the Brussels Agreement for the provisioning of Germany. Thereafter the food blockade of Germany was relaxed until it was finally raised on 12 July 1919 in consequence of her ratification of the peace treaty.

On the same day as the Brussels Agreement, 14 March, Wilson returned to Paris after a month's absence. For as soon as the draft covenant of the League of Nations had been completed and laid before the full conference on 14 February he had left for Washington to face his critics in the Senate, where there was a Republican majority, before Congress adjourned. Wilson's

[1] *British and Foreign State Papers*, vol. CXII, p. 899.
[2] *Op. cit.* vol. CXI, p. 619. English translation of official French text as in H. W. V. Temperley, *A History of the Peace Conference of Paris* (London, 1920f.), vol. I, p. 468.

concentration on the League of Nations was not, however, the only, or even perhaps the chief, psychological factor which combined with executive distractions to delay the primary task of concluding peace with Germany. For many, including the keen young experts on the British and American delegations, the main interest lay less in the stern reckoning with Germany than in the benevolent creation of new nationalities like the Czecho-slovaks and Yugoslavs in fulfilment of wartime allied propaganda which had made of their liberation an idealistic war-aim such as Anglo-Saxon peoples generously crave. The time of the Council of Ten was much taken up with wearisome hearings of Central European and Near Eastern dele-gates and as late as 17 March Wilson 'insisted that peace should be made simultaneously with Germany, Austria-Hungary, Bulgaria, and Turkey'.[1] This impractical attitude was supported by Italy for practical reasons of self-interest in the dissolution of the Austro-Hungarian empire. It was partially reflected in the constitution, early in February, of the territorial commissions of the conference. There were commissions for Czecho-slovak affairs, for Polish affairs, for Roumanian and Yugoslav affairs, for Greek and Albanian affairs, for Belgian and Danish affairs, but none specifically for German or Austrian affairs. Nor was this deficiency very satisfactorily remedied by the creation at the end of the month of the co-ordinating Central Territorial Committee and of later committees for considering enemy representations.

The effective improvement in organisation came in the last week of March when the Council of Ten contracted into the more secret and in-formal Council of Four, much as a century earlier at the Congress of Vienna the Committee of Eight had been effectively superseded by the Committee of Five. And on 25 March Lloyd George presented in his Fontainebleau Memorandum the first conspective review of the salient problems of peacemaking. At last they were hammered out between the four of them: Clemenceau, very old, in suede gloves, Wilson who 'believed in mankind but...distrusted all men',[2] Lloyd George who 'argued like a sharpshooter',[3] and Orlando, the only one who did not speak English. Subordinate to the Council of Four there was constituted a council of foreign ministers or Council of Five; and indeed Wilson and Clemenceau, more even than Lloyd George, did treat their respective foreign ministers, Lansing and Pichon, strictly as subordinates.

The conference now reached its crux over the claims of France in that Rhineland region disputed between Frenchmen and Germans since the middle kingdom of Lothair was cast up in the wreck of Charlemagne's empire more than a thousand years before. The main French claims, already advanced in their clearest form in 1917, were two: first, that

[1] Note by Colonel House. C. Seymour, op. cit. vol. IV, p. 401.
[2] D. Lloyd George, op. cit. vol. I, p. 234.
[3] André Tardieu, La Paix (Paris, 1921), p. 113.

'Alsace and Lorraine must be restored to us not in the mutilated condition in which they were left by the treaty of 1815, but with the frontiers as they existed before 1790. We shall thus have the geographic and mineral basin of the Saar'.[1] Secondly, the French government 'desire to see the territory to the west of the Rhine separated from the German Empire and erected into something in the nature of a buffer state'[2] against their more prolific German neighbours who had invaded France twice in one lifetime, in Clemenceau's. Wilson and Lloyd George opposed these claims, being rightly afraid of repeating in reverse Germany's provocation in annexing Alsace-Lorraine. Concentrated negotiation brought a sensible settlement by mid-April. It was decided that the territory of the Saar valley should be slightly enlarged and placed under a special administration of the League of Nations for fifteen years, after which its sovereignty should be determined by plebiscite; the mines of the Saar basin were given to France in compensation for her ruined coalfields. Clemenceau reluctantly and to the dismay of President Poincaré and Marshal Foch abandoned the demand for a buffer territory in return for three guarantees of security: first, a military guarantee by Great Britain and the United States of immediate assistance to France in the event of German unprovoked aggression; secondly, the demilitarisation of the west bank of the Rhine and of a fifty-kilometre belt on the east bank; thirdly, allied occupation of the west bank and bridgeheads in three zones, one of which might be evacuated each five years up to fifteen years, or sooner if Germany had before then completely fulfilled her obligations. Wilson and Lloyd George were especially doubtful about allied occupation but finally on 15 April Wilson agreed. That same day Clemenceau, in the presence of his friend House, instructed his secretary that the French press must cease its jeering attacks upon the thin-skinned president. They promptly ended. It was commonly supposed that this was more than coincidence and that Wilson had stooped to a disillusioning bargain. Meanwhile Lloyd George was temporarily absent in London; he did not much like the Wilson–Clemenceau agreement on occupation that he found upon return, but consented to it on 22 April.

Already on 18 April the German government had received an invitation to send plenipotentiaries to Versailles and on 7 May the draft treaty of peace was there communicated to Count Brockdorff-Rantzau, German foreign minister. Initially the general idea had been that some sort of 'preliminary peace conference' of the allied powers would serve as a prelude to a full congress, which might include enemy delegates. Here, however, there prevailed even more than the usual haziness over pro-

---

[1] French note of 12 January 1917. *Papers respecting negotiations for an Anglo-French Pact*, Cmd. 2169 of 1924, p. 2.
[2] Balfour, British Foreign Secretary, to the British Ambassador in Paris in connection with the foregoing note, 2 July 1917, *ibid.* pp. 3–4.

cedure. For instance, Balfour had spoken in February of 'the final military proposals', which had originated in connection with renewing the armistice, as facilitating 'an important instalment of the Preliminary Peace'.[1] When nearly a month later the first report from a territorial commission, the Polish, was under discussion Lloyd George asked 'whether the Council proposed to define the frontiers of Germany finally on *ex parte* evidence alone. The other side had not been heard. It was not only a question of fairness to Germany but of establishing a lasting peace in Europe.'[2] But the idea of hearing the Germans before the treaty was in draft receded into the background, and when the first meeting did come on 7 May it was inauspicious. Count Brockdorff-Rantzau spoke sitting, unlike Clemenceau who preceded him, and said: 'We know the force of the hatred which confronts us here, and we have heard the passionate demand that the victors should both make us pay as vanquished and punish us as guilty. We are required to admit that we alone are war-guilty; such an admission on my lips would be a lie.'[3]

In his preceding speech Clemenceau had given the German plenipotentiaries fifteen days, subsequently prolonged by a week, in which to present observations in writing upon the draft terms. There followed a spate of German memoranda, often skilfully, sometimes speciously, argued. The main arguments were that 'the exactions of this treaty are more than the German people can bear'[4] and that in many respects they were in contradiction with the stipulated fourteen points. This comeback jolted the British representatives, who for one thing had tended, with their allied colleagues, to compile the treaty piecemeal without always appreciating the heavy sum of the provisions. ('Instead of drawing the picture with big lines, they are drawing it like an etching', commented House.[5]) Also, the fourteen points had sometimes been rather lost from sight since Wilson had failed to follow them up with a detailed plan and had transferred his enthusiasm to the League of Nations, thus relaxing the American diplomatic initiative which House had secured at the armistice. Now, however, it was apparent that on some questions the Germans could make out 'an awkward case', as Balfour remarked at the session in Paris on 1–2 June of the British Imperial Cabinet at which the German observations were considered. A sincere and honourable desire to deal justly with Germany and a fear of renewed hostilities, if Germany should refuse the terms, combined to render the cabinet unanimous in charging the British prime minister to exert strong pressure to secure large concessions to Germany. These were resisted not only by Clemenceau but also by Wilson, who complained that the British were now afraid of the

---

[1] *The Paris Peace Conference 1919*, vol. IV, p. 86.
[2] D. Lloyd George, *op. cit.* vol. II, p. 984.
[3] *The Paris Peace Conference 1919*, vol. III, p. 417.
[4] *Op. cit.* vol. VI, p. 795.   [5] C. Seymour, *op. cit.* vol. IV, p. 418.

'things that they insisted upon at the time of the writing of the treaty; that makes me very sick....They are all unanimous, if you please, in their funk. Now that makes me very tired.'[1]

Nevertheless Lloyd George obtained important modifications. Back in March he had already secured the revision of the Polish Commission's territorial proposals, which were unduly drastic towards Germany according to the Wilsonian principle of ethnic self-determination; now he returned to the charge. Besides obtaining further modifications of the Polish frontier in Germany's favour, he overcame Wilson's reluctance to apply the process of self-determination to Upper Silesia, and met one of Germany's chief and legitimate grievances by insisting upon a plebiscite there instead of outright cession to Poland. Lloyd George failed, however, to overcome Clemenceau's refusal to reduce the fifteen-year period of allied occupation in the Rhineland. Nor did he get very far in his enlightened .plea for the early admission to the League of Nations of Germany, who had offered to surrender the permitted remnant of her navy if this were granted her forthwith. Popular passions here as elsewhere complicated the task of the democratic peacemakers who, unlike their predecessors at Vienna, worked under the direct pressure of powerful criticism in press and parliament. It was the same with the question of reparation concerning which Lloyd George had been instructed by the cabinet to aim at a modification 'in the direction of fixing the liability of the Germans to the Allies at a definite amount'[2] in place of the stipulation that the Allied Reparation Commission, which was to supervise the execution of Germany's financial obligations, would inform Germany by 1 May 1921 of her total liability.

Other things being equal, there was evident advantage, as the American delegation urged, in inserting the total in the treaty, and in the subsequent event its execution was gravely prejudiced by adding a delay in fixing the figure to the inevitable delay in paying a great indemnity. But other things were not equal. Lloyd George was well aware that Germany's capacity to pay was limited and furthermore that she must mainly pay by exports which would be particularly liable to injure the trade of her industrial competitor, Britain, stripped by war of foreign markets which had underpinned her nineteenth-century supremacy. The British prime minister, however, was saddled with his electioneering assurance that Germany 'must pay to the uttermost farthing'.[3] Politics took precedence over economics so that Lloyd George argued in the Council of Four that 'if figures were given now they would frighten rather than reassure the Germans. Any figure that would not frighten them would be below

---

[1] Wilson at a meeting of the American Commission to Negotiate Peace, 3 June 1919 (stenographic report): *The Paris Peace Conference 1919*, vol. XI, p. 222.

[2] D. Lloyd George, *op. cit.* vol. I, p. 719.

[3] Winston S. Churchill, *The World Crisis: the Aftermath* (London, 1929), p. 50.

the figure with which he and M. Clemenceau could face their peoples in the present state of public opinion':[1] time, he now hoped, would promote moderation.

The British share in reparation would, under the terms of the Lansing Note, have been exiguous except for shipping had it not been that British argument, largely, and in particular the memorandum of 31 March 1919 by high-minded General Smuts of South Africa, had secured the inclusion of service pensions and allowances in the category of damage done to civilians. Under cover of dubious reasoning which tarnished the allied reputation, Germany's liability was thus at least doubled from somewhere about £2000–3000 million, which was what the British Treasury and Board of Trade had estimated that she could and should pay, to the much more uncertain region upwards of £6000 million. The German delegation had in its observations mentioned the impressive-looking figure of £5000 million as a possible maximum, but subject to such far-reaching conditions as the retention of colonies and foreign assets and to such technical qualifications that the amount actually to be paid would have been reduced out of recognition. This was considered an insidious and unacceptable offer. The provision for the determination of Germany's liability by 1 May 1921 was maintained, though Lloyd George secured agreement on 10 June that Germany might submit to the Allies within four months of the signature of the treaty any proposals for payment she chose to make in the way of offering either a lump sum, or labour and materials or 'any practicable plan'.[2] Germany did not avail herself of this concession.

The vigorous and voluminous allied reply of 16 June to the German observations, while mainly controverting them, bore witness to the British initiative not only as regards reparation and Upper Silesia but also in a number of minor concessions to Germany as to the Pomeranian frontier, purchase of Silesian coal, the rate of German disarmament and, for instance, the international control of Germany's main waterways, which was a feature of the treaty. This allied note gave Germany five days, subsequently extended to seven, in which to signify her acceptance of the revised treaty, failing which the armistice would lapse and the Allies would 'take such steps as they think needful to enforce their terms'.[3] These steps were to be in the first instance an advance 'in two bounds' by thirty-nine Allied divisions from the Rhine to the Weser and up the valley of the Main with the object of severing southern from northern Germany. Foch was authorised 'to commence his advance immediately on the expiration of the armistice'[4] at seven o'clock on the evening of

[1] Meeting of 9 June 1919: *The Paris Peace Conference 1919*, vol. VI, p. 261.
[2] Allied reply of 16 June 1919 to the German observations: *British and Foreign State Papers*, vol. CXII, p. 285.   [3] *Ibid.* vol. CXII, p. 253.
[4] Decision of the Council of Four, 20 June 1919: E. L. Woodward and Rohan Butler, *Documents on British Foreign Policy 1919–1939* (H.M. Stationery Office, London, 1946f.), First Series, vol. I, p. 18.

23 June 1919. Meanwhile there was passionate opposition in Germany to the terms, and a cabinet crisis whereby Bauer became chancellor in place of Scheidemann who declared that the hand that signed such a treaty must wither. On 22 June the Supreme Council shook the new German government by rejecting its offer to sign under specific reserve as to those articles (227–31) concerning German war-guilt and the surrender of Germans accused of war crimes. On the morning of 23 June the Supreme Council, incensed by the scuttling two days previously of the German battle-fleet interned at Scapa Flow, refused a German request for a further 48-hour extension of the time limit. The Supreme Council was again in session at five o'clock that afternoon, having not yet received a German reply. The meeting concluded during an observation by Balfour, recorded as follows by the adept secretary, Sir Maurice Hankey: 'As to squeezing the Germans...(At this point M. Dutasta, followed by Colonel Henri and Captain Portier, entered the room, with a note from the German Delegation expressing willingness on behalf of the German Republic to sign, under compulsion, a dishonourable peace....Orders were given for guns to be fired. No further discussion took place)'.[1]

At twelve minutes past three on the afternoon of 28 June 1919 in the *Galerie des Glaces* at Versailles the German plenipotentiaries signed the great treaty of 440 articles and sealed the defeat of that Second German Empire which had been inaugurated in the same room, in victory, not fifty years before. And it was five years to a day since the assassination at Sarajevo.

By the Treaty of Versailles Germany in the west ceded to Belgium the small districts of Eupen and Malmédy subject to conditions concerning popular consultation, and returned to France the Alsace-Lorraine of 1870, accepting also the provisions with regard to the Saar and the Rhineland. In the south Germany 'acknowledges and will respect strictly the independence of Austria' (article 80); the old frontier with the Austro-Hungarian empire was retained with the minor exception of a wedge in Upper Silesia ceded to the new Czechoslovakia. In the east Germany conceded to reconstituted Poland a roughly ethnic frontier giving her Posen and West Prussia with a corridor to the Baltic on the eighteenth-century model in fulfilment of the stipulation in the fourteen points that Poland 'should be assured a free and secure access to the sea' (point XIII). In this connection the German port of Danzig was constituted an outlet for Poland as a free city under the auspices of the League of Nations, but with no provision for subsequent revision as in the case of the Saar. On the other side of East Prussia, Germany lost Memel, which eventually passed to Lithuania. Plebiscites were prescribed to determine the attribution of Upper Silesia and of the East Prussian districts of Allenstein and Marienwerder; this provision, like that concerning Danzig, was sub-

[1] *Loc. cit.*

stituted largely at British instance for the originally proposed cession to Poland. The result of the plebiscites, held under allied administration, justified the British stand. Allenstein and Marienwerder were assigned almost entire to Germany as a result of overwhelming votes in July 1920, and in the Silesian plebiscite in March 1921 Germany secured approximately 60 per cent of the votes against 40 for Poland. The consequent division of Upper Silesia provoked a Polish insurrection under Korfanty and acute Anglo-French dissension before an award by the League of Nations in October 1921 partitioned the territory so that the smaller, but economically much the richer, part went to Poland (see ch. xvii). This difficult award satisfied neither party, but then the whole determination of Germany's eastern frontier on ethnic lines was highly complex, and in the main a creditably fair compromise was achieved. This did not, however, prevent especial resentment in Germany against a frontier which afforded so much to the hated Poles. The Silesian difficulty did not arise in Schleswig since for that borderland the treaty specifically provided for a plebiscite to be held in two zones, the northern of which went to Denmark and the southern to Germany. In all, Germany lost, including Alsace-Lorraine, about $13\frac{1}{2}$ per cent of her territory, a roughly similar proportion of her economic productivity, and a little over 10 per cent of her population, some seven millions. She also lost all her colonies—a notable severity—all her merchant vessels over 1600 tons gross and half those between 1600 and 1000 tons.

The Treaty of Versailles further provided for the disarmament of Germany. Conscription there was abolished, chiefly at the instance of Lloyd George against Foch, who saw danger in the resultant professional army, consequently limited to a mere 100,000 men. This miniature force was deprived of heavy artillery and tanks. The German navy was reduced to minor proportions, without submarines, and an air force was forbidden. (Wilson, however, had insisted, against the majority recommendation of the Aeronautical Commission of the peace conference, upon Germany's being permitted a civil aviation.) The disarmament was to be supervised by inter-allied commissions of control. The former German emperor was arraigned 'for a supreme offence against international morality' (article 227), but the Netherlands persistently refused to surrender him from his neutral asylum. Article 228 bound the German government to hand over for trial before allied military tribunals all persons accused of complicity in the atrocities wherewith Germans had smirched their conduct of the war. The German government from the first did its utmost to evade this obligation and ultimately twelve accused were tried by the German Supreme Court at Leipzig. There they were either acquitted or received such inadequate sentences that in January 1922 an Allied juridical commission of inquiry recommended that the remaining accused be handed over for trial by the Allies. They, however, let the matter drop.

The other article which aroused the fiercest German resentment was the so-called 'war-guilt clause' whereby 'the Allied and Associated Governments affirm and Germany accepts the responsibility of Germany and her allies for causing all the loss and damage to which the Allied and Associated Governments and their nationals have been subjected as a consequence of the war imposed upon them by the aggression of Germany and her allies' (article 231). The Allies not unnaturally did consider this to be an affirmation of the truth, but it was intended to establish the potential extent of German responsibility in its financial bearing before proceeding to limit that financial liability along the lines of the Lansing Note. The article had been drafted, largely by the young American expert, John Foster Dulles, with the intention of achieving a compromise between the American viewpoint, adhering to the Note, and that of France and Great Britain, resigning themselves to its limitations. It was German propaganda which expatiated upon moral war-guilt in connection with an article which provoked no equivalent outcry from Austria or Hungary. The reparation settlement with Germany which this article introduced was as indicated, and included the short-term provision that, pending the fixing of the total liability by 1 May 1921, Germany should pay the equivalent of £1000 million from which, however, there were to be deducted the expenses of the allied armies of occupation and, with allied approval, such supplies of food and raw material as they might judge 'to be essential to Germany to meet her obligations for reparation' (article 235).

Such were the main, but far from the entire, terms of the Treaty of Versailles. They were a severe imposition upon the new democratic regime of Weimar which had been stimulated in its origin by Wilson's objection before the armistice to treating with representatives of 'arbitrary power'. But as Wilson said, 'the real case was that justice had shown itself overwhelmingly against Germany'.[1] That was the central verdict which most Germans would not accept, that and the sheer fact of defeat. They developed a telling propaganda against the treaty, bringing out wherever possible its inconsistencies, real and alleged, with the fourteen points. Attention was averted from the greedy and vindictive war aims which German arms had endeavoured to secure. In the peace-making of the Allies, though, the measure of their good intentions was that they had sincerely adopted so high a standard in the first instance, and that a reproachful propaganda based upon it should have made them, as it did, apologetic. Seldom indeed has so stringent a treaty been framed with such idealistic intent, a dichotomy which suggested to its prescient French critic, Bainville, that it was 'too mild for its severity'.[2] The opening for

[1] Meeting of Council of Four, 3 June 1919. *The Paris Peace Conference 1919*, vol. VI, p. 159.
[2] 'Une paix trop douce pour ce qu'elle a de dur'—8 May 1919. Jacques Bainville, *L'Allemagne* (Paris, 1939), p. 250.

charges of allied hypocrisy over a dictated peace was widened by the mismanagement of concluding an armistice with the enemy negotiated upon ambiguous terms and then, after permitting him to state his case in writing, indeed, but not in oral negotiation, imposing upon him the allied rendering of those terms.

The full significance of the peace can only be appreciated, however, if the settlement of Versailles be extended to embrace the treaties of peace with Austria (St Germain-en-Laye, 10 September 1919), Bulgaria (Neuilly, 27 November 1919) and Hungary (Trianon, 4 June 1920). This last was delayed first by a Hungarian lapse into communism under Bela Kun (21 March–1 August 1919) and then by the ensuing Roumanian occupation of Budapest, which provoked admonitions from the Council of Heads of Delegations. These 'lawful heirs of the Council of Four' (Balfour, the British representative) toiled on for the second half of the peace conference, from the signature of the Treaty of Versailles until its entry into force on 10 January 1920; they mainly completed what Balfour called 'the immense operation of liquidating the Austrian Empire'.[1]

The resultant map of Europe was startlingly different from the old one. The empire was parcelled out among half a dozen 'succession states'. The German remnant of Austria became a top-heavy and economically precarious state of under $6\frac{1}{2}$ million inhabitants of whom nearly a third were concentrated in Vienna. Austria lost the South Tyrol to Italy but retained Klagenfurt by plebiscite and was awarded the Burgenland where, however, Hungary managed to wrest back Sopron. Hungary was due to lose most of all under the doctrine of self-determination; Croatia and Slovenia went, along with Bosnia and Herzegovina, to join with Serbia and later Montenegro in the new Yugoslavia; in the north Hungary yielded Slovakia, including a Magyar minority, to the new Czechoslovak republic, and in the east Transylvania, including another and less avoidable Magyar minority, to Roumania. (Here as elsewhere, special arrangements were concluded to protect the rights of national minorities under the supervision of the League of Nations—see ch. XVII.) Roumania was further aggrandised by gains in the Banat, Bukovina and, uneasily from Russia, in Bessarabia. This expansion could be mainly justified by ethnic arguments but they were scarcely applicable to Roumanian retention of the Dobrudja at the expense of Bulgaria, who also ceded to Greece her Thracian outlet to the Aegean. If Roumania did well from the settlement so did Poland, back on the map after more than a century of suppression. Having gained from Germany in the west, she now, with pent-up chauvinism, pushed out her frontiers in the east beyond the Curzon Line to include Eastern Galicia and adjacent territories after she had defeated the Soviet drive on Warsaw in the summer of 1920 (see

[1] Meeting of the Council of Heads of Delegations, 19 August 1919: E. L. Woodward and Rohan Butler, *op. cit.* First Series, vol. I, p. 432.

ch. xiv); the following autumn General Zeligowski's raid snatched Vilna from the Lithuanians and presented the great allied powers with another Polish accomplished fact; they eventually sanctioned both these Polish gains in March 1923. The Polish dispute with Czechoslovakia over Teschen had been settled for the time being by an allied award of 28 July 1920 partitioning the little duchy and thereby adding a small Polish minority to the Czech, Slovak, German, Hungarian and Ruthenian national groups which combined to make Czechoslovakia an ominous miniature of the defunct Habsburg monarchy.

Such, most briefly, was the balkanisation of central Europe with which the peacemakers were later reproached, not with full justice. For the settlement did, despite shortcomings, unravel a horrid tangle of conflicting claims and considerations broadly according to fresh concepts of ethnic self-determination. This principle was not, indeed, the invariable panacea which people then tended to suppose: much depended for instance upon the size and choice of the units selected for self-determination. Yet its strength in general was suggested by the way that the network of new frontiers on the whole survived the fluctuations of time; and where they were later altered it was not always for the better. Furthermore, the main features of this new national determination were already present when the settlement came to be drafted, since 1918–19 marked the disruptive success throughout the Austro-Hungarian empire of that national-liberal uprising which had been damped down seventy years before. Thus the responsibility of the great Allies might be held to lie less in their peacemaking than in their wartime propaganda which had so successfully preached the empire's dissolution. Nor were the drafters of the settlement so unmindful of wider economic considerations as was sometimes supposed. On 26 August 1919, for instance, they discussed a proposal involving 'a customs union from Danzig to Sicily'. Balfour remarked, however, that 'the proposal of establishing an entirely new customs system over half Europe alarmed him'.[1] And the American attitude discouraged initiatives of the European Allies towards reviewing the economic position of Europe as a whole in relation to America, especially as regards currency, and drawing upon the experience of the Supreme Economic Council to constitute subsequent organs of economic co-operation.

The settlement did, however, contain elements of inherent weakness, especially as regards the main flaw in the logical application of self-determination. For while this doctrine was applied to Germany's detriment in Poland and elsewhere she was not allowed the benefit of it in the Sudetenland and Austria, where on 12 November 1918 the German-Austrian Republic had been constituted specifically as 'a component part of the German Republic', and claiming to include the Sudetenland. Article 80 of the Treaty of Versailles, matched in that of Saint Germain,

[1] Woodward and Butler, op. cit. First Series, vol. I, pp. 547–9.

did not prevent the framers of the new Weimar Constitution from providing for consultative Austrian participation in the German parliament preceding Austria's 'junction with the German Reich' (article 61). On 22 September 1919 Germany was accordingly compelled by the Allies to sign a declaration nullifying any article in the constitution which conflicted with the treaty. It would have been exceedingly difficult for the Allies to sanction such fresh additions to German territory and power but, as it was, Germany was left with a sense of injustice that could appeal to the victors' own principle of self-determination: a moral weakness in the allied position which found its lodgment within twenty years.

Lloyd George had written in his Fontainebleau Memorandum: 'I cannot conceive any greater cause of future war than that the German people, who have certainly proved themselves one of the most vigorous and powerful races in the world, should be surrounded by a number of small States, many of them consisting of people who have never previously set up a stable government for themselves, but each of them containing large masses of Germans clamouring for reunion with their native land.'[1] Yet that was just what Lloyd George and his colleagues found it impossible to avoid. Smuts had written earlier, in 1918: 'Europe is being liquidated, and the League of Nations must be the heir to this great estate.'[2] It was a heavy heritage for so new and experimental an authority.

The unfashionable balance of power had broken down. The Concert of Europe had contracted by the autumn of 1919 to an uneasy western alliance. Attempts were then being made in Paris to strengthen this alliance by promoting the co-ordination of Belgian and Dutch defence against any eventual renewal of German aggression. This preoccupation already underlay the deliberations of the Commission for the revision of the Treaties of 1839, of that 'scrap of paper' torn up by the German invasion of Belgium in 1914. Within two months of the signature of peace a British military representative informed members of this commission that the danger for Belgium of a repetition seemed to him 'to be chiefly for the time when Germany should have been able to arm herself anew and perhaps conclude an alliance with Russia, which might give birth to a rival of the League of Nations. This danger could not, however, arise for twenty or thirty years.... The fact that the French frontier had been retraced towards the north along the Rhine made it more and more necessary for Germany to attack in Limburg. Germany would, therefore, become...more liable to oblige Holland to make war.'[3] The stubborn Dutch, however, were suspicious of Belgian aspirations in regard to Limburg and Dutch Flanders and, more solidly, to freer navigation of

---

[1] *Papers respecting negotiations for an Anglo-French Pact*, Cmd. 2169 of 1924, p. 77.
[2] D. Lloyd George, *op. cit.* vol. I, p. 622.
[3] Lieut.-Colonel Twiss at a meeting of great powers on the commission, 22 August 1919. Woodward and Butler, *op. cit.* First Series, vol. v, pp. iii–iv and 277–8.

the Scheldt. A comprehensive revision of the settlement of 1839 was also stultified, partly owing to British refusal to guarantee Belgium unless she resumed her profitless neutrality.

As to the east, the allied powers, hastily demobilised, were left with barely strength enough to evict from the new Baltic states of Latvia and Lithuania the ruthless German freebooters under General von der Goltz who, even after the peace treaty was signed, aimed at clamping down a teutonic domination there and so resuming the German drive to the east. The Supreme Council at Paris doubted its power to coerce, if necessary, even Hungary or Bulgaria. Balfour opined on 26 July 1919 that 'the Powers, which, eight months ago, were the conquerors of the world, could not, at the present moment, impose their will on an army of 120,000 men'.[1] Of the European conquerors Britain was bent upon reducing her continental commitments, France was wearied and Italy embittered by her treatment at the peace conference.

If Italy's allies were unenthusiastic about her military performance in the war, Italy understandably resented the way in which they had concluded the Sykes–Picot Agreement behind her back, and was further put out when at the peacemaking she found herself less popular with them than her Adriatic rival, Yugoslavia, largely comprising Croats and Slovenes from the Austro-Hungarian empire, her main enemy. But Italy alienated her friends by her 'blinkered greed' (Lloyd George) in pressing not only her extensive claims under the secret Treaty of London (see ch. XIII) but also her vociferous demand for Fiume, which that treaty had assigned to Croatia. The question of Fiume was accorded a symbolic significance beyond its intrinsic importance both by Italy, whose poet D'Annunzio seized it in a filibustering raid on 12 September 1919, and on the other side by Wilson who, in refusing to concede it to Italy, matched Sonnino in stubbornness and had provoked the Italian delegation to temporary withdrawal from the conference by issuing an unseemly manifesto on 23 April 1919. After much commotion the question was eventually left for direct settlement between Italy and Yugoslavia and dragged on until 1924 when most of Fiume was secured by Italy, who had earlier acquired Zara and Lagosta while renouncing her wider claims to Dalmatia under the Treaty of London. This Italian concentration on the Adriatic diminished her activity, if not her appetite, in other regions such as Africa where her interest in the direction of Abyssinia was indicated by her claim to British and French Somaliland and to the French holdings in the Djibouti–Addis Ababa railway. This claim being resisted, Italy in May 1919 offered to swap it for a mandate over the former German colony of Togoland on the other side of Africa. This also was unpalatable to Britain and France, who divided Togoland and the Cameroons between them, eventually under mandates. Italy had to be content, or discontent,

---

[1] Woodward and Butler, *op. cit.* First Series, vol. I, p. 207.

with Jubaland in East Africa, ceded by Britain in 1924, and minor concessions from France on the Libyan border.

The Italian prime minister wrote to the British on 25 May 1919:

I cannot look forward without grave apprehensions to the future of continental Europe; the German longing for revenge must be considered in conjunction with the Russian position. We can thus see even now that the settlement to be arrived at will lack the assent of more than half the population of the European continent. If we detach from the block on which the new European system will have to rely for support forty million Italians, and force them into the ranks of the malcontents, do you think that the new order will rest on a firm basis?[1]

The might of Russia had for the present fallen away to the east and now that of America was to be withdrawn in the west so that, despite the residual League of Nations, European policies throughout the 1920's tended, with exceptions, to be cast upon a reduced scale. Wilson, back in America, suffered a paralytic stroke at the end of September 1919 and lingered on a broken man. Events swiftly demonstrated his partisan error in provoking the Republican Party in the congressional elections of 1918 and in rejecting advice to include one of its leading members in the American Commission to Negotiate Peace. Strong opposition to the Treaty of Versailles had developed among those to whom a policy of splendid isolation seemed as desirable for America in the twentieth century as it had for Britain in the nineteenth. On 19 March 1920 the treaty finally failed to secure the ratification by the Senate required by the constitution. Such was the repudiation of the policy of the President who had assured his staff during their voyage to the peace conference that 'the men whom we were about to deal with did not represent their own people'.[2] America, having constrained the European allies to make peace upon the basis of an American programme, now left them to it.

Along with this repudiation went the American treaty of military guarantee to France which in turn, under the terms of agreement, released Britain from her undertaking so that France found herself deprived of one of the main guarantees of security accorded her in return for renunciation of her demands in the Rhineland. No promising Anglo-French attempt to remedy this situation was made until the end of 1921 and even then negotiations flagged and eventually petered out, England having tried among other things to link them with lesser questions and France contending that the original guarantee of 1919 was humiliating to her because unilateral and inadequate since it did not cover German 'indirect aggression' in Eastern Europe. As the French ambassador said in December 1921 to Lord Curzon, the edgy successor to the urbane Balfour: 'It would not cover us against a Polish Sadowa, which for Germany

[1] D. Lloyd George, *op. cit.* vol. II, p. 883.
[2] Bowman Memorandum of 10 December 1918: C. Seymour, *op. cit.* vol. IV, p. 291.

would be the best preparation for a new Sedan.'[1] If Poland was 'the linch-pin of the Treaty of Versailles' (Churchill), yet Balfour had earlier prophesied that, were she reconstituted, 'France would be at the mercy of Germany in the next war, for this reason, that Russia could not come to her aid without violating the neutrality of Poland'.[2] That, however, still rested with the future, as did the implications of Curzon's refusal now to pledge immediate British military aid to France if Germany should violate the demilitarised zone of the Rhineland. He admitted that the eastern frontier of France was 'in a sense the outer frontier of Great Britain herself', but refused to go beyond or undertake commitments in eastern Europe. France, deprived of her former Russian alliance, was left to seek such security as she could find in her traditional alternative, alliance with Poland (1921), and in association with the Little Entente, formed against Hungary in 1920-1 by Czechoslovakia, Roumania and Yugo-slavia. Italy's rivalry with France in central Europe and the Balkans was indicated by her tendency to support Hungary, Bulgaria and Albania against these powers. This rivalry was significantly reduced in scale from the pre-war antagonism between Austria-Hungary and Russia, but was also the forerunner of a graver division. Already in August 1922, two months before Mussolini inaugurated the fascist era in Italy, an Austrian statesman had put it to Lord D'Abernon, British ambassador in Berlin, that 'the real fact was that two incompatible alliances were fighting for the mastery in Central Europe: A North and South Alliance between Germany, Austria, and Italy. An East and West Alliance between France, Czecho-Slovakia, and Poland.'[3]

Britain viewed this French activity with a coolness verging on disfavour and there was ill-judged talk of a French domination of Europe: in fact the power of France was fragile. This was early suggested in the Near East, where the positions were rather reversed, Britain being the principal exponent of a forward policy. Britain at the peace conference, secure in her basic gains and dominant in Persia, indulged in two somewhat gratui-tous and emotional policies, both calculated to antagonise Muslim populations. The first was a modern edition of ancient Greek colonisation upon the Ionian shores: a Greek expedition to Smyrna, largely Hellenic in population, was promoted in May 1919 by Wilson, Lloyd George and Clemenceau in accord with Venizelos, the persuasive Greek premier; this was during Italian absence owing to Wilson's manifesto of 23 April, and in order to forestall a repetition at Smyrna of independent Italian

---

[1] *Documents relatifs aux négociations concernant les garanties de sécurité contre une agression de l'Allemagne, 10 janvier 1919–7 décembre 1923.* French Yellow Book of 1924, p. 92.

[2] Balfour in a conversation between Colonel House and Lloyd George, Balfour and Sir Edward Grey, 14 February 1916. Louis L. Gerson, *Woodrow Wilson and the Rebirth of Poland 1914–1920* (New Haven, 1953), pp. 27–8.

[3] Lord D'Abernon, *An Ambassador of Peace* (London, 1929–30), vol. II, p. 101.

landings at other points in the zone allotted her by the secret Agreement of Saint-Jean-de-Maurienne. This agreement of 1917 was a corollary, in respect of Italy's rights, to the Sykes–Picot Agreement, but its validity was held by her allies to have lapsed owing to the defection of Russia. An unlikely project for affording Italy compensation in the Caucasus was turned down by the government of the shrewd Nitti, who had succeeded Orlando in June 1919.

The second British policy was the constitution in biblical Palestine of a Jewish national home, after centuries of Jewish dispersion, in accordance with the Balfour Declaration of 2 November 1917. Britain's attempt in Palestine to reconcile her obligations to the Arabs and to the Jews is a long, sad and separate story. A related problem, too, was how to reconcile her obligations to the Arabs under the Hussein–McMahon correspondence of 1915–16 (see ch. IX) with those to the French under the Sykes–Picot Agreement, which was difficult since they were, in spirit at least, inconsistent. The French authorities wrongly suspected that their position in Syria was being disloyally undermined by the British, who in fact urged their Arab adherent, the Emir Feisal, to come to terms with them. In March 1920, however, Feisal defiantly assumed the title of King of Syria and Palestine and was expelled after France had, despite fierce Arab opposition, been designated as the mandatory for Syria at the allied Conference of San Remo on 25 April 1920. Then also British interests in Palestine and Mesopotamia emerged as mandates and an Anglo-French oil agreement was concluded, to be subsequently modified, however, in favour of the United States, which stood out for a share of the economic spoils of the Turkish empire, with which they had not been at war, by pressing the principle of the Open Door stipulated for mandatory regimes. Such was the delicate adjustment in the Near East of national ambitions with the new international idealism.

The renunciation by Turkey of her Arab territories and of her suzerainty over Egypt and Cyprus was notable as being among the lasting provisions of the impermanent Treaty of Sèvres whereby the Allies made peace with Turkey on 10 August 1920. The details of this treaty, which left the Turks in Constantinople and the Greeks in Smyrna, both contrary to Curzon's judgment, and of the accompanying agreement allocating French and Italian spheres of influence in Turkey, are perhaps of more interest in relation to the Eastern Question of the nineteenth century than to the peace settlement of the twentieth. For the treaty, delayed because the Allies waited upon the improbable event of America's deciding to assume a mandate for Constantinople or Armenia, remained unratified and stultified by the nationalist uprising which had meantime gathered momentum under Mustafa Kemal, largely impelled by the Greek occupation of Smyrna. This occupation was generally recognised at the time but never by its philhellenic champion, Lloyd George, to be a lamentable blunder.

The ascendant Kemal set up a nationalist government in Angora over against that of the moribund sultanate in Constantinople, and by the Franklin–Bouillon Agreement of October 1921 France concluded with the nationalists a new and separate peace agreement apart from Great Britain. France failed to comprehend, and therefore mistrusted, British motives in maintaining what Curzon himself called 'the precarious and as I think worthless alliance of the Greeks'.[1] France and Italy now favoured the Turkish nationalists who finally routed the Greeks and entered Smyrna early in September 1922. This victory in turn menaced the small allied forces still stationed upon the Asiatic shores of the Straits, a region where France and Italy habitually suspected British designs. They both withdrew their contingents from Chanak on 21 September 1922, leaving the British to make a stand alone. This they did with such fortunate effect that Mustafa Kemal agreed to a conference at Mudania on 3 October 1922, the prelude to peace negotiations at Lausanne.

Lloyd George's eastern policy brought disaster to his favourite Greeks and an end to his own government on 19 October 1922. Curzon, however, remained as foreign secretary in the conservative government of Bonar Law and, despite French intrigue, retrieved Britain's position by a personal triumph at the Lausanne Conference. As regards the two main British interests, satisfactory solutions were reached over the Straits and, eventually, Mosul. Thus by the Treaty of Lausanne of 24 July 1923 Britain after all came off at least as well in the Turkish settlement as did France or Italy.

The series of Anglo-French squabbles in those post-war years seemed almost to justify Paul Cambon when he wrote at the close of his twenty-years embassy for France in London: 'I do not believe in the possibility of a rupture but everywhere, on every point, there is disagreement and the misfortune is that neither in Paris nor in London are they intelligent enough to reduce the disagreements to the essential points and disregard the trifles. It is easier to settle the big questions than the baubles. But men like Curzon or Leygues only care about the baubles.'[2] Certainly personalities played a part as always. The French came to distrust Lloyd George as being too pro-German and pro-Russian, and the British were alienated by the ungenerous legalism of Poincaré, French prime minister from January 1922 till June 1924. But these rubs were indications of a deeper psychological divergence which made the really big question, the treatment of Germany, not at all easy to solve. Briefly, Briand, prime minister between Leygues and Poincaré, spoke for war-scarred France in declaring (21 November 1921) that she could not disarm physically

---

[1] Letter to Austen Chamberlain, 27 September 1922. The Earl of Ronaldshay, *The Life of Lord Curzon* (London, 1928), vol. III, p. 305.
[2] Letter to his son, 14 October 1920. Paul Cambon, *Correspondance 1870–1924* (Paris, 1940 f.), vol. III, p. 386.

till Germany disarmed morally; whereas British statesmen sought a more cordial security through German goodwill by favouring her rehabilitation. They were impelled thereto by motives psychological, the British being poor haters, political, being afraid of Russia, and economic, seeking to stimulate that world trade which was Britain's mainstay. Time alone could, and did, demonstrate which thesis was the more nearly correct.

This divergence was thrown into relief by episodes in the execution of the peace treaty, as in Upper Silesia, and especially by the negotiations concerning reparation at the series of allied conferences which distinguished the period 1920–2. Germany did not help Britain to help her. Her representatives created a bad impression upon their first appearance at the Conference of Spa in July 1920 with inadequate proposals regarding reparation backed by a most offensive speech by Stinnes, the German coal magnate; and again on 1 March 1921 at the London Conference they proposed 'indefensible' terms (D'Abernon), rejected the demands of the incensed Allies, and consequently provoked an extension of the Allied occupation to Düsseldorf, Duisburg and Ruhrort on 8 March, a sanction of marginal legality under the treaty. On 27 April 1921 the Reparation Commission announced its decision fixing Germany's total liability for reparation at the severe figure of £6600 million. Also it found that as regards the initial £1000 million (20,000 million gold marks) which Germany was bound to pay by 1 May 1921, she was in default by at least 12,000 million marks. On 5 May the allied governments communicated to Germany a 'schedule of payments' prescribing methods for discharging her obligations which in practice mitigated them, but included a demand for the payment of £50 million (one milliard marks) by the end of the month; a covering ultimatum stated that if a satisfactory reply were not made within six days, the Allies would on 12 May occupy the Ruhr. After a governmental crisis in Germany, Wirth's administration accepted the Allied terms on 11 May, and had by August paid the first milliard marks, Germany's first cash payment. In these critical events allied unity had been maintained, but so precariously as to promise ill for further strains ahead.

It was increasingly borne in upon allied statesmen that the question of German reparation was closely related to that of allied debts. They had been sharply warned off this delicate ground by the American Treasury in March 1919, but that July House wrote to Wilson in a prescient letter on Anglo-American relations: 'Do you not think also that our people should be warned not to expect complete payment of loans to the Entente? Should they not be asked to consider a large share of these loans as a part of our necessary war expenditures, and should not an adjustment be suggested by us and not by our debtors?'[1] Wilson did not think so. Nor did Congress, which in February 1922 appointed a World War Foreign

[1] *The Paris Peace Conference 1919*, vol. XI, p. 623.

Debt Commission to collect the allied debts by 1947 and impose a rate of interest not less than 4¼ per cent. Here the case of Britain was a special one, as being both debtor and creditor. For after America had entered the war she took over the traditional British position as banker of the alliance and Britain acted as broker for her European allies, contracting heavy debts in the United States, largely on their behalf. The Balfour Note of 1 August 1922 to the allied powers reminded them that, exclusive of interest, they together owed Great Britain about £1300 million, in addition to the £650 million due to her from Russia and £1450 million as German reparation; for her part Great Britain owed £850 million to the United States. The note explained that American insistence upon payment compelled Britain to abandon her previous policy of refraining from asking for any allied payments to her; the British government would nevertheless still prefer to remit all allied war debts due to it, and the British share of repartion, as part of an all-round cancellation of war-indebtedness in 'one great transaction'. This statesmanlike proposal got a bad reception. The linking of war debts with reparations was opposed, for different reasons, both by the French and by the Americans, whose materialistic mood was reflected in President Coolidge's remark, 'They hired the money, didn't they?' The British government accordingly sent Stanley Baldwin and Montagu Norman, governor of the Bank of England, to Washington, where the American negotiators imposed such stringent terms that the British premier, Bonar Law, nearly resigned rather than accept them. Overborne, however, by considerations of party loyalty, he acquiesced. The British funded debt was fixed at 4600 million dollars repayable over sixty-two years and subject to an average rate of 3⅓ per cent interest.

France had been a main beneficiary from the American loans which Britain was required to repay but Poincaré resented her trying to pass on the pinch. It added to the resentment which France already felt at being denied any priority of reparation for her devastated regions: their reconstruction, plus war-pensions, was costing the French government half of its total yearly expenditure. In this heavy situation Poincaré was determined to secure 'productive pledges' from Germany, where inflation was mounting during 1922 and the government applying for, and partially obtaining, a moratorium on reparations. Productive guarantees chiefly meant for Poincaré the long-contemplated occupation of the Ruhr. At the end of December 1922 the Reparation Commission, by a vote of the French, Italian and Belgian representatives against the vigorous protest of the British, Sir John Bradbury, declared Germany in default on an insignificant delivery of timber, and on 9 January 1923, under the same conditions, declared a default in coal deliveries. Two days later French and Belgian forces marched into the Ruhr.

Bradbury had in the preceding August, as D'Abernon noted, gone 'out of his way to tell the Germans that, in the event of France taking isolated action, England would not interfere, but would adopt an attitude of "surly neutrality". The phrase has stuck in the German mind.'[1] It was a forecast as accurate as it was impolitic. With no united front against them, the German government ordered passive resistance in the Ruhr. This measure created dislocation and severely hampered the French in their attempt to draw economic benefit from an occupation which they compromised politically by fostering the separatist movement, by then weak, in the Rhineland, and by imprisoning local industrialists, who preferred inflation to providing reparation. The French, however, reckoned that they extracted over 1300 million francs from Germany that year while the German government's recklessly defiant subsidising of idle hands in the Ruhr sent inflation rocketing, with values gone crazy with noughts—4,200,000,000,000 marks to the dollar at the peak in November 1923. This, more than 1918, was the true social revolution in Germany. But events were already on the turn. That November also witnessed the failure in Munich of Hitler's national-socialist coup, the climax of a year of extremist disturbance in Germany. Already on 27 September the ruinous policy of passive resistance had been abandoned by the new German government under Stresemann, formerly an intense nationalist, now a secret romantic with an unusual sense of practical moderation. By the end of November the Schacht–Luther financial reforms had already begun a feat of rapid recovery almost as remarkable as the inflation itself, and on 30 November the French government agreed to participate in an expert inquiry, favoured by the other allied governments and by the United States, into the central question of Germany's capacity to pay reparation.

The inquiry was presided over by the American General Dawes and on 9 April 1924 it presented its report, known as the Dawes Plan. French delay in evacuating the Ruhr levered Germany into accepting the plan, and its adoption by France was facilitated by Herriot's succeeding Poincaré on 1 June. The resultant agreement between Germany and the Allies was signed in London on 16 August. The Dawes Plan was based upon the interrelated prerequisites of a balanced budget and a stabilised currency in Germany, the bank of issue being free from governmental control but subjected to supervision to protect foreign interests. The system of supervision was agreeable to France, less so the accompanying demotion of the Reparation Commission. By a similar adjustment, while the theoretical total of reparation due remained unaltered, Germany was in practice to pay on a much more moderate scale rising in five years from £50 million to the standard rate of £125 million, with special provision for the transfers to be operated by the recipients as a safeguard against a collapse of the exchange. In order to tide Germany over, a foreign loan of 800 million gold marks was raised, mostly in America. Foreign, especially American, capital was pumped into Germany, so that during

[1] Lord D'Abernon, *op. cit.* vol. II, p. 91.

the period 1924–8 she achieved an insecure prosperity and punctually discharged her obligations under the Dawes Plan. This seemingly satisfactory solution thus represented a financial roundabout whereby America lent to Germany who paid reparation to the European Allies who repaid debts to America. Such was the tangled legacy of war in which the nations had got caught up.

The Dawes Plan, however, marked the end of the worst of the post-war hangover. In 1925 European primary production first surpassed the level of 1913. Politically, the prospect of overcoming the frustration of Anglo-French friction was improved in October 1924 when the Francophil Austen Chamberlain became British Foreign Secretary in Baldwin's new conservative government. That government rejected, indeed, the Geneva Protocol which its Labour predecessor had helped to elaborate (see ch. XVII), but there was a swift demonstration of the beneficial effects of Anglo-French collaboration, in the interests of which Chamberlain revived the idea of a defensive alliance. Stresemann, who directed Germany's foreign policy from 1923 to 1929, perceived that 'a security agreement without Germany would have been a security agreement against Germany'.[1] On 9 February 1925 the German government presented to the French government a memorandum suggesting a pact for a considerable period between the powers interested in the Rhine, especially England, France, Italy and Germany, whereby they would undertake not to make war upon one another. This was a revised revival of an abortive proposal made by the German Chancellor Cuno in December 1922, and it was now blended with that of an Anglo-French alliance to constitute the Locarno Treaty of Mutual Guarantee, concluded together with pendant arrangements on 16 October 1925. By this treaty Britain, France, Italy, Germany and Belgium severally and collectively guaranteed the western frontier of Germany and the provisions of Versailles concerning the demilitarised zone. This agreement morally strengthened the peace settlement of 1919, since Germany now freely underwrote its attribution of Alsace-Lorraine, Eupen-Malmédy and the disarmed Rhineland, but materially weakened it since, in accordance with Stresemann's design, it circumscribed its military enforcement. Western Europe emerged for a space into 'the pale sunlight of Locarno' (Churchill).

The Pact of Locarno was to enter into force when Germany entered the League of Nations, which she did on 10 September 1926. A week later Stresemann and Briand lunched privately at a little hostelry with first-rate cooking at Thoiry near Geneva, and there waxed expansive over Stresemann's favourite theme of Franco-German economic collaboration, even, according to him, projecting it into Russia. Stresemann probed towards further relaxations of the Treaty of Versailles in return for German

[1] Note by Stresemann, 1 July 1925. Eric Sutton, *Gustav Stresemann, his diaries, letters, and papers* (London, 1935–40), vol. II, p. 98.

bolstering of the French economy. This did not commend itself, though, either to Schacht, the power of the Reichsbank, or to American interests.

American initiative, however, encouraged Briand towards a notable achievement in another direction. In 1927 he communicated to Kellogg, the American Secretary of State, a draft treaty for the renunciation of war between their two countries. After waiting six months to reply, Kellogg suggested in December that the proposed treaty be made multilateral. The outcome was the Pact of Paris or Kellogg Pact of 27 August 1928, whereby fifteen powers renounced war as an instrument of national policy, subject to some limited reservations, Great Britain for instance entering one concerning 'certain regions' in which she was vitally interested— a pointer towards the Suez Canal. By 1933 sixty-five nations had subscribed to this well-intentioned if somewhat indefinite undertaking.

These events illustrated the anxious preoccupation of the powers with regard to security in the aftermath of the war to end war. At the centre of the problem of security lay that of disarmament. Reparation and disarmament were the two main long-term obligations of Germany under the Treaty of Versailles, and the supervision of their fulfilment, respectively through the Reparation Commission and the Control Commissions working under the Conference of Ambassadors in Paris, was in the forefront of the policy of the Allies. In disarming Germany they had to reckon above all with General von Seeckt, a brilliant Prussian staff-officer, cultivated and withdrawn. Chief of the German army directorate (*Chef der Heeresleitung*) since the second quarter of 1920, Seeckt had begun by instructing commanders to cease measures for reducing the German army to the stipulated strength of 100,000 men since the German government were opposed to it. Seeckt, however, failed to induce the Allies at the Conference of Spa to permit double that number and eventually the reduction was effected, at least on paper. For Seeckt emulated Scharnhorst's subterfuge after Jena when he had secretly reconstituted the Prussian army in defiance of Napoleonic disarmament. Volunteers were rapidly passed through the army despite the limitation of enlistments to regulars for a twelve-year period under article 174. The recruitment of the so-called Black Reichswehr embraced the development of paramilitary organisations such as the Einwohnerwehr and Arbeitskommandos in violation of article 177 of the treaty. This was matched by illegal militarisation of the police, who were, indeed, liable to be especially important for maintaining internal order if military disarmament had been scrupulously observed, rather than evaded. Any loophole in the treaty was in fact ingeniously exploited: for instance, while it limited the number of officers to 4000, it omitted to do likewise for non-commissioned officers, who were accordingly increased out of all proportion to the needs of a small army in accordance with Seeckt's aim of building up a military elite (*Führerheer*). Similarly, at the top, the general staff, prohibited by article 160, was maintained under a rich variety of subterfuges and engaged in equally forbidden activities such as plans for general mobilisation (violation of article 178) and for promoting military aviation, prohibited by article 198. Stocks of arms due for surrender were often hidden and the work of the allied control commissions generally rendered difficult and unpleasant. Graver still, the German army was trained in the use of forbidden weapons such as armoured cars and tanks, Seeckt being a far-sighted exponent of mobile warfare. Nor were manœuvres with dummy guns and cardboard tanks a smiling matter when directed by the author of the grim definition: 'Warlike is meant not in the sense of the imitation of war, but in that of a preparation for a war.'[1]

By all-round evasion and violation of the treaty Seeckt created not a small army but a great army in miniature, its danger lying in its potentialities. Here considerations both psychological and economic entered in. Seeckt was determined to combat 'moral disarmament', of which, already in March 1922, D'Abernon, a good friend of Germany, wrote in Berlin: 'I not only doubt the existence of this at the present moment, but its bare possibility at any date. No one that I have met here would think a successful war morally reprehensible.'[2] On the economic side Seeckt perceived that what mattered was less the accumulation of obsolescent armaments than the co-ordination of manufacturing potential for military requirements. Here he secured the backing of Chancellor Wirth, who secretly subsidised the Krupp armament enterprise. That formidable concern concluded a formal agreement on 25 January 1922 with the German ministry of defence 'jointly to circumvent...the provisions of the Treaty of Versailles'.[3] This activity was extended abroad, beyond allied reach. By 1925 Krupp held a controlling interest in the Bofors arms-works in Sweden, and was projecting the latest thing in heavy guns and tanks. German submarines were secretly built and crews trained in Holland, Spain and Finland. Even before the Russo-German treaty of Rapallo in 1922 (see ch. xiv) there were afoot clandestine arrangements foreshadowing the development in the Soviet Union of German artillery, tanks at Kasan, poison-gas at Saratov, and at Lipezk airbase fighters and dive-bombers. Training extended to staff-courses with Soviet officers. Seeckt considered that resurgent Germany should especially work with Russia, to destroy Poland. So did Wirth. He told Brockdorff-Rantzau, setting out after Rapallo as German ambassador to Moscow: 'Poland must be disposed of. My policy is set towards this goal....It is....with my agreement that many things, too, have happened relative to the eastern frontier which are known only to a few besides

---

[1] General von Seeckt. Cited, General Friedrich von Rabenau, *Seeckt: aus seinem Leben 1918–1936* (Leipzig, 1940), p. 503.

[2] Lord D'Abernon, *op. cit.* vol. I, p. 279.

[3] Cited, Gordon A. Craig, *The Politics of the Prussian Army 1640–1945* (Oxford, 1955), p. 406.

myself. On this point I am in complete agreement with the military, especially with General von Seeckt.'[1]

In these views Seeckt, probably the most considerable soldier of the 1920's, was not, however, at one with their most eminent statesman, Stresemann, whose name stamped the pacific period of fulfilment and Locarno. Yet the divergence was rather less than might appear. Stresemann was aware of Seeckt's illicit rearmament, notably in Russia, and lied to D'Abernon in order to shield it. Pacific Stresemann was, though, in that in the time of German weakness he aimed at achieving his policy without war; but it was deep policy, deep and wide. It embraced 'the protection of Germans abroad, those 10 to 12 millions of our kindred who now live under a foreign yoke in foreign lands'.[2] In this connection Stresemann held as regards the South Tyrol, for instance, that 'the German qualities of Walther von der Vogelweide bear witness that Bozen (Bolzano) is within the German cultural community'.[3] Stresemann aimed at regaining Eupen from Belgium, and for him 'the recovery of the German colonies is an object, and a very present object, of German policy'.[4] For him too, moreover, a principal objective was 'the readjustment of our eastern frontiers; the recovery of Danzig, the Polish corridor, and a correction of the frontier in Upper Silesia'.[5] In negotiating the pact of Locarno Stresemann was able to exploit Britain's standing refusal to underwrite French commitments in eastern Europe; he resisted all French attempts to secure in favour of her allies there a German undertaking 'to abstain from any attack. This obligation we undertook in the West, but we refused it in the East. Membership of the League does not exclude the possibility of war.'[6] D'Abernon's earlier suggestion to Stresemann of a 'reciprocal iron curtain'[7] between Germany and France in the Rhineland began to assume an ominous significance, and Stresemann saw 'in Locarno the preservation of the Rhineland, and the possibility of the recovery of German territory in the East'.[8] The settlement, as so often in German foreign policy, wore a two-faced aspect, fair to west, grim to east. There France's weakened position despite significant new treaties with Poland and Czechoslovakia was emphasised not only by Stresemann's ugly gibes at those two countries but also by the further Russo-German treaty of friendship signed at Berlin on 24 April 1926. It was in pursuance of this

[1] Cited, Herbert Helbig, 'Die Moskauer Mission des Grafen Brockdorff-Rantzau', in *Forschungen zur Osteuropäischen Geschichte* (ed. H. Jablonowski and W. Philipp; Berlin, 1954 f.), vol. II, p. 306.
[2] Letter from Stresemann to the former German Crown Prince, 7 September 1925. Eric Sutton, *op. cit.* vol. II, p. 503.
[3] Speech in the Reichstag, 9 February 1926; *ibid.* vol. II, p. 454.
[4] Speech of 29 August 1925; *ibid.* vol. II, p. 314.
[5] Letter to the former Crown Prince, *ibid.* vol. II, p. 503.
[6] Speech of 14 December 1925; *ibid.* vol. II, p. 217.
[7] Lord D'Abernon, *op. cit.* vol. III, p. 101.
[8] Letter to Dr von Keudell, 27 November 1925. Eric Sutton, *op. cit.* vol. II, pp. 231–2.

'fierce friendship' (Lloyd George) that Stresemann at Locarno had secured a critical weakening of article 16 of the Covenant of the League of Nations.

Stresemann, who exploited diplomatically the nationalist opposition against him in the German parliament, crowned his success against France at Locarno by presenting it as a concession to the Allies in return for which they adopted favourable 'reactions' towards Germany, notably by evacuating the Cologne zone by 31 January 1926. This first instalment of the evacuation of the Rhineland had been refused by the Allies the year before owing to 'the numerous defaults of the German government'[1] as regards disarmament. During 1926 the Allied Military Control Commission rendered a final report which indicated persistent German bad faith in refusing to disarm. This report now jarred upon official optimism and was weakly discounted by the allied governments. Their control commission was withdrawn by 31 January 1927 despite the fact that only a fortnight earlier the new British ambassador in Berlin, Sir Ronald Lindsay, had expressed to Stresemann his 'fears that there was still a strong spirit of militarism and revenge in Germany'.[2] In 1928 the German cabinet specifically endorsed illicit German rearmament. By the Hague Agreement of August 1929, Stresemann's last big achievement before his death that October, the Allies undertook to complete the evacuation of the whole of the Rhineland by 30 June 1930. This evacuation was related to the adoption of the short-lived Young Plan whereby Germany's obligations for reparation were further reduced below those which she had assumed under the Dawes Plan with an eye to promoting the French evacuation of the Ruhr. Such was the outstanding success of Stresemann's policy of 'driving France back from trench to trench, as I once expressed it, since no general attack is feasible'.[3]

Germany pressed her 'peace offensive' (Stresemann) wherever she saw an opening, as in the preamble to Part V of the Treaty of Versailles wherein the disarmament of Germany was imposed 'in order to render possible the initiation of a general limitation of the armaments of all nations'. This, and a gloss upon it in the allied reply of 16 June 1919 to the Germans, did not lay a contractual obligation upon the Allies to disarm, as German propaganda tried to make out, but they did constitute a moral obligation. This moral obligation was cancelled by German measures of rearmament in violation of the treaty. The victorious powers nevertheless displayed a well-intentioned desire to work towards general disarmament. At first this desire was, however, mainly manifest in the field which least affected Germany, the naval. The central issue here was Anglo-American competition since during the war the United States had been building their navy up towards British strength and had, during the

---

[1] *Note presented to the German Government by the British, French, Italian, Japanese and Belgian Ambassadors at Berlin, 4 June, 1925.* Cmd. 2429 of 1925, p. 3.
[2] Note by Stresemann, 15 January 1927. Eric Sutton, *op. cit.* vol. III, p. 105.
[3] Letter to Lieut.-General von Schoch, 27 July 1925, Sutton, *op. cit.* vol. II, p. 58.

peace conference, disregarded British representations against continuing construction. American preoccupation with Japan in this connection was evident at the Washington Conference of naval powers in 1921–2 which achieved both a political settlement in the Far East, where the Anglo-Japanese alliance was terminated in deference to American and Dominion wishes (see ch. xv), and an important agreement limiting naval armaments, signed on 6 February 1922. This pointed to the end of the naval supremacy of the Pax Britannica, gracefully accepted by a poorer, less ardent Britain, imaginatively exploited by the rival thrust of America. The agreement fixed a ratio in total tonnages for American, British, Japanese, French and Italian capital ships (see ch. xv), prescribed a ten-year naval holiday in their construction, and limited their size along with total tonnages for aircraft-carriers; but it failed to secure any limitation by ratio for submarines, light cruisers and auxiliaries, chiefly owing to French obstruction which further strained Anglo-French relations. Anglo-American dissension, however, frustrated another attempt to reach agreement with the Japanese in these last categories at a naval conference in Geneva in the summer of 1927. A further naval conference was opened in London in January 1930 and after intricate negotiation produced on 22 April a three-power agreement between Great Britain, the United States and Japan whereby Japan had the right to build up to 70 per cent of British and American tonnage in cruisers and destroyers, with parity at a low level in submarines. Franco-Italian rivalry in the Mediterranean defeated all efforts to include those powers in this agreement, and indicated the limitations to the considerable success achieved in naval disarmament. Another indication was the contemporary construction by Germany of the first 'pocket battleship', ingeniously designed to conform to the letter of the 10,000-ton limit imposed by the peace treaty while defeating its object by its unorthodox and powerful armament.

Military and aeronautical disarmament was more difficult to achieve than naval, both intrinsically and in its special relation to the problem of Germany. The protracted negotiations within the framework of the League of Nations which began with the appointment of the preparatory commission on disarmament in 1925 issued in a disarmament conference which opened at Geneva on 2 February 1932 (see ch. xvii). The success of this conference was ominously prejudiced from the start by Japanese aggression in Manchuria and in the end by the aggressive ascendancy of national-socialism in Germany.

The strength of the Nazi party jumped up in the elections of September 1930 from 800,000 votes to 6½ millions, to a peak of 13¾ millions in July 1932. Behind this phenomenon loomed the American slump on Wall Street in October 1929, the month that Stresemann died, and the ensuing economic blizzard which swept across Europe in renewed proof of the dependence of the old world upon the riches of the new. Swept away was the Young Plan of the preceding summer. The withdrawal of American credits revealed the insecurity of the German economy. The Austrian finances, in which German banks were closely interested, were apt to be delicate at the best of times, and in March 1931 the German government of Brüning tried to combine a bolstering of both economies together with a bold stroke of foreign policy by the surprise announcement of agreement to establish an Austro-German customs union. The project had to be dropped in the face of Anglo-French opposition. On 11 May 1931 the largest Austrian bank, the Credit-Anstalt, failed and precipitated the 'crisis within the crisis'. This spread across Germany to England where the Labour government fell and the pound was forced off the gold standard on 21 September. Already in July the main European powers had, after some haggling by France who had built up much the largest gold reserve after America, accepted President Hoover's timely proposal for a one-year moratorium on all payments of reparation and war-debts. In June 1932 a conference met at Lausanne to consider the situation upon the expiry of the Hoover Moratorium. There Von Papen's 'Cabinet of Barons', which had just succeeded that of Brüning, secured an important success for Germany whereby reparation was at last abolished, subject to German delivery of bonds to the amount of £150 million. A 'gentleman's agreement' reached on 2 July by Germany's creditors made ratification of this settlement contingent upon a satisfactory settlement between them and their creditors, namely the United States. But America refused to cancel or reduce allied war-debts and squashed the expedient adopted by Britain in 1933 of making token payments only. Thereafter the British government joined the French and others in defaulting on its payments, refusing, in effect, that the financial burden of the first world war should be inequitably shifted from Germany, no longer paying reparation, to the European Allies. And indeed even when Germany was paying reparation she had paid in practice not from her own substance and sacrifice, but from her loans and investments from abroad which amounted up to 1931 to some 35–8 milliard marks as against the total of 21 milliards which she had paid to the Allies during the same period according to the books of the Reparation Commission. Such was the sterile yield of a peace settlement which, after first applying the sanction of military intervention to enforcing reparation rather than disarmament, had come to rely, in the financial field even more than in others, upon the accommodating application of stringent terms instead of the reverse.

In the face of the economic blizzard the European powers huddled away from the expansive internationalism of the 'twenties, last manifest in Briand's plan for European union, into national economics behind tariff barriers, especially after America introduced the very stiff Hawley–Smoot tariff in 1929–30. This frustrated the conference which met at Geneva in February 1930 to devise a tariff truce. The era of free trade was finishing;

and, in totalitarian nations, the era of free thought. They were now joined by Germany who, in the time of economic stress, turned to a creed which transcended economics, transformed politics and came to smash the settlement of Versailles.

Thus was the peace settlement after the first world war largely undermined in three waves, successive but overlapping, political, economic and psychological. Almost from the beginning it was compromised politically not only by errors of judgment which the peacemakers made at times in framing a very complex whole, but even more by the power-vacuum left, to German advantage, by the collapse of the Austro-Hungarian and Russian empires upon the one hand and by the falling away of the United States upon the other: a void too great to fill by the hopeful innovation of the League of Nations. This political insecurity was sharply accentuated in the 'twenties by economic crises of quite unforeseen extent, first the German inflation, the greatest in history, and then the world-wide slump. These not only vitiated the whole structure of German reparation and Allied war-debts but also demonstrated that, with the economic balance now tilted towards America in what was possibly the greatest shift of geopolitical stress since its discovery four centuries before, the victorious powers had failed to achieve an economic ordering of international relations which would afford stability to liberal societies in the twentieth-century phase of industrial capitalism. The 'thirties in turn demonstrated that the maintenance of the peace settlement was gravely menaced by unexpected phenomena not only economic but also psychological, ideological. The aftermath of the war to make the world safe for democracy witnessed a retreat from its liberalism into communism in Russia, into fascism in Italy and, most promptly disruptive, into national-socialism in Germany. Wilson, who had sought to make the Treaty of Versailles the palladium of international democracy, had intended that it should subject the Germans to 'a generation of thoughtfulness'.[1] But with many of them their thoughts turned largely inwards, obscure and festering, less to repentance than to revenge. And whereas the allied victors mainly came to look to politicians of rather ordinary capacity, the German vanquished found a leader of deep and evil inspiration. His mouthpiece proclaimed in advance (April 1928):

> We enter parliament in order to supply ourselves in the arsenal of democracy with its own weapons. We are becoming deputies in order to paralyse the Weimar sentiment with its own assistance. If democracy is so stupid as to give us free tickets and salaries for this purpose, that is its own affair....We come as enemies! As the wolf bursts into the flock, so we come.[2]

So they came. On 30 January 1933 Adolf Hitler became Chancellor of Germany, of the Third German Empire.

[1] Meeting of Council of Ten, 12 February 1919. *The Paris Peace Conference 1919*, vol. III, p. 1002.　　[2] Dr Joseph Goebbels, *Der Angriff* (Munich, 1935), pp. 71–3.

CHAPTER XVII

THE LEAGUE OF NATIONS

THE Covenant of the League of Nations formed Part I of each of the treaties of peace concluded after the first world war, and when the first of these, the Treaty of Versailles, entered into force on 10 January 1920, the League began to exist. The incorporation of the Covenant in the treaties was a point on which President Wilson had strongly insisted at the peace conference; he looked to the League as a means whereby injustices and imperfections in the treaties would at some future time be corrected, and he probably foresaw that if the making of the League were postponed until after the treaties came into force there would almost certainly be no League at all. For the League this course had both disadvantages and advantages. On the one hand it led to the League's sharing in the unpopularity which assailed the peace treaties, for it could be represented by hostile or ignorant critics as merely an instrument which the victors had devised in order to rivet on the vanquished the injustices of the settlement. On the other hand the treaties had many provisions to which effect could only be given by a continuing organisation such as the League was intended to be, and by using the League for this purpose they ensured that it would at once be called on to play a part in great affairs and not be relegated to the obscurity to which, as Wilson had reason to suspect, some of his colleagues would have liked to consign it.

The drafting committee at the peace conference worked on the basis of a draft prepared by Mr Cecil Hurst and Mr David Hunter Miller, and under Wilson's forceful chairmanship it accepted the main lines of this without engaging in any preliminary discussion of the fundamental principles on which the new organisation was to be founded. Thus from the outset it was inevitable that the finished Covenant would reflect British and American rather than continental ideas, and though both the French and the Italians produced drafts, they received practically no consideration. The League emerged from the committee possessed of no powers which could be described as supra-national or even in a strict sense governmental, with little more than the bare outlines of a constitution and free therefore to develop as experience might direct. But its fundamental character had been determined in accordance with the Anglo-American view. It was to be an association of separate states, each retaining its sovereignty, but each pledging itself to co-operate with the others for certain purposes. The core of the Covenant lay in these undertakings which each of the members had given to the others that it would act or refrain from acting in certain specified ways, and everything would

475

depend upon their ability and willingness to honour their word. The institutions of the League were more in the nature of machinery designed to make it as easy as possible for the members to agree and act together than organs through which corporate action was to be taken, and 'the League' itself was little more than a name serving to describe the members collectively. It was clear too that the League would be an association more political than juridical in character, more in the tradition of the Concert of Europe, which, as the founders of the League believed, had served Europe well in the nineteenth century, than in that of the Hague Conferences, the work of which had counted for practically nothing in the war just ended. British opinion in particular hoped to find in the League an organisation in which the great powers would meet regularly and whenever an emergency made it desirable for them to confer, but in which the membership and the functions would no longer be limited to Europe: they would be served by a permanent secretariat, and they would accept some measure of accountability to the rest of the world.

The original members of the League were the signatories of the treaties of peace and a few other states invited in the treaties to accede to the Covenant. There was to be an Assembly in which all the members were represented, a Council, and a Secretariat in which Sir Eric Drummond was to be the first Secretary-General. Under the Hurst–Miller draft the Council should have consisted of representatives of the great powers only, but in deference to the strong opposition of the smaller powers it was decided that while the great powers should be permanent members the Assembly should elect four others from time to time, and the number of these non-permanent members was progressively raised to eleven. A few functions were specifically assigned respectively to the Assembly or the Council, but the Covenant did not define their relations, and either of them was authorised to deal with 'any matter within the sphere of action of the League or affecting the peace of the world'. This lack of differentiation was typical of the absence of rigidity in the Covenant as a whole, and it led to no inconvenient results. The Assembly, contrary probably to the expectations of the founders, became the dominant organ, partly because it was able to secure control of the budget; it provided something wholly new in the intercourse of states and only possible in an atmosphere of courtesy and restraint such as normally prevailed at Geneva, a forum in which the smaller powers were free to criticise the great and the great did not refuse to explain and justify their conduct before the world. The Council, being a smaller body, meeting more frequently and therefore better able to act promptly, came to serve as a sort of executive committee of the Assembly, working out the details and supervising the execution of policies which the Assembly had accepted in principle. In conformity with the ordinary rule of international conferences the decisions of either body had normally to be unanimous, but this rule was subject to certain exceptions of which the most important were that matters of procedure might be decided by a majority, and that when a dispute was under consideration the votes of the parties were not counted. This rule of unanimity, however, had less influence on the practical working of the League than is sometimes supposed; it was mitigated by the acceptance of certain conventions which had the effect of making it difficult for a small minority to persist in opposition, and by the fact that, as already mentioned, the effective working of the League depended less on the ability of its organs to reach decisions than on the fulfilment by each member of its own particular obligations. The effect was not to create a right of veto making it possible for any dissenting member to bring the action of the League to a standstill, but rather to safeguard the independence of the members and the co-operative basis of their association by ensuring that rights and obligations could not be varied without their own consent.

The Secretariat was the most original element in the constitution of the League. The previous practice of international conferences had usually been to rely for secretarial assistance on officials temporarily assigned to the work by the participating states, and the disadvantages of this method are obvious; it gave little chance for the development of a sense of corporate responsibility, and it left no machinery in being to give effect to the decisions of the conference. Sir Eric Drummond decided at the outset that the Secretariat of the League should follow a different plan; it was not to consist of national delegates, but of international servants whose first loyalty should be to the League. That ideal could not always be completely realised. It was not practicable, nor perhaps even desirable, always to treat questions of nationality as irrelevant in such matters as the recruitment of the members or the allocation of posts within the Secretariat, and some governments, especially after the rise of totalitarianism, sought to undermine the independence of the members by pressure which it was virtually impossible to resist. None the less, it is for its success rather than for its partial failure that this first experiment in the construction of a truly international civil service is chiefly remarkable.

The Council was directed by Article XIV of the Covenant to formulate plans for the establishment of a Permanent Court of International Justice, and one of its first acts was to set up a committee of jurists to advise it on this matter. The committee prepared a draft which the Assembly accepted as the basis of the statute of the court, and the court came into existence in the latter part of 1921. Its jurisdiction comprised 'all cases which the parties refer to it and all matters specially provided for in treaties and conventions in force'. Submission of disputes to the court was therefore voluntary, but the statute contained a provision, the so-called 'Optional Clause', by accepting which the members might, if they chose, recognise the jurisdiction as compulsory in the classes of disputes enumerated in the clause. As confidence in the court grew, after a few years' experience, this clause was widely accepted, though acceptances were often accompanied by reservations which seriously reduced their value. The court was in effect the judicial organ of the League and there were constitutional links between them. The judges were elected by the Assembly and the Council; the expenses of the court were borne on the League budget; and besides its jurisdiction in contentious cases it was empowered to give an advisory opinion on any dispute or question referred to it by the Assembly or the Council. These links, however, never impaired the complete judicial independence of the court.

Another autonomous body in the League was the International Labour Organisation established by a special chapter of the peace treaties to further the improvement of conditions of labour by international action. It comprised (a) a General Conference consisting of four representatives of each member, two being government delegates, and two, representing employers and work-people respectively, chosen by governments in agreement with industrial organisations in their respective countries. Its functions were the making of recommendations for national legislation and the preparation of draft conventions requiring to be ratified by states before taking effect; (b) an International Labour Office, which was the secretariat of the organisation and was controlled by a governing body consisting of twelve government, six employers' and six work-people's representatives. Expenses were paid out of League funds, and membership of the League carried membership of the organisation, though non-League members might also be elected. It was happily shielded by the nature of its work from the political storms which the main body of the League had to meet.

The League had two great purposes: the achievement of international peace and security through collective action, and the promotion of international co-operation in matters of general social and economic welfare. The second of these was an afterthought, in part inspired by the thought that the problem of war might be attacked indirectly as well as directly by eliminating some of the causes of friction that make wars more probable, and it owed much to a famous pamphlet of General Smuts, *The League of Nations: A Practical Suggestion*, in which he urged that the League should be 'a great organ of the ordinary peaceful life of civilisation, part and parcel of the common life of states'. For its original and paramount purpose of creating a system of collective security the Covenant brought together, without fusing into a single coherent plan, a number of differing lines of thought which were derived from various preliminary drafts, official and unofficial, of the Covenant. The arrangement was almost haphazard, but in the result it had the advantage of providing the League with a choice of alternative procedures for dealing with the cases brought before it which often proved useful. Three main ideas can be distinguished. (1) The League was to be a system of mutual guarantee. This was the

478

effect of Article X in which the members undertook 'to respect and preserve as against external aggression the territorial integrity and existing
political independence of all members of the League'. President Wilson
regarded this article as the very core of the Covenant, and it was mainly
because he refused to accept any compromise on it that he failed to induce
the American Senate to accept the League. Actually, partly because of
ambiguities in the drafting which made it doubtful whether it did more
than assert a principle without creating a definite obligation, the article
never played more than a secondary part in the work of the League.
(2) The League was to act as a commission of conciliation. This was its
function under Article XI which provided that 'any war or threat of war'
was to be a 'matter of concern to the whole League' which was to take
'any action that may be deemed wise and effectual to safeguard the peace
of nations'. This article, which passed through the drafting committee
with very little discussion, proved unexpectedly important, and in the
early years all the disputes that came before the League were dealt with
under it. (3) The League was to exercise a quasi-arbitral function over
disputes and in the last resort it was to be an instrument for enforcing
the peace. Articles XII to XVII, which set out these functions, were taken
with only slight alteration from the report of a committee appointed by
Mr Balfour as foreign secretary under the chairmanship of Lord Philli-
more. They did not absolutely exclude war, but they aimed at making it
extremely improbable by providing that the members should not resort
to it without having exhausted the resources of peaceful settlement enumerated in the Covenant. They bound themselves to submit any 'dispute
likely to lead to a rupture' to one of three alternative procedures: to
settlement by the Permanent Court of International Justice, to arbitration,
or to inquiry by the Council; and in no case were they to resort to war
until three months after the judicial decision, the arbitrators' award, or
the report of the Council as the case might be, provided in the last case
that the Council, apart from the disputing parties, had been unanimous.
If in disregard of any of these undertakings a state should resort to war,
the so-called sanctions were to become applicable to it. All the other
members were then to sever all trade and financial relations with it, to
prohibit all intercourse between its nationals and their own, to prevent all
intercourse between its nationals and those of any other state whether
a member of the League or not, and the Council was to recommend what
armed forces the members should severally contribute to protect the
covenants of the League. These provisions reflected what was believed
to be one of the lessons of the war, namely the overwhelming power of
economic pressure, and therefore, whilst the provisions for economic
measures were detailed and peremptory, those for military measures were
left so obscure that it was never certain whether or not they imposed any
actual obligation on the members.

Before the League had even begun to exist it was dealt a grievous blow by the refusal of the American Senate to consent to the ratification of the peace treaties. The refusal meant much more than that the United States would be absent from the counsels of the League, serious as that alone would have been. It meant for League members, and for Britain and France in particular, that the League in being would be a different League from that which they had had in view when they accepted the Covenant. When the Covenant was before the British parliament not a single member expressed doubt as to the wisdom of accepting the sanctions provisions, though evidently their burden would be heaviest for a naval power; but these provisions took on a different aspect when it was seen that not only would the burden not be shared with the United States, but that it might easily lead to Anglo-American friction. Anxiety on this score introduced into the British attitude towards the League a constant appearance of uncertainty and half-heartedness which gravely impeded the growth of that general confidence upon which the success of any system of collective security depends. For France the American withdrawal was equally disastrous. France had most reluctantly agreed to give up her demand for a strategic frontier on the Rhine in return for treaties of guarantee with Britain and the United States, but these treaties were interdependent, and when the United States refused to ratify that with her, Britain, legitimately though perhaps unwisely, allowed hers to lapse. The French felt that they had been cheated by their allies, and they proceeded to look for safeguards for their security in a system of defensive alliances which, even if it was not formally inconsistent with the Covenant, was a reversion to ideas of national defence which the League was designed to supersede. They also adopted an uncompromising attitude to questions of German recovery which alienated British sympathy and widened the disastrous rift between two countries on whose ability to work together the success of the whole experiment chiefly depended.

The security provisions of the Covenant came under fire at the first meeting of the Assembly in 1920, when the Canadian representative proposed the elimination of Article X. The proposal was rejected, but it was renewed in the two following years, and in 1923 it led to an interpretative resolution which declared that it was for each state to decide for itself how far it was bound to employ its military forces in executing its obligations under the article. In 1921 the attack was extended to Article XVI and certain 'rules of guidance' were adopted for its application which had the effect of weakening its obligations. All this was evidence of a trend of opinion which had already come to regard the collective security provisions as a dangerous experiment, and which, if it should prevail, would lead inexorably to a return to the pre-League system of every state relying for its defence on its own armed forces. It was clear also that it endangered a cause to which the League had already set its hand, that of the reduction of national armaments 'to the lowest point consistent with national safety and the enforcement by common action of international obligations', for the prospects of disarmament were inextricably bound up with those of security (see ch. XVI).

The Allies had justified the disarmament of Germany in the Treaty of Versailles as being necessary to make possible a general reduction of armaments, and the Covenant had expressly charged the Council to formulate plans for this purpose. It was therefore inevitable, though it may have been unfortunate, that this problem should be among the first to be taken up by the League. A permanent military commission had been established by the Covenant to advise the Council, but it soon became evident that a professional body was more easily impressed by the difficulties than by the urgency of reducing armaments, and the first Assembly decided to establish another body to include lay as well as service members which became known as the Temporary Mixed Commission. The difficulties were not at first generally realised. Disarmament was a popular cause both on idealistic and on economic grounds, and there was a tendency to believe that armaments, instead of being merely a sign that wars are still possible, are an independent cause of war and therefore capable of being dealt with in the main as a technical question. The success of the Naval Conference of Washington in 1921 seemed to confirm this view and its exceptionally favourable circumstances were underestimated. It had been concerned with a very restricted subject-matter, that of capital ships; it had been a conference of five powers only, among which only the United States was economically able to engage in competitive building; and it had been preceded by agreements which at least for the time had removed outstanding political difficulties. The League was confronted with a very different problem.

The Temporary Mixed Commission first attempted to apply the Washington method to land armaments by fixing the numbers to be allowed to each state, but the military members easily showed that a direct attack on the problem on these lines would lead nowhere. The political aspect was seen to be fundamental, and in 1923 the Commission attempted a political approach in the draft of a treaty of mutual assistance which ingeniously combined the system of regional alliances which already existed and would, it was practically certain, have to be accepted, with a general system of security. The Council was to have power to determine an aggressor, but the obligation to use armed force against aggression was limited to states on the continent on which it occurred, and there was to be a guarantee for those states only which agreed to disarm. The Treaty was rejected by the British government for various reasons, but chiefly because of the difficulty of reconciling the regional basis of the obligations with the relations between members of the British Commonwealth and with the world-wide responsibilities of the British navy, and though the British was not the only rejection it was decisive for the fate of the draft. The Assembly of 1924 therefore tried a different approach. The rejected treaty would have set up a security system side by side with that of the Covenant but on a different basis; the Protocol of 1924 accepted the Covenant, but sought to strengthen it. Britain and France, which this year for the first time were represented by their prime ministers, Mr Ramsay Macdonald and M. Herriot, presented a joint resolution which became the basis of the Assembly's work. It was thought that a new key to the problem might be found in compulsory arbitration, the acceptance of which would offer a quasi-automatic test of aggression; in short, arbitration would make possible security, and security would then lead to disarmament. Compulsory arbitration would close what were coming to be called the 'gaps' in the Covenant. For the Covenant had not made it certain that all disputes would be settled; theoretically it was possible in certain circumstances for a member to resort to war without breaking its obligations and therefore without exposing itself to sanctions. The 'gaps' existed if the Council failed to reach unanimity in its report on a dispute, or if it found that a dispute arose out of a matter solely within the domestic jurisdiction of one of the parties (in which case it might make no recommendations for a settlement) or if at the end of the three months' 'cooling-off' period neither party accepted the decision of the Court or the arbitrators or the report of the Council. The Protocol proposed to close these 'gaps'. All disputes were to be settled by one means or other, in the last resort by arbitrators whose decision would be final. It did not actually strengthen the sanctions of the Covenant, but it declared that each member was bound to co-operate loyally and effectively 'in the degree which its geographical position and its particular situation as regards its armaments allow', and the closing of the 'gaps' would have had the effect of making the sanctions applicable to every resort to war and not merely, as hitherto, to war in breach of the Covenant. The whole plan, however, was to take effect only after a conference had adopted a disarmament plan, and the complexity of that problem was yet so little realised that it was proposed that the conference should meet in the following year and that in the meantime the Council should produce a draft plan for its consideration. In fact it proved impossible to convene this conference until 1932.

During the debates on the Protocol the Labour government of Mr Macdonald had been in power in Britain, but before the British attitude was declared it had been succeeded by the government of Mr Baldwin, and this decided to reject the proposals. It is unlikely that the change of government affected the issue, for when the Protocol came to be examined at leisure defects became apparent which had been overlooked or underestimated in the enthusiastic atmosphere of the Assembly. The claim of its authors that it ensured the final settlement of all disputes without exception was not justified by its terms; the most dangerous disputes are those which arise out of matters which fall within the domestic juris-diction of one of the parties or in which one of the parties claims some advantage to which it has no legal right, and under the Protocol these could only have been decided on the basis of the existing legal situation, leaving them to continue on the plane of interests even though disposed of on that of law. Indeed, to some members of the League this was one of the merits of the Protocol, for it seemed to place an obstacle in the way of any revision of the territorial settlement. But the main reason for the British rejection was not the defects of the document but the opposi-tion of the Dominions, and of that a British government of whatever party must have taken account. Some of this opposition may have arisen from a mistaken idea that the Protocol would impair their domestic control over such matters as immigration, but it was also significant of their fixed resolve on no account to increase the sanctions obligations to which they had committed themselves in the Covenant. The British rejec-tion decided the fate of the Protocol as it had that of the treaty of the previous year, but it is improbable that it could in any case have satisfied for long the demands of those members of the League that felt themselves insecure. The guarantees that it offered them were for practical purposes only those of the Covenant, and France and the countries associated with her had never regarded these as sufficient. It was founded on a diagnosis of the causes of the weakness of the League which was fundamentally mistaken; that weakness was not due to any juridical defect in the Coven-ant, but to the doubt whether, if the challenge should come, the League powers would, or in the absence of the United States whether they even could, confront an aggressor with the overwhelmingly superior force on which an effective security system depends.

Mr Austen Chamberlain announced the rejection of the Protocol at Geneva in a speech, of which Mr Balfour was believed to be the author, which caused some consternation by seeming to imply that in the absence of the United States the enforcement provisions of the Covenant had become unworkable. But he ended by suggesting that the Covenant might be supplemented by special arrangements 'knitting together the nations most immediately concerned and whose differences might lead to a renewal of strife by treaties for maintaining between themselves an unbroken peace', a cryptic formula which seemed to foreshadow a new approach to the security problem. The speech was made at a time when the prospects for a general pacification had been greatly improved by the removal, at least for the time being, of the question of German repara-tions from the field of controversy through the acceptance in the closing months of 1924 of the plan of the Dawes Committee, and the consequent withdrawal of the last French and Belgian troops from the occupation of the Ruhr. The special arrangements which Mr Chamberlain had in mind took shape at the close of 1925 in the Treaties of Locarno, the negotiations for which necessarily took place outside the League since Germany, one of 'the nations most immediately concerned', was not yet a member; but if France and Germany could be 'knit together' the whole outlook for the League would evidently be transformed. The main provisions of the treaties were that France and Germany, and Belgium and Germany, undertook not to resort to war against each other, that Britain and Italy would immediately come to the help of the party attacked if this undertaking should be broken and would guarantee the frontiers between Germany and France and between Germany and Belgium, that commissions of conciliation would be set up between Germany on the one hand and France, Belgium, Poland and Czechoslovakia on the other, and that France, but not Britain or Italy, would guarantee the frontiers between Germany and Poland and between Germany and Czechoslovakia.

Locarno had a profound effect on the European situation and Mr Chamberlain was justified in calling it 'the real dividing line between the years of war and the years of peace'. But its importance did not lie in its terms. The British guarantee added little if anything to their existing obligations under the Covenant, and by refusing to extend it to the eastern frontiers of Germany they shut their eyes to what was, even at that date, the probability that if aggression came it would come in the east, and that if it did they would be drawn in, guarantee or no guarantee. Nor did it give France the additional security for which she was always looking. Its importance was that it opened a prospect that the chief danger to the peace of Europe, the age-long hostility between France and Germany, might at last be assuaged. For the first time since the war Germany had made a negotiated treaty with her former enemies; she had accepted the loss of Alsace and Lorraine as final; and it had been arranged that she should enter the League and be elected to a permanent seat on the Council at a special Assembly to be held in March 1926. Unfortunately a hitch occurred in this arrangement at the last moment. Three other powers, Spain, Poland and Brazil, came forward as candidates for permanent seats, and as Spain and Brazil were already non-permanent members of the Council their votes were necessary for the election of Germany. It was generally felt that for any other member to be elected to a permanent seat would be a breach of faith towards Germany, and the Assembly dispersed without having reached any decision. Before the regular meeting of the Assembly, however, a compromise was arranged. The number of elected members of the Council was to be raised to nine; there was to be a new class of semi-permanent members who were to be re-eligible at the end of their normal three-year term, and it was understood that Poland would be one of these. Spain and Brazil withdrew their opposition to the election of Germany, but gave notice of withdrawal from the League; Spain retracted her notice before the two years' interval required by the Covenant had elapsed, but Brazil left the League.

For some years after the peace settlement the mentality of war persisted over much of Europe, and the League, with no force at its command and no accumulated reserve of prestige behind it, was often unable to make its writ run when a state attempted to snatch by force or by fraud some advantage for itself and to face the world with a *fait accompli*. Its difficulties were increased by the existence of rival authorities, first in the Supreme Council of the Allies and later in the Conference of Ambassadors which they had set up in Paris to deal with matters left outstanding by the treaties. There was no clear demarcation of function between these bodies and the League, and the latter sometimes found itself excluded from matters which properly belonged to it, or else called in to deal with problems on which its rivals had been unable to agree and at a stage when they had become nearly insoluble. The first dispute to be brought before it was one between Sweden and Finland in 1920, and in this, which related to sovereignty over the Aaland Islands, it succeeded in arranging a settlement which both parties accepted. But a few weeks later a more difficult case arose. A Polish free-lance commander, Zeligowski, had seized the disputed city of Vilna in breach of an armistice which had left it in Lithuanian possession; he was in fact acting, though this was denied at the time, with the approval of the Polish government. The League tried vainly to induce the Poles to give up the city, but in the end, in 1923, the Ambassadors awarded it to Poland. Another successful act of aggression which the League had to accept was the seizure by Lithuania in January 1923 of Memel, which was held by the Allies pending a decision as to its fate, but here it was able to effect an arrangement which secured a measure of autonomy to the mainly German inhabitants of the city.

In August 1923 the League machinery was called upon to deal for the first time with an aggression by a great power. General Tellini, the Italian member of a commission which had been surveying the Greco-Albanian frontier on behalf of the Ambassadors, had been murdered, and the Italians, without waiting for any inquiry into the circumstances, demanded an indemnity from Greece and seized the island of Corfu after a bombardment causing serious loss of life. The Greeks appealed to the League, at the same time declaring their readiness to accept any decision that the Ambassadors might make and thereby providing Italy with some technical justification for arguing that, as the dispute was in course of settlement by another authority, the League should refrain from interfering. The Council, however, declined to accept this argument and proceeded to negotiate a settlement under which the dispute was to be referred to the Permanent Court and Greece was to deposit a sum of 50 million lire to await the decision. Both the Ambassadors and the two parties accepted this settlement and it looked as though the League was about to win a resounding success, when suddenly the Ambassadors, without giving any reason, withdrew their acceptance and ordered Greece to pay the indemnity to Italy forthwith. It was only too clear that this was the price that Italy had exacted for the evacuation of Corfu which she had seized in flagrant disregard of the Covenant undertakings, and that the League had failed to hold the scales of justice even between a strong and a weak power. On the other hand it was generally felt that the League had acted with unexpected vigour, that it had come near to success, and that at least it had shown that a forum now existed before which even a great power might have to defend itself at the bar of world opinion. The results of the incident therefore were not wholly discouraging, and there seemed still to be a hope that with a fair field the machinery of the League might prove effective, and this hope seemed to be confirmed by the manner in which the League dealt with the next dispute to come before it. In October 1925, in consequence of an incident on the frontier between Greece and Bulgaria, Greek troops crossed into Bulgarian territory and Bulgaria at once appealed to the League. The Council happened to be sitting in Paris at the time and it acted with great promptitude. It reminded both parties of their duties under the Covenant and ordered the military attachés of the great powers in Athens to proceed to the scene of action and report on the facts. The Greeks thereupon after a short hesitation countermanded an offensive which they were on the point of launching, and the Council, having secured its immediate object, a cease-fire, proceeded to inquire into the merits of the dispute. A diplomatic mission which it sent out reported that the Greeks were in fault and the Council then fixed a sum which Greece was to pay by way of reparation. The complete success of the League on this occasion raised a hope that it had created a precedent which might be followed in future cases with equally good results. But the circumstances had been exceptionally favourable. Greece was a small power, the great powers had for once been united, and there were no political complications; the Council had acted much as the Concert had sometimes acted in the nineteenth century, Greece had been overawed and had submitted. Circumstances such as these were not destined to recur in the later history of the League.

The years that followed the Dawes Plan and the Locarno Treaties were years of high promise for the League and there were signs that it had established itself as a normal and necessary part of international relations. The foreign ministers of the three principal League powers, Sir Austen Chamberlain, M. Briand, and Herr Stresemann, found it worth their while to attend in person practically every meeting of the Assembly or the Council, and the mutual confidence that grew up amongst these three became an important stabilising influence on the European situation. Most of the other European foreign ministers followed their example and became regular attendants at Geneva. The United States, though she showed no signs of being willing to join the League, had begun to look more benevolently on its work and to take part in many of its non-political activities, and in 1927 the U.S.S.R. began to do the same. For some years no major crisis occurred to test the soundness of the League's structure; and though none of the great controversial questions —reparations, security, disarmament—had been solved, in the friendlier atmosphere that had begun to prevail they were ceasing to seem insoluble.

Locarno had, however, made disarmament more urgent than ever, for if Germany was now to be treated as the equal of the other great powers the unilateral disarmament provisions of Versailles, even if they had never been effectively enforced, could not be left unrevised. In December 1925, therefore, the Council set up a preparatory commission for the conference which it was still hoped to hold in 1926, but this was soon in difficulties. It found that on many questions of fundamental principle there was no sort of agreement among the states. Its technical sub-committees wrestled vainly with matters which might seem technical on the surface but were really rooted in widely divergent national interests. Even on the question of what the term 'armaments' should include, opinions differed widely; if armament potential were to be included it was difficult to see where to draw any line, for almost every feature of a state's situation—economic, geographic, demographic and so on—tends either to increase or to reduce its military strength, whilst to exclude war potential altogether from the calculation would be grossly unfair. Other questions on which opinions differed were whether only men actually serving should be counted in a state's military forces or whether trained reserves should be included; whether there should be a budgetary limitation on the size of armaments; whether naval armaments should be reckoned on a basis of total tonnage or by categories of ships; how far some form of international supervision could be devised to watch over the observance of any agreement that might be reached. There loomed also behind all these particular differences the shadow of the known determination of certain states to demand a firmer guarantee of their security as the price of any reduction in their armaments. The failure of the three chief naval powers, the United States, Britain and Japan, at a conference in June 1927 to reach agreement as to the limitation of non-capital ships, added a new source of discouragement. It began to be evident that the preparatory commission was not far from a deadlock, and indeed it was not until 1930 that it succeeded, and even then only by a majority which did not include Germany, Italy, or the U.S.S.R., in producing a draft statement of principles to serve as a basis for the work of a disarmament conference.

Meantime, however, an event had occurred outside the League which seemed to open up once again the possibility of advancing towards disarmament by the political instead of the technical line of approach. Shortly before the meeting of the Assembly of 1928 the Pact of Paris for the Renunciation of War, the so-called Kellogg–Briand Pact, had been signed in Paris, and League members were now in the rather anomalous position of being parties to two systems for maintaining peace which were in some respects inconsistent with one another. The Pact forbade any resort to war 'as an instrument of national policy', but the Covenant, owing to the existence of the 'gaps', allowed this in certain cases; the Pact declared that the settlement of disputes should never be sought except by pacific means, but the Covenant did not absolutely ensure that every dispute should be settled in this way or even that it should be settled at all. If war, therefore, was now to be excluded, what, it began to be asked, was to be done about disputes which could not be settled peacefully? These questions had very little real importance, but on formal grounds there was no doubt a case for implementing the Pact either by incorporating it in the Covenant or by setting up outside the Covenant a system for the settlement of disputes which might perhaps be accepted by signatories of the Pact who were not also members of the League. The former of these courses would have involved the closing of the gaps and thereby extending the sanctions to all wars, and although the British government, departing for once from its policy of refusing further commitments, supported a plan to this effect, it was not accepted. Instead, the Assembly produced a plan for implementing the Pact without amending the Covenant by a General Act for the Pacific Settlement of International Disputes which provided for conciliation commissions to be set up by each of the parties with every other party, for legal disputes to be submitted to the Permanent Court and non-legal disputes to arbitration. The Act was widely accepted, though in many cases with extensive reservations, but it was completely ineffective. It was a thoroughly doctrinaire document, prepared in haste and full of ambiguities. The conciliation commissions which the Act proposed were never found useful, and it was a retrograde step to substitute them for the Council, which was what the framers hoped would be the effect of the Act. For the Council had advantages which these commissions could never possess; it had prestige, its members were men of international reputation who were accustomed to working together, and it had means of informing itself on the facts and the law of the cases brought before it which had proved their value and which these ephemeral commissions could never command.

With the coming of the great economic depression of 1929 and the following years the League's short period of optimism came to an end. The German elections of 1930, in which the National Socialist party won more than a hundred seats, made it clear that Locarno had failed in its main purpose despite the fact that the evacuation of the Rhineland had been speeded up and that reparations had again been scaled down by the Young Plan of that year. But however discouraging the outlook might be, it had become impossible to postpone much longer the meeting of the long-delayed disarmament conference, and it was definitely fixed for February 1932. Before that date the position had deteriorated still farther, for Japan was now defying the League in China. When the conference did at last meet, the German claim to equality overshadowed all its debates, and in June 1932 Germany threatened to withdraw. The rift was temporarily patched by an ambiguous formula which recognised in principle both Germany's right to equality and France's right to security, but did not show how the two were to be reconciled. Before the conference met again Hitler had become Chancellor of the Reich, and a few days later Japan resigned from the League, though she continued to take part in the conference. Mr Ramsay Macdonald attempted to save the conference from the impending wreck by a new draft of which the chief proposals were that a conference of the powers should be held in the event of a breach or threatened breach of the peace, that limitations should be put on the calibre of certain specified weapons, that the numbers of aircraft should be reduced as a step towards the eventual abolition of air warfare, that chemical and bacteriological warfare should be banned, and that a permanent disarmament commission with powers of inspection should be created. After some difficult negotiations the plan was accepted as a basis for the future work, and a further gleam of hope was introduced by a declaration by President Roosevelt that the United States would be willing to consult with other powers in the event of a breach of the peace and that she would not impede action taken by them provided she agreed that the state against which it was taken was in fact an aggressor. The conference adjourned for the summer of 1933 in a fairly hopeful mood and with no warning of the blow that was impending, but on the day that it met again it learnt that Germany had withdrawn and was giving notice of her resignation from the League. The conference was never formally dissolved, but this was its death warrant. For the League the rise of Hitler had another sequel a year later in a complete reversal of the attitude of the U.S.S.R. In September 1934 the U.S.S.R. was elected to the League, with a permanent seat on the Council, and from that date until the outbreak of the second world war there was no more eloquent advocate at Geneva of the principles of the Covenant than her representative, M. Litvinov.

Meanwhile, however, the League had been facing the most dangerous challenge which it had so far met. In September 1931 Japanese troops guarding the South Manchurian railway attacked and rapidly disarmed the Chinese garrisons in Mukden and neighbouring towns and drove out the provincial Chinese government. They claimed to be acting in self-defence against a threatened Chinese attack, and at first the facts were so obscure that the full purpose of Japan was not realised in the West. Her record in the League had hitherto been a good one, and the western powers, which had themselves had recent experience of the capacity of the Chinese to be exasperating, were not disposed to condemn her out of hand. Her troops were in Manchuria by right of a treaty, and if, as she alleged, their safety was in danger they would be justified in defending themselves. It was only gradually that the smoothness and speed with which the operations were carried out and extended made it clear that they must have been carefully planned.

By the end of the year Japanese troops had overrun the whole of Manchuria and the full seriousness of the situation was revealed. As soon as the trouble started the Chinese appealed to the League under Article XI of the Covenant and the Council set itself to secure the withdrawal of the Japanese into the railway zone. It seemed likely at first to succeed in this object for it was assured by the Japanese member that the withdrawal would take place and that his country had no intention of making a permanent occupation. Support for the Council came from the United States, for the action of Japan had raised a question of the observance of two treaties to which the United States was a party, the Nine Power Treaty of Washington of 1922 which recognised the independence and territorial integrity of China, and the Kellogg Pact of 1928. But as the real intentions of Japan became more and more evident the attitude of her representative on the Council hardened, and when towards the end of October the Council proposed to fix a date for completing the withdrawal he refused to concur and claimed that his dissent invalidated the decision. This was a novel claim which could only be supported by a pedantically literal interpretation of the Covenant, and it was argued that it reduced to practical futility the procedure under Article XI on which, ever since the Greco-Bulgarian incident of 1924, the Council had mainly relied in its handling of disputes. The Council accepted the claim, but what the incident really showed was that the Article XI procedure, based as it was on conciliation without any sanction other than moral behind it, could not be effective against a great power determined to have its way. The Council had been in almost continuous session ever since the trouble started until December, when it decided, this time with the concurrence of the Japanese representative, to send out a commission of representatives of the five great powers under the chairmanship of Lord Lytton to inquire into the situation on the spot.

Before the commission started the situation had deteriorated. Early in 1932 an anti-Japanese boycott and riots broke out in Shanghai, and Japan retaliated by bombing and landing troops which were not withdrawn for several months. The Chinese too had decided to appeal under Articles X and XVI as well as XI, thereby confronting the League with the problem of honouring the guarantee of territorial integrity in Article X, and, since Article XV was the gateway to the sanctions of Article XVI, with the possibility of the members finding themselves obligated to impose sanctions on Japan. They asked also, as the Covenant entitled them to do, that the appeal should be transferred to the Assembly, no doubt because the smaller powers, on whose sympathies they could rely, would there be in a large majority. A special Assembly met accordingly in March and decided, as it could hardly fail to do, to await the report of the Lytton Commission. All these delays facilitated the maturing of the Japanese plans, and when at last the commission arrived in Manchuria it learnt that Japan had established a puppet government and had formally recognised the existence of an independent state of Manchukuo. The commission's report was received in Geneva in September and considered successively by the Council and the Assembly. It was, in general, condemnatory of Japan, but it gave full and fair consideration to the anomalous situation in Manchuria, recognised that the *status quo* had become unworkable, and recommended the setting up of a new autonomous regime under League auspices. The report was accepted in its main lines by the Assembly in February 1933, and Japan thereupon gave notice of resignation from the League. The failure had been complete and the weakness of the collective security system had been mercilessly exposed. It was true that the Assembly did not expressly find that Japan had 'resorted to war' in disregard of her Covenant obligations, but it was obvious that that was what she had done and that here, if ever, was a case to which the sanctions of Article XVI were intended to apply. Yet from first to last the question of sanctions had never been raised. Mr Stimson, the American secretary of state, had indeed announced a doctrine of 'non-recognition' of situations brought about by means contrary to the Kellogg Pact, but Japan could safely disregard a refusal to recognise facts when it was certain that neither the United States nor any other power would take any positive action to alter them. Britain, for her part, was painfully aware that the brunt of any operations which sanctions might entail would fall upon a naval power, and Japan knew that the Washington Treaties had placed her in a practically impregnable position in Far Eastern waters.

While the League was still dealing with the Manchurian affair its attention had also to be turned to two outbreaks of hostilities in South America. One of these arose out of a long-standing frontier dispute between Bolivia and Paraguay in the Chaco area, and fighting began there in June 1932. In May of the following year Paraguay formally declared war. A commission sent out by the League had no success, but the League did succeed in arranging an embargo on the supply of arms, at first against both belligerents, and later, after Bolivia had belatedly appealed to the League and offered to accept the recommendations of the Assembly, against Paraguay only. The embargo, although the United States supported it, was never completely effective, and each side in turn became obdurate as the shifting fortunes of the war favoured its cause. Finally the war ended in June 1935, not through any efforts of the League, but through the exhaustion of both sides.

In the other South American dispute the intervention of the League was more successful. In June 1932 a party of Peruvians, at first repudiated but later supported by their own government, seized a strip of undoubtedly Colombian territory near the village of Leticia, and Colombia having appealed to the League, the Council adopted a report calling for the immediate withdrawal of the Peruvians. There was a refusal to comply at first, but a change of government occurred in Peru and the two parties agreed to invite the League to send a commission to administer the disputed area while the withdrawal took place.

But any hope that still remained that the security system might be restored was destroyed by the war of 1935-6 between Italy and Ethiopia. The relations between these two countries first came before the League as a result of a clash between their troops in December 1934, at Walwal, a place near the undelimited frontier between Ethiopia and Italian Somaliland, when, on Italy's demanding compensation, Ethiopia appealed to the League under Article XI of the Covenant. At a meeting of the Council the next month it was arranged that the matter should be referred to arbitrators in accordance with a treaty between the two countries and that meanwhile consideration by the Council should be postponed. Italy delayed the appointment of the arbitrators and the tribunal did not meet until July, and in September it gave an award which exonerated both sides from blame. But long before this the Walwal incident had lost all importance, for Italy's warlike preparations were on a scale which made concealment of their purpose no longer possible, and as early as March Ethiopia had asked to have the dispute considered under Article XV as being 'likely to lead to a rupture'. Unfortunately her appeal coincided with the repudiation by Germany of the disarmament provisions of the Treaty of Versailles and Britain and France were exceedingly reluctant to take any action which might estrange Italy. The Council therefore several times postponed the matter and it was still engaged in preparing a report which would have contained the recommendations which it considered 'just and proper' for a settlement when, on 4 October, the Italian troops invaded Ethiopia.

Thus when the war began the dispute had been before the League in one form or another for about ten months, and there had been ample time for the 'cooling-off' process, in which the founders of the League security system had placed much confidence, to take effect. Here, however, the system had to deal with an aggression for which, as the Italian commander-in-chief, Marshal De Bono, later revealed, plans had been laid two years before, and the leisurely pace of the League had resulted not in a cooling of tempers but in facilitating the completion of the aggressor's arrangements. Nothing had been done during all these months at Geneva to prevent the catastrophe, and the principal League powers had given no sign that they were likely to take their obligations any more seriously than they had in the Manchurian affair. The rapidity therefore with which events now began to move came as a surprise to the world in general and perhaps particularly to Mussolini himself. The evidence that Italy had 'resorted to war in disregard of her covenants' was overwhelmingly clear, and on 7 October the Council, and four days later the Assembly, passed resolutions to that effect, Italy only dissenting in the former, and Austria, Hungary and Albania, all under Italian influence, in the latter. The resolutions meant that in the view of the great majority of League members the sanctions of Article XVI had now become applicable, and they proceeded to set up a committee to co-ordinate their further action. Literally applied the article required the immediate severance of all trade and financial relations with Italy, the prohibition of intercourse with Italian nationals, and the prevention of intercourse between these and the nationals of any other state whether a member of the League or not. But the Co-ordination Committee decided instead of this policy of complete non-intercourse to act under the Resolutions of 1921 which have been referred to above. Members were advised in the first instance to ban imports from and loans to Italy, and also the export of certain raw materials; but these had the appearance of having been chosen so as not too seriously to inconvenience the Italians, and they did not include an embargo on oil which, in the opinion of some competent judges, might have had a decisive effect on their operations. It may have been thought that, if time were given, the limited sanctions already being applied would be effective even without an oil embargo, and it is also possible that public opinion would sooner or later have forced the governments to impose it in spite of the risks of reprisal that it might have involved. But the events of the campaign moved more quickly than had been expected and soon made the discussion academic. Early in 1936 the Ethiopian resistance collapsed, thanks to the indiscriminate use of poison gas by the Italians on troops and civilians wholly without protection against it, and after that it was clear that nothing short of military sanctions, which the League powers were firmly determined not to use, would affect the issue. At a meeting of the Assembly at the end of June it was decided to lift the sanctions, and in November 1937 Italy resigned from the League.

Thus once again the security system had failed, as decisively as in Manchuria but with far less excuse, and the disaster was the more crushing because of the high hopes with which the enterprise had been started. On the eve of the war Sir Samuel Hoare had declared in the Assembly 'my country stands for the collective maintenance of the Covenant in its entirety and particularly for steady and collective resistance to all acts of unprovoked aggression', and it was naturally assumed that the government which had authorised this categorical statement must have weighed its possible consequences, one of which was obviously the risk of an armed clash with Italy. M. Laval afterwards stated that on the day before the speech Sir Samuel and he had agreed to rule out any sanctions which might lead to war, and although Sir Samuel was doubtless justified in denying any such agreement there can be little doubt that it represented the policy of the British, as it certainly did that of the French, government. The notorious Hoare–Laval Plan resulting from this meeting, which proposed that peace should be made on the basis of the cession to Italy of nearly two-thirds of Ethiopia, much more than the Italians had at that date overrun, showed to what lengths Britain and France were prepared to go in order to avoid a breach, and although the Plan was received in parliament and by public opinion with such a storm of indignation that the British government hastily repudiated it and accepted the resignation of Sir Samuel Hoare, its mere publication had done irreparable harm. It was no longer possible to believe in the sincerity of the professed determination of the two principal League powers to uphold the Covenant.

The defeat of the League had been so decisive that never again was it seriously suggested that the peace enforcement provisions should be put into operation, and except for the expulsion of the U.S.S.R. after her attack on Finland in December 1939 the League remained henceforth a passive witness of the aggressions of the totalitarian powers. Its reaction to Hitler's annexation of Austria in 1938 was to strike Austria off the list of League members, and neither Czechoslovakia in 1938, nor Poland in 1939, thought it worth while to bring its case to Geneva. During these years there was a general feeling that some revision of articles of the Covenant which it was clear that the members did not intend to observe ought to be undertaken, and a number of different suggestions were brought forward. But the fundamental question at issue was whether the League should still be armed with some sort of coercive powers, possibly on a regional instead of a universal basis, or whether it should henceforth be merely a machinery for facilitating consultation and co-operation. That issue was still undecided when the war of 1939 broke out and no change had been made in the Covenant.

The second of the two great objects of the League was the promotion of international co-operation and in this field it achieved important successes; it was responsible, as Mr Cordell Hull, the American secretary of state, has written of it, for the development of mutual exchange and discussion of ideas and methods to a greater extent and in more fields of humanitarian and scientific endeavour than any other organisation in history. That was a just tribute, and the achievement was the more remarkable because the League was handicapped from first to last by the extreme parsimony of the financial provision which the members were willing to make for it. The average annual cost of the whole League, including the International Labour Organisation and the Permanent Court, and including the capital expenditure on its buildings, was about £1,600,000, of which the share of the United Kingdom was about £150,000.

The first of the technical organisations to be set up was one on communications and transit, and in its main lines the constitution of this became a model for the later ones. It consisted of a General Conference which met at intervals of about four years and was composed of delegates of the governments, not all of which were necessarily members of the League; an Advisory and Technical Committee, meeting more often, and composed of individual experts not representing their governments; and a section of the Secretariat. The Committee advised the League, and when so requested individual governments, on matters within its competence; it was available to be used as a conciliation commission for the settlement of disputes on traffic questions; and it conducted investigations and prepared draft agreements for consideration by the General Conference. It formed a number of specialist committees dealing with rail transport, inland navigation, ports, electric power, and other special aspects of communications. The General Conference promoted international agreements on communications questions, and from time to time it convened special conferences on particular topics. The general object of the Organisation had been laid down in Article XXIII (e) of the Covenant as 'to secure and maintain freedom of communications and transit', and though that ideal was far from being realised it had some successes. Some of the conventions which it promoted were accepted and put into operation, but on the whole communications proved to be a difficult subject for international treatment. Political considerations cannot always be excluded from them, and the political organs of the League were never willing to allow the Organisation the independence which it needed to make its work completely successful.

In the economic field the League had some early successes in handling some immediately urgent problems of reconstruction, notably in its work in the rehabilitation of the finances of Austria. Various countries had made relief loans to Austria, but these had served only as palliatives, there was no possibility of further loans, and it had become clear that nothing but a plan of radical reconstruction could avert a complete collapse of the Austrian economy. It was essential, however, before any such plan could be launched that states having reparation claims against Austria should agree to their deferment so as to enable her to offer the security necessary for any loan on an adequate scale. The League carried through the difficult negotiations which were necessary for this purpose, and it was then able to put into operation a comprehensive plan, under the supervision of a League commissioner, of retrenchment and budgetary reform. This brought about a rapid improvement in the Austrian situation and kept the economy on an even keel until, with most of the rest of the world, it was engulfed in the great economic breakdown of the middle inter-war years. A reconstruction scheme modelled on that for Austria was later applied to Hungary.

The League was less successful in its efforts to introduce long-term improvements in the conduct of international economic relations. Everywhere a tendency towards more and more nationalistic economic policies was in the ascendant, and against this the League could make little headway. Moreover, the two most crucial matters of international economic policy in the early years of the League were reparations and inter-allied debts, and from both of these it was excluded. The first important enterprise of a general character was the organisation of a conference of financial experts at Brussels to consider remedies for the monetary chaos left by the war, but though the experts were practically unanimous in their recommendations these would have required, as the report pointed out, fundamental changes in the policies of nearly every state which governments were not willing, and perhaps not even able, to make. One result of this conference was, however, a decision to turn the provisional committee which had prepared it into a standing economic and financial expert committee with a section of the Secretariat to serve it. This was later divided into two separate committees for finance and economics respectively. In 1927 a World Economic Conference was held at Geneva after long and very thorough preparation, and this again resulted in an admirable report and recommendations, but any chance there may have been of effect being given to the recommendations was wrecked by the onset of the great depression two years later. A second World Economic Conference met in London in 1930, but the preparation for this had been quite inadequate and it resulted in a complete failure. The most valuable legacy left by the League in the economic field is, however, the series of studies and the collection and diffusion of economic information by its Economic Intelligence Service. The League could diagnose the causes of economic ills and prescribe the appropriate remedies, but it could not force those remedies on the patients.

Probably the work of the Health Organisation was the most permanently valuable of all the social services of the League. It began with the work of an Epidemics Commission formed to combat an outbreak of typhus and cholera which war and revolution had loosed upon eastern Europe, and this commission was soon afterwards used to assist the Greek government in the health problems arising from the influx of refugees driven from their homes in Asia Minor by the Turkish victories there. A permanent Health Organisation consisting of an Advisory Council of government representatives, a smaller Health Committee of specialists, and a section of the Secretariat, was created in 1923, and thereafter its work developed rapidly. The Epidemics Commission was enlarged into a permanent epidemiological service on a scale never before attempted for the collection of information on certain diseases and its distribution to national and port health authorities all over the world. Another branch of the Organisation's work was the standardisation of drugs, sera, vaccines and vitamins, which is essential to efficient collaboration between scientific workers in different countries, and the standards recommended have now been largely incorporated into national pharmacopoeias. An important new subject was taken up in 1935 when the Assembly asked the Organisation to collaborate with the International Labour Organisation and the International Institute of Agriculture in preparing a report on nutrition. When this report was issued in 1937 it revealed in a startling fashion how vast was the number of human beings who were either underfed or wrongly fed, and it led to the setting up of national nutrition committees in many countries to work towards the attainment of the standards recommended, which incidentally were soon to be found useful in the framing of war rationing schemes. Lastly the Organisation was able, when requested, to advise and help particular countries desiring to improve their health services; China in particular received invaluable help of this kind in a comprehensive programme of reforms involving the reorganisation of her quarantine service, the training of doctors and nurses, and the direction of a campaign against cholera and smallpox.

There were many other more limited but important fields in which the League promoted international co-operation. One great humanitarian work of the early days was that of Dr Nansen, who became the League's commissioner for refugees in 1921 and devoted the last years of his life to organising the resettlement of the scores of thousands of unfortunate people who had lost their homes and nationalities through the war or the peace settlement. On an appeal from the Greek government this work was extended to grapple with the appalling problem created by the influx of more than a million persons from Asia Minor after the Turkish victories there. Among the social evils attacked by the League were the traffic in women and children, on which a conference was held and a convention reached in 1921, and the traffic in dangerous drugs. The drug traffic creates problems on which purely national measures have been found to be almost wholly ineffective, for drugs are easily smuggled and the trade is very lucrative. Its details were obscure, and the League first set itself to collect the facts; it then secured agreement on a system of licences for the export from and the import into each country of certain specified drugs, and this licensing system was then supplemented by limiting the manufacture in the producing countries as closely as possible to medical and scientific needs. The administration of the scheme was supervised by a Permanent Central Opium Board and an Advisory Committee.

In the last years of the League the breakdown of the security system and the hostility of the totalitarian powers made it necessary to change the methods of working of the technical organisations. It had become useless to plan the holding of large general conferences or to hope for the conclusion of conventions on matters of interest to states in general. Instead a practice grew of holding meetings of limited groups of states or of individual experts for the study of particular problems; sugar and wheat were among the subjects treated in this way. Interest shifted also from the action of governments to the interests of the individual, and besides the question of nutrition already mentioned questions taken up in this way included the causes of economic and financial troubles, depressions, the trade cycle, the gold standard, and questions of hygiene and housing. There developed also an opinion in favour of greater independence for the social and technical organs, and on the eve of the second world war a committee under the chairmanship of Viscount Bruce proposed that a new central committee should be established to take over the responsibilities of the Assembly and the Council for these bodies, including the approval of their plans of work and their budgetary demands. A plan on these lines was subsequently adopted in the Economic and Social Council which the Charter of the United Nations constituted as one of its 'principal organs'.

Outside its two great functions of promoting international co-operation and achieving international peace the League had many and very various duties placed upon it by the treaties of peace. It was given, for instance, power to revise some few of the articles of the treaties and to settle some differences of interpretation; it had a part to play in settlir.g the terms of agreements into which Germany was required to enter; its consent was necessary to any alienation of the independence of Austria. But apart from particular acts such as these which it was required or empowered to perform it was given certain tasks of a continuing administrative character. One of these, contained in the Covenant itself, was the supervision of the mandate system, whereby colonies and territories of which the defeated powers were being deprived 'which are inhabited by people not yet able to stand by themselves under the strenuous conditions of the modern world' were to be placed under the 'tutelage' of more advanced nations as 'mandatories on behalf of the League'. The Covenant created a Permanent Mandates Commission to advise the Council and to receive an annual report from each of the mandatory powers, and in course of time this Commission accumulated a great store of experience of colonial problems; its members, who were individuals appointed for their special qualifications for the work and not as representatives of governments, learnt to appreciate the difficulties of colonial administration, and the colonial administrators often found the suggestions and criticisms of the Commission useful and came to realise that they were inspired by a genuine wish to co-operate and not by any captious spirit. Neither the Council nor the Commission had any power to coerce a mandatory power, but on the whole the system worked well.

The League was less successful in another somewhat similar task, that of supervising the observance of the Minorities Treaties made between the great powers and certain states, such as Poland, Czechoslovakia, Roumania, and others, which owed either their independence or an enlargement of their territory to the victory of the Allies. These treaties required the states concerned to accord certain rights to racial, religious, or linguistic minorities within their territories, and placed the observance of these rights under the 'guarantee' of the League. But they gave the League no means of enforcing this guarantee other than by the pressure of persuasion or publicity, and its effectiveness therefore tended to vary with the rise and fall of the League's own prestige. The Council evolved a procedure for dealing with petitions from the minorities which was reasonably good in view of the difficulties of the task; it laid down rules as to the receivability of petitions to be applied by the Secretariat, and it instituted a system of standing committees to examine those found receivable and to decide which of them it was necessary to bring before the full Council. This procedure was more effective than has sometimes been supposed, for it is usually judged by its failures, and these were publicly known; but when, as often happened, a grievance was settled without being brought before the Council, the matter was treated as confidential and the League did not always receive the credit to which it was entitled. But a fully effective system of minority protection is possible only if both the state in which the minority finds itself and the minority have learnt to be tolerant of differences, and in most of the countries with which the League had to deal this condition was far from being realised. The treaties ran counter to the sentiments of nationalism prevailing in most of the states bound by them, and it is possible that they sometimes encouraged irredentist feelings which could be represented as endangering the stability of the territorial settlement. They were resented too because they were felt to mark an inferior national status, especially since none of the great powers had been subjected to similar obligations, and one of them, Italy, was notoriously pursuing an opposite policy in the territories acquired from Austria-Hungary. Confidence in the system naturally declined in the last years of the League, and in 1934 Poland announced that she would no longer recognise the jurisdiction of the Council in minority matters.

Another difficult task laid upon the League by the treaties related to the settlement in the Danzig area. Danzig was a mainly German city, but its situation and its port facilities made it the obvious place for a Polish access to the sea. The Allies therefore sought to reconcile this important Polish interest with the principle of self-determination which they had accepted as the basis of the settlement by detaching it from Germany and constituting it a free city 'under the protection of the League'; its constitution was to be drawn up in agreement with a High Commissioner appointed by the League, and it was then to be placed 'under the guarantee' of the League. The arrangement included provisions limiting the autonomy of Danzig in the interests of Poland; she was to have the free use of the Danzig docks, to control the Vistula and the railway system within the city, to conduct Danzig's foreign relations, and to include Danzig within her customs frontiers. A high commissioner resident in Danzig was to represent the League.

In view of the extreme complexity of the conflicting interests the settlement was probably as intrinsically fair as any that could have been devised, but it was only likely to work if both parties accepted it as definitive or, failing that, if it were backed by some powers of enforcement. Neither of these conditions was satisfied. The high commissioner's function was to mediate in disputes and to act as a guardian of the constitution, but he had no powers of government in Danzig; the League heard appeals from his decisions, and when disputes were taken to Geneva it often happened that a settlement was found possible in the calmer atmosphere prevailing there. But neither the League nor its commissioner could enforce a decision if either of the parties was obdurate. Fundamentally, Danzig–Polish relations were never more than one aspect of the relations between Germany and Poland; when these were good the affairs of Danzig ran smoothly; when German policy towards Poland became aggressive they deteriorated. In the last years before 1939 it was notorious that Berlin had assumed the direction of affairs in Danzig; the Nazi party had step by step established a dictatorship over the city, and the treaty settlement had completely broken down.

As compensation for the destruction of the coal mines of northern France the Treaty of Versailles required Germany to renounce the government of the Saar basin in favour of the League of Nations as trustee and to cede its coal mines to France outright. The League was directed to set up a governing commission of five persons—one Frenchman, one Saarlander, and three from countries other than France and Germany; and after fifteen years a plebiscite was to be held to decide between the maintenance of the treaty regime, union with France, and reunion with Germany, and if the latter were chosen Germany was to re-purchase the mines from France. The commission made a rather unpromising start; the first chairman was a Frenchman, and some of his colleagues were suspected of a too Francophil bias. But even a perfectly constituted commission might have been daunted by the difficulties of the task entrusted to it. It had to organise an administration out of nothing in a politically backward area; it had been imposed on a resentful population which was kept in a state of perpetual unsettlement by the uncertainties of the plebiscite; and it was exposed to a constant stream of hostile propaganda from Berlin attempting to undermine its authority. With a change in the chairmanship and the entry of Germany into the League in 1926 the atmosphere improved and the commission succeeded in organising an honest and highly efficient system of government under which the territory prospered economically and financially. As the date for the plebiscite approached the position again deteriorated, and after Hitler's accession to power in 1933 the Nazis organised a reign of terror which seemed likely to make a fair conduct of the plebiscite impossible. In the end, however, thanks to the protection afforded at the last moment by an international force, the plebiscite passed off without disorder in January 1935 and resulted in an overwhelming vote in favour of reunion with Germany. On the whole the commission had successfully discharged a very difficult task, and incidentally had demonstrated that an efficient international government is not in all circumstances impossible.

After the meeting at which the U.S.S.R. was expelled in December 1939 the Assembly did not meet again while the war lasted, but the economic and social work was carried on, though necessarily on a restricted scale, and every effort was made to preserve the structure of the League and of its institutions intact and to assure the continuance of essential work. The International Labour Organisation moved to Montreal, the health section and the Central Opium Board to Washington, and the economic, financial, and transit work to Princeton, New Jersey. But as the war drew towards an end it became clear that the League would be replaced by a new organisation, and after the adoption of the Charter of the United Nations at San Francisco the chief concern of those responsible for the destinies of the League was to see that its activities were terminated in a manner worthy of the part it had played in world affairs. Representatives of the League and of the United Nations worked out a plan which was later approved by the twenty-first and last Assembly. The buildings and the Library at Geneva were transferred to the United Nations at an agreed valuation to become its European headquarters; the secretary-general was directed to afford every facility for the assumption by the United Nations of such of the non-political activities of the League as the new body might decide to assume; the Permanent Court was formally dissolved and replaced by a new International Court of Justice with a statute in almost identical terms; and provision was made for the continued existence of the International Labour Organisation as an autonomous institution in close relation with the United Nations. The League was dissolved by a resolution of the Assembly on 18 April 1946.

CHAPTER XVIII

ECONOMIC INTERDEPENDENCE AND
PLANNED ECONOMIES

THE twenty years before the outbreak of the first world war in 1914 have frequently been described as the golden age of international economic specialisation and exchange. Improvements in transport facilitated an increased flow of goods through the world markets, and political obstacles to trade did not obstruct to any serious extent the network of business relations.

The world economy was an expanding multilateral system. Trade movements and financial clearings were roundabout, and the tangled mesh of transfer routes revealed the extent to which more and more countries had been drawn into the international economy. The central place in the interdependent world was occupied by Europe. In 1913 50 per cent of total world trade consisted of the imports and exports of seven European countries—the United Kingdom, Germany, France, Belgium, Holland, Switzerland and Denmark. What is more, a large share of the total foreign trade of these countries consisted of an interchange of goods amongst themselves. The United Kingdom and Germany, although industrial rivals, were practically each other's best customers, and the former was the only country in Europe to do more trade outside the Continent than within. Germany sent three-quarters of its exports to nearby countries and received over half its imports from them (see ch. II).

There was no question, however, of the self-sufficiency either of Germany or of Europe as a whole. The central network of European trade depended on the regular supply of raw materials and foodstuffs from areas great distances away. Between 1890 and 1914 Germany became increasingly dependent on net imports of primary products from other continents while the United Kingdom, a special case, obtained less than one-third of its imports from Europe. The economic frontier overseas was a moving frontier, and the export of capital from Europe made possible spectacular foreign development. Europe was the world's banker as well as the world's workshop, and inside the credit empire the United Kingdom took the leading place. In the seven years before 1914 it alone provided £600 million for the construction of railways in countries supplying it with foodstuffs and raw materials.

If the growth of great entrepôt cities like Liverpool, Hamburg, Alexandria and Shanghai registered the vigorous expansion of international commodity trade, so the growth of London as a central financial and insurance centre indicated both the interdependence and unity of the world economy. London was a world financial centre more than it was a national investment centre, and the services which it provided were dependent on a far more extensive trade than that which concerned the United Kingdom alone, either as an importer or an exporter. The financial institutions of the City had world-wide connections and provided investment opportunities both for long-term capital through the new-issues market and short-term capital through the bill market. Sterling acted as a common trade currency, and the cheapness and security of London's financial services encouraged regular international dealings.

The United Kingdom was the pivot of the international gold standard mechanism which was generally established in the last quarter of the nineteenth century. The working of the system has frequently been described in terms of deceptive simplicity, but it seems clear that the relative success of the mechanism as an international economic instrument depended less on the mechanism itself than on the conditions in which it was applied. The most important of the conditions was the position of the United Kingdom in the structure of multilateral trade and its relations with the rest of the system.

There were two features of the international economic position of the United Kingdom which were of outstanding importance. It was the world's largest creditor country, but at no time was this position exploited to accumulate a large stock of gold which would drain the resources of other countries in the system. There were no political obstacles to the free export of capital and British investors looked eagerly for investment outlets overseas. The 'sterling standard' was thus maintained in the interests of world stability, and small countries were able to rest content with keeping their rates of exchange on London in the neighbourhood of par without concerning themselves closely with the working of the mechanism. Stable exchange rates and the 'legal order' provided by the gold standard facilitated international commodity trade.

The second feature of the position of the United Kingdom was its dependence on imports from overseas. The free and open British market absorbed a large proportion of the world's total exports of staple products and enabled debtors to meet their obligations with goods. Furthermore, continental countries and the United States could finance their growing purchases of primary products from overseas by net exports to the United Kingdom. It was the existence of this national market which made the international system work. Even during financial crises British-organised wholesale markets absorbed temporary surpluses of world production. Thus both in financial terms and in real terms the United Kingdom was, in a phrase of Keynes, 'the conductor of the orchestra'.[1] In the story of the disintegration of the multilateral system and the rise of planned economies, the change in the position of the United Kingdom

[1] J. M. Keynes, *Treatise on Money* (London, 1930), vol. II, p. 307.

between 1914 and 1945 and the parallel shifts in economic and financial power are central themes.

Yet even before 1914 the working of the international system did not preclude periods of stagnant trade and the unemployment of resources, and the economics of the interdependent world economy did not rest unchallenged. Beneath the system there were certain tacit assumptions on which it was based, concerning the relationships of countries to each other and of governments to their peoples. The separation of economics and politics, reflected in the limited extent to which politicians interfered with international economic specialisation, depended largely upon the social framework and social pressures inside their countries. As the framework changed and the pressures varied, governments found it increasingly necessary to interfere in economic relations both internally and externally. There were some spheres of economic organisation, like foreign investment, central banking and railways, which had important and obvious political and strategic implications encouraging governments to interfere. In consequence, before 1914, if there was no attempt to plan the economy as a whole, there was some attempt to plan *within* the economy or at least to regulate certain sectors of it. If there was no direct formulation of national income policy, there was a growing interest in budget policy as a means of social adjustment. If quantitative import restrictions had not been developed, tariffs were freely employed. Although the United Kingdom stood firmly by the principles of free trade, in 1900 45 per cent of its exports went to protectionist countries, and some of these, like Germany, conceived of tariffs as instruments of general national policy.

The historical origins of twentieth-century planning can be discerned in the pre-1914 world. The first moves *within* economies began with the attack of the underprivileged against the inequalities of income distribution and the impersonalism of market forces. The extension of the suffrage was followed, and in some cases anticipated, by popular demands for increased social security. The victories of liberal democracy produced new mass pressures. Some of their effects can be noted in the substitution of government spending policies for those based on retrenchment finance. In the United Kingdom in the fifteen years before 1914 government expenditure doubled a budget which had previously taken fifty years to double itself. By 1908 Lloyd George could say that no one need be afraid of any taxes being taken off in his time, and three years later he could offer the working-classes 9d. for 4d. In 1909 Winston Churchill could declare that if he had to sum up the immediate future of democratic politics in a single word, he would say 'insurance'.

The early stages in the gradual transformation of Lassalle's 'nightwatchman state' into the twentieth-century Welfare State can be traced in many parts of Europe before 1914. British insurance legislation was by no means the first of such ventures on the part of governments. The German system of social insurance was inaugurated in 1881 by Bismarck's Accident Insurance Bill and crowned in 1911 by the promulgation of the Workmen's Insurance Code of nearly 2000 articles, the *Reichs-Versicherungsordnung*. The German scheme, designed in part to 'save' the German working-classes from 'the siren song of socialism', was copied by other countries, often for very different reasons. By 1914 there were more or less elaborate social insurance systems in the United Kingdom, France, Belgium, Holland, Italy, Denmark, Austria, Norway, Sweden and Switzerland. Social insurance was the spearhead of spending policy, and even when it was financed out of contributions, it marked a most important advance in the regulation of the labour market by the state. It was conceived of by many writers as a protective device, which heralded the beginning of a period of extended collectivisation.

There was one other important development within economies, which was to prove important in the subsequent history of planning—the growth of large-scale private enterprises which depended for their success upon efficient internal planning, including market planning. Between 1890 and 1914 there was considerable concentration of industry in bodies like the German *Stahlwerksverband*, set up in 1904, or the United States Steel Corporation, set up in 1901. Under the control of powerful industrial titans, who have been described as the true pace-makers of planning, big business became a 'system of organised power'.[1] In the United States, by 1904, trusts controlled two-fifths of the manufacturing capital of the country, while in Germany there was a continuous line of development from private cartellisation and government assistance given to cartels before 1914 down to the economic planning by the state in the 1930's. Before 1914 many German economists already conceived of the state as the central regulator of the economic life of the community and of big business as a model of efficient organisation. During the first world war in Germany and in the United States, as elsewhere, state control had to be exercised through the mediation of business men and business organisations, and Walther Rathenau, who did much to build up the war-time apparatus in Germany, is reported to have said that he learned all that he knew about the planned economy from his father, the managing director of the *Allgemeine Elektrizitäts Gesellschaft*. Rathenau was himself the director of at least sixty-eight business concerns.

It is important to trace one branch of the pedigree of planning back to such beginnings. While socialism remained a gospel, the so-called socialisation of large-scale enterprise was already a fact. Economists have noted the convergence of capitalism and socialism with a 'twilight zone'[2] of intermediate and transitional forms like the *Rheinisch-West-*

[1] R. A. Brady, *Business as a System of Power* (New York, 1943).
[2] A. H. Hansen, *Economic Stabilization in an Unbalanced World* (New York, 1932), p. 329.

fälisches Elektrizitätswerk, which gave shares and seats on one of its boards of directors to municipal corporations like Essen and Gelsenkirchen. By 1914 in Germany there were seventy-five town corporations participating in ninety-five mixed enterprises. In other countries also, although the interpenetration of business and politics had not approached the German standard, joint enterprises and municipal ownership had taken root by 1914, and a liberal economist could write in 1911 that the future of democracy depended upon its success in dealing with the problems of public ownership and regulation.[1] Certainly the monopolistic structure of industry already contained organisations pointing towards planning and central control, and it was clear that dissatisfaction with private ownership coupled with central control would generate new schemes for control in the name of the community.

The first challenge to the pre-war system came from within the individual economies, but there was also an implicit challenge in the relations between them. Even before 1914 the balance of economic power was shifting. The first world war, while it marked a violent break in the process of economic change, was not entirely responsible for the subsequent strains and stresses within the world economy. In particular the sharp distinction between European workshops and overseas granaries had become blurred by 1914, although it was the first world war which was responsible for making the trend clear. Changes in the technique of industrial production, making industries less dependent on highly trained and specialised labour and on specialised raw material supplies like coal, were being commented on before 1914. Between 1895 and 1914 Japanese industry in particular, assisted by foreign capital, made spectacular advances in industries such as textiles, where the number of machine looms increased in the ten years before the war from 19,000 to 123,000. Industrialisation was beginning to be regarded as one of the basic tests of national progress; and it appeared just as unlikely that smaller countries would accept indefinitely the international economic order, which had been built up in the nineteenth century, as that underprivileged social groups would accept the internal distribution of income and property, which had made possible vast capital accumulation and expansion of trade. The relationship between industrialisation, investment and protection was already being underlined by politicians in 'new' countries, and in Australia, to take one example, there was a fundamental alliance between nationalism, including economic nationalism, and democracy. Tariffs were valued not only as symbols of autonomy but also as instruments in the construction of a national system of political economy.

There was a further change in the international economy, which was to upset the balance of the whole system. The position of the United Kingdom was changing. Although in 1914 it retained its position as

[1] F. W. Taussig, *Principles of Economics* (London, 1911 ed.), vol. II, p. 411.

the hub of the international system, its position was increasingly vulnerable. The reasons for this were both internal and external. Internally there was a falling rate of industrial growth, compared with the first three quarters of the nineteenth century, and in the coal, cotton and iron and steel industries there were ominous signs of decline. British industrialists gained ground at the expense of landowners, but Britain's industrial leadership was shaking. Externally the United Kingdom faced increasing competition, and although world trade was expanding rapidly, the United Kingdom's share was diminishing. At the same time, imports began to increase more rapidly than exports, partly as a result of falling transport costs and partly as a result of a slightly more equal internal distribution of incomes. Despite the enormous capital exports of the decade before 1914, payments for imports were always greater than current earnings from the sale of goods and services. The prosperity of the United Kingdom depended on the possibility of maintaining a large and growing income from interest payments overseas and on the continued rapid exploitation of overseas territories which produced the world 'boom' of 1900–14. Even had there been no world war between 1914 and 1918 to diminish the United Kingdom's foreign assets, it is likely that the collapse of this boom would have had serious effects on the structure of the world economy.

While the position of the United Kingdom was changing, so too was that of the United States. Although in 1914 the United States was still a debtor country and played a relatively minor part in world trade in manufactured goods, it was already ahead in output figures for coal, of which it produced over 42 per cent of the world's supply; steel, of which it produced over 41 per cent; and new industries, like the motor-car industry, in which it produced more cars than the rest of the world put together. With a vast and well-protected home market and up-to-date industrial equipment, the United States was in a strong strategic position in world industry, and the trend of relative productivity was in its favour as against the United Kingdom and Europe from the time that the first calculations were made for the period beginning in 1907. There was a shift in economic power, and the position in the international system not only of the United Kingdom but also of Europe was becoming increasingly precarious.

These shifts in economic power did not prevent the resumption of pre-war multilateralism at the end of the conflict, nor did they destroy the existing pattern of trade, but they did prevent a return to the balance of the pre-war world. The maladjustments of the succeeding period, which culminated in the Great Depression of 1929, had their origins in the period before the war, just as the ideas and first crude instruments of national planning did. Against a background of international transformation and, after 1929, breakdown, the demand for planning grew in intensity.

Conscious national planning was contrasted with 'automatic' international interdependence, politics was thought to offer redress for the failures of economics, and governments were called to the assistance both of sectional interests and of whole economies. In the experiments which were mooted or tried, the experience of the war years was frequently invoked, for it was the war years which first taught the need for national planning and provided some of the techniques for making the planning produce results.

The violent break in the continuity of economic development and the shattering of the links in the network of world trade compelled single countries or groups of countries to fall back on their own resources. Germany in particular, where the process of cartellisation and business planning had gone farthest, was a 'beleaguered fortress', cut off by the allied blockade, which was proclaimed immediately after the outbreak of war but which did not become fully effective until after the entry of the United States into the struggle in 1917. The Allies too faced a serious shipping problem, which was made more serious by the German submarine offensive. From the time of David Hume onwards economists had held that the conditions of siege justified the imposition of controls like rationing. The world war posed a production problem, however, as well as a distribution problem, and in this field too the belligerents found it necessary to plan from the centre. Once economics became the controlling factor in war, economies had to be controlled. The longer the war lasted the more politicians found it difficult to reconcile the objective of winning the war with that of maintaining inviolate the autonomy of private business. Market mechanisms could not operate unchecked. But the transition to controlled systems was slow and hesitant, not usually the work of deliberate design, but shaped by the pressure of tightening scarcity and the insatiable needs of war production. Before 1914 there had been no detailed discussion, even in Germany, of the special 'political economy of war'. By the time that the war ended, administrators like von Möllendorff were talking about *Planwirtschaft*, while business men were sighing for a return to 'normalcy'.

The same essential problems faced all the belligerents, although the shape of the problems could not be perceived in many cases until emergencies and crises endowed them with urgent clarity. Large-scale modern wars involve organising the full employment of all available national resources, allocating them to various producers not only in the right order of priority but also in the right proportions at the right time, and so arranging financial and price policies that real resources are transferred rapidly to the war effort. All these implications of large-scale organised violence were less clear in 1914 than they were in 1918, and less clear in 1918 than they were in 1945. The first world war was full of surprises.

The generals could not end it quickly, the factories could not produce sufficient munitions, civilians could not be neglected in the distribution of supplies, and the financial problem bore no resemblance at all to pre-war financial questions. In trying to deal with these problems governments faced all kinds of resistances, even resistances within their own ranks from those committed to doctrines of free trade and individualism. Although business men had to be associated with the framework of control in most countries, the *Politisierung* of economic life was not received with universal enthusiasm. A widely-felt sentiment was expressed by Karl Helfferich, the director of the Anatolian Railway and the Deutsche Bank, when he wrote on being appointed to a new German economic department that the office would understand its task best if it returned as soon as possible to pre-war economic conditions.

It was Rathenau and not Helfferich who was most responsible for planning the economy of war-time Germany, the first of the belligerents to accept the challenge of full economic mobilisation. In August 1914 he was given extensive powers. As a result of his warning about problems of continuous supply, the War Raw Materials Department (*Kriegs-Rohstoff Abteilung*) was set up in August 1914 to deal with problems of conservation, production of substitutes and planned distribution. By the end of the year a whole range of technical offices for materials like metals, wool and timber, was in being. *Kriegswirtschafts-gesellschaften*, war-work agencies, acted as connecting links between government and business. In 1916 all the various branches of centralised authority were co-ordinated in a Supreme War Office (*Oberster Kriegsamt*) under the direct orders of General Groener. The economic system now operated as a whole under close central direction. The Labour Laws of 1916 (*Hilfsdienstgesetz*) regulated manpower, while measures to control prices operated through a chain of price-control offices (*Preisprüfungsstellen*).

More important than this new economic structure were the attitudes it created. Rathenau himself claimed that the economic task was no longer a private one but the task of the community. He saw the war not as a battle between armies but as a prolonged contest between two economic rivals who, except for a few enclaves, had divided the globe between themselves into two gigantic state-socialistic organisations. The final issue in the war was not the victory or defeat of the German army but the victory or defeat of the German economy (*Bedarfsorganisation*). If the result should be victory, the task would be to go forward in peace as in war from private to collective economy, *Gemeinwirtschaft*.

In the United Kingdom there was less clear-cut formulation of new doctrines, although there was increasing resort to new expedients. Although many steps were taken to control the economy before the crisis of December 1916, it was from that date onwards that key ministries like those of Food and Shipping began to function and the small War Cabinet provided a compact agency for central co-ordination. The War Cabinet reported that the war, and especially the year 1917, had brought about a transformation of the social and administrative structure of the state, 'much of which is bound to be permanent',[1] and that the vast majority of the people were working directly or indirectly on public service. The process was a cumulative one. In the case of munitions, the War Office turned down a proposal in October 1914 that the government should take over the big armament firms and run them as a branch of the public service, and it was not until May 1915 that a Ministry of Munitions was formed. It faced problems concerning priorities, allocations, prices and employment which were met by extensions of control first vertically to cover raw material supplies and second horizontally to cover civilian needs as well as military requirements. In the organisation of food supplies and shipping, steps were slow, but final ramifications were wide. Market mechanisms could never have accomplished what was urgent and necessary. The Ministry of Food, 'suppressing private enterprise completely, accomplished what private enterprise in the country could never have accomplished'.[2] The Ministry of Shipping focused attention on the necessity for a national import policy, which would provide for the needs of the economy as a whole. From the questions raised and the answers tentatively suggested to them a scheme of planning emerged. 'Hundreds of improvisations originating in shortages of sand-bags or shells or food, and the more fundamental scarcities of shipping and manpower had fallen together into a pattern. Very few people saw them as a pattern; fewer still saw the logic that informed it.'[3]

That there was a pattern is best revealed by examining the experience of the one belligerent which failed to build up a satisfactory machinery of war-time planning, Russia. Within a few months of the outbreak of the war there was an acute shortage of guns and ammunition and insufficient industrial potential to provide for current military requirements. By the winter of 1916 economic disorganisation had reached an advanced stage. In that year, despite increased war demand, iron and steel production was down by 16 per cent and coal production by 10 per cent on the 1914 figures. There was no manpower policy. The direction of 37 per cent of the Russian population to the army seriously crippled what was already an inadequate industrial effort. The food situation was disastrous. Although in 1916 the government adopted measures for controlling the grain trade, and in March 1917 the new regime proclaimed the grain trade a state monopoly, there were acute food shortages particularly in the towns and there was consequent increased political discontent. By 1917 it was clear that no measures taken from the centre could be effective without a

---

[1] Cmd. 9005 (1918).
[2] W. H. Beveridge, *British Food Control* (1928), p. 338.
[3] W. K. Hancock and M. M. Gowing, *British War Economy* (1949), p. 29.

revolutionary impetus to drive them forward. Allied planning efforts had depended above all else on consent: planning in the revolutionary Russian situation would have to depend on force. The solutions the Bolshevik revolutionaries worked out for meeting problems of prolonged emergency and civil war were to have an important influence in the history of planning in the post-war years (see ch. XIV).

There was one other type of war-time planning which was important. To replace the multilateral market systems of pre-war years the Allies built up an extensive apparatus of international economic co-operation. In the early stages of the war an International Food Commission was set up in London to secure an orderly distribution of supplies instead of a competitive scramble. Later developments led to the evolution of two main groups of commodity organisations, one under a Food Council and the other under a Munitions Council. In addition the Allied Maritime Transport Council aimed at applying the same principles of shipping-pooling and allocation which had already been developed by the United Kingdom. It became the hub of the Allied war machine.

This structure of Allied organisations involved no usurpation of the distinctive tasks of the separate national governments. 'The international machine was not an external organisation based on delegated authority. It was the national organisations linked together for international work, and themselves forming the instruments for that work.'[1] When the machinery was destroyed in the holocaust of controls at the end of the war, all that remained were the separate national economic policies of the various individual states, and they too, influenced by demands from business interests, were anxious to abandon the structure of planning and in the words of the *Journal Officiel* in France in December 1918 'to re-establish freedom of business transactions with the utmost possible rapidity'.

The result was a general movement against war-time planning in face of which most governments were prepared to retreat. In the case of both the United Kingdom and Germany, the governments during the war had captured the commanding heights of the economy without taking part in any direct frontal movement. When the war ended, the purpose which had inspired the creation of the framework of control disappeared. First the post-war boom and then the sharp contraction generated a new set of responses. The boom 'stirred starved appetites to new and clamourous life';[2] the slump destroyed the last vestiges of solidarity and threw all relics of war-time schemes into the melting pot. The work of de-control was carried out thoroughly. Some controls merely lapsed and nothing was done to renew them, others were jettisoned. In the international

[1] J. A. Salter, *Allied Shipping Control* (1921), p. 179.
[2] R. H. Tawney, 'The Abolition of Economic Controls' (*Economic History Review*, vol. XIII, p. 1, 1943).

field, the United States exerted all its influence behind the drive to abolish inter-Allied control of raw materials. 'This government', wrote Hoover, 'will not agree to any programme that even looks like inter-Allied control of our resources after peace.'[1] The result was that not only did bodies like the Coal Control Department in Britain and the *consortiums* in France disappear, but also the Allied Maritime Transport Council. The disappearance of the international agencies made the task of world reconstruction more difficult. War conditions did not end with the end of hostilities, and collective disorganisation still called for collective effort. The fact that this was not forthcoming led to many of the problems of the following six or seven years.

If the machinery of planning was abruptly put out of action, it did not go without leaving a trace. In many governments there were some people or groups in favour of continued control. Möllendorff's plans in Germany for continued planning were defeated, but the Constitution of the Weimar Republic placed considerable emphasis on economic matters, and laid down a system of workers' and economic councils with a National Economic Council (*Reichswirtschaftsrat*) at the top of the pyramid. Although the Council only functioned on a provisional basis after it came into being in 1920, the idea remained important in Germany. In France, where some attempt was made to convert war-machinery to peace-time purposes, a National Economic Council was set up in 1925. In the United Kingdom some members of the government in the last stages of the war were in favour of continued state action, and there were important groups, particularly among organised labour, who demanded continued state intervention in times of peace.

There was one other legacy of war-time experience. When it became clear that the world after 1918 was very different from the world before 1914 and that there could be no mere restoration, the metaphors of war began to reappear in peace-time and were employed in the planning 'campaigns' of the 1930's. In the Soviet Union there continued to be agrarian and industrial 'fronts', 'battles' of production, 'brigade leaders' in the collective farms and 'shock' workers. In Italy a 'Battle of the Grain' was pushed forward from 1925 onwards 'to free the Italian people from the slavery of foreign bread'. In National Socialist Germany a similar battle of agricultural production was waged in 1934, while the Labour Front abandoned the old differentiations of the trade union movement and organised groups in the industrial plants to provide 'a soldier-like kernel' to labour organisation. Compulsory labour service was developed on military lines, and soldiers of labour were urged to become replicas of soldiers of war. All these schemes attempted to re-create the community of purpose and solidarity of interests which had made war-time planning possible.

[1] A. Zimmern, *The League of Nations and the Rule of Law* (London, 1938), p. 157.

The effects of the world war on the development of planning went much farther, however, than the occasional continuity of institutions or the rebirth of metaphors. The post-war world, despite the apparent revival of multilateral trade between 1925 and 1929, was inherently unstable. There were important changes both in the pace and in the direction of economic expansion. Some of these changes were the result of long-term trends, others were the consequence in part at least of the post-war settlement. The break-down of world trade in the years of the Great Depression from 1929–32 diverted the attention of individual countries to their own immediate problems. Each country took steps which its government thought might be favourable to its own recovery, paying small regard to their possible international repercussions. The single world economy, which had already been disrupted by the first world war, was replaced in the 1930's by a multiplicity of national economies each concerned with the well-being of its own members. In the change of government policies the Great Depression was the watershed.

The instabilities of the 1920's were not always immediately plain. As a result of the war and the treaties, powerful large economic units were broken up and the number of nation-states multiplied. Whereas before 1914 the population of Germany and Austro-Hungary taken together substantially exceeded that of the United States, after 1919, of the twenty-nine European states, only five had more than 40 million inhabitants and ten had less than 5 million. While economic forces were making for continued economic interdependence, political forces were re-emphasising the importance of sovereignty and of national frontiers. In central Europe, the large free-trade area of the Austro-Hungarian empire was split up into a number of succession states each with its own currency and tariffs. On ten German finished goods in 1913, the Austro-Hungarian tariff had amounted to 16–25 per cent. In Hungary in 1927 it was up to 34–54 per cent and in 1931 to 42–61 per cent. Farther east, partly for reasons of revenue, Roumania and Bulgaria built high tariff walls very quickly after 1919.

Even more important in the 1920's than tariffs or re-drawing of boundaries was the changed balance of debtor-creditor relationships. During the war the United Kingdom had sold about £1000 million of foreign investments and although by 1929 total investments were higher than in 1913, there was a significant contraction in the frontiers of the British 'empire of investment' and considerable dangerous long-term lending out of short-term funds attracted to London from overseas. London was no longer the directing market in international finance, and rival centres, particularly New York, were growing in importance. The disintegration of the central financial nucleus of the pre-1914 world was well advanced by 1929.

While the position of the United Kingdom was increasingly subject to strain, the position of the United States became dominant. While the United Kingdom was passing through an uneasy period of under-employment and industrial maladjustment, the United States galloped through the roaring boom of 1922-9. At the same time it reinforced the position it had secured during the war of being the world's biggest creditor. American foreign investments rose from $2000 million in 1913 to $15,000 million in 1930, 30 per cent of them being located in Europe. Many of the maladjustments in the post-war economy were concealed by the high level of United States capital exports in the decade after the end of the war. The cessation of American lending during the Great Depression contributed greatly to the international collapse.

Without American loans it would have proved impossible to pay either reparations or war-debts, the two complicating political factors in the European economy. German payments under the Dawes Plan of 1924 were met out of American loans and the net import of capital into Germany during the period of the Plan was more than twice the amount of German reparations payments. German reparation payments to the ex-Allies were used by them to pay annual war-debt sums to the United States. 'Reparations and Inter-allied debts', wrote Keynes in 1926, 'are being mainly settled in paper and not in goods. The United States lends money to Germany, Germany transfers its equivalent to the Allies, the Allies pass it back to the United States Government. Nothing real passes —no one is a penny the worse.'[1]

The continued existence of this circular flow depended on American capital, and American lending was less reliable than the pre-war British lending which had held the system together. From 1925 to 1929 there was apparent recovery from the difficult period of post-war reconstruction —world production of foodstuffs and raw materials was increased by 11 per cent, of manufactures by 26 per cent and world trade by 19 per cent —but the prosperity contained within itself the seeds of decay. In 1928 the United States diverted short-term funds for speculative investment in the home boom: in 1929 it recalled them in face of a break in confidence, a contraction in home demand and a falling price-level. As the flow dried up the world economy collapsed, and even after the revival of the 1930's, international financing remained very small. The collapse was general, affecting men, money and materials. Out of it national planning of many types emerged.

The subsequent break-down of the international monetary system was of fundamental importance. Pre-war multilateral trade had been based on the relatively stable order of the gold standard. The war disrupted the system, but after the end of hostilities there was a general desire to return to gold. Sweden in 1924, the United Kingdom (on unfavourable terms) in 1925, France (de facto) in 1926, Belgium in 1927, Italy in 1928 and

---

[1] In *The Nation and Athenaeum*, 11 September 1926.

many other countries were back on the standard by 1929. The formal restoration of the gold standard was accomplished without the conditions for its smooth and safe working being assured. Gold was and became increasingly unevenly distributed, and the quest for large gold reserves led to 'gold nationalism' in many centres. Those countries which most needed gold as a buffer stock to safeguard insecure balances of payments often possessed the most inadequate supply. The holding of foreign exchange in addition to gold, secured largely as a result of short-term borrowing, was particularly vulnerable in times of depression and strain. After 1929 there were large and disturbing movements of short-term capital, 'hot money', pressing dangerously on national gold and foreign exchange reserves. Wage-rigidities, war-debts, reparations and badly chosen parities made the stable working of the system still more difficult.

The working of the gold exchange standard imposed particularly heavy strains on London, for the United Kingdom had to hold a bigger gold reserve than before 1914 if it was to absorb international shocks. The position proved untenable. In the financial crisis of 1931 it was not the current balance of payments which constituted the immediate danger to the pound but the speculative movements of large foreign short-term balances in London. In September 1931 the Bank of England was forced to suspend gold payments. The following day the standard was abandoned. This was the prelude to a general movement off gold. Apart from the 'sterling bloc' countries, twelve countries left the gold standard between September 1931 and August 1932. In 1933 the dollar went off the gold standard and finally in September 1936 France abandoned the attempt to 'save the franc' and also went off gold.

The instability of the system and its subsequent breakdown depended in large measure on the United States. In addition to clinging to war debts, even after the Lausanne Conference of July 1932 put an end to reparations claims, the United States followed a protectionist policy in international trade. After the beginning of the depression the Hawley–Smoot Act of 1930 raised the already high protective duties imposed by the Fordney–McCumber tariff of 1922. It provoked a series of retaliatory measures in many parts of the world. 'The debts of the outside world to us', wrote the President of the Chase National Bank in 1930, 'are ropes about their necks, by means of which we pull them towards us. Our trade restrictions are pitchforks pressed against their bodies, by means of which we hold them off.'[1] Such contradictions reflected the large extent to which American economic policy was closely bound up with internal sectional pressures, which put obstacles in the way of international interdependence. The contradictions persisted. The dollar was devalued in 1933 although the United States maintained a large favourable balance of trade and continued to attract gold from other countries. Devaluation

---

[1] *Chase Economic Bulletin*, 14 March 1930.

had the effect of increasing disequilibrium and raising tariffs to foreign sellers. It made international economic agreement increasingly difficult just at the time when the World Monetary and Economic Conference was meeting in London.

The end of the international gold standard meant that individual countries or groups of countries had to *manage* their own currencies. The problems of management involved deliberate control of credit and exchange. The controls imposed were often tighter than they had been during the first world war and began to be identified with control of other branches of policy as well. In some countries, like Germany, there was a direct link between exchange control and national economic planning. Out of the monetary crisis more positive lines of policy were taken up.

There were two other important extensions of government action which became increasingly important during and after the Great Depression— first, the control of agriculture, and second, the control of unemployment. In neither case was government intervention entirely new. State planning of agriculture had frequently been considered as a special case. The doctrine of 'due balance' of writers like Adolf Wagner in the 1890's had emphasised that the state should not allow industrialisation to go too far. After 1929 the argument was sometimes stood on its head on the grounds that agricultural economies needed the balancing influence of industry if they were to maintain their stability. In both formulations the farmers played an important part. In addition to their being an important political force particularly in the 'green international countries' of eastern and southern Europe, they were often taken to represent a 'way of life' which it deemed important for governments to protect and to maintain. At the same time industrial countries like the United Kingdom took steps to protect farmers in the interests of stability and ultimately of defence, while Germany and Italy went forward with schemes for encouraging self-sufficiency.

The Great Depression exposed the primary-product markets to exceptionally fierce strains and stresses. Before 1914 trade in primary products had increased *pari passu* with the index of world manufacturing. The result was a great increase in the world's producing areas, particularly in the decade before 1914. Improvements in productivity and government encouragement to agriculture during the war led to an increased flow of primary products. After 1919 demand failed to keep pace with supply. A slackening off in rates of population growth in north-west Europe and North America was coupled with a change in tastes induced by increasing income. Improvements in the standard of living led less to an increase in the consumption of bulky foodstuffs and more to an increase in the demand for light manufactured goods, services and luxuries. The fall in the rate of growth of demand hit countries specialising in the production of primary products. Their vulnerable position was concealed in the 1920's by loans and a high level of demand maintained during the boom, but there were signs as early as 1927 that there would be a break in agricultural prices. The calamitous price fall was held back by accumulation of stocks and by continued industrial prosperity, until the contraction of United States demand in 1929 and the release of stocks accelerated the collapse of the markets. The price fall upset the already precarious balance-of-payments positions of the primary producing countries—Australia had balance-of-payments difficulties as early as 1928—and encouraged protectionism and restrictionism. In such conditions industrial producers were bound to suffer also. Between 1929 and the third quarter of 1932 the value of international trade shrank by more than 65 per cent while the international trade of non-European countries fell to less than 30 per cent of its 1929 level.

Just as the collapse of the international gold standard made it essential for countries to manage their own currencies, so the price fall and the extreme poverty and hardship among primary producers provoked various forms of government action. Traditional instruments like tariffs proved inadequate, and controls of marketing, price formation, capital development and distribution were introduced in many countries. In National Socialist Germany agriculture was the most completely regulated sector of the economy and the Reich Food Estate (*Reichsnährstand*) along with marketing associations (*Marktverbände*) directed the home food-markets, while State Boards (*Reichsstellen*) were given a monopolistic control over the import and export of the principal foodstuffs. In the United Kingdom, the Agricultural Marketing Act of 1933 provided for the organisation of marketing schemes for commodities like milk, potatoes and hops. In recommending that imports of bacon should fluctuate with the level of national production, the Pig Reorganisation Commission conceived of quotas as instruments of long-term agricultural planning. In the United States the First Agricultural Adjustment Act of 1933 aimed at raising farmers' incomes by restricting agricultural output and controlling marketing, while the Second Act of 1938 maintained the apparatus of parity prices and agreed quotas. Once agricultural quotas were introduced there was considerable temptation to extend their scope and use. In Roumania, for example, quotas were first employed in November 1932 on 120 articles. In July 1933 the number of articles was increased to 500, covering 80 per cent of Roumania's imports. French quotas covered one-seventh of tariff items in July 1932: by 1934, one-half were covered. This extension of quantitative import restrictions was one of the most important features of the 'thirties.

Most of the international schemes for dealing with the world market in primary products were producers' schemes aimed at restricting production or dividing markets at a fixed and agreed price level. Some of them like the Stevenson Scheme in rubber and the Copper Exporters' Incorporated were applied before 1929, others, like the International Steel Cartel, were set up in the 1930's. Although these bodies have been described as transitional institutions linking the international expansion of business enterprises and the growth of economic planning, they grew out of the unhealthy restrictive environment of economic blizzard.

In one case at least the reaction against the price fall and the traditional deflationary measures for dealing with the consequent monetary crisis produced an experiment not in restrictionism but in welfare 'planning'. In New Zealand the collapse of farm prices threatened the whole economy, for agriculture accounted for 65 per cent of total production in 1928 and the pastoral products for 92 per cent of total exports. After a deflationary period of 'all-round sacrifice', the policy was adopted of pushing forward social security legislation and developing a 'welfare state'. The liberal spending policy embarked upon provoked serious exchange problems and a crisis was only averted by credits from the United Kingdom in 1939. The history of the New Zealand revolt against 'the impersonal international price system' showed the difficulties of reconciling national aims with international stability.

If the pressure of primary producers and of primary producing countries led to various forms of planning in the 1930's, that of the unemployed was equally important. The existence of large-scale involuntary unemployment was the most alarming symptom of the Great Depression. The United Kingdom peak was reached in 1932 (nearly 3 millions); there were over 13 million unemployed in the United States in 1933 when President Roosevelt came into power; in 1933 there were 6–7 million unemployed in Germany. The existence of these large numbers of unemployed provided a political and an economic challenge, and in the United States and Germany in particular the provision of full employment appeared as the primary objective of government economic policy.

The National Socialist regime began with a series of stop-gap measures to end the social consequences of the policy of deflation. President Roosevelt offered a 'new deal'. There was nothing revolutionary in its philosophy or purposes. Its first object was to pull the United States out of the slump, its second to widen the concept of social justice, its third to balance the economic system. None of these objectives involved any long-term over-all plan, but they all involved the increased intervention of government and optimistic hopes that an economy founded on scarcity would give way to an economy based on abundance. The American 'experiment' stimulated interest in the problems of planning both in the United States and Europe, and the view was widely held that Roosevelt's 'strivings towards reconstruction and revival are as surely the outstanding example of reformed Capitalism as the Russian Five Year Plans are of Socialist planning in the world of today'.[1]

[1] G. D. H. Cole, *Practical Economics* (1937), p. 145: see also ch. VII.

National proposals for collective action in the interests of stability in matters of money, materials and employment varied according to their country of origin and its social philosophy. There was never a pure technique of planning, although there were 'technocrats' who believed in a new science of social engineering, and all governments had to employ larger numbers of expert economic advisers to study problems of income and outlay. The breakdown of the international economic system produced a series of different national reactions varying from *sauve qui peut* devices to comprehensive schemes for transforming the whole social structure. 'We may not all be socialists now,' wrote Robbins in 1934, 'but we are certainly (nearly) all planners.'[1]

There were only two planning schemes which were general in character —those of the Soviet Union and Germany. There was frequent talk of planning elsewhere. President Roosevelt, in introducing the Tennessee Valley Scheme in May 1933, claimed that it was time to extend planning to a wider field as part of a return to the spirit and vision of the pioneer. Fascist economists talked of *corporativismo* as a new order in which the distribution of labour and capital as well as the system of production would be planned in advance. Neither the United States nor Italy, however, could be described as a planned economy in the same sense that Germany and the Soviet Union could. In the United States there was only very limited central control: in Italy there was a façade of control, but it was not until 1936 and 1937 that Mussolini emphasised the significance of increasing state intervention in industry. As late as 1938 there was little co-ordination of the national economy through the action of the corporations.

At the beginning of the Great Depression the one comprehensive planning scheme in operation was that of the Soviet Union. As a result of the revolution and the formulation of economic policy in the 1920's, the Soviet Union had virtually disappeared from the international economic stage, and during the depression remained insulated from the world economy.

The Soviet planning system set out in a phrase of Trotsky's to bring aim and plan into the very basis of society, although at the beginning of the revolution the mechanisms of planning were still to be thought out as well as worked out. 'There was nothing written about such matters in the Bolshevik textbooks, or even in those of the Mensheviks', wrote Lenin six months after the October Revolution. The machinery of planning in the Soviet Union, as in the case of war-time economic organisation, was the product of national emergency. It was at first tentative and hesitant, but it improved as a result of actual experience

---

[1] L. Robbins, *The Great Depression* (1934), p. 145.

of economic administration, first in emergency conditions and then in the period of transformation under the First and Second Five Year Plans. There was continual adaptation and change, and even such a fundamental problem as that of relating central 'steering' to local managerial effort was tackled by trial and error rather than by deliberate design.

The basic problem of the Soviet economy was that of transforming a backward country into an extensively industrialised state without having to depend on private capitalists at home or on foreign investors overseas. The history of the transformation has been divided into four main phases—first, the period of war-communism from the revolution of 1917 down to March 1921, during which in emergency conditions the state set out to capture the commanding heights of the existing economic system; second, the period of recovery and restoration, accomplished within the framework of the New Economic Policy, aiming at increasing the flow of goods to the markets; third, the period of intensive industrialisation and agricultural collectivisation, beginning with the First Five Year Plan in 1928; and fourth, the period of trade expansion, which followed the abolition of rationing in 1934–5. In the late 1930's the shadow of war affected the orientation of Soviet planning in a way that the Great Depression never had done.

In all these phases of development the idea of planning a new society from the centre by use of all the available instruments of the party and the state became much more concrete. Strategic questions concerning the rate of investment, the location of industry, the development of new sources of power and the balance between industrial and agricultural prices and production demanded firm answers. Drawing up plans could not be disassociated from 'plan fulfilment'. 'Planning is no mere piling up of tables and figures unrelated to the course of fulfilment of the plan', said Molotov in 1939.[1] Nor could long-term 'perspective planning' overshadow the need for current planning in terms of immediately available resources. 'There is too much talk of electrification, and too little about *current* economic plans', Lenin wrote to the Chairman of the Gosplan in 1921.[2] The practical tasks of immediate policy-making and supervision of actual production demanded efficient state machinery, which could only be tested by experience. 'Socialist construction cannot proceed otherwise than gropingly, and, wherever practice is in advance of theory, faultless creativeness is impossible.'[3]

The first important plan projected in the Soviet Union was drawn up in 1920. It was a 'perspective' economic plan anticipating extensive electrification of industry in the future. Current planning developed slowly. In February 1921 *Gosplan* was set up as an advisory body attached to the

---

[1] *The Third Five Year Plan of the National Economy of the U.S.S.R.* (Moscow, 1939), pp. 20–1.   [2] Lenin, *Collected Works*, vol. XXVI, p. 296.
[3] *Control Figures of the National Economy* (1928–9), p. 2.

Council of Labour and Defence, drafting plans for controlling crisis sectors of the national economy, such as fuel supply and the corn trade, and passing judgment on departmental plans drawn up independently. In 1925 *Gosplan* began to issue economic 'control figures' for the whole of the Soviet economy, but it was not until 1931, after long controversies, that the series of figures taken from separate industries became a system of figures related to an over-all plan for the ensuing year. The setting up of a Central Administration of Economic Accounting of the *Gosplan* in 1931 improved the collection and use of available statistical information, without which effective planning would have been impossible.

By 1931 the First Five Year Plan was well advanced. It began as a 'perspective' plan, but was discussed and reshaped frequently before it was put into practice. Its keynote was a high rate of investment, particularly in heavy industry and in agriculture. During the first two years of the plan the objectives were secured without great difficulty, but in 1929 and 1930 many problems arose as a result of inflationary pressure and a deliberate attempt by the government to force the pace. In the case of agriculture, enforced collectivisation was pushed by vigorous coercion. At the beginning of June 1929 only 4 per cent of the farmers were employed on collective farms. By the beginning of March 1930 the figure had risen to 55 per cent and by 1936 to 90 per cent. Coercion solved most of the government's agricultural problems, which had proved so difficult during the 1920's, and at the cost of great immediate hardship agriculture was integrated into the general planning system. The years 1929–31 marked the final capture by the state of the whole of the economic system. In 1929 the trade unions were reformed and the old leaders were dismissed, factory discipline became stricter and the new unions became state agencies for raising productivity in the interests of the plan. A year later credit and fiscal reforms made possible more effective central planning.

The First Five Year Plan set the model, and its successor, the Second Five Year Plan, extending from 1933 to the end of 1937, stressed practical advance and consolidation rather than gigantic leaps forward. The economic atmosphere in which it was carried through was favourable. By 1935 it was considered safe to abandon rationing. Agriculture had been reorganised to meet national requirements. Industrial productivity was rising at a remarkable rate. New factories were well established. In 1937 four-fifths of industrial output came from plants that were newly built or that had been reconstructed since 1928, while two metallurgical plants alone, Magnitogorsk and Stalinsk, had a productive capacity equal to that of the entire pre-1914 iron and steel industry.

During the 1930's refinements were made in the apparatus of economic planning. The *Gosplan* was reformed on two occasions, in 1935 and in 1938. In 1935 the Praesidium of the *Gosplan* was abolished and a chairman was appointed with far wider powers than before. A departmental distinction was drawn between planning for co-ordination, including financial and allocation planning, and planning for separate branches of the national economy. Increasing attention was paid to the method of balancing estimates as a means of checking the correctness of the planned relations between different industries. In 1938 the leadership role of the *Gosplan* was stressed and its Commissioners were made responsible for plan supervision and fulfilment on the spot. The core of the Gosplan was to be eleven members selected by the Council of People's Commissars from the leading planning workers in the country. The eleven members were to be assisted by a council of ninety, a large administrative staff and a number of subsidiary functional bodies. Although economic administration was still left to other agencies, *Gosplan* had established its position as the central headquarters of Soviet planning.

The size of the Soviet economic system enabled it to pay smaller attention to foreign trade than would have been possible for a country more dependent on supplies of imports. On the basis of a great variety of agricultural and non-agricultural materials, the Soviet Union was able to set up and operate plants which turned out most of the manufacturing products necessary for the development of the economy. From 1918 onwards international trade was monopolised by the state Commissariat for Foreign Trade (*Narcomvneshtorg*). The monopoly enabled the government to maintain the rouble at an artificial value in terms of foreign currencies and to insist on an extremely rigid import programme. From 1929 to 1932 almost 90 per cent of imports consisted of goods for use in industry.

The volume of foreign trade remained low. 1930 was the peak year, when it reached 73 per cent of the 1913 level. The Second Five Year Plan limited exports to 'surplus products of the national economy' and imports to whatever level was reached by exports. In 1938 the total volume of foreign trade amounted to only 24 per cent of the 1913 level. Soviet planning was thus as independent as possible of world economic movements—indeed at times it could run directly counter to them as in the case of the 'dumping' on foreign markets during the Great Depression of exports sold at prices well below costs. Insulation from the world economy meant that trade could be used as a political instrument, with long-term foreign contracts and agreements acting as useful political counters.

It is difficult to evaluate the efficiency of the Soviet planning system, but its appeal, particularly to backward areas of Asia and south-east Europe, neglected by economically 'advanced' countries, was plain before 1939. The successes of the Soviet experiment aroused new hopes among many 'undeveloped countries'. The Turkish Five Year Plan and the Mexican Six Year Plan were influenced by it, and the Polish scheme, begun in 1936 and interrupted in 1939, to plan an industrial central district within fifteen years showed signs of Soviet influence. Foreign exchange control was introduced in April 1936, and foreign trade was placed on a quota and clearance basis, although it was west towards Germany and not east towards the Soviet Union that Poland looked.

German planning, unlike Soviet planning, accepted private enterprise and the economic institutions of capitalism. Within this framework the government assumed a powerful control over manpower and production, distribution and banking, consumption and investment, and foreign exchange and trade. The aim of the government was to direct the economic machine for political purposes, ultimately for the needs of war. The means at its disposal were flexible. 'Economic policy in the national socialist state', wrote one commentator, 'is determined by considerations of expediency, and, without prejudice, applies such means as are necessary in every given case for the welfare of the people.'[1] The term 'welfare' was elastic, but the effect of government policy was to limit the freedom both of the wage-earner and of the entrepreneur. The wage-stop was coupled with strict limitations on the distribution of dividends among shareholders. 'Private enterprises have become public trusts,' wrote the *Deutsche Volkswirt* in 1937, 'the state is for all practical purposes a partner in every German enterprise.'

When the National Socialists took over in 1933 they found in existence the two necessary components of their later policy—first, a highly organised industrial structure, which had already been affected by the propaganda of 'rationalisation' in the 1920's, and second, exchange control, which became a point of departure for more extensive economic regulation. They had no satisfactory economic theory, but they had the determination to make the economic system fit their political aims. The existence of large-scale unemployment gave them an immediate objective in the shape of the promise of work for all.

Without the existing co-ordination of German business they could not have evolved their own institutional structure. The Central Committee of Entrepreneurial Associations had been set up in 1920. The National Union of German Industry (*Reichsverband der Deutschen Industrie*), its most important member, was formed in 1919 from a union of two older organisations, one going back to 1876 and the other to 1895. The influence and scope of the *Reichsverband* was wide-ranging, and its organisation, under the leadership of the most powerful industrialists in Germany, was complex, based on dual units, regional and functional. The National Socialist government, in establishing the National Economic Chamber (*Reichswirtschaftskammer*) and the Co-operative Council of Chambers of Industry and Commerce, conceived its task merely as the limited one of

[1] L. Barth, *Wesen und Aufgaben* (Berlin, 1936), p. 26.

'co-ordinating with the present national government the existing organisa-tion of the vast field of German business administration'.[1]

Early National Socialist legislation, especially the Law on the Organic Structure of German Industry of February 1934 (*Gesetz zur Vorbereitung des organischen Aufbaus der deutschen Wirtschaft*) made membership of the Chamber and subordinate groups compulsory for all entrepreneurs. The leadership principle operated throughout the whole structure from the local territorial and functional units to the *Reichswirtschaftskammer* itself, 'the great conciliator' at the centre.[2] The guiding rule of all the bodies was 'never to act against the wishes of the government of the Reich'.[3] Principles and rules were established for the organisation of the market. Compulsory cartellisation was introduced as early as 1933 and existing cartels strengthened. As the economy developed, the cartels became agencies of government policy, facilitating effective central control (for example, price control) and speeding up the creation of a war economy.

The government itself had a number of agencies of its own at its dis-posal. A Ministry of Economics had been set up in 1919. In 1938 it was reorganised and placed under the direction of Dr Funk, the President of the Reichsbank. In the meantime, in 1936, the Office of the Four Year Plan was set up under the personal control of General Goering, and the army had built up its own economic departments from the top level downwards. When war broke out in 1939 the German economic system was already mobilised on a war footing, although co-ordination was improved by the setting up of a Ministerial Council for the Defence of the Reich (*Ministerrat für die Reichsverteidigung*).

More important than the elaborate structure of German planning, the efficiency of which it is difficult to assess, was the experiment in regulating employment and the methods it entailed. Between 1933 and 1939 the German economy enjoyed what most of the private enterprise economies were proclaiming as the main goal of economic planning—full employ-ment. In December 1932 a Commissioner for the Creation of Employment was appointed, and two days before the beginning of the National Socialist regime an 'urgency programme' was put into operation involving heavy public expenditure on roads, housing, public utilities and inland water transport. In May 1933 Hitler announced his Four Year Plan for the abolition of unemployment. Partly as a result of the policies of public works expenditure, government encouragement to private investment through loans, subsidies and tax remissions, reduction of labour redun-dancy and measures for increasing consumption, there was a rise in

---

[1] Dr Kurt Schmitt in 1934. See R. A. Brady, *The Spirit and Structure of German Fascism* (1937), p. 266.

[2] O. Nathan, *The Nazi Economic System* (Durham, North Carolina, 1944), p. 38.

[3] Barth, *op. cit.* p. 13.

effective demand. From the late autumn of 1936 to the beginning of the spring of 1938 there was full or near-full employment. By the autumn of 1939 the free reserves of unemployed labour were becoming exhausted, and from 1938 onwards Germany was running on war-economy lines.

The pursuit of full employment was coupled with extensive measures of labour and price control to try to maintain the economy stable in a way in which it certainly would not have been had the social consequences of full employment in a capitalist society been allowed to follow 'naturally'.

Labour control prevented wage-earners from pressing for wage increases in a sellers' market. The Law concerning the Regulation of National Labour, promulgated in January 1934, and the Order of October 1934 substituted for the existing trade-union organisation a Labour Front (*Arbeitsfront*) and for collective bargaining and the right to strike 'enterprise communities' (*Betriebsgemeinschaften*) and 'enterprise rules'. Trustees of Labour (*Treuhänder der Arbeit*) were given wide powers to regulate the labour market as a whole, including the drawing up of both individual enterprise rules and sets of rules fixing conditions of work in whole industries. These controls made the government's policy of a wage-stop effective. Money wages were held firm even after the reserves of unemployed labour had been absorbed, and there was a 6 per cent fall in real wages between 1933 and 1938. From July 1934 onwards government policy encouraged a longer working day and from February 1935 onwards the Employment Book (*Arbeitsbuch*) provided the necessary information for labour conscription.

Price control was also considered necessary to safeguard workers' loyalty and morale. As early as December 1931 a Reich Commissioner for the Supervision of Prices was appointed. Various changes were made until in October 1936 a new office, the Office of the Reich Commissioner for Price Formation, was set up. Previously the emphasis had been placed on the supervision of prices, now it was placed on price formation. Wagner, the first Commissioner, insisted that supply and demand no longer regulated prices—they were now to be fixed to enable entrepreneurs to supply planned outputs at an 'economically justified' profit. In November 1936 the Price-Stop Decree pegged prices to the arbitrarily chosen date, 17 October 1936, and prohibited all further increases in response to rising demand. The Commissioner was given wide powers to raise prices but usually claimed that he only did so when higher production costs sprang from higher import costs or from the high costs of substitute materials. National Socialist price policy was more effective in the highly cartellised investment goods sector of the economy than it was in the consumption goods sector, and although complete evidence is lacking it seems clear that the policy maintained a high share of profits in the national income.

This elaborate framework of internal control would not have worked at all without rigorous control of foreign trade. Exchange control was the foundation of the whole system. It was introduced in July 1931 in order to deal with the flight of capital. Between 1931 and 1934 the balance-of-trade position deteriorated. In 1934 itself there was a heavy fall in exports and a rise in imports. The government decided against devaluation, and in September 1934 introduced Schacht's 'New Plan', a detailed programme of foreign trade control. Licences had to be obtained for any transactions involving an outflow of foreign exchange. All incoming payments from abroad had to be handed over to the Reichsbank, and as a check exporters were compelled to declare to the authorities the nature and value of all goods transferred out of the country. Imports were kept to a minimum, substitutes were encouraged, and interest and dividend payments to foreigners were first reduced and then restricted to payments out of export surpluses. Within the framework of regulation, trade discrimination was developed to its extreme practical limits. Wherever possible, imports were only received from countries willing to hold balances in marks and not in freely convertible currency. Special mark rates were adjusted in terms of the structure of each separate market. A regional bloc, mainly in south-east Europe, was built up on the basis of bilateral agreements providing bulk turnover and long-term contracts.

There was no spectacular recovery of German exports as a result of these measures; indeed, in relation to total industrial production exports declined from 22·5 per cent in 1933 to 13·1 per cent in 1938. By that year, however, only about one-fifth of Germany's foreign trade required and produced foreign exchange. The lines of trade were regulated in the interests of state policy, and in the business recession of 1938 it was not only the Soviet Union but also Germany which was insulated from the rest of the world.

The disintegration of the formerly integrated world economy in the 1930's led to the growth of blocs and bilateral transfers. The wiring system of the world economy was short-circuited. Partly as a result of the national drives for self-sufficiency and partly for more fundamental reasons, there was a decline in international specialisation, reflected in the shift in commodity trade from foodstuffs to raw materials and in the increased variety of exports of the leading primary producing countries. There was also an increased withdrawal into restricted trading groups within the boundaries of empires or spheres of economic influence. The Ottawa Agreements of 1932 marked the extent to which the United Kingdom was falling in with world trends.

There were still clear-cut patterns of trade. Europe's trade was characterised by a large import surplus into the United Kingdom and a large export surplus from Germany. World trade depended on a European import surplus from the United States and a United States import surplus from the rest of the world, but the size of the balances showed the contraction of trade. Problems of balance of payments were largely responsible for restrictive trade policies, and much remaining foreign trade was a 'desperate expedient to maintain employment at home by forcing sales on foreign markets and restricting purchases',[1] thereby shifting unemployment to other countries. The United States, which maintained a large annual export surplus throughout the 1930's (except in 1936) drained gold from the rest of the world and thus contributed towards the trend towards bilateralism. In 1929 the United States owned 38 per cent of the world's monetary gold: in 1939 the stock had risen to 59 per cent. At the same time the domestic economy of the United States was thrown out of gear and American economists pessimistically explained internal stagnation in terms of the declining rates of growth of a 'mature economy'.

It was the reduction in international investment which retarded the continued growth of the world economy. The specialisation of the late nineteenth century was not simply a device for using to the greatest effect the labour of a given number of human beings: it was above all an engine of growth.[2] In the 1930's the continued depression in international trade reduced the yield on foreign investments and discouraged capital exports on which the continued growth of the system depended. The risks of private foreign investment were considered too high, and political uncertainty on the one hand and instability of exchange rates on the other created unfavourable conditions for expansion.

In face of both internal and international obstacles to natural growth the demand for planning grew in intensity. Internally there were demands for sectional advantages in the name of special interests, and bodies like the British Iron and Steel Federation, set up in 1934, were examples of a union of protectionism and 'a considerable measure of reorganisation',[3] which fell far short of general or even specific economic planning. Internally also there were vociferous demands from workers for new mass remedies to meet the problems of unemployment, social insecurity and the 'paradox' of poverty in a world of plenty. The fulfilment of these demands was incompatible with the traditional mechanisms of deflation or with the separation of business and politics. They all involved increased government control of the economy. In the elucidation of a technique of control for democratic societies, Keynes's *General Theory of Employment, Interest and Money* (1936) proved a landmark in non-socialist economic literature. Its influence was delayed. Between 1936 and 1939 there were internal forces in many countries relating *Wehrwirtschaft* to *Kriegswirtschaft* and planning not for welfare but for war.

[1] J. M. Keynes, *General Theory* (1936), pp. 382–3.
[2] D. H. Robertson, 'The Future of International Trade', *Economic Journal*, vol. xlviii, 1938.   [3] Cmd. 4066, 4181 (1932).

In the international field the frequent international conferences held in the 'twenties and the early 'thirties were mainly preoccupied with the narrow question of trying to reduced trade obstacles and not with the bigger problems of expanding world trade. Even in the limited field of tariff- and quota-reduction the many attempts made from the Brussels Conference of 1920 to the Van Zeeland Report of 1938 met with little success. From 1934 onwards Cordell Hull made energetic attempts to promote freer trade by means of national agreements, and the League of Nations published various reports advocating the abolition of national controls and a return to multilateral trade, but the creation of a new international framework to make this possible failed. Germany, Italy, the Soviet Union and Japan stood for different conceptions of international trade in which exchange control, quotas and bulk purchase agreements were employed as instruments of planned national economies. Even apart from these countries other states were unwilling to jeopardise the success of their own internal or group policies by accepting limited and often negative international action. From 1937 onwards defence expenditure began to dominate the world economy, and the trade revival of 1939 mainly featured commodities which it was thought would be useful in a new war.

The second world war raised all the familiar problems of the war of 1914–18 on a yet bigger scale but in a more precise form. Much of the war-time planning looked back to the past and relied on the instruments which had been forged before 1939. Germany, for instance, completed the integration of the trade of continental Europe into a closed system of exchanges dependent on the German clearing network. At the same time other forms of planning anticipated the developments of the post-1945 period. The scheme of mutual aid worked out step by step by the 'United Nations' reflected the high degree of allied interdependence during the war and underlined the necessity for international action in peace-time to promote an expanding world economy.

In 1945 the frontiers of planning did not everywhere roll back; they served as a strategic base for new advances. Much of the established planning process became a routine. Economists, however, disagreed about the form which planning should take and whether the state should work through the price mechanism or in supersession of it. The two big practical problems which persisted and which had their roots in the period before 1939 were those of reconciling social aspirations with internal social peace and national aspirations with international interdependence. The word 'planning' remained a powerful slogan: it was the issues behind the problems of reconciliation which provided the practical test.

CHAPTER XIX

THE BRITISH COMMONWEALTH
OF NATIONS

NEVER had the British empire been more unpopular in the world than it was when the nineteenth century passed over into the twentieth; never indeed had the idea of empire been more questionable in the eyes even of a number of the subjects of that empire; but never did the majority of Britons feel more justified in taking pride in the dominance which it exerted over so large a part of the earth's surface—its 'dominion over palm and pine'. The extraordinary, the frightful happenings in South Africa, where for a few months the British army was so ubiquitously beaten by elusive bands of bearded farmers, gave delight to those Europeans who now saw perfidious Albion in decline and fall. But Albion, though puzzled and perturbed, did not think of decline and fall; it sighed over its generals, sent out others, accepted help from the colonies ('the lion's cubs', in the language of the time, 'rallying to the dam'); and with tedious inevitability wore the farmers down. On 31 May 1902 the Boer leaders accepted the Peace of Vereeniging and British sovereignty. The readers of Kipling were reassured; the Union Jack, fluttering above the veldt, marked the triumph of civilisation and efficiency; the way stood open for the pacifying efforts of Lord Milner's 'kindergarten', the young men from Oxford whose minds were suffused with the light of a liberal empire; and colonial prime ministers, like New Zealand's Richard John Seddon, released the ample folds of their homespun eloquence, congratulating and advising, upon a Mother Country that was both gratified and embarrassed.

Yet at that peak of victory men might well have been touched by anxious questionings. The disappointed enemies of Albion, could they have seen farther, might yet have had their comfort. For all was not lost to the overwhelmed and obscurantist old man, Kruger, to his defeated yet hopeful juniors Botha and Smuts. The Boer mind was not conquered, the treaty had promised self-government. The conquerors, it seemed, had at last learned the lesson proclaimed by Burke, that a great empire and little minds go ill together. They intended to be magnanimous; and the magnanimous empire, it became plain in the next fifty years, would cease to be an empire at all in any sense intelligible to older centuries. Even to the mid-nineteenth century, which had made the remarkable discovery of 'responsible government for colonies', the development of that responsible government might perhaps have seemed too extravagantly logical. Dominion, it was to become plain, could not be exercised over Dominions.

Certainly the phrase 'dominion status' had not, in 1902, been invented. They were few, after all, who gazed on the word 'empire' with queasy stomachs. Earnest federalists there were who showed worry about the future of the empire. But to most people, Britons or colonials, imperial stability, like European stability, was in the order of things. Amid reasserted stability they did not pause to consider the implications for empire of the other British ideal of freedom: freedom, the instrument of magnanimity. There were Victorians, no doubt, who would have accepted as natural the Statute of Westminster, 1931; but would they have understood the extraordinary cohesive power that has gone with this flight from *imperium*?

The Victorian theory of empire was not, of course, simple, and was not static. It had dropped close economic control as one of its ingredients and objects. From a free-trade, still *laissez-faire* Britain the imperial statesmen looked out tolerantly enough, though a little uneasily, on self-governing colonies which had become steadily protectionist—and some of which, like New Zealand and its Australian sister, by 1900 had ceased to regard *laissez-faire* as at all a tolerable social rule. In the imperial economy these communities, with Canada and Newfoundland, were still preponderantly 'primary producers'—the role of the southern ones accentuated by the brilliant success obtained in the refrigeration of meat and butter. But that did not affect the variety of their political development, under the benevolent metropolitan eye. The unitary system of small New Zealand or smaller, sparsely settled Newfoundland, had little in common—save responsible government—with the thirty-year-old federalism of Canada, or with that other federalism which came into operation in the brand-new Australian Commonwealth on the first day of 1901. Nor were the two federations at all identical in design, in distribution of powers or in the power to adjust and amend: Australia was determined that necessary change should be as exclusively as possible an Australian concern,[1] while the Judicial Committee had been, and was still to be, one of the great interpreters of Canadian constitutionalism, and amendments to the British North America Act, 1867, could be made only by Parliament at Westminster. Different from federal and unitary governments alike, different also in its place in world economics, was the Cape Colony, with its South African neighbours; poor in agricultural resources, leaning heavily on gold and diamonds, its politics complicated by the status of a governor who had at once to work with responsible ministers and, as High Commissioner, to control relations with Boers whether independent or conquered, and with native peoples under British rule inside South

---

[1] Nevertheless the decisions of the Judicial Committee of the Privy Council on some Australian cases, involving federal powers, carried to it on appeal have been of marked significance—for example, the judgments on marketing of 1936, and on the nationalisation of banks of 1949.

African geographical limits; a governor who was at once constitutional head of a self-governing colony and an administrative and diplomatic official responsible to England. But, though this was so at the beginning of the century, within a decade war, magnanimity, and economic necessity had done their work; and the Union of South Africa Act, 1909, created still another constitutional variant of that self-government which, according to Campbell-Bannerman's paradox of statesmanship, was better than 'good' government. It was neither federalism, nor, in the New Zealand sense, quite unitary, for the South African provinces had real powers. It could, by men like Botha and Smuts, be worked as good government; and the Union, in its relations to the imperial power, took its place securely enough as another of those dominions beyond the seas which owed allegiance to the Crown but were, certainly, no longer simply colonies of England. An index of that subtle but far-reaching change had been the formal enlargement of the status of New Zealand from 'colony' to 'dominion' in 1907; though what precisely might be implied in that status, beyond compliment, was for legal conference. The Dominion of Canada was a Dominion; so, now, was New Zealand; so was Newfoundland; Australia was a Commonwealth; South Africa was a Union. Was there any difference, within the ambit of the empire?

Whatever the answer to that question might be, there was no doubt of the difference between them and other parts of the empire: those parts that before long were to be called in general, in distinction from Commonwealth and Dominions, 'the colonial empire': the moribund West Indies, into the economy of which Joseph Chamberlain had recently injected the stimulus of an Imperial Department of Agriculture; the large areas of the upper and lower Niger, just ceded by a commercial company to the Crown, and the other territories of West Africa, fatal with fevers, waiting on the schools of tropical medicine founded in England in 1899; the Rhodesias, still smelling somewhat to tender consciences of the blood of the Matabele; the great Bechuanaland and Nyasaland protectorates; the other protectorates of Uganda and British East Africa, where the Foreign Office presided over economic penetration; the virtual protectorate of Egypt, and the Sudan, the 'joint possession' of Egypt and Great Britain; Ceylon; the native states of Malaysia, and Singapore and Hong Kong, those two nodal points of an immense commerce, polyglot empires in themselves; in the great ocean to the south, a spatter of islands Polynesian, Micronesian, Melanesian—more or less exploited, more or less missionised, less rather than more administered. Here was an odd assemblage of bits and pieces, almost entirely the product of Victorian expansion; and very clearly, so the Edwardians as well as Victorians thought, unfit for self-government. Without civilised or scientific tradition, unacquainted with the amiable conventions of parliamentary debate, only a few years earlier large numbers of their peoples had stumbled in the long sad

531   34-2

fettered lines of the slave trade, had speared one another or had their brains knocked out in fantastic varieties of savage experience; or had merely fished and picked coconuts. It was indeed clear that for them good government was better than self-government; that for them young empire-builders should drive the road and bridge the ford, direct plantation-labour and impose the Law. But was it—altogether—clear? What, after all, was good government? What was the Law? The decades immediately in the future were to see some questioning, some diversity of answer, on these points; and the lapse of another fifty years made it begin to seem improbable that a sharp line could be forever drawn, in constitutional status, between the dominions and the colonies, the free communities and the dependent empire.

And there was India. For India the division of centuries was to be a division of epochs, economic as well as political. Autocracy virtually untouched was attended in Lord Curzon's viceroyalty with uproar and indignation. What change would there be? How far was the Indian tradition inimical to self-government?

The historian, gazing back, can see change and at least some of the determinants of change. Most of the imperial fabric had been raised in a remarkably short space of time, in a world that strongly affected the fashion of building, and could not cease to affect it in a new century. Economic and social development on a world scale, two world wars and a vast depression, political and social revolution, the ground-swell of Asian unrest, were among the determinants. So also was political wisdom, in despite of vested interests: magnanimity in spite of the arguments of fear. In a remarkably short space of time the Victorian—or Edwardian —empire was gone, utterly destroyed, the insubstantial pageant of its imperial vision faded. And yet something remained for a future historian to define; the extraordinary British paradox remained; a 'Commonwealth' —whatever that term really meant—remained.

The development of the twentieth-century empire, then, on a basis of 'determinants', is a psychological development. The change of mind displays itself, for example, in unease at the speaking of the very word 'empire'. Men did not wish to be dominated—that had long been true in the settled colonies; it was to become true in a very short time in India, and rather more slowly, irregularly indeed, in large parts of the 'dependent empire'. But also they no longer wished to dominate. The imperialism of the 'nineties, part crude, part liberal, a good deal romantic, began to give way to a new attitude, rather sceptical, increasingly critical. The literature of imperialism began to be a literature of research, critical certainly, in which nineteenth-century humanitarianism was linked increasingly to a new ethnological approach, and to a determination to take full account of economic factors. Its critical role stimulated controversy (where the

African colonies were concerned) reminiscent of the great days of Abori-
gines Protection a hundred years before. There was this difference, that
in the course of the century it had become rather difficult for the reformer
to be self-righteous; human association of all kinds had become too much
the object of exhaustive examination.

It remains true that in the greater part of the period now being considered constitutional interest centres on the development of the relations
of that group of communities which came to be called the British Commonwealth of Nations—of the United Kingdom and the dominions, the
imperial metropolis and the semi-British societies who were exploiting
the possibilities of responsible self-government. 'Semi-British' it is necessary to write; for however much some dominions might glory in their
British blood and tradition, the French-Canadians of Quebec, the Afri-
kaners of the Union, the Irish of the Free State (or Eire) made the problem
of relations a perpetually unfinished one. The position of 'racial' minorities within the whole had been by no means so happily arranged for as
enthusiastic persons were wont to assume in the early days of the century;
the general British community as a reconciler of national differences had
still some way to go.

It is this fact which is one of the underlying causes of the growing feeling
of nationality in more than one dominion. French-Canadians showed
no sign of being assimilated; their birth-rate was high, they were virtually
a colonising people, as they spilled over into the other provinces of Canada;
and wherever they went they carried the demand for special provision
for their needs. Quebec remained a corner-stone of federal politics; its
views of the world at large were a determinant in Canadian foreign policy
that ministers would have ignored with peril certainly, and probably with
disaster. But at least the French-Canadian was in a federation that managed to get along fairly peaceably within itself as the decades passed;
he was not a republican; he was not tempted to take advantage of crisis
by armed rebellion. In South Africa, on the other hand, there was an
element never reconciled to British hegemony or even to British association; the war of 1899 threw off a last flurry in the rebellion of 1914; and
this Afrikaner irreconcilability was the despair of many people who
considered themselves reasonable. The Dutch Reformed Church was a
focus of tradition as compelling as the Catholicism of Quebec; in Afri-
kaans there was a language susceptible of literary development, and, as
in Quebec, an infant native literature began to be consciously cultivated.
The material unification of the world was to be offset, it seemed, by
increasing cultural fission. In South Africa there was the added factor
that the Afrikaner, with his distaste for the British association, considered
himself also a member of a master-race, the rock and fortress of European
civilisation in the midst of the inferior millions of the native tribes. Here
was complete intransigence, implacability emotional as well as political.

Compared to this, the influence of an Irish strain in the population of eastern Australia might seem quite negligible; yet, counting up the causes of Australian nationalism it would be wrong to omit that strain, with its determination not to be taken in by any branch of English policy anywhere. On the whole, however, the national sentiment of Australia was Australian, owing something to the continental nature and democratic social development of the country, and marked by a literature that was sometimes almost belligerently self-conscious in its cultivation of local colour. Only in New Zealand was national status uncomplicated by the existence of a national minority; for the Maori people, though in this period working out a sort of cultural and economic renaissance of extreme importance to itself, was not in the least concerned with status in an empire or commonwealth. A real feeling of New Zealand nationality, a thing felt in the bones, born of time and isolation, came only in the 'thirties and 'forties—or perhaps the first individual expression of it came only then. There were New Zealanders before.

For more than one reason, beyond national tradition, these communities began to feel, and to press, a separate identity; and in the complex twentieth-century world there was ample scope for difference of opinion. To speak in general terms, for fifty years their life was becoming steadily more complex, was being lived steadily on a larger scale. Economically by no means self-sufficient, they were yet building a wider basis for wealth, and were producing more of it. The old simple theory of imperial preference was going with the old simple relation of primary producer to metropolitan manufacturer and financier; even where, as in the case of New Zealand, that relation essentially remained, the impact of the Great Depression, followed by world war, urged a determination to manufacture; and the material of manufacture, even if not local, might not necessarily come from Great Britain. To take an example, the steel used in New Zealand towards the end of this period was largely the product of Australia. Australia, still with wheat and wool as fundamental exports, created heavy as well as light industries which had reached major importance by 1939; and while the prairie provinces of Canada stood deep in their ocean of wheat, its industrialised eastern provinces joined the great manufacturing countries of the world. Populations were increasing, though the centre of white population still remained the United Kingdom; but more important, they were increasing as native-born Canadians or Australians, with family ties concentrated in the one country, and with less and less tendency to think in terms of a 'mother-country', as the nineteenth-century sentiment of 'Home' steadily dwindled. To all this, in a world of trouble and strategic calculations, were added the facts and the implications of geography: the fact that Canada, sharing the economic life and philosophy of the United States, was becoming an American power; the fact that Australia, almost unconsciously, was becoming a Pacific power; the fact that Great Britain could no longer control all the oceans of the world; the fact, explicit as the decade of the 'forties opened, that not merely were the days of expansion over, but the imperial power was in retreat.

This dispersed nationalism in itself, even in its early days, would have been enough to render null the theory of imperial federation that had attracted so many well-meaning people in the last twenty years of Victoria's reign: when the fourth Colonial Conference met in London in 1902 the issue was dead, and no later agitation, however ingenious and plausible the reasoning, could breathe life into it. The proposal brought before the Imperial Conference of 1911 by Sir Joseph Ward, the prime minister of New Zealand, was notable for the unanimity and scorn with which it was pulverised by his fellow statesmen. Yet in retrospect this proposal has a significance which is lost if it is regarded merely as an attempt to revive the dead cause. For Ward was not thinking merely of constitution-building, nor even of defence—which had already concerned Imperial Conferences a good deal. In 1902 Canada, breaking away from the general meagre support of the British navy, proposed to build a fleet of its own, an example followed with more immediate effect by Australia in 1907. In that year, however, there was common agreement over the foundation of the Imperial General Staff. Ward wished to improve on this, and to create a sort of 'Imperial Parliament of defence', which should control not merely naval and military matters, but the whole scope of foreign policy. His lower chamber elected on a population basis would certainly have deprived any partner except the United Kingdom of real power; and apart from other details, the sacrifice of autonomy was too great a price to pay. Nor, argued Mr Asquith, could the United Kingdom possibly share control of foreign policy: there sovereignty must be unimpaired. But the desire for a share was precisely what lay behind Ward's imprecise scheme. Not merely was he conscientiously anxious for participation in the burden of defence: he was anxious also that dominions which might be called on to shed blood as a result of British policy should have some say in its formation.

Nor was New Zealand alone in this feeling, or, indeed, generally the most prominent in expressing it. Ward's inadequate exercise in federalism was, paradoxically enough, only one offshoot in a general growth of autonomy, which was leading the dominions inevitably, though hardly as deliberate choosers, towards an individual international status. (Nothing ever more admirably illustrated Cromwell's dictum that no man goes farther than he who knows not where he is going.) Their right to separate withdrawal from or adherence to British trade treaties was followed in 1907 by recognition of their right to negotiate their own trade treaties, subject only to final signature by a Foreign Office-accredited plenipotentiary. Then came the Anglo-American arbitration treaty of 1908, which bound Canada only with Canadian concurrence, extending thus the principle far beyond matters of trade. Nevertheless, in the drafting of the Declaration of London 1909 (covering contraband and neutral trade in time of war, a result of the 1907 Hague Conference) the dominions were not consulted; and some dominion statesmen brooded. Thus, though Canada in 1910 legislated for itself over a fishery dispute with America, the 1911 Imperial Conference witnessed more than Ward's discontent. Australia protested at the failure to consult the dominions, and suggested, without pressing, direct communication between them and the Foreign Office. Canada differed: consultation, Sir Wilfrid Laurier seems to have felt, would argue commitment, and commitment was exactly what French-Canadians would refuse. Nevertheless, in spite of Mr Asquith's *non possumus*, some steps were taken. It was decided that in future the dominions would be consulted over the instructions to delegates to conferences, and over the signature of agreements which might concern them; while upon other international agreements, if time and circumstances permitted, their views would also be invited. The assembled statesmen were then given by the foreign secretary an intimate and comprehensive view of the subject-matter of European diplomacy which sent them home, having created a Committee of Imperial Defence, thinking furiously—not so much about the elasticity of the British constitution as about trouble to come.

The development of consultation was to be marked by hesitations, contradictions and nervous withdrawals. No one, it seems, can have suspected the total implications of the word; or measured against the brute facts of international relations a theory which involved all the circumlocutory possibilities of the sequence foreign secretary or cabinet —Colonial Office (dominions branch)—governor or governor-general —dominion prime minister and cabinet and back again. The brute facts proclaimed themselves in the summer of 1914, when the dominions found themselves at war, without motion of their own, as completely and unequivocally as if their autonomy had reached no farther than that of the Isle of Wight. Paradox, however, is always round the corner. The war, begun in what might be described as so constitutionally reactionary a way, itself turned out to be a singular constitutional forcing ground. For the empire that seemed to calculating outside observers to be on the point of dissolution proved to have extraordinary powers of coherence, a tough inner spirit capable of creating new institutions according to its needs. Those needs brought dominion prime ministers to London, where their membership of the Imperial War Cabinet made consultation immediate and effective. So great was the success of this experiment, and so lively the feelings of unity that the common effort aroused, that when the war-time Imperial Conference of 1917 met, there was general determination that somehow this happy state must be continued in time of peace. The dominions must be fully recognised as 'autonomous nations of an Imperial Commonwealth'. At a later conference the theory of an empire, in which unity and autonomy had been so markedly reconciled, must be somehow re-shaped in accordance with reality.

But what was the nature of reality? It appears that even then there were different interpretations—that Mr Massey from New Zealand, for instance, had been impressed chiefly by the unity possible in the midst of autonomy, Sir Robert Borden from Canada by the autonomy possible in the midst of unity; and Mr Massey as politician was no more conservative than Sir Robert Borden. It was Sir Robert Borden who insisted that the dominions, having devoted themselves so unrelentingly to the purposes of war, and been consulted so freely, should be consulted as freely in the making of peace; that dominion leaders could not simply trail subordinate in a British delegation, but must have an independent status of their own. Could the importance conceded to the lesser European countries be denied to these dominions? Could Smuts, who spoke the language of a new and better world, and was listened to, be ignored; could the astute and obstinate Australian Hughes be ignored? So dominion prime ministers signed the Treaty of Versailles, as somehow British, but also independent, negotiators; so their countries became members in their own right of the League of Nations created by that anomalous instrument. There seemed, to other people, to be a sort of gross cynicism about these proceedings, perfidiousness in Albion as ever; for were they not merely a means of gaining Britain five votes in the world parliament instead of one? They were not, but to Europeans whose theories of sovereignty were logical and tight, to Americans whose continental federal system issued in a single foreign policy, the disclaimers might well seem hollow though bland. It was difficult for others to understand a system which many in Britain and in the dominions themselves tended to regard as dangerous nonsense; which was anyhow highly dubious in law; which was, as we can now see, merely constitutional work in progress. Nevertheless, irretraceable steps had been taken. New Zealand might refuse to accept the mandate for western Samoa except through a channnel provided by the United Kingdom; Sir John Salmond, that extremely able constitutional lawyer, might return to New Zealand from the Washington Conference in 1922 insisting that the empire had undergone no essential change; but Canada and South Africa, at least, were quite convinced that a new status existed, and that it should continue to exist, and that British statesmen should not be allowed to forget it. And, by a miracle of convenience, this status seemed to provide a solution, at last, for the problem of Ireland.

The constitutional conference that had been anticipated after the war was not held. There were too many conferences, too many problems. Ireland was on the hands of the British government, an Ireland in which nationality was certainly a leading emotion, raised to heights of undefeatable stubbornness by the abortive rebellion of Easter 1916; in July 1921 Mr Lloyd George abandoned hope of reducing Ireland to quietude by force. The Irish were invited to London to 'ascertain how the association of Ireland with the community of nations known as the British Empire¹ can best be reconciled with Irish nationalist aspirations'. To the dominions the answer seemed easy; but they did not have Ireland's history. Nor has it been easy for any state not a dominion to feel quite sure of the virtues of dominion status. So to this conference came Irish proposing what was virtually a republic in 'external association' with the empire—not 'in' the empire, but acting with it in matters of peace and war and defence and all other common concerns; to meet British ready for autonomy though insisting on symbols of sovereignty, on the supremacy of the king, acting through a personally-appointed governor-general, on an oath of allegiance. Here doctrinaire met doctrinaire, but it was the republicans who compromised: twenty-six of the thirty-two counties of Ireland became the Irish Free State, and Arthur Griffith and Michael Collins went home to face civil war. Northern Ireland remained, unredeemed and perhaps unredeemable, still part of the United Kingdom and yet, oddly enough, enjoying responsible government as well.

The Treaty of December 1921 and the Government of Ireland Act, 1922, did not prove, exactly, to have solved the problem. For the Irish wanted clean definition, and that they could not be given in anything short of their republic. True, they were given the same constitutional status as 'the Dominion of Canada, the Commonwealth of Australia, the Dominion of New Zealand and the Union of South Africa', with more special reference to Canada: 'the law, practice and constitutional usage governing the relationship of the Crown and of the Imperial Parliament to the Dominion of Canada shall govern their relationship to the Irish Free State'. But what, again, was that law, practice and constitutional usage? What, to repeat, was the nature of reality? Certainly, if one were to judge from history, 'dominion status' could not be deemed to be static. Was its secret, then, development? And if it was development, how far and how fast could it be allowed to develop? Was there in fact any theoretical limit, or might 'law, practice and constitutional usage' be in the end a sort of floating figment, 'a cloud that's dragonish'?

While such questions stirred uneasily in a number of minds, Canada affirmed its international position by negotiating a treaty with the United States for the protection of the North Pacific halibut fishery, signed at Washington by a Canadian minister alone, without the intervention of a British ambassador. This led to discussion at the Imperial Conference of 1923 about the mode of negotiating treaties, whence came general agreement over principles of consultation or information, whether the United

¹ *sic*: not simply with Great Britain.

Kingdom or a dominion should be primarily concerned. This in its turn was followed, within a year, by entire forgetfulness on the British part to consult the dominions over the Treaty of Lausanne; and the month of June 1924 saw almost simultaneously the Canadian prime minister re-asserting the broken principle, and the Irish Free State dispatching its own minister to Washington. This latter step, an important one, though it again gave pause to the uneasy, was followed shortly by Canada; followed too, as convenience dictated, by the other dominions, in America, Europe and the Far East; so that in twenty years each one of them had its minia-ture Diplomatic List, and its problem of training young persons for the diplomatic life. In the meantime the uneasy were still further disturbed; and in 1926 a number of arguments were carried to London for settlement at the Imperial Conference of that year—the post-war constitutional conference at last, much more complicated than had seemed likely in 1917.

Constitutional advance within the Commonwealth (a term it was now becoming the habit to use) had been traditionally led by Canada. Canada was still advancing, but had at this stage been joined by the Irish Free State and South Africa. Each, or a considerable party in each, was deeply concerned about its status. The Irish found it impossible to reconcile their interpretation of dominion autonomy with treaty limitations. In South Africa the hegemony exercised for so long by Botha and then Smuts had been overthrown by the Nationalists—for whom, it seems, it was very necessary to assert the right of South Africa to secede from the empire if it so wished. Party feelings were displayed more noisily over the design of a new South African flag, and the manner of flying it, a controversy which issued naturally enough from the thorough-going nationalism of the Union. The Commonwealth, or the empire, could stand any number of flags, but could it admit secession? Canada had more than one trouble. In politics it had experienced a first-class crisis, and in law a serious rebuff. The crisis concerned the governor-general's prerogative. Had that personage still, when advised by his prime minister to dissolve parliament, a right to discretionary refusal, or was he bound to obey? Lord Byng, by refusing a dissolution to one minister and granting it to another, outraged Mr Mackenzie King, who had been denied—and who denounced such procedure as a blow at the very heart of dominion freedom, a return to colonialism, a jeopardising of all the fruits of constitutional progress. For if Canadian autonomy was real, then the governor-general's pre-rogative, his discretion to bind or loose, could be no more real than that of the king in Great Britain. (The true measure of constitutional advance is indicated by the subsequent controversy, which centred not on any difference of degree in prerogative, but on whether the king himself had discretion or not.) In the legal sphere, feelings, though less excited, were no less upset. The issue arose on a criminal case, *Nadan* v. *the King*, carried on appeal to the Judicial Committee of the Privy Council. A

Canadian act of 1888 had purported to abolish appeal to the Privy Council in criminal cases. The Privy Council now declared this abolition void: first, because appeals were regulated by the Judicial Committee Acts of 1833 and 1844—British legislation—and abolition by a Canadian act infringed the Colonial Laws Validity Act, 1865; while, secondly, if that famous measure were not enough, the Canadian act assumed extra-territorial power, which the Privy Council would not concede. Canadian laws, or the laws of any other dominion, could have force only within the dominion which enacted them; they could not affect a court elsewhere domiciled. So—concluded Canadian lawyers—Canadian justice was to be determined ultimately not by Canadian laws in Canadian courts, but by a clutter of transatlantic anachronisms, applied by transatlantic judges whose regime many Canadians already disliked. The load of discontents was enough to ensure that that Imperial Conference of 1926 would not escape some difficult constitutional thinking. It is notable that neither Australia nor New Zealand nor Newfoundland had registered any dismay.

The celebrated Conference set up an 'Inter-Imperial Relations Committee', with a celebrated dialectician as its chairman. But it took the Committee a fortnight's hard work, as well as all the subtlety of Lord Balfour, to arrive at the point where it 'readily defined' the 'position and mutual relation of the group of self-governing communities composed of Great Britain and the Dominions'—which had 'as regards all vital matters, reached its full development'. Carefully italicised, the definition proceeded. Its members were *autonomous Communities within the British Empire, equal in status, in no way subordinate one to another in any aspect of their domestic or external affairs, though united by a common allegiance to the Crown, and freely associated as members of the British Commonwealth of Nations'*. But, the report went on, the principles of equality and similarity, appropriate to *status*, did not universally extend to function. Diplomacy and defence demanded flexible machinery. The committee had endeavoured not only to state political theory, but to apply it to the common needs; that is, two aspects of what we may now, following the custom of the 'twenties, call 'dominion status', the domestic and the external—or, perhaps, status looked at from within the Commonwealth and from outside it—were both to be considered.

On the domestic side administrative, legislative, and judicial forms admittedly were out of date. It was easy enough to alter the royal title, now that Ireland was no longer part of a United Kingdom. 'His Majesty's Government in Great Britain' certainly had now no wish to impose the Judicial Committee on any of His Majesty's Governments elsewhere. As for the governor-general, the committee could but generalise. The governor-general, certainly no longer the agent of the imperial government, personally represented the king, holding the same constitutional position (with, one assumes, whatever dubieties attached) as that held by the king in Great Britain; and it was accordingly thought fit that henceforth communication between government and government should be direct, and not through the royal representative. What should be done about the legislative powers of the dominions it was less easy to say, though some things were obvious, and expert legal examination was recommended. In the sphere of external relations there was further definition of treaty-making procedure, and of dominion representation at international conferences—the general intent of which was that any dominion might have its own plenipotentiaries commissioned by the king on the advice of its own government. 'It was frankly recognised' that in foreign policy, as in defence—matters of 'function'—responsibility mainly rested, and must for some time continue to rest, with 'His Majesty's Government in Great Britain'. Nevertheless, as practically all the dominions were involved in some foreign relations, it was felt that neither they nor Great Britain could be committed to active obligations except with the definite assent of their own governments. And, indeed, none of the dominions was committed to the guarantee of French or German frontiers which Britain had given under the Treaty of Locarno. The appointment of dominion ministers in foreign capitals was approved, with the proviso that in their absence existing diplomatic channels should be used. But what of day-to-day consultation between His Majesty's Government in Great Britain and His Majesty's Governments elsewhere? Failing the governor-general, some other functionary would have to be instituted.

The prime ministers separated with varying degrees of cheerfulness. The famous italicised formula gave pleasure in Canada, South Africa, and the Free State, where it, and the deductions drawn from it, seemed to concede with reasonable adequacy the main points then claimed by those communities—though certainly nothing had been said about secession. In the other dominions satisfaction was not marked. Newfoundland, small in population and resources, could hardly make an effect in constitutional controversy, but neither Australia nor New Zealand was prepared at that moment for further advance into the doubtful region of autonomy, and New Zealand was indeed alarmed. To this dominion, in its colonial days so critical of British policy, Canadian, Irish and South African behaviour seemed to invoke the disruption of the empire. Distrusting the new term Commonwealth, it wished neither for plenipotentiaries nor for political theory; into the proceedings of the next five years its political leaders were drawn with reluctance, and to the great enactment which was the crown of those proceedings, and indeed of the whole legal development of responsible government, it was stubbornly opposed.

That enactment was the Statute of Westminster, 1931. It was the logical result of the further consideration of administrative, legislative and judicial forms which the 1926 Committee had seen to be necessary—consideration given by the experts of the Conference on the Operation of Dominion Legislation and Merchant Shipping Legislation which met at London in 1929. It did not touch the Privy Council, however, except by implication; what the experts were concerned with were the limits on the legislative competence of the dominion parliaments—limits which had been imposed by, and did not exist for, the imperial parliament; limits which must be abolished if equality of status was to be real. These limits were drawn partly in the statutes by which the dominions had gained their constitutions, or in other statutes which by particular wording affected them; partly (as Canada had found) in that other fundamental statute, the Colonial Laws Validity Act, 1865; and partly in the obscure doctrine of extra-territoriality. There had been further limits on colonial autonomy, reaching far back into the history of imperial expansion, but these had disappeared in the process of conventional change. Under statute, for example, the Crown could (except in the case of the Irish Free State) disallow dominion legislation—though such power had not been exercised since 1873; and statute provided for 'reservation', discretionary or obligatory, by a governor—that is, the withholding of his assent to a bill till the sanction of Whitehall should be obtained. Discretionary reservation had lapsed; obligatory reservation in some cases remained. Under the Colonial Laws Validity Act no dominion legislature could thrust aside these limits, even as no dominion legislature could (for instance) abolish appeals to the Judicial Committee; so that not merely was an abstract equality undermined but there was practical inconvenience. As for extra-territoriality, legal learning conflicted both as to the existence of the limitation and as to its extent. Something would undoubtedly have to be done to bring certainty into such spheres of law as fisheries, shipping, air navigation, marriage; while dominion shipping was affected still by imperial legislation. The Conference saw no way of removing the mass of anomalies except through an act of parliament at Westminster, and punctuated its report with draft clauses.

The draft clauses, discussed again at the Imperial Conference of 1930, were referred to the individual legislatures, who added further clauses to conciliate Canadian provinces and Australian states, always touchy over suspected federal aggrandisement; and in December 1931 the act was passed. Like many statutes of profound constitutional importance, it does not illustrate by the nobility of its language or the rhythms of its prose its quite remarkable place in the development of an empire: as an application of a political theory which might well have exploited the combined eloquence of a Burke, a Chatham and a Fox, it was indeed remarkably flat. Its importance is not that of the memorable phrase but of the memorable deed. It is the final fracturing of the sovereignty of a centralised empire, with the remains of which unhappy legal conception the constitutional lawyers—confronted with the spectacle of one king advised by a multiplicity of governments—had to do their best. The very title of the act was significant: 'An Act to give effect to certain resolutions passed by Imperial Conferences held in the years 1926 and 1930.' It annulled for the dominions the Colonial Laws Validity Act, and declared the power of any dominion parliament to make laws having extra-territorial operation; it did away with all reservation; it declared that no future act passed at Westminster should apply to any dominion, unless a clause therein expressly stated that enactment had been requested and consented to by that dominion. The Canadian, Australian and New Zealand constitution acts were, at the request of those countries, excepted from the operations of the Statute. Australia, New Zealand and New-foundland were excepted, indeed, altogether from the operation of the Statute until they should choose to adopt it through their own legislatures; so that loosing and binding were both voluntary. But how odd and irregular is constitutional development! It was in the year of the Statute that Australia, which held back from the operation of the Statute, yet, taking advantage of new procedure in the appointment of a governor-general, was the first dominion to elevate a native son to that post: for though, it was agreed in 1930, the governor-general represented the king, he must be appointed by the king on the advice of responsible ministers, and those ministers must be the ministers of the dominion concerned. As convention, that was as damaging to the old theory of empire as any statute could be. But before long the first fruits of the Statute of Westminster appeared in the abolition by Canada and the Irish Free State of appeals to the Privy Council; while South Africa, with a milder approach, opened its campaign by doing away with disallowance.

So went the accent on separateness—an accent hardened in the Free State by its abolition of the oath of allegiance and of the governor-generalship, and its other successive denunciations of Commonwealth ties. The Free State (or Eire), however, was the odd example among dominions; an artificial creation, rather than a natural growth, it was driven by a psychological necessity different from the rather more muddled spirit of its partners. It had a certain willingness to co-operate—on its own terms, terms which were (from 1932, under Mr de Valera) stringent and uncompromising. The peculiarity of the Commonwealth relationship, indeed, may be measured on the one hand by the Irish move outwards, and on the other by the fate which in 1934 overtook Newfoundland. That unhappy child of circumstance, smitten by economic depression as well as irresponsible administration, then saw no alternative to putting itself into the hands of receivers. Its relinquishment of dominion status was designed to be a temporary measure; in fact, having after some years of government by commission become again solvent, it found its post-war constitutional destiny not in resumption of its place as a dominion but in incorporation as a province of Canada. Meanwhile separateness was mitigated by other facts of Commonwealth life. Whatever the difficulties of regular consultation, information could be given, and the flow of information from the centre to the perimeter and back again steadily increased in volume. The governor-general, decorating a formal niche, was superseded as government representative in his dominion by a high commissioner for the United Kingdom (the first such official had in fact gone to Ottawa in 1928); and though there was less business done directly between dominion governments, it was found useful for some of them to be politically represented in one another's capitals also. Thus each dominion was building up a sort of diplomatic pattern for itself, a reflection of its own needs, without doctrinaire extension, both inside and outside the Commonwealth. Inside the Commonwealth, as a sort of test case both of fundamental theory and of procedure, men studied the constitutional history of the Abdication; for with so much divided sovereignty and such a multiplicity of advisers, on an issue which connoted emotion, it was important to steer opinion and legislation all the same way at the same time. The machinery worked; and the Commonwealth was spared the embarrassment of more than one monarch.

The British, though they may be a self-governing people, are also a conferring people. Nothing could be more striking, sometimes, than the determination of this fragmented and disparate empire, or the greater part of it, to work out a common policy; just as sometimes nothing could be more striking than the determination of the individuals to go their own way; so that to the outside observer the whole presents the perpetual possibility of surprise, or of annoyance. Annoyance came from the Ottawa Conference of 1932. It is interesting to mark the diverse implications of the latest great revolution in British fiscal policy, the abandonment of free trade under the impact of the Great Depression, and of that previous revolution, the abandonment of protection nearly ninety years earlier. For while free trade came before the colonies were their own masters, yet left them virtually at liberty to adopt what fiscal policy they liked—was part, even, of the foundation of their political freedom—the later event seemed to those same colonies, their autonomy sealed and blessed, almost the return of a prodigal mother to the home. Was not there, at last, to be introduced that system of Imperial Preference which had gilded the colonial fancy three decades before, to pursue which Chamberlain had abandoned office, which now, in an unstable world, might shore up the staggering Commonwealth? The Ottawa Conference did not redeem these high hopes, and the eloquence which played round that not very exactly defined concept, 'the spirit of Ottawa', died away from a stage that was being set for a different and more agonising performance. For the Ottawa agreements, though they marked a considerable degree of determination to work out a joint economic policy, and though they did materially help certain groups—for instance, the coffee-growers of Kenya—were essentially opposed to the greatest possible recovery of world trade. The best that could be argued for them as a whole, perhaps, was that as it seemed beyond the competence, or goodwill, of men to organise a rational economic system for the world, it was at least preferable to organise rationally a smaller unit than to concede general chaos. But there could be no large economic salvation for Britain merely in the empire, and the economic life of the dominions had become so elaborated with industry that British manufacturers, who were to have been encouraged, not infrequently felt rebuffed instead. Nor did the Australian and New Zealand producer of butter and meat feel more confident that his problems had been solved. The return of prosperity came with a world return; and there were critics who held that that return was impeded by the manful though not single-minded efforts of the statesmen of 1932. At least the historian may contemplate with some interest the process, without being involved too deeply in economic hypothesis.

This Ottawa Conference, with its underlying conception of an empire closing its ranks against the outside world, could not help implying a general foreign policy. Nevertheless, as the decade advances, what claims attention is again separateness. Or, to be more precise, as the international situation became more and more violently complicated and European politics more and more charged with doom, we see the dominions more and more struggling to work out their own foreign policies, which would reconcile their national interests with some sort of responsibility to civilisation in general; and at the same time, or perhaps alternately, to maintain as a permanent and desirable thing the power and unity of the British association. This individuality might be the expression of a traditional attitude, as with Canada's reluctance to become caught in foreign entanglements; or it might be due to the emergence, with change of government, of strong personalities with convictions on international morality, as in New Zealand; or to the Australian realisation that potential markets and potential danger lay in the north; and in any case it went with a determination to scrutinise the foreign policy of the United Kingdom with care before giving it support. Naturally, in the mid-'thirties, dominion representatives found the League of Nations at once a peg for policy and a platform for its enunciation. They were certainly not dragged in the English wake; they reached their own conclusions about the application of sanctions to Italy during her Ethiopian adventure. In a time when collective security was greatly talked about and little heeded, when in 1936 the reform of the League was being considered, with no general determination either to reform it or to stand by it, Australia declared for automatic sanctions, economic and financial, and for regional pacts of mutual assistance; New Zealand and South Africa believed in taking the Covenant literally; while Canada deprecated the idea of force, or the notion that the League's central purpose was to maintain the *status quo*, and suggested the perfecting of the machinery of mediation and conciliation. They were all struggling against forces that took little account of dominion sentiments on collective security, or morality; in the last dreadful crises they fell silent; and in due course the blood of their sons and daughters was spilt.

Almost six years of hostilities completed, for the dominions, the assertion of their international status; some of them made independent declarations of war, and in 1939 South Africa decided only after war and neutrality had hung for some days in the balance. Constitutionally even more decisive, perhaps, was the neutrality of Eire. It was regarded as an unhappy stand by the remainder of the Commonwealth, but it was respected; and the scrupulous respect exercised, above all, by the United Kingdom made plain as nothing else could do the reality of autonomy. The Irish problem was not even then 'solved'; Eire could not by now reconcile its national freedom, its peculiar sovereignty, either with status as a dominion, or with the tenuous bond of external association; it had to become an independent republic, and it was not impeded. Nothing could more clearly register the change in the idea of empire over fifty years than the difference in the British attitude to the South African Republic in 1899, and the Republic of Ireland in 1949.

The war forced both Australia and New Zealand into greater legal autonomy. Australia found it necessary to put the powers of the Commonwealth beyond dispute by adopting the Statute of Westminster in 1942; New Zealand, after being entangled in complications which were a crown lawyer's nightmare, finally took the step in 1947. Dominions, too, were thrown into what was almost a new sense of geography, and what was certainly a new outlook on strategy, by the war's very course. Canada, besides sending an army to England and Europe, found itself interlocked with the United States in an Arctic strategy; Australia and New Zealand, with Singapore gone and the British navy vanished from the Pacific, found themselves interlocked with the United States in an oceanic strategy. Only South Africa found its traditional strategic position unchanged, with its interest in the Suez Canal, and its midway position, by a different route, between England and the East. For the others, this American interlocking gave new modes of 'consultation', with Washington sometimes the centre rather than London; or remoteness from England stimulated a greater sense of regional burdens, so that it was natural for the two Pacific dominions to work out their own Australian–New Zealand Agreement of 1944, the so-called 'Canberra pact', which insisted not only on a future common defence, but on common responsibility for the welfare of the island groups. They, it is notable, and none of the great powers, brought into existence the South Pacific Commission, with its accent on a new and more knowledgeable trusteeship. Nor is it unworthy of remark that after the war the British representative on the Allied

Council in Japan—a rather powerless body, to be sure—was no English general or diplomatist, but an Australian. This was an autonomy and a co-operation undreamed of even in 1939. And still, amid the wreck and the reclamation of financial systems, as western Europe fought for stability, the process of consultation went on, the feeding of Britain proceeded; while once again the dominions, so different from the colonies of the nineteenth century, nevertheless began to think in terms of population and of labour, and of new experiments in migration.

The dominions? Some of them were beginning to reluct, to be restive, at the use of that convenient word. Was there in even it, for tender minds, some subtle angularity? With Canada the term dated from 1867, with New Zealand from 1907.[1] Did it carry with it, in spite of all that had passed, the shadow, almost imperceptible but lingering, of the equality of status that was not equality of function? In fifty years, indeed, the whole world-entangled British complex had changed, in the facts and the philosophy of its constitution, in its general politics and its general economics, in its social structure and its social relations—had changed so much that nothing that could happen to it in the future could be more surprising or more paradoxical than its past. But then were not the paradoxes logical after all?

To the consideration of this development must be added consideration of the colonies of the dependent empire—a history exceedingly complicated and as interesting as that of the sovereign dominions. For if the dominions may be regarded, on the whole, from an agreed basis of objectivity, whence passion has departed, the controversy that attends the relations of dominating and dominated societies has not ceased to brood over colonies and dependencies, whatever their status in the hierarchy of empire. None of these, whatever their stage of social development, has had till recently responsible government: that, even at the end of fifty years, in almost every case remained an ideal. There was much difference between Ceylon, which became a dominion, and the communities of East and West Africa; Ceylon's constitutional problem was very different from that of Malaya or of the West Indies. Yet, no less than among the partners of the Commonwealth, the history is one of government, on a basis of social and economic life, and of changing relations between colonies and imperial centre.

In all that history the overmastering fact is the poverty of the colonial peoples, though it was not for poverty but for the potentiality of wealth

[1] Changes in susceptibility are nicely balanced by changes in the administrative organisation of Whitehall. In 1907 the Colonial Office produced a Dominions Department. In 1925 this became the Dominions Office with a separate Secretary of State for the Dominions. In 1947 a further change of name resulted in the Commonwealth Relations Office, and a Secretary for Commonwealth Relations; and in these, within a few months, were absorbed the India Office and the Secretary of State for India.

that adventurers first toiled up their rivers and through their forests; and certainly wealth has been extracted from them. Or, as in the West Indies, they exchanged outright slavery for slavery to world economics, and while demand for their products fell, saw their population increased beyond any possibility of providing for it at home. Thus whether a colony were old or recently acquired, and whatever its administration, the spectacle it presented was almost always one of quite inadequte subsistence agriculture, on soil of diminishing fertility, for the overwhelming majority of its people. Not quite always; for in some cases a single crop for export revolutionised material life and involved its diversification, as cocoa did on the Gold Coast. Alternatively, mining by European companies, for copper in Northern Rhodesia or gold in the mandated territory of New Guinea might, in draining off male population, both complicate and impoverish the pattern of village life, without increasing real material prosperity. Poverty meant lack of community services—health, education, agricultural research and organisation, communications. Even where things were best, as in Nigeria or the Gold Coast of the African continent, the problems were enormous; where they were worst, as in Kenya, the twentieth-century model of 'colonies of exploitation', English plantation owners prospered only at the expense of a native population dispossessed of fertile soil. The historical generalisations are not altered, essentially, by the importance of particular colonial exports in the world's economy— by the fact that the plantations of Malaya, for example, produced before the last war half the world's rubber and half its tin. And politically speaking, for the 60 million people in British colonial or mandated territories at the outset of that war (of whom 80 per cent were in Africa) the Statute of Westminster, 1931, was certainly void of meaning.

On this material basis of colonial life were worked out two conceptions of great importance for British policy, that of the 'dual mandate' and that of 'indirect rule'. The first, the twentieth-century variant of the 'nineties' idea of 'the white man's burden', is prior logically though not chronologically to the second. On administration, it argues, a double burden is laid: to see that the government of native peoples is directed to the interests of those peoples themselves; and to see that in this process the natural resources of the colonies concerned are not denied to the world. The conception was criticised as hypocritical or at best an attempt to reconcile incompatibles, but it was certainly an advance on naked exploitation. It received its classic exposition by one whose practice was fundamental also to the development of indirect rule, Lord Lugard. As a young soldier Lugard had been instrumental in the acquisition and pacification of much of Nigeria, where his great talent for administration, first awakened in East Africa, fastened on the possibilities of ruling through native agencies and institutions—throwing responsibility, that is, where it had always been, and placing on the officers of the colonial service the tasks of supervision, advice, and superior justice, together with policy-making for the colony as a whole. Indirect rule proved capable of brilliant success, as with the northern emirates of Nigeria or the kingdoms of Uganda, and was extended elsewhere to tribal and village government all over the world. In some parts of East Africa, indeed, where the peoples were nomadic or tribal institutions were inchoate, native councils or chiefs had to be created before power could be conferred upon them. The principal disadvantage of the system was its tendency to acceptance of a *status quo*, however mediocre—to impotence in the face of economic and social change, to the perpetuation of native vested interests, to a general lack of imagination on the part of administrators: indeed, as the century wore on, close students of African life were to think that as a constitutional safety measure it had perhaps been overdone. But sanctification of stalemate was not inevitable, as not a few district officers proved in the face of government poverty; and at the worst it could be said that direct government in such old-established colonies as the West Indies was certainly no more enterprising or skilful. At least peace and good order were maintained; native life was not broken up and destroyed in the name of an alien efficiency; able chiefs were not forced into despairing idleness; for the higher ranks there was even some formal western education; so that certain advanced colonies were able to acquire the nucleus of a native civil service, and to make use of indigenous wisdom and experience through native membership of legislative councils. The condition of the native peoples of Bechuanaland, Uganda, or Nigeria, was a happy contrast to that of those subject to the rule of a white minority in Kenya or the Rhodesias, however the Colonial Office strove there to impose its safeguards and its benevolence; or of those hapless millions whose fate was determined by the segregation policy of the Union of South Africa.

The first world war afflicted Britain with fresh problems under the mandate system—problems, even though the doctrine of trusteeship seemed to the optimistic to have enough sanction in existing practice to minimise them in British hands. But it was one thing to deal, relatively successfully, with Iraq and Transjordan, which were not colonies at all; it was quite another to handle Palestine, a country which was being colonised, and presented a problem quite insoluble in colonial terms—a problem finally to be abandoned. The old German colonies, on the other hand, split up between members of the Commonwealth, could certainly be treated on traditional lines. To Britain went German East Africa or Tanganyika (where for some years standards of social service were lower than under the Germans), and part of the Cameroons and Togoland in West Africa; these, as 'B' mandates, were virtually indistinguishable from British colonies. To South Africa went German South-West Africa—which the South Africans, without any pedantic regard to the terms of the mandate, before long wished to incorporate completely in the Union; to Australia went the German part of New Guinea, which was administered, without good results, quite independently of the adjoining Australian territory of Papua—where results had been good; and to New Zealand went Western Samoa, the charming and difficult people of which made clear the inadequacy, for successful government, of mere good intentions. Nevertheless, under a later dispensation, it was Western Samoa that was the subject of the first Trusteeship agreement with the United Nations in 1947.

Between the two world wars came a period notable for discussion and development in both constitutional and economic spheres, discussion and development stimulated by the depression of the 'thirties, with the subsequent inquiries into the causes of misery and riot; stimulated not less by the second war—during which, indeed, a forward step of major social and economic importance took place. Constitutionally, legislative councils were given greater non-official membership—a process carried much farther in the late 1940's in both East and West Africa. Southern Rhodesia, formally annexed as a colony to the Crown in 1923, was in the same year granted responsible government though without dominion status. Such advance indeed—so great are the contradictions of autonomy—might have dubious value; for it was the small minority of white Rhodesians who proceeded to deny all civil rights to the overwhelming majority of Africans. A number of movements for the amalgamation or federation of colonies were considered, sometimes by royal commissions, without much effect. (Without much effect, that is, in the period under discussion. The year 1945, however, in all this is a singularly poor dividing point: it is merely a year of unfinished business. The following decade saw a great deal of constitutional change, both federal and non-federal, in Africa as elsewhere.) One tentative scheme, which was put forward in 1936, but which did not gain the blessing of the Colonial Office, was for the union of the two Rhodesias as a single dominion. Another was for closer union of the East African protectorates and territories, a movement supported mainly by European communities and opposed by natives and by the commercial Indian minority; favoured by the imperial government for certain limited purposes, discouraged as a whole in the absence of sufficient guarantees of native interests; and reaching no farther within our period than an annual Governors' conference, which met first in 1926. The West Indies, with its queer congeries of representative and crown-colony governments, and its history of abortive federal plans, was the scene of a developing West Indian consciousness; but a commission in 1932 could make no more of a scheme for federation, even on a small scale, than could its predecessors. There was greater hope from the conference of seven colonies which met at Jamaica in 1947 and set up a standing committee to work on details. A startling contrast to this was the indignation aroused all over Malaya by the British post-war plan for a Malayan Union, to replace the loose and sprawling federation, admittedly out of date, under which Malays, Chinese, Indians, Europeans and Eurasians had been governed, both indirectly and directly. Only in Ceylon, a country well fitted for unitary government, with a relatively high literacy level and an able educated class, and without bitter communal feuds, was there a change both rapid and successful. Since 1910, in Ceylon as a crown colony, increasing popular representation had been accorded on the legislative council; the official majority was abolished in 1920; and in 1931 adult suffrage and a measure of responsible government were both granted. But there was too much reservation of power, too little real autonomy; nationalist demands were strong, and the new and considerably improved constitution of 1946 was followed rapidly by dominion status.

Economically and socially the great step forward was the Colonial Welfare and Development Act of 1940. This act provided for free grants to the colonies, up to £120 millions spread over ten years—an expansion of the small and restricted Colonial Development Fund of 1929—for expenditure under approved development plans on research, education, health and agricultural services, training of civil servants, labour and co-operative organisation, the development of local industries and communications—for, in fact, a systematic overhauling and re-shaping of colonial resources. Large schemes were to be managed through development corporations in each area, an Economic and Development Council being established in London to advise the Colonial Office. Though the total was certainly inadequate for colonial needs, it was regarded not as a discharge of liability, but rather as a mode of breaking the vicious circle of poverty which stultified all self-help, a stimulation of potentialities as much as a particular grant-in-aid. The motive behind this new and hopeful advance harmonised with a movement for international collaboration over specific problems of trusteeship, designed to give badly needed improvement to the old mandates system. It was this movement that in different ways produced the Anglo-American Caribbean Commission in 1942, with its organs the Caribbean Research Council (which included French and Netherlands representation) and the advisory West Indian Conference; and, in the Pacific, the South Pacific Commission that was initiated by Australia and New Zealand, joined by those powers which were concerned also in the Caribbean, and inaugurated in 1947. Here, it could be said, was the working out of formulated intention where earlier had been only wishes and vague hopes.

India, more than any other part of the empire, was the land of formulated intentions. But, by a sort of desperate fatality, the imperial formulation always came too late, it was aimed to meet a situation which had already passed away, the forward step was always in the rear of necessity. Nowhere was social and political complexity more knotted and strained, nor good intentions ruined by such lack of imagination, nor lack of imagination confronted by such demands for an imaginative act of faith. The British in India were not an imaginative people; and, devoted to the ideal of good administration, they were not able, generally, to convey an impression of magnanimity. Self-government, they felt, could not be good government, and their duty was to ensure good government. They were, by the second half of this period, in a false position brought about, through a vast irony, largely by their own virtues—by their capacity to give India a firm basis of material and administrative order; by their bestowal, on the classes most able to lead a revolution, of western political ideas and education and a lingua franca; and they were met, not merely by political abilities of a very high order, not merely by a refusal to compromise which was the despair of the English tradition, but by a philosophy and a strategy which were singularly alien to the English mind. The dominating influence in India over these critical decades was the Mahatma Gandhi, who was both a saint and, by a sort of divine instinct, an extremely practical man; and to that combination of qualities the administrator had no effectual reply. Nor could India be isolated, be treated as a self-contained, though complicated problem; it was part of Asia, and all Asia was in an unrest which was one of the major phenomena of human history. It was no mere accident that the year of Japanese triumph over Russia, 1905, was the year in which Lord Curzon's partition of Bengal raised Indians to an astonishing height of fury, the year indeed which marked the beginning of modern Indian nationalism.

That movement, as an articulate thing, centred on the Indian National Congress, a predominantly Hindu and middle-class organisation. Not till the 1930's did it make a strong effort to call on the support of the peasants of India; yet devotion to Gandhi as a leader—and Gandhi was also for years the unchallenged leader of Congress—was deep in the heart of those peasant millions. Mass support for a new India had to come, if from anywhere, from them; for Indian industrialism, though after the first world war it rose in importance enormously,[1] utilised a labour force small in comparison with that of the land, and its organisation tended naturally to be of trade union type, socially more radical; there only, apart from the mind of the young intellectual, did the doctrine of communism tend to get a footing, not in the poverty-stricken multitudinous villages. The general poverty, the consequent general lack of political interest, the appalling Indian ignorance, determined the very cautious

[1] By the middle of the twentieth century India was one of the eight principal industrial countries of the world represented on the governing body of the International Labour Organisation.

approach to constitutional change of the Morley–Minto reforms of 1907—
a grant, in answer to the new demand of *swaraj*, or national freedom,
merely of Indian representation on legislative councils. By no means
could this be regarded as more than a beginning, its inadequacy emphasised by the first world war, a war which both illuminated the importance
of India as a reservoir of men and supplies, and cast increasing administrative and military duties upon Indians; so that Indian self-consciousness
was not unaccompanied by British gratitude. It was in 1917 that Mr E. S.
Montagu, the secretary of state for India, made the famous declaration
that Indian self-government should be gradually developed to the stage
of responsible government within the empire, and that 'substantial steps'
should be taken towards this as soon as possible—a declaration important in its time, even though the development was to be 'gradual'.
Psychologically even more important was the affirmation that 'the British
Government and the Government of India...must be judges of the time
and measure of each advance'; for when was ever any revolutionary
movement satisfied by authoritarian conviction that it had gone far
enough? or where was ever any man bent on freedom prepared to accept
limits on that freedom defined by a parliament at Westminster? More
than once, in the decades that followed, might British governments have
learnt from British colonial history; but one department of state, it seems,
was insulated from the experience of another.

Thus the year of the Government of India Act, 1919, was also the year
in India of the Rowlatt Act which, superseding war emergency measures,
provided among other things for imprisonment without trial. Murder and
riots were the prelude to the shooting down of a crowd at Amritsar in
the Punjab, and to measures of humiliation that deeply affected the Indian
mind. Congress under Gandhi's leadership replied with the 'non-cooperation' movement—a boycott of the new legislatures, the law courts,
government schools, and foreign cloth. When there was violence Gandhi
ordered the cessation of the movement; nevertheless, he was sentenced
to gaol for six years, and so became a martyr. In this atmosphere a new
constitution could hardly work efficiently; the new constitution indeed
seemed to be designed not to work. It set up both central and provincial
legislatures; the central legislature without trace of responsible government, and the provincial bodies, including one for Burma, intended to
function on a peculiar system of 'dyarchy'—a dual system of responsibility in certain departments (such as education) but not in others, all the
key departments (such as finance) being reserved; while both viceroy and
provincial governors were given an emergency power to rule against the
will of their legislatures altogether. This gift of conditional freedom called
forth no thanks; and though there were able Indians who did their best
as ministers and councillors, there were few indeed who regarded the
system as anything but a monstrous birth. At least the Act provided for

inquiry into its working within ten years. So widespread had distrust become that Congress refused to co-operate even with the Simon Commission, which, after making this inquiry, in 1930 recommended further and considerable reforms.

Change was inevitable. What stood in the way was not any administrative problem; the greater part of the civil service was now effectively Indian. The problem was one of constitutional relations and of deep-seated distrusts. Three difficult Round Table Conferences were held in London in 1930–2, succeeded by a White Paper of government proposals and the unfortunately long and bitter debates over the Government of India Act, 1935. The Act provided for a federal India (excluding Burma), this time with dyarchy at the centre but abolished provincially, and for the representation of the princely states in the central legislature. Once again latent powers were reserved to governors, and the power of the parliament of the United Kingdom to legislate for British India was specifically declared. In the provinces representation was to be based on religious and racial communities; for communalism was becoming a major concern and fear of government in India, and a bedevilling agent in any reform, however whole-hearted. Meanwhile Congress had pursued a policy of passive resistance and civil disobedience, its principal leaders spent more time in prison than out of it, and when the new provincial elections were first held in 1937, its candidates stood on a platform of non-participation in provincial governments, gained a majority of votes— and took office. Truly the demands on the English imagination were becoming—so the English thought—outrageous. It should perhaps be emphasised that the British people, if one may distinguish between them and certain of their political leaders and publicists, were anxious that government in India should be transferred as soon as the transfer was workable. But for the ordinary man the issues could become very confused. The amount of plausible writing, pro and con, was very great; yet the popularity in Great Britain of Jawarharlal Nehru's noble autobiography was an index of the real goodwill that existed.

With so much conceded, dissension between right and left wings of Congress could hardly be avoided. Social reform in India also was coming to seem as important as merely political reform; peasant movements in the states were hailed as a new dawn. Indeed, the princes were not popular figures in British India. At the same time the Muslim League of Mr Jinnah, uncompromisingly opposed to majority Hindu rule, appeared as a large political factor. On this unsatisfactory scene burst the war of 1939. Into it India was carried automatically and, as matter of constitutional form, simply by declaration of the viceroy. No comment upon promises of dominion status could have been more cutting, except possibly Mr Churchill's explanation that the Atlantic Charter, with its accent on national freedom, did not apply to India; when Congress offered full co-operation in the war it was now only at the price of the unequivocal concession of independence; and the proposals borne by Sir Stafford Cripps in 1942 of a constituent assembly 'immediately upon the cessation of hostilities' for the creation of an Indian Union, with full equality in the Commonwealth, were met by diverse, argumentative and mutually contradictory answers. Indians, determined to accept no further promises, unhappily could not agree on what realities they would find acceptable. The grim stalemate was ended by a new British prime minister, Mr Attlee; Britain, he announced in 1947, would leave India not later than June 1948; let Indians themselves solve their constitutional problems. Here at last was magnanimity, here at last were words which carried conviction, made effective by parliament in the Indian Independence Act of July 1947. But there was to be no Indian Union; there were to be the Hindu India of Nehru and the Muslim Pakistan of Jinnah, separated in mutual massacre and terror; a Pakistan clinging still, for almost a decade, to the national and political status of the dominions, a republican India linked with the Commonwealth in something like 'external association'. Burma had chosen independence. In the moment of freedom the Mahatma Gandhi was slain by a young Hindu who charged him with the betrayal of India; and when that light went out a period of history ended.

CHAPTER XX

EUROPEAN CIVILISATION IN THE TWENTIETH CENTURY

THIS volume has been concerned with the processes of change which made Europe of the mid-twentieth century different in its internal political, economic and social structure, and in its external relations with the other continents of the world, from Europe of the late nineteenth century.[1] These changes in the content and the context of European civilisation were both rapid and profound. They occurred at an uneven pace because of the three great cataclysmic events which dominate the history of this half-century: two world wars and the intervening world economic crisis. Indeed 'crisis' is the most over-used yet unavoidable term in all historical studies of the period, and it is tempting to present this 'era of violence' as a concatenation of crises, each in turn producing a situation of instability and a nexus of forces which led remorselessly to further crises.

There is some truth in this image of a sequence of crises, interrelated by links of cause and effect. The first task of the historian is to define and explain such connections between events. But since the present is always the outcome of the whole of the past, and not merely of the recent past, his further task is to uncover the continuities and more long-term tendencies which underlay the whole course of events. The surge of history pays little heed to such nominal breaks as the ends of centuries or decades, and most of the formative institutions, movements and ideas of the twentieth century had their roots deep in the revolutionary changes of the nineteenth century. During the first half of the twentieth century the peoples of Europe took over the whole legacy of the nineteenth century and developed very much farther both its propensity for great material progress and its tendency (noted apprehensively by many nineteenth-century critics) towards violence and dehumanisation. The very ambivalence of this legacy, and its contrary potentialities as revealed in experience of two world wars and their aftermaths, make generalisations about contemporary Europe peculiarly difficult, if also peculiarly necessary.

By 1919 universal male suffrage and a nation's rights to independence and self-determination were accepted throughout most of Europe as the best bases of government. National communities and states were brought into close reciprocal relationship as a result of the triumphs of democracy and nationalism in the first world war. It was hoped that the spread of democratic ideals and the prestige of democratic institutions, combined

[1] See above, ch. I, for a general survey of these changes.

556

with a territorial settlement of Europe's frontiers that approximated as closely as possible to the ideal of independent nation-states, would make possible the organisation of peace. Nineteenth-century tensions between liberal and nationalist movements, as between social-democratic and nationalist movements, seemed capable of being ended within a peace-loving and increasingly prosperous community of free peoples. The League of Nations existed and attracted high hopes. Men dreamed of achieving disarmament, free trade, social justice, and an end of poverty in a decade which followed the most destructive war in European history and preceded the world's worst economic depression. This was the twilight of the nineteenth century. The liberal dream of progress in harmony lasted until half-way through the half-century.

The few years around 1925 were the height of the post-war economic boom, when Europe's output as a whole again became as great as it had been in 1913. The time of chronic inflation in Germany, Austria and France seemed to be past. Prosperity was real, if fragile. Production, trade and personal incomes were expanding. It was the era of Locarno and of generally improving relations between the great powers. Contacts were again made with the Soviet Union, and in 1926 Germany was admitted as a member of the League of Nations. 'Normalcy' seemed to be returning. By 1929 Europe's share in total world production was as great as before the first world war.

Then the dream faded, and the obverse side of the legacy became apparent. It was not that democratic ideals had ever triumphed completely. There had been the Bolshevik revolution in 1917, and fear of communism was ever-present. Admiral Horthy's regime in Hungary dated from 1919, Mussolini's in Italy from 1922, General Primo de Rivera's dictatorship in Spain from 1923. The process of peacemaking had itself lasted until 1923, when Turkey signed the Treaty of Lausanne. But now a recession in democracy preceded the economic recession. In 1926 General Carmona in Portugal, Marshal Pilsudski in Poland, and President Smetona in Lithuania all gained dictatorial power. Already in 1925 Field-Marshal von Hindenburg, the 'wooden Titan', had succeeded Friedrich Ebert as President of the Weimar Republic. Elsewhere, too, more nationalistic and militaristic forces gained ascendancy, whilst the men of Locarno left the stage. In France Raymond Poincaré replaced Briand and Herriot. In Britain the general strike of 1926 exposed and sharpened deep social tensions. In the Soviet Union the feud between Stalin and Trotsky reached its climax. The economic blizzard of 1929 struck a continent already drifting away from the era of optimism, pacification and hope of smooth social advancement. More authoritarian government, civil strife and social schism, widespread unemployment and economic hardship, were already realities of the European scene. The Great Depression led to conditions which favoured further growth, in still more extreme forms, of the single-party totalitarian state. But it did not originate, neither can it entirely explain, this novel version of tyranny.

The decade of the 1930's brought accumulating crises in economic life, domestic politics, and international relations. The shrinkage of international trade caused mass unemployment, on a scale larger than ever before. By 1932 Germany had six million unemployed, and the slump helped to bring the National Socialists to power. In France it exacerbated civil strife and political divisions, and led to the crisis of February 1934 in which the parliamentary republic nearly foundered. In Italy it spurred Mussolini to imperialist adventure in Ethiopia, and so to further defiance of the League of Nations. In nearly all European countries the economic depression created conditions in which extremist political movements gained ground and disrupted parliamentary government. Communism and fascism became more clearly movements international in character, each thriving in the fertile soil of popular frustration and social distress, and on fears aroused by the other. After 1933, when the National Socialists took absolute control of Germany, the accumulating crises merged into one supreme crisis: the direct challenge of unbridled organised violence to all that men had tried to achieve in 1919 and had still hoped to achieve in 1925.

In these ways the idea of a concatenation of events, leading from world war to economic crisis to dictatorship, and thence to a second world war, has some historical validity. But it was a vast and complex process, within which simple relationships of cause and effect between the major events can hardly ever be drawn. It is as valid, for example, to trace the genesis of the later Welfare State as it is to trace the origins of Hitler's power, and so of the second world war, to these years of mass unemployment. It was experience of the slump that quickened the interest of governments and peoples alike in methods of providing greater economic security. The first determined efforts to control and regulate the economy—especially in the United States where conventional opinion was strongest against such federal interference—date from the middle 1930's. The revolution in economic thought, from Keynes to Beveridge, belongs to these years. It sprang from the conviction, forced upon economists by events, that capitalism itself had run into crisis, rendering inoperative the old reliance on the working of free competitive enterprise and a free market to yield a healthy economy.

Meanwhile the new dichotomy in Europe, between democracies and dictatorships, hardened into a conflict of ideologies as well as of great powers. The conditions in which single-party dictatorships could flourish were, in large part, a consequence of the upheavals of the first world war and of the economic instability and depression a decade later. The economic foundations of democracy had cracked, at the same time as its political institutions were challenged and disrupted. But if it was these

peculiar circumstances that made possible the rise of aggressive dictatorship in the inter-war years, it was an intensification and an extension of
nineteenth-century trends which gave these regimes their special nihilistic
character. They were a conscious reversal of liberal doctrines of the
sanctity of human personality and of individual or group rights, a total
reaction against the bases of European civilisation so far as these meant
regarding the rule of law and belief in human reason as components of
progress. This reaction dated continuously from the end of the nineteenth
century itself.

A writer to whom Hitler avowedly owed some of his racial doctrines
was Houston Stewart Chamberlain, whose study of *The Foundations of
the Nineteenth Century* first appeared in German in 1899. Chamberlain
saw the century then ending as

essentially a century of accumulation, an age of transition and of the provisional;
in other respects it is neither fish nor flesh; it dangles between empiricism and
spiritism, between *liberalismus vulgaris*, as it has been wittily called, and the impotent
efforts of senile conservatism, between autocracy and anarchism, doctrines of infallibility and the most stupid materialism, worship of the Jew and Anti-Semitism,
the rule of the millionaire and proletarian government. Not ideas, but material
gains, are the characteristic feature of the nineteenth century.[1]

The quotation is significant less for its emphasis on the ambivalence of
the legacy of the nineteenth century than for its implicit nihilism—its
rejection of all the ideas derived from the passing age. Thirty years later
the Spanish philosopher Ortega y Gasset noted prophetically that violence would come to be regarded as characteristic of the era and that the
cult of violence dated from the very beginning of the twentieth century.

When the reconstruction of the origins of our epoch is undertaken, it will be
observed that the first notes of its special harmony were sounded in those groups
of French syndicalists and realists of about 1900, inventors of the method and the
name of 'direct action'....Civilisation is nothing else than the attempt to reduce
force to being the *ultima ratio*...'direct action' consists in inverting the order and
proclaiming violence as *prima ratio*, or strictly as *unica ratio*.[2]

The urge to violence as the solvent of social as well as international
tensions was abundantly evident long before 1914: and if Ortega y Gasset
is right in regarding Georges Sorel and his colleagues as prophets of the
new age, then the single-party dictatorships of Lenin, Mussolini and Hitler
spring from a common set of ideas, and the tendency for fascist leaders
to be drawn from men originally of the extreme Left has some explanation.[3]

---

[1] H. S. Chamberlain, *Grundlagen des Neunzehnten Jahrhunderts*, Eng. trans. as *The
Foundations of the Nineteenth Century*, 2 vols., translated by John Lees (1911), vol. I,
p. xcvi.

[2] J. Ortega y Gasset, *La Rebelión de las Masas* (1930), Engl. trans. as *The Revolt of the
Masses*, 1950, pp. 53 f.

[3] Mussolini, Gregor Strasser, Pierre Laval, Marcel Déat, Jacques Doriot, Sir Oswald
Mosley, are among the obvious examples, and Sorel himself supported the *Action française*
for a time.

The paradox of nineteenth-century developments became apparent in the twenty years before 1914. Rapid advance towards universal suffrage, universal primary education, municipal self-government, social legislation and reforms, coincided with an increasing recourse to violence in social life. In the most democratic countries—Britain, France, Belgium, Sweden, the United States, the Dominions—these were years of large and often violent strikes. In Russia comparable strikes and unrest precipitated the revolution of 1905. This was the theory of 'direct action' in operation, though the syndicalist movement itself was 'merely that branch of a world-wide unrest that was equipped with a particular philosophy'.[1] In Edwardian Britain three other political issues added to the crescendo of violence: the suffragette movement in its later stages, the battle between Unionists and Home Rulers over the Irish question, and the prolonged and bitter quarrel between conservatives and liberals which culminated in conflict between the two Houses of Parliament and led to the Parliament Act of 1911. So ferocious were class and party schisms that when Britain went to war in 1914 she was on the brink of a general strike and of civil war in Ireland.[2] France of these years was rent first by the Dreyfus Affair, and then by the separation of church and state. 'Direct action' and 'militancy', anti-semitism and anti-clericalism, were the domestic counterparts to militarism and imperialism in international affairs. It is not mere coincidence that Bolshevism, the prototype of revolutionary movements aiming at single-party dictatorship, dated also from 1903, and the ideas of Lenin were shaped during the twenty years before 1914.

In these years, too, international diplomacy became more continuously raucous and violent. Beset with periodic war-scares, feverish competition in military and naval rearmament, and sabre-rattling, snarling behaviour on the part of imperial governments, the great powers, now grouped in hostile armed camps, made the threat and imminence of war an ever-present factor of inter-state relations. In eastern Europe insurgent nationalities, bent upon asserting their independence and unity whatever the cost, added more inflammable material to the antipathies of the powers. Although war in Europe was avoided between 1900 and 1912, these were years of wars and revolutions on the periphery of Europe or overseas: the South African War which exacerbated Anglo-German relations, the Russo-Japanese War of 1904, and revolutions in Russia (1905), Turkey (1908), Persia (1909) and China (1911).

So much was violence a feature of European civilisation in the twenty years before 1914 that the increasing recourse to it during the inter-war years cannot be attributed entirely to the after-effects of the first world war.

---

[1] W. Milne-Bailey, *Trade Unions and the State* (1934), p. 30.
[2] George Dangerfield, in *The Strange Death of Liberal England* (1936), has amassed evidence that violence was the outstanding feature of political life in England between 1910 and 1914.

There are countless strands of continuity and affinity between pre-war and post-war tendencies in the politics, social life and international behaviour of European states. The war itself, in some aspects, was a consistent if vastly exaggerated form of a nihilistic, destructive trend inherent in European civilisation.

Likewise the second general cataclysm of the period, the Great Depression, cannot be interpreted as exclusively a product of post-war conditions. Historians have not yet reached complete agreement about how far it should rank as an especially virulent form of the secular trend of boom and slump, related to movements of the trade and business cycle, which can be traced back into the mid-nineteenth century. Periodic depressions, affecting large areas of Europe, had become a recurrent feature of economic development long before 1914. Persistent unemployment was a fact of world economy before the first world war. The existence of communities which concentrated on producing only a few commodities in large quantities, in order to sell them abroad, was a phenomenon of the later nineteenth century. Thus Australasia and Argentina became great meat-producing areas, dependent for their prosperity almost entirely on international exchange. Although the war brought somewhat greater diversification and industrialisation in such countries, they were still preponderantly producers of primary commodities. It was not only changes attributable to the war and its immediate aftermath that caused a depression in such countries. If there was over-production in some countries, there was under-consumption in others.

There was a general difficulty that the labour force engaged in primary production for the market was increasing much faster than the population of the major consuming areas, that supplies were further augmented by the use of better technical methods, that increases of income in the wealthier countries were not devoted to the purchase of larger quantities of basic foodstuffs, and that in other countries which were physically in need of more of these foods, incomes were not growing enough to make it possible to purchase the available supplies.[1]

Many elements in the whole complex of circumstances which produced the Great Depression were not attributable to the war, but were rooted deep in the subsoil of European economic development as a whole: in growth of population, overseas expansion, and the effects of new technologies. At most the war altered the incidence or significance of such elements. It did not create them.

It was significant that the first sector of the world's economy to suffer from the economic blizzard was American and Canadian agriculture. Throughout the North American continent agricultural prices began to fall sharply after 1926. Grain was a commodity in which Europe as a continent could be almost self-sufficing once its agriculture had recovered from the disruptions of war, and for which its demand was relatively

---

[1] W. Ashworth, *A Short History of the International Economy, 1850–1950* (1952), p. 200.

inelastic. The decade before 1929 had been a time of chronic depression in agriculture all over the world, but especially in those large areas which specialised in primary products for export: North American grain, Australian fruit and meat, Brazilian coffee, Javanese sugar. In these areas further contraction of world trade had speedy and disastrous results. The inter-connected world economy bequeathed by the nineteenth century left such sectors sensitive and exposed to any shrinkage of world trade. The disturbances of world trade caused not only by the war itself, but by post-war protectionist policies and other impediments to the free flow of gold, struck the world's economy in its most vulnerable spots. The repercussions upon industry and investment built up into a general economic crisis that engulfed the world.

Between the two world wars themselves there are many obvious links of cause and effect. That both began as essentially European wars occasioned by conflicts in eastern Europe, and as a clash between France and Britain on one side, Germany on the other, suggests a common basis. It has been suggested by participants as eminent as General Smuts and Sir Winston Churchill that they should be seen as but two stages of one great conflict—a new 'Thirty Years War' for German domination of Europe, with only a twenty-year truce between them. Marshal Foch remarked in 1919, 'This is not Peace. It is an Armistice for twenty years.' But the issues involved in each are too varied, complex and multiple to justify so simple a generalisation. Just as the first hinged too much upon the Austro-Serbian and Austro-Russian conflicts to make it merely a war of German aggression, so the second became too world-wide in its scope to be interpreted in parochially European terms.

The second, indeed, was caused much more by deliberate policies of aggression and conquest than was the first. There was no 'war guilt' controversy after the second, because there could be no doubts now about which governments had precipitated war. The National Socialist government of Germany, under the dictatorship of Adolf Hitler, pursued an avowed and consistent policy of aggression from the moment it attained power in 1933, and more especially after German remilitarisation of the Rhineland in 1936. By its carefully prepared *Anschluss* with Austria in March 1938, its annexation of the Sudetenland from Czechoslovakia in the Munich crisis of September 1938, its cynical occupation of the remainder of Bohemia in March 1939, and its attack upon Poland six months later, it rushed headlong into war with a remorselessness seldom equalled in history. Hitler's dictatorship was devised to wage war. It rested on a lust for power that was insatiable and self-destructive. The National Socialist movement as a 'revolution of destruction' was the apotheosis of the whole half-century of violence, its racialist ideology the total denial of all traditional values of European civilisation. Its exploitation of every instrument of power, from mass hysteria and terror to mass extermination and war, made it the most significant and revealing phenomenon for the historian of the twentieth century. Auschwitz and Belsen were the grotesque and tragic climax of Hitler's 'New Order' in Europe.

A subsidiary aggressor, of considerable diplomatic importance after the formation of the 'Rome–Berlin Axis' in 1936, was Mussolini's Italy. As early as 1923 Mussolini had defied the League of Nations by bombarding Corfu, and in October 1935 he successfully resisted League action against his attack on Ethiopia (see above, ch. xvii). Italian aggressions paved the way for German aggressions by proving that the system of 'collective security' did not avail to defend a weak member of the League. But thereafter Italian policy was overshadowed in significance by the dominant impulse of German aggression. A more important aggressor than Italy was Japan, the counterpart to Germany in the Far East in that her government shared a similar fixed resolve to expand her territories on the mainland. Japan also enjoyed a comparable degree of power and of strategic advantages with which to accomplish her purposes. She had shaken the world's confidence in the League, and disrupted the settlement in the Pacific, by her attack on Manchuria in September 1931 and her withdrawal from the League in May 1933. A month after the Rome–Berlin Axis was formed Japan signed with Germany (on 27 November 1936) the Anti-Comintern Pact, to which Italy adhered a year later. These were not formal alliances, and included no specific military commitments. But they were an ominous diplomatic *rapprochement* of the three most actively aggressive states. From the end of 1936 onwards, the world was set on a course heading directly towards a general war.

There were many factors which postponed the outbreak of general war for another three years. Each aggressor aimed at procuring every strategic and material advantage first, if need be by local hostilities. None had any interest in precipitating a general war until it had accumulated the maximum advantage. Meanwhile there were plenty of troubled waters in which they could fish: in Spain or in China, internally divided by civil strife; in states like Czechoslovakia or Yugoslavia, burdened with large national minorities; in weak or isolated countries, such as Abyssinia or Albania, where pickings might be expected to be easy and safe. Above all, they were able to exploit differences of policy and interest that kept their future victims at variance with one another—France and Britain, the United States and the Soviet Union. Democratic governments favoured policies of 'appeasement'. Heavy charges have been brought against the political leaders of these countries for their failure to appreciate soon enough their common peril and to sink minor differences in face of self-avowed aggressors, their short-sighted cowardice of sacrificing smaller nations in efforts to postpone the day of reckoning. Such charges are heavy and cannot in all cases be rebutted. But the heaviest of such charges do not amount to an accusation of 'war guilt'. The drive to make national gains, even at the calculated cost of general war, came entirely from Germany, Italy and Japan. Human intention had a much larger share in bringing about the second war than in bringing about the first.

In one respect, especially, were the two world wars alike: in their demonstration that violence, as expressed in general wars of unlimited commitment, has a propensity to produce totally unintended results which are liable to disappoint the aims and hopes of even the victorious belligerents. The powers did not go to war in 1914 to produce a Bolshevik revolution in Russia or a nationalist revolution in Turkey, to restore the Polish state or make an Irish Free State, to set up a Jewish national home in Palestine or new Arab kingdoms, or even to found a League of Nations. That the war-aims of defeated powers should be frustrated was natural enough: but that the avowed aims of the victorious powers, to destroy German militarism and check German supremacy in Europe, and to establish greater respect for the rights of smaller nations, should be so completely unfulfilled by the outcome of the war, was an ominous warning. Yet again, in 1939, the powers did not go to war to subject eastern Europe to communism, to precipitate a communist revolution in China or national independence in colonial territories, to create a new world schism between East and West: whereas the disarmament of Germany and the restoration of independence to Czechoslovakia and Poland, the creation of an effective organisation to ensure world security and prevent future aggressions, avowed war-aims of the victorious powers, within a decade crumbled to dust.

The two wars were alike, too, in producing progressive deterioration in the importance of Europe in the world. If the first exalted the relative power in the world of the United States and Japan, the second exalted the relative power of the United States, the Soviet Union and China. The colonial revolution, encouraged by the first and greatly advanced by the second, altered the whole relationship between European powers and the peoples of Asia and Africa. The demotion of even the greatest European states in the hierarchy of world power was accompanied by a contraction of Europe overseas—the reversal of a process of expansion that had lasted for more than four centuries.

The overshadowing of Europe by semi-European powers dated, perhaps, from 1815. The continental empire, like the continental system, of Napoleon had been overthrown mainly by the alliance of Great Britain and Russia, the two great peripheral powers then involved in European affairs. Twice within a generation this alliance was repeated, despite the difference each time in the political regimes and ideologies of the two countries. Between 1914 and 1918, and again between 1941 and 1945, it was alliance between Britain and Russia which confronted Germany with a war on two fronts and took a large part in frustrating German domination of Europe. On each occasion the allies fell apart soon after they had removed the common threat to the balance of power in Europe. But each time, too, still greater reserves of power from the new world had to be drawn upon to redress the balance of the old. In the first world war the resources of the Commonwealth and, after 1917, of the United States, proved a decisive element in ensuring German defeat. In the second the resources of the Commonwealth and the United States were needed on a much more extensive scale before Hitler's 'New Order' in Europe could be destroyed. The North Atlantic Treaty Organisation and the maintenance of American bases in Europe were the mid-century counterpoise to Soviet power, now extended as far into Europe as the Elbe and the Danube. They perpetuated that overshadowing of Europe by the Americas and by Asia which was one of the major outcomes of the two world wars.

There was a further important consequence of the changing nature of warfare in the twentieth century. After 1815 France could still be regarded as, and still was, a necessary component of Europe whose place was one of parity with the other great powers. After 1918, because of the things it had been thought necessary to do in order to win a modern total war, it became impossible to treat the defeated enemy in the same way. Germany had to regain her status among the great powers by force of arms. After 1945 the still more intensive and comprehensive nature of modern warfare led to the partition of Germany and her prolonged occupation. Total war led to demands for unconditional surrender and an attempt to achieve total victory. These were concepts alien to the nineteenth century but natural to the twentieth. Because the partition of Germany was accompanied by the partition of Europe and by the coming of the cold war between the American and the Soviet Unions, the result of attempts to attain total victory was an exhaustion of Europe which left her peoples more exposed to the rival pulls of the giant non-European powers. Realisation of this weakness led, in turn, to attempts to unify large areas of Europe into regional or functional groupings which transcended traditional national frontiers. By mid-century, when the Soviet Union as well as the United States held the secret of the atomic bomb, the world passed into a new age when the destruction of mankind ceased to be rhetoric and became a real possibility. European peoples had to adjust themselves to this new and supremely perilous circumstance at a time when their destiny, more completely than ever before, was liable to be determined by powers outside the geographical orbit of Europe itself.

So many, so subtle, and so intricately interwoven are the strands of continuity that compose the tapestry of the twentieth-century tragedy that no final historical judgment is yet possible. It is evident that the three great cataclysms of the two world wars and the intervening economic crisis were not only interconnected in many ways, and linked together by complex interplay of cause and effect: they can also be seen, in retrospect, as in some sense three different expressions of permanent tendencies and forces in European civilisation. The lacerations inflicted by these violent events went deep. They went deepest, perhaps, in the souls of men, where the historian of culture or the social psychologist is better able to trace their full consequences than is the political and economic historian. In material terms the wounds they made healed surprisingly fast, for the impetus of material progress—in many ways accelerated by the more intense efforts of nations at war—speedily overtook the losses and setbacks of war. In spite of the immense damage, deterioration and misery occasioned by these major upheavals, the peoples of Europe were in general richer and more prosperous, and their prosperity was more evenly spread, in 1950 than in 1900. They enjoyed a higher standard of living, longer life, greater amenities, more social security and welfare after these three calamities had happened than they had enjoyed before they happened. It is the paradox of the century that the crescendo of violence reached in 1945—with the last-ditch resistance of Hitler's *Reich*, the use of V I and V 2 (rocket) missiles, and the dropping of the first atom bombs on Hiroshima and Nagasaki—coincided with the well-prepared merciful missions of the United Nations Relief and Rehabilitation Administration, extensive care for displaced persons and refugees, and the beginnings of the most solicitous activities of the Welfare State in arranging social security for each citizen 'from the cradle to the grave'.

This dramatic juxtaposition of opposites was only a particularly vivid example of a larger characteristic of twentieth-century civilisation: the connection between warfare and welfare. It is here that the interplay of the great nineteenth-century movements towards mass democracy, national unity, industrialism and applied science can be most clearly discerned. States deriving their authority from universal suffrage, their power from conscription of the whole of a nation's resources and manpower for purposes of war, and their wealth from taxation, felt it necessary to elicit national sacrifices by promising prospects of social improvement. Mr Lloyd George's promise of 'homes fit for heroes to live in' had its sequel in cradle-to-grave social security. Moreover, modern states attain an absoluteness of power in the exigencies of war which is not entirely dissipated in peace, and peoples accustomed to high taxation in war, as well as to ubiquitous state activity, more readily tolerate these things in peace if they are believed to promote greater social justice. To the economic difficulties which beset Europe a decade after 1919 no answer could be found except still greater activities on the part of public authorities. The trend towards economic planning originated not in Soviet Russia after the revolution, but in imperial Germany during the British blockade, and in this respect Walter Rathenau is a more significant figure than Lenin.

The mighty invasion of governments into economic life, one of the most fundamental contrasts between the twentieth century and the nineteenth, is a direct consequence of the three great crises of the half-century. From this much else derives. The choice, so often posed by publicists of these years, between 'guns or butter', was a dilemma that forced itself upon men's attention only when economic depression threatened. Normally, it seemed, twentieth-century man could afford both. The greatest advances in the standard of living, in productivity, and in the provision of social services and social security, were associated historically with the three great crises of the period. In most European countries the inter-war curse of heavy unemployment was lifted only when governments embarked upon extensive armaments programmes. The twice-repeated experience of speedy recovery after war was connected with expanded activity during war: for ploughshares could be made quickly and plentifully in peace only because so many swords had been in production for war. Preventive and curative medicine made its fastest advances in time of war. If social discipline and sacrifice were peculiarly stimulated and demanded by war, so the 'comradeship of the trenches' came to be valued by many who had lacked such experience in peace.

These associations of apparent opposites prompt the most tantalising of all riddles that confront the historian of the period: was there some inherent but hidden interconnection between them? Were democracy and dictatorship, welfare and warfare, plenty and poverty, the completely antithetical concepts they were usually assumed to be? Was it, in twentieth-century conditions, possible to get social security without national insecurity, atomic energy without the atomic bomb? Were economic aims incompatible, such as expanding productivity without periodic dislocation, full employment without inflation? Might it be that the apparently opposite potentialities of European civilisation were not so much alternatives as concomitants, and the best man could hope for was a dangerous endowment of both? And was it only a hangover of nineteenth-century faith in inevitable progress that made men imagine that they could choose between these concomitant consequences of their dedication to science, technology, material advancement and organised power?

Some have seen an explanation of these paradoxes in an inherent tendency, within the mass democracy of universal suffrage, towards totalitarianism and an absolute state authority. 'It looks as though the advance of the State is a means to the advance of the individual. Here is the main reason for the endless complicity of subjects in the designs of Power: it is the true secret of Power's expansion.'[1] Others have found an explanation in the incompatibility of nationalist enthusiasm with an industrial civilisation. 'To keep to the broadest phenomena, the present crisis is not the direct and inevitable result of industrial civilisation, but

---

[1] Bertrand de Jouvenel, *Du Pouvoir, 1945*, Eng. trans. as *Power: The Natural History of its Growth* (1948), p. 117; and see J. L. Talmon, *The Origins of Totalitarian Democracy* (1952).

of its collision with certain long-standing facts of history....The eternal rivalry of nations has continued into the age of infernal machines; and nations, in their pursuit of power, have not found a way to agree either to a common law or to moderation and compromise.'[1] To marry these views together is to approach the truth.

Of the many predicaments of the age, theologians, philosophers, economists, social theorists and artists could each give their varied explanations. The historian can at least record that the capacity of nations and governments to generate and accumulate power and wealth in more mighty agglomerations than ever before in human history had in this period far exceeded their ability to harness such power and wealth for constructive and creative ends alone. The capacity of applied science, technology and mechanisation to produce material wealth, together with the capacity of human organisation to concentrate power, resulted also in the enhanced ability and tendency of modern societies to destroy one another, and of modern governments to establish inhuman tyranny.

Can he also record signs of the ability and will of European peoples to adjust their ideas and their organisations of public life to the new circumstances and needs that confronted them? Human societies pre-eminent in adaptability, ingenuity and inventiveness might be expected to apply these talents to their mid-century predicaments: and there were signs that in organisation, at least, efforts were being made to overcome the results of the 'collision' between industrial civilisation and the hand of history that lay so heavy on the nations of Europe. New forms of international co-operation proliferated. They included the formation of a very close union between Belgium, the Netherlands and Luxemburg ('Benelux') which, beginning in 1944 as a customs union, developed into a habit of acting as one unit for purposes of international agreements; the extension of this unity to include close co-operation with France and the United Kingdom through the Brussels Treaty of Economic, Social and Cultural Collaboration and Collective Self-Defence, signed in March 1948; the further extension of this regional grouping into the wider economic grouping of the Organisation for European Economic Co-operation (O.E.E.C.) set up in April 1948 to administer American aid provided by the Marshall Plan, and into the looser Council of Europe on one hand, the tighter and supra-national European Coal and Steel Community on the other. Although the United Kingdom held aloof from the Coal and Steel Community, Italy and western Germany participated. The North Atlantic Treaty Organisation of 1949 not only linked the defence organisations of the United States and Canada with those of the United Kingdom and the western European powers, but came to include also such remote states as Greece and Turkey. In 1949 the states of eastern Europe formed

[1] Raymond Aron, *Les Guerres en chaîne* (1951), Eng. trans. as *The Century of Total War* (1954), pp. 164–5.

a Council for Mutual Economic Aid; the League of Arab States dated from 1945, and included Egypt, Iraq, Saudi Arabia, Syria, Lebanon, Jordan and Yemen. In addition to these regional groupings which, in aggregate, wove a new network of co-operative relationships between European states, most countries participated in the many functional agencies wherein governments concerted action for specific purposes: the International Labour Organisation which had survived since 1919, the Food and Agriculture Organisation, the World Health Organisation, the International Bank and Monetary Fund, the United Nations Educational, Scientific and Cultural Organisation, and several other agencies of earlier date. The United Nations itself came to be less the security provider than had been originally intended, and more a general framework within which all such specialised bodies could operate.

International co-operation after 1945 suffered from no lack of facilities. Multiplication of agreements and organisations was such as to betray a lack of assurance that they could be relied upon, especially in the sphere of national defence. The all-pervading fact was the sense of mistrust bequeathed by inter-war experiences and the feeling of insecurity fostered by the cold war. Adjustment of ideas and habits of mind proved more difficult to accomplish than adjustments of organisation.

There was urgent need for greater readjustments in the conceptual framework of European thought. This was reflected by the spiritual and intellectual confusion manifest in theology, philosophy and artistic taste. Conventional categories and accepted ideas had become increasingly outdated and irrelevant to existing conditions. Traditional distinctions between war and revolution meant little when war and revolution had become so intimately interconnected. The distinction between internal and international affairs was blurred by the actual interdependence of nations. Even the most traditional dichotomies, such as that between war and peace, lost much of their meaning in the endemic crisis of the years 1936–9, and in the conditions of 'cold war' after 1947. Of all the social sciences economics made the readiest readjustments of ideas. Postulates previously accepted as true—such as the belief that a high degree of social security and freedom from risk must militate against high productivity—were belied by events and increasingly discarded in theory.[1] Cut adrift from so many intellectual moorings, civilisation was entering a world of relativity in which old absolutes, whether of truth or value, seemed no longer operative.

[1] For example, J. K. Galbraith, *The Affluent Society* (1958), p. 92: '...measures to minimise insecurity comprise a considerable part of what economists have come to call the "built-in stabilisers" of the economy. Thus measures thought by the conventional wisdom to be hostile to productivity all support it at the most critical point.'

INDEX

'Abd al-Ḥamīd II, of Turkey, 207, 209
Abyssinia, 174, 307–8, 459, 563
  Italian aggression, 210, 267–8, 284, 558
  appeal to League of Nations against Italy, 492–3
Adler, Dr Victor, Austrian statesman, 62
Adrian, Edgar Douglas, Baron, of Cambridge, physiologist, 110
Aehrenthal, Count Alois von, Austro-Hungarian diplomat, 321, 322
Afghanistan, 320
Africa
  population, 18
  North, 271–2, 306, see also Morocco
  East, desert warfare in, 271–2; German, 372, 549; British, 531, 547, 549, 550
  Transvaal, 306–7
  Union of South, in British Commonwealth: nationalism, 529, 533, 539, 541; status, 531, 537, 538; and Statute of Westminster, 543; and League of Nations, 545; and autonomy, 546; and mandates, 549
  West, British, 547, 549, 550
  South-West, German, 549
Agadir, 326, 328
Agriculture
  European, effects on, of urban industrial civilisation, 26–7, of war, 27, 29–30; increase in output by exporting countries (after 1918), 29–30; recovery from Great Depression, 30; world surpluses, 30, 119
  peasant, in eastern Europe, 89–90, 94, see also Russia; in Latin America, see separate countries
  and world population, 119
Alamein, El, battle of, 271
Albania
  as a monarchy, 73
  as a satellite of U.S.S.R., 74, 93
  nationalist unrest, 86, 333
  question of her independence, 304, 335, 336
  Serbian invasion, 335, 337
Albert I, king of Belgium, 79
Alcock, Sir John William, aviator, 114, 281
Alessandri, Arturo, Chilean president, 193
Alexander, Samuel, philosopher, 138
Alexei, Tsarevich (Alexis Nikolaevich), 392
Alexeiev, Yevgeni Ivanovich, Russian admiral and statesman, 314
Algeciras, conference of, 8, 153, 319; Act, 319, 325, 326

Allenby, Edmund Henry Hynman, General, 209, 260, 377
Alsace-Lorraine, 300, 339, 449, 453, 454, 484
Amau Declaration, 234
Ambassadors, conferences of: in London (1912), 335; in Paris, after treaty of Versailles, 485–6
America, Latin
  population, 17, 191; immigration, 189–90, 191, 199
  decline of European influence, 178
  and Pan-Americanism, 178–9, 200–2
  and United States: increased North American influence, 178; U.S. annexes Puerto Rico, 186; grants conditional independence to, then reoccupies, Cuba, 186, 187; takes part in 'Isthmian Canal' negotiations, 186–7; forestalls Colombian authorities in Panama revolt, 186; Theodore Roosevelt's corollary to the Monroe doctrine, 152, 187; Washington conference for peacemaking in Central America, 182, 187; armed interventions by U.S., 187; widespread distrust of U.S. 'dollar diplomacy', 187–8; increase in trade with U.S. (1914–18), 190; U.S. resentment of barter agreements, 200; the 'good neighbour' policy, 201–3
  economy: economic and political features common to major republics, 182; dependence on foreign capital, 182, 190; economic consequences of first world war, 189–91; prosperity from oil, 191–2; impact of Great Depression, 194–5; nationalist discrimination against foreign capital, 199–200
  political conditions: constitutional government, 183, 193–4; abuse of constitutional forms, 194; growth of political stability in 'twenties, 191–4; political activity of student population, 193; widespread revolution in 'thirties, 195–9; growth of authoritarian forms of government, 199; differences between Russian communism and agrarismo and aprismo, 203
  religious life, 183
  intellectual life, 183–4
  world status, 188, 204
  in world wars: first, 188–9; second, 202
  and League of Nations, 189, 200
  social reform: welfare schemes, 192–3
  nationalism, growth of, 199

America, United States of (*cont.*)
   training of native army, 221; grant of independence, 228
   and the League of Nations: refusal of support for, 158, 162, 460, 480; more favourable attitude to, 486–7, and to Disarmament Conference (1933), 489
   and peace conference at Versailles, 445–6, 460, 462; sets up World War Foreign Debt Commission, 464–5; loans to Germany under Dawes plan, 466–7, 514; the Hoover moratorium, 473

Anatolia, 304, 305

Anderson, Carl David, physicist, 107

Andorra, 73

Anglo-American Arbitration Treaty, 535–6

Annam, 219, 225, 226, 227

Anti-Comintern Pact, 563

Antonov-Ovseenko, Russian Bolshevik leader, 411

'Apis', *see* Dimitrievic

Aquinas, St Thomas, scholastic philosopher, 141, 142

Arab States, League of, 569

Argentina
   population, 17; immigration, 21, 22 (restrictive legislation on), 199
   agriculture, 29
   commerce and industry: beef and grain exports, 180; improved methods, 184; crisis in beef industry after first world war, 191; movement to improve labour conditions, 192; Roca-Runciman agreement with Great Britain, 199
   social structure, 180
   economic structure: dependence on foreign capital, 180; attempts to achieve economic independence, 199–200
   political structure: concentration of political power in Buenos Aires, 180; radical constitutional change, 184–5, 193; presidency of Irigoyen, 185, 193–4, 195; setting up of department of labour, 192; National Democratic government, 195; dictatorship of Perón, 203
   railway system, 184, 199, 204
   and United States, 188, 201, 202
   in world wars: attitude in first, 188, 189; in second, 202

Armenia, 304

Arrow war, 228

Asia, South-East
   population, 17
   colonial exploitation of, 220
   nationalism, 221
   expansion of rubber and tin production, 223
   Dutch empire in: extent of, 219; 'ethical policy', 220, 222–3; exploitation,
222; beginnings of nationalism, 222; of communism, 222–3; revolutionary post-war government, 227; establishment of an independent republic, 228
   British empire in: extent of, 219; administration in Malaya, 224; in Burma, 225; granting of Burmese independence, 227; new Federation of Malaya, 228
   American dominion in Philippines: annexation, 150, 219; grant of self-government, 156, 171, 221; retention of bases, 221; training of native army, 221; grant of independence, 228
   French empire in: extent of, 219; impotence of native royal houses, 225; exploitation, 225–6; rise of communism, 226; Annamite nationalism, 226; revolutionary post-war government, 227; setting up of independent states, 228

Asquith, Herbert Henry, earl of Oxford and Asquith, British prime minister, 373, 535, 536

Aston, F. W., physicist and chemist, 105

Astronomy, advances in, 102–3

Atlantic, Battle of the, 252; Charter, 554

Attlee, Clement R., British prime minister, 555

Auden, W. H., poet, 129, 133, 134

Aung San, commander of Burmese national army, 227

Auschwitz, 563

Australia
   population, 16, 17, 19; immigration, 20–1
   agriculture, industry, and trade, 29, 30, 119, 534
   political economy, 62, 506, 517
   nationalisation, 62
   warfare: voluntary enlistment, 262; naval activity in Pacific (1914), 416, 417–18, 427; plans for own navy, 535
   mandate in Pacific islands, 429, 550
   in British Commonwealth: status, 530, 531; nationalism, 543, 545; and consultation, 536; and autonomy, 540, 541; and Statute of Westminster, 542, 543, 546; and Ottawa Conference, 545
   as a Pacific power, 534
   and United States of America, 546

Austria
   social conditions: suffrage, 52, 78; social services, 57; social insurance, 505
   taxation, 58
   political developments: strength of Social Democratic Party (before 1914), 62–3, (in 1933), 68; conflict between Socialist loyalties and nationalist divisions, 63; the Vienna or 'Two-and-a-Half' International, 67; socialist government

Foch, Ferdinand (*cont.*)
 at Versailles, 443, 449; and proposed
 enforcement of armistice terms, 452;
 on issue of conscription, 454; on peace,
 562
Food and Agriculture Organisation, 569
Ford, Henry, automobile manufacturer,
 161, 173
Fordney–McCumber tariff, 160, 515
Formosa, 302, 420
Foundations of the Nineteenth Century
 (H. S. Chamberlain), 559
Four-Power Treaty, 438–9, 441
Fourier, Charles, socialist writer, 70
France
 population, 16, 17, 19, 20; infant mortality, 48
 economy, industry and trade: export of
 capital, 26; the Great Depression, 33,
 34; industrialisation (before 1914), 43;
 world trade (before 1914), 502; and
 gold standard, 514, 515; economic
 planning, 517
 social conditions: urbanisation, 46; *rapprochement* between town and country
 life, 47; suffrage, 52; social insurance,
 505, 560
 nationalisation, 59–60
 education, 54, 55
 religion: conflict of Church and State
 over education, 55, 560; new bond between democratic politics and Church,
 84
 taxation, 58
 political developments: unification of
 socialist and trade unionist movements,
 62; formation of Unified Socialist
 Party, 62; the second-ballot election
 system, 75–6, 77, 80; similarities (1902)
 with *Reichstag*, 78; the *Mouvement
 Républicain Populaire*, 84
 trade unionism: formation of *Conféder-
 ation générale du travail*, 62
 status as a great power, 73
 literature, 132
 in Latin America, decline of influence, 178
 and Near and Middle East: the Entente
 with Britain, 207, 208; mandate over
 Syria, 208, 210, 211, 212, 462; Anglo-
 Franco-Turkish alliance, 210; menace
 of Italian and German propaganda,
 210–11
 and Great Britain: the Entente (1904),
 207, 208, 237, 315–16, 316–17; friction
 in Siam, 219–20; struggle for control
 of Upper Nile, 306; military and naval
 talks (1906), 319; secret letters on naval
 matters (1912), 331–2; British royal
 visit, 340; British guarantee of military

aid against German aggression, 449,
 480; discussions on military aid (1921),
 460–1; disagreements in 'twenties,
 460–4; oil agreement in Near East
 (1920), 462
 reaction to Austrian ultimatum to Serbia,
 349
 in South-East Asia: extent of empire
 (early 1900's), 219; stimulus to creation
 of French Indo-China, 225; powerless-
 ness of native royal houses, 225;
 establishment of École Française
 d'Extrême-Orient, 225; exploitation
 of native economy, 225–6; measures
 against Annamite nationalism, 226;
 founding of University of Hanoi, 226
 and China: Franco-Russian railway
 scheme in, 228, 302; occupation of
 Kwang Chow Wan, 303
 warfare, military: 'Napoleonic legacy' of
 assault tactics, 258, 266; casualties in
 first world war, 262, 263; military
 power (after 1918), 265; concentration
 on defence (after 1918), 266, 269; collapse (in 1940), 270
 warfare, air: early lead in aerial navigation, 277–8; superiority in strength
 (after 1918), 280; creation of separate
 air force, 284
 and Russia: alliances with (1891 and
 1892), 301, 309, 310, 311, 329, 332;
 Poincaré's reaffirmation of obligation
 of, 333
 and Italy, secret agreement (1900), 309–10
 and Spain: negotiations over North
 Africa, 315, 316
 and Germany: clash of interests in
 Morocco, 317; agreements thereon,
 326–7, 329; tension (1913), 339; inter-
 parliamentary conference (1913), 339;
 the Rhineland question, 448–9, 453,
 460–1, 465–6; insistence on 'productive
 pledges' (1922), 465–6; the Saar question, 500–1
 and first world war: numbers of men
 available (1914), 359; naval position,
 360; strategic intentions, 360–1; defeat
 of Ardennes offensive (1914), 361;
 German advance halted outside Paris,
 362; effects of British unpreparedness,
 365; offensive in west (1915), 368,
 (1916) 370, 371; new strategy of Gen.
 Nivelle, 373–5; replacement by Pétain,
 375–6; deterioration of morale in
 forces, 376; Foch succeeds Pétain, 380;
 successful counter-attacks, 381–2
 and peace settlement of Versailles, 446,
 459, 460; claims in Rhineland, 448–9,
 453, 460–1, 465–6

India
 population, 17, 20
 British rule, 22, 512; policy of Lord
 Curzon, 212–13, 532; slowness of Indian reaction against, 213; rise of
 Hindu and Muslim reform movements,
 213, 214; first moderate requests for
 share in government, 213; British attitude, 213–14; agitation over proposed
 division of Bengal, 214, 552; challenge
 in Congress of extremist Hindu groups,
 214; reforms by Morley and Minto,
 214–15, 552–3; granting of separate
 electorates to Muslims, 214; Government of India Act (1919), 215, 216, 553,
 (1935) 554; remodelling of central and
 provincial governments, 215, 553–4;
 opposition of majority of Indian
 opinion, 216; emergence of Gandhi,
 216, 553; political rivalry of Muslims
 and Hindus, 216–17; British present
 revised constitution (1935), 217; sweeping Congress victory in general election,
 217; Muslim resentment of Congress
 policy, 218–19; communal rioting, 219;
 Muslim demand for Pakistan, 218;
 Congress–Muslim League deadlock
 (1939–45), 218, 554–5; partition and
 British withdrawal, 218, 555
Indian Independence Act, 555
Indies, West, 531, 547, 548, 549, 550; West
 Indian Conference, 551
Industrialisation
 spread of, in twentieth century, 23–7, 42
 international economics, influence on, 43
 technological advance, 42–3
 urbanisation, 45–6; lessening difference
 between town and country life, 47
Inge, Dr W. R., philosopher, 126, 141, 147
International Justice, Permanent Court of,
 see League of Nations
International Labour Organisation, see
 League of Nations
Iraq, 210, 211
 British mandate in, 208, 462, 549
 prosperity from oil, 208
 Anglo-Iraq treaty, 282
 see also Mesopotamia
Ireland
 population, 17
 Southern: becomes an independent re-
 public, 74, 87, 537–8, 543, 546, 564; and
 world economic crisis, 82
Irigoyen, Hipólito, president of Argentina,
 185, 189, 193–4, 195
'Iron curtain', 85
Ishii, Viscount Kikujiro, Japanese states-
 man, 425–6
Israel, 6, 210, 564

'Isthmian Canal', 152–3, 186
Iswolsky (Izvolsky), Alexandr Petrovich,
 Russian diplomat, 320, 321, 322, 335
Italy
 population, 17
 industry and economy: benefits of new
 techniques, 43; economic planning,
 512; and gold standard, 514
 social conditions: suffrage, 52; social
 services, 57; social insurance, 505
 education, 55
 taxation, 58
 nationalisation, 59
 trade unionism, 62
 political developments: adoption of constitution on Russian lines between
 wars, 74; Mussolini's dictatorship,
 80–1, 82, 83; growth of Christian
 Democrat Party, 84
 status as a European power, 73, 74
 church and state, 95
 philosophy, 140–1
 in Libya, suzerainty, 210–11
 and Abyssinia: aggression against, 210,
 267–8, 492–3; defeat by (1896), 307–8
 warfare: casualties in first world war,
 263; methods used against Abyssinia,
 267–8, 284, 493; inferior training in
 desert warfare, 271; test of air equipment in Spanish Civil War, 284; defeat
 of air force in North Africa, 288–9
 and France: secret agreement (1900),
 309–10
 and Russia: Treaty of Racconigi, 324
 and Turkey: war with (1911), 328, 333
 reaction to Austrian ultimatum to Serbia,
 349
 entry into first world war, 368
 in 'Fourteen Points', 444
 and peace settlement of Versailles, 459–60,
 461–2
 and Yugoslavia: dispute over Fiume,
 459–60
 and Treaty of Locarno, 467, 484
 and Greece: bombardment of Corfu,
 485–6, 563
 and League of Nations, 485–6, 492–3
Ito, Prince, of Japan, 313
Izvolsky, see Iswolsky

Jagow, Gottlieb von, German statesman,
 340, 344, 352
Jamaica, 550
James, William, philosopher, 136, 139
Jameson raid, 307
Japan
 population, 17, 19
 industry and commerce: the Great Depression, 33; recovery, 35; industrial

Japan (*cont.*)
  advance (after 1918), 44, (before 1914) 506
  rearmament, 35; war-preparation economy, 39
  and Russia: war (1904-5), 152-3, 230, 236-7, 256, 314-15, 316; Treaty of Portsmouth, 153, 314; relations over China, *see* Manchuria, Shantung
  and America, 152-3, 229-30, 425-6; attack on Pearl Harbor, 235, 293-4
  and South-East Asia: the 'New Order' announcement, 226, 234, 235; failure to interest Netherlands in co-prosperity scheme, 226; invasion, 226-7; aspiration to leadership of Asia, 229
  and China: war (1894), 228; Treaty of Shimonoseki, 302; presentation of Twenty-One Demands, 232, 419-22, 440; attempted extension of control in, after Russian revolution, 232, 425-6; war (1937), 235, 268; financial domination over, after outbreak of first world war, 422; attitude to entry of, into war (1917), 423; *see also* Manchuria, Shantung
  and Korea, 228, 302
  and Great Britain: treaty of alliance with, 229, 313, 416, 435, 438; offer of services in first world war, 416-17; secret agreements on German Pacific islands, 418, 429
  military warfare: maintenance of standing army (before 1914), 256; fanaticism, 274, 275; jungle tactics, 275
  air warfare: attack on Pearl Harbor, 293-4; attack on Manila, 294; occupation of Philippine Islands, 294; sinking of British warships, 294; suicide pilots, 294
  and Germany, 417, 418, 419; conflict of interests in China, *see* Shantung
  and Peace Conference of Versailles, 428-35
  and Washington Conference, 436-42
  and League of Nations, 446, 490-1, 563
Jaspers, Karl, psychiatrist and philosopher, 140
Jaurès, Jean, French socialist leader, 62, 70
Java, 222-3, 227
Jellicoe, John Rushworth, earl, Admiral, 372, 373, 384
Jews, 50, 87, 92, 210-1, 462, 564
Jinnah, Muhammad Ali, leader of All-India Muslim League, 218, 554, 555
Joffre, Joseph, French commander-in-chief, 258, 362, 365, 371, 373, 374, 383
Johnson, Hugh A., American general, 169
Joyce, James, novelist, 129, 130

Judicial Committee Acts, 540
Jugoslavia, *see* Yugoslavia
Jung, Carl Gustav, psychologist and psychiatrist, 98
Justo, Agustín, Argentine general and president, 195
Jutland, Battle of, 246, 249, 372-3

Kafka, Franz, novelist, 130
Kamenev, Lev Borisovich, Russian politician, 399, 406, 409, 413
Kant, Immanuel, philosopher, 139
Kartini, Raden Adjeng, Indonesian nationalist leader, 222
Kellogg Pact (Pact of Paris), 162, 468, 488, 490, 491
Kemal, Mustafa, Turkish soldier and statesman, 54, 462-3
Kendall, Edward Calvin, American biochemist, 108
Kenya, 548, 549
Kerensky, Alexandr, leader of Russian Social Revolutionary Party, 398, 412, 413, 426
  Minister of Justice in provisional government (1917), 392; Minister for War, 401, 405
  premier of second coalition government, 395, 396, 406-7
  forms Directory, 396, 407
  convenes Democratic Conference, 408
  forms third coalition government, 408
  orders redistribution of military forces, 410
  overthrow of his government, 411
Keynes, John Maynard, economist, 44, 70, 167, 503, 514, 558
Kiderlen-Wächter, Alfred von, German diplomat, 326, 327
Kierkegaard, Sören, philosopher, 5, 135, 140
Kipling, Rudyard, poet, 129, 220, 529
Kitchener, Horatio, earl, of Khartoum and of Broome, British general, 262, 306, 364, 373
Kluck, Alexander von, German general, 278, 361, 362
Knox, Frank, American newspaper publisher and public official, 188
Kokovtsov, Count V. N., Russian premier, 339
Kolchak, Alexandr, Russian admiral and counter-revolutionary, 427
Kollontai, Alexandra, Russian revolutionary, 406
Koo, V. K. Wellington, Chinese statesman, 432
Korea
  Russian and Japanese designs on, 228

Salisbury, earl of (Robert Arthur Talbot
Gascoyne-Cecil, Marquis of Salisbury),
British statesman and prime minister,
304, 311, 312
Salmond, Sir John, New Zealand lawyer
and statesman, 537
Salvador, El, 188
Salonika, 332, 368
Samoa, German, 417, 418, 429, 537, 550
San Martín, Grau, ruler of Cuba, 201
San Remo, conference of (1920), 462
Sandler, Rickard, politician, 70
Sanders, Liman von, German general, 338-9
Sarajevo, 341-2, 344, 345, 453
Sarawak, 219
Sarekat Islam, Javanese popular movement,
222
Sarrail, Maurice, French general, 372
Sartre, Jean-Paul, author, 140
Saudi Arabia, 210, 282
Savinkov, Boris, leader of Russian Social
Revolutionary Party, 398
Sayers, Dorothy, poet and novelist, 127,
134
Sazonov, Sergei Dimitrievich, Russian dip-
lomat, 332, 348, 353
admonition to Montenegro, 336
advice to Serbia, 337
attitude to German military dominance,
338, 341, 346
attitude to Austrian ultimatum to Serbia,
349, 351
Scapa Flow, 241
Schacht, Hjalmar, German financier, 526
Scharnhorst, German cruiser, 253, 417, 418
Scheer, Reinhard von, German naval commander, 372
Scheidemann, Philipp, German political
leader, 68, 453
Schiller, F. C. S., philosopher, 137
Schleiermacher, Friedrich Ernst, philosopher and theologian, 146
Schlieffen, Count Alfred von, German army
commander, 360, 362
Schoen, Baron Wilhelm von, Bavarian politician, 344-5
Schuschnigg, Dr Kurt von, Austrian chancellor, 68
Schweitzer, Albert, Christian philosopher,
145-6
Science
alliance with technology, 4, 120
'revolutions' in scientific thought (before
1900), 100-1
radio-activity, discovery of, 100; and
geology, 111
cathode rays, discovery of, 100
speed of advance, in twentieth century,
100-1

cosmic system, investigation of, 102-3
atoms, structure of, 100-1, 103-7; atomic
fission, 116-17
physics: atomic and chemical, 107; biochemistry and bio-physics, 108; discovery of vitamins and hormones, 108,
110; viruses, 108
organic chemistry, 108-9
new drugs, 109
crystallography, 110
physiology, histology, X-ray and microscopic technique, 110
geology, geochemistry, study of the
atmosphere, 110; geophysics, 111; and
radio-activity: the atomic bomb, 111
meteorology, 111
Special and General Theory of Relativity,
112
genetics, 112-14
application of science to medicine:
malaria research, blood transfusion,
114
internal combustion; land, air, and space
travel, 114-15
electricity, 115
wireless telephony, radio-broadcasting,
television, 115-16
technological developments, 117-20
agricultural production, increase in, 119
refrigeration, 119
scientific education, organisation of,
120-3
societies and periodicals, 123-4
Scutari, 336
Seddon, Richard John, prime minister of
New Zealand, 529
Seeckt, Hans von, Chief of German army
directorate, 468-70
Senegambia, 316
Serbia, 8, 88, 89, 340
and Austria-Hungary: deteriorating relations, 321, 334-5; Austrian ultimatum
(1913) over Albania, 337; the Sarajevo
murder, 341-2, 345; Austrian ultimatum (1914), 348-50; Austrian attacks (1914), 363
contention over, between Austria and
Russia, 321, 322, 323
and Bulgaria: treaty with (1912), 332,
333; disagreement over Macedonia,
337
entry into Balkan war, 334
Russian sponsorship, 334, 335
and Adriatic Sea, 335
and Scutari crisis, 336
collapse (1915), 369
becomes part of Yugoslavia, 456
Sèvres, Treaty of, 462
Shakespeare, William, 128

Stalin (*cont.*)
    as member of Council of People's Commissars, 412
    feud with Trotsky, 557
Stanley, Wendell M., biochemist, 108
Starling, Ernest Henry, physiologist, 108
Stimson, Henry L., American statesman, 170, 491
Stinnes, Hugo, German mining engineer and businessman, 464
Stolypin, Piotr Arkadevich, tsarist statesman, 94
Stone, Harlan F., American Chief Justice, 173
Strachey, Lytton, author, 131
Strassmann, Fritz, physicist, 116
Stresemann, Gustav, German statesman, 11, 466, 467, 470–1, 486
Strutt, John William (Baron Rayleigh), 107
Sudan, 531
Sudetenland, 457, 562
Suez Canal, 207, 546
    in world wars, 293, 363
    British interest in, 468
Sukhomlinov, Vladimir Alexandrovich, Russian general, 339
Sumatra, 219
Sun Yat-sen, founder of Chinese national movement, 230–1, 232, 233
Supreme Council for Supply and Relief, 447
Supreme Economic Council, 446–7, 457
Supreme War Council, 378, 447, 453
Sweden
    population, 16, 17, 19; infant mortality, 48
    suffrage, 52, 54, 73, 560
    political institutions: achievement of Social Democratic Party, 69–70; proportional representation, 79
    association with Norway, 87
    neutrality, 93
    dispute with Finland, 485
    social insurance, 505
    currency 514
Swinton, Sir Ernest Dunlop, soldier and writer, 371
Switzerland
    population, 17
    social conditions: suffrage, 52; social services, 57; social insurance, 505
    industrialisation, 43, 45
    status in Europe, 73, 93
    and world trade, 44, 502
Sykes–Picot Agreement, 459, 462
Syria
    French mandate over, 208, 210, 211, 212
    nationalist movement, 209
Sze, S. K. Alfred, Chinese diplomat, 432
Szögyény, Count, Austro-Hungarian diplomat, 342, 343, 344, 352

Taft Robert Alphonso, American lawyer and politician, 175
Taft, William Howard, American president chosen as successor by Theodore Roosevelt, 153
    elected, 154
    tariff revision, 154
    unpopularity in Republican party, 154–5
    renomination and defeat, 155
    relations with Central America, 187–8
Takahashi, Viscount Korekiyo, Japanese diplomat and premier, 441
Takamine, Jokichi, chemist, 108
Tampico, 156, 185
Tanganyika, 549
Taylor, A. E., philosopher, 141, 142
Tellini, Enrico, Italian general, 485
Temple, William, archbishop of Canterbury, 146
Ten Years Rule, 268
Tennant, F. R., theologian, 142, 143
Tennyson, Alfred, Lord (Baron Tennyson), poet, 127, 129
Theology
    close relation with philosophy, 142
    changes in theological currents, 143
    Liberal Protestantism, 143–4
    modernist movement, 144–5
    controversy on 'historical Jesus', 145–6
    orthodox doctrines re-stated, 146
    mysticism, 146–7
    Barth's theology of crisis, 147–8
Theology, 2
    Russian and Eastern theological writers, 148
Thibaw, last king of Burma, 219
Thomson, Sir J. J., physicist, 100, 104, 105
Three Emperors' League, 300, 321
Tibet, 320
Tilak, Bal Gangadher, Hindu revolutionary, 214
Tirpitz, Alfred von, German naval commander, 312, 325, 330, 331, 348, 357
Tisza, Kálmán, Hungarian statesman, 342
Tobruk, 271
Togoland, 549
Tongking, 219, 226
Toynbee, Arnold, historian, 142
Trade unions
    links with socialist parties throughout Europe, 61–3, 65, 67, 69, 70
    attitude to war in 1914, 66
    International Federation of Trade Unions, 66–7
    Red International of Labour Unions, 67
Trafalgar, battle of, 237
Transjordan, 208, 211, 549
Transvaal, 307
Transylvania, 337, 456

War of 1914–18 (*cont.*)
  armistice, 382
  capitulation of Bulgaria and Turkey; col-
    lapse of Austria-Hungary, 382
  innovations of the war, 383
  retrospect over the war, 384–5
Ward, James, philosopher, 135
Ward, Sir Joseph, New Zealand prime
  minister, 535
Washington, Conference and Treaties of,
  161, 232, 234, 537
  American proposal of ten-year holiday in
    naval building, 437, 441, 481
  Japanese condition on Pacific bases, 437–8
  problems of the Anglo-Japanese Alliance:
    the Four-Power Treaty, 438–9, 441
  question of Yap, 438–9
  nine-power treaty on China, 439, 490, 491
  problem of Shantung discussed outside
    conference, 439–40
  discussion on Group Two of the Twenty-
    One Demands, 440
  achievement of the conference, 440–2
Webb, Clement C. J., theologian, 142
Webb, Sidney, socialist writer, 96; and
  Beatrice Webb, 98
Weber, Max, philosopher, 139
Wegener, Alfred, geophysicist and meteoro-
  logist, 111
Wei-hai-Wei, 233, 303, 440
Weimar Republic, 52, 68, 455, 512, 557
  see also Germany
Welfare State, 3, 52, 57–9, 72, 98, 504, 558,
  566
Wells, Herbert George, author, 97, 129–30,
  131, 259
Westminster, Statute of, 530, 541–3, 546,
  548
Whitehead, A. N., philosopher, 138
Wigforss, Ernest, politician, 70
Wilhelm II, German emperor, 301, 322, 357,
  454
  and 'Kruger telegram', 307, 311
  visit to Tangier, 317
  meeting with tsar at Björkö, 318
  and naval programme, 325, 330
  negotiations with Haldane, 330–1
  supports Austria over Serbia (1913), 337
  political outlook, 338, 341
  conference with Archduke Francis Ferdi-
    nand, 341
  message from Francis Joseph of Austria,
    342–3
  and Serbian reception of Austrian ulti-
    matum (1914), 350
  telegraphic exchange with tsar (1914),
    351–2
Wilkie, Wendell, American politician, 175
Williams, Charles, poet, 134

Wilson, Sir Henry, British C.I.G.S., 378
Wilson, Woodrow, American president, 88
  elected, 155
  programme of legislation, 155–6
  wartime leadership, 157
  'fourteen points' speech, 157, 443–5, 455,
    450
  loss of control of Congress, 158, 447
  and League of Nations: insistence on
    incorporation of Covenant in peace
    treaties, 158, 475; failure to secure
    American support in this, 158, 460,
    479; and drafting of Covenant, 430, 431
  and Peace Settlement of Versailles, 438,
    448, 449, 461, 464
Wingate, Orde, British general, 275
Wirth, Joseph, German statesman, 464, 469,
  471
Witte, Count Sergei, tsarist statesman, 90
Wittgenstein, Ludwig, philosopher, 139
Wood, Leonard, American soldier, 157
Woolf, Virginia, novelist, 130
World Health Organisation, 569
World War, first, *see* War of 1914; similari-
  ties between two world wars, 562, 564
Wright brothers, aviators, 114, 277

Yap Island, 418, 438–9
Yeats, William Butler, poet, 133
Young Plan, 161, 471, 473, 488
Young Turks, 207, 209
Youth organisations, in dictatorships, 83,
  93, 96
Yuan Shih-kai, first president of the republic of China, 230, 231–2, 420, 422
Yugoslavia
  population, 17, 44
  agriculture, 45
  status in Europe, 73; components, after
    first world war, 88, 89; after second,
    456, 459
  and Russian communism, 74, 93
  German invasion, 289
  disagreements with Italy, 459–60
  and Little Entente, 461
Yussupov, Prince, assassin of Rasputin, 390

Zapata, Emiliano, Mexican Indian agrarian
  agitator, 185
Zeeland, Paul van, economist, 69, 528
Zelaya, José, Nicaraguan dictator, 187
Zeligowski, Lucian, Polish general, 485
Zeppelin, Count Ferdinand von, 239
Zimmermann, Arthur, German statesman,
  326, 344
Zinoviev, Grigory, Russian revolutionary
  statesman, 406, 409, 413, 415
Zionism, 87, 210, 462, 564
Zola, Émile, French novelist, 132